# Mastering
# AutoCAD® 2008
# and AutoCAD LT® 2008

# Mastering
# AutoCAD® 2008
# and AutoCAD LT® 2008

**George Omura**

BICENTENNIAL
1807
WILEY
2007
BICENTENNIAL

Wiley Publishing, Inc.

Acquisitions Editor: Willem Knibbe

Development Editor: David Ziegler

Technical Editor: Paul Richardson

Production Editor: Martine Dardignac

Copy Editor: Tiffany Taylor

Production Manager: Tim Tate

Vice President and Executive Group Publisher: Richard Swadley

Vice President and Executive Publisher: Joseph B. Wikert

Vice President and Publisher: Neil Edde

Book Designers: Maureen Forys and Judy Fung

Compositor: Craig Woods, Happenstance Type-O-Rama

Proofreader: Nancy Riddiough

Indexer: Ted Laux

Anniversary Logo Design: Richard Pacifico

Cover Designer: Ryan Sneed

Cover Image: © Pete Gardner / Digital Vision / gettyimages

Dear Reader,

Thank you for choosing *Mastering AutoCAD 2008 and AutoCAD LT 2008*. This book is part of a family of premium quality Sybex books, all written by outstanding authors who combine practical experience with a gift for teaching.

Sybex was founded in 1976. More than thirty years later, we're still committed to producing consistently exceptional books. With each of our titles we're working hard to set a new standard for the industry. From the paper we print on, to the authors we work with, our goal is to bring you the best books available.

I hope you see all that reflected in these pages. I'd be very interested to hear your comments and get your feedback on how we're doing. Feel free to let me know what you think about this or any other Sybex book by sending me an email at nedde@wiley.com, or if you think you've found a technical error in this book, please visit http://sybex.custhelp.com. Customer feedback is critical to our efforts at Sybex.

Best regards,
Neil Edde

Vice President and Publisher
Sybex, an Imprint of Wiley

To my two wonderful sons, Arthur and Charles, and to Susan, who helps me to put things in perspective.

# Acknowledgments

Many talented and hardworking folks gave their best effort to produce Mastering AutoCAD 2008 and AutoCAD LT 2008. I offer my sincerest gratitude to those people who helped bring this book to you.

Heartfelt thanks go to the editorial and production teams at Sybex for their efforts. Willem Knibbe made sure things got off to a great start and was always there for support. Martine Dardignac kept a watchful eye on the progress of the book. David Ziegler kept things running smoothly and always had a positive attitude. Tiffany Taylor made sure I wasn't trying out new uses of the English language. Paul Richardson did an excellent job of ensuring that I didn't make any glaring mistakes and offered suggestions based on his own training experience.

You can see the handiwork of Paul Richardson (not the same Paul Richardson who did the technical editing) and Christine Merredith of Technical Publications in the sidebars that discuss the San Francisco Main Library. Thanks also go to the architectural firms of Pei Cobb Freed & Partners and Simon Martin-Vegue Winkelstein Morris Associated Architects for generously granting permission to reproduce drawings from their design of the San Francisco Main Library.

At Autodesk, a special thanks goes to Abhi Singh, AutoCAD Production Manager, for taking the time from his busy schedule to write the foreword. Thanks for the kind words, Abhi. Thanks also go to Denis Cadu, who has always given his steadfast support of my efforts over many projects. Jim Quanci always gives his generous and thoughtful assistance to us author types—I'd be lost without your help, Jim. Finally, as always, a big thanks to Shaan Hurley for generously allowing us to have a look at the pre-release software.

And a great big thank you to my family and friends, who have always been a source of inspiration and understanding.

# Foreword

Congratulations!

As someone interested in AutoCAD or AutoCAD LT, or as someone who uses one of those products to make a living as many do, you have truly made a worthwhile investment.

First of all, it's all there. You are not going to get a more comprehensive guide than the one you hold in your hands. Everything from the basics of AutoCAD to programming in AutoLISP and VBA to installing and setting up AutoCAD is covered.

Moreover, the information is well-organized. Both the contents at a glance and a comprehensive index make retrieving information you need a cinch.

My personal favorites are the real-world AutoCAD drawings that are available for download. As every designer knows, there is no better way to learn than by doing, and the drawings are an excellent tool to guide you through a series of exercises available with each chapter in the book.

Don't let the size of the book intimidate you. The book is written to be comprehensive, but I don't believe anyone uses all the features in AutoCAD. Pick out the tools that you want to learn about and proceed from there, or if you are interested in learning new things, pick a different topic each week to learn about.

Whether you're new to AutoCAD or a veteran, you will undoubtedly find this book to be an excellent resource.

Now the only question left is: what will you design?

Abhi Singh
AutoCAD Product Manager
Autodesk, Inc.

# Contents

# Contents

# Introduction

Welcome to *Mastering AutoCAD 2008 and AutoCAD LT 2008*. As many readers have already discovered, this book is a unique blend of tutorial and reference that includes everything you need to get started and stay ahead with AutoCAD. With this edition, you get coverage of the latest features of both AutoCAD 2008 and AutoCAD LT 2008, plus the latest information on new features.

## How to Use This Book

Rather than just showing you how each command works, this book shows you AutoCAD 2008 in the context of a meaningful activity. You'll learn how to use commands while working on an actual project and progressing toward a goal. This book also provides a foundation on which you can build your own methods for using AutoCAD and become an AutoCAD expert. For this reason, I haven't covered every single command or every permutation of a command response. You should think of this book as a way to get a detailed look at AutoCAD as it's used on a real project. As you follow the exercises, I encourage you to also explore AutoCAD on your own, applying the techniques you learn to your own work.

Both experienced and beginning AutoCAD users will find this book useful. If you aren't an experienced user, the way to get the most out of this book is to approach it as a tutorial—chapter by chapter, at least for the first two parts of the book. You'll find that each chapter builds on the skills and information you learned in the previous one. To help you navigate, the exercises are shown in numbered steps. To address the needs of all readers worldwide, the exercises provide both U.S. (feet/inches) and metric measurements.

After you've mastered the material in Parts 1 and 2, you can follow your interests and explore other parts of the book in whatever order you choose. Part 3 takes you to a more advanced skill level. There, you'll learn more about storing and sharing drawing data and how to create more complex drawings. If you're interested in 3D, check out Part 4. If you want to start customizing right away, go to Part 5. You can check out Chapters 27 and 28 at any time because they give you general information about sharing AutoCAD files with your coworkers and consultants. Chapter 28 focuses on AutoCAD's Sheet Set Manager, which offers a way to organize your multisheet projects.

You can also use this book as a ready reference for your day-to-day problems and questions about commands. Optional exercises at the end of each chapter will help you review and look at different ways to apply the information you've learned. Experienced users will also find this book a handy reference tool.

Finally, if you run into problems using AutoCAD, see the "When Things Go Wrong" section in Appendix B. You'll find a list of the most common issues that users face when first learning AutoCAD.

## AutoCAD 2008 and AutoCAD LT 2008

Autodesk has released both AutoCAD 2008 and AutoCAD LT 2008 simultaneously. Not surprisingly, they're nearly identical in the way they look and work. You can share files between the two programs with complete confidence that you won't lose data or corrupt files. The main differences are that LT doesn't support all the 3D functions of AutoCAD 2008, nor does it support the customization tools of AutoLISP and VBA. But LT still has plenty to offer in both the productivity and customization areas. And because they're so similar, I can present material for both programs with only minor adjustments.

When a feature is discussed that is available only in AutoCAD 2008, you'll see the AutoCAD Only icon.

You'll also see warning messages when tutorials vary between AutoCAD 2008 and LT. If only minor differences occur, you'll see either a warning message or directions embedded in the tutorial indicating the differences between the two programs.

In the few instances in which LT has a feature that isn't available in AutoCAD 2008, you'll see the LT Only icon.

I've also provided work-around instructions wherever possible when LT doesn't offer a feature found in AutoCAD 2008.

## Getting Information Fast

I've included plenty of tips and warnings:

**TIP**    Tips are designed to make practice easier.

**WARNING**    Warnings steer you away from pitfalls.

Also, in each chapter you'll find more extensive tips and discussions in the form of sidebars set off from the main text. To encourage you along the way, some of the sidebars show you how topics in each chapter were applied to a real-world project, the San Francisco Main Library. Together, the tips, warnings, and sidebars provide a wealth of information I have gathered over years of using AutoCAD on a variety of projects in different office environments. You may want to browse through the book, just reading these notes, to get an idea of how they might be useful to you.

Another quick reference you'll find yourself turning to often is Appendix C, which contains descriptions of all the dimension settings with comments on their uses. If you experience any problems, you can consult the "When Things Go Wrong" section in Appendix B.

## What to Expect

*Mastering AutoCAD 2008 and AutoCAD LT 2008* is divided into five parts, each representing a milestone in your progress toward becoming an expert AutoCAD user. Here is a description of those parts and what they will show you.

### Part 1: The Basics

As with any major endeavor, you must begin by tackling small, manageable tasks. In this first part, you'll become familiar with the way AutoCAD looks and feels. Chapter 1, "Exploring the AutoCAD and AutoCAD LT Interface," shows you how to get around in AutoCAD. In Chapter 2, "Creating Your First Drawing," you'll learn how to start and exit the program and how to respond to AutoCAD commands. Chapter 3, "Setting Up and Using AutoCAD's Drafting Tools," tells you how to set up a work area, edit objects, and lay out a drawing. In Chapter 4, "Organizing Objects with Blocks and Groups," you'll explore some tools unique to CAD: symbols, blocks, and layers. As you're introduced to AutoCAD, you'll also get a chance to make some drawings that you can use later in the book and perhaps even in future projects of your own. Chapter 5, "Keeping Track of Layers, Blocks, and Files" shows you how to use layers to keep similar information together and object properties such as linetypes to organize things visually.

## Part 2: Mastering Intermediate Skills

After you have the basics down, you'll begin to explore some of AutoCAD's more subtle qualities. Chapter 6, "Editing and Reusing Data to Work Efficiently" tells you how to reuse drawing setup information and parts of an existing drawing. In Chapter 7, "Mastering Viewing Tools, Hatches, and External References," you'll learn how to use viewing tools and hatches and how to assemble and edit a large drawing file. Chapter 8, "Introducing Printing, Plotting, and Layouts," shows you how to get your drawing onto hard copy. Chapter 9, "Understanding Plot Styles," discusses methods for controlling lineweights and shading in your printer output. Chapter 10, "Adding Text to Drawings," tells you how to annotate your drawing and edit your notes. Chapter 11, "Using Fields and Tables," shows you how to add spreadsheet functionality to your drawings. Chapter 12, "Using Dimensions," gives you practice in using automatic dimensioning (another unique CAD capability).

## Part 3: Mastering Advanced Skills

At this point, you'll be on the verge of becoming a real AutoCAD expert. Part 3 is designed to help you polish your existing skills and give you a few new ones. Chapter 13, "Using Attributes," tells you how to attach information to drawing objects and how to export that information to database and spreadsheet files. In Chapter 14, "Copying Pre-existing Drawings into AutoCAD," you'll learn techniques for transferring paper drawings to AutoCAD. In Chapter 15, "Advanced Editing and Organizing," you'll complete the apartment building tutorial. During this process you'll learn how to integrate what you've learned so far and gain some tips on working in groups. Chapter 16, "Laying Out Your Printer Output," shows you the tools that let you display your drawing in an organized fashion. Chapter 17, "Using Dynamic Blocks," shows you how you can create blocks that can be edited with grips without having to redefine them. Chapter 18, "Drawing Curves and Solid Fills," gives you an in-depth look at some special drawing objects, such as splines and fitted curves. In Chapter 19, "Getting and Exchanging Data from Drawings," you'll practice getting information about a drawing and learn how AutoCAD can interact with other applications, such as spreadsheets and desktop-publishing programs. You'll also learn how to copy and paste data.

## Part 4: 3D Modeling and Imaging

Although 2D drafting is AutoCAD's workhorse application, AutoCAD's 3D capabilities give you a chance to expand your ideas and look at them in a new light. Chapter 20, "Creating 3D Drawings," covers AutoCAD's basic features for creating three-dimensional drawings. Chapter 21, "Using Advanced 3D Features," introduces you to some of the program's more powerful 3D capabilities. Chapter 22, "Rendering 3D Drawings," shows how you can use AutoCAD to produce lifelike views of your 3D drawings. Chapter 23, "Editing and Visualizing 3D Solids," takes a closer look at 3D solids and how they can be created, edited, and displayed in AutoCAD 2008.

## Part 5: Customization and Integration

One of AutoCAD's greatest strengths is its openness to customization. Chapter 24, "Using the Express Tools," gives you a gentle introduction to the world of AutoCAD customization. You'll learn how to load and use existing Express tools that expand AutoCAD's functionality, and you'll be introduced to AutoLISP as a tool to create macros. Chapter 25, "Introducing AutoLISP," is a primer to AutoCAD's popular macro language. You'll learn how you can create custom commands built on existing ones and how you can retrieve and store locations and other data. Chapter 26, "Customizing Toolbars, Menus, Linetypes, and Hatch Patterns," shows you how to customize menus, toolbars, linetypes, and hatch patterns. Chapter 27, "Managing and Sharing Your Drawings," shows you how to adapt AutoCAD to your own work style. You'll learn about the tools that help you exchange drawings with others and how to secure your drawings to prevent tampering. Chapter 28, "Keeping a Project Organized with Sheet Sets," shows you how to use the new Sheet Set Manager to simplify your file management. By using the Sheet Set Manager, you can automate some of the more tedious drawing coordination tasks.

### The Appendices

Finally, this book has three appendices. Appendix A, "Installing and Setting Up AutoCAD," contains an installation and configuration tutorial. If AutoCAD isn't already installed on your system, follow the steps in this tutorial before starting Chapter 1. Appendix B, "Hardware and Software Tips," provides information about hardware related to AutoCAD. It also provides tips on improving AutoCAD's performance and troubleshooting and provides more detailed information on setting up AutoCAD's plotting feature. Appendix C, "System Variables and Dimension Styles," provides a reference to dimension style settings.

### The Sample Files from Our Website

For the first part of the book, you're asked to create new files, and each chapter builds on the files you create in the previous chapters. You also have the option to use ready-made sample files. When you see a comment in the book that refers to a sample file, you can download the file from our website at the following location:

> www.sybex.com/go/masteringautocad2008

There you will also find some extra sample files that you can download and play with without the worry of accidentally changing original files. As you progress into later chapters, you'll definitely want to download the sample files, because they're required for many of the exercises.

## The Minimum System Requirements

This book assumes you have an IBM-compatible computer with at least a Pentium IV or equivalent CPU. Your computer should have at least one CD drive and a hard disk with 2GB or more of free space for the AutoCAD program files and about 120MB of additional space for sample files and workspace. In addition to these requirements, you should have enough free disk space to allow for a Windows virtual memory page file that is about 1.5 times the amount of installed RAM. Consult your Windows manual or Appendix B of this book for more on virtual memory.

AutoCAD 2008 runs best on systems with at least 2GB or more of RAM, although you can get by with 512MB. Your computer should also have a high-resolution monitor and an up-to-date display card. An SVGA display with a resolution of 1024 × 768 or greater will work fine with AutoCAD, but if you want to take full advantage of AutoCAD's new 3D features, you should have a 128MB or greater, OpenGL -capable, workstation-class graphics card. If you intend to use a digitizer tablet, you'll need one free USB, or serial, port available. I also assume you're using a mouse and have the use of a printer or a plotter. A CD or DVD reader is needed to install AutoCAD and the software from this book. Finally, you'll need an Internet connection to take full advantage of the support offerings from Autodesk.

If you want a more detailed explanation of hardware options with AutoCAD, see Appendix B. You'll find a general description of the available hardware options and their significance to AutoCAD.

**TIP**    If you don't have AutoCAD, you can download a trial version from the Autodesk website. Go to the Autodesk home page, and follow the links to AutoCAD. The trial download is approximately 1.8GB, so be prepared to wait a while to complete the download. Also be aware that the trial is good for only 30 days—don't start to use it until you're certain you'll have plenty of free time to practice using AutoCAD.

## Doing Things in Style

Much care has been taken to see that the stylistic conventions in this book—the use of uppercase or lowercase letters, italic or boldface type, and so on—are the ones most likely to help you learn AutoCAD. On the whole, their effect should be subliminal. However, you may find it useful to be conscious of the following rules:

- Drop-down menu selections are shown by a series of options separated by the ➤ symbol (for example, choose File ➤ New).

- Keyboard entries are shown in boldface (for example, enter **Rotate**).

- Command-line prompts are shown in a monospaced font (for example, `Select objects:`).

For most functions, this book describes how to select options from toolbars and the menu bar. In addition, where applicable, I include related keyboard shortcuts and command names in parentheses. These command names provide continuity for readers accustomed to working at the Command prompt.

## New Features of AutoCAD 2008

AutoCAD has a fresh new look and several new features that will help make your work easier and faster. If you've used AutoCAD before, you'll notice that the look has changed. Dig a little deeper, and you'll find that some new features have been added to simplify your work so you don't have to keep track of so many details. Here are some of the new features you'll be covering in this book:

- New Dashboard interface that puts most of the tools you need in a single panel

- Annotation scale that simplifies the scale of text and other graphics to fit the scale of your drawing

- New Daylight lighting feature to create more realistic outdoor renderings of your 3D models

- Better links between AutoCAD tables and external spreadsheets

- Improved text-editing tools and features

## Contact the Author

I hope that *Mastering AutoCAD 2008 and AutoCAD LT 2008* will be of benefit to you and that, after you've completed the tutorials, you'll continue to use the book as a reference. If you have comments, criticisms, or ideas about how the book can be improved, you can e-mail me at the following address:

`george.omura@gmail.com`

If you find errors, please let my publisher know. At `www.sybex.com`, navigate to the catalog page for this book, and click the Errata link to find a form on which you can identify the problem. And thanks for choosing *Mastering AutoCAD 2008 and AutoCAD LT 2008*.

# Part 1

# The Basics

**In this part:**
- Chapter 1: Exploring the AutoCAD and AutoCAD LT Interface
- Chapter 2: Creating Your First Drawing
- Chapter 3: Setting Up and Using AutoCAD's Drafting Tools
- Chapter 4: Organizing Objects with Blocks and Groups
- Chapter 5: Keeping Track of Layers, Blocks, and Files

# Chapter 1

# Exploring the AutoCAD and AutoCAD LT Interface

Before you can start to use AutoCAD 2008's new capabilities, you'll need to become familiar with the basics. If you're completely new to AutoCAD, you'll want to read this first chapter carefully. It introduces you to many of AutoCAD's basic operations, such as opening and closing files, getting a close-up look at part of a drawing, and changing a drawing. If you're familiar with earlier versions of AutoCAD, you should review this chapter anyway to get acquainted with features you haven't already used.

Autodesk has recently changed its AutoCAD update strategy to release new versions every year. Part of this strategy is to introduce new items that focus on a particular category of features. This latest version, AutoCAD 2008, includes several new features focused on 2D drafting. AutoCAD now sports a new tool panel called a *dashboard* which includes the most common tools needed to produce technical drawings of all types. The ability to setup the scale of drawings has been improved and there are more learning resources at your fingertips.

You'll get a chance to explore these new features in Part 4 as you work through this book; but for now, let's get started with some basics.

Topics in this chapter:

- ◆ Using the AutoCAD Window
- ◆ Opening an Existing File
- ◆ Getting a Closer Look with the Zoom Command
- ◆ Saving a File as You Work
- ◆ Making Changes and Opening Multiple Files

**TIP** In this chapter, and throughout the rest of the book, when I say AutoCAD, I mean both AutoCAD and AutoCAD LT. Some topics apply only to AutoCAD. In those situations, you'll see an icon indicating that the topic applies only to AutoCAD and doesn't apply to AutoCAD LT. If you're using AutoCAD 2008 LT, these icons can help you focus on the topics that are more relevant to your work.

## Taking a Guided Tour

In this section, you'll get a chance to familiarize yourself with the AutoCAD screen and how you communicate with AutoCAD. As you do the exercises in this chapter, you'll also get a feel for how to work with this book. Don't worry about understanding or remembering everything you see in this chapter. You'll get plenty of opportunities to probe the finer details of the program as you work through the later chapters. To help you remember the material, you'll find a brief exercise at the end of each chapter. For now, just enjoy your first excursion into AutoCAD.

**NOTE**    AutoCAD 2008 is designed to run on Windows 2000, Windows XP and Windows Vista. This book was written using AutoCAD 2008 on Windows XP Professional with a Windows Classic desktop theme.

If you already installed AutoCAD and are ready to jump in and take a look, proceed with the following steps to launch the program:

1. Choose Start ➤ All Programs ➤ Autodesk ➤ AutoCAD 2008 ➤ AutoCAD 2008. You can also double-click the AutoCAD 2008 icon on your Windows Desktop. LT users will use AutoCAD LT 2008 in place of AutoCAD 2008.

2. The opening greeting, called a *splash screen,* tells you which version of AutoCAD you're using, to whom the program is registered, and the AutoCAD dealer's name and phone number, should you need help. If this is the first time you've started AutoCAD after installing it, you'll also see a dialog box asking you to register the product.

3. After the splash screen closes, you see the Workspace screen. (You won't see this in LT.) This screen allows you to select between the 2D drawing workspace called 2D Drafting & Annotation and the 3D workspace called 3D Modeling. A third option called AutoCAD Classic offers the 2D drawing workspace from earlier versions of AutoCAD. Workspaces are saved arrangements of the AutoCAD window. You'll explore the 3D Modeling workspace in Part 4.

4. You may also see the New Features Workshop screen, which offers a set of tutorials showing you the new features of AutoCAD 2008. Click the No, Don't Show Me This Again or Maybe Later radio button, and click OK. You can always get to the New Features Workshop screen from the AutoCAD help menu by choosing Help ➤ New Features Workshop.

5. The AutoCAD window displays a blank default document named `Drawing1.dwg`, as shown in Figure 1.1. AutoCAD users may see the Sheet Set Manager palette to the left of the AutoCAD window, which doesn't appear in Figure 1.1, to show more of the drawing area. LT users may see the Info palette to the left of the AutoCAD window.

**FIGURE 1.1**

A typical arrangement of the elements in the AutoCAD window. The Sheet Set Manager palette (or Info palette for LT) is closed for clarity.

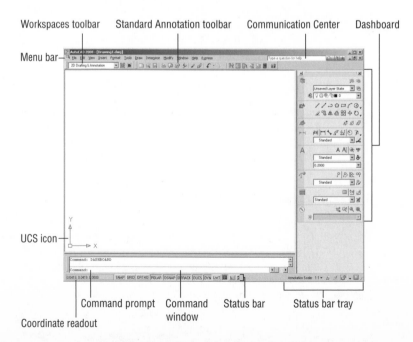

Workspaces toolbar    Standard Annotation toolbar    Communication Center    Dashboard

Menu bar

UCS icon

Command prompt    Command window    Status bar    Status bar tray

Coordinate readout

If this is the first time you've started AutoCAD since you installed it, you're asked to register and authorize AutoCAD in step 2. If you're using the Trial version, you can use the default serial number 000-00000000 for the one-month trial. After you've entered the registration information, you see the New Features Workshop window described in step 4.

Let's look at the AutoCAD window in detail. Don't worry if it seems like a lot of information. You don't have to memorize it, but by looking at all the parts, you'll be aware of what is available in a general way.

---

**IF YOUR AUTOCAD WINDOW DOESN'T LOOK LIKE FIGURE 1.1**

As you saw in step 3 in the opening exercise, you have a choice between three workspaces when you start AutoCAD. If you didn't see the Workspace screen, and your drawing opens to a 3D Modeling workspace (see Figure 1.2, later in this chapter), do the following to get to the 2D Drafting & Annotation workspace:

1. Click the Workspaces list in the upper-left corner of the AutoCAD window, and select 2D Drafting & Annotation. LT users can select 2D Drafting & Annotation from the floating Workspaces toolbar.

2. AutoCAD users, choose File ➢ New. Then, in the Select Template dialog box, choose acad.dwt and click Open. LT users can skip this step.

If you did step 2, the default filename is Drawing2.dwg instead of Drawing1.dwg. Aside from that, your AutoCAD window will look similar to Figure 1.1, which shows AutoCAD in a moderate resolution screen.

## The AutoCAD Window

The AutoCAD program window is divided into six parts:

◆ Menu bar

◆ Toolbars

◆ Drawing area

◆ Command window

◆ Status bar

◆ Dashboard

Figure 1.1, shown earlier in this chapter, shows a typical layout of the AutoCAD program window. Along the top is the *menu bar,* and just below that are the Workspaces and Standard Annotation toolbars. At the bottom are the *Command window* and the *status bar.* To the right is the Dashboard. The *drawing area* occupies the rest of the screen. AutoCAD calls the window layout a *workspace;* you can save and recall a workspace at any time using the Workspaces toolbar. The workspace in Figure 1.1 is called the 2D Drafting & Annotation workspace.

**TIP**    Your screen may show the drawing area in black. You can set the drawing area background color by using the Options dialog box. Appendix A describes how to do this. The figures in this book show the drawing area background in white for clarity.

Figure 1.2 shows AutoCAD's 3D Modeling workspace, which has a different set of screen elements. Figure 1.2 also shows a standard AutoCAD drawing file with a few setting changes to give it a 3D appearance. Beneath these external changes, the underlying program is the same.

**TIP**    You'll learn more about workspaces later in this chapter and in Chapter 26.

**FIGURE 1.2**

The 3D Modeling workspace offers an alternative arrangement of the elements in the AutoCAD window.

The menu bar at the top of the drawing area (as shown in Figure 1.3) includes drop-down menus from which you select commands in a typical Windows fashion. The toolbars and Dashboard provide a variety of commands through tool buttons and drop-down lists.

**FIGURE 1.3**

The menu bar, the Workspaces toolbar, and the Standard Annotation toolbar. LT users may see a floating Workspaces toolbar instead of the docked version shown at far right.

The drawing area occupies most of the screen. Everything you draw appears in this area. As you move your mouse around, crosshairs appear to move within the drawing area. This is the drawing cursor that lets you point to locations in the drawing area.

At the bottom of the drawing area is a set of tabs. These tabs give you access to the Layout views of your drawing. These views let you lay out your drawing as in a desktop publishing program. You'll learn about the Layout tabs in Chapter 8. The arrows to the left of the tabs let you navigate the tabs when there are more tabs than can fit in the AutoCAD window.

---

**TURNING ON THE TABS**

If you don't see the tabs, don't worry. AutoCAD can be set up to hide the tabs, but you can easily restore them to view. To turn them on, locate the Model tool in the status bar at the bottom of the AutoCAD window.

Right-click the Model tool, and then select Display Layout and Model Tabs. The tabs will appear just below the drawing area. To hide the tabs, right-click any tab, and select Hide Layout and Model Tabs.

---

The Command window, located just below the Layout tabs, gives you feedback about AutoCAD's commands as you use them. You can move and resize this window just as you move and resize toolbars. By default, the Command window is in its docked position, as shown in Figure 1.4.

**FIGURE 1.4**

The Command window and the status bar

Below the Command window is the status bar (see Figure 1.4). The status bar gives you information at a glance about the state of the drawing. For example, the coordinate readout toward the far left of the status bar tells you the location of your cursor.

### PICKING POINTS IN THE DRAWING AREA

Now that you've seen the general layout of AutoCAD, try using the coordinate readout and the drawing cursor to get a sense of how the parts of the AutoCAD screen work together:

1. Move the cursor around in the drawing area. As you move it, notice how the coordinate readout changes to tell you the cursor's location. It shows the coordinates in an X, Y, Z format.

2. Place the cursor in the middle of the drawing area, and click the left mouse button. Move the cursor, and a rectangle follows. This is a *window selection;* you'll learn more about this window in Chapter 2. You also see a coordinate readout following the cursor and a message asking you to Specify opposite corner:. This display at the cursor is called the *dynamic input.* You'll learn more about it a little later in this chapter.

**TIP**    If you don't see the dynamic input display, click the button labeled DYN in the status bar to turn it on.

3. Move the cursor a bit in any direction; then, click the left mouse button again. Notice that the window selection disappears, as does the dynamic input display.

4. Try picking several more points in the drawing area. Notice that as you click the mouse, you alternately start and end a window selection.

If you happen to click the right mouse button, a shortcut menu appears. A right-click frequently opens a menu containing options that are *context sensitive.* This means the contents of the shortcut menu depend on the location where you right-click as well as the command that is active at the time of your right-click. If there are no appropriate options at the time of the right-click, AutoCAD treats the right-click as an ↵. You'll learn more about these options as you progress through the book. For now, if you happen to open this menu by accident, press the Esc key to close it.

### THE UCS ICON

In the lower-left corner of the drawing area, you see an L-shaped arrow. This is the *User Coordinate System (UCS)* icon, which tells you your orientation in the drawing. This icon becomes helpful as you start to work with complex 2D drawings and 3D models. The X and Y arrows indicate the X and Y axes of your drawing. The little square at the base of the arrows tells you that you're in what is called the *World Coordinate System.* Chapter 21 discusses this icon in detail. For now, you can use it as a reference to tell you the direction of the axes.

---

### IF YOU CAN'T FIND THE UCS ICON

The UCS icon can be turned on and off, so if you're on someone else's system and you don't see the icon, don't panic. If you don't see the icon or it doesn't look as it does in this chapter, see Chapter 21 for more information.

---

#### THE COMMAND WINDOW

At the bottom of the screen, just above the status bar, is a small horizontal window called the *Command window*. Here, AutoCAD displays responses to your input. By default, it shows two lines of text. The bottom line shows the current messages, and the top line shows messages that have scrolled by or, in some cases, components of the current message that don't fit in a single line. Right now, the bottom line displays the message Command (see Figure 1.4, earlier in this chapter). This *prompt* tells you that AutoCAD is waiting for your instructions. When you click a point in the drawing area, you see the message Specify opposite corner:. At the same time, the cursor starts to draw a window selection that disappears when you click another point. The same message appears in the dynamic input display at the cursor.

As a new user, pay special attention to messages displayed in the Command window and the dynamic input display because this is how AutoCAD communicates with you. Besides giving you messages, the Command window records your activity in AutoCAD. You can use the scroll bar to the right of the Command window to review previous messages. You can also enlarge the window for a better view. (Chapter 2 discusses these components in more detail.)

Now, let's look at AutoCAD's window components in detail.

**TIP**   The Command window and the dynamic input display allow AutoCAD to provide text feedback to your actions. You can think of these features as a chat window to AutoCAD—as you enter commands, AutoCAD responds with messages. As you become more familiar with AutoCAD, you may find you don't need to rely on the Command window and dynamic input display as much. For new and casual users, however, the Command window and dynamic input display can be helpful in understanding what steps to take as you work.

## The Drop-Down Menus

As in most Windows programs, the drop-down menus on the menu bar provide an easy-to-understand way to access AutoCAD's general controls and settings. In these menus, you'll find the commands and functions that are the heart of AutoCAD. By clicking menu items, you can cut and paste items to and from AutoCAD, change the settings that make AutoCAD work the way you want it to, set up the measurement system you want to use, access the help system, and much more.

The drop-down menu options perform three basic functions:

◆ Display a dialog box that contains settings you can change.

◆ Issue a command to create or modify your drawing.

◆ Offer an expanded set of the same tools found in the Draw and Modify toolbars.

As you point to commands and options in the menus, AutoCAD provides additional help for you in the form of brief descriptions of each menu option, which appear in the status bar.

Here's an exercise to let you practice with the drop-down menus and get acquainted with the way you issue AutoCAD commands:

1. Click View in the menu bar. The list of items that appears includes the commands and settings that let you control the way AutoCAD displays your drawings. Don't worry if you don't understand them yet; you'll get to know them in later chapters.

**WARNING**   LT users won't see the Render option in the View menu.

2. Move the highlight cursor slowly down the list of menu items. As you highlight each item, notice that a description of it appears in the status bar at the bottom of the AutoCAD window. These descriptions help you choose the menu option you need.

**TIP**   If you look carefully at the command descriptions in the status bar, you'll see an odd word at the end. This is the keyboard command equivalent to the highlighted option in the menu or toolbar. You can type these keyboard commands to start the tool or menu item that you're pointing to. You don't have to memorize these command names, but knowing them will be helpful to you later if you want to customize AutoCAD.

3. Some of the menu items have triangular pointers to their right. This means the command has additional choices. For instance, highlight the Zoom item, and another set of options appears to the right. This second set of options is called a *cascading menu*. Whenever you see a drop-down menu item with the triangular pointer, you know that this item opens a cascading menu offering a more detailed set of options.

4. Other drop-down menu options are followed by an ellipsis (…). This indicates that the option displays a dialog box. For instance, move the highlight cursor to the Tools option in the menu bar.

**TIP**   If you prefer, you can click and drag the highlight cursor over the drop-down menu to select an option.

**ACAD only**

**5.** Click the Draw option from the menu bar, and then click the Rectangle command. Notice that the Command window now shows the following prompt:

```
Specify first corner point or [Chamfer/Elevation/Fillet/Thickness/Width]:
```

AutoCAD is asking you to select the first corner for the rectangle, and, in brackets, it's offering a few options that you can take advantage of at this point in the command. Don't worry about those options right now. You'll have an opportunity to learn about command options in Chapter 2. You also see the same prompt, minus the bracketed options, in the dynamic input display at the cursor.

**6.** Click a point roughly in the lower-left corner of the drawing area, as shown in Figure 1.5. Now, as you move your mouse, a rectangle follows the cursor, with one corner fixed at the position you just selected. You also see the following prompt in the Command window, with a similar prompt in the dynamic input display:

```
Specify other corner point or [Area/Dimensions/Rotation]:
```

**FIGURE 1.5**

Selecting the first point of a rectangle

**7.** Click another point anywhere in the upper-right region of the drawing area. A rectangle appears (see Figure 1.6). You'll learn more about the different cursor shapes and what they mean in Chapter 2.

At this point, you've seen how most of AutoCAD's commands work. Many drawing and editing functions display messages in the Command window. These messages are also displayed in the dynamic input display. You'll find that dialog boxes are displayed when you want to change settings. Also, be aware that many of the drop-down menu items are duplicated in the toolbars, which you'll explore next.

**FIGURE 1.6**

After you've selected
the first point of the
rectangle, you see
a rectangle follow the
motion of your mouse.

## COMMUNICATING WITH THE COMMAND WINDOW AND DYNAMIC INPUT DISPLAY

AutoCAD is the perfect servant: It does everything you tell it to, and no more. You communicate with AutoCAD by using the drop-down menus and the toolbars. These devices invoke AutoCAD commands. A *command* is a single-word instruction you give to AutoCAD, telling it to do something, such as draw a line (the Line tool in the Draw toolbar) or erase an object (the Erase tool in the Modify toolbar). Whenever you invoke a command, by either typing it or selecting a menu or toolbar item, AutoCAD responds by presenting messages to you in the Command window and the dynamic input display or by displaying a dialog box.

The messages in the Command window often tell you what to do next, or they display a list of options, usually shown in square brackets. A single command often presents a series of messages, which you answer to complete the command. These messages serve as an aid to new users who need a little help. If you ever get lost while using a command or forget what you're supposed to do, look at the Command window for clues. As you become more comfortable with AutoCAD, you'll find that you won't need to refer to these messages as frequently.

As an additional aid, you can right-click to display a context-sensitive shortcut menu. If you're in the middle of a command, this menu displays a list of options specifically related to that command. For example, if you right-click your mouse before picking the first point for the rectangle command in the previous exercise, a menu opens, displaying the same options that are listed in the Command prompt plus some additional options.

Finally, the dynamic input display allows you to enter dimensional data of objects as you draw them. Besides echoing the command-line messages, the dynamic input display shows the coordinates and angles of objects you're drawing and editing. As you enter coordinate or angle values through the keyboard, they appear in the dynamic input display. If you're used to earlier versions of AutoCAD, you can easily turn off the dynamic input display by clicking the DYN button in the status bar. When the dynamic input display is turned off, your keyboard input appears in the Command window.

## The Dashboard

The menu bar provides most of the commands you need in a format that most Windows users will find easy to understand, and many users are more comfortable using the menu bar. If you prefer using toolbars with their graphic icons, you can start to use the Dashboard. The Dashboard offers many of the same commands as the menu bar but in a more compact format that is quicker to access.

The Dashboard is a collection of lists, buttons, and tools that invoke commands. These tools are grouped into eight *control panels*, each with an icon that shows its function (see Figure 1.7). In typical Windows fashion, each tool offers a *ToolTip* that provides a short description, which helps you understand what the icons represent.

**FIGURE 1.7**

The control panels of the Dashboard

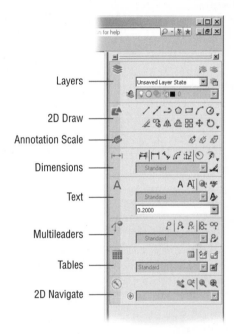

Layers

2D Draw

Annotation Scale

Dimensions

Text

Multileaders

Tables

2D Navigate

**NOTE**  If the Dashboard doesn't appear on the screen, you can choose Tools ➤ Palettes ➤ Dashboard to restore it to the window.

If you move the arrow cursor onto one of the control-panel tools and leave it there for a moment, you'll see a ToolTip appear just below the cursor. As a new user, you'll find these ToolTips helpful because they show you the name of the tool. In addition, when I ask you to select a tool, I'll use the name shown in the ToolTip. For example, if you hover over the icon in the upper-left corner of the Dashboard, you'll see a ToolTip appear with the name of the control panel, 2D Draw.

Take a moment to examine the top portion of the Dashboard where the 2D Draw control panel resides. You'll be instructed to use the tools in this control panel frequently throughout the early part of this book, so it will be helpful for you to get a feel for their arrangement and what they contain. You'll get a closer look at the Dashboard and control panels in Chapter 2.

In addition to the visible tools, a few tools are hidden from view. You can expand the list of tools to select more tools. Click and hold the downward-pointing arrow to the far right of the row of tools (see Figure 1.8). The set of tools expands into a fly-out toolbar. While continuing to hold down the mouse button, you can point to the tool you want in the fly-out toolbar and then release the mouse.

**FIGURE 1.8**
Click and hold the downward-pointing arrow to open the fly-out toolbar.

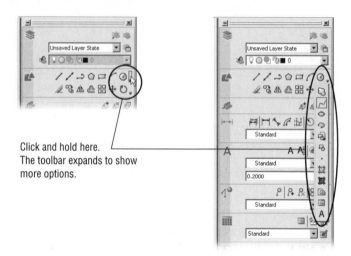

Click and hold here.
The toolbar expands to show more options.

In most cases, you'll be able to guess what each tool does by looking at its icon. The icon with an arc in the 2D Draw control panel, for instance, indicates that the tool draws arcs; the one with the circle shows that the tool draws circles; and so on. For further clarification, the ToolTip gives you the name of the tool.

## The Toolbars

The menu bar and Dashboard offer the most frequently used tools, but you'll eventually find that you need to use a set of tools geared toward a specific task. AutoCAD offers a number of toolbars that contain tools for specific types of drawing functions. For example, the View toolbar offers a set of tools that quickly give you a 3D view. The Inquiry toolbar contains tools that display information about your drawing.

AutoCAD displays the Workspaces and Standard Annotation toolbars in its default 2D Drafting & Annotation workspace. As you work though this book, occasionally you'll be asked to open other toolbars. To get familiar with the process, try opening a one now.

1. Right-click the Workspaces or Standard Annotation toolbar. A shortcut menu of toolbars appears, displaying a long list of toolbars, as shown in Figure 1.9.

2. Locate and select View in the shortcut menu (see Figure 1.9). The View toolbar appears.

**FIGURE 1.9**

The toolbar shortcut menu

**3.** You won't need the View toolbar right now, so go ahead and close it by clicking the X in the upper-right corner of the toolbar.

You may have noticed that the shortcut menu displays a check mark next to the name of a toolbar that is currently open (see Figure 1.9). You can click a checked toolbar name to close the toolbar. AutoCAD remembers your toolbar arrangement between sessions. When you exit and then reopen AutoCAD later, the AutoCAD window appears just as you left it.

**NOTE**  If your drawing becomes too cluttered with toolbars, you can drag a toolbar to the border of the AutoCAD window, and it will automatically merge with the border. This is called its *docked* position. If you don't want the toolbar to dock but instead want it to appear floating near the border of the AutoCAD window, you can do the following: First, change the shape of the toolbar to conform to the orientation of the border. Do this by clicking and dragging the toolbar's border. Next, press and hold the Ctrl key as you click and drag the toolbar into position near the border. This prevents the toolbar from automatically falling into a docked position.

---

### MENUS VERSUS THE KEYBOARD

Throughout this book, you'll be told to select commands and command options from the drop-down menus and toolbars. For new and experienced users alike, menus and toolbars offer an easy-to-remember method for accessing commands. If you're an experienced AutoCAD user who is used to the earlier versions of AutoCAD, you can type commands directly from the keyboard. Most of the keyboard commands you know and love still work as they did.

Another method for accessing commands is to use *accelerator keys,* which are special keystrokes that open and activate drop-down menu options. You may have noticed that the commands in the menu bar and the items in the drop-down menus all have an underlined character. By pressing the Alt key followed by the key corresponding to the underlined character, you activate that command or option without having to engage the mouse. For example, to choose File ➢ Open, press Alt, then F, and then finally O (Alt+F+O).

Many tools and commands have keyboard shortcuts; *shortcuts* are one-, two-, or three-letter abbreviations of a command name. As you become more proficient with AutoCAD, you may find these shortcuts helpful. As you work through this book, the shortcuts will be identified for your reference.

Finally, if you're feeling adventurous, you can create your own accelerator keys and keyboard shortcuts for executing commands by adding them to the AutoCAD support files. Chapter 25 discusses how to customize menus, toolbars, and keyboard shortcuts.

### SAVING YOUR PREFERRED WORKSPACE

You may find that you prefer a specific arrangement of toolbars that you'd like to be able to recall at will. You can rearrange the toolbars and then save the arrangement as a named *workspace*. Doing so can be useful if you must share your AutoCAD workstation with someone else who prefers their own AutoCAD window layout or if you want to set up different arrangements for different types of work. For example, you might want to save the current AutoCAD window layout with the Tool palettes out of the way, while someone else prefers the default AutoCAD setup. To save the current setup under a new name, do the following:

1. In the Workspaces toolbar, click in the drop-down list, and select Save Current As to open the Save Workspace dialog box.

2. Enter **My Custom Layout** in the text box, and click Save. The current arrangement of AutoCAD components is saved under the name My Custom Layout.

3. To recall a workspace, select the name of the saved workspace from the drop-down list in the Workspaces toolbar.

You may have noticed a house icon in the Workspaces toolbar. This is the My Workspace tool, which offers a quick way to restore your favorite workspace. You can customize the My Workspace tool to recall any AutoCAD window layout you like. You'll learn more about creating and customizing workspaces in Chapter 26.

# Working with AutoCAD

Now that you've been introduced to the AutoCAD window, you're ready to try using a few AutoCAD commands. First, you'll open a sample file and make a few modifications to it. In the process, you'll become familiar with some common methods of operation in AutoCAD.

## Opening an Existing File

In this exercise, you'll get a chance to see and use a typical Select File dialog box. To start, you'll open an existing file:

1. From the menu bar, choose File ➢ Close. A message appears, asking whether you want to save the changes you've made to the current drawing. Click No.

**2.** Choose File ➢ Open to open the Select File dialog box. This is a typical Windows file dialog box, with an added twist: The large Preview box on the right lets you preview a drawing before you open it, thereby saving time while searching for files. To the left is a panel known as the Places List in which you can find frequently used locations on your computer or the Internet.

**TIP** If you don't see a Preview box in the Select File dialog box, click the word Views in the upper-right corner, and then select Preview from the list that appears.

**3.** In the Select File dialog box, open the Look In drop-down list, and locate the 2008acad2008\samplefiles\Mastering AutoCAD 2008\Projects\Chapters 01 folder. (You may need to explore the list to find it.) The file list changes to show the contents of the \AutoCAD 2008\Projects\Chapter 01 folder.

**4.** Move the arrow cursor to the clip.dwg file, and click it. Notice that the clip.dwg filename now appears in the File Name input box above the file list. Also, the Preview box now shows a thumbnail image of the file. Be aware that files from older versions of AutoCAD may not show a thumbnail.

**TIP** The clip.dwg drawing is included on the companion website. If you can't find this file, be sure you installed the sample drawings from the companion website. See the Readme file on the book's website for installation instructions.

**5.** Click the Open button at the bottom of the Select File dialog box. AutoCAD opens the clip.dwg file, as shown in Figure 1.10.

The clip.dwg file opens to display a Layout tab view of the drawing. You'll know this by looking at the tabs at the bottom of the AutoCAD window. Currently, the Layout1 tab is highlighted.

**FIGURE 1.10**
The Layout1 view of
the `clip.dwg` file

You may recall that a *layout* is a type of view that lets you lay out different views of your drawing in preparation for printing. Also notice that the AutoCAD window's title bar displays the name of the drawing. This offers easy identification of the file.

This particular file contains both 2D drawings and a 3D model of a typical locking clip. The Layout1 tab view shows a top, front, and right-side view as well as an isometric view.

## Getting a Closer Look

One of the most frequently used commands is Zoom, which gives you a closer look at part of your drawing. This command offers a variety of ways to control your view. In this section, you'll enlarge a portion of the clip drawing to get a more detailed look. To tell AutoCAD which area you want to enlarge, you use what is called a *zoom window*.

You'll start by switching to a Model Space view of the drawing. The Model tab places you in a workspace where you do most of your drawing creation and editing. Follow these steps:

1. Click the Model tab at the bottom of the AutoCAD window.

Your view changes to show the full 3D model with the 2D representations of the model.

**2.** Choose View ➢ 3D Views ➢ Plan View ➢ World UCS. You can also type **PLAN↵W↵**. Your display changes to a two-dimensional view looking down on the drawing, as shown in the top image of Figure 1.11.

Click the Zoom Window button on the Standard toolbar.

You can also choose View ➢ Zoom ➢ Window from the drop-down menu or type the command **Z↵W↵**.

**3.** The Command window and the dynamic input display show the Specify first corner: prompt. Look at the top image in Figure 1.11. Move the crosshair cursor to a location similar to the one shown in the figure; then, left-click the mouse. Move the cursor, and the rectangle appears with one corner fixed on the point you just picked; the other corner follows the cursor.

**4.** The Command window and dynamic input display now show the Specify first corner: and Specify opposite corner: prompts. Position the other corner of the zoom window so it encloses the lower image of the clip, as shown in the top image in Figure 1.11, and left-click the mouse again. The clip enlarges to fill the screen (see the bottom image in Figure 1.11).

In this exercise, you used the Window option of the Zoom command to define an area to enlarge for your close-up view. You saw how AutoCAD prompts you to indicate first one corner of the window selection and then the other. These messages are helpful for first-time users of AutoCAD. You'll use the Window option frequently—not just to define views, but also to select objects for editing.

**FIGURE 1.11**

Placing the zoom window around the clip

Click here for the first corner.          Click here for the opposite corner.

Getting a close-up view of your drawing is crucial to working accurately, but you'll often want to return to a previous view to get the overall picture. To do so, choose View ➤ Zoom ➤ Previous from the menu bar.

Do this now, and the previous view—the one showing the entire clip—returns to the screen.

You can quickly enlarge or reduce your view by clicking the Zoom Realtime button in the 2D Navigate control panel. Follow these steps to change your view with the Zoom Realtime button:

1. Click the Zoom Realtime button on the 2D Navigate control panel of the Dashboard.

You can also right-click and choose Zoom from the shortcut menu. The cursor changes to a magnifying glass.

2. Place the Zoom Realtime cursor slightly above the center of the drawing area, and then click and drag downward. Your view zooms out to show more of the drawing.

3. While still holding the left mouse button, move the cursor upward. Your view zooms in to enlarge your view. When you have a view similar to the one shown in Figure 1.12, release the mouse button. (Don't worry if you don't get *exactly* the same view as the figure. This is just for practice.)

4. You're still in Zoom Realtime mode. Click and drag the mouse again to see how you can further adjust your view. To exit, you can select another command besides a Zoom or Pan, press the Esc key, or right-click your mouse and choose Exit from the shortcut menu.

5. Right-click now, and choose Exit from the shortcut menu to exit the Zoom Realtime command.

**FIGURE 1.12**
The final view you want to achieve in step 3 of the exercise

As you can see from this exercise, you have a wide range of options for viewing your drawings, just by using a few buttons. These buttons are all you need to control the display of 2D drawings.

## Saving a File as You Work

It's a good idea to save your file periodically as you work on it. As with any Windows program, you can save it under its original name (choose File ➢ Save) or under a different name (choose File ➢ Save As), thereby creating a new file.

By default, AutoCAD automatically saves your work at 10-minute intervals under a name that is a combination of the current filename plus a number and that ends with the .sv$ filename extension; this is known as the *Automatic Save* feature. Using settings in the Options dialog box or system variables, you can change the name of the autosaved file and control the time between autosaves. See Chapter 3 for details.

**TIP**  By default, in Windows XP, the Automatic Save file is stored in C:\Documents and Settings\ *User Name*\Local Settings\Temp\. You can find the exact location for your system by typing **Savefilepath**⏎ at the Command prompt. This file location is often set as a hidden folder, so you may need to set up Windows Explorer to display hidden folders before you can get to the Automatic Save file. See Appendix A for information on how to do this.

## Making Changes

You'll frequently make changes to your drawings. One of AutoCAD's primary advantages is the ease with which you can make changes. The following exercise shows you a typical sequence of operations involved in changing a drawing:

1. Use the File ➢ Save As menu option to save the current Clip.dwg file under the name **MyFirst**. For convenience, you can save your files in the My Documents folder.

2. From the 2D Draw control panel, click the Erase tool (the one with a pencil eraser touching paper). This activates the Erase command. You can also choose Modify ➢ Erase from the drop-down menu.

   Notice that the cursor has turned into a small square; this square is called the *pickbox.* You also see Select objects: in the Command window and the dynamic input display. This message helps remind new users what to do.

3. Move the pickbox over the drawing, placing it on various parts of the clip. Don't click anything yet. Notice that as you hover over objects with the pickbox, they're highlighted. This helps you see the objects the pickbox is likely to select, should you click the left mouse button.

4. Place the pickbox on the crosshatch pattern of the clip (see Figure 1.13), and click. The crosshatch changes in appearance from a dark highlight to a light highlight. The pickbox and the Select objects: prompt remain, indicating that you can continue to select objects.

5. Press ⏎. The crosshatch disappears. You've just erased a part of the drawing.

In this exercise, you first issued the Erase command, and then you selected an object by using a pickbox to click it. The pickbox tells you that you must select items on the screen, and it shows you what you're about to select by highlighting objects as you hover over them. Once you've clicked an object or a set of objects, press ⏎ to move on to the next step. This sequence of steps is common to many of the commands you'll work with in AutoCAD.

**TIP**  You can also click an object or a set of objects and then press the Delete key without using the Erase tool.

**FIGURE 1.13**
Erasing a portion
of the clip

Click here.

## Opening Multiple Files

You can have multiple documents open at the same time in AutoCAD. This can be especially help-ful if you want to exchange parts of drawings between files or if you want another file open for reference. Try the following exercise to see how multiple documents work in AutoCAD:

1. Choose File ➢ New to open the Select Template dialog box.

**NOTE** If you see the Create New Drawing dialog box after step 1, click the Start from Scratch but-ton and select Imperial; then, click OK, and AutoCAD will display a default document. You'll learn more about the Create New Drawing dialog box in Chapter 2.

2. Make sure acad.dwt is selected, and then click Open.

3. Choose Window ➢ Tile Vertically to get a view of both drawing files. The options in the Window drop-down menu act just like their counterparts in other Windows programs that allow multiple-document editing.

**TIP** When you create a new file in AutoCAD, you're actually opening a copy of a template file, as you saw in step 1. A *template file* is a blank file that is set up for specific drawing types. The acad.dwt file is a generic template set up for Imperial measurements. Another template file called acadiso.dwt is a generic template useful for metric measurements. Other templates are set up for specific drawing-sheet sizes and measurement systems. You'll learn more about tem-plates in Chapter 6.

4. Let's see what can be done with these two files. Click in the window with the clip drawing to make it active.

5. Choose View ➢ Zoom ➢ All to get an overall view of the drawing.

6. Click the 2D version of the clip at the bottom of the drawing to select it. A series of squares and arrows appears on the drawing. These are called *grips*, and you'll learn more about them in the next chapter.

7. Click and hold the mouse button on the selected object, but avoid clicking any of the blue squares. Also avoid dragging the object. You'll see a small rectangle appear next to the cursor.

8. While still holding the left mouse button, drag the cursor to the new file window. When you see the clip appear in the new drawing window, release the mouse button. You've just copied part of a drawing from one file to another.

9. This ends the exercises for this chapter. Save the file and then exit AutoCAD.

**NOTE** You can also use the standard Windows Copy and Paste options (Edit ➢ Copy *and* Edit ➢ Paste from the menu bar) to copy objects from one window to the other.

Now you've had two files open at once. You can have as many files open as you want, as long as your computer has adequate memory to accommodate them. You can control the individual document windows as you would any window, using the Window drop-down menu or the window control buttons in the upper-right corner of the document window.

## Adding a Predrawn Symbol with the Tool Palette

In the preceding exercise, you saw how you can easily copy an object from one file to another by using a click-and-drag method. AutoCAD offers a Tool Palettes window that lets you click and drag predrawn objects into your drawing.

You can open the Tool Palettes window by clicking the Tool Palettes Window tool in the Standard Annotation toolbar. Once it's open, you can select a tab containing the predrawn objects you want to use and then click the specific object you want to add. The object appears at the cursor, ready for you to select a location.

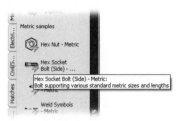

In addition to predrawn objects, the Tool palettes offer a way to quickly add fill patterns and other components to your drawing. They're great tools to help you manage your library of custom, predrawn symbols. Chapter 25 shows you how to use and customize the Tool palettes.

## The Bottom Line

**Using the AutoCAD Window**    AutoCAD is a typical Windows graphics program that makes use of menus, toolbars, and palettes. If you've used other graphics programs, you'll see at least a few familiar tools.

**Master It**    Name the components of the AutoCAD window that let you select a function.

**Solution**    AutoCAD offers the menu bar, toolbars, and the Dashboard to give you access to the most common functions.

**Getting a Closer Look with the Zoom Command**    One of the first things you'll want to learn is how to manipulate your views. The Zoom command is a common tool in graphics programs.

**Master It**    Name two ways of zooming into a view.

**Solution**    Choose View ➢ Zoom ➢ Window, and then click two points to define a zoom window. Another option is to use the Realtime tool in the 2D Navigate control panel.

**Saving a File as You Work**    Nothing is more frustrating than having a power failure cause a loss of hours of work. It's a good idea to save your work frequently. AutoCAD offers an autosave feature that can be a lifesaver if you happen to forget to save your files.

**Master It**    How often does the AutoCAD autosave feature save your drawing?

**Solution**    Autosave saves a copy of a drawing every 10 minutes by default. This interval can be set by the user.

**Making Changes and Opening Multiple Files**    As with other Windows programs, you can have multiple files open and exchange data between them.

**Master It**    With two drawings open, how can you copy parts of one drawing into the other?

**Solution**    Select the parts you want to copy, and click and hold on any selected part. When you see a small rectangle appear below the cursor, drag the parts into the other drawing. Alternately, you can use the standard Windows Copy and Paste functions.

# Chapter 2

# Creating Your First Drawing

This chapter examines some of AutoCAD's basic functions. You'll get a chance to practice with the drawing editor by building a simple drawing to use in later exercises. You'll learn how to give input to AutoCAD, interpret prompts, and get help when you need it. This chapter also covers the use of coordinate systems to give AutoCAD exact measurements for objects. You'll see how to select objects you've drawn and how to specify base points for moving and copying.

If you're not a beginning AutoCAD user, you may want to move on to the more complex material in Chapter 3. You can use the files supplied on the companion website to continue the tutorials at that point.

Topics in this chapter include the following:

◆ Getting to Know the 2D Draw Control Panel

◆ Starting Your First Drawing

◆ Specifying Distances with Coordinates

◆ Interpreting the Cursor Modes and Understanding Prompts

◆ Selecting Objects and Editing with Grips

◆ Using Dynamic Input

◆ Getting Help

◆ Displaying Data in a Text Window

◆ Displaying the Properties of an Object

## Getting to Know the 2D Draw Control Panel

Your first task in learning how to draw in AutoCAD is simply to draw a line. But before you begin drawing, take a moment to familiarize yourself with the feature you'll be using more than any other to create objects with AutoCAD: the 2D Draw control panel. Try these steps:

1. Start AutoCAD just as you did in Chapter 1, by choosing Start ➢ All Programs ➢ Autodesk ➢ AutoCAD 2008 ➢ AutoCAD 2008. If you see the Workspace dialog box, select 2D Drafting & Annotation, and click OK. If you see the Startup dialog box, click Cancel to go directly to the default Drawing1 document. If the default Drawing1.dwg file shows a gray 3D workspace, choose File ➢ New, select acad.dwt from the Select Template dialog box, and click Open.

**2.** Make sure the Workspace toolbar shows 2D Drafting & Annotation. If it doesn't, click the Workspace toolbar, and select 2D Drafting & Annotation.

**3.** Close any open palettes except the Dashboard.

**4.** In the AutoCAD window, move the arrow cursor to the Line tool in the 2D Draw control panel, which is near the top of the Dashboard at the far right of the AutoCAD window, and rest it there so that the ToolTip appears.

**5.** Slowly move the arrow cursor to the right over the other tools in the 2D Draw control panel, and read each ToolTip.

In most cases, you'll be able to guess what each tool does by looking at its icon. The icon with an arc, for instance, indicates that the tool draws arcs; the one with the ellipse shows that the tool draws ellipses; and so on. For further clarification, the ToolTip gives you the name of the tool.

You see two rows of tools in the 2D Draw control panel. The top row includes the Draw tools; they correspond to the Draw menu. The lower row contains the Modify tools, which offer many of the same tools from the Modify menu. In Chapter 1, you saw that if you click and hold the downward-pointing arrow to the far right of the rows of tools, the row expands to offer additional tools (see Figure 2.1).

## Starting Your First Drawing

In Chapter 1, you looked at a preexisting sample drawing. This time. you'll begin to draw your own drawing by creating a door that will be used in later exercises. First, though, you must learn how to tell AutoCAD what you want, and, even more important, you must understand what AutoCAD wants from you.

**TIP**   In this chapter, you'll start to see instructions for both Imperial and metric measurement. In general, you'll see the instructions for Imperial measurement first, followed by the metric instructions. You won't be dealing with inches or centimeters yet, however. You're just getting to know the AutoCAD system.

FIGURE 2.1

The 2D Draw control panel tools

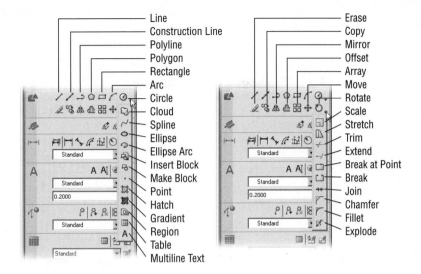

You'll start by opening a new drawing and setting the size of the work area, known as the drawing *limits*. These limits aren't fixed in any way, and you aren't forced to stay within the bounds of the drawing limits, but they can help to establish a starting area from which you can expand your drawing:

1. Choose File ➢ Close to close the current file. In the Save Changes dialog box, click No. Notice that the toolbars disappear. and the AutoCAD drawing window appears blank when no drawings are open.

2. Choose File ➢ New to open the Select Template dialog box.

3. Select the Acad.dwt template, and click Open.

You have a brand-new blank file, but it's a little difficult to tell how big your drawing area is. Next, you'll set up the work area so you have a better idea of the space you're working with:

1. Choose Format ➤ Drawing Limits.

2. At the `Specify lower left corner or [ON/OFF] <0.0000,0.0000>:` prompt, press ↵.

3. At the `Specify upper right corner <12.0000,9.0000>:` prompt, metric users should enter **40,30**↵. If you use Imperial units (feet and inches), then press ↵ to accept the default of 12.0000,9.0000.

4. From the menu bar, choose View ➤ Zoom ➤ All.

In the last step, View ➤ Zoom ➤ All uses the limits you set up in steps 2 and 3 to determine the display area. In a drawing that contains objects, View ➤ Zoom ➤ All displays the limits plus the area occupied by the objects in the drawing if they happen to fall outside the limits. Now give your file a unique name.

1. Choose File ➤ Save As to open the Save Drawing As dialog box.

2. Type **Door**. As you type, the name appears in the File Name text box.

3. Save your file in the `My Documents` folder; or, if you prefer, save it in another folder of your choosing. Just remember where you put it, because you'll use it later.

4. Click Save. You now have a file called `Door.dwg`, located in the `My Documents` folder. Of course, your drawing doesn't contain anything yet. You'll take care of that next.

**WARNING** The new file shows a drawing area roughly 12 inches wide by 9 inches high. Metric users have a file that shows an area roughly 40 mm wide by 30 mm high. This area is your workspace, although you're not limited to it in any way. No visual clues indicate the size of the area. To check the area size for yourself, move the crosshair cursor to the upper-right corner of the drawing area, and observe the value in the coordinate readout in the lower-left corner. The coordinate readout won't show exactly 12 inches by 9 inches, or 40 mm by 30 mm for metric, because the proportions of your drawing area aren't likely to be exactly 12 × 9 or 40 × 30. AutoCAD does try to optimize the display for the drawing area when you choose View ➤ Zoom ➤ All.

You're almost ready to do some drawing. Before you begin, turn off the Dynamic Input display. The Dynamic Input display is a great tool, but while you're learning how to enter coordinates, it can be a distraction:

1. Locate the DYN button in the status bar.

2. Click the DYN button so it's in the up, or off, position.

You'll get a chance to work with Dynamic Input display a bit later in this chapter.
Now you can begin to explore the drawing process. To begin a drawing, follow these steps:

1. Click the Line tool on the 2D Draw control panel, or type **L**↵.

You've just issued the Line command. AutoCAD responds in two ways. First, you see the message

```
Specify first point:
```

in the Command prompt, asking you to select a point to begin your line. Also, the cursor changes its appearance; it no longer has a square in the crosshairs. This is a clue telling you to pick a point to start a line.

**TIP**   Throughout this book, you'll be given the option to use the keyboard shortcuts for commands. For example, in step 1, you were given the option to type **L↵** in the Command window to start the Line command.

2. Using the left mouse button, select a point on the screen near the center. After you select the point, AutoCAD changes the prompt to

```
Specify next point or [Undo]:
```

Now, as you move the mouse around, notice the line with one end fixed on the point you just selected and the other end following the cursor (see the first image in Figure 2.2). This action is called *rubber-banding.*

3. Move the cursor to a location directly to the left or right of the point you clicked, and you'll see a dotted horizontal line appear, along with a message at the cursor. This action also occurs when you point directly up or down. Your cursor seems to jump to a horizontal or vertical position.

This feature is called *Polar Tracking.* Like a T-square or triangle, it helps to restrict your line to an exact horizontal or vertical direction. You can turn Polar Tracking on or off by clicking the Polar button in the status bar. If you don't see it, chances are it's been turned off. You'll learn more about Polar Tracking in Chapter 3.

4. Continue with the Line command: Move the cursor to a point below and to the right of the first point you selected, and click the left mouse button again. The first rubber-banding line is now fixed between the two points you selected, and a second rubber-banding line appears (see the second image in Figure 2.2).

5. If the line you drew isn't the exact length you want, you can back up during the Line command and change it. To do this, type **U↵**. The line you drew previously rubber-bands as if you hadn't selected the second point to fix its length.

**TIP**   The Undo tool in the Standard Annotation toolbar offers an Undo drop-down list from which you can select the exact command you want to undo. See the "Getting Out of Trouble" sidebar in this chapter for more information.

**FIGURE 2.2**
A rubber-banding line

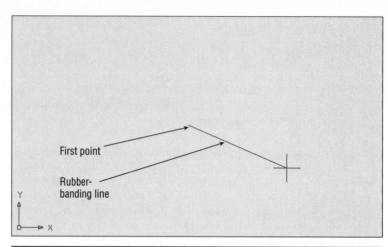

First point

Rubber-
banding line

Y

X

Rubber-
banding line

Line segment

Y

X

You've just drawn, and then undrawn, a line of an arbitrary length. The Line command is still active. Two onscreen clues tell you that you're in the middle of a command. If you don't see the word Command in the bottom line of the Command window, a command is still active. Also, the cursor is the plain crosshair without the box at its intersection.

**TIP**   From now on, I'll refer to the crosshair cursor without the small box as the Point Selection mode of the cursor. If you look ahead to Figure 2.8, you'll see all the modes of the drawing cursor.

## Specifying Distances with Coordinates

Next, you'll continue with the Line command to draw a plan view (an overhead view) of a door, to no particular scale. Later, you'll resize the drawing to use in future exercises. The door will be 3.0 units long and 0.15 units thick. For metric users, the door will be 9 units long and 0.5 units thick. To specify these exact distances in AutoCAD, you can use either relative polar coordinates or Cartesian coordinates.

## GETTING OUT OF TROUBLE

Beginners and experts alike are bound to make a few mistakes. Before you get too far into the tutorial, here are some powerful but easy-to-use tools to help you recover from accidents:

**Backspace**   If you make a typing error, press the Backspace key to back up to your error, and then retype your command or response. The Backspace key is in the upper-right corner of the main keyboard area.

**Escape (Esc)**   This is perhaps the single most important key on your keyboard. When you need to quickly exit a command or a dialog box without making changes, press the Esc key in the upper-left corner of your keyboard. Before AutoCAD 2000, you had to press Esc twice in some instances. In more recent versions, you need to press Esc only once, although it won't hurt to press it twice. (Press Esc before editing with grips or issuing commands through the keyboard.)

**U**   If you accidentally change something in the drawing and want to reverse that change, click the Undo tool in the Standard Annotation toolbar (the left-pointing curved arrow). You can also type U↵ at the Command prompt. Each time you do this, AutoCAD undoes one operation at a time, in reverse order. The last command performed is undone first, then the next-to-last command, and so on. The prompt displays the name of the command being undone, and the drawing reverts to its state prior to that command. If you need to, you can undo everything back to the beginning of an editing session.

**Undo**   If you decide that you want to back up a few steps of an operation you just performed, you can use the Undo tool (the left-pointing curved arrow) in the Standard Annotation toolbar. Or, type Undo↵. Each click of the Undo tool steps you back one operation. You can also select the exact command to back up to by using the Undo drop-down list

You can open the Undo drop-down list by clicking the downward-pointing arrow found to the right of the Undo tool.

**Redo**   If you accidentally undo one too many commands, you can redo the last undone command by clicking the Redo tool (the right-pointing curved arrow) in the Standard Annotation toolbar. Or, type Redo↵. In AutoCAD 2008, you can redo several operations that you may have undone with the Undo command. You can also select the exact command to redo to by using the Redo drop-down list. To open the Redo drop-down list, click the downward-pointing arrow found to the right of the Redo tool

**WARNING** The Imperial and metric distances aren't equivalent in the exercises in this chapter. For example, 3 units in the Imperial-based drawing isn't equal to 9 metric units. These distances are arbitrary and based on how they appear in the figures in this chapter.

## Specifying Polar Coordinates

To enter the exact distance of 3 (or 9 metric) units to the right of the last point you selected, do the following:

1. Type **@3<0**. Metric users should type **@9<0**. As you type, the letters appear at the Command prompt.

2. Press ↵. A line appears, starting from the first point you picked and ending 3 units to the right of it (see Figure 2.3). You've just entered a relative polar coordinate.

**FIGURE 2.3**

Notice that the rubber-banding line now starts from the last point selected. This indicates that you can continue to add more line segments.

Rubber-banding line

Line segment,
3 units in length or
9 units for metric users

The "at" sign (@) you entered tells AutoCAD that the coordinate you're specifying is from the last point you selected. The 3 (or 9 metric) is the distance, and the less-than symbol (<) tells AutoCAD that you're designating the angle at which the line is to be drawn. The last part is the value for the angle, which in this case is 0 for 0°. This is how to use polar coordinates to communicate distances and directions to AutoCAD.

**TIP** If you're accustomed to a different method for describing directions, you can set AutoCAD to use a vertical direction or downward direction as 0°. See Chapter 3 for details.

Angles are given based on the system shown in Figure 2.4, in which 0° is a horizontal direction from left to right, 90° is straight up, 180° is horizontal from right to left, and so on. You can specify degrees, minutes, and seconds of arc if you want to be that exact. I'll discuss angle formats in more detail in Chapter 3.

## Specifying Relative Cartesian Coordinates

For the next line segment, let's try another method for specifying exact distances:

1. Enter **@0,0.15**↵. Metric users should enter **@0,0.5**↵. A short line appears above the endpoint of the last line. Once again, @ tells AutoCAD that the coordinate you specify is from the last

point picked. But in this example, you give the distance in X and Y values. The X distance, 0, is given first, followed by a comma, and then the Y distance, 0.15. This is how to specify distances in relative Cartesian coordinates.

**FIGURE 2.4**
AutoCAD's default system for specifying angles

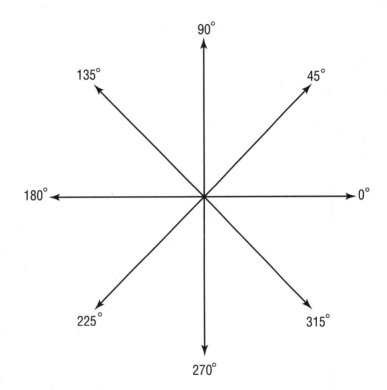

**TIP** Step 1 indicates that metric users should enter **@0,0.5**↵ for the distance. Instead, you could enter **0,.5** (zero comma point five). The leading zero is included for clarity. European metric users should be aware that the comma is used as a separator between the X and Y components of the coordinate. In AutoCAD, commas aren't used for decimal points; you must use a period to denote a decimal point.

2. Enter **@-3,0**↵. Metric users should enter **@-9,0**↵. This distance is also in X,Y values, but here you use a negative value to specify the X distance. The result is a drawing that looks like Figure 2.5.

   Positive values in the Cartesian coordinate system are from left to right and from bottom to top (see Figure 2.6). (You may remember this from your high school geometry class!) If you want to draw a line from right to left, you must designate a negative value. It's also helpful to know where the origin of the drawing lies. In a new drawing, the origin, or coordinate 0,0, is in the lower-left corner of the drawing.

3. Type **C**↵. This C stands for the Close command. It closes a sequence of line segments. A line connecting the first and last points of a sequence of lines is drawn (see Figure 2.7), and the Line command terminates. The rubber-banding line also disappears, telling you that AutoCAD has finished drawing line segments. You can also use the rubber-banding line to indicate direction while simultaneously entering the distance through the keyboard. See the upcoming sidebar "A Fast Way to Enter Distances."

**TIP** To finish drawing a series of lines without closing them, you can press Esc, ↵, or the spacebar.

**FIGURE 2.5**

These three sides of the door were drawn by using the Line tool. Points are specified by using either relative Cartesian or polar coordinates.

**FIGURE 2.6**

Positive and negative Cartesian coordinate directions

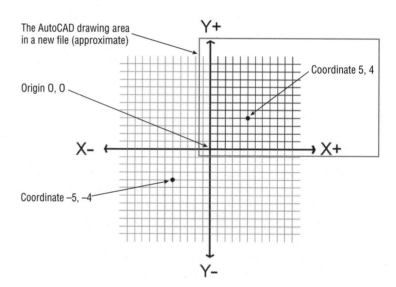

**FIGURE 2.7**

Distance and direction input for the door. Distances for metric users are shown in brackets.

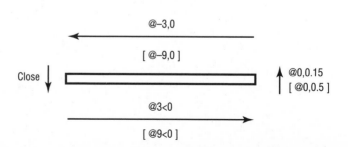

# Interpreting the Cursor Modes and Understanding Prompts

The key to working with AutoCAD successfully is understanding the way it interacts with you. This section will help you become familiar with some of the ways AutoCAD prompts you for input. Understanding the format of the messages in the Command window and recognizing other events on the screen will help you learn the program more easily.

---

### A FAST WAY TO ENTER DISTANCES

A third method for entering distances is to point in a direction with a rubber-banding line and then enter the distance through the keyboard. For example, to draw a line 3 units long from left to right, click the Line tool on the 2D Draw control panel, click a start point, and then move the cursor so the rubber-banding line points to the right at some arbitrary distance. With the cursor pointing in the direction you want, type **3↵**. The rubber-banding line becomes a fixed line 3 units long.

Using this method, called the Direct Distance method, along with the Ortho mode or Polar Tracking described in Chapter 3, can be a fast way to draw objects of specific lengths. Use the standard Cartesian or polar coordinate methods when you need to enter exact distances at angles other than those that are exactly horizontal or vertical. If you have the Dynamic Input display turned on, you can set the angle of the rubber-banding line using the angle display as a guide and then enter the distance you want through the keyboard followed by a ↵. Lines are drawn to the nearest whole degree shown in the Dynamic Input display.

On some systems, the AutoCAD Blipmode setting may be turned on. This causes tiny cross-shaped markers, called *blips*, to appear where you select points. These blips can be helpful to keep track of the points you've selected on the screen.

Blips aren't part of your drawing and don't print. Still, they can interfere with your work. To clear the screen of blips, choose View ➤ Redraw, or type **R↵**. The screen quickly redraws the objects, clearing the screen of the blips. As you'll see later in this book, Redraw can also clear up other display problems.

Another command, Regen, does the same thing as Redraw, but it also updates the drawing-display database—which means it takes a bit longer to restore the drawing. Regen is used to update certain types of changes that occur in a drawing. You'll learn about Regen in Chapter 6.

To turn Blipmode on and off, type **blipmode↵** at the Command prompt, and then enter ↵ or **off.↵**.

---

## Understanding Cursor Modes

As the Command window aids you with messages, the cursor gives you clues about what to do. Figure 2.8 illustrates the various modes of the cursor and gives a brief description of the role of each mode. Take a moment to study this figure:

**The Standard cursor** tells you that AutoCAD is waiting for instructions. You can also edit objects by using grips when you see this cursor. *Grips* are squares that appear at endpoints and at the midpoint of objects when they're selected. (You might know them as *workpoints* from other graphics programs.)

**The Point Selection cursor** appears whenever AutoCAD expects point input. It can also appear in conjunction with a rubber-banding line. You can either click a point or enter a coordinate through the keyboard.

**FIGURE 2.8**
The drawing
cursor's modes

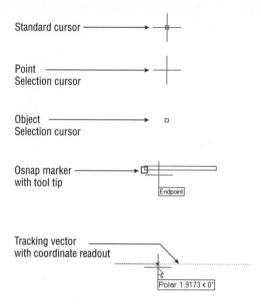

Standard cursor

Point
Selection cursor

Object
Selection cursor

Osnap marker
with tool tip

Endpoint

Tracking vector
with coordinate readout

Polar: 1.9173 < 0°

**The Object Selection cursor** tells you that you must select objects—either by clicking them or by using any of the object-selection options available.

**The Osnap (object snap) marker** appears along with the Point Selection cursor when you invoke an osnap. Osnaps let you accurately select specific points on an object, such as endpoints or midpoints.

**The tracking vector** appears when you use the Polar Tracking or Object Snap Tracking feature. Polar Tracking aids you in drawing orthogonal lines, and Object Snap Tracking helps you align a point in space relative to the geometry of existing objects. Object Snap Tracking works in conjunction with osnaps. You'll learn more about the tracking vector in Chapters 3 and 4.

**TIP**  If you're an experienced AutoCAD user, you may prefer to use the old-style crosshair cursor that crosses the entire screen. Choose Tools ➤ Options to open the Options dialog box, and then click the Display tab. Set the Crosshair Size option near the bottom left of the dialog box to 100. The cursor then appears as it did in previous versions of AutoCAD. As the option name implies, you can set the crosshair size to any percentage of the screen you want. The default is 5 percent.

## Choosing Command Options

Many commands in AutoCAD offer several options, which are often presented to you in the Command window in the form of a prompt. This section uses the Arc command to illustrate the format of AutoCAD's prompts.

Usually, in a floor-plan drawing in the United States, an arc is drawn to indicate the direction of a door swing. Figure 2.9 shows a drawing that includes other standard symbols used in architectural-style drawings.

**FIGURE 2.9**
Samples of standard
symbols used in archi-
tectural drawings

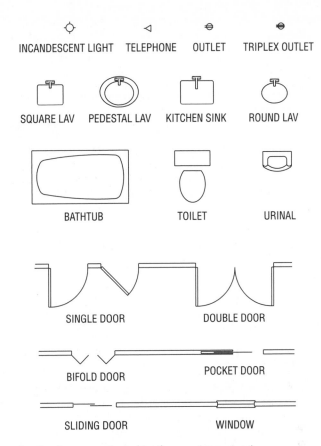

Here, you'll draw the arc for the door you started in the previous exercise:

1.  Click the Arc tool in the 2D Draw control panel. The prompt `Specify start point of arc or [Center]:` appears, and the cursor changes to Point Selection mode.

    Examine this `Specify start point of arc or [Center]:` prompt. The start point contains two options. The default option is the one stated in the main part of the prompt. In this case, the default option is to specify the start point of the arc. If other options are available, they appear within square brackets. In the Arc command, you see the word `Center` within brackets telling you that if you prefer, you can also start your arc by selecting a center point instead of a start point. If multiple options are available, they appear within the brackets and are separated by slashes (/). The default is the option AutoCAD assumes you intend to use unless you tell it otherwise.

2.  Type **C↵** to select the Center option. The prompt `Specify center point of arc:` appears. Notice that you had to type only the *C* and not the entire word *Center*.

**TIP**   When you see a set of options in the Command window, note their capitalization. If you choose to respond to prompts by using the keyboard, these capitalized letters are all you need to enter to select that option. In some cases, the first two letters are capitalized to differentiate two options that begin with the same letter, such as LAyer and LType.

3. Pick a point representing the center of the arc near the upper-left corner of the door (see Figure 2.10). The prompt `Specify start point of arc:` appears.

4. Type **@3<0**↵. Metric users should type **@9<0**↵. The prompt `Specify end point of arc or [Angle/chord Length]:` appears.

5. Move the mouse, and a temporary arc appears, originating from a point 3 units to the right of the center point you selected and rotating about that center, as in Figure 2.10. (Metric users will see the temporary arc originating 9 units to the right of the center point.)

   As the prompt indicates, you now have three options. You can enter an angle, a chord length, or the endpoint of the arc. The prompt default, to specify the endpoint of the arc, picks the arc's endpoint. Again, the cursor is in Point Selection mode, telling you it's waiting for point input. To select this default option, you only need to pick a point on the screen indicating where you want the endpoint.

6. Move the cursor so that it points in a vertical direction from the center of the arc. You'll see the Polar Tracking vector snap to a vertical position.

7. Click any location with the Polar Tracking vector in the vertical position. The arc is now fixed in place, as in Figure 2.10.

This exercise has given you some practice working with AutoCAD's Command window prompts and entering keyboard commands—skills you'll need when you start to use some of the more advanced AutoCAD functions.

As you can see, AutoCAD has a distinct structure in its prompt messages. You first issue a command, which in turn offers options in the form of a prompt. Depending on the option you select, you get another set of options, or you're prompted to take some action, such as picking a point, selecting objects, or entering a value.

As you work through the exercises, you'll become intimately familiar with this routine. After you understand the workings of the toolbars, the Command window prompts, and the dialog boxes, you can almost teach yourself the rest of the program!

### SELECTING OPTIONS FROM A SHORTCUT MENU

Now you know that you can select command options by typing them. You can also right-click at any time during a command to open a shortcut menu containing those same options. For example, in step 2 in the previous exercise, you typed **C**↵ to tell AutoCAD that you wanted to select the center of the arc. Instead of typing, you can also right-click the mouse to open a menu of options applicable to the Arc command at that time.

**FIGURE 2.10**
Using the Arc command

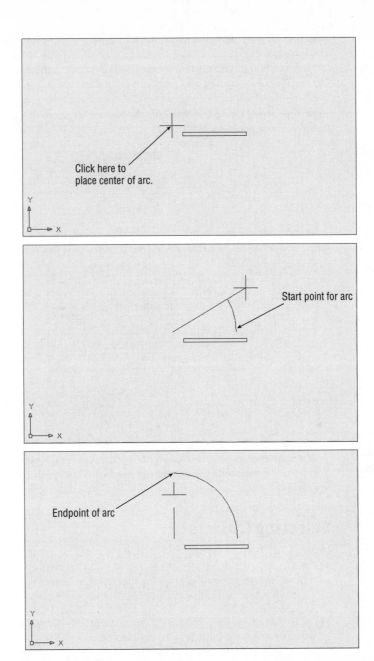

Notice that in addition to the options shown in the Command prompt, the shortcut menu also shows you a few more options: Enter, Cancel, Pan, and Zoom. The Enter option is the same as pressing ↵. Cancel cancels the current command. Pan and Zoom let you adjust your view as you're working through the current command.

The shortcut menu is context sensitive, so you see only those options that pertain to the command or activity that is currently in progress. Also, when AutoCAD is expecting a point, an object selection, or a numeric value, right-clicking doesn't display a shortcut menu. Instead, AutoCAD treats a right-click as ⏎.

The location of your cursor when you right-click determines the contents of the shortcut list. You've already seen that you can right-click a toolbar to get a list of other toolbars. A right-click in the Command window displays a list of operations you can apply to the command line, such as repeating one of the last several commands you've used or copying the most recent history of command activity to the Clipboard.

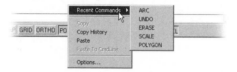

A right-click in the drawing area when no command is active displays a set of basic options for editing your file, such as Cut, Paste, Undo, Repeat the last command, Pan, and Zoom, to name a few.

If you're ever in doubt about what to do in AutoCAD, you can right-click to see a list of options. You'll learn more about these options later in this book. For now, let's move on to the topic of selecting objects.

## Selecting Objects

In AutoCAD, you can select objects in many ways. This section has two parts: The first part covers object-selection methods unique to AutoCAD, and the second part covers the more common selection method used in most popular graphic programs, the Noun/Verb method. Because these two methods play a major role in working with AutoCAD, it's a good idea to familiarize yourself with them early on.

**TIP**    If you need to select objects by their characteristics rather than by their location, see Chapter 15, which describes the Quick Select and Object Selection Filters tools. These tools let you easily select a set of objects based on their properties, including object type, color, layer assignment, and so on.

### Selecting Objects in AutoCAD

Many AutoCAD commands prompt you to Select objects:. Along with this prompt, the cursor changes from crosshairs to a small square (look back at Figure 2.8). Whenever you see the Select objects: prompt and the square Object Selection cursor, you have several options while making your selection. Often, as you select objects on the screen, you'll change your mind about a selection or accidentally select an object you don't want. Let's look at most of the selection options available in AutoCAD and learn what to do when you make the wrong selection.

Before you continue, you'll turn off two features that, although extremely useful, can be confusing to new users. These features are called Running Osnaps and Osnap Tracking. You'll get a chance to explore these features in depth later in this book, but for now follow these steps to turn them off:

1. Check to see if either Running Osnaps or Osnap Tracking is turned on. Look at the Osnap and Otrack buttons in the status bar at the bottom of the AutoCAD window. If they're turned on, they look like they're pressed.

2. To turn off Running Osnaps or Osnap Tracking, click the Osnap or Otrack button in the status bar. When turned off, they look like they aren't pressed.

Now, let's see how to select an object in AutoCAD:

1. Choose Move from the 2D Draw control panel, or type **M**↵.

2. At the Select objects: prompt, click each of the two horizontal lines that constitute the door. As you know, whenever AutoCAD wants you to select objects, the cursor turns into the small square pickbox. This tells you that you're in Object Selection mode. As you place the cursor over an object, it appears thicker to give you a better idea of what you're about to select. As you click an object, it's highlighted, as shown in Figure 2.11.

**WARNING**    If objects don't become "thicker" as you roll over them with your selection cursor, the Selection preview system variable may be turned off. You can turn it back on by entering **selection-preview**↵ **3**↵. This setting can also be found in the Selection tab of the Options dialog box. See Appendix A for more on the Options dialog box and Appendix C for more on system variables.

**FIGURE 2.11**
Selecting the lines of the door and seeing them highlighted

3. After making your selections, you may decide to deselect some items. Enter **U**↵ from the keyboard. Notice that one line is no longer highlighted. When you type **U**↵, objects are deselected, one at a time, in reverse order of selection.

**4.** You can deselect objects in another way. Hold down the Shift key, and click the remaining highlighted line. It reverts to a solid line, showing you that it's no longer selected for editing.

**5.** By now, you've deselected both lines. Let's try another method for selecting groups of objects. To select objects with a window selection, type **W⏎**. The cursor changes to a Point Selection cursor, and the prompt changes to

```
Specify first corner:
```

**6.** Click a point below and to the left of the rectangle representing the door. As you move your cursor across the screen, a selection window appears and stretches across the drawing area. Also notice that the window has a blue tint.

**7.** After the selection window completely encloses the door but not the arc, click this location to highlight the entire door. This window selects only objects that are completely enclosed by the window, as shown in Figure 2.12.

**FIGURE 2.12**
Selecting the door in a selection window

**TIP**    Don't confuse the selection window you're creating here with the zoom window you used in Chapter 1, which defines an area of the drawing you want to enlarge. Remember that the Window option works differently under the Zoom command than it does for other editing commands.

**8.** Press ⏎. This tells AutoCAD that you've finished selecting objects. It's important to remember to press ⏎ as soon as you finish selecting the objects you want to edit. A new prompt, `Specify base point or [Displacement] <Displacement>:`, appears. The cursor changes to its Point Selection mode.

Now you've seen how the selection process works in AutoCAD—but you're in the middle of the Move command. The next section discusses the prompt that's on your screen and describes how to enter base points and displacement distances.

### PROVIDING BASE POINTS

When you move or copy objects, AutoCAD prompts you for a base point, which is a difficult concept to grasp. AutoCAD must be told specifically *from* where and *to* where the move occurs. The *base point* is the exact location from which you determine the distance and direction of the move. After the base point is determined, you can tell AutoCAD where to move the object in relation to that point.

Follow these steps to practice using base points:

1. To select a base point, hold down the Shift key, and right-click. A menu appears, displaying the Object Snap (Osnap) options.

**WARNING** When you right-click the mouse, make sure the cursor is within the AutoCAD drawing area; otherwise, you won't get the results described in this book.

2. Choose Intersection from the Osnap menu. The Osnap menu closes.

3. Move the cursor to the lower-right corner of the door. Notice that as you approach the corner, a small x-shaped graphic appears on the corner. This is called an *Osnap marker*.

4. After the x-shaped marker appears, hold the mouse motionless for a second or two. A Tool-Tip appears, telling you the current Osnap point AutoCAD has selected.

5. Click the left mouse button to select the intersection indicated by the Osnap marker. Whenever you see the Osnap marker at the point you want to select, you don't have to point exactly at the location with your cursor. Just left-click the mouse to select the exact Osnap point (see Figure 2.13). In this case, you selected the exact intersection of two lines.

6. At the `Specify second point of displacement or <use first point as displacement>:` prompt, hold down the Shift key, and click the right mouse button again. You'll use the Endpoint osnap this time, but instead of clicking the option with the mouse, type **E↵**.

7. Pick the lower-right end of the arc you drew earlier. (Remember that you only need to move your cursor close to the endpoint until the Osnap marker appears.) The door moves so that the corner of the door connects exactly with the endpoint of the arc (see Figure 2.14).

As you can see, the osnap options let you select specific points on an object. You used Endpoint and Intersection in this exercise, but other options are available. Chapter 3 discusses some of the other osnap options. You may have also noticed that the Osnap marker is different for each of the options you used. You'll learn more about osnaps in Chapter 3. Now, let's continue with our look at point selection.

**FIGURE 2.13**
Using the Point
Selection cursor and
Osnap marker

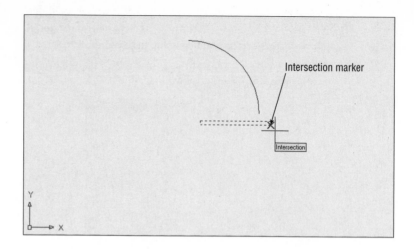

**FIGURE 2.14**
Moving the rectangle to
its new position using
the Endpoint osnap

**TIP** You may have noticed the statement Use first point as displacement in the prompt in step 6. This means that if you press ↵ instead of clicking a point, the object will move a distance based on the coordinates of the point you selected as a base point. If, for example, the point you click for the base point is at coordinate 2,4, the object will move 2 units in the X axis and 4 in the Y axis.

If you want to specify an exact distance and direction by typing a value, select any point on the screen as a base point. Or, you can type @ followed by ↵ at the base point prompt; then, enter the second point's location in relative coordinates. Remember that @ means the last point selected. In the next exercise, you'll try moving the entire door an exact distance of 1 unit at a 45° angle. Metric users will move the door 3 units at a 45° angle. Here are the steps:

1. Click the Move tool on the 2D Draw control panel.

2. Type P↵. The set of objects you selected in the previous exercise is highlighted. P is a selection option that selects the previously selected set of objects.

## CONTROLLING THE STATUS BAR DISPLAY

To the far right of the status bar, you'll see a downward-pointing arrow. This arrow opens a menu that controls the display of the status bar. You use this menu to turn the items in the status bar on or off. A checkmark by an item indicates that it's currently on. If for some reason you don't see all the buttons mentioned in the previous exercise, check this menu to make sure all the status-bar options are turned on. Note that LT doesn't have an Otrack option in the status bar.

3. You're still in Object Selection mode, so click the arc to include it in the set of selected objects. The entire door, including the arc, is highlighted.

4. Press ↵ to tell AutoCAD that you've finished your selection. The cursor changes to Point Selection mode.

5. At the `Specify base point or [Displacement] <Displacement>:` prompt, choose a point on the screen between the door and the left side of the screen (see Figure 2.15).

**FIGURE 2.15**
The highlighted door and the base point just to the left of the door. Note that the base point doesn't need to be on the object that you're moving

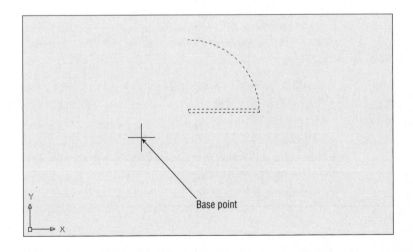

Base point

6. Move the cursor around slowly, and notice that the door moves as if the base point you selected were attached to the door. The door moves with the cursor, at a fixed distance from it. This demonstrates how the base point relates to the objects you select.

7. Type @1<45↵. (Metric users should type @3<45↵.) The door moves to a new location on the screen at a distance of 1 unit (3 for metric users) from its previous location and at an angle of 45°.

**TIP** If AutoCAD is waiting for a command, you can repeat the last command used by pressing the spacebar or pressing ↵. You can also right-click in the drawing area and select the option at the top of the list. If you right-click the Command window, a shortcut menu offers the most recent commands.

This exercise illustrates that the base point doesn't have to be on the object you're manipulating; it can be virtually anywhere on your drawing. You also saw how to reselect a group of objects that were selected previously without having to duplicate the selection process.

## Using Noun/Verb Selection

Nearly all graphics programs today allow the Noun/Verb method for selecting objects. This method requires you to select objects before you issue a command to edit them—that is, you identify the "noun" (the object you want to work on) before the "verb" (the action you want to perform on it). The exercises in this section show you how to use the Noun/Verb method in AutoCAD.

You've seen that when AutoCAD is waiting for a command, it displays the crosshair cursor with the small square. As mentioned, this square is a pickbox superimposed on the cursor. It indicates that you can select objects even while the Command prompt appears at the bottom of the screen and no command is currently active. The square momentarily disappears when you're in a command that asks you to select points.

### OTHER SELECTION OPTIONS

There are several other selection options you haven't tried yet. You'll see how these options work in exercises later in this book. Or, if you're adventurous, try them now on your own. To use these options, type their keyboard abbreviations (shown in brackets in the following list) at any Select objects: prompt.

**Add [add↵]** Switches from Remove mode to the Add mode. See "Remove", later in this sidebar.

**All [all↵]** Selects all the objects in a drawing except those in frozen or locked layers. (See Chapter 4 for information on layers.)

**Box [r↵]** Forces the standard selection window whereby a left-to-right selection uses a standard window and a right-to-left selection uses a crossing window.

**Crossing [c↵]** Similar to the Window selection option but selects anything that crosses through the window you define.

**Crossing Polygon [cp↵]** Acts exactly like Window Polygon (see later in this sidebar) but, like the Crossing selection option, selects anything that crosses through a polygon boundary.

**Fence [f↵]**   Selects objects that are crossed by a temporary line called a *fence*. This operation is like using a line to cross out the objects you want to select. After you invoke this option, you can then pick points, as when you're drawing a series of line segments. After you finish drawing the fence, press ↵, and then go on to select other objects or press ↵ again to finish your selection.

Use a Fence selection to extend a set of lines to a spline.

Fence                    Result

**Group [g↵]**   Allows you to select a group by name.

**Last [l↵]**   Selects the last object you entered.

**Multiple [m↵]**   Lets you select several objects first, before AutoCAD highlights them. In a large file, selecting objects individually can cause AutoCAD to pause after each selection while it locates and highlights each object. The Multiple option can speed things up by letting you first select all the objects quickly and then highlight them all by pressing ↵. This has no menu equivalent.

**Previous [p↵]**   Selects the last object or set of objects that was edited or changed.

**Remove [r↵]**   Switches to a selection mode whereby the objects you click are removed from the selection set.

**Window [w↵]**   Forces a standard window selection. This option is useful when your drawing area is too crowded to use the Autoselect feature to place a window around a set of objects. (See the Auto entry later in this sidebar.) It prevents you from accidentally selecting an object with a single pick when you're placing your window.

**Window Polygon [wp↵]**   Lets you select objects by enclosing them in an irregularly shaped polygon boundary. When you use this option, you see the prompt First polygon point:. You then pick points to define the polygon boundary. As you pick points, the prompt Specify endpoint of line or [Undo]: appears. Select as many points as you need to define the boundary. You can undo boundary line segments as you go by pressing U↵. With the boundary defined, press ↵. The bounded objects are highlighted and the Select objects: prompt returns, allowing you to use more selection options.

A window polygon selection

The following two selection options are also available but are seldom used. They're intended for use in creating custom menu options or custom toolbar tools:

**Auto [au⏎]** Forces the standard automatic window or crossing window when a point is picked and no object is found. (See the "Using Autoselect" section later in this chapter.) A standard window is produced when the two window corners are picked from left to right. A crossing window is produced when the two corners are picked from right to left. After this option is selected, it remains active for the duration of the current command. Auto is intended for use on systems on which the Automatic Selection feature has been turned off.

**Single [si⏎]** Forces the current command to select only a single object. If you use this option, you can pick a single object; then, the current command acts on that object as if you had pressed ⏎ immediately after selecting the object. This has no menu equivalent.

**TIP** In addition to Noun/Verb selection, AutoCAD offers other selection options that let you use familiar GUI techniques. See Appendix B to learn how you can control object-selection methods. This appendix also describes how to change the size of the standard cursor.

Try moving objects by first selecting them and then using the Move command:

1. Press the Esc key twice to make sure AutoCAD isn't in the middle of a command you might have accidentally issued. Then, click the arc. The arc is highlighted, and you may also see squares appear at its endpoints, center point, and midpoint. As stated earlier, these squares are called *grips*. You'll get a chance to work with them later.

2. Choose Move from the 2D Draw control panel. The cursor changes to Point Selection mode. Notice that the grips on the arc disappear, but the arc is still selected.

3. At the `Specify base point or [Displacement] <Displacement>:` prompt, pick any point on the screen. The following prompt appears:

```
Specify second point or
<use first point as displacement>:
```

4. Type @1<0⏎. Metric users should type @3<0⏎. The arc moves to a new location 1 unit (3 units for metric users) to the right.

**WARNING** If this exercise doesn't work as described here, chances are the Noun/Verb setting has been turned off on your copy of AutoCAD. To turn on the Noun/Verb setting, choose Tools ➣ Options to open the Options dialog box, and click the Selection tab. In the Selection Modes group, place a checkmark in the check box next to the Noun/Verb Selection option, and click OK.

In this exercise, you picked the arc *before* issuing the Move command. Then, when you clicked the Move tool, you didn't see the `Select objects:` prompt. Instead, AutoCAD assumed you wanted to move the arc that you selected and went directly to the `Specify base point or [Displacement] <Displacement>:` prompt.

### USING AUTOSELECT

Next, you'll move the rest of the door in the same direction by using the Autoselect feature:

1. Pick a point just above and to the left of the rectangle representing the door. Be sure not to pick the door itself. A selection window appears that you can drag across the screen as you move the cursor. If you move the cursor to the left of the last point selected, the window appears dotted with a green tint (see the first image in Figure 2.16). If you move the cursor to the right of that point, it appears solid with a blue tint (see the second image in Figure 2.16).

2. Pick a point below and to the right of the door so that the door is completely enclosed by the window but not the arc, as shown in the bottom image in Figure 2.16. The door is highlighted (and again, you may see grips appear at the lines' endpoints and midpoints).

**FIGURE 2.16**
The dotted window (first image) indicates a crossing selection; the solid window (second image) indicates a standard selection window.

Crossing window

Standard window

3. Click the Move tool again. Just as in the preceding exercise, the `Specify base point or [Displacement] <Displacement>:` prompt appears.

4. Pick any point on the screen; then, enter **@1<0**↵. Metric users should enter **@3<0**↵. The door joins with the arc.

The two selection windows you've just seen—the blue solid one and the dotted green one—represent a standard window and a crossing window. If you use a *standard window,* anything completely within the window is selected. If you use a *crossing window,* anything that crosses through the window is selected. These two types of windows start automatically when you click any blank portion of the drawing area with a Standard cursor or a Point Selection cursor; hence the name *Autoselect.*

Next, you'll select objects with an automatic crossing window:

1. Pick a point below and to the right of the door. As you move the cursor left, the crossing (dotted) window appears.

2. Select the next point so that the window encloses the door and part of the arc (see Figure 2.17). The entire door, including the arc, is highlighted.

3. Click the Move tool.

4. Pick any point on the screen; then, enter **@1<180**↵. Metric users should type **@3<180**↵. The door moves back to its original location.

**FIGURE 2.17**
The door enclosed by
a crossing window

You'll find that in most cases, the Autoselect standard and crossing windows are all you need when selecting objects. They really save you time, so you'll want to become familiar with these features.

Before continuing, choose File ➤ Save to save the Door file. You won't want to save the changes you make in the next section, so saving now stores the current condition of the file on your hard disk for safekeeping.

### RESTRICTIONS ON NOUN/VERB OBJECT SELECTION

For many of the modifying or construction-oriented commands, the Noun/Verb selection method is inappropriate because for those commands, you must select more than one set of objects. You'll know whether a command accepts the Noun/Verb selection method right away. Commands that don't accept the Noun/Verb selection method clear the selection and then ask you to select an object or set of objects.

If you'd like to take a break, now is a good time to do it. If you want, exit AutoCAD, and return to this point in the tutorial later. When you return, start AutoCAD and open the Door file.

# Editing with Grips

Earlier, when you selected the door, grips appeared at the endpoints, center points, and midpoints of the lines and arcs. You can use grips to make direct changes to the shape of objects or to quickly move and copy them.

**WARNING**    If you didn't see grips on the door in the previous exercise, your version of AutoCAD may have the Grips feature turned off. To turn them on, refer to the information on grips in Appendix B.

So far, you've seen how operations in AutoCAD have a discrete beginning and ending. For example, to draw an arc, you first issue the Arc command and then go through a series of operations, including answering prompts and picking points. When you're finished, you have an arc, and AutoCAD is ready for the next command.

The Grips feature, on the other hand, plays by a different set of rules. Grips offer a small yet powerful set of editing functions that don't conform to the lockstep command/prompt/input routine you've seen so far. As you work through the following exercises, it's helpful to think of grips as a subset of the standard method of operation in AutoCAD.

To practice using the Grips feature, you'll make some temporary modifications to the door drawing.

## Stretching Lines by Using Grips

In this exercise, you'll stretch one corner of the door by grabbing the grip points of two lines:

1. Press the Esc key to make sure you're not in the middle of a command. Click a point below and to the left of the door to start a selection window.

2. Use the Zoom tool to adjust your view so the size of the door is similar to what is shown in Figure 2.18.

3. Click above and to the right of the rectangular part of the door to select it.

4. Place the cursor on the lower-left corner grip of the rectangle, *but don't press the mouse button yet*. Notice that the cursor jumps to the grip point and that the grip changes color.

5. Move the cursor to another grip point. Notice again how the cursor jumps to it. When placed on a grip, the cursor moves to the exact center of the grip point. This means, for example, that if the cursor is placed on an endpoint grip, it's on the exact endpoint of the object.

6. Move the cursor to the upper-left corner grip of the rectangle, and click. The grip becomes a solid color and is now a *hot grip*. The prompt displays the following message:

```
**STRETCH**
Specify stretch point or [Base point/Copy/Undo/eXit]:
```

This prompt tells you that Stretch mode is active. Notice the options in the prompt. As you move the cursor, the corner follows, and the lines of the rectangle stretch (see Figure 2.18).

**TIP**    You can control the size and color of grips by using the Selection tab in the Options dialog box; see Appendix B for details.

**FIGURE 2.18**

Stretching lines by using hot grips. The first image shows the rectangle's corner being stretched upward. The next image shows the new location of the corner at the top of the arc.

**7.** Move the cursor upward toward the top end of the arc, and click that point. The rectangle deforms, with the corner placed at your pick point (see Figure 2.18).

Here you saw that a command called Stretch is issued by clicking a grip point. As you'll see in these next steps, a handful of other hot-grip commands are also available:

**1.** Notice that the grips are still active. Click the grip point that you moved before to make it a hot grip again.

**2.** Right-click the mouse to open a shortcut menu that contains a list of grip edit options.

**TIP** When you click the joining grip point of two contiguous line segments, AutoCAD selects the overlapping grips of two lines. When you stretch the corner away from its original location, the endpoints of both lines follow.

3. Choose Base Point from the list, and then click a point to the right of the hot grip. Now, as you move the cursor, the hot grip moves relative to the cursor.

4. Right-click again, choose Copy from the shortcut menu, and enter @1<-30↵. (Metric users should enter @3<-30↵.) Instead of moving the hot grip and changing the lines, copies of the two lines are made, with their endpoints 1 unit (or 3 units for metric users) below and to the right of the first set of endpoints.

5. Pick another point just below the last. More copies are made.

6. Press ↵ or enter X↵ to exit Stretch mode. You can also right-click again and choose Exit from the shortcut menu.

In this exercise, you saw that you can select a base point other than the hot grip. You also saw how you can specify relative coordinates to move or copy a hot grip. Finally, you saw that with grips selected on an object, right-clicking the mouse opens a shortcut menu that contains grip edit options.

## Moving and Rotating with Grips

As you've just seen, the Grips feature is an alternative method for editing your drawings. You've already seen how you can stretch endpoints, but you can do much more with grips. The next exercise demonstrates some other options. You'll start by undoing the modifications you made in the preceding exercise:

1. Type U↵. The copies of the stretched lines disappear.

2. Press ↵ again. The deformed door snaps back to its original form.

**TIP** Pressing ↵ at the Command prompt causes AutoCAD to repeat the last command entered—in this case, U.

3. Select the entire door by first clicking a blank area below and to the right of the door.

4. Move the cursor to a location above and to the left of the rectangular portion of the door, and click. Because you went from right to left, you created a crossing window. Recall that the crossing window selects anything enclosed and crossing through the window.

5. Click the lower-left grip of the rectangle to turn it into a hot grip. Just as before, as you move your cursor, the corner stretches.

6. Right-click, and choose Move from the shortcut menu. The Command window displays the following:

```
**MOVE**
Specify move point or [Base point/Copy/Undo/eXit]
```

Now, as you move the cursor, the entire door moves with it.

7. Position the door near the center of the screen, and click. The door moves to the center of the screen. Notice that the Command prompt returns, but the door remains highlighted, indicating that it's still selected for the next operation.

8. Click the lower-left grip again, right-click, and choose Rotate from the shortcut menu. The Command window displays the following:

```
**ROTATE**
Specify rotation angle or [Base point/Copy/Undo/Reference/eXit]:
```

As you move the cursor, the door rotates about the grip point.

9. Position the cursor so that the door rotates approximately 180° (see Figure 2.19). Then, Ctrl+click the mouse (hold down the Ctrl key, and press the left mouse button). A copy of the door appears in the new rotated position, leaving the original door in place.

**FIGURE 2.19**
Rotating and copying the door by using a hot grip. Notice that more than one object is affected by the grip edit, even though only one grip is hot.

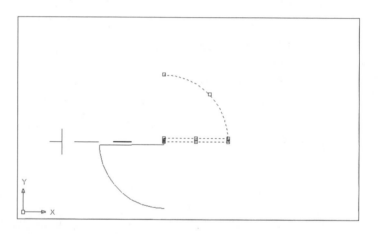

10. Press ↵ to exit Grip Edit mode.

**TIP**   You've seen how the Move command is duplicated in a modified way as a hot-grip command. Other hot-grip commands (Stretch, Rotate, Scale, and Mirror) have similar counterparts in the standard set of AutoCAD commands. You'll see how those work in Chapters 12 and 14.

After you complete any operation by using grips, the objects are still highlighted with their grips active. To clear the grip selection, press the Esc key.

In this exercise, you saw how hot-grip options appear in a shortcut menu. Several other options are available in that menu, including Exit, Base Point, Copy, and Undo. You can also adjust an object's properties by using the Properties option.

You can access many of these grip edit options by pressing the spacebar or ↵ while a grip is selected. With each press, the next option becomes active. The options then repeat if you continue to press ↵. The Ctrl key acts as a shortcut to the Copy option. You have to use it only once; then, each time you click a point, a copy is made.

### SCALING WITH GRIPS

Grips can be used to graphically scale an object to fit between two other objects. For example, a door can be scaled to fit within a door frame. Place the door so its hinge side is at the door frame and the door is oriented properly for the frame. With the door selected, click the grip at the hinge side. Right-click, and select Scale. Type **R.↵**, and then click the grip at the hinge again. Click the grip at the end of the arc representing the door swing. Finally, click the opposite side of the door frame.

Click the grip at the hinge.   Right-click and select Scale.   Type R↵ and Click these grips hinge side first.   Click the endpoint of the frame to scale the door.

### A QUICK SUMMARY OF THE GRIPS FEATURE

The exercises in this chapter include only a few of the grips options. You'll get a chance to use other hot-grip options in later chapters. Meanwhile, here is a summary of the Grips feature:

◆ Clicking endpoint grips stretches those endpoints.

◆ Clicking midpoint grips of lines moves the entire line.

◆ If two objects meet end to end, and you click their overlapping grips, both grips are selected simultaneously.

◆ You can select multiple grips by holding down the Shift key and clicking the desired grips.

◆ When a hot grip is selected, the Stretch, Move, Rotate, Scale, and Mirror options are available to you; right-click the mouse.

◆ You can cycle through the Stretch, Move, Rotate, Scale, and Mirror options by pressing ↵ while a hot grip is selected.

◆ All the hot-grip options let you make copies of the selected objects by either using the Copy option or holding down the Ctrl key while selecting points.

◆ All the hot-grip options let you select a base point other than the originally selected hot grip.

## Using Dynamic Input

Earlier in this chapter, you turned off the Dynamic Input display so you could get an uncluttered view of what was going on in AutoCAD's display. In this section, you'll get a chance to explore the Dynamic Input display through grip editing.

You'll start by going back to the original version of the Door.dwg drawing that you saved earlier:

1. Choose File ➢ Close.

2. When you're asked if you want to save changes, click No.

3. Choose File ➢ Open, and then locate and select the door.dwg file you saved earlier. You can also open the doorsample.dwg file from the sample files you installed from this book's companion website.

4. The door appears in the condition you left it when you last saved the file.

5. Turn on Dynamic Input display by clicking the DYN button in the status bar. It should look like it's in the down position.

6. Click the arc to expose its grips.

7. Place the cursor on the outward-pointing arrow grip at the middle of the arc, but don't click it. (This is called *hovering* over a grip.) You see the dimensions of the arc appear. This feature is useful when you need to check the size of objects you've drawn.

8. Click the arrow you're hovering over. The Command prompt appears at the cursor, and the radius dimension changes to a text box.

9. Move the cursor toward the upper-right corner of the drawing area. The radius dimension changes as you move the cursor.

10. Enter 4↵. Metric users enter 130↵. As you type, the new value appears in the radius dimension. When you press ↵, the arc changes to the new radius.

11. Click the Undo button to revert to the original arc size.

Here you saw the basic methods for using the Dynamic Input display. You can hover over an object's grip to display its dimensions. Click the grip, and, if available, those dimensions can be edited directly through the keyboard. In this example, you were able to change the radius of the arc to an exact value. Depending on the grip you click, you can change a dimension through direct keyboard input. For example, if you want to change the degrees the arc covers instead of its radius, you can click the arrow grip at either end of the arc.

Next, try Dynamic Input display on a line:

1. Click the bottommost line of the door, as shown in Figure 2.20; hover over the rightmost grip on the selected line. Just as with the arc, you can see the dimensions of the line, including its length and directional angle.

**FIGURE 2.20**

Selecting a line on the door

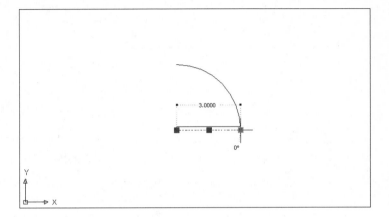

2. Click the grip you're hovering over, and then move the cursor upward and to the right. You see two dimensions: One indicates the overall length, and the other shows the change in length of the line. You also see the Command prompt at the cursor. Notice that the dimension indicating the change in length is highlighted.

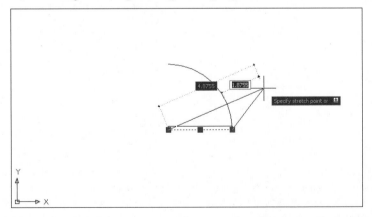

3. Enter **1** and press the Tab key to increase the length of the line by 1 unit. Metric users should enter **30** and press the Tab key. Now, as you move the cursor, the line is locked at a new

length that is 1 or 30 units longer than its original length. Also notice that the overall dimension is highlighted. You also see a lock icon on the length dimension.

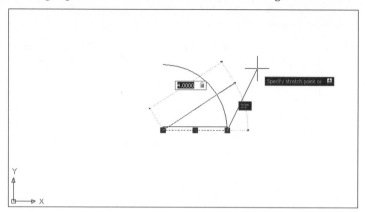

4. Press the Tab key again. The angle value is highlighted.

5. Enter **45** and press the Tab key to lock the angle of the line at 45°.

6. Make sure the cursor isn't too close to the locked endpoint of the line, and then click the left mouse button. The line is now in its new orientation with a length of 4 (130 for metric users) and an angle of 45°, as shown in Figure 2.21.

**FIGURE 2.21**
The line's new length and orientation

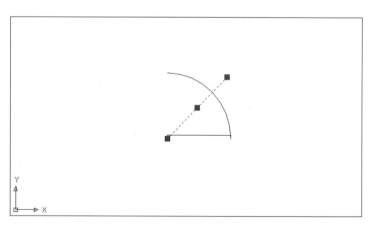

You can see that the Dynamic Input display lets you enter specific dimensions for the selected object, making possible precise changes in an object's size.

You can also use the Dynamic Input display while using other grip-editing features. Try the following exercise to see how the Dynamic Input display works while moving objects:

1. Click above and to the right of the door drawing to start a crossing selection window.

2. Click below and to the left to select the entire door drawing.

3. Click the middle grip of the arc.

**4.** Right-click, and choose Move. You see the Command prompt at the cursor with the distance value highlighted. As you move the cursor, you can see the distance and angle values in the Dynamic Input display change.

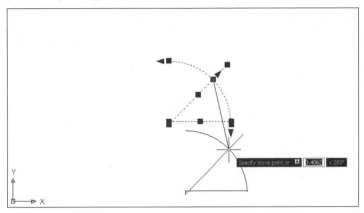

**5.** Enter **4**, and then press the Tab key. As you move the cursor, the distance from the original location of the arc's midpoint is locked at 4 units. The angle value is now highlighted and available for editing.

**6.** Enter **225**, and then press the Tab key to lock the angle at 225°.

**7.** Click a location away from the door drawing. The door moves to its new location exactly 4 units from its original location.

As you can see from these exercises, the Dynamic Input display adds some helpful methods for editing objects. To summarize, here is a rundown of the basic Dynamic Input display features:

◆ You can easily turn the Dynamic Input display on or off by clicking the DYN button in the status bar.

◆ You can quickly check the dimensions of an object by selecting it and then hovering over a grip.

◆ You can alter an object's dimensions by entering values into the highlighted dimensions of the Dynamic Input display.

◆ To highlight a different dimension, press the Tab key.

◆ To accept any changes you've made using Dynamic Input display, click the mouse at a location away from the grip you're editing. You can also press ↵ or the spacebar.

Not all grips offer dimensions that can be edited. If you click the midpoint grip on the line, for example, you won't see the dimensions of the line, although you'll see the Command prompt and you'll be able to enter a new coordinate for the midpoint.

As you've seen in the arc and line examples, each object offers a different set of dimensions. If you like the way the Dynamic Input display works, you can experiment on other types of objects. AutoCAD offers a number of settings that let you control the behavior of the Dynamic Input display. You'll learn about those settings later in Appendix A.

## Getting Help

Eventually, you'll find yourself somewhere without documentation, and you'll have a question about an AutoCAD feature. AutoCAD provides an online help facility that gives you information on nearly any topic related to AutoCAD. Here's how to find help:

1. Choose Help ➤ Help from the menu bar to open the AutoCAD 2008 Help window.

2. If it isn't already selected, click the Contents tab. This tab contains a table of contents. The other two tabs—Index and Search—provide assistance in finding specific topics.

3. Scan down the screen until you see the topic Command Reference, and double-click it. Both panels of the Help window change to show more topics.

4. In the panel on the right, click the item labeled C just to the right of the Commands listing. The panel expands to display a list of command names that start with the letter C.

5. Look down the list, and click the word *Copy*. A description of the Copy command appears in the panel to the right.

**TIP** You can also press F1 to open the AutoCAD Help window.

You also have the Concepts and Procedures tabs along the top of the panel on the right. These options provide more detailed information about the use of the selected item. If you want to back up through the steps you've just taken, click the Back button on the toolbar.

## Using the InfoCenter

If you want to find information about a topic based on a keyword, you can use the Info Center in the upper-right corner of the AutoCAD window. Follow these steps:

1. Type **change** in the InfoCenter text box at the top right of the AutoCAD window, and then click the InfoCenter tool to the right of the input box.

**2.** The InfoCenter expands to display a list of resources for the word *change*.

This list is a bit overwhelming. You can use Boolean AND, OR, NEAR, and NOT in conjunction with other keywords to help filter your searches, just as in a typical search engine that you might use in your web browser. After you've found a topic you want, select it from the Select Topic list, and then click the Display button to display information related to the topic in the panel on the right.

Besides using a keyword for searches, you can also use phrases or questions. Try the following steps to see how you can use a question:

**1.** In the InfoCenter text box, type **How do I zoom into my view.**↵. The list below the text box changes to show several items that relate to adjusting views in AutoCAD.

**2.** Click Pan or Zoom a View - Concept from the list. The Help window opens to display a description of how the Zoom command works.

You'll notice three tabs in the right panel: Concepts, Procedures, and Commands. Concepts covers the general description of the topic. Procedures shows you methods for using the command, and Commands provides more detailed information about the command and its options.

## Using Context-Sensitive Help

AutoCAD also provides *context-sensitive help* to give you information related to the command you're currently using. To see how this works, try the following:

1. Close or minimize the Help window, and return to the AutoCAD window.

2. Click the Move tool in the 2D Draw control panel to start the Move command.

3. Press the F1 function key, or choose Help from the menu bar to open the Help window. A description of the Move command appears in the panel on the right.

4. Click the Help window's Close button, or minimize the Help window.

5. Press the Esc key to exit the Move command.

## Finding Additional Sources of Help

The InfoCenter is the main online source for reference material, but you can also find answers to your questions through the other options in the Help menu. Here is a brief description of them:

**New Features Workshop**   The New Features Workshop offers descriptions and tutorials focused on the new features in AutoCAD 2008. You can update this unique support tool through the Autodesk website.

**Additional Resources**   Here you'll find several options to choose from. The Support Knowledge Base opens your browser to Autodesk's own knowledge base. This is an excellent source for finding answers to problems you may encounter while using AutoCAD.

Online Training Resources takes you to the Autodesk Training site, where you'll find further information on where to get training and tutorial information.

If you're a developer, you'll be interested in the Online Developer Center. This option takes you to the Autodesk Developer Center website, where you can find more information about getting started with your own AutoCAD-related application.

If you're already customizing AutoCAD, the Developer Help option takes you to the Developer Help section of the AutoCAD Help window. Here, you'll find specific information about how to use the customization tools built into AutoCAD.

Finally, if you would like to join an established community of AutoCAD users, the Autodesk User Group International option takes you to the AUGI website. AUGI offers a wide range of resources for users of Autodesk products. You can join a forum to discuss issues with other AutoCAD users. AUGI also offers its own knowledge base.

**About**   This option provides information about the version of AutoCAD you're using.

## Staying Informed with the Communication Center

Another feature that can help you stay informed about the latest news on AutoCAD is the Communication Center. To the far right of InfoCenter, you'll see the Communication Center icon.

Click the Communication Center icon to open the Communication Center list.

The Communication Center offers a way to stay informed about the latest software updates and support issues for AutoCAD. Click the Settings button at the bottom of the Communication Center list to open the Info Center Settings dialog box.

You may need to minimize the size of some of the panels to get to the Settings button. Here, you can select your country from the Country/Region drop-down list to ensure that the information is correct for your country. The Check For New Content option lets you select the frequency at which the Communication Center checks for new information; you can choose Daily, Weekly, Monthly, or On Demand. If you want to turn off the balloon message, clear the Enable Balloon Notification For New Announcements check box at the bottom of the dialog box.

The Communication Center works best if you use an "always on" Internet connection such as DSL or high-speed cable. If you don't have such a connection, you can set the Check For New Content option to On Demand. You can then check for updates when you connect to the Internet.

## Displaying Data in a Text Window

You may have noticed that as you work in AutoCAD, the activity displayed in the Command window scrolls up. Sometimes, it's helpful to view information that has scrolled past the view shown in the Command window. For example, you can review the command activity from your session to check input values or to recall other data-entry information. Try the following exercise to see how the Text Window works:

1. Choose Tools ➤ Inquiry ➤ List.

2. At the `Select objects:` prompt, click the arc, and press ↵. Information about the arc is displayed in the AutoCAD Text Window (see Figure 2.22). Toward the bottom is the list of the arc's properties. Don't worry if the meaning of some listed properties isn't obvious yet; as you work through this book, you'll learn what the properties of an object mean.

**FIGURE 2.22**
The AutoCAD Text Window showing the data displayed by the List tool

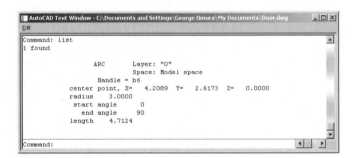

3. Press F2 to close the AutoCAD Text Window.

**TIP**   Pressing F2 is a quick way to switch between the drawing editor and the AutoCAD Text Window.

The scroll bar to the right of the AutoCAD Text Window lets you scroll to earlier events. You can even set the number of lines that AutoCAD retains by using the Options dialog box, or you can have AutoCAD record the AutoCAD Text Window information in a text file.

When you have more than one document open, the AutoCAD Text Window displays a listing for the drawing that is currently active.

# Displaying the Properties of an Object

While we're on the subject of displaying information, you'll want to know about the Properties palette. In the preceding exercise, you saw how the List command showed some information regarding the properties of an object, such as the location of an arc's center and endpoints. You can also double-click an object to display a Properties palette that shows similar information. (You might accidentally display the Properties palette from time to time!)

**TIP**   Since the Properties palette is so useful, you may want to consider leaving it open all the time.

To see what this palette is for, try the following exercise:

1.  Select the arc in the drawing, right-click it, and select Properties to open the Properties palette, which displays a list of the arc's properties. Don't worry if many of the items in this palette are undecipherable; you'll learn more about this palette as you work through the early chapters of this book. For now, just be aware that this palette appears whenever you double-click an object and that it displays the object's properties. You can also use it to modify many of the properties listed.

2.  Click the small Auto-Hide box at the bottom left of the Properties palette: It's the icon that looks like a double arrow. The icon changes to a single arrow. The Auto-Hide option in the Properties palette lets you keep the palette open without having it take up too much of the drawing area. This can be useful when you need to edit the properties of many objects.

3.  Move the cursor away from the Properties palette. The Properties palette collapses so that only the title bar remains.

4.  Hover the cursor on the Properties palette title bar. The Properties palette opens to display all the options again.

5. Click the Auto-Hide box again to restore the "always open" mode of the palette.

6. Close the Properties palette by clicking the X in its upper corner. (The X appears in the upper-left or upper-right corner, depending on the placement of the palette in the AutoCAD window.) You can also right-click the title on the side of the Properties palette and then choose Close from the shortcut menu.

7. You're finished with the door drawing, so choose File ➢ Close.

8. In the Save Changes dialog box, click the No button. (You've already saved this file just as you want it, so you don't need to save it again.)

**TIP**   In many cases, you can open the Properties palette by double-clicking an object. Some objects, however, display a dialog box to allow you to edit the object.

## The Bottom Line

**Specifying Distances with Coordinates**   One of the most basic skills you need to learn is how to indicate exact distances through the keyboard. AutoCAD uses a simple annotation system to indicate distance and direction.

**Master It**   What would you type to indicate a relative distance of 14 units at a 45 degree angle?

**Solution**   @14<45

**Interpreting the Cursor Modes and Understanding Prompts**   AutoCAD's cursor changes its shape depending on the command that is currently active. These different cursor modes can give you a clue regarding what you should be doing.

**Master It**   Describe the Point Selection cursor and the Object Selection cursor.

**Solution**   The Point Selection cursor is a simple crosshair. The Object Selection cursor is a small square or pickbox.

**Selecting Objects and Editing with Grips**   Grips are small squares that appear at key points on the object when they're selected. These grips offer a powerful way to edit objects.

**Master It**   How do you select multiple grips?

**Solution**   Hold down the Shift key while clicking the grips.

**Using Dynamic Input**   Besides grips, objects display their dimensional properties when selected. These dimensional properties can be edited to change the object's shape.

**Master It**   How do you turn on Dynamic Input? And once it's on, what key lets you shift between the different dimensions of an object?

**Solution**   The DYN button on the AutoCAD status bar turns Dynamic Input on and off. When an object is selected, you can move between the dimensional properties by pressing the Tab key.

**Getting Help**   AutoCAD's help window is thorough in its coverage of AutoCAD's features. New and experienced users alike can often find answers to their questions thorough the help window, so it pays to become familiar with it.

**Master It**   What keyboard key do you press for context-sensitive help?

**Solution**   F1.

**Displaying Data in a Text Window**   AutoCAD offers a Text Window that keeps a running account of the commands you use. This can be helpful in retrieving input that you've entered when constructing your drawing.

**Master It**   Name a command that displays its results in the AutoCAD Text Window.

**Solution**   The List command.

**Displaying the Properties of an Object**   The Properties palette is one of the most useful sources for drawing information. Not only does it list the properties of an object, but it also lets you change the shape, color, or other property of objects.

**Master It**   How do you open the Properties palette for a particular object?

**Solution**   Select the object whose properties you want to view. Right-click the object, and select Properties.

# Chapter 3

# Setting Up and Using AutoCAD's Drafting Tools

Chapters 1 and 2 covered the basic information you need to understand the workings of AutoCAD. Now, you'll put this knowledge to work. In this architectural tutorial, which begins here and continues through Chapter 15, you'll draw an apartment building composed of studios. The tutorial illustrates how to use AutoCAD commands and gives you a solid understanding of the basic AutoCAD package. With these fundamentals, you can use AutoCAD to its fullest potential, regardless of the kinds of drawings you intend to create or the enhancement products you may use in the future.

In this chapter, you'll start drawing an apartment's bathroom fixtures. In the process, you'll learn how to use AutoCAD's basic tools. You'll also be introduced to the concept of drawing scale and how the size of what you draw is translated into a paper sheet size.

Topics in this chapter include the following:

◆ Setting Up a Work Area

◆ Exploring the Drawing Process

◆ Planning and Laying Out a Drawing

◆ Using the AutoCAD Modes as Drafting Tools

## Setting Up a Work Area

Before beginning most drawings, you should set up your work area. To do this, determine the *measurement system*, the *drawing sheet size*, and the *scale* you want to use. The default work area is roughly 16″ × 9″ at full scale, given a decimal measurement system in which 1 unit equals 1 inch. Metric users will find that the default area is roughly 550 mm × 300 mm, in which 1 unit equals 1 mm. If these are appropriate settings for your drawing, you don't have to do any setting up. It's more likely, however, that you'll make drawings of various sizes and scales. For example, you might want to create a drawing in a measurement system in which you can specify feet, inches, and fractions of inches at 1″ = 1′ scale and print the drawing on an 8½″× 11″ sheet of paper.

In this section, you'll learn how to set up a drawing exactly the way you want.

## Specifying Units

You'll start by creating a new file called Bath. Then, you'll set up the unit style.

Use these steps to create the file:

1. If you haven't done so already, start AutoCAD. If AutoCAD is already running, choose File ➢ New.

2. In the Select Template dialog box, select Acad.dwt, and click Open. Metric users should select Acadiso.dwt and then click Open.

3. Choose View ➢ Zoom ➢ All.

4. Choose File ➢ Save As.

5. In the Save Drawing As dialog box, enter **Bath** for the filename.

6. Check to make sure you're saving the drawing in the My Documents folder or in the folder where you've chosen to store your exercise files, and then click Save.

---

### USING THE IMPERIAL AND METRIC EXAMPLES

Many of the exercises in this chapter are shown in both the metric and Imperial measurement systems. Be sure that if you start with the Imperial system, you continue with it throughout this book.

The metric settings described in this book are only approximations of their Imperial equivalents. For example, the drawing scale for the metric example is 1:10, which is close to the 1″=1′-0″ scale used in the Imperial example. In the grid example, you're asked to use a 30-unit grid, which is close to the 1′ grid of the Imperial example. Dimensions of objects are similar, but not exact. For example, the Imperial version of the tub measures 2′-8″×5′-0, and the metric version of the tub is 81 cm × 152 cm. The actual metric equivalent of 2′-8″×5′-0″ is 81.28 cm×152.4 cm. Measurements in the tub example are rounded to the nearest centimeter.

Metric users should also be aware that AutoCAD uses a period as a decimal point instead of the comma used in most European nations, South Africa, and elsewhere. Commas are used in AutoCAD to separate the X, Y, and Z components of a coordinate.

---

The next thing you want to tell AutoCAD is the *unit style* you intend to use. So far, you've been using the default, which is decimal inches. In this unit style, whole units represent inches, and decimal units are decimal inches. If you want to be able to enter distances in feet, you must change the unit style to a style that accepts feet as input. You'll do this through the Drawing Units dialog box, shown in Figure 3.1.

**TIP**  If you're a civil engineer, you should know that the Engineering unit style lets you enter feet and decimal feet for distances. For example, the equivalent of 12′-6″ is 12.5′. If you use the Engineering unit style, you'll ensure that your drawings conform to the scale of drawings created by your architectural colleagues.

**FIGURE 3.1**

The Drawing Units
dialog box

Follow these steps to set a unit style:

1. Choose Format ➢ Units or type **Un**↵ to open the Drawing Units dialog box.

2. Let's look at a few of the options available. Click the Type drop-down list in the Length group. Notice the unit styles in the list.

3. Click Architectural. The Sample Output section of the dialog box shows you what the Architectural style looks like in AutoCAD. Metric users should keep this setting as Decimal.

**TIP**    You can also control the Drawing Units settings by using several system variables. To set the unit style, you can type **'lunits.**↵ at the Command prompt. (The apostrophe lets you enter this command while in the middle of other commands.) At the Enter new value for Lunits <2>: prompt, enter **4** for Architectural. See Appendix C for other settings.

4. Click the Precision drop-down list just below the Type list. Notice the options available. You can set the smallest unit AutoCAD will display in this drawing. For now, leave this setting at its default value of ¹⁄₁₆″. Metric users will keep the setting at 0.0000.

5. Press the Esc key to close the drop-down list, and then click the Direction button at the bottom of the Drawing Units dialog box to open the Direction Control dialog box. The Direction Control dialog box lets you set the direction for the 0° angle. For now, don't change these settings—you'll read more about them in a moment.

6. Click the Cancel button.

7. Click the drop-down list in the Insertion Scale group. The list shows various units of measure.

8. Click Inches; or, if you're a metric user, choose Centimeters. This option lets you control how AutoCAD translates drawing scales when you import drawings from outside the current drawing. You'll learn more about this feature in Chapter 27.

9. Click OK in the Drawing Units dialog box to return to the drawing.

If you use the Imperial system of measurement, you selected Architectural measurement units for this tutorial, but your work may require a different unit style. You saw the unit styles available in the Drawing Units dialog box. Table 3.1 shows examples of how the distance 15.5 is entered in each of these styles.

**TABLE 3.1:**      Measurement Systems Available in AutoCAD

| MEASUREMENT SYSTEM | AUTOCAD'S DISPLAY OF MEASUREMENT |
|---|---|
| Scientific | 1.55E+01 (inches or metric) |
| Decimal | 15.5000 (inches or metric) |
| Engineering | 1´-3.5″ (input as 1´3.5″) |
| Architectural | 1´-3½″ (input as 1´3-½″) |
| Fractional | 15½″ (input as 15-½″) |

In the previous exercise, you needed to change only two settings. Let's look at the other Drawing Units settings in more detail. As you read, you may want to refer to Figure 3.1.

## Fine-Tuning the Measurement System

Most of the time, you'll be concerned only with the units and angles settings of the Drawing Units dialog box. But as you saw in the preceding exercise, you can control many other settings related to the input and display of units.

**TIP**    To measure the distance between two points, choose Tools ➢ Inquiry ➢ Distance from the menu bar, or type **Di**↵, and then click the two points. (Di is the shortcut for entering **Dist**↵.) If this command doesn't give you an accurate distance measurement, examine the Precision option in the Drawing Units dialog box. If it's set too high, the value returned by the Dist command may be rounded to a value greater than your tolerances allow, even though the distance is drawn accurately.

The Precision drop-down list in the Length group lets you specify the smallest unit value that you want AutoCAD to display in the status bar and in the prompts. If you choose a measurement system that uses fractions, the Precision list includes fractional units. You can also control this setting with the Luprec system variable.

The Angle group lets you set the style for displaying angles. You have a choice of five angle styles: Decimal Degrees, Degrees/Minutes/Seconds, Grads, Radians, and Surveyor's Units. In the Angle group's Precision drop-down list, you can specify the degree of accuracy you want AutoCAD to display for angles. You can also control these settings with the Aunits and Auprec system variables.

**TIP** You can find out more about system variables in the Help window. Select the Contents tab of the Help window, and then expand the Command Reference listing. Locate and expand the System Variable listing under Command Reference.

You can tell AutoCAD which direction is positive, either clockwise or counterclockwise. This book uses the default, which is counterclockwise. You can also control these settings with the Angbase and Angdir system variables. The Direction Control dialog box lets you set the direction of the 0 base angle. The default base angle (and the one used throughout this book) is a direction from left to right. However, at times you may want to designate another direction as the 0 base angle.

The Insertion Scale setting in the Drawing Units dialog box lets you control how blocks from the Tool palettes or DesignCenter are scaled as they're imported into your current drawing. A *block* is a collection of drawing objects that form a single object. Blocks are frequently used to create standard symbols. You'll learn more about blocks in Chapter 4. The Insertion Scale setting lets you compensate for drawings of different scales by offering an automatic scale translation when importing blocks from an external file. The Insunits system variable also controls the Insertion Scale setting. You'll learn more about this setting in Chapter 27.

**TIP** If you're new to AutoCAD, don't worry about the Insertion Scale setting right now. Make a mental note of it. It may come in handy in your work in the future.

## Setting Up the Drawing Limits

One of the big advantages in using AutoCAD is that you can draw at full scale; you aren't limited to the edges of a piece of paper the way you are in manual drawing. But you may find it difficult to start drawing without knowing where the drawing boundaries are. You can set up some arbitrary boundaries using the Limits feature. You got a taste of the Limits feature in Chapter 1. You'll use it again here to set up a work area for your next drawing.

### THINGS TO WATCH FOR WHEN ENTERING DISTANCES

When you're using Architectural units, you should be aware of two points:

◆ Use hyphens only to distinguish fractions from whole inches.

◆ You can't use spaces while specifying a dimension. For example, you can specify eight feet, four and one-half inches as 8´4-½″ or 8´4.5, but not as 8´-4½″.

These idiosyncrasies are a source of confusion to many architects and engineers new to AutoCAD because the program often displays architectural dimensions in the standard architectural format but doesn't allow you to enter dimensions that way.

Here are some tips for entering distances and angles in unusual situations:

◆ When entering distances in inches and feet, you can omit the inch (″) sign. If you're using the Engineering unit style, you can enter decimal feet and forgo the inch sign entirely.

◆ You can enter fractional distances and angles in any format you like, regardless of the current unit style. For example, you can enter a distance as **@½<1.5708r**, even if your current unit system is set for decimal units and decimal degrees (1.5708r is the radian equivalent of 90°).

◆ If you have your angle units set to degrees, grads, or radians, you don't need to specify g, r, or d after the angle. You do have to specify g, r, or d, however, if you want to use these units when they aren't the current default angle system.

◆ If your current angle system is set to something other than degrees, but you want to enter angles in degrees, you can use a double less-than symbol (<<) in place of the single less-than symbol (<) to override the current angle system of measure. The << also assumes the base angle of 0° to be a direction from left to right and the positive direction to be counterclockwise.

◆ If your current angle system uses a different base angle and direction, and you want to specify an angle in the standard base direction, you can use a triple less-than symbol (<<<) to indicate angles. Note that this works only if Dynamic Input is turned off.

◆ You can specify a denominator of any size when specifying fractions. However, be aware that the value you've set for the maximum number of digits to the right of decimal points (under the Precision setting in the Length group of the Drawing Units dialog box) restricts the fractional value AutoCAD reports. For example, if your units are set for a maximum of two digits of decimals, and you give a fractional value of 5/32, AutoCAD rounds this value to 3/16, or 0.1875. Note that this doesn't affect the accuracy of the actual drawing dimensions.

◆ You can enter decimal feet for distances in the Architectural unit style. For example, you can enter 6′-6″ as **6.5′**.

You'll be drawing a bathroom that is roughly 8 feet by 5 feet (230 cm by 150 cm for metric users). You'll want to give yourself some extra room around the bathroom, so your drawing limits should be a bit larger than that actual bathroom size. You'll use an area of 11′ by 8′6″ for the limits of your drawing. Metric users will use an area 297 cm by 210 cm. These sizes will accommodate your bathroom with some room to spare.

Now that you know the area you need, you can use the Limits command to set up the area:

**1.** Choose Format ➢ Drawing Limits.

**2.** At the Specify lower left corner or [ON/OFF] <0′-0″,0′-0″>: prompt, specify the lower-left corner of your work area. Press ↵ to accept the default.

**3.** At the Specify upper right corner <1′0″,0′9″>: prompt, specify the upper-right corner of your work area. (The default is shown in brackets.) Enter **132,102**. Or if you prefer, you can enter **11′,8′6**, because you've set up your drawing for architectural units. Metric users should enter **297,210**.

**4.** Choose View ➢ Zoom ➢ All, or type **Z↵A↵**. Although it appears that nothing has changed, your drawing area is now set to a size that will enable you to draw your bathroom at full scale.

**TIP** You can toggle through the Coordinate Readout modes by repeatedly pressing Ctrl+I or by clicking the coordinate readout on the status bar. For more on the Coordinate Readout modes, see Chapter 1.

**5.** Move the cursor to the upper-right corner of the drawing area, and watch the coordinate readout. Notice that now the upper-right corner has a Y coordinate of approximately 8′-6″, or 210 for metric users. The X coordinate depends on the proportion of your AutoCAD window. The coordinate readout also displays distances in feet and inches.

In step 5, the coordinate readout shows you that your drawing area is larger than before, but no visual clues tell you where you are or what distances you're dealing with. To help you get your bearings, you can turn on Grid mode, which you'll learn about toward the end of this chapter. Grid mode displays an array of dots that help you visualize distances and the limits of your drawing.

## An Alternative to Limits

As an alternative to setting up the drawing limits, you can draw a rectangle that outlines the same area used to define the drawing limits. For example, in the previous exercise, you could use the Rectangle tool to draw a rectangle that has its lower-left corner at coordinate 0,0 and its upper-right corner at 132,102 (297,210 for metric users). You can set up the rectangle to be visible without printing using the Layer feature. You'll learn more about layers in Chapter 5.

---

**COORDINATING WITH PAPER SIZES**

At this point, you may have questions about how your full-scale drawing will fit onto standard paper sizes. AutoCAD offers several features that give you precise control over the scale of your drawing. These features offer industry-standard scales to match your drawing with any paper size you need. You'll learn more about these features as you work through the chapters of this book; but if you're anxious to find out about them, look at the sections on layouts in Chapters 8 and 16 and also check out the Annotation Scale feature in Chapter 10.

---

## Understanding Scale Factors

When you draft manually, you work on the final drawing directly with pen and ink or pencil. With a CAD program, you're a few steps removed from the finished product. Because of this, you need a deeper understanding of your drawing scale and how it's derived. In particular, you need to understand *scale factors*. For example, one of the more common uses of scale factors is translating the size of a graphic symbol, such as a section symbol in an architectural drawing, to the final plotted text size. When you draw manually, you draw your symbol at the size you want. In a CAD drawing, you need to translate the desired final symbol size to the drawing scale.

When you start adding graphic symbols to your drawing (see Chapter 4), you have to specify a symbol height. The scale factor helps you determine the appropriate symbol height for a particular drawing scale. For example, you may want your symbol to appear ½″ high in your final plot. But if you draw your symbol to ½″ in your drawing, it appears as a dot when plotted. The symbol has to be scaled up to a size that, when scaled back down at plot time, appears ½″ high. So, for a ¼″ scale drawing, you multiply the ½″ text height by a scale factor of 48 to get 24″. Your symbol should be 24″ high in the CAD drawing in order to appear ½″ high in the final plot. Where did the number 48 come from?

The scale factor for fractional inch scales is derived by multiplying the denominator of the scale by 12 and then dividing by the numerator. For example, the scale factor for ¼″ = 1′-0″ is (4 × 12)/1, or 48/1. For 3/16″ = 1′-0″ scale, the operation is (16 × 12)/3, or 64. For whole-foot scales such as 1″ = 10′, multiply the feet side of the equation by 12. Metric scales require simple decimal conversions.

You can also use scale factors to determine your drawing limits. For example, if you have a sheet size of 11″ × 17″, and you want to know the equivalent full-scale size for a 1/4″-scale drawing, you multiply the sheet measurements by 48. In this way, 11″ becomes 528″ (48 × 11″), and 17″ becomes 816″ (48 × 17″). Your work area must be 528″ × 816″ if you intend to have a final output of 11″ × 17″ at 1/4″ = 1′. You can divide these inch measurements by 12″ to get 44′ × 68′.

Table 3.2 shows scale factors as they relate to standard drawing scales. These scale factors are the values by which you multiply the desired final printout size to get the equivalent full-scale size. If you're using the metric system, you can use the drawing scale directly as the scale factor. For example, a drawing scale of 1:10 has a scale factor of 10; a drawing scale of 1:50 has a scale factor of 50; and so on. Metric users need to take special care regarding the base unit. The examples in this book use centimeters as a base unit, which means that if you enter a distance as 1, you can assume the distance to be 1 cm.

**TABLE 3.2:**     Scale Conversion Factors

| SCALE FACTORS FOR ENGINEERING DRAWING SCALES | | | | | | | | |
|---|---|---|---|---|---|---|---|---|
| $n = 1''$ | 10´ | 20´ | 30´ | 40´ | 50´ | 60´ | 100´ | 200´ |
| Scale factor | 120 | 240 | 360 | 480 | 600 | 720 | 1200 | 2400 |
| **Scale Factors for Architectural Drawing Scales** | | | | | | | | |
| $n = 1'\text{-}0''$ | ⅟₁₆" | ⅛" | ¼" | ½" | ¾" | 1" | 1½" | 3" |
| Scale factor | 192 | 96 | 48 | 24 | 16 | 12 | 8 | 4 |

If you're working on a drawing from an older version of AutoCAD, you'll use scale factors to specify text height and dimension settings, so understanding them now will pay off later. Plotting to a particular scale is also easier with an understanding of scale factors.

## Using Polar Tracking

In this section, you'll draw the first item in the bathroom: the toilet. It's composed of a rectangle representing the tank and a truncated ellipse representing the seat. To construct the toilet, you'll use Polar Tracking, which is one of the more versatile drafting tools. Polar Tracking helps you align your cursor to exact horizontal and vertical angles, much like a T-square and triangle.

In this exercise, you'll use Polar Tracking to draw a rectangular box:

1. Start your line at the coordinate 5´-7˝, 6´-3˝ by entering **5´7˝,6´3˝**⏎. Metric users should enter **171,189**⏎ as the starting coordinate. This starting point is somewhat arbitrary, but by entering a specific starting location, you're coordinated with the figures and instructions in this book.

2. Make sure Polar Tracking is on (the Polar button in the status bar should be in the on position), and then point the cursor directly to the right of the last point. The Polar Tracking cursor appears, along with the Polar Tracking readout.

3. With the cursor pointing directly to the right, enter **1´-10˝**⏎. Metric users should enter **56**⏎.

**NOTE**    You can use the spacebar in place of the ⏎ key when entering distances in this way.

4. Point the cursor downward, enter **0´-9˝**⏎, and click this point. Metric users should enter **23**⏎.

5. Continue drawing the other two sides of the rectangle by using Polar Tracking. After you've completed the rectangle, press ⏎ or the Esc key to exit the Line tool. You should have a drawing that looks like Figure 3.2.

**FIGURE 3.2**

A plan view of the toilet tank

As you can see from the exercise, you can use Polar Tracking to restrain your cursor to horizontal and vertical positions, just like a T-square and triangle. Later, you'll learn how you can set up Polar Tracking to set the angle to any value you want in a way similar to an adjustable triangle.

In some situations, you may find that you don't want Polar Tracking on. You can turn it off by clicking the Polar button in the status bar. You can also press the F10 function key to turn Polar Tracking on or off.

Although this exercise tells you to use the Line tool to draw the tank, you can also use the Rectangle tool. The Rectangle tool creates what is known as a *polyline,* which is a set of line or arc segments that acts like a single object. You'll learn more about polylines in Chapter 18.

By using the Snap modes in conjunction with the coordinate readout and Polar Tracking, you can locate coordinates and measure distances as you draw lines. This is similar to the way you draw when using a scale. The smallest distance registered by the coordinate readout and Polar Tracking readout depends on the area you've displayed on your screen. For example, if you're displaying an area the size of a football field, the smallest distance you can indicate with your cursor may be 6″ or 15 cm. On the other hand, if your view is enlarged to show an area of only one square inch or centimeter, you can indicate distances as small as 1/1000 of an inch or centimeter by using your cursor.

## Setting the Polar Tracking Angle

You've seen how Polar Tracking lets you draw exact vertical and horizontal lines. You can also set Polar Tracking to draw lines at other angles, such as 30° or 45°. To change the angle Polar Tracking uses, you use the Polar Tracking tab in the Drafting Settings dialog box.

Right-click the Polar button in the status bar, and then choose Settings from the shortcut menu to open the Drafting Settings dialog box. Or, you can choose Tools ➢ Drafting Settings from the menu bar and then click the Polar Tracking tab.

---

### ORTHO MODE

In addition to using Polar Tracking mode, you can further restrain the cursor to a vertical or horizontal direction by using Ortho mode. To use Ortho mode, hold down the Shift key while drawing. You can also press F8 or click Ortho in the status bar to keep Ortho mode on while you draw. When you move the cursor around while drawing objects, the rubber-banding line moves only vertically or horizontally. With Ortho mode turned on, Polar Tracking is automatically turned off.

---

To change the Polar Tracking angle, enter an angle in the Increment Angle text box, or select a predefined angle from the drop-down list. You can do this while drawing series of line segments, for example, so that you can set angles on the fly.

Numerous other settings are available in the Polar Tracking tab. Here is a listing of their functions for your reference:

**Additional Angles**   This setting lets you enter a specific angle for Polar Tracking. For example, if you want Polar Tracking to snap to 12″, click the New button next to the Additional Angles list box, and enter **12**. The value you enter appears in the list box, and when the Additional Angles check box is selected, Polar Tracking snaps to 12″. To delete a value from the list box, highlight it, and click the Delete button.

The Additional Angles option differs from the Increment Angle setting in that the Increment Angle setting causes Polar Tracking to snap to every increment of its setting, whereas Additional Angles snaps only to the angle specified. You can enter as many angles as you want in the Additional Angles list box.

**Object Snap Tracking Settings**   These settings let you control whether Object Snap Tracking uses strictly orthogonal directions (0°, 90°, 180°, and 270°) or the angles set in the Polar Angle Settings group in this dialog box. (See the "Aligning Objects by Using Object Snap Tracking" section later in this chapter.)

**Polar Angle Measurement**   These radio buttons let you determine the zero angle on which Polar Tracking bases its incremental angles. The Absolute option uses the current AutoCAD setting for the 0° angle. The Relative To Last Segment option uses the last drawn object as the 0° angle. For example, if you draw a line at a 10° angle and the Relative To Last Segment option is selected with the Increment Angle set to 90°, Polar Tracking snaps to 10, 100°, 190°, and 280°, relative to the actual 0° direction.

## Exploring the Drawing Process

This section presents some of the more common AutoCAD commands and shows you how to use them to complete a simple drawing. As you draw, watch the prompts and notice how your responses affect them. Also notice how you use existing drawing elements as reference points.

While drawing with AutoCAD, you create simple geometric forms to determine the basic shapes of objects, and you can then modify the shapes to fill in detail.

AutoCAD offers 14 basic 2D drawing object types: lines, arcs, circles, text, dimensions, traces, polylines, points, ellipses, elliptical arcs, spline curves, regions, hatches, and multiline text. All drawings are built on these objects. In addition, there are five 3D meshes, which are three-dimensional surfaces composed of 3D faces. You're familiar with lines and arcs; these, along with circles, are the most commonly used objects. As you progress through the book, you'll learn about the other objects and how they're used. You'll also learn about 3D objects in the section on AutoCAD 3D.

## Locating an Object in Reference to Others

To define the toilet seat, you'll use an ellipse. Follow these steps:

1. Click the Ellipse tool in the 2D Draw control panel, or type **El**↵. You can also choose Draw ➤ Ellipse ➤ Axis, End.

2. At the `Specify axis endpoint of ellipse or [Arc/Center]:` prompt, pick the midpoint of the bottom horizontal line of the rectangle. Do this by opening the Osnap pop-up menu and selecting Midpoint; then, move the cursor toward the bottom line. (Remember, Shift+click the right mouse button to open the Osnap menu.) When you see the Midpoint Osnap marker on the line, click the left mouse button.

3. At the `Specify other endpoint of axis:` prompt, point the cursor downward, and enter **1′-10″**↵. Metric users should enter **55**↵.

4. Pick this as the second axis endpoint.

5. At the `Specify distance to other axis or [Rotation]:` prompt, point the cursor horizontally from the center of the ellipse, and then enter **8″**↵. Metric users should enter **20**↵. Your drawing should look like Figure 3.3.

**TIP**   As you work with AutoCAD, you'll eventually run into NURBS. NURBS stands for *Non-Uniform Rational B-Splines*—a fancy term meaning that curved objects are based on accurate mathematical models. When you trim the ellipse in a later exercise, it becomes a NURBS curve known as a *spline* in AutoCAD. You'll learn more about polylines and spline curves in Chapter 18.

**FIGURE 3.3**
The ellipse added to the tank

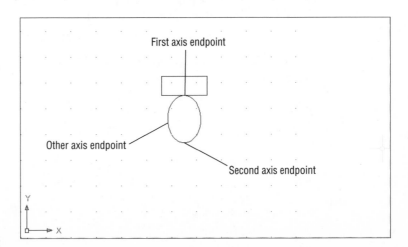

## Getting a Closer Look

During the drawing process, you'll often want to enlarge areas of a drawing to edit its objects. In Chapter 1, you saw how to use the Zoom capability for this purpose. Follow these steps to enlarge the view of the toilet:

1. Click the Zoom Window tool on the 2D Navigate control panel, or type **Z↵W↵**. You can also choose View ➢ Zoom ➢ Window.

2. At the Specify first corner: prompt, pick a point below and to the left of your drawing, at or near coordinate 5′-0″, 3′-6″. Metric users should use the coordinate 150.0000,102.0000.

3. At the Specify opposite corner: prompt, pick a point above and to the right of the drawing, at or near coordinate 8′-3″, 6′-8″ (246.0000,195.0000 for metric users). The toilet should be completely enclosed by the zoom window. To obtain this view, use the Zoom Window tool. You can also use the Zoom Realtime tool in conjunction with the Pan Realtime tool. The toilet enlarges to fill more of the screen. Your view should look similar to Figure 3.4.

**TIP** To start the Zoom Realtime tool from the keyboard, type **Z↵↵**. If you have a mouse with a scroll wheel, you can avoid using the Zoom command altogether; just place the cursor on the toilet, and turn the wheel to zoom into the image.

## Modifying an Object

Now, let's see how editing commands are used to construct an object. To define the back edge of the seat, let's put a copy of the line defining the front of the toilet tank 3″ (7 cm for metric users) toward the center of the ellipse:

1. Click the Copy tool in the 2D Draw control panel, or type **co↵**. You can also choose Modify ➢ Copy from the drop-down menu.

**TIP** You can also use the Grip Edit tools to make the copy. See Chapter 2 for more on grip editing.

2. At the Select objects: prompt, pick the horizontal line that touches the top of the ellipse. The line is highlighted. Press ↵ to complete your selection.

3. At the Specify base point or [Displacement] <Displacement>: prompt, pick a base point near the line. Then, point the cursor down, and enter **3″↵** or **7↵** for metric users.

4. Press ↵ to exit the Copy command. Your drawing should look like Figure 3.4.

Notice that the Copy command acts exactly like the Move command you used in Chapter 2, except that Copy doesn't alter the position of the objects you select and you must press ↵ to exit Copy.

### TRIMMING AN OBJECT

Now you must delete the part of the ellipse that isn't needed. You'll use the Trim command to trim off part of the ellipse:

1. Turn off Snap mode by pressing F9 or clicking Snap on the status bar. Snap mode can be a hindrance at this point in your editing session because it can keep you from picking the points you want. Snap mode forces the cursor to move to points at a given interval, so you'll have difficulty selecting a point that doesn't fall exactly at one of those intervals.

**FIGURE 3.4**

The line copied down

2. Click the Trim tool in the 2D Draw control panel. You'll see this prompt:

```
Current settings: Projection=UCS Edge=None
Select cutting edges ...
Select objects or <select all>:
```

3. Click the line you just created—the one that crosses through the ellipse—and press ↵ to finish your selection.

4. At the `Select object to trim or shift-select to extend or [Fence/Crossing/Project/Edge/eRase/Undo]:` prompt, pick the topmost portion of the ellipse above the line. This trims the ellipse back to the line.

5. Press ↵ to exit the Trim command.

**TIP**   By holding down the Shift key in step 4, you can change from trimming an object to extending an object. You'll learn about the Extend command in Chapter 18.

In step 2 of the preceding exercise, the Trim command produces two messages in the prompt. The first prompt, `Select cutting edges...`, tells you that you must first select objects to define *the edge to which you want to trim an object.* In step 4, you're again prompted to select objects, this time to select the *object to trim.* Trim is one of a handful of AutoCAD commands that asks you to select two sets of objects: The first set defines a boundary, and the second is the set of objects you want to edit. The two sets of objects aren't mutually exclusive. You can, for example, select the cutting-edge objects as objects to trim. The next exercise shows how this works.

First, you'll undo the trim you just did; then, you'll use the Trim command again in a slightly different way to finish the toilet:

1. Click the Undo button in the Standard Annotation toolbar, or enter **U**↵ at the command prompt. The top of the ellipse reappears.

2. Start the Trim tool again by clicking it in the 2D Draw control panel.

3. At the `Select objects or <select all>:` prompt, click the ellipse and the line crossing the ellipse. (See the first image in Figure 3.5.)

**FIGURE 3.5**

Trimming the ellipse
and the line

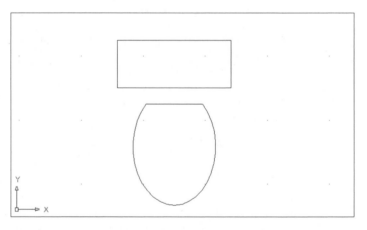

**4.** Press ↵ to finish your selection and move to the next step.

**TIP** These Trim options—Fence, Crossing, Project, Edge, eRase, and Undo—are described in the section "Exploring the Trim Options" next in this chapter.

**5.** At the Select object to trim or [Fence/Crossing/Project/Edge/eRase/Undo]: prompt, click the top portion of the ellipse, as you did in the previous exercise. The ellipse trims back.

**6.** Click a point near the left end of the trim line, past the ellipse. The line trims back to the ellipse.

**7.** Click the other end of the line. The right side of the line trims back to meet the ellipse. Your drawing should look like the second image in Figure 3.5.

**8.** Press ↵ to exit the Trim command.

**9.** Choose File ➤ Save to save the file in its current state, but don't exit the file. You may want to get in the habit of doing this every 20 minutes.

Here you saw how the ellipse and the line are both used as trim objects as well as the objects to be trimmed.

### EXPLORING THE TRIM OPTIONS

AutoCAD offers six options for the Trim command: Fence, Crossing, Project, Edge, eRase, and Undo. As described in the following paragraphs, these options give you a higher degree of control over how objects are trimmed:

**Edge [E]**   Lets you trim an object to an apparent intersection, even if the cutting-edge object doesn't intersect the object to be trimmed. (See the top of Figure 3.6.) Edge offers two options: Extend and No Extend. You can also set these options by using the Edgemode system variable.

**FIGURE 3.6**
The Trim command's options

Imagined extension of line

Actual extent of line

Result

With the Extend option, objects will trim even if the trimmed object doesn't actually intersect with the object to be trimmed.

Trimmed Portion

With the UCS option, objects in 3D space will trim on a plane perpendicular to the current UCS...

but when viewed in 3D or in another UCS, may appear to be trimmed incorrectly.

With the View option, objects in 3D space will trim according to your point of view...

but when they are viewed in plan, they may appear to be trimmed incorrectly.

**Project [P]** Useful when you're working on 3D drawings. It controls how AutoCAD trims objects that aren't coplanar. Project offers three options: None, UCS, and View. The None option causes Trim to ignore objects that are on different planes so that only coplanar objects are trimmed. If you choose UCS, the Trim command trims objects based on a plan view of the current UCS and then disregards whether the objects are coplanar. (See the middle of Figure 3.6.) View is similar to UCS but uses the current view's "line of sight" to determine how non-coplanar objects are trimmed. (See the bottom of Figure 3.6.)

**eRase [R]** Allows you to erase an object while remaining in the Trim command.

**Fence/Crossing [F or C]** Lets you use a Fence or Crossing window to select objects.

**Undo [U]** Causes the last trimmed object to revert to its original length.

You've just seen one way to construct the toilet. However, you can construct objects in many ways. For example, you can trim only the top of the ellipse, as you did in the first Trim exercise, and then use the Grips feature to move the endpoints of the line to meet the endpoints of the ellipse. As you become familiar with AutoCAD, you'll start to develop your own ways of working, using the tools best suited to your style.

If you'd like to take a break, now is a good time. You can exit AutoCAD and then come back to the Bath drawing file when you're ready to proceed.

## Planning and Laying Out a Drawing

For the next object, the bathtub, you'll use some new commands to lay out parts of the drawing. This will help you get a feel for the kind of planning you must do to use AutoCAD effectively. You'll begin the bathtub by using the Line command to draw a rectangle 2′-8″ × 5′-0″ (81 cm × 152 cm for metric users) on the left side of the drawing area. For a change this time, you'll use a couple of shortcut methods built into AutoCAD: the Line command's keyboard shortcut, and the Direct Distance method for specifying distance and direction.

First, though, you'll go back to the previous view of your drawing and arrange some more room to work. Follow these steps:

1. Return to your previous view, shown in Figure 3.7. A quick way to do this is to choose View ➢ Zoom ➢ Previous. Your view returns to the one you had before the last Zoom command.

**FIGURE 3.7**
The view of the finished toilet after using the Zoom Previous tool. You can also obtain this view by using the Zoom All tool from the Zoom Window flyout.

**2.** Type **L↵**, and, at the `Specify first point:` prompt, enter **9,10↵** to start the line at the 0´-9″, 0´-10″ coordinate. Metric users should enter **24,27↵** for the coordinate 24.0000,27.0000.

**3.** Place your cursor to the right of the last point selected so that the rubber-banding line is pointing directly to the right, and type **2´8″**; then, press ↵ for the first side of the tub. Metric users should enter **81↵**. Notice that the rubber-banding line is now fixed at the length you typed.

**4.** Point the rubber-banding line upward toward the top of the screen, and type **5´**; then, press ↵ for the next side. Metric users should enter **152↵**.

**5.** Point the rubber-banding line directly to the left of the last point, and type **2´8″** (81 for metric users); then, press ↵ for the next side.

**6.** Type **C↵** to close the rectangle and exit the Line command.

**TIP** Instead of pressing ↵ during the Direct Distance method, you can press the spacebar or right-click, and choose Enter from the shortcut menu.

Now you have the outline of the tub. Notice that when you enter feet and inches from the keyboard, you must avoid hyphens or spaces. Thus, 2 feet 8 inches is typed as **2´8″**. Also notice that you don't have to enter the at sign (@) or angle specification. Instead, you use the Direct Distance method to specify direction and distance. You can use this method for drawing lines or moving and copying objects at right angles. The Direct Distance method is less effective if you want to specify exact angles other than right angles.

Some of the keyboard shortcuts for tools or commands you've used in this chapter are CO (Copy), E (Erase), EL (Ellipse), F (Fillet), M (Move), O (Offset), and TR (Trim). Remember that you can enter keyboard shortcuts, such as keyboard commands, only when the Command prompt is visible in the Command window.

## Making a Preliminary Sketch

In this section, you'll see how planning ahead will make your use of AutoCAD more efficient. When drawing a complex object, you'll often have to do some layout before you do the actual drawing. This is similar to drawing an accurate pencil sketch using construction lines that you later trace over to produce a finished drawing. The advantage of doing this in AutoCAD is that your drawing doesn't lose any accuracy between the sketch and the final product. Also, AutoCAD enables you to use the geometry of your sketch to aid you in drawing. While you're planning your drawing, think about what you want to draw, and then decide which drawing elements will help you create that object.

You'll use the Offset command to establish reference lines to help you draw the inside of the tub. This is where the Osnap overrides are useful. (See the sidebar "The Osnap Options," later in this chapter.)

You can use the Offset tool on the 2D Draw control panel to make parallel copies of a set of objects, such as the lines forming the outside of your tub. Offset is different from the Copy command; Offset allows only one object to be copied at a time, but it can remember the distance you specify. The Offset option doesn't work with all types of objects. Only lines, arcs, circles, ellipses, splines and 2D polylines can be offset.

Standard lines are best suited for the layout of the bathtub in this situation. In Chapter 6, you'll learn about two other objects, construction lines (Xlines) and rays, which are specifically designed to help you lay out a drawing. In this exercise, you'll use standard lines:

**1.** Click the Offset tool in the 2D Draw control panel, or type **O↵**. You can also choose Modify ➢ Offset from the drop-down menu.

2. At the `Specify offset distance or [Through/Erase/Layer] <Through>:` prompt, enter **3↵**. This specifies the distance of 3″ as the offset distance. Metric users should enter **7** for 7 cm, which is roughly equivalent to 3 inches.

3. At the `Select object to offset or [Exit/Undo] <Exit>:` prompt, click the bottom line of the rectangle you just drew.

4. At the `Specify point on side to offset or [Exit/Multiple/Undo]:` prompt, pick a point inside the rectangle. A copy of the line appears. You don't have to be exact about where you pick the side to offset; AutoCAD wants to know only on which side of the line you want to make the offset copy.

5. The prompt `Select object to offset or [Exit/Undo] <Exit>:` appears again. Click another side to offset; then, click again on a point inside the rectangle.

6. Continue to offset the other two sides; then, offset these four new lines inside the rectangle toward the center. You'll have a drawing that looks like Figure 3.8.

7. When you're done, exit the Offset command by pressing ↵.

**FIGURE 3.8**

The completed layout

## Using the Layout

Now, you'll begin to draw the inside of the tub, starting with the narrow end. You'll use your offset lines as references to construct the arcs that make up the tub. Also in this exercise, you'll set up some of the Osnap tools to be available automatically whenever AutoCAD expects a point selection. Here are the steps:

1. Choose Tools ➢ Drafting Settings, and click the Object Snap tab. You can also type **Os↵** or right-click the Osnap button on the status bar and then choose Settings from the shortcut menu.

2. Click the Clear All button to turn off any options that may be selected.

**TIP** Look at the graphic symbols next to each of the Osnap options in the Object Snap tab. These are the Osnap markers that appear in your drawing as you select Osnap points. Each Osnap option has its own marker symbol. As you use the osnaps, you'll become more familiar with how they work.

3. Click the Endpoint, Midpoint, and Intersection check boxes so that a check mark appears in each box, and make sure the Object Snap On option is selected. Click OK.

You've just set up the Endpoint, Midpoint, and Intersection osnaps to be on by default. This is called a *Running Osnap;* AutoCAD automatically selects the nearest Osnap point without your intervention. Now, let's see how a Running Osnap works:

1. In the 2D Draw control panel, click the Arc tool or type **a**↵. See Figure 3.9 for other Arc options available when you choose Draw ➢ Arc.

2. For the first point of the arc, move the cursor toward the intersection of the two lines, as indicated in the top image in Figure 3.10. Notice that the Intersection Osnap marker appears on the intersection.

3. With the Intersection Osnap marker on the desired intersection, click the left mouse button.

4. Move the cursor to the midpoint of the second horizontal line near the top. When the Midpoint Osnap marker appears at the midpoint of the line, click the left mouse button.

5. Use the Intersection Osnap marker to locate and select the intersection of the two lines at the upper-left side of the bathtub.

**FIGURE 3.9**

If you look at the Arc cascading menu, you'll see some additional options for drawing arcs. These options provide canned responses to the Arc command so that you only have to select the appropriate points as indicated in the drop-down menu option name.

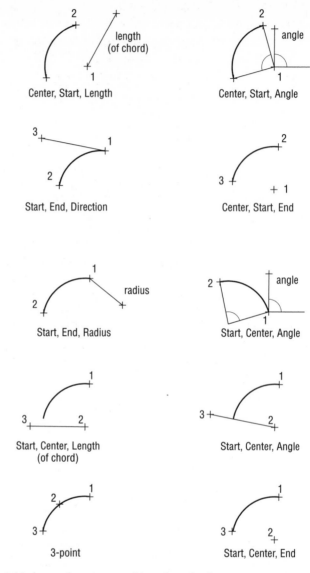

Center, Start, Length

Center, Start, Angle

Start, End, Direction

Center, Start, End

Start, End, Radius

Start, Center, Angle

Start, Center, Length (of chord)

Start, Center, Angle

3-point

Start, Center, End

The top image in Figure 3.10 shows the sequence I just described.

**TIP** When you see an Osnap marker on an object, you can have AutoCAD move to the next osnap point on the object by pressing the Tab key. If you have several Running Osnap modes on (Endpoint, Midpoint, and Intersection, for example), pressing the Tab key cycles through those osnap points on the object. This feature can be especially useful in a crowded area of a drawing.

**FIGURE 3.10**
Drawing the top, left side, and bottom of the tub

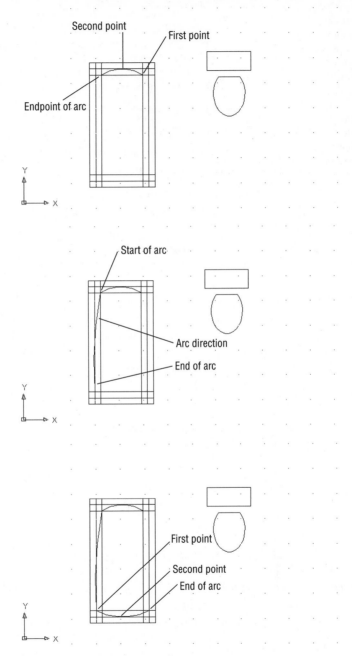

Next, you'll draw an arc for the left side of the tub:

1. In the 2D Draw control panel, click the Arc tool again.

2. Type @↵ to select the last point you picked as the start of the next arc.

### ADJUSTING THE AUTOSNAP FEATURE

When you click the Options button in the Object Snap tab of the Drafting Settings dialog box, you'll see the Drafting Settings tab of the Options dialog box. This tab offers a set of options pertaining to the AutoSnap feature. AutoSnap looks at the location of your cursor during osnap selections and locates the osnap point nearest your cursor. AutoSnap then displays a graphic called a *marker* showing you the osnap point it has found. If it's the one you want, you left-click your mouse to select it.

The AutoSnap settings enable you to control various features:

**Marker** turns the graphic marker on or off.

**Magnet** causes the Osnap cursor to jump to inferred osnap points.

**Display AutoSnap Tooltip** turns the Osnap ToolTip on or off.

**Display AutoSnap Aperture Box** turns the old-style Osnap cursor box on or off.

**AutoSnap Marker Size** controls the size of the graphic marker.

**Colors** controls the color of the AutoSnap marker. This option opens the Drawing Window Colors dialog box, which lets you select a color.

**WARNING** It's easy for new users to select points inadvertently. If you accidentally select additional points after the last exercise and prior to step 1, you may not get the results described here. If this happens, issue the Arc command again; then, use the Endpoint Osnap, and select the endpoint of the last arc.

3. Type **E↵** to tell AutoCAD that you want to specify the other end of the arc instead of the next point. Or, you can right-click anywhere in the drawing area and choose End from the shortcut menu.

4. At the `Specify end point of arc:` prompt, use the Intersection osnap to pick the intersection of the two lines in the lower-left corner of the tub. See the middle image in Figure 3.10 for the location of this point.

5. Type **D↵** to select the Direction option. You can also right-click anywhere in the drawing area and then choose Direction from the shortcut menu. The arc drags as you move the cursor, along with a rubber-banding line from the starting point of the arc.

6. Move the cursor to the left of the dragging arc until it touches the middle line on the left side of the tub. Pick that, as shown in the middle image in Figure 3.10.

**TIP** In step 3, the rubber-banding line indicates the direction of the arc. Be sure Ortho mode is off, because Ortho mode forces the rubber-banding line and the arc in a direction you don't want. Check the status bar; if the Ortho button looks like it's pressed, press F8 or click the Ortho button to turn off Ortho mode.

Now, you'll draw the bottom of the tub:

1. Click the Arc tool in the 2D Draw control panel again. You can also press ↵ to replay the last command.

2. Using the Endpoint Osnap marker, pick the endpoint of the bottom of the arc just drawn.

3. Using the Midpoint Osnap marker, pick the middle horizontal line at the bottom of the tub.

4. Pick the intersection of the two lines in the lower-right corner of the tub (see the image at the bottom in Figure 3.10).

Next, create the right side of the tub by mirroring the left side:

1. Click the Mirror tool on the 2D Draw control panel. You can also choose Modify ➤ Mirror or enter **mi**↵ at the Command prompt.

2. At the `Select objects:` prompt, pick the long arc on the left side of the tub to highlight the arc. Press ↵ to indicate that you've finished your selection.

3. At the `Specify first point of mirror line:` prompt, pick the midpoint of the top horizontal line. By now, you should know how to use the automatic osnap modes you set up earlier.

4. At the `Specify second point of mirror line:` prompt, use Polar Tracking mode to pick a point directly below the last point selected.

5. At the `Erase source objects? [Yes/No] <N>:` prompt, press ↵ to accept the default (No). A mirror image of the arc you picked appears on the right side of the tub. Your drawing should look like Figure 3.11.

**FIGURE 3.11**
The inside of the tub completed with the layout lines still in place

In this exercise, you were able to use osnaps in a Running Osnap mode. You'll find that you'll use osnaps constantly as you create your drawings. For this reason, you may want Running Osnaps on all the time. Even so, at times Running Osnaps can get in the way. For example, they may be a nuisance in a crowded drawing when you want to use a zoom window. The osnaps can cause you to select an inappropriate window area by automatically selecting osnap points.

Fortunately, you can toggle Running Osnaps on and off easily by clicking the Osnap button in the status bar. If you don't have any Running Osnaps set, clicking the Osnap button opens the Object Snap settings in the Drafting Settings dialog box, enabling you to select your osnaps.

## Erasing the Layout Lines

Next, you'll erase the layout lines you created using the Offset command. But this time, you'll try selecting the lines *before* issuing the Erase command.

**TIP**  If the following exercise doesn't work as described, be sure you have the Noun/Verb selection setting turned on. See Appendix A for details.

Follow these steps:

1.  Click each internal layout line individually.

    If you have problems selecting just the lines, try using a selection window to select single lines. (Remember, a window selects only objects that are completely within the window.).

2.  After all the layout lines are highlighted, enter E↵ to use the keyboard shortcut for the Erase command, or right-click and choose Erase from the shortcut menu. Your drawing will look like Figure 3.12.

If you right-click to use the shortcut menu in step 2, you'll notice that you have several options besides Erase. You can move, copy, scale, and rotate the objects you selected. These options act just like the standard 2D Draw control panel options. Be aware that these commands act somewhat differently from the hot-grip options described in Chapter 2.

**TIP**  If you need more control over the selection of objects, you'll find the Add/Remove Selection Mode setting useful. This setting lets you deselect a set of objects within a set of objects you've already selected. While in Object Selection mode, enter R↵; then, proceed to use a window or other selection tool to remove objects from the selection set. Enter A↵ to continue to add options to the selection set. Or, if you need to deselect only a single object, Shift+click it.

**FIGURE 3.12**
The drawing after erasing the layout lines

**TIP**   When you're preparing to erase an object that is close to other objects, you may want to select the object first, using the Noun/Verb selection method. This way, you can carefully select objects you want to erase before you invoke the Erase command.

---

### THE OSNAP OPTIONS

Earlier, you made several of the osnap settings automatic so they're available without having to select them from the Osnap pop-up menu. Another way to invoke the osnap options is to type their keyboard equivalents while selecting points or to Shift+right-click while selecting points to open the Osnap shortcut menu.

Here is a summary of all the available osnap options, including their keyboard shortcuts. You've already used many of these options in this chapter and in the previous chapter. Pay special attention to those options you haven't yet used in the exercises but may find useful to your style of work. The full name of each option is followed by its keyboard shortcut name in brackets. To use these options, you can enter either the full name or the abbreviation at any point prompt. You can also select these options from the pop-up menu obtained by Shift+clicking the right mouse button.

**Tip:** Sometimes you'll want one or more of these osnap options available as the default selection. Remember that you can set Running Osnaps to be on at all times. Choose Tools ⊁ Drafting Settings from the menu bar, and then click the Object Snap tab. You can also right-click the Osnap button in the status bar and choose Settings from the shortcut menu.

Available osnap options (in alphabetic order):

**Apparent Intersection [app]**   Selects the apparent intersection of two objects. This is useful when you want to select the intersection of two objects that don't actually intersect. You'll be prompted to select the two objects.

**Center [cen]**   Selects the center of an arc or a circle. You must click the arc or circle itself, not its apparent center.

**Endpoint [endp or end]**   Selects all the endpoints of lines, polylines, arcs, curves, and 3D Face vertices.

**Extension [ext]**   Selects a point that is aligned with an imagined extension of a line. For example, you can pick a point in space that is aligned with an existing line but isn't on that line. To use that point, type **ext.⅃** during point selection, or select Extension from the Osnap pop-up menu; then, move the cursor to the line whose extension you want to use, and hold it there until you see a small, cross-shaped marker on the line. The cursor also displays a ToolTip with the word *extension,* letting you know that the Extension osnap is active.

**From [fro]**   Selects a point relative to a picked point. For example, you can select a point that is 2 units to the left and 4 units above a circle's center. This option is usually used in conjunction with another osnap option, such as From Endpoint or From Midpoint.

**Insert [ins]**   Selects the insertion point of text, blocks, Xrefs, and overlays.

**Intersection [int]**   Selects the intersection of objects.

**Mid Between 2 Points [m2p]**   Selects a point that is midway between two other points.

**Midpoint [mid]**   Selects the midpoint of a line or an arc. In the case of a polyline, it selects the midpoint of the polyline segment.

**Nearest [nea]**    Selects a point on an object nearest the pick point.

**Node [nod]**    Selects a point object.

**None [non]**    Temporarily turns off Running Osnaps.

**Parallel [par]**    Lets you draw a line segment that is parallel to another existing line segment. To use this option, type **par⏎** during point selection, or select Parallel from the Osnap pop-up menu; then, move the cursor to the line you want to be parallel to, and hold it there until you see a small, cross-shaped marker on the line. The cursor also displays a ToolTip with the word *parallel*, letting you know that the Parallel osnap is active.

**Perpendicular [per]**    Selects a position on an object that is perpendicular to the last point selected.

**Point Filters**    Not really object snaps, but point-selection options that let you filter X, Y, or Z coordinate values from a selected point. (See Chapter 20 for more on point filters.)

**Quadrant [qua]**    Selects the nearest cardinal (north, south, east, or west) point on an arc or a circle.

**Tangent [tan]**    Selects a point on an arc or a circle that represents the tangent from the last point selected.

**Temporary Track Point**    Provides an alternate method for using the Object Snap Tracking feature described later in this chapter. (See Chapter 15 for more on Temporary Track Point.)

## Putting On the Finishing Touches

The inside of the tub still has some sharp corners. To round out these corners, you can use the versatile Fillet command on the 2D Draw control panel. Fillet enables you to join lines and arcs end to end, and it can add a radius where they join so there is a smooth transition from arc to arc or line to line. Fillet can join two lines that don't intersect, and it can trim two crossing lines back to their point of intersection. Follow these steps:

1. Click the Fillet tool on the 2D Draw control panel, or type **f⏎**. You can also choose Modify ➤ Fillet from the menu bar.

2. At the prompt

   ```
   Current settings: Mode = TRIM, Radius = 0´-0½
   Select first object or [Undo/Polyline/Radius/Trim/Multiple]:
   ```

   enter **R⏎**, or right-click and choose Radius from the shortcut menu.

3. At the `Specify fillet radius <0´-0″>:` prompt, enter **4⏎**. This tells AutoCAD that you want a 4″ radius for your fillet. Metric users should enter **10⏎**.

4. Pick two adjacent arcs. The fillet arc joins the two larger arcs.

5. Press ⏎ again, and fillet another corner. Repeat until all four corners are filleted. Your drawing should look like Figure 3.13.

6. Save and close the Bath file.

**FIGURE 3.13**
A view of the finished toilet and tub with the tub corners filleted

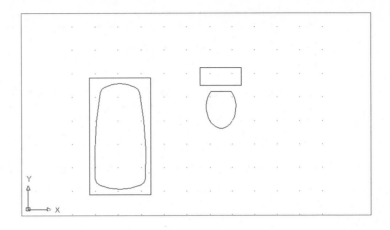

## Aligning Objects by Using Object Snap Tracking

You saw how to use lines to construct an object such as the bathtub. In many situations, using these *construction lines* is the most efficient way to draw, but they can also be a bit cumbersome. AutoCAD 2008 offers another tool that helps you align locations in your drawing to existing objects without having to draw intermediate construction lines. The tool is called *Object Snap Tracking* or *Osnap Tracking*.

Osnap Tracking is like an extension of object snaps that enables you to *align* a point to the geometry of an object instead of just selecting a point on an object. For example, with Osnap Tracking, you can select a point that is exactly at the center of a rectangle.

In the following exercises, you'll draw a plan view of a bathroom sink as an introduction to the Osnap Tracking feature. This drawing will be used as a symbol in later chapters.

**WARNING** The Object Snap Tracking feature isn't available in AutoCAD LT 2008. If you're using LT, follow along with the tutorial until you're asked to draw the ellipse to represent the bowl of the sink. Go ahead and draw an ellipse approximating the shape and size of the one in the tutorial. In Chapter 15, you'll learn about the Temporary Tracking feature, which is available in LT as well as AutoCAD and is similar to the Object Snap Tracking feature.

### A QUICK SETUP

First, as a review, you'll open a new file by using the Create New Drawing Wizard. Because this drawing will be used as a symbol for insertion in other CAD drawings, don't worry about setting it up to conform to a sheet size. Chances are, you won't be printing individual symbols. Here are the steps:

1. Choose File ➢ New to create a new drawing for your bathroom sink. Enter Startup↵ 1↵. This turns on the Quick Setup wizard for new drawings. Next...

**2.** Click the Use A Wizard button in the Create New Drawing dialog box, select Quick Setup from the list that appears below the buttons, and then click OK.

**3.** In the Units screen, choose Architectural; then, click Next. Metric users can use the Decimal option. This option performs the same operation as the Drawing Units dialog box you saw earlier in this chapter.

**4.** In the Area screen, enter **48** for the width and **36** for the length. Metric users should enter **122** for the width and **92** for the length. Click Finish. This option performs the same operation as choosing Format ➢ Drawing Limits from the menu bar.

**5.** Click the Grid button in the status bar, and then choose View ➢ Zoom ➢ All from the menu bar. This enables you to see your entire work area.

**6.** Choose File ➢ Save As to save the file under the name **Sink**.

**7.** Enter Setup↵ 0↵ to turn off the Quick Setup wizard. Or you can leave it turned on, but be aware that later exercises assume that it is turned off.

As you saw in steps 3 and 4, the Create New Drawing Wizard simplifies the drawing setup process by limiting the options you need to work with.

**TIP** If you find that you use the same drawing setup over and over, you can create template files that are already set up to your own, customized way of working. Templates are discussed in Chapter 5.

---

### ALIGNING WITH GRIPS

Osnaps, in conjunction with grips, offer a feature similar to Osnap Tracking that lets you align a grip with the direction of a line or an arc. Here's how it works. Select the line to which you want to be aligned so that its grips are displayed. Select the grip of another object that you want to edit, and then hover over the endpoint grip of the first line you selected. As you move your cursor away from the grip, an alignment vector appears that is aligned with the first line. Your cursor then snaps to the line and the vector it describes. As you move the cursor, it stays along the vector described by the line.

You can also hover over the endpoint grips of two lines or a line and an arc to find their intersection. Or, you can quickly extend the length of a line or an arc using this method. Click the endpoint grip of a line, for example, hover over it until a cross appears, and then drag the endpoint along the direction of the line to lengthen or shorten it. This also works with grips in a polyline.

### DRAWING THE SINK

You're ready to draw the sink. First, you'll draw the sink countertop. Then, you'll make sure Running Osnaps and Osnap Tracking are turned on. Finally, you'll draw the bowl of the sink.

Here are the steps for drawing the outline of the sink countertop:

1.  Click the Grid button in the status bar to turn off the grid. It was helpful to let you see the work area, but you don't need it now.

2.  Click the Rectangle tool in the 2D Draw control panel, or type **rec↵**.

3.  At the prompt

    ```
    Specify first corner point or [Chamfer/Elevation/Fillet/Thickness/Width]:
    ```

    enter **0,0↵**. This places one corner of the rectangle in the origin of the drawing.

4.  At the `Specify other corner point or [Area/Dimensions/Rotation]:` prompt, enter **@2′4,1′6↵**. Metric users should enter **@71,46↵**. This makes the rectangle 2′-4″ wide by 1′-6″ deep, or 71 cm by 46 cm for metric users. The rectangle appears in the lower half of the drawing area.

5.  Choose View ≻ Zoom ≻ Extents to enlarge the view of the sink outline. Then, use the Zoom Realtime tool in the 2D Navigate control panel to adjust your view so it looks similar to the one shown in Figure 3.14.

When you draw the bowl of the sink, the bowl will be represented by an ellipse. You want to place the center of the ellipse at the center of the rectangle you've just drawn. To do this, you'll use the midpoint of two adjoining sides of the rectangle as alignment locations. This is where the Osnap Tracking tool will be useful.

**FIGURE 3.14**
The view of the sink countertop after making some adjustments

You need to make sure Running Osnaps are turned on and that they're set to the Midpoint option. Then, you'll make sure Osnap Tracking is turned on. Use these steps:

1. Right-click the Otrack button in the status bar, and choose Settings from the shortcut menu to open the Drafting Settings dialog box at the Object Snap tab.

2. Make sure the Midpoint check box in the Object Snap Modes group is selected.

3. Also make sure that Object Snap On and Object Snap Tracking On are both selected. Click OK. You'll notice that the Osnap and Otrack buttons in the status bar are now in the on position.

Finally, you're ready to draw the ellipse:

1. Click the Ellipse tool in the 2D Draw control panel, or enter El↵.

2. At the `Specify axis endpoint of ellipse or [Arc/Center]:` prompt, type **C**; or, right-click, and choose Center from the shortcut menu.

3. Move your cursor to the top, horizontal edge of the rectangle, until you see the Midpoint ToolTip.

4. Move the cursor directly over the Midpoint Osnap marker. Without clicking the mouse, hold the cursor there for a second until you see a small cross appear. Look carefully, because the cross is small. This is the Osnap Tracking marker.

**TIP**    You can alternately insert and remove the Osnap Tracking marker by passing the cursor over the Osnap marker.

**5.** As you move the cursor downward, a dotted line appears, emanating from the midpoint of the horizontal line. The cursor also shows a small X following the dotted line as you move it.

**6.** Move the cursor to the midpoint of the left vertical side of the rectangle. Don't click, but hold it there for a second until you see the small cross. Now, as you move the cursor away, a horizontal dotted line appears, with an X following the cursor.

**7.** Move the cursor to the center of the rectangle. The two dotted lines appear simultaneously, and a small X appears at their intersection.

8. With the two dotted lines crossing and the X at their intersection, click the left mouse button to select the exact center of the rectangle.

9. Point the cursor to the right, and enter **8.↵** to make the width of the bowl 16″. Metric users should enter **20.↵** for a bowl 40 cm wide.

10. Point the cursor downward, and enter **6.↵** to make the length of the bowl 12″. Metric users should enter **15.↵** for a bowl with a length of 30 cm. The basic symbol for the sink is complete (see Figure 3.15).

**FIGURE 3.15**
The completed bathroom sink

11. Choose File ➤ Save. You can exit AutoCAD now and take a break.

In this exercise, you saw how Osnap Tracking enables you to align two locations to select a point in space. Although you used only the Midpoint osnap setting in this exercise, you aren't limited to only one osnap setting. You can use as many as you need in order to select the appropriate geometry. You can also use as many alignment points as you need, although in this exercise, you used only two. If you like, erase the ellipse, and repeat this exercise until you get the hang of using the Osnap Tracking feature.

**TIP** As with all the other buttons in the status bar, you can turn Osnap Tracking on or off by clicking the Otrack button.

## Using the AutoCAD Modes as Drafting Tools

Before you finish this chapter, you'll want to know about a few of the other drafting tools that are common to drawing programs. These tools may be compared to a background grid (*Grid mode*), scale (*Coordinate Readout mode*), and a T-square and triangle (*Object Snap Tracking mode* and *Polar Tracking mode*). These drawing modes can be indispensable tools under certain conditions. You won't use them in any exercises, but their use is fairly straightforward. You can experiment with them on your own using the information in this section.

### Using Grid Mode as a Background Grid

Using Grid mode is like having a grid under your drawing to help you with layout. In AutoCAD, Grid mode can also let you see the limits of your drawing, because the grid can be set to display only within the limits setting of your drawing. Grid mode can help you visually determine the distances you're working with in any given view. In this section, you'll learn how to control the grid's appearance. The F7 key toggles Grid mode on and off; you can also click the Grid button in the status bar.

### USING OSNAP TRACKING AND POLAR TRACKING TOGETHER

In addition to selecting as many tracking points as you need, you can also use different angles besides the basic orthogonal angles of 0°, 90°, 180°, and 270°. For example, you can have AutoCAD locate a point that is aligned vertically to the top edge of the sink and at a 45° angle from a corner.

This can be accomplished by using the settings in the Polar Tracking tab of the Drafting Settings dialog box. (See the "Setting the Polar Tracking Angle" section earlier in this chapter.) If you set the increment angle to 45° and turn on the Track Using All Polar Angle Settings option, you'll be able to use 45° in addition to the orthogonal directions. You'll see firsthand how this works in Chapter 5.

To set up the grid spacing, follow these steps:

1. Choose Tools ➢ Drafting Settings, or type **Ds.⏎** to open the Drafting Settings dialog box, showing all the mode settings.

2. Click the Snap And Grid tab. You see five groups: Snap Spacing, Grid Spacing, Polar Spacing, Grid Behavior, and Snap Type. Notice that the Grid X Spacing text box contains a value of ½". Metric users see a value of 10.

**TIP** You can use the Gridunit system variable to set the grid spacing. Enter **Gridunit**⏎, and, at the Enter new value for GRIDUNIT <0´-0 ½˝,0´-0 ½˝>: prompt, enter a grid spacing in X,Y coordinates. You must enter the Gridunit value as an X,Y coordinate.

You can set the grid spacing by entering a value for the Grid X spacing and Grid Y spacing values. In the Grid Behavior group, the Display Grid Beyond Limits check box lets you determine whether the grid displays outside the limits of the drawing.

Click the Grid On check box to make the grid visible. Notice the F7 in parentheses: This tells you that the F7 function key also controls the Grid On/Off function. Click OK to dismiss the Drafting Settings dialog box and save your setting.

Once you've set up your grid, you can now press F7 or click Grid in the status bar to turn the grid on and off. (You can also hold down the Ctrl key and press G.)

## Using the Snap Modes

The *Snap mode* forces the cursor to move in steps of a specific distance. Snap mode is useful when you want to select points on the screen at a fixed interval. Two snap modes are available in AutoCAD: *Grid Snap* and *Polar Snap*. The F9 key toggles Grid Snap mode on and off, or you can click the Snap button in the status bar. Follow these steps to access the Snap mode:

1. Choose Tools ➢ Drafting Settings, or type **Ds**⏎ to open the Drafting Settings dialog box.

2. In the Snap Spacing group of the dialog box, double-click the Snap X Spacing text box, and enter a value for your snap spacing. Then, press the Tab key to move to the next option. AutoCAD assumes you want the X and Y snap spacing to be the same, unless you specifically ask for a different Y setting.

3. You can click the Snap On check box to turn on Snap mode from this dialog box.

4. Click OK to save your settings and close the dialog box.

With Snap mode on, the cursor seems to move in steps rather than in a smooth motion. The Snap button in the status bar appears pressed, indicating that Snap mode is on. Press F9 or click Snap in the status bar (you can also hold down the Ctrl key and press B) to turn Snap mode on or off.

**TIP** You can use the Snapunit system variable to set the snap spacing. Enter ´**Snapunit**⏎. Then, at the Enter new value for SNAPUNIT <0´0˝,0´0˝>: prompt, enter **a snap distance** value as an X,Y coordinate.

Take a moment to look at the Drafting Settings dialog box. The other option in the Snap Spacing group enables you to force the X and Y spacing to be equal (Equal X and Y Spacing).

In the Snap Type group, you can change the snap and grid configuration to aid in creating 2D isometric drawings by clicking the Isometric Snap radio button. The PolarSnap option enables you to set a snap distance for the Polar Snap feature. When you click the PolarSnap radio button, the Polar Distance option at the middle left of the dialog box changes from gray to black and white to allow you to enter a Polar Snap distance.

**NOTE** You can set up the grid to automatically follow the snap spacing. To do this, set the grid X and Y spacing to 0.

# The Bottom Line

**Setting Up a Work Area**   A blank AutoCAD drawing offers few clues about the size of the area you're working with, but you can get a rough idea of the area shown in the AutoCAD window.

**Master It**   Name two ways to set up the area of your work.

**Solution**   You can use the Limits command to define the work area, otherwise known as the limits of the drawing. You can also draw a rectangle of the size of your work area.

**Exploring the Drawing Process**   To use AutoCAD effectively, you'll want to know how the different tools work together to achieve an effect. The drawing process often involves many cycles of adding objects and then editing them.

**Master It**   Name the tool that causes the cursor to point in an exact horizontal or vertical direction.

**Solution**   Polar Tracking. Ortho mode can also perform this function.

**Planning and Laying Out a Drawing**   If you've ever had to draw a precise sketch with just a pencil and pad, you've probably used a set of lightly drawn guidelines to lay out your drawing first. You do the same thing in AutoCAD; but instead of lightly drawn guidelines, you can use any object you want. In AutoCAD, objects are easily modified or deleted so you don't have to be as careful when adding guidelines.

**Master It**   What is the name of the feature that lets you select exact locations on objects?

**Solution**   Object Snap or Osnap.

**Using the AutoCAD Modes as Drafting Tools**   The main reason for using AutoCAD is to produce precision technical drawings. AutoCAD offers many tools to help you produce a drawing with the precision you need.

**Master It**   What dialog box lets you set both the grid and snap spacing?

**Solution**   The Drafting Settings dialog box.

# Chapter 4

# Organizing Objects with Blocks and Groups

Drawing the tub, toilet, and sink in Chapter 3 may have taken what seemed to you an inordinate amount of time. As you continue to use AutoCAD, however, you'll learn to draw objects more quickly. You'll also need to draw fewer of them because you can save drawings as symbols and use them like rubber stamps, duplicating drawings instantaneously wherever they're needed. This saves a lot of time when you're composing drawings.

To make effective use of AutoCAD, begin a *symbol library* of drawings you use frequently. A mechanical designer might have a library of symbols for fasteners, cams, valves, or any type of parts for their application. An electrical engineer might have a symbol library of capacitors, resistors, switches, and the like. A circuit designer will have yet another unique set of frequently used symbols.

In Chapter 3, you drew three objects—a bathtub, toilet, and sink—that architects often use. In this chapter, you'll see how to create symbols from those drawings.

This chapter includes the following topics:

◆ Creating and Inserting a Symbol

◆ Modifying a Block

◆ Understanding the Annotation Scale

◆ Grouping Objects

## Creating a Symbol

To save a drawing as a symbol, you use the Block tool. In word processors, the term *block* refers to a group of words or sentences selected for moving, saving, or deleting. You can copy a block of text elsewhere within the same file, to other files, or to a separate file or disk for future use. AutoCAD uses blocks in a similar fashion. In a file, you can turn parts of your drawing into blocks that can be saved and recalled at any time. You can also use entire existing files as blocks.

You'll start by opening the file you worked on in the last chapter and selecting the objects that will become a block:

1. Start AutoCAD, and open the existing Bath file. Use the one you created in Chapter 3, or open 04-bath.dwg sample file from the Sybex web site. Metric users can use the 04-bath-metric.dwg file. The drawing appears just as you left it in the last session.

**2.** In the Draw toolbar, click the Make Block tool or type **B**↵, the keyboard shortcut for the Make Block tool, to open the Block Definition dialog box. You can also choose Draw ➢ Block ➢ Make.

**3.** In the Name text box, type **Toilet**.

**4.** In the Base Point group, click the Pick Point button. This option enables you to select a base point for the block by using your cursor. (The *insertion base point* of a block is a point of reference on the block that is used like a grip.) When you've selected this option, the Block Definition dialog box temporarily closes.

**TIP** Notice that the Block Definition dialog box gives you the option to specify the X, Y, and Z coordinates for the base point instead of selecting a point.

**5.** Using the Midpoint osnap, pick the midpoint of the back of the toilet as the base point. Remember that you learned how to set up Running Osnaps in Chapter 3; all you need to do is point to the midpoint of a line to display the Midpoint Osnap marker and then left-click your mouse.

After you've selected a point, the Block Definition dialog box reappears. Notice that the X, Y, and Z values in the Base Point group now display the coordinates of the point you picked. For two-dimensional drawings, the Z coordinate should remain at 0.

Next, you need to select the objects you want as part of the block.

**6.** Click the Select Objects button in the Objects group. Once again, the dialog box momentarily closes. You now see the familiar object-selection prompt in the Command window, and the cursor becomes an Object Selection cursor. Click a point below and to the left of the toilet. Then, use a selection window to select the entire toilet. The toilet is now highlighted.

**WARNING**   Make sure you use the Select Objects option in the Block Definition dialog box to select the objects you want to turn into a block. AutoCAD lets you create a block that contains no objects. If you try to proceed without selecting objects, you'll get a warning message. This can cause confusion and frustration, even for an experienced user.

7. Press ↵ to confirm your selection. The Block Definition dialog box opens again.

8. Select Inches from the Block Unit drop-down list. Metric users should select Centimeters.

9. Click the Description list box, and enter **Standard Toilet**.

10. Make sure the Retain radio button in the Objects group is selected, and then click OK. The toilet drawing is now a block with the name Toilet.

11. Repeat the blocking process for the tub, but this time use the upper-left corner of the tub as the insertion base point and give the block the name **Tub**. Enter **Standard Tub** for the description.

**TIP**   You can press ↵ or right-click the mouse and choose Repeat Block from the shortcut menu to start the Make Block tool again.

When you turn an object into a block, it's stored in the drawing file, ready to be recalled at any time. The block remains part of the drawing file even when you end the editing session. When you open the file again, the block is available for your use. In addition, you can access blocks from other drawings by using the AutoCAD DesignCenter and the Tool palettes. You'll learn more about the DesignCenter and the Tool palettes in Chapter 27.

A block acts like a single object, even though it's really made up of several objects. One unique characteristic of a block is that when you modify it, all instances of that block are updated to reflect the modifications. For example, if you insert several copies of the toilet into a drawing and then later decide the toilet needs to be a different shape, you can edit the Toilet block, and all the other copies of the toilet are updated automatically.

You can modify a block in a number of ways after it has been created. In this chapter, you'll learn how to make simple changes to individual blocks by modifying the block's properties. For more detailed changes, you'll learn how to redefine a block after it has been created. Later, in Chapter 17, you'll learn how to use the Block Editor to make changes to blocks.

## Understanding the Block Definition Dialog Box

The Block Definition dialog box offers several options that can help make using blocks easier. If you're interested in these options, take a moment to review the Block Definition dialog box as you read the descriptions of the options. If you prefer, you can continue with the tutorial and come back to this section later.

You've already seen how the Name option lets you enter a name for your block. AutoCAD doesn't let you complete the block creation until you enter a name.

You've also seen how to select a base point for your block. The base point is like the grip of the block: It's the reference point you use when you insert the block back into the drawing. In the exercise, you used the Pick Point option to indicate a base point, but you also have the option to enter X, Y, and Z coordinates just below the Pick Point option. In most cases, however, you'll want to use the Pick Point option to indicate a base point that is on or near the set of objects you're converting to a block.

The Objects group of the Block Definition dialog box lets you select the objects that make up the block. You use the Select Objects button to visually select the objects you want to include in the block you're creating. The QuickSelect button to the right of the Select Objects button lets you filter out objects based on their properties. You'll learn more about QuickSelect in Chapter 15. Once you select a set of objects for your block, you'll see a thumbnail preview of the block's contents in the upper-right corner of the Block Definition dialog box.

Other options in the Objects group and Settings group let you specify what to do with the objects you're selecting for your block. Table 4.1 shows a list of those other options and what they mean:

**TABLE 4.1:**  The Block Definition dialog box options

| OPTION | PURPOSE |
| --- | --- |
| **Objects Group** | |
| Retain | Keeps the objects you select for your block as they are, unchanged. |
| Convert To Block | Converts the objects you select into the block you're defining. It then acts like a single object after you've completed the Block command. |
| Delete | Deletes the objects you selected for your block. This is what AutoCAD did in earlier versions. You may also notice that a warning message appears at the bottom of the Objects group. This warning appears if you haven't selected objects for the block. After you've selected objects, the warning changes to tell you how many objects you've selected. |
| **Behavior Group** | |
| Annotative | Turns on the Annotative scale feature for blocks. This feature lets you use a single block for different scale views of a drawing. With this feature turned on, AutoCAD can be set to adjust the size of the block to the appropriate scale for the drawing. |
| Match Block Orientation To Layout | With the Annotative option turned on, this option is available. This option causes a block to always appear in its normal orientation regardless of the orientation of the layout view. |
| Scale Uniformly | By default, blocks can have a different X, Y, or Z scale. This means they can be stretched in any of the axes. You can lock the X, Y, and Z scale of the block by selecting this option. That way, the block will always be scaled uniformly and can't be stretched in one axis. |
| Allow Exploding | By default, blocks can be exploded or reduced to their component objects. You can lock a block so that it can't be exploded by turning off this option. You can always turn on this option later if you decide that you need to explode a block. |

**TABLE 4.1:**     The Block Definition dialog box options *(CONTINUED)*

| OPTION | PURPOSE |
|---|---|
| **Settings group** | |
| Block Unit | Lets you determine how the object is to be scaled when it's inserted into the drawing using the DesignCenter feature discussed in Chapter 27. By default, this value is the same as the current drawing's insert value. |
| Hyperlink | Lets you assign a hyperlink to a block. This option opens the Insert Hyperlink dialog box, where you can select a location or file for the hyperlink. |
| **Description and Open in Block Editor** | |
| Description | Lets you include a brief description or keyword for the block. This option is helpful when you need to find a specific block in a set of drawings. You'll learn more about searching for blocks later in this chapter and in Chapter 27. |
| Open in Block Editor | If you turn on this option, the block is created and then opened in the Block Editor described in Chapter 17. |

## Inserting a Symbol

You can recall the Tub and Toilet blocks at any time, as many times as you want. In this section, you'll first draw the interior walls of the bathroom, and then you'll insert the tub and toilet. Follow these steps to draw the walls:

1. Delete the original tub and toilet drawings. Click the Erase tool in the Modify toolbar, and then enter **All**↵↵ to erase the entire visible contents of the drawing. (Doing so has no effect on the blocks you created previously.)

2. Draw a rectangle 7′-6″ × 5′. Metric users should draw a 228 cm × 152 cm rectangle. Orient the rectangle so the long sides go from left to right and the lower-left corner is at coordinate 1′-10″,1′-10″ (or coordinate 56.0000,56.0000 for metric users).

   If you use the Rectangle tool to draw the rectangle, make sure you explode it by using the Explode tool. This is important for later exercises. (See the "Unblocking and Redefining a Block" section later in this chapter if you aren't familiar with the Explode tool.) Your drawing should look like Figure 4.1.

**TIP**    The Insert Block tool is also on the Insert toolbar, which you can open by right-clicking any open toolbar and choosing Insert.

**FIGURE 4.1**

The interior walls of the bathroom

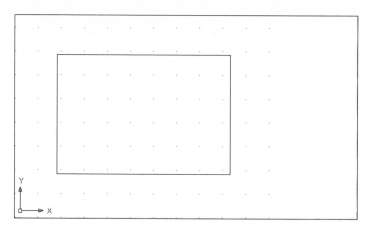

Now you're ready to place your blocks. Start by placing the tub in the drawing:

1. In the Draw toolbar, click the Insert Block tool, or type I↵ to open the Insert dialog box.

2. Click the Name drop-down list to display a list of the available blocks in the current drawing.

3. Click the block name Tub.

4. In the Insertion Point group and Rotation group, click the Specify On-Screen check box. With this option turned on in the Insertion Point group, you're asked to specify an insertion point using your cursor. The Specify On-Screen option in the Rotation group lets you specify the rotation angle of the block graphically as you insert it.

5. Click OK, and you see a preview image of the tub attached to the cursor. The upper-left corner you picked for the tub's base point is now on the cursor intersection.

6. At the Specify insertion point or [Basepoint/Scale/X/Y/Z/Rotate]: prompt, pick the upper-left intersection of the room as your insertion point.

**7.** At the `Specify rotation angle <0>:` prompt, notice that you can rotate the block. This lets you visually specify a rotation angle for the block. You won't use this feature at this time, so press ↵ to accept the default of 0. The tub should look like the one in Figure 4.2.

**FIGURE 4.2**

The bathroom, first with the tub and then with the toilet inserted

You've got the tub in place. Now, place the Toilet block in the drawing:

**1.** Open the Insert dialog box again, but this time select Toilet in the Name drop-down list.

**2.** Clear the Specify On-Screen check box in the Rotation group.

**3.** Place the toilet at the midpoint of the line along the top of the rectangle representing the bathroom wall, as shown in the bottom image in Figure 4.2. Notice that after you select the insertion point, the toilet appears in the drawing; you aren't prompted for a rotation angle for the block.

## Scaling and Rotating Blocks

In step 7 in the previous section, you can see the tub rotate as you move the cursor. You can pick a point to fix the block in place, or you can enter a rotation value. This is the result of selecting the Specify On-Screen option in the Insert dialog box. You may find that you want the Rotation group's Specify On-Screen option turned on most of the time to enable you to adjust the rotation angle of the block while you're placing it in the drawing.

The other options in the Insert dialog box that you didn't use are the Scale group options. These options let you scale the block to a different size. You can scale the block uniformly, or you can distort the block by individually changing its X, Y, or Z scale factor. With the Specify On-Screen option unchecked, you can enter specific values in the X, Y, and Z text boxes to stretch the block in any direction. If you turn on the Specify On-Screen option, you can visually adjust the X, Y, and Z scale factors in real time. Although these options aren't used often, they can be useful in special situations when a block needs to be stretched one way or another to fit in a drawing.

You aren't limited to scaling or rotating a block when it's being inserted into a drawing. You can always use the Scale or Rotate tools or modify an inserted block's properties to stretch it in one direction or another. This exercise shows you how this is done:

1. Click the Toilet block to select it.

2. Right-click, and choose Properties from the shortcut menu to open the Properties palette. Take a moment to study the Properties palette. Toward the bottom, under the Geometry heading, you see a set of labels that show Position and Scale. These labels may appear as Pos and Sca if the width of the palette has been adjusted to be too narrow to show the entire label. Remember that you can click and drag the left or right edge of the palette to change its width. You can also click and drag the border between the columns in the palette.

3. If the first item label under the Geometry heading isn't visible, place the cursor on the label. A ToolTip displays the full wording of the item, which is Position X.

4. Move the cursor down one line to display the ToolTip for Position Y. This shows how you can view the label even if it isn't fully visible.

5. Continue to move the cursor down to the Scale X label. The ToolTip displays the full title.

6. Let's try making some changes to the toilet properties. Double-click the Scale X value in the column just to the right of the Scale X label.

**7.** Enter **1.5**↵. Notice that the toilet changes in width as you do this.

**8.** You don't really want to change the width of the toilet, so click the Undo tool in the Standard toolbar or enter **U**↵.

**9.** Close the Properties palette by clicking the X in the upper-left corner.

**WARNING**   If a block is created with the Scale Uniformly option turned on in the Block Definition dialog box, you can't scale the block in just one axis, as shown in the previous exercise. You can only scale the block uniformly in all axes.

You've just seen how you can modify the properties of a block by using the Properties palette. In the exercise, you changed the X scale of the Toilet block, but you could have just as easily changed the Y value. You may have noticed other properties available in the Properties palette. You'll learn more about those properties as you work through this chapter.

You've seen how you can turn a drawing into a symbol, known as a block in AutoCAD. Now, let's see how you can use an existing drawing file as a block.

## Using an Existing Drawing as a Symbol

You need a door into the bathroom. Because you've already drawn a door and saved it as a file, you can bring the door into this drawing file and use it as a block:

**1.** In the Draw toolbar, click the Insert Block tool, or type **I**↵.

**2.** In the Insert dialog box, click the Browse button to open the Select Drawing File dialog box.

**3.** This is a standard Windows file browser dialog box. Locate the Door file, and double-click it. If you didn't create a door file, you can use the door file from the Chapter 04 project files that you can download from the Mastering AutoCAD web site.

**TIP**   You can also browse your hard disk by looking at thumbnail views of the drawing files in a folder.

**4.** When you return to the Insert dialog box, make sure the Specify On-Screen options for the Insertion Point, Scale and Rotation groups are checked, and then click OK. As you move the cursor around, notice that the door appears above and to the right of the cursor intersection, as in Figure 4.3.

**5.** At this point, the door looks too small for this bathroom. This is because you drew it 3 units long, which translates to 3″. Metric users drew the door 9 cm long. Pick a point near coordinates 7′-2″,2′-4″, so that the door is placed in the lower-right corner of the room. Metric users should use the coordinate 210,70.

**FIGURE 4.3**

The door drawing being inserted in the Bath file

6. If you take the default setting for the X scale of the inserted block, the door will remain 3″ long, or 9 cm long for metric users. However, as mentioned earlier, you can specify a smaller or larger size for an inserted object. In this case, you want a 3′ door. Metric users want a 90 cm door. To get that from a 3″ door, you need an X scale factor of 12, or 10 for metric users. (You may want to look again at Table 3.3 in Chapter 3 to see how this is determined.) At the Enter X scale factor, specify opposite corner, or [Corner/XYZ] <1>: prompt, enter **12**↵. Metric users should enter **10**↵.

7. Press ↵ twice to accept the default Y = X and the rotation angle of 0°.

The Command prompt appears, but nothing seems to happen to the drawing. This is because when you enlarged the door, you also enlarged the distance between the base point and the object. This brings up another issue to be aware of when you're considering using drawings as symbols: All drawings have base points. The default base point is the absolute coordinate 0,0, otherwise known as the *origin*, which is located in the lower-left corner of any new drawing. When you drew the door in Chapter 2, you didn't specify the base point. When you try to bring the door into this drawing, AutoCAD uses the origin of the door drawing as its base point (see Figure 4.4).

**FIGURE 4.4**

By default, a drawing's origin is also its insertion point. You can change a drawing's insertion point by using the Base command.

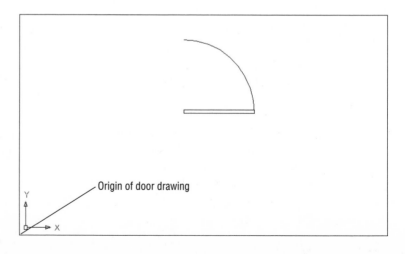

Because the door appears outside the bathroom, you must first choose Zoom ➢ All to show more of the drawing and then use the Move command on the Modify toolbar to move the door to the right-side wall of the bathroom. Let's do this now:

1. Choose View ➢ Zoom ➢ All from the menu bar drop-down menu to display the area set by the limits of your drawing (choose Format ➢ Drawing Limits), plus any other objects that are outside those limits. The view of the room shrinks, and the door is displayed. Notice that it's now the proper size for your drawing (see Figure 4.5).

**FIGURE 4.5**

The enlarged door

2. Choose Modify ➢ Move, or type **M↵**.

3. To pick the door you just inserted, at the `Select objects:` prompt, click a point anywhere on the door, and press ↵. Notice that now the entire door is highlighted. This is because a block is treated like a single object, even though it may be made up of several lines, arcs, and so on.

4. At the `Specify base point or [Displacement] <Displacement>:` prompt, turn on Running Osnaps, and pick the lower-left corner of the door. Remember that pressing the F3 key or clicking Osnap in the status bar toggles Running Osnaps on or off.

5. At the `Specify second point or <use first point as displacement>:` prompt, use the Nearest Osnap override, and position the door so that your drawing looks like Figure 4.6.

**FIGURE 4.6**

The door on the right-side wall of the bathroom

Because the door is an object that you'll use often, it should be a common size so you don't have to specify an odd value every time you insert it. It would also be helpful if the door's insertion base point were in a more convenient location—that is, a location that would let you place the door accurately within a wall opening. Next, you'll modify the Door block to better suit your needs.

## Modifying a Block

You can modify a block in two ways. One way is to completely redefine the block. In earlier versions of AutoCAD, this was the only way to make changes to a block. A second way is to use the Block Editor.

In this chapter, you'll learn how to redefine a block by making changes to the door symbol. Later, in Chapter 17, you'll see how the Block Editor lets you add adjustability to blocks.

**TIP**   Double-clicking most objects displays the Properties palette. Double-clicking a block opens the Edit Block Definition dialog box, which gives you another way to edit blocks. You'll learn more about the Edit Block Definition dialog box in Chapter 17.

### Unblocking and Redefining a Block

One way to modify a block is to break it down into its components, edit them, and then turn them back into a block. This is called *redefining* a block. If you redefine a block that has been inserted in a drawing, each occurrence of that block in the current file changes to reflect the new block definition. You can use this block-redefinition feature to make rapid changes to a design.

To separate a block into its components, use the Explode command:

1. Choose Explode from the Modify toolbar. You can also type **X**↵ to start the Explode command.

2. Click the door, and press ↵ to confirm your selection.

**TIP**   You can simultaneously insert and explode a block by clicking the Explode check box in the lower-left corner of the Insert dialog box.

Now, you can edit the individual objects that make up the door, if you desire. In this case, you want to change only the door's insertion point because you've already made it a more convenient size. You'll turn the door back into a block, this time using the door's lower-left corner for its insertion base point:

1. In the Draw toolbar, select Make Block, or type **B**↵. You can also choose Draw ➤ Block ➤ Make.

2. In the Block Definition dialog box, select Door from the Name drop-down list.

3. Click the Pick Point button, and pick the lower-left corner of the door.

4. Click the Select Objects button, and select the components of the door. Press ↵ when you've finished making your selection.

5. Select the Convert To Block option in the Objects group to automatically convert the selected objects in the drawing into a block.

**6.** Select Inches from the Block Unit drop-down list, and then enter **Standard door** in the Description box.

**7.** Click OK. You see a warning message that reads "Door is already defined. Do you want to redefine it?" You don't want to redefine an existing block accidentally. In this case, you know you want to redefine the door, so click the Yes button to proceed.

**TIP** The Select Objects and Pick Point buttons appear in other dialog boxes. Make note of their appearance, and remember that when you select them, the dialog box temporarily closes to let you select points or objects and otherwise perform operations that require a clear view of the drawing area.

In step 7, you received a warning message that you were about to redefine the existing Door block. But originally, you inserted the door as a file, not as a block. Whenever you insert a drawing file by using the Insert Block tool, the inserted drawing automatically becomes a block in the current drawing. When you redefine a block, however, you don't affect the drawing file you imported. AutoCAD changes only the block in the current file.

You've just redefined the door block. Now, place the door in the wall of the room:

**1.** Choose Erase from the Modify toolbar, and then click the door. Notice that the entire door is one object instead of individual lines and an arc. Had you not selected the Convert To Block option in step 5 of the previous exercise, the components of the block would have remained individual objects.

**2.** Insert the door block again by using the Insert Block tool in the Draw toolbar or by choosing Insert ➤ Block. This time, use the Nearest Osnap override, and pick a point on the right-side wall of the bathroom, near coordinate 9´-4″,2´-1″. Metric users should insert the door near 284,63.4.

**3.** Use the Grips feature to mirror the door, using the wall as the mirror axis so that the door is inside the room. Your drawing will look like Figure 4.7.

**FIGURE 4.7**
The bathroom floor plan thus far

**TIP**  To mirror an object using grips, first be sure the Grips feature is on. (It's usually on by default.) Select the objects to mirror, click a grip, and right-click. Select Mirror from the shortcut menu; then, indicate a mirror axis with the cursor.

Next, you'll see how you can update an external file with a redefined block.

## Saving a Block as a Drawing File

You've seen that, with little effort, you can create a symbol and place it anywhere in a file. Suppose you want to use this symbol in other files. When you create a block by using the Block command, the block exists in the current file only until you specifically instruct AutoCAD to save it as a drawing file on disk. For an existing drawing that has been brought in and modified, such as the door, the drawing file on disk associated with that door isn't automatically updated. To update the Door file, you must take an extra step and use the Export option on the File menu. Let's see how this works.

**TIP**  You can retrieve blocks that are embedded in other drawings by using a feature called the DesignCenter. See Chapter 27.

Start by turning the Tub and Toilet blocks into individual files on disk:

1. Choose File ➤ Export to open the Export Data dialog box, which is a simple file dialog box.

2. Open the Files Of Type drop-down list, and select Block (*.dwg).

**TIP**  If you prefer, you can skip step 2 and instead, in step 3, enter the full filename including the .dwg extension, as in Tub.dwg.

3. Double-click the File Name text box, and enter **Tub**.

4. Click the Save button to close the Export Data dialog box.

5. At the [= (block=output file)/* (whole drawing)] <define new drawing>: prompt, enter the name of the block you want to save to disk as the tub file—in this case, **Tub**↵. The Tub block is now saved as a file.

6. Repeat steps 1 through 5 for the Toilet block. Give the file the same name as the block.

**TIP**  AutoCAD gives you the option to save a block's file under the same name as the original block or with a different name. Usually, you'll want to use the same name, which you can do by entering an equal sign (=) after the prompt.

**TIP**  Normally, AutoCAD saves a preview image with a file. This enables you to preview a drawing file before opening it. Preview images aren't included with files that are exported with the File ➤ Export option or the Wblock command, which is discussed in the next section.

## Replacing Existing Files with Blocks

The Wblock command does the same thing as choosing File ➤ Export, but output is limited to AutoCAD .dwg files. Let's try using the Wblock command this time to save the Door block you modified:

1. Issue the Wblock command by typing **Wblock.↵**, or use the keyboard shortcut by typing **w↵** to open the Write Block dialog box.

2. In the Source group, click the Block radio button.

3. Select Door from the drop-down list. You can keep the old name or enter a different name if you prefer.

4. In this case, you want to update the door you drew in Chapter 2. Click the browse button in the Destination group.

5. Locate and select the original door.dwg file that you inserted earlier.

6. Click OK. A warning message tells you that the Door.dwg file already exists. Go ahead and click Yes to confirm that you want to overwrite the old door drawing with the new door definition.

In this exercise, you typed the Wblock command at the Command prompt instead of choosing File ➢ Export. The results are the same, regardless of which method you use. If you're in a hurry, the File ➢ Export command is a quick way to save part of your drawing as a file. The Wblock option might be easier for new users because it offers options in a dialog box.

### UNDERSTANDING THE WRITE BLOCK DIALOG BOX OPTIONS

The Write Block dialog box offers a way to save parts of your current drawing as a file. As you can see from the dialog box shown in the previous exercise, you have several options.

In that exercise, you used the Block option of the Source group to select an existing block as the source object to be exported. You can also export a set of objects by choosing the Objects option. If you choose this option, the Base Point and Objects groups become available. These options work the same way as their counterparts in the Block Definition dialog box, which you saw earlier when you created the Tub and Toilet blocks.

The other option in the Source group, Entire Drawing, lets you export the whole drawing to its own file. This may seem to duplicate the File ➤ Save As option in the menu bar, but saving the entire drawing from the Write Block dialog box performs some additional operations, such as stripping out unused blocks or other unused components. This has the effect of reducing file size. You'll learn more about this feature later in this chapter.

## Other Uses for Blocks

So far, you've used the Make Block tool to create symbols, and you've used the Export and Wblock commands to save those symbols to disk. As you can see, you can create symbols and save them at any time while you're drawing. You've made the tub and toilet symbols into drawing files that you can see when you check the contents of your current folder.

However, creating symbols isn't the only use for the Make Block, Block, Export, and Wblock commands. You can use them in any situation that requires grouping objects (though you may prefer to use the more flexible Object Group command discussed later in this chapter). You can also use blocks to stretch a set of objects along one axis by using the Properties palette. Export and Wblock also enable you to save a part of a drawing to disk. You'll see instances of these other uses of the Block, Export, and Wblock commands throughout the book.

Make Block, Export, and Wblock are extremely versatile commands and, if used judiciously, can boost your productivity and simplify your work. If you aren't careful, however, you can get carried away and create more blocks than you can keep track of. Planning your drawings helps you determine which elements will work best as blocks and recognize situations in which other methods of organization are more suitable.

Another way of using symbols is to use AutoCAD's external reference capabilities. External reference files, known as *Xrefs*, are files inserted into a drawing in a way similar to blocks. The difference is that Xrefs don't become part of the drawing's database. Instead, they're loaded along with the current file at startup time. It's as if AutoCAD opens several drawings at once: the main file you specify when you start AutoCAD, and the Xrefs associated with the main file.

By keeping the Xrefs independent from the current file, you make sure that any changes made to the Xrefs automatically appear in the current file. You don't have to update each inserted copy of an Xref. For example, if you use the External References option on the Reference toolbar (discussed in Chapter 7) to insert the Tub drawing, and later you make changes to the tub, the next time you open the Bath file, you'll see the new version of the tub. Or, if you have both the tub and the referencing drawing open, and you change the tub, AutoCAD will notify you that a change has been made to an external reference. You can then update the tub Xref using the External Reference palette.

Xrefs are especially useful in workgroup environments, where several people are working on the same project. One person might be updating several files that have been inserted into a variety of other files. Before Xrefs were available, everyone in the workgroup had to be notified of the changes and had to update all the affected blocks in all the drawings that contained them. With Xrefs, the updating is automatic. Many other features are unique to these files; they're discussed in more detail in Chapters 7 and 12.

## Understanding the Annotation Scale

One common use for AutoCAD's block feature is creating *reference symbols*. These are symbols that refer the viewer to other drawings or views in a set of drawings. An example would be a building-section symbol on a floor plan that directs the viewer to look at a location on another sheet to see a cross-section view of a building. Such a symbol is typically a circle with two numbers: one for the drawing sheet number and the other for the view number on the sheet (examples appear a little later, in Figure 4.8).

In the past, AutoCAD users had to insert a reference symbol block multiple times to accommodate different scales of the same view. For example, the same floor plan might be used for a ¼″ = 1′1″ scale view and a ⅛″ = 1′0″ view. An elevation symbol block that works for the ¼″ = 1′1″ scale view would be too small for the ⅛″ = 1′0″ view, so two copies of the same block were inserted, one for each scale. The user then had to place the two blocks on different layers to control their visibility. In addition, if sheet numbers changed, the user had to make sure every copy of the elevation symbol block was updated to reflect the change.

The annotation scale feature does away with this need for redundancy. You can now use a single instance of a block even if it must be displayed in different scale views. To do this, you must take some additional steps when creating and inserting the block. Here's how you do it:

1.  Draw your symbol at the size it should appear when plotted. For example, if the symbol is supposed to be a ¼″ circle on a printed sheet, draw the symbol as a ¼″ circle.

2.  Open the Block Definition dialog box by choosing the Make Block tool from the 2D Draw control panel.

3.  Turn on the Annotative option in the Behavior section of the Block Definition dialog box. You can also turn on the Match Block Orientation To Layout option if you want the symbol to always appear in a vertical orientation.

4.  Select the objects that make up the block, and indicate an insertion point as usual.

5.  Click OK.

After you've followed these steps, you need to apply an annotation scale to the newly created block:

1.  Click the new block to select it.

2.  Right-click, and choose Annotative Object Scale ➤ Add/Delete Scales. The Annotation Object Scale dialog box appears.

**3.** Click the Add button. The Add Scales To Object dialog box appears.

**4.** Select from the list the scale you'll be using with this block. You can Ctrl+click to select multiple scales. When you're finished selecting scales, click OK. The selected scales appear in the Annotation Object Scale dialog box.

**5.** Click OK to close the Annotation Object Scale dialog box.

At this point, the block is ready to be used in multiple scale views. You need only to select a scale from the Model view's Annotation Scale drop-down list or the Layout view's VP (Viewport) Scale drop-down list, which are both in the lower-right corner of the AutoCAD window.

The Annotation Scale drop-down list appears in Model view, and the VP Scale drop-down list appears in Layout view and when a viewport is selected (see Chapter 16 for more about layouts and viewports). In Layout view, you can set the VP Scale value for each individual viewport so the same block can appear at the appropriate size of different scale viewports (see Figure 4.8).

Note that if you want to use several copies of a block that is using multiple annotation scales, you should insert the block and assign the additional annotation scales and then make copies of the block. If you insert a new instance of the block, the block acquires only the annotation scale that is current for the drawing. You'll have to assign additional annotation scales to each new insertion of the block.

If you're uncertain whether an annotation scale has been assigned to a block, you can click the block, and you'll see the different scale versions of the block as ghosted images. Also, if you hover over a block, a triangular symbol appears next to the cursor for blocks that have been assigned annotation scales.

Annotative Scale symbol

**FIGURE 4.8**

A single block is used to create different size building section symbols in this Layout view. Both views show the same floor plan displayed at different scales.

The size of the block adjusts to the viewport scale so its size remains constant.

¼″ scale viewport          ⅛″ scale viewport

If you need to change the position of a block for a particular layout viewport scale, go to Model view, select the appropriate scale from the Annotation Scale drop-down list, and then adjust the position of the block.

## Grouping Objects

**ACAD only**

Blocks are extremely useful tools, but for some situations, they're too restrictive. At times, you'll want to group objects so they're connected but can still be edited individually.

For example, consider a space planner who has to place workstations in a floor plan. Although each workstation is basically the same, some slight variations in each station could make the use of blocks unwieldy. For instance, one workstation might need a different configuration to accommodate special equipment, and another workstation might need to be slightly larger than the standard size. Using a block, you would need to create a block for one workstation and then, for each variation, explode the block, edit it, and create a new block. A better way is to draw a prototype workstation and turn it into a group. You can copy the group into position and then edit it for each individual situation without losing its identity as a group. AutoCAD LT offers a different method for grouping objects. If you're using LT, skip this exercise and continue with the following section, "Grouping Objects for LT Users."

The following exercise demonstrates how grouping works:

1. Save the Bath file, and then open the drawing Office1.dwg from the sample files from the Sybex web site. Metric users should open Office1-metric.dwg.

2. Use the Zoom command to enlarge just the view of the workstation, as shown in the first image in Figure 4.9.

**FIGURE 4.9**
A workstation in an
office plan

3. Type **G**↵ or **Group.**↵ to open the Object Grouping dialog box.

4. Type **Station1**. As you type, your entry appears in the Group Name text box.

5. Click New in the Create Group group, about midway in the dialog box. The Object Grouping dialog box temporarily closes to let you select objects for your new group.

6. At the Select objects: prompt, window the entire workstation in the lower-left corner of the plan, and press ↵ to display the Object Grouping dialog box. Notice that the name Station1 appears in the Group Name box at the top of the dialog box.

7. Click OK. You've just created a group.

Now, whenever you want to select the workstation, you can click any part of it to select the entire group. At the same time, you can still modify individual parts of the group—the desk, partition, and so on—without losing the grouping of objects.

## Grouping Objects for LT Users

LT users have to use a slightly different method to create a group. If you're using AutoCAD 2007 LT, do the following:

1. Open Office1.dwg from the downloaded sample files. Metric users should open Office1-metric.dwg.

2. Use the Zoom command to enlarge just the view of the workstation, as shown in the first image in Figure 4.9.

3. Type G↵ or Group↵ to open the Group Manager dialog box.

4. Move the dialog box so that you have a clear view of the workstation; then, use a selection window to select all the objects of the workstation. You can also click the individual objects of the workstation to make the selection.

5. In the Group Manager dialog box, click the Create Group button. A new listing appears in the Group Manager list box.

6. Type Station1↵ in the text box that appears in the group list.

7. Close the Group Manager dialog box.

Now, whenever you want to select the workstation, you can click any part of it to select the entire group. At the same time, you can still modify individual parts of the group—the desk, partition, and so on—without losing the grouping of objects.

## Modifying Members of a Group

Next, you'll make copies of the original group and modify the copies. Figure 4.10 is a sketch of the proposed layout that uses the new workstations. Look carefully, and you'll see that some of the workstations in the sketch are missing a few of the standard components that exist in the Station1 group. One pair of stations has a partition removed; another station has no desk.

The exercises in this section show you how to complete your drawing to reflect the design requirements of the sketch.

**FIGURE 4.10**
A sketch of the new
office layout

Start by making a copy of the workstation:

1. Click Copy on the Modify toolbar, or type **Co↵**, and click the Station1 group you just created. Notice that you can click any part of the station to select the entire station. If only a single object is selected, press Shift+Ctrl+A and try clicking another part of the group.

2. Press ↵ to finish your selection.

3. At the `Specify base point or [Displacement] <Displacement>:` prompt, enter **@↵**. Then, enter **@8′2″<90** to copy the workstation 8′-2″ vertically. Metric users should enter **@249<90**. Press ↵ to exit the Copy command.

**TIP** In step 3, you can also use the Direct Distance method by typing **@↵** and then pointing the rubber-banding line 90° and typing **8′2″ ↵**. Metric users should type **249↵**.

4. Issue the Copy command again, but this time click the copy of the workstation you just created. Notice that it too is a group.

5. Copy this workstation 8′-2″ (249 cm for the metric users) vertically, just as you did the original workstation. Press ↵ to exit the Copy command.

Next, you'll use grips to mirror the first workstation copy:

1. Click the middle workstation to highlight it, and notice that grips appear for all the entities in the group.

2. Click the grip in the middle-left side, as shown in Figure 4.11.

3. Right-click the mouse, and choose Mirror from the shortcut menu. Notice that a temporary mirror image of the workstation follows the movement of your cursor.

**FIGURE 4.11**
Mirroring the new group by using grips

Click this grip to mirror the workstation.

4. Turn on Ortho mode, and pick a point directly to the right of the hot grip you picked in step 2. The workstation is mirrored to a new orientation.

5. Press the Esc key twice to clear the grip selection. Also, turn off Ortho mode.

Now that you've got the workstations laid out, you need to remove some of the partitions between the new workstations. If you had used blocks for the workstations, you would first need to explode the workstations that have partitions you want to edit. Groups, however, let you make changes without undoing their grouping.

Use these steps to remove the partitions:

1. At the Command prompt, press Shift+Ctrl+A. You should see the `<Group off>` message in the command line. If you see the `<Group on>` message instead, press Shift+Ctrl+A until you see `<Group off>`. This turns off groupings so you can select and edit individual objects within a group.

2. Using a window, erase the short partition that divides the two copies of the workstations, as shown in Figure 4.12.

**FIGURE 4.12**
Remove the partitions between the two workstations.

Erase this partition.

3. Press Shift+Ctrl+A again to turn groupings back on.

4. To check your workstations, click one of them to see whether all its components are high-lighted together.

**TIP** Pickstyle is a system variable that controls how groups are selected. See Appendix C for more information about Pickstyle and other system variables.

## Working with the Object Grouping Dialog Box

Each group has a unique name, and you can also attach a brief description of the group in the Object Grouping dialog box. When you copy a group, AutoCAD assigns an arbitrary name to the newly created group. Copies of groups are considered unnamed, but you can still list them in the Object Grouping dialog box by clicking the Include Unnamed check box. You can click the Rename button in the Object Grouping dialog box to name unnamed groups appropriately.

Objects in a group aren't bound solely to that group. One object can be a member of several groups, and you can have nested groups.

**NOTE** AutoCAD LT users have a different set of options. See the "Working with the LT Group Manager" section.

Table 4.2 gives a rundown of the options available in the Object Grouping dialog box:

**TABLE 4.2:**   Object Grouping Dialog Box Options

| OPTION | PURPOSE |
| --- | --- |
| Group Identification | Use the Group Identification group to identify your groups, using unique elements that let you remember what each group is for. |
| Group Name | This text box lets you create a new group by naming it first. |
| Description | This text box lets you include a brief description of the group. |

**TABLE 4.2:**     Object Grouping Dialog Box Options *(CONTINUED)*

| OPTION | PURPOSE |
| --- | --- |
| Find Name | Click this button to find the name of a group. The Object Grouping dialog box temporarily closes so you can click a group. |
| Highlight | Click this button to highlight a group that has been selected from the Group Name list. This helps you locate a group in a crowded drawing. |
| Include Unnamed | This check box determines whether unnamed groups are included in the Group Name list. Check this box to display the names of copies of groups for processing by this dialog box. |
| Create Group | Here's where you control how a group is created. |
| New | Click this button to create a new group. The Object Grouping dialog box closes temporarily so that you can select objects for grouping. To use this button, you must have either entered a group name or selected the Unnamed check box. |
| Selectable | This check box lets you control whether the group you create is selectable. See the description of the Selectable button in the Change Group group in the section that follows. |
| Unnamed | This check box lets you create a new group without naming it. |
| Change Group | These buttons are available only when a group name is highlighted in the Group Name list at the top of the dialog box. |
| Remove | Click this button to remove objects from a group. |
| Add | Click this button to add objects to a group. While using this option, grouping is temporarily turned off to allow you to select objects from other groups. |
| Rename | Click this button to rename a group. |
| Re-Order | Click this button to change the order of objects in a group. The order refers to the order in which you selected the objects to include in the group. You can change this selection order for special purposes such as tool-path machining. |
| Description | Click this button to modify the description of a group. |

**TABLE 4.2:**      Object Grouping Dialog Box Options *(CONTINUED)*

| OPTION | PURPOSE |
|---|---|
| Explode | Click this button to separate a group into its individual components |
| Selectable | Click this button to turn individual groupings on and off. When a group is selectable, it's selectable only as a group. When a group isn't selectable, the individual objects in a group can be selected, but not the group. |

**TIP**    If a group is selected, you can remove individual items from the selection with a Shift+click. In this way, you can isolate objects within a group for editing or removal without having to temporarily turn off groups.

## Working with the LT Group Manager

If you're using AutoCAD LT, you use the Group Manager to manage groups. Table 4.3 offers a rundown of the tools that are available in the Group Manager.

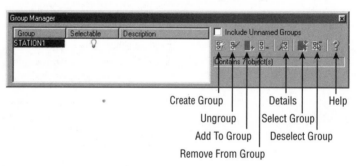

**TABLE 4.3:**      AutoCAD 2008 LT Group Manager Options

| OPTION | PURPOSE |
|---|---|
| Create Group | Lets you convert a set of objects into a group. Select a set of objects, and then click Create Group. |
| Ungroup | Removes the grouping of an existing group. Select the group name from the list, and then select Ungroup. |
| Add To Group | Lets you add an object to a group. At least one group and one additional object must be selected before this option is available. |
| Remove From Group | Lets you remove one or more objects from a group. To isolate individual objects in a group, first select the group, and then Shift+click to remove individual objects from the selection set. After you isolate the object you want to remove, click Remove From Group. |

**TABLE 4.3:**    AutoCAD 2008 LT Group Manager Options *(CONTINUED)*

| OPTION | PURPOSE |
|---|---|
| Details | Lists detailed information about the group, such as the number of objects in the group and whether it's in Model Space or a layout. Select the group name from the group list, and then click Details. |
| Select Group | Lets you select a group by name. Highlight the group name in the group list, and then click Select Group. |
| Deselect Group | Removes a group from the current selection set. Highlight the group name in the group list, and then click Deselect Group. |
| Help | Opens the AutoCAD LT Help dialog box, and displays information about the Group Manager |

**TIP**    You've seen how you can use groups to create an office layout. You can also use groups to help you keep sets of objects temporarily together in a complex drawing. Groups can be especially useful in 3D modeling when you want to organize complex assemblies together for easy selection.

## The Bottom Line

**Creating and Inserting a Symbol**    If you have a symbol that you use often in a drawing, you can draw it once and then turn it into an AutoCAD block. A block can be placed in a drawing multiple times in any location, like a rubber stamp. Blocks are stored in a drawing as a block definition, which can be called up at any time.

**Master It**    Name the dialog box used to create a block from objects in a drawing, and also name the tool to open this dialog box.

**Solution**    The Block Definition dialog box can be opened using the Make Block tool.

**Modifying a Block**    Once you've created a block, it isn't set in stone. One of the features of a block is that you can change the block definition, and all the copies of the block are updated to the new definition.

**Master It**    What is the name of the tool used to "unblock" a block?

**Solution**    You can use the Explode tool to break a block down to its component objects. Once this is done, you can modify the objects and then redefine the block.

**Understanding the Annotation Scale**    In some cases, you'll want to create a block that is dependent on the drawing scale. You can create a block that adjusts itself to the scale of your drawing through the annotation scale feature. When the annotation scale feature is turned on for a block, the block can be set to appear at the correct size depending on the scale of your drawing.

**Master It**    What setting in the Block Definition dialog box turns on the annotation scale feature, and how do you set the annotation scale of a block?

**Solution**    The Annotative option in the Block Definition dialog box turns on the annotation scale feature. You can set the scales for a block by selecting the block, right-clicking, and selecting Object Scale ➤ Add/Delete Scales.

**Grouping Objects**   Blocks can be used as a tool to group objects together, but blocks can be too rigid for some grouping applications. AutoCAD offers groups, which are collections of objects that are similar to blocks but aren't as rigidly defined.

**Master It**   How are groups different from blocks?

**Solution**   Objects in a group can be easily edited by turning groups off with a Shift+Ctrl+A keystroke. Also, unlike blocks, groups don't have a single definition stored in the drawing that defines the group's appearance. You can copy a group, but each copy is independent of the other groups.

# Chapter 5

# Keeping Track of Layers and Blocks

Imagine a filing system that has only one category into which you put all your records. For a handful of documents, such a filing system might work; but as soon as you start to accumulate more documents, you would want to start separating them into meaningful categories, perhaps alphabetically or by their use, so you could find them more easily.

The same is true for drawings. If you have a simple drawing with only a few objects, you can get by without using layers. But as soon as your drawing gets the least bit complicated, you'll want to start sorting your objects into layers to keep track of what's what. Layers don't restrict your editing of objects such as blocks or groups, and you can set up layers so that you can easily identify which object belongs to which layer.

In this chapter, you'll learn how to create and use layers to keep your drawings organized. You'll learn how color can play an important role while you're working with layers, and you'll also learn how to include linetypes such as dashes and center lines through the use of layers.

Topics in this chapter include the following:

- ◆ Organizing Information with Layers
- ◆ Keeping Track of Blocks and Layers

## Organizing Information with Layers

You can think of layers as overlays on which you keep various types of information (see Figure 5.1). In a floor plan of a building, for example, you want to keep the walls, ceiling, plumbing fixtures, wiring, and furniture separate so that you can display or plot them individually or combine them in different ways. It's also a good idea to keep notes and reference symbols, as well as the drawing's dimensions, on their own layers. As your drawing becomes more complex, you can turn the various layers on and off to allow easier display and modification.

For example, one of your consultants might need a plot of just the dimensions and walls, without all the other information; another consultant might need only a furniture layout. Using manual drafting, you would have to redraw your plan for each consultant or use overlay drafting techniques, which can be cumbersome. With AutoCAD, you can turn off the layers you don't need and plot a drawing containing only the required information. A carefully planned layering scheme helps you produce a document that combines the types of information needed in each case.

Using layers also lets you modify your drawings more easily. For example, suppose you have an architectural drawing with separate layers for the walls, the ceiling plan, and the floor plan. If any change occurs in the wall locations, you can turn on the ceiling plan layer to see where the new wall locations will affect the ceiling and then make the proper adjustments.

AutoCAD allows an unlimited number of layers, and you can name each layer anything you want.

**FIGURE 5.1**
Placing drawing
elements on
separate layers

## Creating and Assigning Layers

You'll start your exploration of layers by using a dialog box to create a new layer, giving it a name, and assigning a color. Then, you'll look at alternate ways of creating a layer through the command line. Next, you'll assign the new layer to the objects in your drawing. Start by getting familiar with the Layer Properties Manager dialog box:

1. Open the Bath file you created in Chapter 4. (If you didn't create one, use the file 04b-bath.dwg or 04b-bath-metric.dwg.)

2. To display the Layer Properties Manager dialog box, click the Layer Properties Manager tool in the Layers control panel, or choose Format ➤ Layer from the drop-down menu. You can also type **LA.↵** to use the keyboard shortcut.

**TIP** The Layer Properties Manager dialog box shows you at a glance the status of your layers. Right now, you have only one layer, but as your work expands, so will the number of layers. You'll then find this dialog box indispensable.

**3.** Click the New Layer button at the top of the dialog box. The button has an icon that looks like a star next to a sheet.

A new layer named Layer1 appears in the list box. Notice that the name is highlighted. This tells you that by typing, you can change the default name to something better suited to your needs.

**4.** Type **Wall**. As you type, your entry replaces the Layer1 name in the list box.

**5.** With the Wall layer name highlighted, click the Color icon in the Wall layer listing to display a dialog box in which you can assign a color to the Wall layer. The Color icon can be found under the Color column and currently shows White as its value. The icon is just to the left of the word *white*.

The Select Color dialog box opens.

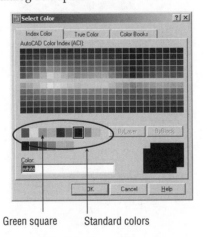

Green square    Standard colors

**6.** In the row of standard colors next to the ByLayer button, click the green square, and then click OK. Notice that the color swatch in the Wall layer listing is now green.

**7.** When the Layer Properties Manager dialog box returns, click OK to close it.

From this point on, any object assigned to the Wall layer will appear green unless the object is specifically assigned a different color.

### USING TRUE OR PANTONE COLORS

In the preceding exercise, you chose a color from the Index Color tab of the Select Color dialog box. Most of the time, you'll find that the Index Color tab includes enough colors to suit your needs. But if you're creating a presentation drawing in which color selection is important, you can choose colors from either the True Color or the Color Books tab of the Select Color dialog box.

The True Color tab offers a full range of colors through a color palette similar to the one found in Adobe Photoshop and other image-editing programs.

You have the choice of using hue, saturation, and luminance, which is the HSL color model, or you can use the RGB (red, green, blue) color model. You can select HSL or RGB from the Color Model drop-down list in the upper-right corner of the dialog box.

You can also select from a PANTONE *color book* by using the Color Books tab. The Color Book option lets you match colors to a PANTONE color book for offset printing.

**TIP** The Files tab of the Options dialog box (choose Tools ➤ Options) contains the Color Book Locations option, which tells AutoCAD where to look for the Color Book settings.

Let's continue with our look at layers in AutoCAD.

### UNDERSTANDING THE LAYER PROPERTIES MANAGER DIALOG BOX

The Layer Properties Manager dialog box conforms to the Windows interface standard. The most prominent feature of this dialog box is the layer list box, as you saw in the preceding exercise. Notice that the bar at the top of the list of layers offers several buttons for the various layer properties. Just as you can adjust Windows Explorer, you can adjust the width of each column in the list of layers by clicking and dragging either side of the column head buttons. You can also sort the layer list based on a property by clicking the property name at the top of the list. And, just as with other Windows list boxes, you can Shift+click names to select a block of layer names, or you can Ctrl+click individual names to select multiple layers that don't appear together. These features will become helpful as your list of layers grows.

Above the layer list, you can see a box displaying the current layer. Just to the left of the current layer name are four tool buttons.

You've already seen how the New Layer tool works. The tool next to the New Layer tool, the New Layer VP Frozen In All Viewports tool, looks similar to the New Layer tool and performs a similar function. The main difference is that the New Layer VP Frozen tool freezes the newly created layer. To delete layers, you select a layer or group of layers and then click the Delete Layer tool. Be aware that you can't delete layer 0, locked layers, or layers that contain objects. The Set Current tool enables you to set the current layer on which you want to work. You can also see at a glance which layer is current by the green check mark in the Status column of the layer list.

**TIP** Another way to create or delete layers is to select a layer or set of layers from the list box and then right-click. A menu appears, offering the same functions as the tools above the layer list.

You'll also notice another set of three tools farther to the left of the Layer Properties Manager dialog box. Those tools offer features to organize your layers in a meaningful way. You'll get a closer look at those tools a little later in this chapter.

### CONTROLLING LAYERS THROUGH THE LAYER COMMAND

You've seen how the Layer Properties Manager dialog box makes it easy to view and edit layer information and how you can easily select layer colors from an on-screen toolbar. But you can also control layers through the Command prompt.

**WARNING** You won't see the Pstyle option in the layer prompt or the Truecolor/True Color/Color Books options in the color option prompt unless you're using named plot styles. See Chapter 9 for more on plot styles.

Use these steps to control layers through the Command prompt:

1. Press the Esc key to make sure any current command is canceled.

2. At the Command prompt, enter **–Layer.**↵. Make sure you include the minus sign in front of the word *Layer*. The following prompt appears:

```
Enter an option
```

[?/Make/Set/New/ON/OFF/Color/Ltype/LWeight/MATerial/Plot/ Freeze/Thaw/ LOck/Unlock/stAte].

You'll learn about many of the options in this prompt as you work through this chapter.

3. Enter **N**↵ to select the New option.

4. At the `Enter name list for new layer(s):` prompt, enter **Wall2**↵. The [?/Make/ Set/New/ON/OFF/Color/Ltype/LWeight/MATerial/Plot/Freeze/Thaw/LOck/Unlock/ stAte]: prompt appears again.

5. Enter **C**↵.

6. At the `New color [Truecolor/COlorbook]:` prompt, enter **Yellow**↵. Or, you can enter **2**↵, the numeric equivalent of the color yellow in AutoCAD.

7. At the `Enter name list of layer(s) for color 2 (yellow) <0>:` prompt, enter **Wall2**↵. The [?/Make/Set/New/ON/OFF/Color/Ltype/LWeight/MATerial/Plot/Freeze/Thaw/ LOck/Unlock/stAte]: prompt appears again.

8. Press ↵ to exit the Layer command.

Each method of controlling layers has its own advantages. The Layer Properties Manager dialog box offers more information about your layers at a glance. On the other hand, the Layer command offers a quick way to control and create layers if you're in a hurry. Also, if you intend to write custom macros, you'll want to know how to use the Layer command as opposed to using the Layer Properties Manager dialog box, because dialog boxes can't be controlled through custom toolbar buttons or scripts.

### ASSIGNING LAYERS TO OBJECTS

When you create an object, that object is assigned to the current layer. Until now, only one layer has existed—layer 0—which contains all the objects you've drawn so far. Now that you've created some new layers, you can reassign objects to them by using the Properties palette:

1. Select the four lines that represent the bathroom walls. If you have trouble singling out the wall to the left, use a window to select the wall line.

2. With the cursor in the drawing area, right-click, and choose Properties from the shortcut menu to open the Properties palette. This palette lets you modify the properties of an object or a set of objects. (See the upcoming "Understanding Object Properties" sidebar for more on the properties of objects.)

3. Click the Layer option on the list in the Properties palette. Notice that an arrow appears in the layer name to the right of the Layer option.

4. Click the downward-pointing arrow to the far right of the Layer option to display a list of all the available layers.

5. Select the Wall layer from the list. Notice that the wall lines you selected change to a green color. This tells you that the objects have been assigned to the Wall layer. (Remember that you assigned a green color to the Wall layer.)

6. Close the Properties palette by clicking the X button in the upper-left corner.

The bathroom walls are now on the new layer called Wall, and the walls are changed to green. Layers are more easily distinguished from one another when you use colors to set them apart.

Next, you'll practice the commands you learned in this section and try some new ones by creating new layers and changing the layer assignments of the rest of the objects in your bathroom:

1. Open the Layer Properties Manager dialog box (choose Format ➢ Layer, or click the Layer Properties Manager button in the Layers control panel). Create a new layer called Fixture, and give it the color blue.

**TIP** You can change the name of a layer by clicking it in the Layer Properties Manager dialog box. After it's highlighted, click it again so that a box surrounds the name, or press the F2 function key. You can then rename the layer. This works in the same way as renaming a file or folder in Windows.

2. Click the Tub and Toilet blocks, and then right-click and choose Properties from the shortcut menu to open the Properties palette.

3. Click Layer in the list of properties, and then select Fixture from the drop-down list to the right of the layer listing.

4. Click the X in the upper-left corner of the Properties palette to dismiss it, and then press the Esc key to clear your selection.

5. Create a new layer for the door, name the layer Door, and make it red.

**TIP** In a block, you can change the color assignment and linetype of only those objects that are on layer 0. See the sidebar "Controlling Colors and Linetypes of Blocked Objects," later in this chapter.

6. Just as you've done with the walls and fixtures, use the Properties palette to assign the door to the Door layer.

**7.** Use the Layer Properties Manager dialog box to create three more layers for the ceiling, door jambs, and floor, as shown in Table 5.1. Remember that you can open the Select Color dialog box by clicking the color swatch of the layer listing.

**TABLE 5.1:** Create These Layers, and Set Their Colors as Indicated

| LAYER NAME | LAYER COLOR (NUMBER) |
| --- | --- |
| Ceiling | Magenta (6) |
| Jamb | Green (3) |
| Floor | Cyan (4) |

### UNDERSTANDING OBJECT PROPERTIES

It helps to think of the components of an AutoCAD drawing as having properties. For example, a line has geometric properties, such as its length, and coordinates that define its endpoints. An arc has a radius, a center, and beginning and ending coordinates. And even though a layer isn't an object you can grasp and manipulate, it can have properties such as color, linetypes, and lineweights.

By default, objects take on the color, linetype, and lineweight of the layer to which they're assigned, but you can also assign these properties directly to individual objects. These general properties can be manipulated through both the Properties palette and the Properties toolbar.

Although many of the options in the Properties palette may seem cryptic, don't worry about them at this point. As you work with AutoCAD, these properties will become more familiar. You'll find that you won't be too concerned with the geometric properties, because you'll be manipulating them with the standard editing tools in the Modify toolbar. The other properties will be explained in the rest of this chapter and in other chapters.

In step 3 of the previous exercise, you used the Properties palette, which offered several options for modifying the block. The options displayed in the Properties palette depend on the objects you've selected. With only one object selected, AutoCAD displays options that apply specifically to that object. With several objects selected, you'll see a more limited set of options because AutoCAD can change only those properties that are common to all the objects selected.

### CONTROLLING COLORS AND LINETYPES OF BLOCKED OBJECTS

Layer 0 has special importance to blocks. When objects assigned to layer 0 are used as parts of a block, and that block is inserted on another layer, those objects take on the characteristics of their new layer. On the other hand, if those objects are on a layer other than layer 0, they maintain their original layer characteristics even if you insert or change that block to another layer. For example, suppose the tub is drawn on the Door layer, instead of on layer 0. If you turn the tub into a block and insert it on the Fixture layer, the objects the tub is composed of will maintain their assignment to the Door layer, although the Tub block is assigned to the Fixture layer.

It may help to think of the block function as a clear plastic bag that holds together the objects that make up the tub. The objects inside the bag maintain their assignment to the Door layer even while the bag itself is assigned to the Fixture layer. This may be a bit confusing at first, but it should become clearer after you use blocks for a while.

AutoCAD also enables you to have more than one color or linetype on a layer. For example, you can use the Color and Linetype buttons in the Properties palette (the Properties button on the Standard toolbar) to alter the color or linetype of an object on layer 0. That object then maintains its assigned color and linetype—no matter what its layer assignment. Likewise, objects specifically assigned a color or linetype aren't affected by their inclusion in blocks.

## Working on Layers

So far, you've created layers and then assigned objects to those layers. In this section, you'll learn how to use the Layer drop-down list in the Properties toolbar to assign layers to objects. In the process, you'll make some additions to the drawing.

The current layer is still layer 0, and unless you change the current layer, every new object you draw will be on layer 0. Here's how to change the current layer:

1. Click the arrow button next to the layer name on the Layers control panel. A drop-down list opens, showing you all the layers available in the drawing.

   Notice the icons that appear next to the layer names; these control the status of the layer. You'll learn how to work with these icons later in this chapter. Also notice the box directly to the left of each layer name. This shows you the color of the layer.

**TIP** Momentarily placing the cursor on an icon in the Layer drop-down list displays a ToolTip that describes the icon's purpose.

2. Click the Jamb layer name. The drop-down list closes, and the name Jamb appears in the toolbar's layer name box. Jamb is now the current layer.

**TIP** You can also use the Layer command to reset the current layer. To do this here, enter **–Layer** (be sure to include the minus sign) at the Command prompt, and at the ?/Make/Set/New/ON/OFF/ Color/Ltype/LWeight/MATerial/Plot/Freeze/Thaw/LOck/Unlock/stAte]: prompt, enter **S** for Set. At the Enter layer name to make current or <select object>: prompt, enter **Jamb,** and then press ↵ twice to exit the Layer command.

3.  Zoom in on the door, and draw a 5″ line; start at the lower-right corner of the door, and draw toward the right. Metric users should draw a 13 cm line.

4.  Draw a similar line from the top-right end of the arc. Your drawing should look like Figure 5.2.

**FIGURE 5.2**

Door at wall with door jamb added

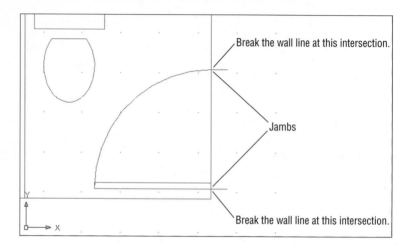

Because you assigned the color green to the Jamb layer, the two lines you just drew to represent the door jambs are green. This gives you immediate feedback about which layer you're on as you draw.

Now, you'll use the part of the wall between the jambs as a line representing the door header (the part of the wall above the door). To do this, you'll have to cut the line into three line segments and then change the layer assignment of the segment between the jambs:

1.  In the Modify toolbar, click the Break At Point tool.

2.  At the Select object: prompt, click the wall between the two jambs.

3.  At the Specify first break point: prompt, use the Endpoint osnap override to pick the endpoint of the door's arc that is touching the wall, as shown previously in Figure 5.2.

4.  Click Break At Point on the Modify toolbar, and then repeat steps 2 and 3, this time using the jamb near the door hinge location to locate the break point (see Figure 5.2).

Although it may not be obvious, you've just broken the right-side wall line into three line segments: one at the door opening and two more on either side of the jambs. You can also use the Break tool (below the Break At Point tool) to produce a gap in a line segment.

**TIP**    The Break At Point tool won't work on a circle. You can, however, use the Break tool to place a small gap in the circle. If you create a small enough gap, the circle will still look like a full circle.

Next, you'll change the Layer property of the line between the two jambs to the Ceiling layer. But instead of using the Properties tool, as you've done in earlier exercises, you'll use a shortcut method:

1.  Click the line between the door jambs to highlight it. Notice that the layer listing in the Layers control panel changes to Wall. Whenever you select an object to expose its grips, the Color, Linetype, Lineweight, and Plot Style listings in the Properties toolbar change to reflect those properties of the selected object.

2. Click the layer name in the Layers control panel to open the Layer drop-down list.

3. Click the Ceiling layer. The list closes, and the line you selected changes to the magenta color, showing you that it's now on the Ceiling layer. Also notice that the color list in the Properties toolbar changes to reflect the new color for the line.

4. Press the Esc key twice to clear the grip selection. Notice that the layer returns to Jamb, the current layer.

5. Click the Zoom Previous tool in the Standard toolbar, or choose View ➢ Zoom ➢ Previous to return to the previous view.

In this exercise, you saw that when you select an object with no command active, the object's properties are immediately displayed in the Properties toolbar under Color Control, Linetype, Lineweight, and Plot Style. Using this method, you can also change an object's color, linetype, lineweight, and plot style independent of its layer. Just as with the Properties palette, you can select multiple objects and change their layers through the Layer drop-down list. These options in the Properties toolbar offer a quick way to edit some of the properties of objects.

Now, you'll finish the bathroom by adding a sink to a layer named Casework:

1. Open the Layer Properties Manager dialog box, and create a new layer called Casework.

2. With the Casework layer selected in the layer list, click the Set Current button at the top of the dialog box.

3. Click the color swatch for the Casework layer listing, and then select Blue from the Select Color dialog box. Click OK to exit the dialog box.

4. Click OK in the Layer Properties Manager dialog box. Notice that the layer listing in the Layers control panel indicates that the current layer is Casework.

Next, you'll add the sink. As you draw, the objects will appear in blue, the color of the Casework layer.

5. Choose View ➢ Zoom ➢ All.

6. Click the Insert Block tool on the Draw toolbar, and then click the Browse button in the Insert dialog box to open the Select Drawing File dialog box.

7. Locate the Sink file, and double-click it.

8. In the Insert dialog box, make sure the Specify On-Screen options in both the Scale and Rotation groups aren't selected; then, click OK.

9. Place the sink roughly in the upper-right corner of the bathroom plan, and then use the Move command to place it accurately in the corner, as shown in Figure 5.3.

## Controlling Layer Visibility

I mentioned earlier that you'll sometimes want to display only certain layers to work with in a drawing. In this bathroom is a door header that would normally appear only in a reflected ceiling plan. To turn off a layer so that it becomes invisible, you click the Off button in the Layer Properties Manager dialog box, as shown in these steps:

1. Open the Layer Properties Manager dialog box by clicking the Layer Properties Manager button in the Layers control panel.

2. Click the Ceiling layer in the layer list.

**FIGURE 5.3**

The bathroom with sink and countertop added

3. Click the lightbulb icon in the layer list, next to the Ceiling layer name. The lightbulb icon changes from yellow to gray to indicate that the layer is off.

4. Click the OK button to exit the Layer Properties Manager dialog box. When you return to the drawing, the door header (the line across the door opening) disappears because you've made it invisible by turning off its layer.

You can also control layer visibility by using the Layer drop-down list on the Layers control panel:

1. On the Layers control panel, click the Layer drop-down list.

2. Find the Ceiling layer, and notice that its lightbulb icon is gray. This tells you that the layer is off and not visible.

3. Click the lightbulb icon to make it yellow.

4. Click the drawing area to close the Layer drop-down list; the door header reappears.

Figure 5.4 explains the roles of the other icons in the Layer drop-down list.

**FIGURE 5.4**

The Layer drop-down list icons

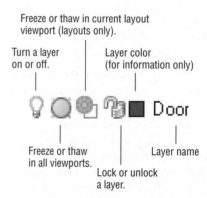

**NOTE** When you start to work with layouts in Chapters 8 and 16, you'll learn about *viewports*. A viewport is like a custom view of your drawing. You can have multiple viewports in a layout, each showing a different part of your drawing. Layer properties can be controlled for each viewport independently, so you can set up different linetypes, colors, and layer visibility for each viewport.

## Finding the Layers You Want

With only a handful of layers, it's fairly easy to find the layer you want to turn off. It becomes much more difficult, however, when the number of layers exceeds 20 or 30. The Layer Properties Manager dialog box offers some useful tools to help you quickly find the layers you want.

Suppose you have several layers whose names begin with C, such as C-lights, C-header, and C-pattern, and you want find those layers quickly. You can click the Name button at the top of the layer list to sort the layer names in alphabetic order. (You can click the Name button again to reverse the order.) To select those layers for processing, click the first layer name that starts with C; then, scroll down the list until you find the last layer of the group, and Shift+click it. All the layers between those layers are selected. If you want to deselect some of those layers, hold down the Ctrl key while clicking the layer names you don't want to include in your selection. Or, Ctrl+click other layer names you do want selected.

The Color and Linetype buttons at the top of the list let you control which layers appear in the list by virtue of their color or linetype assignments. Other buttons sort the list by virtue of status: On/Off, Freeze/Thaw, Lock/Unlock, and so forth. (See the "Other Layer Options" sidebar later in this chapter.)

Now, try changing the layer settings again by turning off all the layers except Wall and Ceiling, leaving just a simple rectangle. In this exercise, you'll get a chance to experiment with the On/Off options of the Layer Properties Manager dialog box:

1. Click the Layer Properties Manager button in the Layers control panel, or choose Format ➢ Layer.

2. Click the top layer name in the list box; then, Shift+click the last layer name. All the layer names are highlighted.

**TIP** Another way to select all the layers at once in the Layer Properties Manager dialog box is to right-click the layer list and then choose the Select All option from the shortcut menu. If you want to clear your selections, right-click the layer list, and choose Clear All.

3. Ctrl+click the Wall and Ceiling layers to deselect them and thus exempt them from your next action.

4. Click the lightbulb icon of any of the highlighted layers.

5. A message appears, warning you that the current layer will be turned off. Click No in the message box. The lightbulb icons turn gray to show that the selected layers have been turned off.

6. Click OK. The drawing now appears with only the Wall and Ceiling layers displayed. It looks like a simple rectangle of the room outline.

7. Open the Layer Properties Manager dialog box again, select all the layers as you did in step 2, and then click any of the gray lightbulbs to turn on all the layers at once.

8. Click OK to return to the drawing.

In this exercise, you turned off a set of layers with a single click on a lightbulb icon. You can freeze/thaw, lock/unlock, or change the color of a group of layers in a similar manner by clicking the appropriate layer property. For example, clicking a color swatch of one of the selected layers opens the Select Color dialog box, in which you can set the color for all the selected layers.

## Taming an Unwieldy List of Layers

Chances are, you'll eventually end up with a fairly long list of layers. Managing such a list can become a nightmare, but AutoCAD provides some tools to help you organize layers so you can keep track of them more easily.

On the left side of the Layer Properties Manager dialog box is a set of tools and a list box designed to help you with your layer-management tasks.

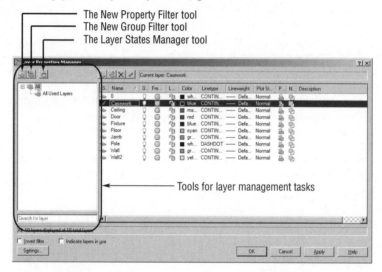

In the upper-left corner of the dialog box is a toolbar with three tools:

**The New Property Filter tool** lets you filter your list of layers to display only layers with certain properties, such as specific colors or names.

**The New Group Filter tool** lets you create named groups of layers that can be quickly recalled at any time. This tool is helpful if you often work with specific sets of layers. For example, you might have a set of layers in an architectural drawing that pertains to the electrical layout. You could create a group filter called Electrical that filters out all layers except those pertaining to the electrical layout. The filters don't affect the layers in any way; they just limit which layers are displayed in the main layer list.

**The Layer States Manager tool** lets you create sets of layer states. For example, if you want to save the layer settings that have only the wall and door layer turned on, you can do so by using this tool.

### FILTERING LAYERS BY THEIR PROPERTIES

Below these three tools is a filter list, which is a hierarchical list displaying the different sets of layer properties and group filters. Right now, you don't have any filters in place, so you see only All and All Used Layers.

## OTHER LAYER OPTIONS

You may have noticed the Freeze and Thaw buttons in the Layer Properties Manager dialog box. These options are similar to On and Off buttons. However, Freeze not only makes layers invisible, but it also tells AutoCAD to ignore the contents of those layers when you use the All response to the `Select objects:` prompt. Freezing layers can save time when you issue a command that regenerates a complex drawing. This is because AutoCAD ignores objects on frozen layers during Regen. You'll get first-hand experience with Freeze and Thaw in Chapter 7.

Another pair of Layer Properties Manager options, Lock and Unlock, offer functionality similar to Freeze and Thaw. If you lock a layer, you can view and snap to objects on that layer, but you can't edit those objects. This feature is useful when you're working on a crowded drawing and you don't want to accidentally edit portions of it. You can lock all the layers except those you intend to edit and then proceed to work without fear of making accidental changes.

Three more options—Lineweight, Plot Style, and Plot—offer control over the appearance of printer or plotter output. Lineweight lets you control the width of lines in a layer. Plot Style lets you assign plotter configurations to specific layers. (You'll learn more about plot styles in Chapter 9.) Plot lets you determine whether a layer gets printed in hard-copy output. This can be useful for setting up layers you may use for layout purposes only. The Linetype option lets you control line patterns, such as dashed or center lines.

Finally, you can save layer settings for later recall by using the Layer States Manager tool in the upper-left corner of the Layer Properties Manager dialog box. This feature is extremely useful when you want to save different layer combinations. Chapter 15 shows you how to use this feature. This option is also accessible from the State option in the command-line version of the Layer command.

In this section, you'll learn how the tools and the filter list box work. You'll start with a look at the New Property Filter tool:

1. Open the Layer Properties Manager dialog box by clicking the Layer Properties Manager button in the Layers control panel. You can also choose Format ➤ Layer from the toolbar.

2. Click the New Property Filter tool in the upper-left corner of the dialog box to open the Layer Filter Properties dialog box. You see two list boxes. The Filter Definition list box at the top is where you enter your filter criteria. The Filter Preview list box below is a preview of your layer list based on the filter options. Right now, there are no filter options, so the Filter Preview list shows all the layers.

3. In the Filter Definition list box, click the blank box just below the Color label. A button appears in the box.

Click the box under the Color column.

**4.** Click in the blank box again; then, enter **red**⏎. The Filter Preview changes to show only layers that are red. In the current drawing, only one layer has been assigned the color red.

**5.** Click twice in the blank box below the one you just edited. Again, a button appears.

**6.** This time, enter **green**⏎. The layers that are green appear in the Filter Preview list.

**TIP** You can also select a color from the Select Color dialog box by clicking the button that appears in the box.

**7.** In the Filter Definition list, click in the Name column in the third row down. A cursor appears, followed by an asterisk.

**8.** Enter **F**⏎. Two new layers are added to the Filter Preview list that have names beginning with F.

**9.** In the Filter Name text box at the upper-left corner of the dialog box, change the name Properties Filter 1 to **My List**. Then, click OK.

Now you see the My List filter in the list box on the left side of the Layer Properties Manager dialog box.

The layer list shows only the layers that have properties conforming to those you selected in the Layer Filter Properties dialog box. Notice that My List is highlighted in the filter list to the left. This tells you that My List is the current layer property filter being applied to the layer list to the right. You can change the layer list display by selecting different options in the filter list. Try these steps:

**1.** Click the All option in the filter list at the left side of the dialog box. The layer list to the right changes to display all the layers in the drawing. Also note that a brief description of the current layer filter is displayed at the bottom of the dialog box.

**2.** Click the All Used Layers option in the filter list. Now only layers that contain objects are displayed.

**3.** Click My List. The layer list changes back to the limited set of layers from your filter list.

**4.** Double-click My List. The Layer Filter Properties dialog box opens and displays the list of layer properties you set up earlier for My List. You can edit the criteria for your filter by making modifications in this dialog box.

**5.** Click Cancel to exit the Layer Filter Properties dialog box.

## CREATING LAYER GROUPS

The preceding exercise shows how you can filter out layer names based on the properties you specify in the Layer Filter Properties dialog box. But suppose you want to create a layer filter list by graphically selecting objects on the screen. You can use the New Group Filter tool to do just that:

1. Click the New Group Filter tool in the upper-left corner of the Layer Properties Manager dialog box, and then press ↵ to accept the default name for the group. You see a new listing appear called Group Filter1.

2. Right-click the Group Filter1 listing panel to the left, and then choose Select Layers ➢ Add from the shortcut menu. The Layer Properties Manager dialog box temporarily closes to enable you to select objects in your drawing. Notice that your cursor is now an Object Selection cursor.

3. Click a line representing a wall of the bathroom; then click the door. Press ↵ when you're finished with your selection. The Layer Properties Manager dialog box reappears, and the layers of the two objects you selected are displayed in the layer list. Also note that Group Filter1 is highlighted in the filter list to the left.

**TIP** You may have noticed the Select Layers ➢ Replace option in the shortcut menu in step 2. This option lets you completely replace an existing group filter with a new selection set. It works just like the Select Layers ➢ Add option.

Earlier, you saw how you can double-click a properties filter to edit a properties filter list. But group filters work in a slightly different way. If you want to add layers to your group filter, you can click and drag them from the layer list to the group filter name. Here's how it's done:

1. In the Layer Properties Manager dialog box, select All from the filter list to the left.

2. Click the Fixture layer in the layer list; then, Ctrl+click the Jamb layer in the list. These are the layers you'll add to the Group Filter1 layer group.

3. Click and drag the Fixture layer to the Group Filter1 listing in the filter list.

4. To check the addition to Group Filter1, click it in the filter list. The Fixture and Jamb layers have been added to the Group Filter1 list.

If you want to delete a layer from a group filter, you can use the shortcut menu, as shown in these steps:

1. With the Group Filter1 list selected, select the Jamb layer from the layer list, and then right-click it.

2. Select Remove From Group Filter in the shortcut menu. (Make sure you don't select Delete Layer.) Jamb is removed from the Group Filter1 list.

**TIP**   You can also convert a layer property filter into a group filter. Select the layer property filter from the filter list, right-click, and then select Convert To Group Filter. The icon for the layer property filter changes to a group filter icon, indicating that it's now a group filter.

You've seen how you can add property and group filters to the Layer Properties Manager dialog box by using the tools on the left side of the dialog box. One tool you haven't explored yet is the Layer States Manager. To understand how this tool works, you'll need to learn a little more about AutoCAD; look for a discussion of the Layer States Manager in Chapter 15.

Before you move on, you'll want to know about the options just below the filter list:

The **Invert Filter check box** changes the list of layers to show all layers *excluding* those in the selected filter. For example, if the My List filter contains layers that are red, and you select Invert Filter, the layer list will display all layers *except* those that are red.

The **Indicate Layers In Use check box** changes the icon in the status column of the list of layers to indicate layers that have no objects assigned to them. If you turn this option on, "empty" layers will display a gray icon in the Status column.

The **Settings button** opens the Layer Settings dialog box. This dialog box controls the way you're notified when new layers are added to a drawing.

In the next section, you'll find some tips for how to use layer names so that you can use text filters more effectively.

### NAMING LAYERS TO STAY ORGANIZED

In the previous section, you saw how to create a layer property filter by using the name of a layer. If you name layers carefully, you can use them as a powerful layer-management tool. For example, suppose you have a drawing whose layer names are set up to help you easily identify floor-plan data versus ceiling-plan data, as in the following list:

◆   A-FP-WALL-JAMB

◆   A-FP-WIND-JAMB

- A-CP-WIND-HEAD
- A-CP-DOOR-HEAD
- L-FP-CURB
- C-FP-ELEV

The first character in the layer name designates the discipline related to that layer: *A* for architectural, *L* for landscape, *C* for civil, and so on. In this example, layers with names containing the two characters *FP* signify floor-plan layers. *CP* designates ceiling-plan information.

**TIP**   These layer examples are loosely based on a layer-naming convention devised by the American Institute of Architects (AIA). As you can see from this example, careful naming of layers can help you manage them.

If you want to isolate only those layers that have to do with floor plans, regardless of their discipline, enter **??FP\*** in the Name column of the Layer Filter Properties dialog box. You can then give this layer property filter the name Floor Plan by entering **Floor Plan** in the Filter Name text box.

After you've created the Floor Plan layer properties list, you can pick Floor Plan from the filter list on the right side of the Layer Properties Manager dialog box, and only those layers with names containing the letters *FP* as their third and fourth characters will appear in the list of layers. You can turn off all these layers, change their color assignment, or change other settings quickly, without having to wade through layers you don't want to touch. You can create other filter properties to isolate other groups of layers. AutoCAD keeps these filter lists for future use until you delete them by using the Delete option in the shortcut menu. (Right-click the name of the properties filter, and choose Delete.)

In the ??FP\* example, the question marks (??) tell AutoCAD that the first two characters in the layer name can be anything. The *FP* tells AutoCAD that the layer name must contain *F* and *P* in these two places of the name. The asterisk (\*) at the end tells AutoCAD that the remaining characters can be anything. The question marks and asterisk are known as *wildcard characters*. They're commonly used filtering tools for both the Unix and Windows operating systems.

As the number of layers in a drawing grows, you'll find layer filters an indispensable tool. But bear in mind that the successful use of layer filters can depend on a careful layer-naming convention. If you're producing architectural plans, you may want to consider the AIA layering guidelines.

**TIP**   Check out Chapter 24 for some additional tools that will help you manage layer settings.

## Assigning Linetypes to Layers

You'll often want to use different linetypes to show hidden lines, center lines, fence lines, or other noncontinuous lines. You can assign a color and a linetype to a layer. You then see International Organization for Standardization (ISO) and complex linetypes, including lines that can be used to illustrate gas and water lines in civil work or batt insulation in a wall cavity.

AutoCAD comes with several linetypes, as shown in Figure 5.5. ISO linetypes are designed to be used with specific plotted line widths and linetype scales. For example, if you're using a pen width of 0.5 mm, set the linetype scale of the drawing to 0.5 as well. (See Chapter 16 for more information on plotting and linetype scale.) You can also create your own linetypes (see Chapter 26).

**FIGURE 5.5**

Standard, ISO, and complex AutoCAD linetypes

Linetypes that contain text, such as the gas line sample at the bottom of Figure 5.5, use the current text height and font to determine the size and appearance of the text displayed in the line. A text height of zero displays the text properly in most cases. See Chapter 10 for more on text styles.

AutoCAD stores linetype descriptions in an external file named Acad.lin, or Acadiso.lin for metric users. You can edit this file in a text editor like Notepad to create new linetypes or to modify existing ones. You'll see how this is done in Chapter 26.

## Adding a Linetype to a Drawing

To see how linetypes work, you'll add a dash-dot line in the bathroom plan to indicate a shower curtain rod:

1. Open the Layers Properties Manager dialog box, and select All from the filter list.

2. Click New, and then type **Pole** to create a new layer called Pole.

**TIP** If you're in a hurry, you can simultaneously load a linetype and assign it to a layer by using the Layer command. In this exercise, you enter **–Layer**↵ at the Command prompt. Then, enter **L**↵, **dashdot**↵, **pole**↵, and press ↵ to exit the Layer command.

3. In the Pole layer listing, under the Linetype column, click the word *Continuous* to open the Select Linetype dialog box. To find the Linetype column, you may need to scroll the list to the right by using the scroll bar at the bottom of the list.

**WARNING** The word *Continuous* truncates to *Contin* when the Linetype column is at its default width and the Continuous option is selected.

4. The Select Linetype dialog box offers a list of linetypes to choose from. In a new file such as the Bath file, only one linetype is available by default. You must load any additional linetype you want to use. Click the Load button at the bottom of the dialog box to open the Load Or Reload Linetypes dialog box. Notice that the list of linetype names is similar to the Layer drop-down list. You can sort the names alphabetically or by description by clicking the Linetype or Description heading at the top of the list.

5. In the Available Linetypes list, scroll down to locate the Dashdot linetype, click it, and then click OK.

6. Notice that the Dashdot linetype is added to the linetypes available in the Select Linetype dialog box.

7. Click Dashdot to highlight it; then, click OK. Dashdot appears in the Pole layer listing under Linetype.

8. With the Pole layer still highlighted, click the Set Current button to make the Pole layer current.

9. Click OK to exit the Layer Properties Manager dialog box.

10. Turn off Running Osnap mode; then, draw a line across the opening of the tub area, from coordinate 4′-4″,1′-10″ to coordinate 4′-4″,6′-10″. Metric users should draw a line from coordinate 133,56 to 133,208.

### CONTROLLING LINETYPE SCALE

Although you've designated this as a dashdot line, it appears solid. Zoom in to a small part of the line, and you'll see that the line is indeed as you specified.

Because you're working at a scale of 1″ = 1′, you must adjust the scale of your linetypes accordingly. This too is accomplished in the Linetype Manager dialog box. Here are the steps:

1. Choose Format ≻ Linetype from the drop-down menu.

2. The Linetype Manager dialog box opens. Click the Show Details button in the upper-right corner of the dialog box. Some additional options appear at the bottom.

**TIP** The Linetype Manager dialog box offers Load and Delete buttons that let you load or delete a linetype directly without having to go through a particular layer's linetype setting.

3. Double-click the Global Scale Factor text box, and then type **12** (metric users type **30**). This is the scale conversion factor for a 1″ = 1′ scale (see "Understanding Scale Factors" in Chapter 3).

4. Click OK. The drawing regenerates, and the shower curtain rod is displayed in the linetype and at the scale you designated.

5. Click the Zoom Previous tool so your drawing looks like Figure 5.6.

**TIP** You can also use the Ltscale system variable to set the linetype scale. Type **Ltscale**↵, and at the Enter new linetype scale factor <1.0000>: prompt, enter **12**↵.

**TIP** If you change the linetype of a layer or an object, but the object remains a continuous line, check the Ltscale system variable. It should be set to your drawing scale factor. If this doesn't work, set the Viewres system variable to a higher value (see Appendix C). (Viewres can also be set by the Arc And Circle Smoothness option in the Display tab of the Options dialog box.) The behavior of linetype scales depends on whether you're in Model Space or in a drawing layout. If your efforts to control linetype scale have no effect on your linetype's visibility, you may be in a drawing layout. See Chapter 16 for more on Model Space and layouts.

**FIGURE 5.6**
The completed
bathroom

Shower curtain rod

Remember that if you assign a linetype to a layer, everything you draw on that layer will be of that linetype. This includes arcs, polylines, circles, and traces. As explained in the "Assigning Colors, Linetypes, and Linetype Scales to Individual Objects" sidebar later in this chapter, you can also assign different colors and linetypes to individual objects, rather than relying on their layer assignment to define color and linetype. However, you may want to avoid assigning colors and linetypes directly to objects until you have some experience with AutoCAD and a good grasp of your drawing's organization.

In the previous exercise, you changed the global linetype scale setting. This affects all noncontinuous linetypes within the current drawing. You can also change the linetype scale of individual objects by using the Properties button on the Properties toolbar. Or you can set the default linetype scale for all new objects with the Current Object Scale option in the Linetype Manager dialog box.

When individual objects are assigned a linetype scale, they're still affected by the global linetype scale set by the Ltscale system variable. For example, say you assign a linetype scale of 2 to the curtain rod in the previous example. This scale is then multiplied by the global linetype scale of 12, for a final linetype scale of 24.

**TIP**   You can also set the default linetype scale for individual objects by using the Celtscale system variable. After it's set, only newly created objects are affected. You must use the Properties palette to change the linetype scale of individual existing objects.

If the objects you draw appear in a different linetype from that of the layer they're on, check the default linetype by using the Linetype Control drop-down list on the Properties toolbar. You can also choose Format ➤ Linetype. Then, in the Linetype Manager dialog box, highlight ByLayer in the Linetype list, and click the Current button. In addition, check the linetype scale of the object itself, by using the Properties palette. A different linetype scale can make a line appear to have an assigned linetype that might not be what you expect. (See the sidebar "Assigning Colors, Linetypes, and Linetype Scales to Individual Objects.")

**NOTE**   A system variable called Psltscale affects how layout viewports display linetypes. When the Psltscale system variable is set to 1, layout viewports display linetypes at the Ltscale setting, which is usually incorrect for the 1-to-1 scale of the layout. When Psltscale is set to 0, linetypes appear in layout viewports in the same way they appear in the Model tab.

### ADDING THE FINAL DETAIL

If you're working through the tutorial, your final task is to set up an insertion point for the current drawing, to facilitate its insertion into other drawings in the future. Follow these steps:

1. Type **Base**.⏎.

2. At the Enter base point <0´-0″,0´-0″,0´-0″>: prompt, pick the upper-left corner of the bathroom. The bathroom drawing is complete.

3. Choose File ➢ Save to record your work up to now.

## Controlling Lineweights

You may have noticed a Lineweight column in the Layer Properties Manager dialog box. If you click this option for a given layer, the Lineweight dialog box opens, where you can control the plotted thickness of your lines. Plotted lineweights can also be set through direct object property assignment. You can view lineweights as they will appear in your final plot by making setting changes in the Lineweights Settings dialog box, which you'll learn about in Chapter 16.

With the Lineweight option and Lineweight Settings dialog box, you have greater control over the look of your drawings. This can save time because you don't have to print your drawing just to check for lineweights. You'll be able to see how thick or thin your lines are as you edit your drawing. You'll get a chance to delve into lineweights in Chapter 16.

# Keeping Track of Blocks and Layers

The Insert and Layer Properties Manager dialog boxes let you view the blocks and layers available in your drawing by listing them in a window. The Layer Properties Manager dialog box also includes information about the status of layers. However, you may forget the layer on which an object resides. You've seen how the Properties option on the shortcut menu shows you the properties of an object. The List option in the Tools ➢ Inquiry menu also enables you to get information about individual objects.

Use these steps to see an alternate way to view the properties of a block:

1. Choose Tools ➢ Inquiry ➢ List from the menu bar.

**TIP** If you just want to quickly check which layer an object is on, click it. Its layer will appear in the Layer list of the Layers control panel.

2. At the Select objects: prompt, click the Tub block, and then press ⏎ to open the AutoCAD Text Window.

3. In the AutoCAD Text Window, a listing appears that shows not only the layer the tub is on, but also its space, insertion point, name, rotation angle, and scale.

The information in the Text Window, except the handle listing, is duplicated in the Properties palette you see when you right-click and choose Properties. But having the data in the AutoCAD Text Window gives you the flexibility to record the data in a text file, in case you need to store data about parts of your drawing. You can also use the AutoCAD Text Window to access and store other types of data regarding your drawings.

**TIP** The Space property listed for the Tub block designates whether the object resides in Model Space or Paper Space. You'll learn more about these spaces in Chapters 8 and 16.

## Getting a Text File List of Layers or Blocks

With complex drawings, it can be helpful to get a text file that lists the layers or blocks in your drawing. You can do this by using the log-file feature in AutoCAD. At the command prompt, enter **Logfilemode**↵, and then enter **1**↵. Type **–La**↵**?**↵↵ (don't forget the minus sign at the beginning of the La command). If your list of layers is extensive, you may be asked to press ↵ to continue. Do so. Your list of layers appears in the Command window. Press the F2 key to view an expanded version of the Command window. For a list of blocks, enter **–Insert**↵ **?**↵↵. When you've obtained your list, close the log-file feature by typing **Logfilemode**↵ **0**↵.

Once the log-file feature is closed, you can use Windows Notepad to open the AutoCAD log file located in the `C:\Documents and Settings\`*YourName*`\Local Settings\Application Data\ Autodesk\AutoCAD 2008\R17.1\enu\` folder. The name of the log file will start with the name of the current drawing, followed by a series of numbers and the `.log` filename extension, as in `04c-bath-metric_1_1_6500.log`.

If you have difficulty finding the log file, enter **(getvar "logfilepath")** at the AutoCAD Command prompt to get a listing of the log-file location. The log file may also be in a hidden folder, so you may have to turn off the hidden folder setting in Windows Explorer. See Appendix A for instructions on how to do this.

With the log-file feature, you can record virtually anything that appears at the Command prompt. You can even record an entire AutoCAD session. The log file can also be helpful in constructing script files to automate tasks. (See Chapter 26 for more information on scripts.) If you want a hard copy of the log file, print it from an application such as Windows Notepad or your favorite word processor.

---

### ASSIGNING COLORS, LINETYPES, AND LINETYPE SCALES TO INDIVIDUAL OBJECTS

If you prefer, you can set up AutoCAD to assign specific colors and linetypes to objects, instead of having objects take on the color and linetype settings of the layer on which they reside. Normally, objects are given a default color and linetype called ByLayer, which means each object takes on the color or linetype of its assigned layer. (You've probably noticed the word *ByLayer* in the Object Properties toolbar and in various dialog boxes.)

Use the Properties toolbar to change the color or linetype of existing objects. This toolbar lets you set the properties of individual objects. For new objects, use the Color control drop-down list on the Properties toolbar to set the current default color to red (for example) instead of ByLayer. Then, everything you draw will be red, regardless of the current layer color. The Color control drop-down list also offers a Select Color option that opens the Select Color dialog box you saw earlier in this chapter.

For linetypes, you can use the Linetype Control drop-down list in the Properties toolbar to select a default linetype for all new objects. The list shows only linetypes that have already been loaded into the drawing, so you must first load a linetype before you can select it.

Another possible color and linetype assignment is ByBlock, which you also set with the Properties toolbar. ByBlock makes everything you draw white, until you turn your drawing into a block and then insert the block on a layer with an assigned color. The objects then take on the color of that layer. This behavior is similar to that of objects drawn on layer 0. The ByBlock linetype works similarly to the ByBlock color.

Finally, if you want to set the linetype scale for each individual object, instead of relying on the global linetype scale (the Ltscale system variable), you can use the Properties palette to modify the linetype scale of individual objects. In place of using the Properties button, you can set the Celtscale system variable to the linetype scale you want for new objects.

As mentioned earlier, stay away from assigning colors and linetypes to individual objects until you're comfortable with AutoCAD; even then, use color and linetype assignments carefully. Other users who work on your drawing may have difficulty understanding your drawing's organization if you assign color and linetype properties indiscriminately.

## The Bottom Line

**Organizing Information with Layers**    Layers are perhaps the most powerful feature in AutoCAD. They help to keep drawings well organized and they give you control over the visibility of objects. They also let you control the appearance of your drawing by setting colors, lineweights, and linetypes.

**Master It**    Describe the process of creating a layer.

**Solution**    First, click the Layer Properties Manager tool in the Layers control panel. Second, click the New Layer button at the top of the dialog box. Finally, type the name for your new layer.

**Controlling Layer Visibility**    When a drawing becomes dense with information, it can be difficult to edit. If you've organized your drawing using layers, you can reduce the complexity of a drawing by turning off layers that aren't important to your current session.

**Master It**    Describe two methods for hiding a layer.

**Solution**    Open the Layer Properties Manager, select a layer, and click the Freeze icon for the layer. Then, open the Layer drop-down list in the Layers control panel, and click the Freeze icon for the layer you want to hide.

**Keeping Track of Blocks and Layers**    At times, you may want a record of the layers or blocks in your drawing. You can create a list of layers using the log file feature in AutoCAD.

**Master It**    Where do you go to turn on the log file feature?

**Solution**    The Options dialog box.

# Part 2

# Mastering Intermediate Skills

**In this part:**

# Chapter 6

# Editing and Reusing Data to Work Efficiently

At least 5 AutoCAD commands are devoted to duplicating objects—10, if you include the Grips options. Why so many? If you're an experienced drafter, you know that you frequently have to draw the same item several times in many drawings. AutoCAD offers a variety of ways to reuse existing geometry, thereby automating much of the repetitive work usually associated with manual drafting.

In this chapter, as you finish drawing the studio apartment unit, you'll explore some of the ways to exploit existing files and objects while constructing your drawing. For example, you'll use existing files as prototypes for new files, eliminating the need to set up layers, scales, and sheet sizes for similar drawings. With AutoCAD, you can also duplicate objects in multiple arrays. In Chapter 3, you saw how to use the Object Snap (Osnap) overrides on objects to locate points for drawing complex forms. This chapter describes other ways of using lines to aid your drawing.

Because you'll begin to use the Zoom command more in the exercises in this chapter, you'll review this command as you go along. You'll also discover the Pan command—another tool to help you get around in your drawing.

You're already familiar with many of the commands you'll use to draw the apartment unit. So, rather than going through every step of the drawing process, the exercises will sometimes ask you to copy the drawing from a figure, using notes and dimensions as guides, and put objects on the indicated layers. If you have trouble remembering a command you've already learned, go back and review the appropriate section of the book.

Topics in this chapter include the following:

- ◆ Creating and Using Templates
- ◆ Copying an Object Multiple Times
- ◆ Developing Your Drawing
- ◆ Finding an Exact Distance along a Curve
- ◆ Changing the Length of Objects
- ◆ Creating a New Drawing by Using Parts from Another Drawing

## Creating and Using Templates

Most programs today include what are called templates. A *template* is a file that is already set up for a specific application. For example, in your word processor, you might want to set up letters with a logo, a return address, and a date so you don't have to add these elements each time you create a letter. You might also want to format invoices in a slightly different way. You can set up a template for the needs of each type of document. That way, you don't have to spend time reformatting each new document you create.

Similarly, AutoCAD offers templates, which are drawing files that contain custom settings designed for a particular function. Out of the box, AutoCAD has templates for ISO, ANSI, DIN, GB, and JIS standard drawing formats that include generic title blocks. But you aren't limited to these "canned" templates. You can create your own templates for your particular style and method of drawing.

If you find that you use a particular drawing setup frequently, you can turn one or more of your typical drawings into a template. For example, you might want to create a set of drawings with the same scale and sheet size as an existing drawing. By turning a frequently used drawing into a template, you can save a lot of setup time for subsequent drawings.

## Creating a Template

The following exercise guides you through creating and using a template drawing for your studio's kitchenette. Because the kitchenette will use the same layers, settings, scale, and sheet size as the bathroom drawing, you can use the Bath file as a prototype. Follow these steps:

1. Start AutoCAD in the usual way.

2. Choose File ➢ Open to open the Select File dialog box.

3. Locate the Bath file you created in the last chapter. You can also use the file 06-bath.dwg.

4. Click the Erase button on the Modify toolbar, or enter **e**↲; then, type **all**↲. This erases all the objects that make up the bathroom; but other elements, such as layers, linetypes, and stored blocks, remain in the drawing.

5. Choose File ➢ Save As to open the Save Drawing As dialog box. Open the File Of Type dropdown list, and select AutoCAD Drawing Template (*.dwt). The file list window changes to display the current template files in the \Template\ folder.

**TIP** When you choose the AutoCAD Drawing Template option in the Save Drawing As dialog box, AutoCAD automatically opens the folder containing the template files. The standard AutoCAD installation creates the folder named Template to contain the template files. If you want to place your templates in a different folder, you can change the default template location by using the Options dialog box (choose Tools ➢ Options). Click the Files tab, double-click to expand Template Settings, and then double-click Drawing Template File Location in the list. Double-click the folder name that appears just below Template Drawing File Location; then, select a new location from the Browse For Folder dialog box that appears.

6. In the File Name text box, enter the name **Arch8x11h**. If you're a metric user, enter the name **A4plan**.

7. Click Save to open the Template Description dialog box.

8. Enter the following description: **Architectural one inch scale drawing on 8½ by 11 inch media**. Metric users should enter the description **Architectural 1:10 scale drawing on A4 media**.

9. Select English or Metric from the Measurement drop-down list, depending on the unit system you're using.

10. Click OK to save your new file and create a template. The template file you saved becomes the current file. (As with other Windows programs, choosing File ➢ Save As makes the saved file current.) This also shows that you can edit template files just as you would regular drawing files.

11. Close the template file.

### Using a Template

Now, let's see how a template is used. You'll use the template you just created as the basis for a new drawing you'll work on in this chapter:

1. Choose File ➢ New to open the Select Template dialog box. If you don't see the Select Template dialog box, press the Esc key and then enter Startup↵ 1↵ Choose File ➢ New again.

2. In the Select Template list box, click the filename `Arch8x11h.dwt`. Metric users should click the filename `A4plan.dwt`. Because this file is blank, you won't see anything in the preview window. Notice that the description you entered earlier in the Template Description dialog box appears in the Template Description area below the list.

3. Click OK. It may not be obvious, but your new file is set up with the same architectural units and drawing limits as the bathroom drawing. It also contains the Door, Toilet, and Tub blocks.

4. You need to give your new file a name. Choose File ➢ Save As to open the Save Drawing As dialog box. (Make sure you choose Save As, or you won't get the Save Drawing As dialog box.) Enter **Kitchen** for the filename, and select the appropriate folder in which to save your new kitchen file.

5. Click Save to create the `Kitchen` file and close the dialog box.

You've created and used your own template file. Later, when you've established a comfortable working relationship with AutoCAD, you can create a set of templates that are custom-made to your particular needs.

However, you don't need to create a template every time you want to reuse settings from another file. You can use an existing file as the basis or prototype for a new file without creating a template. Open the prototype file, and choose File ➢ Save As to create a new version of the file under a new name. You can then edit the new version without affecting the original prototype file.

## Copying an Object Multiple Times

Let's explore the tools that let you quickly duplicate objects. In this section, you'll begin to draw parts of a small kitchen. The first exercise introduces the Array command, which you can use to draw the gas burners of a range top.

As you'll see, an array can be in either a circular pattern, called a *polar array*, or a matrix of columns and rows, called a *rectangular array*.

## Making Circular Copies

To start the range top, first set the layer on which you want to draw, and then draw a circle representing the edge of one burner:

1. Set the current layer to Fixture.

**TIP** Because you used the Bath file as a template, Running Osnaps for Endpoint, Midpoint, and Intersection are already turned on and available in this new file.

2. Click the Circle tool on the Draw toolbar, or type C↵.

3. At the Specify Center point for circle or [3P/2P/Ttr (tan tan radius)]: prompt, pick a point at coordinate 4´,4´. Metric users should pick a point at coordinate 120,120.

4. At the Specify radius of circle or [Diameter]: prompt, enter **3**↵. Metric users should enter **7.6**↵. The circle appears.

Now you're ready to use the Array command to draw the burner grill. You'll first draw one line representing part of the grill and then use the Array command to create the copies:

1. Turn off both Polar Snap and Grid Snap modes by clicking the Snap button in the status bar, and draw a 4″ line starting from the coordinate 4´-1″,4´-0″ and ending to the right of that point. Metric users should draw a 9 cm line starting at coordinate 122,120 and ending to the right of that point.

2. Zoom into the circle and line to get a better view. Your drawing should look like Figure 6.1.

**FIGURE 6.1**
A close-up of the circle and line

You've got the basic parts needed to create the burner grill. You're ready to make multiple copies of the line. For this part, you'll use the Array dialog box:

1.  Click Array on the Modify toolbar, or type **AR**↵ to open the Array dialog box.

2.  Click the Select Objects button. The dialog box temporarily closes, enabling you to select objects.

3.  Type **L**↵ to select the last object drawn, or click the object you want to array.

4.  Press ↵ to confirm your selection. The Array dialog reopens.

5.  Click the Polar Array radio button at the top of the dialog box to tell AutoCAD you want a circular array. The Array dialog box displays the Polar Array options.

6.  Click the Pick Center Point button to temporarily close the Array dialog box.

7.  Pick the point that represents the center of the circular array. Use the Center osnap to select the center of the circle. After you've indicated a point, the Array dialog box returns.

**TIP**  Remember that to access osnaps other than those set up as Running Osnaps, you Shift+right-click the mouse and then select the osnap you want to use from the resulting menu.

At this point, you've selected an object to array, and you've indicated the center location of the array. If you've selected the wrong object or the wrong center point, you can go back and specify these options again.

Now, to complete the process, tell AutoCAD the number of copies in the array and the extent of the array through the circle:

1. In the Array dialog box, enter **8** in the Total Number Of Items text box. This tells AutoCAD to make eight copies including the original.

2. Accept the default of 360 for the Angle To Fill text box. This tells AutoCAD to spread the copies evenly over the full 360 degrees of the circle. Of course, you can enter other values here. For example, if you enter 180, the array will fill half the circle.

**TIP** You can click the Pick Angle To Fill button to the right of the Angle To Fill text box to graphically select an angle in the drawing.

3. Make sure the Rotate Items As Copied check box in the lower-left corner of the dialog box is selected. This ensures that the arrayed object is rotated about the array center. If you clear this option, the copies will all be oriented in the same direction as the original object.

4. Click the Preview button. AutoCAD shows you the results of your array settings plus a dialog box that offers Accept, Modify, and Cancel.

5. Click Accept. The circular array appears in the drawing, as shown in Figure 6.2.

**FIGURE 6.2**
The completed
gas burner

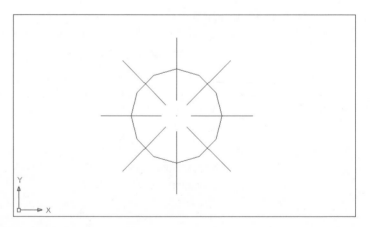

In step 5, you could select the Modify option to return to the Array dialog box and change settings before committing to a final array pattern, or you could click Cancel to cancel the whole process. The Array dialog box gives you a lot of leeway in creating your array copies.

**TIP** If you're a veteran AutoCAD user and you prefer the command-line version of the Array command, you can type **–Array.**↵ or **–Ar.**↵ at the Command prompt and then answer the prompts as you would in earlier versions of AutoCAD.

## Making Row and Column Copies

Now, you'll draw the other three burners of the gas range by creating a rectangular array from the burner you just drew. You'll first zoom back a bit to get a view of a larger area. Then, you'll proceed with the Array command.

Follow these steps to zoom back:

1. Choose View ➤ Zoom ➤ Scale, or type **Z⏎ S⏎**.

2. Enter **.5x⏎**. Your drawing will look like Figure 6.3.

**TIP** If you're not too fussy about the amount you want to zoom out, you can choose View ➤ Zoom ➤ Out to quickly reduce your view, or you can click the Zoom Realtime tool on the Standard toolbar.

Entering .5x for the Zoom Scale factor tells AutoCAD you want a view that reduces the width of the current view to fill half the display area, enabling you to see more of the work area. If you specify a scale value greater than 1 (5, for example), you'll magnify your current view. If you leave off the *x*, your new view will be in relation to the drawing limits rather than the current view.

**FIGURE 6.3**
The preceding view reduced by a factor of 0.5

Next, you'll finish the range top. You'll get a chance to use the Rectangular Array option to create three additional burners:

1. Click the Array tool on the Modify toolbar again, or type **AR⏎** to open the Array dialog box.

2. Click the Select Objects button to temporarily close the Array dialog box.

3. Select the entire burner, including the lines and the circle, and then press ⏎ to confirm your selection.

4. In the Array dialog box, click the Rectangular Array radio button.

5. Change both the Rows and Columns text boxes to 2.

6. Change the Row Offset text box value to 1´-2″ (35.5 for metric users) and the Column Offset text box value to 1´-4″ (40.6 for metric users).

7. Click OK. Your screen will look like Figure 6.4.

**FIGURE 6.4**
The burners arrayed

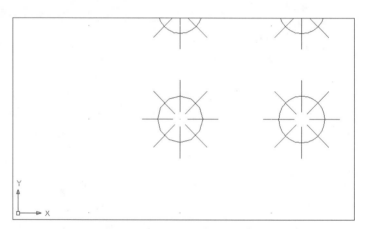

AutoCAD usually draws a rectangular array from bottom to top and from left to right. You can reverse the direction of the array by giving negative values for the distance between columns and rows.

**TIP** At times, you may want to create a rectangular array at an angle. To accomplish this, enter the desired angle in the Angle Of Array text box in the Array dialog box. You can also select the angle graphically by clicking the Pick Angle Of Array button just to the right of the Angle Of Array text box.

If you need to graphically indicate an array cell, you can do so by using options in the Offset Distance And Direction group of the Array dialog box (see the bottom image in Figure 6.5). An *array cell* is a rectangle defining the distance between rows and columns (see the top image in Figure 6.5). You may want to use this option when objects are available to use as references from which to determine column and row distances. For example, you might draw a crosshatch pattern, as on a calendar, within which you want to array an object. You use the intersections of the hatch lines as references to define the array cell, which is one square in the hatch pattern.

In the Offset Distance And Direction group, the Pick Both Offsets button lets you indicate the row and column distance by placing an array cell graphically in the drawing, as shown in the bottom image in Figure 6.5. You can also indicate a row or column distance graphically by using the Pick Row Offset or Pick Column Offset button to the right of the Pick Both Offsets button.

**FIGURE 6.5**

An array cell and the Array dialog box options that let you graphically indicate array cells

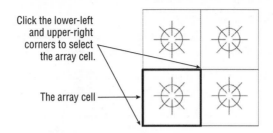

Click the lower-left and upper-right corners to select the array cell.

The array cell

## Fine-Tuning Your View

Back in Figure 6.4, you may have noticed that parts of the burners don't appear on the display. To move the view over so you can see all the burners, use the Pan command. Pan is similar to Zoom in that it changes your view of the drawing. However, Pan doesn't alter the magnification of the view the way Zoom does. Rather, Pan maintains the current magnification while moving your view across the drawing, just as you would pan a camera across a landscape.

---

### QUICK ARRAY COPIES WITH GRIPS

Sometimes the Array tool can be overkill if you only need to make a few evenly spaced copies. Fortunately, grip editing offers a feature that lets you quickly make evenly spaced copies. Here's how it's done:

1. Press the Esc key to make sure you aren't in the middle of a command; then, select the objects you want to copy.

2. Click a grip point as your base point.

3. Right-click your mouse, and select Move.

4. Ctrl+click a location to place a copy of the selected object. This first copy will determine the interval distance for additional copies.

5. Continue to hold down the Ctrl key and select additional points to make copies at regularly spaced intervals.

The copies snap to the distance you indicate with the first Ctrl+click point in step 4. You can use osnaps to select a distance based on the position of another object. Once you've made the first copy with the Ctrl+click, you can release the Ctrl key to make multiple copies at random intervals. Another option is to use Polar Snap while making grip edit copies. With Polar Snap, you can enter a specific distance for the intervals. See Chapter 3 for more on Polar Snap.

To activate the Pan command, follow these steps:

1. Click the Pan Realtime tool on the Standard toolbar, choose View ➤ Pan ➤ Realtime, or type P↵. You can also right-click and choose Pan from the shortcut menu. A small hand-shaped cursor appears in place of the AutoCAD cursor.

2. Place the hand cursor in the center of the drawing area, and then click and drag it downward and to the left. The view follows the motion of your mouse.

3. Continue to drag the view until it looks similar to Figure 6.6; then, release the mouse button.

**FIGURE 6.6**
The panned view of the range top

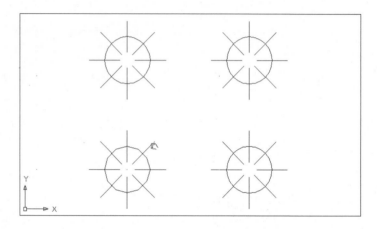

4. To finish the kitchen, you want a view that shows more of the drawing area. Right-click to open the Zoom/Pan shortcut menu, and then choose Zoom. The cursor changes to the Zoom Realtime cursor. The Zoom/Pan shortcut menu also appears when you right-click during the Zoom Realtime command.

5. Place the cursor close to the top of the screen, and click and drag the cursor downward to zoom out until your view looks like the top panel of Figure 6.7. You may need to click and drag the Zoom Realtime cursor a second time to achieve this view.

6. Right-click the mouse again, and choose Exit from the shortcut menu. You're now ready to add more information to the kitchen drawing.

**TIP** To exit the Pan Realtime or Zoom Realtime command without opening the shortcut menu, press the Esc key.

This exercise showed how you can fine-tune your view by easily switching between Pan Realtime and Zoom Realtime. After you get the hang of these two tools working together, you'll be able to quickly access the best view for your needs. The other options in the shortcut menu—Zoom Window, Zoom Original, and Zoom Extents—perform the same functions as the options in the View drop-down menu.

**TIP** The Zoom Window option in the Zoom/Pan shortcut menu functions in a slightly different way from the standard Zoom Window option. Instead of clicking two points, you click and drag a window across your view.

**FIGURE 6.7**

The final view of the range top burners (top image) and the finished kitchen (bottom image). Metric dimensions are shown in brackets.

Base Point

Corner Coordinate: 0'-11",3'-6" [26,105]

Put Entire Kitchen on Fixture Layer.

While we're on the subject of display tools, don't forget the scroll bars to the right and bottom of the AutoCAD drawing area. They work like any other Windows scroll bars, offering a simple way to move up, down, left, or right in your current view. They also come in handy for quickly panning your view in one direction or another.

If for some reason the scroll bars don't appear in AutoCAD, or if you prefer to turn them off, open the Options dialog box (choose Tools ➢ Options), click the Display tab, and make sure that the Display Scroll Bars In Drawing Window option is either selected to turn them on or cleared to turn them off.

## Finishing the Kitchenette

Before you save and close the `Kitchen` file, you need to do one more thing. You'll be using this drawing as a symbol and inserting it into the overall plan of the studio apartment unit. To facilitate accurate placement of the kitchen, you'll change the location of the base point of this drawing to the upper-left corner of the kitchen. This will then be the drawing's *grip*:

1. Complete the kitchenette as indicated in the bottom panel of Figure 6.7, shown earlier in this chapter. As the figure indicates, make sure you put the kitchenette on the Fixture layer. This will help you control the visibility of the kitchenette in future edits of this file. Draw the sink roughly as shown in the figure.

2. Choose Draw ➢ Block ➢ Base from the drop-down menu.

3. At the `Enter base point:` prompt, pick the upper-left corner of the kitchen, as indicated in the bottom image of Figure 6.7. The kitchen drawing is complete.

4. Choose File ➢ Save, and exit the file.

## Developing Your Drawing

As mentioned briefly in Chapter 3, when you're using AutoCAD, you first create the basic geometric forms used in your drawing; and then you refine them. In this section, you'll create two drawings—the studio apartment unit and the lobby—that demonstrate this process in more detail.

First, you'll construct a typical studio apartment unit by using the drawings you've created thus far. In the process, you'll explore the use of lines as reference objects.

You'll also further examine how to use existing files as blocks. In Chapter 4, you inserted a file into another file. The size and number of files you can insert are limitless. As you may already have guessed, you can also *nest* files and blocks; that is, you can insert blocks or files in other blocks or files. Nesting can help reduce your drawing time by enabling you to build one block out of smaller blocks. For example, you can insert your door drawing into the bathroom plan. In turn, you can insert the bathroom plan into the studio unit plan, which also contains doors. Finally, you can insert the unit plan into the overall floor plan for the studio apartment building.

### Importing Settings

In this exercise, you'll use the Bath file as a prototype for the studio unit plan. However, you must make a few changes to it first. After the changes are made, you'll import the bathroom and thereby import the layers and blocks contained in the bathroom file.

As you go through this exercise, observe how the drawings begin to evolve from simple forms to complex, assembled forms.

Use these steps to modify the Bath file:

1. Open the Bath file. If you skipped drawing the Bath file in Chapter 5, use the file 05c-bath.dwg (or 05c-bath-metric.dwg).

2. Use the Base command and select the upper-left corner of the bathroom as the new base point for this drawing, so you can position the Bath file more accurately.

3. Save the Bath file. If you use the online file, choose File ➤ Save As and save it as Bath.

4. Choose File ➤ Close to close the Bath drawing.

Next, you'll create a new file. But this time, instead of using the Start From Scratch or Use A Template option in the Create New Drawing dialog box, you'll try the Use A Wizard option:

1. Choose File ➤ New to open the Select template dialog box.

2. Locate and select the Acad.dwt template file. Metric users should locate the Acadiso.dwt template file.

3. Click Open to open the new file.

4. If you're using Imperial measurements, choose Format ➤ Units; then, in the Drawing Units dialog box, select Architectural from the Length group's Type drop-down list, and click OK. Metric users, use the default decimal length type.

5. Choose Format ➤ Drawing Limits. At the Specify lower left corner or [ON/OFF] <0.0000,0.0000>: prompt, press ↵ to accept the default drawing origin for the lower-left corner.

6. If you're using Imperial measurements, enter **528,408** at the next prompt. These are the appropriate dimensions for an 8½″ × 11″ drawing at ¼″ = 1′-0 ″ scale. Metric users should enter **1485,1050**. This is the work area for a 1:50 scale drawing on an A4 sheet.

7. Choose View ➢ Zoom ➢ All.

Let's continue by laying out a typical studio unit. You'll discover how importing a file also imports a variety of drawing items such as layers and linetypes. Follow these steps:

1. Begin the unit by drawing two rectangles, one 14′ long by 24′ wide, and the other 14′ long by 4′ wide. Metric users should make the rectangles 426 cm wide by 731 cm long and 426 cm wide by 122 cm long. Place them as shown in Figure 6.8. The large rectangle represents the interior of the apartment unit, and the small rectangle represents the balcony. The size and location of the rectangles are indicated in the figure.

**FIGURE 6.8**
The apartment unit interior and balcony. Metric locations and dimensions are shown in brackets.

**TIP** If you used the Rectangle tool to draw the interior and balcony of the apartment unit, make sure you use the Explode tool on the Modify toolbar to explode the rectangles. The Rectangle tool draws a polyline rectangle instead of simple line segments, so you need to explode the rectangle to reduce it to its component lines. You'll learn more about polylines in Chapter 18.

2. Click the Insert Block tool on the Draw toolbar to open the Insert dialog box.

3. Click the Browse button, and locate and select the bathroom drawing by using the Select Drawing File dialog box. Then, click Open. If you haven't saved a Bathroom drawing from earlier exercises, you can use 05c-bath.dwg.

**TIP** If you're using the 05c-bath.dwg file, do the following: After selecting 05c-bath.dwg in step 3, change the name that appears in the Block text box to Bath instead of 05c-bath before you click OK in step 4. This gives the inserted file a block name of Bath, even though its originating filename is 05c-bath.

4. Click OK in the Insert dialog box, and then click the upper-left corner of the unit's interior as the insertion point (see Figure 6.9). You can use the Endpoint osnap to place the bathroom accurately. Use a scale factor of 1.0 and a rotation angle of 0°.

**FIGURE 6.9**
The unit after the
bathroom is inserted

**TIP**    If Running Osnaps haven't been set up in this file, you need to use the Osnap shortcut menu (Shift+right-click) to access the Endpoint osnap. You can set up Running Osnaps to take advantage of AutoCAD's AutoSnap functions by right-clicking the Osnap button in the status bar. Set the Running Osnaps as described in Chapter 3.

5.  Assign the two rectangles that you drew earlier to the Wall layer. To do this, select the two rectangles so they're highlighted, and then open the Layer drop-down list in the Layers toolbar and select Wall. Press the Esc key twice to clear the selection.

**TIP**    You can also use the Match Properties tool on the Standard toolbar to change the layer settings of an object to those of another object in the drawing. See Chapter 7.

By inserting the bathroom, you imported the layers and blocks contained in the Bath file. You were then able to move previously drawn objects to the imported layers. If you're in a hurry, this can be a quick way to duplicate layers that you know exist in another drawing. This method is similar to using an existing drawing as a template, but it lets you start work on a drawing before deciding which template to use.

## Using Osnap Tracking to Place Objects

You'll draw lines in the majority of your work, so it's important to know how to manipulate lines to your best advantage. In this section, you'll look at some of the more common ways to use and edit these fundamental drawing objects. The following exercises show you the process of drawing lines, rather than just how individual commands work. While you're building walls and adding doors, you'll get a chance to become more familiar with Polar Tracking and Osnap Tracking.

### ROUGHING IN THE LINE WORK

The bathroom you inserted in the preceding section has only one side of its interior walls drawn. (Walls are usually shown by double lines.) In this next exercise, you'll draw the other side. Rather than trying to draw the wall perfectly the first time, you'll sketch in the line work and then clean it up in the next section, in a way similar to manual drafting.

Use these steps to rough in the wall lines:

1. Zoom in to the bathroom so that the entire bathroom and part of the area around it are displayed, as in Figure 6.10.

**FIGURE 6.10**
The enlarged view of
the bathroom

**TIP** You may notice that some of the arcs in your bathroom drawing aren't smooth. Don't be alarmed; this is how AutoCAD displays arcs and circles in enlarged views. The arcs will be smooth when they're plotted. If you want to see them now as they're stored in the file, you can regenerate the drawing by typing **Regen.⏎** at the Command prompt. Chapter 7 discusses regeneration in more detail.

2. Select Wall from the Layer drop-down list in the Layers toolbar to make Wall the current layer.

3. Make sure that the Otrack and Osnap buttons on the status bar are pressed, indicating that Osnap Tracking and Object Snap are turned on.

ORTHO POLAR OSNAP OTRACK DUCS DYN LWT MODEL

4. Choose Draw ➤ Line, or type L⏎.

5. At the Specify first point: prompt, move your cursor over the lower-right corner of the bathroom so that the Endpoint osnap marker appears, but don't click it. As you move the cursor downward, the tracking vector appears. (If the tracking vector doesn't appear at first, move your cursor over the corner again until it does appear.)

**TIP** Remember that a little cross appears at the osnap location, telling you that Osnap Tracking has "locked on" to that location.

6. With the tracking vector visible, point the cursor directly downward from the corner, and then type **5.⏎**. Metric users should type **13.⏎**. A line starts 5″ (or 13 cm) below the lower-right corner of the bathroom.

**7.** Continue the line horizontally to the left, to slightly cross the left wall of the apartment unit, as illustrated in the top image in Figure 6.11. Press↲.

**FIGURE 6.11**

The first wall line and the wall line by the door

Draw the line to the left past the vertical wall line.

End the line using the Perpendicular Osnap.

Perpendicular

Add wall line from the endpoint of the jamb.

**8.** Draw another line upward from the endpoint of the top door jamb to meet the top wall of the unit (see the second image in Figure 6.11). Use the Perpendicular osnap to pick the top wall of the unit. This causes the line to end precisely on the wall line in perpendicular position, as in the bottom image in Figure 6.11.

**TIP** You can also use the Perpendicular osnap override to draw a line perpendicular to a non-orthogonal line—one at a 45 angle, for instance.

**9.** Draw a line connecting the two door jambs. Then, assign that line to the Ceiling layer. (See the first panel in Figure 6.12.)

**10.** Draw a line 6″ downward from the endpoint of the door jamb nearest the corner. (See the first panel in Figure 6.12.)

**FIGURE 6.12**
The corner of the bathroom wall and the filleted wall around the bathroom

Add a door header and change it to the Ceiling layer.

Add a 6" line. [15cm line]

Fillet

In the previous exercise, Osnap Tracking mode enabled you to specify a starting point of a line at an exact distance from the corner of the bathroom. In step 6, you used the Direct Distance method for specifying distance and direction.

**TIP**   If you prefer, you can choose From on the Osnap shortcut menu, and then open the shortcut menu again and select Endpoint. Select the corner and enter a polar coordinate such as **@5<-90** to accomplish the same task as this exercise.

### CLEANING UP THE LINE WORK

You've drawn some of the wall lines, approximating their endpoint locations. Next, you'll use the Fillet command to join lines exactly end to end and then import the Kitchen drawing.

Follow these steps to join the lines:

1. Click the Fillet tool on the Modify toolbar.

2. Type **R↲0↲** to make sure that the fillet radius is set to 0.

### UNDERSTANDING THE OSNAP TRACKING VECTOR

The Osnap Tracking vector comes into play only after you've placed an Osnap marker on a location—in this case, the corner of the bathroom. It won't appear at any other time. If you have both Running Osnaps and Osnap Tracking turned on, you'll get the tracking vector every time the cursor lands on an osnap location. This can be confusing to novice users, so you may want to use Osnap Tracking sparingly until you become more comfortable with it.

Because Polar Tracking also uses a tracking vector, you may get the two confused. Remember that Polar Tracking lets you point the cursor in a specific direction while selecting points. If you're an experienced AutoCAD user, you can think of it as a more intelligent Ortho mode. On the other hand, Osnap Tracking lets you align points to osnap locations. Experienced AutoCAD users can think of Osnap Tracking as a more intelligent XYZ filter option.

**TIP** The Chamfer command performs a similar function to the Fillet command. Unlike Fillet, the Chamfer command enables you to join two lines with an intermediate beveled line rather than with an arc. Chamfer can be set to join two lines at a corner in exactly the same manner as Fillet.

3. Fillet the two lines by picking the vertical and horizontal lines, as indicated in the second panel in Figure 6.12, shown earlier in this chapter. Notice that these points lie on the portion of the line you want to keep. Your drawing will look like the second panel in Figure 6.12.

4. Fillet the bottom wall of the bathroom with the left wall of the unit, as shown in Figure 6.13. Make sure the points you pick on the wall lines are on the side of the line you want to keep, not on the side you want trimmed.

**FIGURE 6.13**
The cleaned-up wall intersections

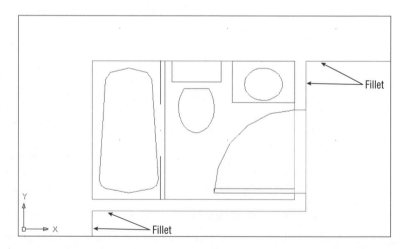

5. Fillet the top wall of the unit with the right-side wall of the bathroom, as shown in Figure 6.13.

**TIP** You can select two lines at once for the fillet operation by using a crossing window; to do so, type **C.⏎** at the Select first object or ...: prompt. The two endpoints closest to the fillet location are trimmed.

The location where you select the lines affects how the lines are joined. As you select objects for Fillet, the side of the line where you click is the side that remains when the lines are joined. Figure 6.14 illustrates how the Fillet command works and shows what the Fillet options do.

**FIGURE 6.14**

The place where you click the object to select it determines which part of an object gets filleted.

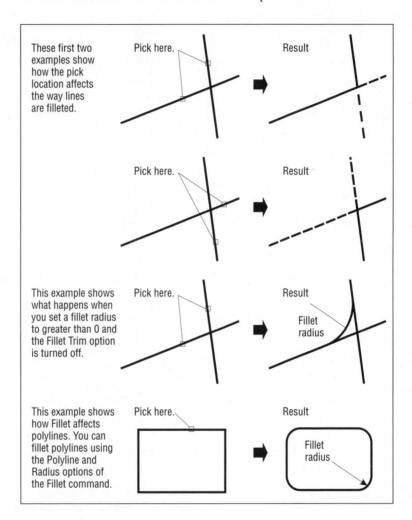

These first two examples show how the pick location affects the way lines are filleted.

Pick here.    Result

Pick here.    Result

This example shows what happens when you set a fillet radius to greater than 0 and the Fillet Trim option is turned off.

Pick here.    Result

Fillet radius

This example shows how Fillet affects polylines. You can fillet polylines using the Polyline and Radius options of the Fillet command.

Pick here.    Result

Fillet radius

**TIP**  If you select two parallel lines during the Fillet command, the two lines are joined with an arc.

Now, import the Kitchen plan you drew earlier in this chapter:

1. Click Insert Block on the Draw toolbar, and then browse to locate the kitchen drawing you created earlier in this chapter. Make sure you leave the Specify On-Screen check box unselected under the Scale and Rotation groups of the Insert dialog box.

2. Place the kitchen drawing at the wall intersection below the bathtub. (See the top image in Figure 6.15.)

**FIGURE 6.15**

The view after using
Pan and Zoom, with
the door inserted
and the jamb and
header added

**FIGURE 6.15**

The view after using
Pan and Zoom, with
the door inserted
and the jamb and
header added

**TIP**    If you didn't complete the kitchen earlier in this chapter, you can insert the 06a-kitchen.dwg
file. Metric users can insert 06 kitchen-metric.dwg.

3. Adjust your view with Pan and Zoom so that the upper portion of the apartment unit is
centered in the drawing area, as illustrated in the top image in Figure 6.15.

### PLACING THE DOOR ACCURATELY

The next step is to add the entry door shown in the bottom image in Figure 6.15. In doing that, you'll
use a number of new tools together to streamline the drawing process.

In this exercise, you'll practice using the Osnap Tracking feature and the From Osnap option to
place the entry door at an exact distance from the upper corner of the floor plan:

1. Right-click the Command window, and choose Recent Commands ➤ Insert from the shortcut
menu to open the Insert dialog box.

2. Select Door from the Name drop-down list.

**3.** Make sure the Specify On-Screen option is checked in the Rotation group but not in the Scale group, and then click OK. You'll see the door follow the cursor in the drawing window.

**4.** Shift+right-click the mouse to open the Osnap shortcut menu, and then choose From.

**5.** Make sure the Osnap and Otrack buttons on the status bar are on; then, use the Endpoint Running Osnap to pick the corner where the upper horizontal wall line meets the bathroom wall.

**6.** Move the cursor over the Osnap marker so that the Osnap Tracking vector appears from the corner. Now, move the cursor to the right, and you'll see the Osnap Tracking vector extend from the corner.

**7.** Continue to move the cursor to the right so that the tracking vector readout shows roughly 6″, or 15 cm for metric users.

**8.** With the cursor in this position, enter **5**↵. Metric users should enter **13**↵. The door is placed exactly 5 (or 13) units to the right of the corner.

**9.** At the `Specify rotation angle <0>:` prompt, enter **270**↵. Or, if you prefer, turn on Polar Tracking to orient the door so that it's swinging *into* the studio. You've now accurately placed the entry door in the studio apartment.

**10.** Make sure the door is on the Door layer.

**TIP** For a shortcut to setting an object's layer, you can select the object or objects and then select a layer from the Layer drop-down list in the Layers toolbar.

Next, add the finishing touches to the entry door:

1. Add 5″ (13 cm for metric users) door jambs, and change their Layer property to the Jamb layer, as shown in the bottom image in Figure 6.15.

2. Choose the Break tool in the Modify toolbar, and then select the header over the entry door. (See the bottom image in Figure 6.15.)

3. Type **F↵** to use the first-point option; then, select the endpoint of one of the door jambs.

4. At the `Specify second break point:` prompt, select the endpoint of the other jamb, as shown in the bottom image in Figure 6.15.

5. Draw the door header on the Ceiling layer, as shown in Figure 6.16.

**FIGURE 6.16**
The other side of the wall

Offset lines 5″ [13cm] up.

Add door header.

6. Click Offset on the Modify toolbar, and offset the top wall lines of the unit and the door header up 5″ (13 cm for metric users) so they connect with the top end of the door jamb, as shown in Figure 6.16. Don't forget to include the short wall line from the door to the bathroom wall.

7. Choose File ➤ Save As to save your file as `Unit`.

---

**OTHER METHODS FOR USING THE BREAK COMMAND**

In the exercise for finishing the Unit plan, you used the Break command to accurately place a gap in a line over the entry door. In Chapter 4, you broke a line at a single point to create multiple, contiguous line segments.

In both cases, you used the F option. You can also break a line without the F option with a little less accuracy. When you don't use the F option, the point at which you select the object is used as the first break point. If you're in a hurry, you can dispense with the F option and place a gap in an approximate location. You can then later use other tools to adjust the gap.

In addition, you can use locations on other objects to select the first and second points of a break. For example, you might want to align an opening with another opening some distance away. After you've selected the line to break, you can then use the F option and select two points on the existing opening to define the first and second break points. The break points will align in an orthogonal direction to the selected points.

### USING POLAR AND OSNAP TRACKING AS CONSTRUCTION-LINE TOOLS

So far, you've been using existing geometry to accurately place objects in the plan. In this section, you'll use the Polar and Osnap Tracking tools to extend the upper wall line 5″ (13 cm for metric users) beyond the right-side interior wall of the unit. You'll also learn how to use the Construction Line tool to accurately locate door jambs near the balcony.

Start by changing the Polar Tracking setting to include a 45° angle:

1. Right-click the Polar button in the status bar at the bottom of the AutoCAD window, and choose Settings to open the Drafting Settings dialog box at the Polar Tracking tab.

2. Select 45 from the Increment Angle drop-down list in the upper-left corner of the dialog box.

3. In the Object Snap Tracking Settings button group, make sure that the Track Using All Polar Angle Settings option is selected, and click OK.

You're ready to extend the wall line. For this operation, you'll use grip editing:

1. Click the wall line at the top of the plan, to the right of the door, to select the line and expose its grips.

2. Click the Ortho button in the status bar to turn on Ortho mode. This keeps the wall line straight as you edit it.

3. Click the rightmost grip of the line to make it hot.

4. Place the cursor on the upper-right corner of the plan until you see the Endpoint osnap marker; then, move the cursor away from the corner at a 45° angle. The Osnap Tracking

vector appears at a 45° angle. Notice the small X that appears at the intersection of the Osnap Tracking vector and the line.

With the Osnap Tracking vector and the line intersecting, click the mouse button. The line changes to extend exactly 5 units beyond the vertical interior wall of the plan.

**5.** Press the Esc key twice to clear your selection. Then, repeat steps 1 through 4 for the horizontal wall line to the left of the door, to extend that line to the left corner.

**6.** Choose View ➤ Zoom ➤ All to view the entire drawing. It looks like Figure 6.17.

**FIGURE 6.17**
The studio unit so far

**TIP**  With Polar Tracking set to 45 and Osnap Tracking turned on in a crowded drawing, you may find that you're selecting points you don't really want to select. Just remember that if a drawing becomes too crowded, you can turn off these options temporarily by clicking the Otrack or Polar button in the status bar.

In this exercise, you used Polar Tracking and Ortho mode to accurately position the two lines used for the exterior walls of the studio unit. This shows how you can take advantage of existing geometry with a combination of tools in the status bar.

**TIP** If you prefer to use a standard line instead of a construction line as a construction tool, you can use a ray (choose Draw ➤ Ray from the menu bar). A *ray* is a line that starts from a point you select and continues off to an infinite distance. You specify the start point and angle of the ray. You can place a ray at the corner at a 45 angle and then fillet the ray to the horizontal wall line to shorten or lengthen the line to the appropriate length.

Now, you'll finish the balcony by adding a sliding-glass door and a rail. This time, you'll use lines for construction as well as for parts of the drawing. First, you'll add the door jamb by drawing a Construction Line. A *Construction Line* is a line that has an infinite length; but unlike a ray, it extends in both directions. After drawing the Construction Line, you'll use it to quickly position the door jambs. Follow these steps:

1. Zoom in to the balcony area.

   Click the Construction Line tool on the Draw toolbar. You can also choose Draw ➤ Construction Line or type **XL**↵. You'll see this prompt:

   ```
   Specify a point or [Hor/Ver/Ang/Bisect/Offset]:
   ```

2. Type **O**↵ to select Offset.

3. At the `Specify offset distance or [Through] <0´-5">:` prompt, type **4´**↵. Metric users should type **122**↵.

4. At the `Select a line object:` prompt, click the wall line at the right of the unit.

5. At the `Specify side to offset:` prompt, click a point to the left of the wall to display the Construction Line. (See the top image of Figure 6.18.)

6. At the `Select a line object:` prompt, click the left wall line, and then click to the right of the selected wall to create another Construction Line. Your drawing should look like the top image in Figure 6.18.

   Next, you'll edit the Construction Lines to form the jambs.

7. Click Trim on the Modify toolbar.

8. Select the Construction Lines and the two horizontal lines representing the wall between the unit and the balcony, and press ↵. You can either use a crossing window or select each line individually. You've just selected the objects to trim to.

**TIP** You can also use the Fence selection option to select the lines to be trimmed. For more information, see Chapter 2 or Chapter 15.

9. Click the horizontal lines at any point between the two Construction Lines. Then, click the Construction Lines above and below the horizontal lines to trim them. Your drawing looks like the bottom image in Figure 6.18.

10. Assign the trimmed Construction Lines to the Jamb layer.

**FIGURE 6.18**
Drawing the
door opening

11. Add lines on the Ceiling layer to represent the door header.

12. Draw lines between the two jambs (on the Door layer) to indicate a sliding-glass door (see Figure 6.19).

The wall facing the balcony is now complete. To finish the unit, you need to show a handrail and the corners of the balcony wall:

1. Offset the bottom line of the balcony 3″ toward the top of the drawing. Metric users should offset the line 7.6 units.

2. Create a new layer called **F-rail**, and assign this offset line to it.

3. Add a 5″ (13 cm for metric users) horizontal line to the lower corners of the balcony, as shown in Figure 6.19.

**FIGURE 6.19**

Finishing the sliding-glass door and the railing

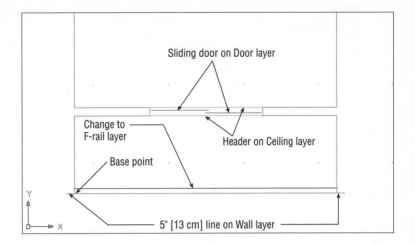

Sliding door on Door layer

Change to F-rail layer

Header on Ceiling layer

Base point

5" [13 cm] line on Wall layer

4. Choose Draw ➤ Block ➤ Base from the drop-down menu to set the base point at the lower-left corner of the balcony, at the location shown in Figure 6.19.

5. Assign the lines indicating walls to the Wall layer, and put the sliding glass door on the Door layer (see Figure 6.19).

6. Zoom back to the previous view. Your drawing should now look like Figure 6.20.

**FIGURE 6.20**

The completed studio apartment unit

7. Choose File ➤ Save to save the drawing, and then close the file.

Your studio apartment unit plan is now complete. The exercises you've just completed demonstrate a typical set of operations you'll perform while building your drawings. In fact, nearly 80 percent of what you'll do in AutoCAD is represented here.

Now, to review the drawing process, and to create a drawing you'll use later, you'll draw the apartment building's lobby. As you follow the steps, refer to Figure 6.21.

**FIGURE 6.21**

Drawing the lobby plan. Metric dimensions are shown in brackets

1. Draw rectangles on Wall layer.

2. Add stairs on Floor layer.

3. Add door and elevator.

4. Add door openings.

---

**THE CONSTRUCTION LINE OPTIONS**

There is more to the Construction Line command than you've seen in the exercises in this chapter. Here is a list of the Construction Line options and their uses:

**Hor** Draws horizontal Construction Lines as you click points

**Ver** Draws vertical Construction Lines as you click points

**Ang** Draws Construction Lines at a specified angle as you pick points

**Bisect** Draws Construction Lines bisecting an angle or a location between two points

**Offset** Draws Construction Lines offset at a specified distance from an existing line

---

As is usual in floor plans, the elevator shaft is indicated by the box with the large X through it, and the stair shaft is indicated by the box with the row of vertical lines through it. If you're in a hurry, use the finished version of this file called Lobby.dwg (Lobby-metric.dwg for metric users). To draw the apartment-building lobby, follow these steps:

1. Create a new file called Lobby, using the Unit file as a prototype. (Open the Unit file, choose File ➢ Save As, and enter **Lobby** for the new filename.)

2. Erase the entire unit (choose Erase ➢ All).

3. Draw the three main rectangles that represent the outlines of the stair shaft, the elevator shaft, and the lobby.

4. To draw the stairs, copy or offset the stair shaft's left wall to the right a distance of 4′ (122 cm). This creates the first line representing the steps.

5. Array this line in one row of 10 columns, using 11″ (28 cm) column offset.

6. Draw the center line dividing the two flights of stairs.

7. Draw the elevator, insert the door, and assign the door to the Door layer. Practice using Construction Lines here.

8. Draw the door jambs. Edit the door openings to add the door jambs and headers.

9. Use the Base command to set the base point of the drawing. Your plan should resemble the one in Figure 6.21, step 4.

10. Save the Lobby file.

## Finding an Exact Distance along a Curve

To find an exact distance along a curve or to mark off specific distance increments along a curve, do the following:

1. Choose Format ➤ Point Style from the drop-down menu to open the Point Style dialog box.

2. Click the X icon in the top row. Also be sure the Set Size Relative To Screen radio button is selected. Then, click OK.

**TIP** You can also set the point style by setting the Pdmode system variable to 3. See Appendix C for more on Pdmode.

3. Choose Draw ➤ Point ➤ Measure from the drop-down menu, or type **me**↵.

**TIP** The Divide command (choose Draw ➤ Point ➤ Divide) marks off a line, an arc, or a curve into equal divisions, as opposed to divisions of a length you specify. You might use Divide to divide an object into 12 equal segments, for example. Aside from this difference in function, Divide works exactly the same way as Measure.

4. At the `Select object to measure:` prompt, click the end of the curve that you want to use as the starting point for your distance measurement.

5. At the `Specify length of segment or [Block]:` prompt, enter the distance you want. A series of Xs appears on the curve, marking off the specified distance along the curve. You can select the exact location of the Xs by using the Node Osnap override (see Figure 6.22).

**FIGURE 6.22**

Finding an exact distance along a spline curve by using points and the Measure command

Distance found by the Measure command

Point entity

> **TIP** The Block option of the Measure command enables you to specify a block to be inserted at the specified segment length, in place of the Xs on the arc. You can align the block with the arc as it's inserted. (This is similar to the polar array's Rotate Objects As They Are Copied option.)

The Measure command also works on most objects including arcs and polylines. You'll get a more detailed look at the Measure command in Chapter 18.

As you work with AutoCAD, you'll find that constructing temporary geometry such as the circle and points in the two previous examples will help you solve problems in new ways. Don't hesitate to experiment! Remember, you've always got the Save and Undo commands to help you recover from mistakes.

## Changing the Length of Objects

Suppose that, after finding the length of an arc, you realize you need to lengthen the arc by a specific amount. Choosing Modify ➤ Lengthen lets you lengthen or shorten arcs, lines, polylines, splines, and elliptical arcs. As an example, here's how to lengthen an arc:

1. Choose Modify ➤ Lengthen, or type **len.↵**.

2. At the `Select an object or [DElta/Percent/Total/DYnamic]:` prompt, type **T↵**.

3. At the `Specify total length or [Angle] <1.0000)>:` prompt, enter the length you want for the arc.

4. At the `Select an object to change or [Undo]:` prompt, click the arc you want to change. Be sure to click at a point nearest the end you want to lengthen. The arc increases in length to the size you specified.

The Lengthen command also shortens an object if it's currently longer than the value you enter.

In this short example, you've learned how to change an object to a specific length. You can use other criteria to change an object's length, using these options available for the Lengthen command:

**DElta**  Lengthens or shortens an object by a specific length. To specify an angle rather than a length, use the Angle suboption.

**Percent**  Increases or decreases the length of an object by a percentage of its current length.

**Total**  Specifies the total length or angle of an object.

**DYnamic**  Lets you graphically change the length of an object using your cursor.

## Creating a New Drawing by Using Parts from Another Drawing

This section explains how to use the Wblock command (which you learned about in Chapter 4) to create a separate staircase drawing by using the staircase you've already drawn for the lobby. Although you haven't turned the existing stairs into a block, you can still use Wblock to turn parts of a drawing into a file.

Follow these steps:

1. If you closed the Lobby file, open it now. If you didn't create the lobby drawing, open the Lobby.dwg (or Lobby-metric.dwg) file.

2. Chose File ➢ Export, or type **export**↵ to open the Export Data dialog box.

3. Enter **stair.dwg** in the File Name text box, and click Save. By including the .dwg filename extension, you let AutoCAD know that you want to export to a drawing file and not some other file format, such as .dxf or .wmf.

4. At the Enter name of existing block or [= (block=output file)/* (whole drawing)] <define new drawing>: prompt, press ↵. When you export to a .dwg format, AutoCAD assumes you want to export a block. Bypassing this prompt by pressing ↵ tells AutoCAD that you want to create a file from part of the drawing, rather than from a block.

5. At the Specify insertion base point: prompt, pick the lower-right corner of the stair shaft. This tells AutoCAD the base point for the new drawing.

6. At the Select objects: prompt, use a window to select the stair shaft, as shown in Figure 6.23.

**FIGURE 6.23**
A selection window enclosing the stair shaft

7. When the stair shaft, including the door, is highlighted, press ↵ to confirm your selection. The stairs disappear.

8. Because you want the stairs to remain in the lobby drawing, click the Undo button to bring them back. Undo doesn't affect any files you might export by choosing File ➢ Export, by using Wblock, or by using the Make Block tool.

### DRAWING PARALLEL LINES WITH MULTILINES

If you need to draw a continuous, straight set of parallel lines, AutoCAD offers multilines (the Multiline command and its equivalent tool on the Draw menu) for this purpose. *Multilines* are multiple parallel lines that you can use to represent walls. You can also customize multilines to display solid fills, center lines, and additional linetypes. You can save your custom multilines as multiline styles, which are in turn saved in special files for easy access from other drawings.

Multilines aren't used often, but if you'd like to learn more about them, use the AutoCAD Help window and look up the Mline, Mledit, and Mlstyle commands.

## Eliminating Unused Blocks, Layers, Linetypes, Shapes, Styles, and More

A template can contain blocks and layers you don't need in your new file. For example, the lobby you just completed contains the bathroom block because you used the Unit file as a prototype. Even though you erased this block, it remains in the drawing file's database. It's considered unused because it doesn't appear as part of the drawing. Such extra blocks can slow you down by increasing the amount of time needed to open the file. They also increase the size of your file unnecessarily. You can eliminate unused elements from a drawing by using the Purge command.

### SELECTIVELY REMOVING UNUSED ELEMENTS

You use the Purge command to remove unused individual blocks, layers, linetypes, shapes, text styles, and other drawing elements from a drawing file. To help keep the file size small and to make layer maintenance easier, you should purge your drawing of unused elements. Bear in mind, however, that the Purge command doesn't delete certain primary drawing elements—namely, Layer 0, the Continuous linetype, and the Standard text style.

Use these steps to practice using the Purge command:

1. Choose File ➢ Open, and open the Lobby.dwg sample file.

2. Choose File ➢ Drawing Utilities ➢ Purge to open the Purge dialog box (see Figure 6.24). You'll see a listing of drawing components that can be purged. If the drawing contains any of the types of components listed, a plus sign appears to the left of the component name.

3. Click the plus sign of the component you want to purge. In this exercise, click the plus sign next to the Blocks listing. The list expands to show the names of the items under the component category.

4. Select the name Bath from the expanded list. If you want to select more than one item, you can Ctrl+click individual names or Shift+click to select a group of names.

5. After the components are selected, click the Purge button in the lower-left corner of the dialog box. You then see a message box asking you to confirm that you want to purge the drawing.

**FIGURE 6.24**

The Purge dialog box

### REMOVING ALL UNUSED ELEMENTS

In the preceding exercise, you selected a single block for removal from the Lobby file. If you want to clear all the unused elements from a file at once, you can click the Purge All button at the bottom of the Purge dialog box (see Figure 6.24).

Here are the steps:

1. Choose File ➤ Drawing Utilities ➤ Purge to open the Purge dialog box.

2. Click the Purge Nested Items check box to turn on this option.

3. Click Purge All to open the Confirm Purge dialog box, which asks whether you want to purge a block.

4. Click Yes. The Confirm Purge dialog box displays the name of another block, asking you to confirm the purge. You can continue to click Yes, and AutoCAD will display the Confirm Purge dialog box for each unused element still in the drawing.

5. Click the Yes To All option to purge everything at once. The Confirm Purge dialog box closes.

6. In the Purge dialog box, click Close.

7. Close and save the Lobby file, and exit AutoCAD.

The Lobby file is now trimmed down to the essential data it needs and nothing else. You may have noticed that when you returned to the Purge dialog box in step 6, the items in the list box no longer showed plus signs. This indicates that there are no longer any unused items in the drawing.

In this last exercise, you used the Purge Nested Items option at the bottom of the dialog box. The Purge Nested Items option automatically purges unused blocks, including those nested within other blocks. If this option isn't checked, you might have to repeat the Purge operation to remove all unused elements in a drawing.

## The Bottom Line

**Creating and Using Templates**   If you find that you're using the same settings when you create a new drawing file, you can set up an existing file the way you like and save it as a template. You can then use your saved template for any new drawings you create.

**Master It**   Describe the method for saving a file as a template.

**Solution**   After setting up a blank drawing with the settings you use most frequently, choose File ➤ Save As. In the Save Drawing As dialog box, choose AutoCAD Drawing Template from the Files Of Type drop-down list. Give your template file a descriptive name, and click Save.

**Copying an Object Multiple Times**   Many tools in AutoCAD allow you to create multiple copies. The Array command offers a way to create circular copies or row and column copies.

**Master It**   What name is given to the two types of arrays in the Array dialog box?

**Solution**   Rectangular and Polar.

**Developing Your Drawing**   When laying down simple line work, you'll use a few tools frequently. The exercises in the early part of this book showed you some of these commonly used tools.

**Master It**   What tool can you use to join two lines end to end?

**Solution**   Fillet.

**Finding an Exact Distance along a Curve**   AutoCAD offers some tools that allow you to find an exact distance along a curve.

**Master It**   Name the two tools you can use to mark off exact distances along a curve.

**Solution**   Point and Measure.

# Chapter 7

# Mastering Viewing Tools, Hatches, and External References

Now that you've created drawings of a typical apartment unit and the apartment building's lobby and stairs, you can assemble them to complete the first floor of the apartment building. In this chapter, you'll take full advantage of AutoCAD's features to enhance your drawing skills, as well as to reduce the time it takes to create accurate drawings.

As your drawing becomes larger, you'll find that you need to use the Zoom and Pan commands more often. Larger drawings also require some special editing techniques. You'll learn how to assemble and view drawings in ways that will save you time and effort as your design progresses. Along the way, you'll see how you can enhance the appearance of your drawings by adding hatch patterns.

This chapter includes the following topics:

◆ Assembling the Parts

◆ Taking Control of the AutoCAD Display

◆ Using Hatch Patterns in Your Drawings

◆ Understanding the Boundary Hatch Options

◆ Using External References

◆ Editing Xrefs in Place

## Assembling the Parts

One of the best time-saving features of AutoCAD is its ability to quickly duplicate repetitive elements in a drawing. In this section, you'll assemble the drawings you've been working on into the complete floor plan of a fictitious apartment project. This will demonstrate how you can quickly and accurately copy your existing drawings in a variety of ways.

Start by creating a new file for the first floor:

1. Create a new file named Plan to contain the drawing of the apartment building's first floor. This is the file you'll use to assemble the unit plans into an apartment building. If you want to use a template file, use Acad.dwt. Metric users can use the Acadiso.dwt template file. (These are AutoCAD template files that appear in the Create New Drawing dialog box when you choose File ➢ New.)

2. Set the Units style to Architectural (choose Format ➢ Units).

3. Set up the drawing for a ⅛″ = 1′-0″ scale on a 24″ × 18″ drawing area (choose Format ➤ Drawing Limits). If you look at Table 3.2 in Chapter 3, you'll see that such a drawing requires an area 2,304 units wide × 1,728 units deep. Metric users should set up a drawing at 1:100 scale on an A2 sheet size. If you look at Table 3.4, you'll see that your drawing area should be 5940 cm × 4200 cm.

4. Create a layer called Plan1, and make it the current layer.

5. In the Drafting Settings dialog box, set the Snap Spacing to 1, and set Grid Spacing to 8′, which is the distance required to display 1″ divisions in a ⅛″ = 1′-0″ scale drawing. Metric users can set the Grid mode to 250.

6. Turn on the grid if it isn't on already.

7. Choose View ➤ Zoom ➤ All, or type Z↵A↵ to get an overall view of the drawing area.

Now you're ready to start building a floor plan of the first floor from the Unit plan you created in the previous chapter. You'll start by creating a mirrored copy of the apartment plan:

1. Make sure Running Osnaps are turned off, and then insert the 07a-unit.dwg drawing at coordinate 31′-5″,43′-8″. Metric users should insert the 07a-unit-metric.dwg drawing at coordinate 957,1330. Accept the Insert defaults. 07a-unit and 07a-unit-metric are the same drawings as the Unit.dwg file you were asked to create in earlier chapters.

**TIP** If you prefer, you can specify the insertion point in the Insert dialog box by removing the check mark from the Specify On-Screen check box. The Input options in the dialog box then become available to receive your input.

2. Zoom in to the apartment unit plan.

3. Click Mirror on the Modify toolbar, select the Unit plan, and press ↵.

4. At the Specify first point of the mirror line: prompt, Shift+right-click the mouse, and choose From.

5. Shift+right-click again, and choose Endpoint.

6. Select the endpoint of the upper-right corner of the apartment unit, as shown in Figure 7.1.

**FIGURE 7.1**
The unit plan mirrored

Select this corner for the Mirror command in step 6.

7. Enter @2.5<0↵. Metric users should enter @6.5<0↵. A rubber-banding line appears, indicating the mirror axis.

8. Turn on Ortho mode, and select any point to point the mirror axis in a vertical orientation.

9. At the `Erase Source Objects? [Yes/No] <N>:` prompt, press ↵. You'll get a 5″ wall thickness between two studio units. Your drawing should be similar to Figure 7.1.

You now have a mirror-image copy of the original plan in the exact location required for the overall plan. Next, make some additional copies for the opposite side of the building:

1. Press ↵ to reissue the Mirror command and select both units.

2. Use the From osnap option again, and, using the Endpoint osnap, select the same corner you selected in step 6.

3. Enter @24<90 to start a mirror axis 24″↵ directly above the selected point. Metric users should enter @61<90.

4. With Ortho mode on, select a point so that the mirror axis is exactly horizontal.

5. At the `Erase source objects? [Yes/No] <N>:` prompt, press ↵ to keep the two unit plans you selected in step 1 and complete the mirror operation.

With the tools you've learned about so far, you've quickly and accurately set up a fairly good portion of the floor plan. Continue with the next few steps to "rough in" the main components of the floor:

1. Choose View ➤ Zoom ➤ Extents, or type Z↵E↵ to get a view of the four plans. You can also use the Zoom Extents tool on the Zoom Window tool fly-out. The Extents option forces the entire drawing to fill the screen at the center of the display area. Your drawing will look like Figure 7.2.

**TIP** If you happen to insert a block in the wrong coordinate location, you can use the Properties palette to change the insertion point for the block.

2. Copy the four units to the right at a distance of 28′-10″ (878 cm for metric users), which is the width of two units from center line to center line of the walls.

**FIGURE 7.2**
The unit plan, duplicated four times

3. Insert the lobby at coordinate 89´-1˝,76´-1˝ (2713,2318 for metric users).

4. Copy all the unit plans to the right 74´-5˝ (2267 cm for metric users), the width of four units plus the width of the lobby.

5. Choose View ➢ Zoom ➢ All, or type Z↵A↵ to view the entire drawing, which should look like Figure 7.3. You can also use the Zoom All tool on the Zoom Window fly-out.

**FIGURE 7.3**
The Plan drawing

6. Choose File ➢ Save to save this Plan.dwg file to disk.

# Taking Control of the AutoCAD Display

By now, you should be familiar with the Pan and Zoom functions in AutoCAD. Many other tools can also help you get around in your drawing. In this section, you'll get a closer look at the ways you can view your drawing.

## Understanding Regeneration and Redrawing

AutoCAD uses two commands for refreshing your drawing display: drawing regeneration (Regen) and Redraw. Each command serves a particular purpose, although it may not be clear to a new user.

To better understand the difference between Regen and Redraw, it helps to know that AutoCAD stores drawing data in two ways:

◆ In a database of highly accurate coordinate information that is part of the properties of objects in your drawing

◆ In a simplified database used just for the display of the objects in your drawing

As you draw, AutoCAD starts to build an accurate, core database of objects and their properties. At the same time, it creates a simpler database that it uses just to display the drawing quickly. AutoCAD uses this second database to allow quick manipulation of the display of your drawing. For the purposes of this discussion, I'll call this simplified database the *virtual display* because it's like a computer model of the overall display of your drawing. This virtual display is in turn used as the basis for what is shown in the drawing area. When you issue a Redraw command, you're telling AutoCAD to reread this virtual display data and display that information in the drawing area. A Regen command, on the other hand, tells AutoCAD to rebuild the virtual display based on information from the core drawing database.

You may notice that the Pan Realtime and Zoom Realtime commands don't work beyond a certain area in the display. When you reach a point where these commands seem to stop working, you've come to the limits of the virtual display data. To go beyond these limits, AutoCAD must rebuild the virtual display data from the core data; in other words, it must regenerate the drawing. You can usually do this by zooming out to the extents of the drawing.

Sometimes, when you zoom in to a drawing, arcs and circles may appear to be faceted instead of smooth curves. This faceting is the result of AutoCAD's virtual display simplifying curves to conserve memory. You can force AutoCAD to display the curves in a smoother curve by choosing View ➢ Regen.

---

### CONTROLLING DISPLAY SMOOTHNESS

As you work in AutoCAD, you may notice that linetypes sometimes appear continuous, even when they're supposed to be dotted or dashed. You may also notice that arcs and circles occasionally appear to be segmented lines, although they're always plotted as smooth curves. A command called Viewres controls how smoothly linetypes, arcs, and circles are displayed in an enlarged view. The lower the Viewres value, the fewer the segments, and the faster the redraw and regeneration. However, a low Viewres value causes noncontinuous linetypes, such as dashes or center lines, to appear continuous, especially in drawings that cover very large areas (for example, civil site plans).

Finding a Viewres value that best suits the type of work you do will take some experimentation. The default Viewres setting is 1000. You can try increasing the value to improve the smoothness of arcs and see if a higher value works for you. Enter **Viewres.⊐⊐** at the command prompt to change the value. If you work with complex drawings, you may want to keep the value at 1000; then, when you zoom in close to a view, use the Regen command to display smooth arcs and complete linetypes.

---

### CREATING MULTIPLE VIEWS

So far, you've looked at ways to help you get around in your drawing while using a single view window. You can also set up multiple views of your drawing, called *viewports*. With viewports, you can display more than one view of your drawing at one time in the AutoCAD drawing area. For example, one viewport can display a close-up of the bathroom, another viewport can display the overall plan view, and yet another can display the unit plan.

When viewports are combined with AutoCAD's Paper Space feature, you can plot multiple views of your drawing. Paper Space is a display mode that lets you paste up multiple views of a drawing, much like a page-layout program. To find out more about viewports and Paper Space, see Chapters 16 and 23.

---

### SAVING VIEWS

Another way to control your views is by saving them. You might think of saving views as a way of creating a bookmark or a placeholder in your drawing.

For example, a few walls in the Plan drawing aren't complete. To add the lines, you'll need to zoom in to the areas that need work, but these areas are spread out over the drawing. AutoCAD lets you save views of the areas you want to work on and then jump from saved view to saved view. This technique is especially helpful when you know you'll often want to return to a specific area of your drawing.

You'll see how to save and recall views in the following set of exercises. Here's the first one:

1. Choose View ➢ Zoom ➢ All, or type **Z↵A↵** to get an overall view of the plan.

2. Choose View ➢ Named Views, or type **V↵** to open the View Manager dialog box.

**TIP** In the View Manager dialog box, you can call up an existing view (Set Current), create a new view (New), or get detailed information about a view. You can also select from a set of predefined views that include orthographic and isometric views of 3D objects. You'll learn more about these options in Chapter 20.

3. Make sure the Current option is selected in the list to the left, and then click the New button to open the New View dialog box. You'll notice some options related to the User Coordinate System (UCS) plus an option called View Category. You'll get a chance to look at the UCS in Chapters 20 and 21. The View Category option relates to the Sheet Set feature described in Chapter 28. Other options, including Visual Style, Background, and Boundary, give you control over the appearance of the background and layout of a saved view. For now, you'll concentrate on creating a new view.

4. Click the Define Window radio button. The dialog boxes momentarily disappear, and the Dynamic input display turns on.

5. At the `Specify first corner:` prompt, click two points to place a selection window around the area around the elevator lobby, as shown in Figure 7.4. Notice that the display changes so that the white area shows the area you selected. If you aren't satisfied with the selection area, you can place another window in the view.

**FIGURE 7.4**
Select this area for
your saved view.

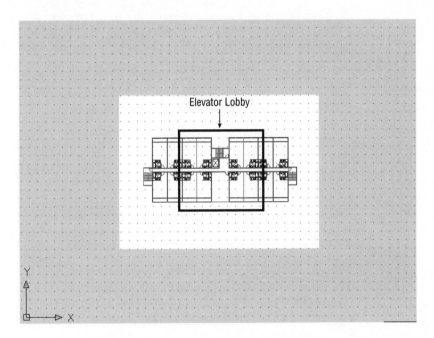

6. When you're satisfied with your selection, press ↵ or right-click. The dialog boxes reappear.

7. Click the View Name input box, and type **Elevator Lobby** for the name of the view you just defined.

8. Click the OK button. The New View dialog box closes, and you see Elevator Lobby in the Views list.

9. Click OK to close the View dialog box.

10. Let's see how to recall the view that you've saved. In the 2D Navigate control panel, click the drop-down list, and select Elevator Lobby.

Your view changes to a close-up of the area you selected in step 5. You can also open the View dialog box, select Elevator Lobby from the view list, click Set Current, and click OK.

**TIP** If you need to make adjustments to a view after you've created it, you can do so by following these steps: Right-click the view name in the View Manager dialog box, select Edit Boundaries, and then select a window as you did in steps 5 and 6.

**TIP** Remember that when no command is active, you can right-click the Command window and then select Recent Commands to repeat a recently issued command. You can also right-click the drawing area when AutoCAD is idle and repeat the last command.

If you prefer, you can use the keyboard to invoke the View command and thus avoid all the dialog boxes:

1. Choose View ➢ Zoom ➢ Extents, or type **Z↵E↵**.

2. Enter **–View↵S↵** at the Command prompt, or use the **–V↵S↵** shortcut. (Don't forget the minus sign in front of View or V.)

3. At the Enter view name to save: prompt, enter **Overall↵**.

4. Save the Plan file to disk.

As you can see, this is a quick way to save a view. With the name Overall assigned to this view, you can easily recall the Overall view at any time. (Choosing View ➢ Zoom ➢ All gives you an overall view too, but it may zoom out too far for some purposes, or it may not show what you consider an overall view.)

**TIP** Another useful tool for getting around in your drawing is the Zoom toolbar. It contains the Zoom Window, Dynamic, Scale, Center, Object In, Out, All, and Extents tools. To open the Zoom toolbar, right-click any toolbar, and choose Zoom from the shortcut menu.

---

### OPENING A FILE TO A PARTICULAR VIEW

The Select File dialog box contains a Select Initial View check box. If you open an existing drawing with this option selected, you're greeted with a Select Initial View dialog box just before the opened file appears on the screen. This dialog box lists any views saved in the file. You can then go directly to a view by double-clicking the view name. If you've saved views and you know the name of the view you want, using Select Initial View saves time when you're opening large files.

---

## Understanding the Frozen Layer Option

As mentioned earlier, you may want to turn off certain layers to plot a drawing containing only selected layers. But even when layers are turned off, AutoCAD still takes the time to redraw and regenerate them. The Layer Properties Manager dialog box offers the Freeze option; this acts like the Off option, except that Freeze causes AutoCAD to ignore frozen layers when redrawing and regenerating a drawing. By freezing layers that aren't needed for reference or editing, you can reduce the time AutoCAD takes to perform regens. This can be helpful in large, multi-megabyte files.

Be aware, however, that the Freeze option affects blocks in an unusual way. Try the following exercise to see firsthand how the Freeze option makes entire blocks disappear.

1. Close the Plan file, and open the 07b-plan.dwg file from the sample files. Metric users should open 07b-plan-metric.dwg. This file is similar to the Plan file you created but with a few additional walls added to finish off the exterior. Also note that the individual units are blocks named 07a-unit-metric. This will be important in a later exercise.

2. In the Layer Properties Manager dialog box, set the current layer to 0.

**TIP** You can freeze and thaw individual layers by clicking the Freeze/Thaw icon (which looks like a sun) in the layer list in the Layers toolbar.

3. Click the yellow lightbulb icon in the Plan1 layer listing to turn off that layer, and then click OK. Nothing changes in your drawing. Even though you turned off the Plan1 layer, the layer on which the unit blocks were inserted, the unit blocks remain visible.

4. Use the Layer Properties Manager dialog box to turn off all the layers. You see a message warning you that the current layer will be turned off. Click No to turn off the current layer, and then close the Layer Properties Manager by clicking OK. Now everything is turned off, including objects contained in the unit blocks.

5. Open the Layer Properties Manager dialog box again, and turn all the layers back on.

6. Click the Plan1 layer's Freeze/Thaw icon. (You can't freeze the current layer.) The yellow sun icon changes to a gray snowflake, indicating that the layer is now frozen.

7. Click OK. Only the unit blocks disappear.

Even though none of the objects in the unit blocks were drawn on the Plan1 layer, the entire contents of the blocks assigned to the Plan1 layer are frozen when Plan1 is frozen.

**TIP** Remember that to select all the layers at once, you can right-click a blank area of the Layer Properties Manager dialog box and then choose Select All from the shortcut menu.

You don't really need the Plan1 layer frozen. You froze it to see the effects of Freeze on blocks. Do the following to turn Plan1 back on:

1. Thaw layer Plan1 by opening the Layer Properties Manager dialog box and clicking the snowflake icon in the Plan1 layer listing.

2. Turn off the Ceiling layer. Exit the dialog box by clicking OK.

The previous exercise showed the effect of freezing on blocks. When a block's layer is frozen, the entire block is made invisible, regardless of the layer assignments of the objects contained in the block.

Keep in mind that when blocks are on layers that aren't frozen, the individual objects that are a part of the block are still affected by the status of the layer to which they're assigned. This means that if some objects in a block are on a layer called Wall, and the Wall layer is turned off or frozen, then those objects become invisible. Other objects with the block that aren't on the layer that is off or frozen remain visible.

## Using Hatch Patterns in Your Drawings

To help communicate your ideas to others, you'll want to add graphic elements that represent types of materials, special regions, or textures. AutoCAD provides hatch patterns for quickly placing a texture over an area of your drawing. In this section, you'll add a hatch pattern to the floor of the studio apartment unit, thereby instantly enhancing the appearance of one drawing. In the process, you'll learn how to quickly update all the units in the overall floor plan to reflect the changes in the unit.

### Placing a Hatch Pattern in a Specific Area

It's always a good idea to provide a separate layer for hatch patterns. By doing so, you can turn them off if you need to. For example, a floor plan might display the floor paving pattern in one drawing, while in another drawing it was turned off so it won't distract from other information.

In the following exercises, you'll set up a layer for a hatch pattern representing floor tile and then add that pattern to your drawing. This will give you the opportunity to learn the different methods of creating and controlling hatch patterns.

Follow these steps to set up the layer:

1. Open the 07a-unit.dwg file. Metric users should open 07a-unit-metric.dwg. These files are similar to the Unit drawing you created in earlier chapters and are used to create the overall plan in the 07b-plan and 07b-plan-metric files. Remember that you also still have the 07b-plan or 07b-plan-metric file open.

2. Zoom in to the bathroom and kitchen area.

3. Create a new layer called Flr-pat.

4. Make Flr-pat the current layer.

Now that you've set up the layer for the hatch pattern, you can place the pattern in the drawing:

**WARNING**    If you're using LT, you won't see the Gradient tab in the Hatch And Gradient dialog box shown in step 1 of the next exercise.

1. Click the Hatch tool on the Draw toolbar, or type **H**↵. Hatch is also located in the Draw drop-down menu. The Hatch And Gradient dialog box opens.

2. In the Type drop-down list box, select User-Defined. The User-Defined option lets you define a simple crosshatch pattern by specifying the line spacing of the hatch and whether it's a single- or double-hatch pattern. The Angle and Spacing input boxes become available, so you can enter values.

3. Double-click the Spacing text box near the bottom, and enter **6** (metric users should enter **15**). This tells AutoCAD you want the hatch's line spacing to be 6 inches or 15 cm. Leave the Angle value at 0 because you want the pattern to be aligned with the bathroom.

4. Click the Double check box (on the left side of the dialog box). This tells AutoCAD that you want the hatch pattern to run both vertically and horizontally. Also notice that the Swatch box displays a sample of your hatch pattern.

5. Click the Add: Pick Points button in the upper-right corner of the dialog box. The dialog box momentarily closes, enabling you to pick a point inside the area you want hatched.

6. Click a point anywhere inside the bathroom floor area, below the toilet. Notice that a high-lighted outline appears in the bathroom. This is the boundary AutoCAD has selected to enclose the hatch pattern. It outlines everything, including the door swing arc.

**TIP** If you have text in the hatch boundary, AutoCAD will avoid hatching over it, unless the Ignore option is selected in the Island Display Style options of the Advanced Hatch settings. See the section "Using Additional Hatch Features," later in this chapter, for more on the Ignore setting.

7. Press ↵ to return to the Hatch And Gradient dialog box.

8. Click the Preview button in the lower-left corner of the dialog box. The hatch pattern appears everywhere on the floor except where the door swing occurs. You also see this prompt:

```
Pick or press Esc to return to dialog or <Right-click to accept hatch>:
```

9. Press Esc or the spacebar to return to the dialog box.

10. Click the Add: Pick Points button again, pick a point inside the door swing, and press ↵.

11. Click Preview again. The hatch pattern now covers the entire floor area.

12. Right-click to place the hatch pattern in the drawing.

The Hatch And Gradient dialog box lets you first define the boundary in which you want to place a hatch pattern. You do this by clicking a location inside the boundary area, as in step 6. AutoCAD finds the boundary for you. Many options give you control over how a hatch boundary is selected. For details, see the section "Understanding the Boundary Hatch Options," later in this chapter.

> **TIP** Say you want to add a hatch pattern that you've previously inserted in another part of the drawing. You might think that you have to guess at its scale and rotation angle. But with the Inherit Properties option in the Hatch And Gradient dialog box, you can select a previously inserted hatch pattern as a prototype for the current hatch pattern. However, this feature doesn't work with exploded hatch patterns.

## Positioning Hatch Patterns Accurately

In the previous exercise, you placed the hatch pattern in the bathroom without regard for the location of the lines that make up the pattern. In most cases, however, you'll want accurate control over where the lines of the pattern are placed.

> **TIP** You can also click the Swatch button in the upper half of the Hatch And Gradient dialog box to browse through a graphical representation of the predefined hatch patterns.

By default, hatch patterns use the drawing origin (0,0) as the pattern origin. This means that the corner of the hatch pattern starts at the 0,0 coordinate, even though the pattern is only displayed in the area you select. The Hatch And Gradient dialog box offers a set of options that give you control over the hatch origin, thereby allowing you to control the exact positioning of the hatch pattern in the area you're hatching. This can be crucial for laying out tile patterns on a floor or ceiling, for example.

The following exercise guides you through the process of placing a hatch pattern accurately, using the example of adding floor tile to the kitchenette. You'll start by drawing the area of the tile pattern and then go on to select a pattern for the tile:

1. Pan your view so that you can see the area below the kitchenette. Using the Rectangle tool in the Draw toolbar, draw the 3'-0" × 8'-0" outline of the floor tile area, as shown in Figure 7.5. Metric users should create a rectangle that is 91 cm × 228 cm. You can also use a closed polyline.

2. Click the Hatch tool in the Draw toolbar.

3. In the Hatch And Gradient dialog box, make sure Predefined is selected in the Type drop-down list box.

**FIGURE 7.5**
The area below the
kitchen, showing
the outline of the floor
tile area

**4.** Click the button labeled with the ellipses (…) just to the right of the Pattern drop-down list.

The Hatch Pattern Palette dialog box opens. This dialog box lets you select a predefined pattern from a graphic that shows what the pattern looks like.

**TIP** If you know the name of the pattern you want, you can select it from the Pattern drop-down list in the Hatch And Gradient dialog box.

**5.** Click the Other Predefined tab, and then locate and click AR-PARQ1.

**6.** Click OK to exit the dialog box.

You've selected the hatch pattern. The next thing is to place the pattern in the drawing. First, you'll select the location for the hatch pattern, and then you'll experiment with the origin settings to see how they affect the positioning of the pattern:

1. Click the Add: Pick Points button in the Hatch and Gradient dialog box.

2. Click the interior of the area to be hatched, and press ↵. Metric users should double-click the Scale input box and enter **2.54** to scale this pattern appropriately to match the proportions of the Imperial measurement example.

3. In the Hatch Origin group, make sure the Use Current Origin option is selected, and then click the Preview button. Notice that the hatch pattern doesn't fit evenly in the hatch area. Some of the tiles along the edges are only partially drawn, as if they were cut off.

4. Press the Esc key to return to the Hatch And Gradient dialog box.

5. In the Hatch Origin group, turn on the Specified Origin option and the Default To Boundary Extents option.

**NOTE**    Another method is to indicate the origin of the hatch pattern. Turn on the Specified Origin option, click the Click To Set New Origin tool, and select the lower-left origin point for your hatch pattern. This can also be accomplished by using the HPORIGIN system variable.

6. Click Preview again. This time, the pattern fits completely in the boundary, with no incomplete tiles appearing around the edges.

7. Right-click the mouse to accept the hatch pattern location. A parquet-style tile pattern appears in the defined area.

8. Save the Unit file but keep it open.

**TIP**    You can use the Solid predefined hatch pattern at the top of the list to create solid fills. And don't forget that you can drag and drop solid fills and hatch patterns from the Tool palettes you saw in Chapter 1.

Notice that each tile is shown whole; none of the tiles are cut off as in the bathroom example. This is the result of using the Specified Origin option and the Default To Boundary Extents option in the Hatch And Gradient dialog box.

The Specified Origin option gives you access to a number of hatch pattern features. In the previous exercise, you used the Default To Boundary Extents feature, which is best suited to rectangular areas. This option assumes you're hatching a rectangular area, and it lets you place the boundary hatch origin in one of the four corners of a rectangle or directly in the center. The default option is Bottom Left, as shown in the drop-down list. The graphic to the right of the list also shows a cross where the origin is located in a rectangular area.

The Click To Set New Origin option lets you select a point in your drawing to specify the hatch origin. When you click this option, the dialog box temporarily closes to allow you to select a point.

Finally, the Store As Default Origin option lets you save your selected origin as the default origin for future hatch patterns in the current drawing.

In the previous exercise, you used a predefined hatch pattern. Figure 7.6 shows you all the patterns available. You can also create your own custom patterns, as described in Chapter 26.

**FIGURE 7.6**
Predefined hatch patterns available in AutoCAD

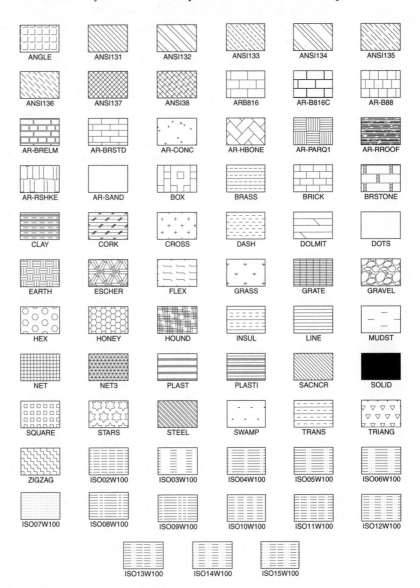

In the next exercise, you'll use this updated 07a-unit file to update all the units in the Plan file.

**TIP**  The predefined patterns with the AR prefix are architectural patterns that are drawn to full scale. In general, you should leave their Scale settings at 1. You can adjust the scale after you place the hatch pattern by using the Properties palette, as described later in this chapter.

## Updating a Block from an External File

As you progress through a design project, you make countless revisions. With traditional drafting methods, revising a drawing such as the studio apartment floor plan takes a good deal of time. If you change the bathroom layout, for example, you have to erase every occurrence of the bathroom and redraw it 16 times. With AutoCAD, on the other hand, revising this drawing can be a quick operation. You can update the studio unit you just modified throughout the overall plan drawing by replacing the current Unit block with the updated Unit file. AutoCAD can update all occurrences of the Unit block. The following exercise shows how this is accomplished:

**NOTE**  For this exercise, remember that the blocks representing the units in the 07b-plan and 07b-plan-metric files are named 07a-unit and 07a-unit-metric.

1. Make sure you've saved the 07a-unit (07a-unit-metric for metric users) file with the changes, and then return to the 07b-plan file that is still open. Choose Window ➤ \*directory path*\07b-plan.dwg. Your full path to the 07b-plan.dwg file is shown in the Windows menu. Metric users should use 07b-plan-metric.dwg.

**WARNING**  This method doesn't update exploded blocks. If you plan to use this method to update parts of a drawing, don't explode the blocks you plan to update. See Chapter 4.

2. Click the Insert Block tool on the Draw toolbar.

3. Click the Browse button. In the Select Drawing File dialog box, double-click the 07a-unit filename (07a-unit-metric for metric users).

4. Click OK in the Insert dialog box. A warning message tells you that a block already exists with the same name as the file. You can cancel the operation or redefine the block in the current drawing.

5. Click Yes. The drawing regenerates (unless you have Regenauto turned off).

6. At the Specify insertion point or [Basepoint/Scale/X/Y/Z/Rotate]: prompt, press the Esc key. You do this because you don't want to insert the Unit file into your drawing; you're just using the Insert feature to update an existing block.

**WARNING**  If Regenauto is turned off, you must use the Regen command to force a regeneration of the drawing before the updated Unit block appears on the display.

7. Zoom in to one of the units. The floor tile appears in all the units as you drew it in the Unit file (see Figure 7.7).

Nested blocks must be updated independently of the parent block. For example, if you modified the Toilet block while editing the 07a-unit file and then updated the 07a-unit drawing in the 07b-plan file, the old Toilet block wouldn't be updated. Even though the toilet is part of the 07a-unit file, it's still a unique, independent block in the Plan file, and AutoCAD won't modify it unless specifically instructed to do so. In this situation, you must edit the original Toilet block and then update it in both the Plan and Unit files.

**FIGURE 7.7**
The Plan drawing with
the tile pattern

**TIP** If you want to substitute one block for another in the current file, type **–Insert**↵. (Don't forget the minus sign in front of Insert.) At the *Block name:* prompt, enter the block name followed by an equal sign (=), and then enter the name of the new block or the filename. Don't include spaces between the name and the equal sign.

Also, block references and layer settings of the current file take priority over those of the imported file. For example, if a file to be imported has layers of the same name as the current file, but those layers have color and linetype assignments that are different from the current file's, the current file's layer color and linetype assignments determine those of the imported file. This doesn't mean, however, that the imported file on disk is changed; only the inserted drawing is affected.

## SUBSTITUTING BLOCKS

In the preceding example, you updated a block in your Plan file by using the Browse option in the Insert dialog box. In that exercise, the block name and the filename were the same. You can also replace a block with another block or file of a different name. Here's how to do this:

1. Open the Insert dialog box.

2. Click the Browse button next to the Name input box, locate and select the file you want to use as a substitute, and then click Open to return to the Insert dialog box.

3. Change the name in the Name input box to the name of the block you want replaced.

4. Click OK. A warning message appears, telling you that a block with this name already exists. Click OK to proceed with the block substitution.

You can use this method of replacing blocks if you want to see how changing one element of your project can change your design. You might, for example, draw three different apartment unit plans and give each plan a unique name. You could then generate and plot three apartment building designs in a fraction of the time it would take you to do so by hand.

Block substitution can also reduce a drawing's complexity and accelerate regenerations. To substitute blocks, you temporarily replace large, complex blocks with schematic versions of those blocks. For example, you might replace the Unit block in the Plan drawing with another drawing that contains just a single-line representation of the walls and bathroom fixtures. You would still have the wall lines for reference when inserting other symbols or adding mechanical or electrical information, but the drawing would regenerate much faster. When you did the final plot, you would reinsert the original Unit block showing every detail.

## Changing the Hatch Area

You may have noticed the Associative option in the Hatch And Gradient dialog box. When this radio button is selected, AutoCAD creates an associative hatch pattern. *Associative* hatches adjust their shapes to any changes in their associated boundary; hence the name. The following exercise demonstrates how this works.

Suppose you want to enlarge the tiled area of the kitchen by one tile. Here's how it's done:

1. Return to the Unit file (choose Window ➢ \\*directory path*\\Unit.dwg); then, click the outline border of the hatch pattern you created earlier. Notice the grips that appear around the hatch-pattern area.

2. Shift+click the grip in the lower-left corner of the hatch area.

**TIP**   If the boundary of the hatch pattern consists of line segments, you can use a crossing window or polygon-crossing window to select the corner grips of the hatch pattern.

3. With the lower-left grip highlighted, Shift+click the lower-right grip.

4. Click the lower-right grip again, but don't Shift+click this time.

5. Enter @12<–90↵↵ (@30<–90 for metric users) to widen the hatch pattern by 1′. The hatch pattern adjusts to the new size of the hatch boundary.

6. Press the Esc key twice to clear any grip selections.

7. Choose File ➢ Save to save the Unit file.

8. Return to the Plan file (choose Window ➢ \\*directory path*\\Plan.dwg), and repeat the steps in the exercise in the "Updating a Block From an External File" section, earlier in this chapter, to update the units again.

The Associative feature of hatch patterns can save time when you need to modify your drawing, but you need to be aware of its limitations. A hatch pattern can lose its associativity when you do any of the following:

- Erase or explode a hatch boundary.

- Erase or explode a block that forms part of the boundary.

- Move a hatch pattern away from its boundary.

These situations frequently arise when you edit an unfamiliar drawing. Often, boundary objects are placed on a layer that is off or frozen, so the boundary objects aren't visible. Or the hatch pattern might be on a layer that is turned off, and you proceed to edit the file, not knowing that a hatch pattern exists. When you encounter such a file, take a moment to check for hatch boundaries so you can deal with them properly.

## Modifying a Hatch Pattern

Like everything else in a project, a hatch pattern may eventually need to be changed in some way. Hatch patterns are like blocks in that they act like single objects. You can explode a hatch pattern to edit its individual lines. The Properties palette contains most of the settings you'll need to make changes to your hatch patterns. Perhaps the most direct way to edit a hatch pattern is to use the Hatch Edit dialog box.

## EDITING HATCH PATTERNS FROM THE HATCH EDIT DIALOG BOX

Follow these steps to modify a hatch pattern by using the Hatch Edit dialog box:

1. Return to the Unit drawing by choosing Window ➤ \\*directory path*\Unit.dwg.

2. Press the Esc key to clear any grip selections that may be active from earlier exercises.

3. Double-click the hatch pattern in the kitchen to open the Hatch Edit dialog box. It's the same as the Hatch And Gradient dialog box.

**TIP** When you double-click a hatch pattern, you don't get the typical Properties palette. Double-clicking complex objects such as text, blocks, attributes, and hatch patterns opens a dialog box in which you can edit the object in a more direct way. You can still access the Properties palette for any object by right-clicking the object and choosing Properties from the shortcut menu.

4. Click the ellipsis button to the right of the Pattern drop-down list to open the Hatch Pattern Palette dialog box at the Other Predefined tab.

5. Locate and double-click the pattern named AR-BRSTD. It's the pattern that looks like a brick wall. The Hatch Pattern Palette dialog box closes, and you see the AR-BRSTD hatch pattern in the Swatch field.

6. Click OK to accept the change to the hatch pattern. The AR-BRSTD pattern appears in place of the original parquet pattern.

7. Exit and save your file.

In this exercise, you were able to change the hatch just by double-clicking it. Although you changed only the pattern type, other options are available. You can, for example, modify a predefined pattern to a user-defined one by selecting User Defined from the Type listing in the Hatch Edit dialog box.

You can then enter angle and spacing values for your hatch pattern in the spaces provided in the Hatch Edit dialog box.

The other items in the Hatch Edit dialog box duplicate some of the options in the Hatch And Gradient dialog box. They let you modify the individual properties of the selected hatch pattern. The upcoming section "Understanding the Boundary Hatch Options" describes these other properties in detail.

If you create and edit hatch patterns frequently, you'll find the Modify II toolbar useful. It contains an Edit Hatch tool that gives you ready access to the Hatch Edit dialog box. To open the Modify II toolbar, right-click any toolbar, and then click Modify II in the pop-up menu.

### EDITING HATCH PATTERNS FROM THE PROPERTIES PALETTE

If you prefer, you can use the older method to edit a hatch pattern. To open the Properties palette, right-click a pattern, and choose Properties from the shortcut menu. The Properties palette displays a Pattern category, which offers a Pattern Name option.

When you click this option, an ellipsis button appears, enabling you to open the Hatch Pattern Palette dialog box, just as in step 4 of the previous exercise. You can then select a new pattern from the dialog box. The Type option in the Properties palette lets you change the type of hatch pattern from Predefined to User Defined or Custom.

**TIP**   If you're working through the tutorial in this chapter, this would be a good place to take a break or stop. You can pick up the next exercise, which is in the "Attaching a Drawing as an External Reference" section, at another time.

## Understanding the Boundary Hatch Options

The Hatch And Gradient dialog box offers many other options that you didn't explore in the previous exercises. For example, instead of selecting the area to be hatched by clicking a point, you can select the objects that bound the area you want to hatch by clicking the Add: Select Objects button. You can use Add: Select Objects to add boundaries to existing hatch patterns as well.

The Swatch box just below the Pattern drop-down list opens the Hatch Pattern Palette dialog box, which lets you select a predefined hatch pattern from a graphic window.

The Hatch Pattern Palette dialog box has several tabs that further divide the types of hatch patterns into four categories: ANSI, ISO, Other Predefined, and Custom. The Custom tab is empty until you create your own set of custom hatch patterns. See Chapter 26 for details on how to create custom hatch patterns.

Other options in the right column of the Hatch And Gradient dialog box include Remove Boundaries, Recreate Boundaries, View Selections, Associative, Create Separate Hatches, Draw Order, and Inherit Properties:

**Remove Boundaries** Lets you remove a bounded area, or *island*, in the area to be hatched. An example is the toilet seat in the bathroom. This option is available only when you select a hatch area by using the Add: Pick Points option and an island has been detected.

**Recreate Boundaries** Draws a region or polyline around the current hatch pattern. When this option is selected, the dialog box temporarily closes. You're then prompted to choose between a region or a polyline and to specify whether to reassociate the pattern with the re-created boundary. (See the Associative option discussed in a moment.)

**View Selections** Temporarily closes the dialog box and then highlights the objects that have been selected as the hatch boundary by AutoCAD.

**Annotative** Allows the hatch pattern to adjust to different scale views of your drawing. With this option turned on, a hatch pattern's size or spacing adjusts to the annotation scale of a viewport Layout or Model Space view. See Chapter 4 for more on annotation scale.

**Associative** Allows the hatch pattern to adjust to changes in its boundary. With this option turned on, any changes to the associated boundary of a hatch pattern cause the hatch pattern to flow with the changes in the boundary.

**Create Separate Hatches** Creates separate and distinct hatches if you select several enclosed areas while selecting hatch areas. With this option off, separate hatch areas behave as a single hatch pattern.

**Draw Order** Allows you to specify whether the hatch pattern appears on top of or underneath its boundary. This is useful when the boundary is of a different color or shade and must read clearly or when the hatch pattern must cover the boundary.

**Inherit Properties** Lets you select a hatch pattern from an existing one in the drawing. This is helpful when you want to apply a hatch pattern that is already used, but you don't know its name or its scale, rotation, or other properties.

---

### ANNOTATIVE HATCH PATTERNS

In Chapter 4, you learned about a new feature in AutoCAD 2008 called *annotation scale*. With this feature, you can assign several scales to certain types of objects, and AutoCAD displays the object to the proper scale of the drawing. Hatches can take advantage of this feature to allow hatch patterns to adjust their spacing or pattern size to the scale of your drawing. The Annotative option in the Options group of the Hatch and Gradient dialog box turns on the annotation scale feature for hatch patterns. Once a hatch pattern has this feature turned on, you can set up the drawing scales that you want to apply to the hatch pattern using the same methods described for blocks in Chapter 4.

## Using Additional Hatch Features

AutoCAD's Boundary Hatch command has a fair amount of "intelligence." As you saw in an earlier exercise, it was able to detect not only the outline of the floor area, but also the outline of the toilet seat that represents an island in the pattern area. If you prefer, you can control how AutoCAD treats these island conditions and other situations by selecting options available when you click the More Options button in the lower-right corner of the Hatch And Gradient dialog box.

This button expands the dialog box to show additional hatch options.

### ISLANDS

The Islands group at the top of the dialog box controls how nested boundaries affect the hatch pattern. The graphics in this group show examples of the effect of the selected option. The Islands options include the following:

**Island Detection** Turns on the Island Detection feature. This check box excludes closed objects within the boundary from being hatched. For example, when you were hatching the bathroom in an earlier exercise, the toilet seat wasn't hatched, because it was an island within the boundary.

**Normal** Causes the hatch pattern to alternate between nested boundaries. The outer boundary is hatched; if there is a closed object within the boundary, it isn't hatched. If *another* closed object is inside the first closed object, *that* object is hatched. This is the default setting.

**Outer** Applies the hatch pattern to an area defined by the outermost boundary and a closed object within that boundary. Any boundaries nested in that closed object are ignored.

**Ignore** Supplies the hatch pattern to the entire area within the outermost boundary, ignoring any nested boundaries.

### BOUNDARY RETENTION

The Boundary Hatch command can also create an outline of the hatch area by using one of two objects: 2D regions, which are like 2D planes; or polyline outlines. Boundary Hatch creates such a polyline boundary temporarily, to establish the hatch area. These boundaries are automatically removed after the hatch pattern is inserted. If you want to retain the boundaries in the drawing, make sure the Retain Boundaries check box is selected. Retaining the boundary can be useful if you know you'll be hatching the area more than once or if you're hatching a fairly complex area.

**TIP** Retaining a hatch boundary is useful if you want to know the hatched area's dimensions in square inches or feet, because you can find the area of a closed polyline by using the List command. See Chapter 2 for more on the List command.

**TIP** The Boundary command creates a polyline outline or region in a selected area. It works much like the Boundary Hatch command but doesn't add a hatch pattern.

### BOUNDARY SET OPTIONS

The Boundary Hatch feature is view dependent; that is, it locates boundaries based on what is visible in the current view. If the current view contains a lot of graphic data, AutoCAD can have difficulty finding a boundary or can be slow in finding a boundary. If you run into this problem, or if you want to single out a specific object for a point selection boundary, you can further limit the area that AutoCAD uses to locate hatch boundaries by using the Boundary Set options:

**New (Select New Boundary Set)**    Lets you select the objects from which you want AutoCAD to determine the hatch boundary, instead of searching the entire view. The screen clears and lets you select objects. This option discards previous boundary sets. It's useful for hatching areas in a drawing that contain many objects that you don't want to include in the hatch boundary.

**Current Viewport**    Tells you that AutoCAD will use the current view to determine the hatch boundary. After you select a set of objects by using the New button, you also see Existing Set as an option in this drop-down list. You can then use this drop-down list to choose the entire view or the objects you select for the hatch boundary.

The Boundary Set options are designed to give you more control over the way a point selection boundary is created. These options have no effect when you use the Add: Select Objects button to select specific objects for the hatch boundary.

### GAP TOLERANCE

This group lets you hatch an area that isn't completely enclosed. The Gap Tolerance value sets the maximum gap size in an area you want to hatch. You can use a value from 0 to 5000.

### INHERIT OPTIONS

This group controls the hatch origin when the Inherit Properties option is used to create new hatch patterns. Select Use Current Origin when you want to use the current default hatch origin. Select Use Source Hatch Origin when you want to use the origin from the inherited hatch pattern.

## Using Gradient Shading

You may have noticed that one of the hatch patterns offered is a solid. The solid hatch pattern lets you apply a solid color instead of a pattern to a bounded area. AutoCAD also offers a set of gradient patterns that let you apply a color gradient to an area.

You can apply a gradient to an area by using the same method you used to apply a hatch pattern; but instead of using the Hatch tab of the Hatch And Gradient dialog box, you use the Gradient tab to select a gradient pattern.

**WARNING** The Gradient Shading feature isn't available in AutoCAD LT.

### CHOOSING A GRADIENT COLOR

Instead of offering hatch patterns, the Gradient tab offers a variety of gradient patterns. It also lets you control the color of the gradient. For example, if you want to set the gradient between shades of blue, you can click the One Color radio button and then double-click the blue color swatch at the top of the dialog box.

When you double-click the color swatch, the Select Color dialog box opens, offering a palette of True Color options.

You can then select the color you want for the gradient. On the Gradient tab of the Hatch And Gradient dialog box, the Shade/Tint slider just below the Two Color radio button lets you control the shade of the single-color gradient.

### USING TWO COLORS

You can choose a gradient that transitions between shades of a single color by clicking the One Color radio button, or you can transition between two entirely different colors by clicking the Two Color radio button. When you select Two Color, the slider below the Two Color option changes to a color swatch. You can double-click the swatch or click the ellipses button to the right of the swatch to open the Select Color dialog box.

### SELECTING GRADIENT PATTERNS

Just below the One Color and Two Color options are the gradient pattern options. You can choose from nine patterns, plus you can select an angle for the pattern from the Angle drop-down list box. The Centered option places the center of the gradient at the center of the area selected for the pattern.

To place a gradient pattern, select a set of objects or a point in a bounded area, just as you would for a hatch pattern. You can then click the Preview button to preview your hatch pattern, or you can click OK to apply the gradient to the drawing.

## Tips for Using the Boundary Hatch

Here are a few tips on using the Boundary Hatch feature:

- ◆ Watch out for boundary areas that are part of a large block. AutoCAD examines the entire block when defining boundaries. This can take time if the block is large. Use the Boundary Set options to focus in on the set of objects you want AutoCAD to use for your hatch boundary.

- ◆ The Boundary Hatch feature is view dependent; that is, it locates boundaries based on what is visible in the current view. To ensure that AutoCAD finds every detail, zoom in to the area to be hatched.

- ◆ If the area to be hatched is large yet requires fine detail, first outline the hatch area by using a polyline. (See Chapter 18 for more on polylines.) Then, use the Add: Select Objects option in the Hatch And Gradient dialog box to select the polyline boundary manually, instead of depending on Boundary Hatch to find the boundary for you.

- ◆ Consider turning off layers that might interfere with AutoCAD's ability to find a boundary.

- ◆ Boundary Hatch works on nested blocks as long as the nested block entities are parallel to the current UCS.

## Space Planning and Hatch Patterns

Suppose you're working on a plan in which you're constantly repositioning equipment and furniture, or you're in the process of designing the floor covering. You might be a little hesitant to place a hatch pattern on the floor because you don't want to have to rehatch the area each time you move a piece of equipment or change the flooring. You have two options in this situation: You can use the Boundary Hatch's associative capabilities to include the furnishings in the boundary set, or you can use the Display Order feature.

### USING ASSOCIATIVE HATCH

Associative Hatch is the most straightforward method. Make sure the Associative option is selected in the Hatch And Gradient dialog box, and include your equipment or furniture in the boundary set. You can do this by using the Add: Select Objects option in the dialog box.

After the pattern is in place, the hatch pattern automatically adjusts to its new location when you move the furnishings in your drawing. One drawback, however, is that AutoCAD attempts to hatch the interior of your furnishings if they cross the outer boundary of the hatch pattern. Also, if any boundary objects are erased or exploded, the hatch pattern no longer follows the location of your furnishings. To avoid these problems, you can use the method described in the next section.

### OVERLAPPING OBJECTS WITH DRAW ORDER

The Draw Order feature lets you determine how objects overlap. In the space-planning example, you can create furniture by using a solid hatch to indicate horizontal surfaces (see Figure 7.8).

**FIGURE 7.8**
Using Draw Order to create an overlapping effect over a hatch pattern

Draw an outline of the furniture or equipment, then use the Hatch tool in the Draw toolbar to fill the outline with a Solid hatch pattern.

In the Hatch And Gradient dialog box, make sure that Send Behind Boundary is selected in the Draw Order drop-down list before you add the hatch pattern.

Place the drawing of the equipment on the floor pattern, then choose Tools > Draw Order > Send to Back and select the floor pattern.

The equipment will appear to sit on top of the floor pattern.

---

**HOW TO QUICKLY MATCH A HATCH PATTERN AND OTHER PROPERTIES**

Another tool to help you edit hatch patterns is Match Properties, which is similar to Format Painter in the Microsoft Office suite. This tool lets you change an existing hatch pattern to match another existing hatch pattern. Here's how to use it:

1. Click the Match Properties tool in the Standard toolbar.

2. Click the source hatch pattern you want to copy.

3. Click the target hatch pattern you want to change. The target pattern changes to match the source pattern.

The Match Properties tool transfers other properties as well, such as layer, color, and linetype settings. You can select the properties that are transferred by opening the Property Settings dialog box.

To open this dialog box, type **S**↵ after selecting the object in step 2, or right-click and choose Settings from the shortcut menu. You can then select the properties you want to transfer from the options shown. All the properties are selected by default. You can also transfer text and dimension style settings. You'll learn more about text and dimension styles in Chapters 10 and 12.

---

You can then place the furniture on top of a floor-covering pattern, and the pattern will be covered and hidden by the furniture. Here's how to do that. (These steps aren't part of the regular exercises of this chapter. They're shown here as general guidelines when you need to use the Draw Order feature.)

1. Draw the equipment outline, and make sure the outline is a closed polygon.

2. Start the Hatch tool described earlier in this chapter to place a solid hatch pattern inside the equipment outline.

3. In the Hatch And Gradient dialog box, make sure that Send Behind Boundary is selected in the Draw Order drop-down list.

4. Complete the rest of the hatch pattern.

5. After you've finished placing the hatch, turn the outline and solid hatch into a block, or use the Group command to group them.

6. Choose Tools ➢ Draw Order ➢ Bring To Front, and select the equipment. When you're done, the equipment covers the floor hatch pattern (see the bottom panel in Figure 7.8).

After you take these steps, you can place the equipment over a hatched floor pattern, and the equipment will appear to rest on top of the pattern. If you create a floor pattern *after* you create the equipment, choose Tools ➢ Draw Order ➢ Send To Back to move the pattern to the back of the display order. You can also change the display order of objects relative to other objects.

The Draw Order options are all part of the Draworder command. As an alternative to the menu, you can type **Draworder↵** at the Command prompt, select an object, and then enter an option at the prompt:

```
Enter object ordering option
[Above objects/Under objects/Front/Back] <Back>:
```

For example, the equivalent of choosing Tools ➢ Draw Order ➢ Send To Back is entering **Draworder↵B↵**. You can also select the object you want to edit, right-click, and then choose Draw Order from the shortcut menu.

If you need to white out an area of a hatch pattern to make text more readable, you can use a solid hatch along with the Display Order option to block out areas behind text.

**TIP**  Draworder settings are maintained through blocks and Xrefs.

You've had a detailed look at hatch patterns and fills in this section. Remember that you can also use the Tool palettes to help organize and simplify access to your favorite hatch patterns, or use the patterns already available in the Tool palettes. The patterns in the Tool palettes can be edited and manipulated in the same way as described in this chapter. If you want to know how to make full use of the Tool palettes, check out the discussion on the AutoCAD DesignCenter in Chapter 27.

## Using External References

AutoCAD allows you to import drawings in a way that keeps the imported drawing independent from the current one. A drawing imported in this way is called an *external reference* (Xref). Unlike drawings that have been imported as blocks, Xref files don't become part of the drawing's database. Instead, they're loaded along with the current file at startup time. It's as if AutoCAD were opening several drawings at once: the currently active file you specify when you start AutoCAD, and any file inserted as an Xref.

If you keep Xref files independent from the current file, any changes you make to the Xref automatically appear in the current file. You don't have to update the Xref file manually as you do blocks. For example, if you used Xref to insert the Unit file into the Plan file, and you later made changes to the Unit file, you would see the new version of the Unit file in place of the old the next time you opened the Plan file. If the Plan file was still open while edits were made, AutoCAD would notify you that a change had been made to an Xref.

**TIP**  You can't Xref a file if the file has the same name as a block in the current drawing. If this situation occurs, but you still need to use the file as an Xref, you can rename the block of the same name by using the Rename command. You can also use Rename to change the name of various objects and named elements. See Chapter 10.

Another advantage of Xref files is that because they don't become part of a drawing's database, drawing size is kept to a minimum. This results in more efficient use of your hard disk space.

**TIP**  Xref files, like blocks, can only be edited using special tools. You can, however, use osnaps to snap to a location in an Xref file, or you can freeze or turn off the Xref file's insertion layer to make it invisible.

## Attaching a Drawing as an External Reference

The next exercise shows how to use an Xref in place of an inserted block to construct the studio apartment building. You'll first create a new unit file by copying the old one. Then, you'll bring a new toolbar, the External References palette, to the screen. Follow these steps to create the new file:

1. Return to the 07a-unit file; choose File ➤ Save As to save it under the name Unitxref.dwg, and then close the Unitxref.dwg file. This will make a copy of the 07a-unit.dwg file for the following steps. Or, if you prefer, you can use the Unitxref.dwg file for the following steps.

2. Return to the 07b-plan file, choose Save As, and save the file under the name Planxref. The current file is now Planxref.dwg.

3. Erase all the Unit plans (enter E↵All↵), and, as described in the next step, purge the Unit plans from the file. (By completing steps 2 and 3, you save yourself from having to set up a new file.)

4. Choose File ➤ Drawing Utilities ➤ Purge to open the Purge dialog box, and then click the Purge All button to open the Confirm Purge dialog box. This purges blocks that aren't in use in the drawing.

5. Click Yes To All.

Now you're ready to use the External References palette:

1. Choose Insert ➤ External References, or type XR↵ to open the External References palette (see Figure 7.9).

2. Click the Attach DWG button in the upper-left corner of the palette to open the Select Reference File dialog box. This is a typical AutoCAD file dialog box complete with a preview window.

**FIGURE 7.9**
The External References palette

3. Locate and select the `Unitxref.dwg` file, and then click Open to open the External Reference dialog box (see Figure 7.10). Notice that this dialog box looks similar to the Insert dialog box. It offers the same options for insertion point, scale, and rotation.

**FIGURE 7.10**

The External Reference dialog box

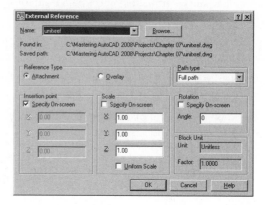

4. You'll see a description of the options presented in this dialog box. For now, click OK.

5. Enter **31´-5˝⏎,43´-8˝⏎** (metric users enter **957,1330**) for the insertion point.

6. After the `Unitxref.dwg` file is inserted, re-create the same layout of the floor plan you created in the first section of this chapter by copying and mirroring the `Unitxref.dwg` external reference.

7. Save the `Planxref` file.

You now have a drawing that looks like the `07b-plan.dwg` file you worked with earlier in this chapter, but instead of using blocks that are detached from their source file, you have a drawing composed of Xrefs. These Xrefs are the actual `Unitxref.dwg` file, and they're loaded into AutoCAD at the same time that you open the `Planxref.dwg` file. An icon in the lower-right corner of the AutoCAD window tells you that the current drawing contains Xrefs.

This icon not only alerts you to Xrefs but also enables you to open the External References palette, as you'll see in the next exercise.

Next, you'll modify the `Unitxref.dwg` file and see the results in the `Planxref.dwg` file:

1. To open the `Unitxref.dwg` file, from the current `Planxref` file, select and then right-click the unit, and choose Open Xref from the shortcut menu. You can also enter **Xopen.⏎** at the Command prompt and then select the unit plan Xref.

**WARNING** Xopen and the Open Xref option in the shortcut menu aren't available in LT. If you're using LT, choose File ➢ Open, and use the Select File dialog box to open the `Unitxref.dwg` file.

2. Erase the hatch pattern and kitchen outline for the floors, and save the `Unitxref.dwg` file.

3. Choose Window ➢ `Planxref.dwg` to return to the `Planxref.dwg` file. You see a message balloon pointing to the Xref icon in the lower-right corner of the AutoCAD window. The balloon warns you that an Xref has changed. Right-click the Manage Xrefs icon in the lower-right corner of the AutoCAD window, and then choose External References from the pop-up menu to open the External References palette.

**4.** Select the Unitxref name in the list box, click Reload, and then click OK. Notice that the units in the Planxref drawing have been updated to include the changes you made to the Unitxref file.

You can open multiple Xrefs at once by selecting more than one Xref while using the Xopen command.

**TIP**   The Open option in the External References palette performs the same function as the Xopen command or the Open Xref option in the shortcut menu. To use this option, select and right-click the Xref files from the list box in the External References palette, and then click Open.

Be aware that when an Xref has been modified, the Manage Xrefs icon at lower-right in the AutoCAD window changes to show an exclamation point. This alerts you to changes in an Xref in the current drawing.

Click the Manage Xrefs icon to open the External References palette. The Xref that has been changed is indicated by a message in the Status column of the list box.

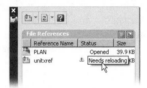

You can then select the Xref that needs to be updated, right-click, and choose the Reload option from the shortcut menu to reload the selected Xref. You can also select multiple Xrefs if more than one needs updating.

Here you saw how an Xref file is updated in a different way than a block. Because Xrefs are loaded along with the drawing file that contains them, the containing file, which in this case was the Planxref file, automatically displays any changes made to the Xref when it's opened. Also, you avoid having to update nested blocks, because AutoCAD updates nested Xrefs as well as non-nested Xrefs. When an Xref is modified while you're editing a file, you're alerted to the change through the Xref icon located in the lower-right corner of the AutoCAD window. You can click the balloon message that appears from that icon to update any modified Xrefs.

## Other Differences between External References and Blocks

Here are a few other differences between Xrefs and inserted blocks that you'll want to keep in mind:

♦   Any new layers, text styles, or linetypes brought in with cross-referenced files don't become part of the current file. If you want to import any of these items, you can use the Xbind command (described in Chapter 15).

♦   If you make changes to the layers of a cross-referenced file, those changes aren't retained when the file is saved unless you checked the Retain Changes To Xref Layers option in the Open And Save tab of the Options dialog box. This option, found in the External References (Xrefs) group, instructs AutoCAD to remember any layer color or visibility settings from one editing session to the next. In the standard AutoCAD settings, this option is on by default.

**TIP**   Another way to ensure that layer settings for Xrefs are retained is to enter **Visretain** ↵ at the Command prompt. At the New value for VISRETAIN <0>: prompt, enter **1**.

**IMPORTING BLOCKS, LAYERS, AND OTHER NAMED ELEMENTS FROM EXTERNAL FILES**

You can use the Xbind command to import blocks and other drawing components from another file. First, use the External References palette to cross-reference a file; type **Xbind** at the Command prompt. In the Xbind dialog box, click the plus sign next to the Xref filename, and then select Block. Locate the name of the block you want to import, click the Add button, and click OK. Finally, open the External References palette, select the Xref filename from the list, right-click, and select Detach to remove the Xref file. The imported block remains as part of the current file. (See Chapter 15 for details on importing drawing components.) You can also use the AutoCAD DesignCenter to import items from external files. DesignCenter is described in Chapter 27.

The Tool Palettes window give you access to frequently used blocks and hatch patterns that reside in other drawings. You can open the Tool palettes by clicking the Tool Palettes icon in the Standard toolbar.

In the standard AutoCAD installations, the Tool Palettes window is configured with sample 3D commands, blocks, and hatch patterns that you can drag and drop into your current drawing. Select a tab for the Tool palette that contains the block or pattern you want, and then click and drag the item into your drawing. In the case of hatch patterns, click and drag the pattern into an area that is bounded on all sides by objects. When you're ready to customize the Tool Palettes window, you do so by clicking and dragging objects or tools into a new or existing palette. See Chapter 27 for more on customizing tool palettes.

♦ To segregate layers in Xref files from layers in the current drawing, the Xref file's layers are prefixed with their file's name. A vertical bar separates the filename prefix and the layer name when you view a list of layers in the Layer drop-down list or the Layer Properties Manager dialog box (as in Unitxref | wall).

♦ You can't explode Xrefs. You can, however, convert an Xref into a block and then explode it. To do this, select the Xref in the External References palette to open another dialog box that offers two ways of converting an Xref into a block. See the section "Other External Reference Options" later in this chapter for more information.

♦ If an Xref is renamed or moved to another location on your hard disk, AutoCAD won't be able to find that file when it opens other files to which the Xref is attached. If this happens, you must select the path in the Found At field in the External References palette and then click the Browse button (the ellipses) to tell AutoCAD where to find the cross-referenced file.

**WARNING**  Take care when retargeting an Xref file with the Browse button. The Browse button can assign a file of a different name to an existing Xref as a substitution.

♦ Xref files are especially useful in workgroup environments in which several people are working on the same project. For example, one person might be updating several files that are inserted into a variety of other files. Using blocks, everyone in the workgroup would have to be notified of the changes and would have to update all the affected blocks in all the drawings that contained them. With cross-referenced files, however, the updating is automatic; you avoid confusion about which files need their blocks updated.

## Other External Reference Options

Many other features are unique to external reference files. Let's briefly look at some of the other options in the External References palette.

**OPTIONS IN THE EXTERNAL REFERENCES PALETTE**

Several options are available when you right-click an external reference name listed in the External References palette, shown in Figure 7.13 earlier in this chapter. You saw the Reload option in an earlier exercise. The following other options are available:

**Attach**   Opens the Select Reference dialog box, in which you can select a file to attach and set the parameters for the attachment.

**Detach**   Detaches an Xref from the current file. The file is then completely disassociated from the current file.

**Reload**   Restores an unloaded Xref.

**Unload**   Similar to Detach but maintains a link to the Xref file so that it can be quickly reattached. This has an effect similar to freezing a layer and can reduce redraw, regeneration, and file-loading times.

**Bind**   Converts an Xref into a block. Bind offers two options: Bind (again) and Insert. Bind's Bind option maintains the Xref's named elements (layers, linetypes, and text and dimension styles) by creating new layers in the current file with the Xref's filename prefix (see Chapter 15). The Insert option doesn't attempt to maintain the Xref's named elements but merges them with named elements of the same name in the current file. For example, if both the Xref and the current file have layers of the same name, the objects in the Xref are placed in the layers of the same name in the current file.

**Open**   Lets you open an Xref. Select the Xref from the list, and then click Open. The Xref opens in a new window when you close the External References palette. This option isn't available in AutoCAD LT.

**Details**   A panel at the bottom of the External References palette. It's similar to the Properties palette in that it displays the properties of a selected external reference and also allows you to modify some of those properties. For example, the Reference Name option in the Details panel lets you give the external reference a name that is different from the Xref filename. Table 7.1 gives you a rundown of the options in the Details panel.

**TABLE 7.1:**      The Details Panel of the External References Palette

| OPTION | FUNCTION |
| --- | --- |
| Reference Name | Lets you give the Xref a name that is different from the Xref's filename. This can be helpful if you want to use multiple external references of the same file. |
| Status | Tells you whether the Xref is loaded, unloaded, or not found (read only). |
| Size | Gives you the file size information (read only). |
| Type | Lets you choose between the Attach and Overlay attachment method for the Xref file. Xrefs attached as overlays don't include nested Xrefs. |
| Date | Gives you the date and time the file was attached (read only). |
| Saved Path | Tells you where AutoCAD expects to find the Xref file (read only). |
| Found At | Lets you select the location of the Xref file. When you click the text box for this option, a Browse button appears to the right. You can click this button to locate a lost Xref or use a different file from the original attached Xref. |

#### THE EXTERNAL REFERENCE DIALOG BOX

The External Reference dialog box, shown in Figure 7.10 earlier in this chapter, offers these options:

**Browse**   Opens the Select Reference File dialog box to enable you to change the file you're importing as an Xref.

**Attachment**   Tells AutoCAD to include other Xref attachments that are nested in the selected file.

**Overlay**   Tells AutoCAD to ignore other Xref attachments that are nested in the selected file. This avoids multiple attachments of other files and eliminates the possibility of circular references (referencing the current file into itself through another file).

**Path Type**   Offers options for locating Xrefs. Xref files can be located anywhere on your system, including network servers. For this reason, links to Xrefs can be easily lost either by moving them or rearranging file locations. To help you manage Xrefs, the Path Type option offers three options: Full Path, Relative Path, and No Path. Full Path retains the current full path. Relative Path maintains paths in relation to the current drawing. The current drawing must be saved before using the Relative Path option. The No Path option is for drawings in which Xrefs are located in the same folder as the current drawing or in the Support File Search Path specified in the Files tab of the Options dialog box (choose Tools ➢ Options).

**Specify On-Screen**   Appears in three places. It gives you the option to enter insertion point, scale factors, and rotation angles in the dialog box or in the Command window, in a way similar to inserting blocks. If you clear this option for any of the corresponding parameters, the parameters change to allow input. If they're selected, you're prompted for those parameters after you click OK to close the dialog box. With all three Specify On-Screen check boxes cleared, the Xref is inserted in the drawing using the settings indicated in the dialog box.

## Clipping Xref Views and Improving Performance

Xrefs are frequently used to import large drawings for reference or backgrounds. Multiple Xrefs, such as a floor plan, column grid layout, and site-plan drawing, might be combined into one file. One drawback to multiple Xrefs in earlier versions of AutoCAD was that the entire Xref was loaded into memory, even if only a small portion of the Xref was used for the final plotted output. For computers with limited resources, multiple Xrefs could slow the system to a crawl.

AutoCAD 2008 offers two tools that help make display and memory use more efficient when using Xrefs: the Xclip command and the Demand Load option in the Options dialog box.

### CLIPPING VIEWS

The Xclip command lets you clip the display of an Xref or a block to any shape you want, as shown in Figure 7.11. For example, you might want to display only an L-shaped portion of a floor plan to be part of your current drawing. Xclip lets you define such a view. To access the command, choose Modify ➢ Clip ➢ Xref.

You can clip blocks and multiple Xrefs as well. And you can specify a front and back clipping distance so that the visibility of objects in 3D space can be controlled. You can define a clip area by using polylines or spline curves, although curve-fitted polylines revert to decurved polylines. (See Chapter 18 for more on polylines and spline curves.)

### CONTROLLING XREF SETTINGS IN THE OPTIONS DIALOG BOX

The External References (Xrefs) group in the Open And Save tab of the Options dialog box offers some tools to help you manage memory use and other features related to Xrefs. If you're working on large projects with others in a workgroup, you should be aware of these settings and what they do.

**FIGURE 7.11**

The first panel shows a polyline outline of the area to be isolated with Xclip. The second panel shows how the Xref appears after Xclip is applied. The last panel shows a view of the plan with the polyline's layer turned off.

The Demand Load Xrefs drop-down list offers three settings: Disabled, Enabled, and Enabled With Copy. Demand Load is set to Enable With Copy by default in the standard AutoCAD drawing setup. In addition to reducing the amount of memory an Xref consumes, Demand Load also prevents other users from editing the Xref while it's being viewed as part of your current drawing. This helps aid drawing version control and drawing management. The Enabled With Copy option creates a copy of the source Xref file and then uses the copy, thereby enabling other AutoCAD users to edit the source Xref file.

Demand loading improves performance by loading only the parts of the referenced drawing that are needed to regenerate the current drawing. You can set the location for the Xref copy in the Files tab of the Options dialog box under Temporary External Reference File Location.

Two other options are also available in the Options dialog box:

**Retain Changes To Xref Layers**   Instructs AutoCAD to remember any layer color or visibility settings of Xrefs from one editing session to the next. In the standard AutoCAD settings, this option is on by default.

**Allow Other Users To Refedit Current Drawing**   Lets others edit the current drawing by choosing Tools ➢ Xref And Block In-Place Editing ➢ Edit Reference In-Place (Refedit). You'll learn about this command in the next section.

## Editing Xrefs in Place

You've seen different methods for editing blocks and Xrefs as external files. There is another way to edit a block or an Xref directly in a file, without having to edit an external file: You can use the Xref And Block In-Place Editing option in the Tools drop-down menu. This option issues the Refedit command.

The following exercise demonstrates how Refedit works:

1. If it isn't already open, open the `Planxref.dwg` file. Also make sure you've closed the `Unitxref.dwg` file.

2. Zoom in to the unit plan in the lower-left corner of the drawing so you see a view similar to Figure 7.12.

3. Double-click the wall of the corner unit. You can also choose Tools ➢ Xref And Block In-Place Editing ➢ Edit Reference In-Place from the menu bar. Then, at the `Select reference:` prompt, click a wall of the corner unit to open the Reference Edit dialog box.

4. The Reference Edit dialog box contains two panels. The right panel shows a thumbnail view of the item that you're editing. The left panel shows a listing of the specific item you selected in the Xref. Notice that the listing shows the hierarchical relationship of the kitchenette block in relation to the Unitxref Xref.

   In the left panel, click the unitxref | KITCHEN listing, and then click OK. The Reference Edit dialog box closes, and the Refedit toolbar appears.

5. Use a selection window to select the entire lower-left corner unit. Notice that only the grips in the kitchenette appear, indicating that the objects in the kitchenette are selected. Although the rest of the unit appears to be selected, it appears lighter in color. This shows you that only the kitchen is available for editing.

**FIGURE 7.12**
The enlarged view of
the Unit Xref in the
Planxref file

6. Press the Esc key to clear your selection.

**TIP** You can open the Refedit toolbar so that it stays on the screen by right-clicking any toolbar and choosing Refedit from the shortcut menu.

---

**SPECIAL SAVE AS OPTIONS THAT AFFECT DEMAND LOADING**

AutoCAD offers a few additional settings that boost the performance of the Demand Load feature. When you choose File ➢ Save As to save a file in the standard .dwg format, you see the Tools button in the upper-right corner. Choosing Tools ➢ Options opens the Save As Options dialog box. Using the options in the Index Type drop-down list in the DWG Options tab can help improve the speed of demand loading. The index options are as follows:

**None**   No index is created.

**Layer**   AutoCAD loads only layers that are both turned on and thawed.

**Spatial**   AutoCAD loads only portions of an Xref or raster image within a clipped boundary.

**Layer & Spatial**   This option turns on both the Layer and Spatial options.

---

In step 5 of the previous exercise, the Refedit command isolates the objects you select for editing. You can't edit anything else in the Xref until you exit the Refedit command and start over.

At this point, you can edit a block in an Xref. Now, let's continue editing the kitchenette:

1. Zoom in on the kitchenette, and move the four burners to the right 8″ (20 cm for metric users).

2. Erase the sink.

3. Click the Save Reference Edits button on the Refedit toolbar, or choose Tools ➢ Xref And Block In-Place Editing ➢ Save Reference Edits.

4. A warning message appears, telling you that the changes you've made to the Xref will be saved. Click OK.

5. Zoom back to your previous view. Notice that the other units reflect the changes you made to the Unitxref Xref (see Figure 7.13).

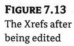

**FIGURE 7.13**
The Xrefs after
being edited

6. Open the `Unitxref.dwg` file. The kitchen reflects the changes you made to the Xref of the unit in the `Planxref` file. This shows you that by choosing to save the reference edit in step 3, you save the changes back to the Xref's source file.

As you saw from these two exercises, it's possible to edit a specific block in an Xref, but to do that you must select the block name in the Reference Edit dialog box.

In these exercises, you edited a block contained in an Xref, but you could have just as easily edited a block in the current drawing. You can also edit nested blocks by using the Refedit command. Changes in blocks in the current file don't affect other files because blocks aren't linked to external files. The changes to blocks remain in the current file until you explicitly export the changed block to a file, as you saw in earlier exercises.

## Adding and Removing Objects from Blocks and Xrefs

In the previous exercises, you removed objects from the Kitchen block by using the Erase command. You can also move objects from a block or an Xref into the current drawing without erasing them. To do this, choose Tools ➢ Xref And Block In-Place Editing ➢ Remove From Working Set while in the Refedit command. This removes the objects from the block or Xref without erasing them. Likewise, you can add new objects to the block or Xref by choosing Tools ➢ Xref And Block In-Place Editing ➢ Add To Working Set. Both menu options invoke the Refset command, with different options applied.

To see how Refset works, try the following exercise:

1. Close the `Unitxref.dwg` file.

2. In the `Planxref` file, zoom in to the kitchenette to get a view similar to the top panel of Figure 7.14.

3. Double-click the unit plan drawing. You can also choose Tools ➢ Xref And Block In-Place Editing ➢ Edit Reference In-Place and then click the unit plan.

4. Click the unitxref|KITCHEN listing in the Reference Edit dialog box, and then click OK.

5. Use the Move tool to move the two burners on the right just to the right of the kitchenette, as shown in Figure 7.14.

**FIGURE 7.14**
Moving the burners
out of the Kitchen
block and adding
the rectangle

**FIGURE 7.14**
Moving the burners
out of the Kitchen
block and adding
the rectangle

6. Click the Remove From Working Set tool in the Refedit toolbar, or choose Tools ➢ Xref And Block In-Place Editing ➢ Remove From Working Set.

7. Select the two burners you just moved, and then press ↵.

Notice that the burners become grayer to show that they're removed from the working set. They remain as part of the Planxref drawing, but they're no longer part of the Kitchen block.

Now, add a rectangle to the Kitchen block in place of the burners:

1. Draw a 7″ × 16″ (18 cm × 40 cm) rectangle in place of the moved burners, as shown in Figure 7.14. Anything you add to the drawing automatically becomes part of the working set.

2. Click Save Reference Edits on the Refedit toolbar, or choose Modify ➢ Xref And Block In-Place Editing ➢ Save Reference Edits. You'll see a warning message stating that "All reference edits will be saved". Click OK.

3. Zoom out enough to see the other units in the drawing (see Figure 7.15).

You can see that the burners have been replaced by the rectangle in all the other Xref units. The burners you moved are still there in the lower-left corner unit, but they have been removed from all the Xrefs. It's as if you extracted them from the block and placed them in the Plan drawing.

During the Refedit command, any new objects you create are added to the working set automatically. When you drew the rectangle in step 1, for example, it was automatically included in the *working set*, which is the set of objects included in the block or Xref you're currently working on. You didn't have to specifically add it to the working set.

**FIGURE 7.15**

The Planxref drawing with the changes made to the Unitxref Xref

If you want to include existing objects in the working set, choose Tools ➤ Xref And Block In-Place Editing ➤ Add To Working Set, or choose Add To Working Set from the Refedit toolbar.

You've completed the exercises in this chapter, so you can exit AutoCAD without saving these changes.

## Understanding the Reference Edit Dialog Box Options

The Reference Edit dialog box offers you the option to isolate specific blocks in the Xref by selecting them from the hierarchy list. You may have noticed the two radio button options: Automatically Select All Nested Objects and Prompt To Select Nested Objects. The default option, Automatically Select All Nested Objects, lets you select any object contained in the selected object in the hierarchy listing. If you select the Prompt To Select Nested Objects option, you're prompted to select objects on the screen before the Refedit toolbar appears.

In addition to the options you used in the exercises, the Reference Edit dialog box also offers the Settings tab with some additional options.

### CREATE UNIQUE LAYER, STYLE, AND BLOCK NAMES

When you use the Refedit command with the Automatically Select All Nested Objects option turned on, you can import nested blocks into the current drawing. For example, if you selected the Bath block in the hierarchy list in the previous exercise, you would have access to the Tub and Toilet blocks in the Bath block. You could then copy either of those blocks into the current file.

When you make a copy of a block from an Xref, AutoCAD needs to assign that block a name. The Create Unique Layer, Style, And Block Names option tells AutoCAD to use the original block name and append a $#$ prefix to the name (# is a numeric value starting with zero). If you were to import the Bath block, for example, it would become $0$bath in the current drawing. This ensures that the block maintains a unique name when it's imported, even if there is a block with the same name in the current drawing. If you turn off the Create Unique Layer, Style, And Block Names option, the original name is maintained. If the current drawing contains a block of the same name, the imported block uses the current file's definition of that block.

### DISPLAY ATTRIBUTE DEFINITIONS FOR EDITING

If your drawing contains attributes (see Chapter 13 for more on attributes), this option is offered. If you turn on this option, you can then edit attribute definitions by using the Refedit command. If you select a block that contains an attribute definition while you're using the Refedit command, the attribute definition is exposed, enabling you to make changes. Changes to attribute definitions affect only new attribute insertions. Except for the attribute of the edited block, existing attributes aren't affected. If you want to update existing attributes to a newly edited definition, use the Sync option of the Block Attribute Manager (choose Modify ➤ Object ➤ Attribute ➤ Block Attribute Manager).

### LOCK OBJECTS NOT IN WORKING SET

In the Refedit exercises, you saw that objects that aren't selected in the Reference Edit dialog box are grayed out and aren't selectable. The Lock Objects Not In Working Set option controls this feature and is turned on by default.

## The Bottom Line

**Assembling the Parts**   Technical drawings are often made up of repetitive parts that are drawn over and over. AutoCAD makes quick work of repetitive elements in a drawing, as shown in the first part of this chapter.

> **Master It**   What is the object used as the basic building block for the unit plan drawing in the beginning of this chapter?

> **Solution**   Blocks of a typical unit plan are used to build a floor plan of an apartment building.

**Taking Control of the AutoCAD Display**   Understanding the way the AutoCAD display works can save you time, especially in a complex drawing.

> **Master It**   Name the dialog box used to save views in AutoCAD. Describe how to recall a saved view.

> **Solution**   The View Manager dialog box lets you save a view. To recall a view, select the view name from the 2D Navigate control panel drop-down list.

**Using Hatch Patterns in Your Drawings**   Patterns can convey a lot of information at a glance. You can show the material of an object, or you can indicate a type of view, like a cross section, by applying hatch patterns.

> **Master It**   How do you open the Hatch and Gradient dialog box?

> **Solution**   Choose Draw ➤ Hatch from the menu bar, or select the Hatch tool from the 2D Draw control panel.

**Understanding the Boundary Hatch Options**  The boundary hatch options give you control over the way hatch patterns fill an enclosed area.

**Master It**  Describe an island as it relates to boundary hatch patterns.

**Solution**  An island is an enclosed object that is found in an area to be hatched.

**Using External References**  External references are drawing files that you've attached to the current drawing to include as part of the drawing. Because external references aren't part of the current file, they can be worked on at the same time as the referencing file.

**Master It**  Describe how drawing files are attached as external references.

**Solution**  Open the External Reference palette, click the Attach DWG button at upper left, and then locate and select the file you want to attach.

# Chapter 8

# Introducing Printing, Plotting, and Layouts

Getting hard-copy output from AutoCAD is something of an art. You'll need to be intimately familiar with both your output device and the settings available in AutoCAD. You'll probably spend a good deal of time experimenting with AutoCAD's plotter settings and with your printer or plotter to get your equipment set up just the way you want.

With the huge array of output options available, this chapter can provide only a general discussion of plotting and printing. As a rule, the process for using a plotter isn't much different from that for a printer; you just have more media size options with plotters. Still, every output device is different. It's up to you to work out the details and fine-tune the way you and AutoCAD together work with your particular plotter or printer. This chapter describes the features available in AutoCAD and discusses some general rules and guidelines to follow when setting up your plots.

I'll start with an overview of the plotting features in AutoCAD and then delve into the finer details of setting up your drawing and controlling your plotter or printer.

Topics in this chapter include the following:

◆ Plotting the Plan

◆ Understanding the Plotter Settings

◆ WYSIWYG Plotting Using Layout Tabs

◆ Adding an Output Device

◆ Storing a Page Setup

◆ Plotter and Printer Hardware Considerations

## Plotting the Plan

To see first hand how the Plot command works, you'll plot the Plan file by using the default settings on your system. You'll start by getting a preview of your plot, before you commit to printing your drawing. As an introduction, you'll plot from the Model tab of an AutoCAD drawing, but be aware that typically you should plot from a Layout tab. The Layout tabs give you a greater degree of control over how your output will look. You'll be introduced to the Layout tab later in this chapter. Now, let's get started!

First, try plotting your drawing to no particular scale:

1. Be sure your printer or plotter is connected to your computer and is turned on.

2. Start AutoCAD, and open the Plan.dwg file.

**3.** Choose View ➢ Zoom ➢ All to display the entire drawing.

**4.** Choose File ➢ Plot to open the Plot dialog box. You can also right-click the Model tab at the bottom of the AutoCAD window and choose Plot.

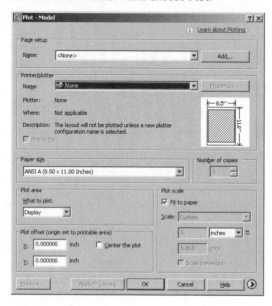

**5.** If the Name option in the Printer/Plotter group shows None, click the drop-down arrow and select your current Windows system printer.

**6.** In the Plot Area group, make sure the Display option is selected in the drop-down list. This tells AutoCAD to plot the drawing as it looks in the drawing window. You also have the option to plot the limits of the drawing or select an area to plot with a window. In addition, you can choose to plot the extents of a drawing or a saved view.

**7.** Make sure the Fit To Paper option is selected in the Plot Scale group.

**8.** Click the Preview button in the lower-left corner of the dialog box. AutoCAD works for a moment and then displays a sample view of how your drawing will appear when printed. Notice that the view also shows the Zoom Realtime cursor. You can use the Zoom/Pan Realtime tool to get a close-up of your print preview.

9. Go ahead and plot the file: Right-click, and choose Plot from the shortcut menu. AutoCAD sends the drawing to your printer.

10. Your plotter or printer prints the plan to no particular scale.

You've just plotted your first drawing to see how it looks on paper. You used the minimal settings to ensure that the complete drawing appears on the paper.

You may notice that a message bubble appears in the lower-right corner of the AutoCAD window.

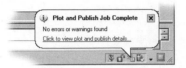

If you click the text that reads *Click to view plot and publish details...*, the Plot And Publish Details dialog box opens to display some detailed information about your plot.

As you become more experienced with AutoCAD and your projects become more demanding, the information presented in the Plot And Publish Details dialog box may be useful to you. For now, make a mental note that this information is available should you need it.

Next, try plotting your drawing to an exact scale. This time, you'll expand the Plot dialog box to show a few more options:

**WARNING**   It's important to make sure you use the appropriate unit settings in this chapter. If you've been using the metric measurements for previous exercises, make sure you use the metric settings in the exercises of this chapter; otherwise, your results won't coincide.

1. Choose File ➢ Plot again to open the Plot dialog box. If the Name option in the Printer/Plotter group shows None, click the drop-down arrow and select your current Windows system printer.

2. Click the More Options button; this is the round button with the > symbol in the lower-right corner of the dialog box. You'll see some additional options appear on the right side of the dialog box.

3. If your last printout wasn't oriented on the paper correctly, select the Landscape option in the Drawing Orientation group.

**TIP** The appearance of the print preview depends on the type of output device you chose when you installed AutoCAD or when you last selected a Plotter Device option (described in the section "WYSIWYG Plotting Using Layout Tabs" later in this chapter). The print preview is also affected by other settings in the Plot dialog box, such as those in the Drawing Orientation, Plot Offset, and Plot Area groups. This example shows a typical preview view using the Windows default system printer in landscape mode.

4. In the Plot Scale group, clear the Fit To Paper check box. Then, select ¹⁄₁₆′ = 1′-0″ from the Scale drop-down list. Metric users should select 1:20. As you can see, you have several choices for the scale of your output.

5. In the Paper Size group, select Letter. Metric users should select A4. The options in this drop-down list depend on your Windows system printer or the output device you configured for AutoCAD.

6. In the Plot Area group, select Limits from the drop-down list. This tells AutoCAD to use the limits of your drawing to determine which part of your drawing to plot.

7. Click the Preview button again to get a preview of your plot.

8. Right-click, and choose Plot from the shortcut menu. This time, your printout is to scale.

Here, you were asked to specify a few more settings in the Plot dialog box. Several settings work together to produce a drawing that is to scale and that fits properly on your paper. This is where it pays to understand the relationship between your drawing scale and your paper's size, discussed in Chapter 3. You also saw how you can expand the options in the Plot dialog box.

**TIP**   The next section is lengthy but doesn't contain any exercises. If you prefer to continue with the exercises in this chapter, skip to the section "WYSIWYG Plotting Using Layout Tabs." Be sure to come back and read the following section while the previous exercises are still fresh in your mind.

## Understanding the Plotter Settings

In this section, you'll explore all the settings in the Plot dialog box. These settings give you control over the size and orientation of your image on the paper. They also let you control which part of your drawing gets printed. All these settings work together to give you control over how your drawing fits on your printed output.

**WARNING**   If you're a veteran AutoCAD user, be aware that AutoCAD 2008 relies mainly on the Windows system printer configuration instead of its own plotter drivers. It also remembers printer settings that are specific to AutoCAD so you don't have to adjust your printer settings each time you use AutoCAD. This gives you more flexibility and control over your output. Be aware that you'll need to understand the Windows system printer settings in addition to those offered by AutoCAD.

### Paper Size

You use the option in this group to select the paper size for your output. You can select a paper size from the Paper Size drop-down list. These sizes are derived from the sizes available from your currently selected system printer. You'll find out how to select a different printer later in this chapter.

AutoCAD 2008 offers sheet sizes in both Imperial and metric measurements with a drop-down list located in the Plot Scale group. AutoCAD assumes that if you pick a metric sheet size such as A4 or A5, you'll want the sheet dimensions specified in metric measurements, and it adjusts the dialog box settings accordingly.

### Drawing Orientation

When you used the Preview button in the first exercise in this chapter, you saw your drawing as it would be placed on the paper. In that example, it was placed in a *landscape orientation*, which places the image on the paper so that the width of the paper is greater than its height. You can rotate the image on the paper 90° into what is called a *portrait orientation* by selecting the Portrait radio button in the Drawing Orientation group. A third option, Plot Upside-Down, lets you change the orientation further by turning the landscape or portrait orientation upside down. These three settings let you print the image in any one of four orientations on the sheet.

In AutoCAD, the preview displays the paper in the orientation that it leaves the printer. For most small-format printers, if you're printing in the portrait orientation, the image appears in the same orientation as you see it when you're editing the drawing. If you're using the landscape orientation, the preview image is turned sideways. For large-format plotters, the preview may be oriented in the opposite direction. The graphic in the Drawing Orientation group displays a capital *A* on a sheet showing the orientation of your drawing on the paper output.

**TIP**    Remember that you need to click the More Options button in the lower-right corner of the Plot dialog box to access the Drawing Orientation group. The More Options button looks like a circle with a greater-than sign. You can also press Alt+Shift+>.

## Plot Area

The What To Plot drop-down list in the Plot Area group lets you specify which part of your drawing you want to plot. You may notice some similarities between these settings and the Zoom command options. Each Plot Area option is described next. Most of these options are used only in a Model tab. Typically, when plotting from a Layout tab, you'll use the Layout option.

### LIMITS

The Limits option (available in Model Space only) uses the limits of the drawing to determine the area to print. If you let AutoCAD fit the drawing onto the sheet (by selecting the Fit To Paper check box in the Plot Scale group), the plot displays exactly the same image that you would see on the screen if you selected View ➢ Zoom ➢ All.

### LAYOUT

The Layout option (available in Layout tabs only) replaces the Limits option when you plot from a Layout tab. (See the section "WYSIWYG Plotting Using Layout Tabs" later in this chapter.) This option plots everything displayed within the paper margins shown in the Layout tab view. Typically, this is the only option you'll use when printing from a layout.

### EXTENTS

The Extents option uses the extents of the drawing to determine the area to print. If you let AutoCAD fit the drawing onto the sheet (by selecting the Fit To Paper check box in the Plot Scale group), the plot displays exactly the same image that you would see on the screen if you chose View ➢ Zoom ➢ Extents.

### DISPLAY

Display is the default option; it tells AutoCAD to plot what is currently displayed on the screen. If you let AutoCAD fit the drawing onto the sheet (that is, you select the Fit To Paper check box from the Plot Scale group), the plot is exactly the same as what you see on your screen, adjusted for the width and height proportions of your display.

### VIEW

The View option is available when you've saved a view in the drawing by using the View command. When you select View from the What To Plot drop-down list, another drop-down list appears, offering a list of views available in the drawing. You can then select the view that you want to plot. If you let AutoCAD fit the drawing onto the sheet (by selecting Fit To Paper from the Plot Scale group), the plot displays exactly the same thing that you would see on the screen if you recalled the view you're plotting. Objects that don't appear in the view are clipped in the plotted view.

**TIP**   Do you get a blank printout, even though you selected Extents or Display? Chances are, the Fit To Paper check box isn't selected, or the Inches = Units setting is inappropriate for the sheet size and scale of your drawing. If you don't care about the scale of the drawing, make sure the Fit To Paper option is selected. Otherwise, make sure the Plot Scale settings are set correctly. The next section describes how to set the scale for your plots.

### WINDOW

The Window option enables you to use a window to indicate the area you want to plot. Nothing outside the window prints. To use this option, select it from the drop-down list. The Plot dialog box temporarily closes to allow you to select a window. After you've done this the first time, a Window button appears next to the drop-down list. You can then click the Window button and then indicate a window in the drawing area. If you let AutoCAD fit the drawing onto the sheet by using the Fit To Paper option in the Plot Scale group, the plot displays exactly the same thing that you enclose in the window.

## Plot Scale

In the previous section, the descriptions of several Plot Area options indicate that the Fit To Paper option can be selected. Bear in mind that when you instead apply a scale factor to your plot, it changes the results of the Plot Area settings, and some problems can arise. This is where most new users have difficulty.

For example, the apartment plan drawing fits nicely on the paper when you use Fit To Paper. But if you try to plot the drawing at a scale of 1″ = 1′, you'll probably get a blank piece of paper because, at that scale, hardly any of the drawing fits on your paper. AutoCAD will tell you that it's plotting and then tell you that the plot is finished. You won't have a clue as to why your sheet is blank.

**TIP**   Remember that the Plan1.dwg file was set up for an 18´ × 24´ (A2, or 594 mm × 420 mm for metric users) sheet at a scale of ⅛´ = 1′-0′ (1:10 for metric users). If, when plotting from the Model tab, you select these settings from the Plot dialog box (provided your printer or plotter supports 18´ × 24´, or A2, paper) and you also select Limits for your plot area, your drawing will fit on the paper and will be at the appropriate scale.

If an image is too large to fit on a sheet of paper because of improper scaling, the plot image is placed on the paper differently, depending on whether the plotter uses the center of the image or the lower-left corner for its origin. Keep this in mind as you specify scale factors in this area of the dialog box.

### SCALE

You can select a drawing scale from a set of predefined scales in the Scale drop-down list. These options cover the most common scales you'll need to use.

You've already seen how the Fit To Paper option enables you to avoid giving a scale and forces the drawing to fit on the sheet when plotting from the Model tab. This works fine if you're plotting illustrations that aren't to scale. If you select another option, such as ⅛′ = 1″-0′, the inches and units input boxes change to reflect this scale. The Inches = input box changes to 0.125, and the Units input box changes to 12.

If you're plotting from a layout, you'll use the 1:1 scale option or perhaps a 1:2 scale if you're plotting a half-size drawing. In a layout, the drawing scale is typically set up through the viewport. While plotting from a layout, AutoCAD automatically determines the area to plot based on the printer and sheet size you select. For more information, see "WYSIWYG Plotting Using Layout Tabs" later in this chapter.

### CUSTOM SCALE

In some cases, you may need to set up a nonstandard scale to plot your drawing. If you can't find the scale you want in the Scale drop-down list, you can select Custom from this list and then enter custom values in the Inches = and Units input boxes.

Through these input boxes, you can indicate how the drawing units in your drawing relate to the final plotted distance in inches or millimeters. For example, if your drawing is of a scale factor of 96, follow these steps:

1. Double-click the Inches = input box, enter **1**, and press the Tab key.

2. Double-click the Units input box, enter **96**, and press the Tab key.

   Metric users who want to plot to a scale of 1:10 should enter **1** in the MM input box and **10** in the Units input box.

If you're more used to the Architectural unit style in the Imperial measurement system, you can enter a scale as a fraction. For example, for a ⅛′ scale drawing:

1. Double-click the Inches = input box, enter **⅛**, and press the Tab key.

2. Double-click the Units input box, enter **12**, and press the Tab key.

If you specify a different scale than the one you chose while setting up your drawing, AutoCAD plots your drawing to that scale. You aren't restricted in any way as to scale, but entering the correct scale is important: If it's too large, AutoCAD will think your drawing is too large to fit on the sheet, although it will attempt to plot your drawing anyway. See Chapter 3 for a discussion of unit styles and scale factors.

**TIP**　If you plot to a scale that is different from the scale you originally intended, objects and text appear smaller or larger than is appropriate for your plot. You'll need to edit your text size to match the new scale. You can do so by using the Properties palette. Select the text whose height you want to change, click the Properties tool on the Standard toolbar, and then change the Height setting in the Properties palette.

### ADDING A CUSTOM SCALE TO THE SCALE DROP-DOWN LIST

If you use a custom scale frequently, you may find it annoying to have to input the scale every time you plot. AutoCAD offers the ability to add your custom scale to the Scale drop-down list shown earlier. You can then easily select your custom scale from the list instead of entering it through the text box.

Here are the steps you use to add a custom scale to the Scale drop-down list:

1. Choose Tools ➢ Options to open the Options dialog box.

2. Select the User Preferences tab, and then click the Edit Scale List button at the bottom of the dialog box.

3. In the Edit Scale List dialog box, click the Add button.

4. In the Add Scale dialog box, enter a name for your custom scale in the Name Appearing In Scale List text box, and then enter the appropriate values in the Scale Properties text boxes.

5. Click OK in each dialog box to close it.

There are several options besides Add in the Edit Scale List dialog box. Clicking the Edit button lets you edit an existing scale in the list. Clicking the Move Up and Move Down buttons lets you change the location of an item in the list. Clicking Delete deletes an item or a set of items from the list. Clicking the Reset button restores the list to its default condition and removes any custom items you may have added.

**TIP** Instead of opening the Options dialog box and clicking Edit Scale List on the User Preferences tab, you can enter **Scalelistedit.⏎** at the Command prompt to open the Edit Scale List dialog box directly.

### SCALE LINEWEIGHTS

AutoCAD offers the option to assign lineweights to objects either by their layer assignments or by directly assigning a lineweight to individual objects. The lineweight option, however, doesn't have any meaning until you specify a scale for your drawing. After you specify a scale, the Scale Lineweights option is available. Select this check box if you want the lineweight assigned to layers and objects to appear correctly in your plots. You'll get a closer look at lineweights and plotting later in this chapter.

## Shaded Viewport Options

Most of your plotting will probably involve 2D technical line drawings, but occasionally you may need to plot a shaded or rendered 3D view. You may need to include such 3D views combined with 2D or 3D Wireframe views. AutoCAD offers Shaded Viewport Options that enable you to plot shaded or rendered 3D views of your AutoCAD drawing. These options give you control over the quality of your rendered output. (LT users don't have the Shaded Viewport Options.)

**TIP**   Remember that you need to click the More Options button in the lower-right corner of the Plot dialog box to get to the Shaded Viewport Options group. The More Options button looks like a circle with a greater-than sign. You also need to select a printer name in the Printer/Plotter group before these options are made available.

### SHADE PLOT

The Shade Plot drop-down list lets you control how a Model Space view is plotted. You can choose from the following options:

**As Displayed** plots the Model Space view as it appears on your screen.

**Wireframe** plots the Model Space view of a 3D object as a wireframe view.

**Hidden** plots your Model Space view with hidden lines removed.

**3D Hidden/3D Wireframe/Conceptual/Realistic** plots the Model Space using one of these visual styles. These selections override the current Model Space visual style. See Chapter 20 for more on visual styles.

**Rendered** renders your Model Space view before plotting (see Chapter 22 for more on rendered views).

**Draft/Low/Medium/High/Presentation** sets the quality of the plot.

The Shade Plot options aren't available if you're plotting from a Layout tab. You can control the way each layout viewport is plotted through the viewport's Properties settings. You'll learn more about layout viewport properties later in this chapter.

### QUALITY AND DPI

The Quality drop-down list determines the dots per inch (dpi) setting for your output. These options aren't available if you select Wireframe or Hidden from the Shade Plot drop-down list:

**Draft** plots 3D views as wireframes.

**Preview** offers 150 dpi resolution.

**Normal** offers 300 dpi resolution.

**Presentation** offers 600 dpi resolution.

**Maximum** defers dpi resolution to the current output device's settings.

**Custom** lets you set a custom dpi setting. When Custom is selected, the DPI input box is made available for your input.

**TIP** If some of the terms discussed for the Shaded Viewport Options are unfamiliar, don't be alarmed. You'll learn about 3D Shaded and Rendered views in Part IV of this book. And when you start to explore 3D modeling in AutoCAD, come back and review the Shaded Viewport Options.

## Plot Offset

Sometimes, your first plot of a drawing shows the drawing positioned incorrectly on the paper. You can fine-tune the location of the drawing on the paper by using the Plot Offset settings. To adjust the position of your drawing on the paper, you enter the location of the view origin in relation to the plotter origin in X and Y coordinates (see Figure 8.1).

**FIGURE 8.1**
Adjusting the image location on a sheet

For example, suppose you plot a drawing and then realize that it needs to be moved 1′ to the right and 3′ up on the sheet. You can replot the drawing by making the following changes:

1. Double-click the X input box, type **1**, and press the Tab key.

2. Double-click the Y input box, type **3**, and press the Tab key.

Now, proceed with the rest of the plot configuration. With the preceding settings, the image is shifted on the paper exactly 1′ to the right and 3′ up when the plot is done.

You can also tell AutoCAD the location from which the offset is to occur. The Plot And Publish tab of the Options dialog box (choose Tools ➢ Options from the menu bar) offers the Specify Plot Offset Relative To button group. This group offers two radio buttons: Printable Area and Edge Of Paper. You can select the option that makes the most sense for you.

## Plot Options

The options in the Plot Options group offer a greater amount of control over your output and require some detailed instruction. Here is a brief description of these options. You'll learn more about them in the next section.

### PLOT IN BACKGROUND

If you think your plot will take some time to complete, this option plots your drawing in the background so that after you begin a plot you can immediately return to your drawing work. You can also control this option through the Backgroundplot system variable.

### PLOT OBJECT LINEWEIGHTS

As mentioned earlier, AutoCAD lets you assign lineweights to objects either through their layer assignment or by directly assigning a lineweight to the object. If you use this feature in your drawing, this option lets you turn lineweights on or off in your output.

### PLOT WITH PLOT STYLES

Plot styles give you a high degree of control over your drawing output. You can control whether your output is in color or black and white, and you can control whether filled areas are drawn in a solid color or a pattern. You can even control the way lines are joined at corners. You'll learn more about these options and how they affect your work in the next section.

### PLOT PAPERSPACE LAST

When you're using a Layout tab, otherwise known as Paper Space, this option determines whether objects in Paper Space are drawn before or after objects in Model Space. You'll learn more about Model Space and Paper Space later in this chapter.

### HIDE PAPERSPACE OBJECTS

This option pertains to 3D models in AutoCAD. When you draw in 3D, you see your drawing as a *Wireframe view*. In a Wireframe view, your drawing looks like it's transparent even though it's made up of solid surfaces. Using hidden-line removal, you can view and plot your 3D drawings so that solid surfaces are opaque. To view a 3D drawing in the editor with hidden lines removed, use the Hide command. To plot a 3D drawing with hidden lines removed, use the Hidden option from the Shade Plot drop-down list.

**WARNING**   Hide Paperspace Objects doesn't work for views in the Layout tab viewport described in the next section. Instead, you need to set the viewport's Shade Plot setting to Hidden. (Click the viewport, right-click, and choose Shade Plot ➤ Hidden from the shortcut menu.)

### PLOT STAMP ON

The Plot Stamp feature lets you place pertinent data on the drawing in a location you choose. This data includes the drawing name, date and time, scale, and other data. When you click the Plot Stamp On check box to turn on this option, an additional button appears.

Click this button to gain access to the Plot Stamp dialog box. This dialog box offers many controls over the plot stamp. This is a fairly extensive tool, so rather than fill this chapter with a description of all its features, see Appendix B for a complete rundown of the Plot Stamp options.

### SAVE CHANGES TO LAYOUT

When this option is turned on, the changes you make to Plot dialog box settings are saved with the current layout. You'll learn more about layouts in the next section.

**TIP**    The Plot dialog box has the usual OK, Cancel, and Help buttons at the bottom. You'll also see the Apply To Layout button. This button lets you save the plot settings you make without sending your drawing to the printer or plotter for output. This option is convenient for those times when you decide halfway through your plot setup not to plot your drawing.

## WYSIWYG Plotting Using Layout Tabs

You've probably noticed the tabs at the bottom of the drawing area labeled Model, Layout1, and Layout2. So far, you've done all your work in the Model tab, also known as Model Space. The other two tabs open views to your drawing that are specifically geared toward printing and plotting. The Layout views enable you to control drawing scale, add title blocks, and set up different layer settings from those in the Model tab. You can think of the Layout tabs as page-layout spaces that act like a desktop-publishing program.

You can have as many Layout tabs as you like, each set up for a different type of output. You can, for example, have two or three Layout tabs, each set up for a different scale drawing or with different layer configurations for reflected ceiling plans, floor plans, or equipment plans. You can even set up multiple views of your drawing at different scales in a single Layout tab. In addition, you can draw and add text and dimensions in Layout tabs just as you would in Model Space.

**TIP**    When you create a new file, you see two Layout tabs. If you open a pre–AutoCAD 2000 file, you see only one Layout tab.

To get familiar with the Layout tabs, try the following exercise:

1.  With the Plan file open, click the Layout1 tab at the bottom of the AutoCAD window. A view of your drawing appears on a gray background, as shown in Figure 8.2. This is a view of your drawing as it will appear when plotted on your current default printer or plotter. The white area represents the printer or plotter paper.

**FIGURE 8.2**
A view of the
Layout1 tab

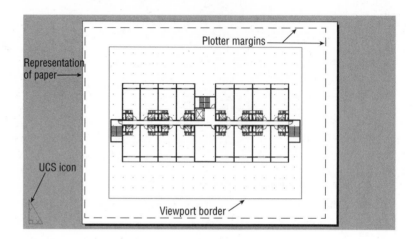

2.  Try zooming in and out using the Zoom Realtime tool. Notice that the entire image zooms in and out, including the area representing the paper.

Layout tabs give you full control over the appearance of your drawing printouts. You can print a Layout tab just as you did the view in the Model tab, by using the Plot option on the Layout1 tab's shortcut menu.

Let's take a moment to look at the elements in the Layout1 tab. As mentioned previously, the white background represents the paper on which your drawing will be printed. The dashed line immediately inside the edge of the white area represents the limits of your printer's margins. Finally, the solid rectangle that surrounds your drawing is the outline of the Layout viewport. A *viewport* is an AutoCAD object that works like a window into your drawing from the Layout tab. Also notice the triangular symbol in the lower-left corner of the view: This is the UCS icon for the Layout tab. It tells you that you're currently in the Layout tab space. You'll see the significance of this icon in the following exercise:

1.  Try selecting part of your drawing by clicking in the lobby area. Nothing is selected.

2.  Click the viewport border, which is the solid rectangle surrounding the drawing, as shown in Figure 8.2. This is the viewport into the Model tab. Notice that you can select it.

3.  Right-click, and choose Properties from the shortcut menu. You can see from the Properties palette that the viewport is just like any other AutoCAD object with layer, linetype, and color assignments. You can even hide the viewport outline by turning off its layer.

4.  Close the Properties palette.

5. With the viewport still selected, click the Erase tool in the Modify toolbar. The view of your drawing disappears with the erasure of the viewport. Remember that the viewport is like a window into the drawing you created in the Model tab. After the viewport is erased, the drawing view goes with it.

6. Type **U↵** or click the Undo button in the Standard toolbar to restore the viewport.

**NOTE**   You can create new viewports using the Vports command (View ➢ Viewports ➢ New Viewports). See "Creating New Paper Space Viewports" in Chapter 16 for more information.

7. Double-click anywhere within the viewport's boundary. Notice that the UCS icon you're used to seeing appears in the lower-left corner of the viewport. The Layout UCS icon disappears.

8. Click the lobby of your drawing. You can now select parts of your drawing.

9. Try zooming and panning your view. Changes in your view take place only within the boundary of the viewport.

10. Choose View ➢ Zoom ➢ All, or type **Z↵A↵** to display the entire drawing in the viewport.

11. To return to Paper Space, double-click an area outside the viewport.

**TIP**   You can also type **PS↵** to return to Paper Space or **MS↵** to access the space within the viewport. Or, click the Paper/Model button in the status bar at the bottom of the AutoCAD window.

This exercise shows you the unique characteristics of the Layout tab. The objects in the viewport are inaccessible until you double-click the interior of the viewport. You can then move about and edit your drawing in the viewport, just as you would while in the Model tab.

The Layout tabs can contain as many viewports as you like, and each viewport can hold a different view of your drawing. You can size and arrange each viewport any way you like, or you can create multiple viewports, giving you the freedom to lay out your drawing as you would a page in a desktop-publishing program. You can also draw in the Layout tab or import Xrefs and blocks for title blocks and borders.

## Plot Scale in the Layout Tab Viewports

In the first part of this chapter, you plotted your drawing from the Model tab. You learned that to get the plot to fit on your paper, you had to either use the Fit To Paper option in the Plot dialog box or indicate a specific drawing scale, plot area, and drawing orientation.

The Layout tab works in a different way: It's designed to enable you to plot your drawing at a 1-to-1 scale. Instead of specifying the drawing scale in the Plot dialog box, as you did when you plotted from the Model tab, you let the size of your view in the Layout tab viewport determine the drawing scale. You can set the viewport view to an exact scale by making changes to the properties of the viewport.

To set the scale of a viewport in a Layout tab, try the following exercise:

1. Press the Esc key to clear any selections. Then, select the viewport border, right-click, and choose Properties from the shortcut menu. The Properties palette for the viewport appears.

2. Scroll down the Properties palette by using the scroll bar on the left side, and locate the Standard Scale option under the Misc category. Click this option. The item to its right turns into a list box.

3. Open the list box, and select ¹⁄₁₆′ = 1″ (metric users should select 1:20). The view in the drawing window changes to reflect the new scale for the viewport. Now most of the drawing fits into the viewport, and it's to scale.

**TIP**  The scale of ¹⁄₁₆′ = 1′ is similar to the metric 1:200 scale, but because you used centimeters instead of millimeters as the base unit for the metric version of the Plan file, you drop the second 0 in 200. The metric scale becomes 1:20.

4. Close the Properties palette.

5. Use the viewport grips to enlarge the viewport enough to display all of the drawing, as shown in Figure 8.3. You need to move only a single corner grip. As you move a corner grip, notice that the viewport maintains a rectangular shape.

**FIGURE 8.3**
The enlarged viewport

6. Choose File ➢ Plot, and, in the Plot dialog box, make sure the Scale option is set to 1:1 and your system printer is selected in the Printer/Plotter group; then, click OK. Your drawing is plotted as it appears in the Layout tab, and it's plotted to scale.

7. After reviewing your plot, close the drawing without saving it.

In step 2, you saw that you can select a scale for a viewport by selecting it from the Properties palette. If you look just below the Standard Scale option, you see the Custom Scale option. Both options work like their counterpart, the Plot Scale group, in the Plot dialog box.

**TIP** Veteran AutoCAD users can still choose View ➢ Zoom ➢ Scale to control the scale of the viewport view.

Layout tabs and viewports work in conjunction with your plotter settings to give you a better idea of how your plots will look. There are numerous plotter settings that can dramatically change the appearance of your Layout tab view and your plots. In the next section, you'll learn how some of the plotter settings can enhance the appearance of your drawings. You'll also learn how Layout tabs can display those settings, letting you see on your computer screen exactly what will appear on your paper output.

## Adding an Output Device

This chapter mentioned that you can set up AutoCAD for more than one output device. You can do this even if you have only one printer or plotter connected to your computer. You might want multiple printer configurations in AutoCAD for many reasons. You might want to set up your system so that you can print to a remote location over a network or the Internet. Some printer configurations are strictly file oriented, such as the AutoCAD .dwf format for Internet web pages or raster file output. (See Chapter 27 for more on .dwf files.)

AutoCAD works best with printers and plotters configured as Windows system devices. Although you can add devices through the AutoCAD Plot Manager, Autodesk recommends that you set up your plotters and printers as Windows devices and then use the System Printer option in AutoCAD to select your output device. (In Windows XP, choose Start ➢ Control Panel ➢ Printers And Other Hardware ➢ Add A Printer to configure a new printer.) You can use the Add-A-Plotter Wizard to create predefined settings for your system printer so that you can quickly choose a printer or plotter setup.

You can also configure additional printers through the AutoCAD Plot Manager; this method also uses the Add-A-Plotter Wizard. Here's how it's done:

1. Choose File ➢ Plotter Manager to open the Plotters window. Your view of the Plotters window may look a little different depending on your operating system, but the same basic information is there.

You can also open this window by clicking the Add Or Configure Plotters button in the Plot And Publish tab of the Options dialog box. It's just an Explorer window showing you the contents of the `Plotters` folder under the `Documents and Settings` folder for your Windows user profile.

2. Double-click the Add-A-Plotter Wizard icon to open the Add Plotter dialog box. You see the Introduction screen, which describes the purpose of the wizard.

3. Click Next. The next screen of the wizard lets you select the type of setup you want. You're offered three options: My Computer, Network Plotter Server, and System Printer. The My Computer and the Network Plotter Server options offer plotter options based on AutoCAD-specific drivers. The main difference between these two options is that the Network Plotter option asks you for a network server name. Otherwise, they both offer the same set of options. The System Printer option uses the existing Windows system printer as the basis for the setup.

4. If you click the My Computer radio button and then click Next, you see a listing of plotter models that are supported by AutoCAD directly through AutoCAD's own drivers. If you use a PostScript device, or if you want to convert drawings to raster formats, this is the place to select those options. You can select the plotter or printer manufacturer name from the Manufacturers list on the left and then select a specific model from the list on the right. If you have a driver for a specific plotter or printer that isn't listed, you can click the Have Disk button to browse to your driver location.

5. After you've made a printer or plotter selection, click Next. You're then asked if you want to use an existing PCP or PC2 configuration file for the selected plotter. PCP and PC2 configurations files are plotter configuration files from earlier releases of AutoCAD.

6. Unless you plan to use one of those files, click Next on the Import PCP Or PC2 screen. If you selected My Computer in step 4, the Ports screen opens. With the Plot To A Port option selected, you can select a port from a list to which your printer or plotter is connected. The Configure Port button lets you set up the port if you have a specific requirement for the port. Or, if you intend to plot to a file instead of to a port, you can select the Plot To File radio button at the top. An AutoSpool option is also offered if your printer requires this feature.

If you selected an option in step 4 that doesn't require a port setup, click the Next button to skip this option; the Plotter Name screen opens. You can enter a descriptive name in the Plotter Name text box. This name will appear in the Printer Name drop-down list of the Plot Or Page Setup dialog box.

**7.** Enter a name for this configuration in the space provided; then, click Next to open the Finish screen.

**8.** This screen gives you the option to make adjustments to the configuration you've just created by clicking the Edit Plotter Configuration button. Click Finish to exit the Add-a-Plotter Wizard. Your new configuration appears in the Plotters window.

This editor lets you fine-tune your plotter settings. For example, you can calibrate your plotter for more accurate scaling of your plots; or, if you're creating a raster file output configuration, you can create a custom page setting for extremely high-resolution raster images.

After you've set up a plotter, the plotter information is stored as a file with the `.pc3` filename extension in the `Plotters` subfolder under the `Documents and Settings` folder for your Windows user profile.

---

**CONTROLLING THE APPEARANCE OF THE LAYOUT TABS**

The Options dialog box offers a set of controls dedicated to the Layout tabs. If you don't like some of the graphics in the Layout tab, you can turn them off. Open the Options dialog box, and click the Display tab to see a set of options in the Layout Elements group.

As you can see, you can control the display of the tabs themselves, the margins, the paper background, and the paper shadow. In addition, you can specify whether AutoCAD automatically creates a viewport or opens the Page Setup dialog box when you open a Layout tab for the first time.

---

## Editing a Plotter Configuration

In step 8 of the previous exercise, you exited the Add-a-Plotter Wizard without editing the newly created plotter configuration. You can always go back and edit the configuration by opening the Plotters window (choose File ➢ Plotter Manager) and double-clicking the configuration you want to edit. You can recognize a plotter configuration file by its `.pc3` filename extension.

Many users use their Windows system printer or plotter for other applications besides AutoCAD, and frequently the AutoCAD settings for that printer are different from the settings used for other applications. You can set up AutoCAD to automatically use its own settings so you don't have to reconfigure your Windows system printer every time you switch applications. To do so, follow these steps:

1. Choose File ➢ Page Setup Manager to open the Page Setup Manager dialog box.

2. Click the Modify button to open the Page Setup dialog box.

3. Select the printer that you want to configure in the Name drop-down list of the Printer/ Plotter group.

4. Click the Properties button just to the right of the drop-down list to open the Plotter Configuration Editor dialog box. A list box displays all the properties of the printer or plotter. Not all these properties are editable, however. Each time you click a property in the list box, the lower half of the dialog box displays the options associated with that property.

5. Click the Custom Properties item in the list box. The lower half of the dialog box displays the Custom Properties button.

6. Click the Custom Properties button. You'll see the Windows system printer options. These are the same options you see when you edit the properties of your printer by choosing Start ➢ Printers And Faxes or Start ➢ Control Panel ➢ Printers And Other Hardware.

7. Adjust these settings the way you want them when you plot from AutoCAD, and click OK.

8. Back in the Plotter Configuration Editor dialog box, click the Save As button. A standard file dialog box appears.

9. Enter the name of the plot configuration you've set up, or accept the default name, which is usually the name of the Windows printer or plotter, and click Save.

10. Click OK in the Plotter Configuration Editor dialog box; then, click OK in the Page Setup dialog box.

The Plotter Configuration Editor offers a wide variety of options that are fairly technical in nature. If you want to know more about the Plotter Configuration Editor, see Appendix B.

---

**PLOTTING IMAGE FILES AND CONVERTING 3D TO 2D**

If your work involves producing manuals, reports, or similar documents, you may want to add the Raster File Export option to your list of plotter configurations. The Raster File Export option lets you plot your drawings to a wide range of raster file formats including CALS, JPEG, PCX, Targa, Tiff, and BMP. You can then import your drawings into documents that accept bitmap images. Images can be up to 8,000 × 8,000 pixels (set through the Plotter Configuration Editor) and can contain as many colors as the file format allows. If you need several raster formats, you can use multiple instances of this or any plotter configuration.

To convert your 3D wireframe models into 2D line drawings, use the Flatshot tool described in Chapter 20. You can then include your 2D line drawings with other 2D drawing for plotting and printing.

---

## Storing a Page Setup

Unlike most other programs, AutoCAD offers hundreds of page setup options. It can be quite a chore to keep track of and maintain all these options. But as you settle into using AutoCAD, you'll probably find that you'll set up a few plotter configurations and stick to them. AutoCAD 2008 lets you save a page setup under a name to help you store and manage the settings you use most.

You've already seen the Page Setup Manager dialog box on your way to preparing a page for printing. In this section, you'll take a closer look at this useful tool.

Follow these steps to create a page setup.

1. In AutoCAD, choose File ➢ Page Setup Manager. You can also right-click a Layout tab and choose Page Setup Manager. The Page Setup Manager dialog box opens. So far, you've used only the Modify option in this dialog box to modify an existing page setup. Now you'll try creating a new setup.

2. Click the New button to open the New Page Setup dialog box.

3. To create a new page setup, first enter a name in the New Page Setup Name input box, and select a setup from the Start With list box. AutoCAD will use the setup you select as the basis for the new setup. Notice that AutoCAD offers the name Setup1 as a default name for a new setup.

4. Click OK when you're finished. AutoCAD opens the Page Setup dialog box, where you can choose the settings for your new page setup.

5. Click OK to return to the Page Setup Manager. Your new page setup is listed in the Current Page Setup list box. From here, you can select a page setup from the list box and then click the Set Current button to make it the current page setup for the layout.

You can also import other user-defined page setups by clicking the Import button. Because page setups are stored in the drawing, the Import button opens a standard file dialog box that displays drawing files. You can then select a file from which you want to import a page setup.

The current page setup applies to the current Layout tab; but after you create a new page setup, it's offered as an option in the Page Setup Manager dialog box for all other Layout tabs. You can also select a page setup directly from the Plot dialog box by using the Name drop-down list in the Page Setup group.

Page setups can be used with the Publish feature described in Chapter 27 to set up batch plots, or in the Sheet Set feature to quickly setup sheet layouts. If you decide that you want to create an entirely new page setup while in the Page Setup dialog box, you can click the Add button. This opens a simple dialog box that enables you to enter a name for your new setup. After you enter a new name and click OK, you can proceed to set up your page settings. Then, click OK again, and the setup will be saved under the new name.

## Plotter and Printer Hardware Considerations

Positioning an AutoCAD drawing on the printer output is something of an art. Before you face a deadline with hundreds of plots to produce, you may want to create some test plots and carefully refine your plotter settings so that you have AutoCAD set up properly for those rush jobs.

Part of the setup process is to understand how your particular printer or plotter works. Each device has its own special characteristics, so a detailed description of printer hardware setup is beyond the scope of this section. However, here are a few guidelines that will make the process easier.

## UNDERSTANDING THE PLOT AND PUBLISH TAB IN THE OPTIONS DIALOG BOX

I mentioned the Plot And Publish tab in the Options dialog box earlier in this chapter. This tab contains several options related to plotting that can be useful. Here's a summary of those options and their purposes.

### DEFAULT PLOT SETTINGS FOR NEW DRAWINGS

The settings in this group let you control the default plot settings for new drawings and for drawings from earlier versions of AutoCAD that are opened for the first time in AutoCAD 2008. The Use As Default Output Device radio button and drop-down list let you select the default plotter or printer to be used with new drawings. When selected, the Use Last Successful Plot Settings radio button uses the last successful plotter settings for subsequent plots. This is how earlier versions of AutoCAD worked. The Add Or Configure Plotters button opens the Plotters window. This is the same as choosing Files ➢ Plot Manager from the AutoCAD menu bar. From the Plotters window, you can launch the Add-A-Plotter Wizard to add new plotter configurations. You can also edit existing plotter configurations.

### GENERAL PLOT OPTIONS

These options control some of the general plotter parameters. The Keep The Layout Paper Size If Possible radio button causes AutoCAD to attempt to plot to the paper size specified in the Plot dialog box, regardless of the paper size in the plotter. If the specified size is larger than the capacity of the plotter, a warning message is displayed. The Use The Plot Device Paper Size option causes AutoCAD to use the paper size specified by the system printer or the PC3 plot configuration file currently in use. Both settings are also controlled by the Paperupdate system variable.

The System Printer Spool Alert drop-down list offers control over printer-spooling alert messages. The OLE Plot Quality drop-down list lets you control the quality of OLE objects embedded in or linked to a drawing. This setting can also be controlled through the Olequality system variable.

When the Use OLE Application When Plotting OLE Objects check box is selected, AutoCAD launches any application that is associated with an OLE object embedded or linked to the AutoCAD drawing that is currently being plotted. This helps improve the plot quality of OLE objects. You can also set this option through the Olestartup system variable.

The Hide System Printers option affects the Printer/Plotter group's Name drop-down list in the Plot and Page Setup dialog boxes. With this option turned on, you see only printers that have a .pc3 file associated with them. These include printers that have been set up using the Add-A-Plotter Wizard discussed earlier in this chapter.

### PLOT TO FILE

You have the option to plot to a file that can be downloaded to your printer or plotter at a later date. The Plot To File group lets you specify the default destination for the plot files.

### PLOT AND PUBLISH LOG FILE

You can maintain a plot log file that records information about each plot you make. This can be helpful when you must keep records of hard-copy output for billing purposes. The location of the plot and publishing log file can be specified in the Files tab of the Options dialog box under the Plot And Publishing Log File Location listing. The log file has a .csv filename extension.

### BACKGROUND PROCESSING OPTIONS

AutoCAD performs background plots so that after you begin a plot you can immediately return to your drawing work instead of waiting for the plot to be completed. The options in this group let you turn on this feature either for standard plotting or for the Publish feature discussed in Chapter 27. You can also control this option through the Backgroundplot system variable.

### PLOT STAMP SETTINGS

This button opens the Plot Stamp dialog box, which you saw earlier in the "Plot Options" section of this chapter. The Plot Stamp dialog box lets you determine what information is displayed in a plot stamp, which is a label placed on the print of a drawing to provide information about the source file.

### PLOT STYLE TABLE SETTINGS

When you click this button, the Plot Style Table Settings dialog box opens. This dialog box controls the type of plot styles used in AutoCAD. In the case of named plot styles, you can also select a default plot style for Layer 0 and a default plot style for objects. Note that the Use Color Dependent Plot Styles and Use Named Plot Styles radio buttons don't have an effect on the current drawing; they affect only new drawings and pre–AutoCAD 2000 drawings being opened for the first time. The Default Plot Style Table drop-down list lets you select a default plot style table for new and pre–AutoCAD 2000 drawings. These settings are also controlled by the Pstylepolicy system variable.

The Add Or Edit Plot Style Tables button opens the Plot Styles dialog box. From there, you can double-click an existing plot style table file or start the Add-A-Plot Style Table Wizard to create a new plot style.

### SPECIFY PLOT OFFSET RELATIVE TO

Here you can determine whether the plot offset is set in relation to the printable area of your printer or the edge of the paper. The printable area is determined by the printer margin.

## Understanding Your Plotter's Limits

If you're familiar with a word-processing or desktop-publishing program, you know that you can set the margins of a page, thereby telling the program exactly how far from each edge of the paper you want the text to appear. With AutoCAD, you don't have that luxury. To accurately place a plot on your paper, you must know the plotter's hard clip limits. The *hard clip limits* are like built-in margins, beyond which the plotter won't plot. These limits vary from plotter to plotter (see Figure 8.4).

**FIGURE 8.4**
The hard clip limits of a plotter

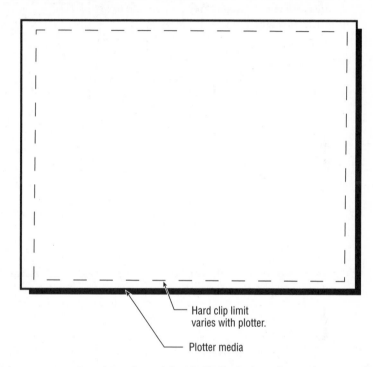

Hard clip limit
varies with plotter.

Plotter media

It's crucial that you know your printer's or plotter's hard clip limits in order to place your drawings accurately on the sheet. Take some time to study your plotter manual and find out exactly what these limits are. Then, make a record of them and store it somewhere, in case you or someone else needs to format a sheet in a special way.

Hard clip limits for printers often depend on the software that drives them. You may need to consult your printer manual or use the trial-and-error method of plotting several samples to see how they come out.

After you've established the limits of your plotter or printer, you'll be better equipped to fit your drawing in those limits. You can then establish some standard drawing limits based on your plotter's limits. You'll also need to know the dimensions of those hard clip limits to define custom sheet sizes. Although AutoCAD offers standard sheet sizes in the Paper Size button group of the Page Setup and Plot dialog boxes, these sizes don't take into account the hard clip limits.

## Knowing Your Plotter's Origins

Another important consideration is the location of your plotter's origin. For example, on some plotters, the lower-left corner of the plot area is used as the origin. Other plotters use the center of the plot area as the origin. When you plot a drawing that is too large to fit the sheet on a plotter that uses a corner for the origin, the image is pushed toward the top and to the right of the sheet (see Figure 8.5). When you plot a drawing that is too large to fit on a plotter that uses the center of the paper as the origin, the image is pushed outward in all directions from the center of the sheet.

**FIGURE 8.5**
Plotting an oversized image on a plotter that uses the lower-left corner for its origin

Plot orgin        Clipped portion of drawing

In each situation, the origin determines a point of reference from which you can relate your drawing in the computer to the physical output. After you understand this, you're better equipped to accurately place your electronic drawing on the physical medium.

---

### USING BATCH AND ELECTRONIC PLOTS

The focus of this chapter so far has been printer or plotter hard-copy output. But a major part of your work will involve the transmission of electronic versions of your documents. More than ever, architects and engineers are using the Internet to exchange documents of all types, so AutoCAD offers several tools to make the process easier.

I've mentioned that you can control some of your output settings thorough the Plot And Publish tab of the Options dialog box. The Publish features includes items that enable you to "print" your drawings as a file that can be e-mailed to clients and consultants or posted on an FTP site or website. The Publish features let you create a single file that contains multiple pages so you can combine several drawing sheets into one file.

The Publish feature also enables you to plot several drawings at once without having to load and print each one individually. This can be helpful when you've finished a set of drawings and want to plot them during a break or overnight. Chapter 27 gives you a detailed look at the Publish feature.

# The Bottom Line

**Understanding the Plotter Settings**    Unlike other types of documents, AutoCAD drawings can end up on nearly any size sheet of paper. To accommodate the range of paper sizes, the AutoCAD plotter settings are fairly extensive and give you a high level of control over your output.

**Master It**    Name a few of the settings available in the Plot dialog box.

**Solution**    Paper size, plot area, plot scale and printer/plotter name are a few of the settings available in the Plot dialog box.

**WYSIWYG Plotting Using Layout Tabs**    The layout tabs in AutoCAD offer a way to let you set up the way a drawing will be plotted. You can think of the layout tabs as a kind of paste up area for your drawings.

**Master It**    Name some of the items that you see in a layout tab.

**Solution**    The layout tab shows the paper orientation, plotter margins, and the location of your drawing on the final plotted output.

**Adding an Output Device**    Typically, AutoCAD will use the Windows system printer as an output device, but often you will find that the printer you use is a dedicated plotter that is not connected to Windows in the usual way. AutoCAD lets you add custom plotter and prints through the Add-A-Plotter wizard.

**Master It**    How do you start the Add-A-Plotter wizard?

**Solution**    Choose File ➤ Plotter Manager, double-click the Add-A-Plotter Wizard application in the Plotters window.

**Storing a Page Setup**    Most of the time, you will use the same set of plotter settings for your drawings. You can save plotter settings using the Page Setup feature.

**Master It**    Describe a way to create a page setup. Describe how to retrieve a setup.

**Solution**    Choose File ➤ Page Setup Manager then click New at the Page Setup Manager dialog box. Enter a name for your page setup in the New Page Setup dialog box, then click OK. You can retrieve a page setup by selecting it from the Page Setup drop-down list in the Plot dialog box.

# Chapter 9

# Understanding Plot Styles

To gain full control over the appearance of your output, you'll want to know about plot style tables. By using *plot style tables*, you can control how colors are translated into plotted lineweights and how area fills are converted into shades of gray or screened colors in your printer or plotter output. You can also control other aspects of how the plotter draws each object in a drawing.

If you don't use plot style tables, your plotter will produce output as close as possible to what you see in the drawing editor, including colors. With plot style tables, you can force all the colors to print as black, or you can also assign a fill pattern or a screen to a color. This can be useful for charts and maps that require area fills of different gradations. You can create multiple plot style tables to produce plots that fit the exact requirements of your project.

This chapter will show you firsthand how you can use plot style tables to enhance your plotter output. You'll look at how to adjust the lineweight of the walls in the Plan file and make color changes to your plotter output. Topics in this chapter include:

- ◆ Choosing between Color-Dependent and Named Plot Style Tables
- ◆ Creating a Color Plot Style Table
- ◆ Editing and Using Plot Style Tables
- ◆ Assigning Named Plot Styles Directly to Layers and Objects

## Choosing between Color-Dependent and Named Plot Style Tables

You can think of a plot style as a virtual pen that has the attributes of color, width, shape, and screen percentage. A typical drawing may use several different line widths, so you use a different plot style for each line width. Multiple plot styles are collected into *plot style tables* that allow you to control a set of plot styles from one dialog box.

AutoCAD offers two types of plot style tables: color and named. *Color plot style tables* enable you to assign plot styles to the individual AutoCAD colors. For example, you can assign a plot style with a 0.50 mm width to the color red so that anything that is red in your drawing is plotted with a line width of 0.50 mm. You can, in addition, set the plot style's color to black so that everything that is red in your drawing is plotted in black.

*Named plot style tables* let you assign plot styles directly to objects in your drawing, instead of assigning a plot style in a more general way through a color. Named plot style tables also enable you to assign plot styles directly to layers. For example, with named plot styles, you can assign a plot style that is black and has a 0.50 mm width to a single circle or line in a drawing, regardless of its color.

Named plot styles are more flexible than color plot styles; but if you already have a library of AutoCAD drawings set up for a specific set of plotter settings, the color plot styles are a better choice when you're opening files that were created in AutoCAD R14 and earlier. This is because color plot styles are more similar to the older method of assigning AutoCAD colors to plotter pens. You may also want to use color plot style tables with files that you intend to share with an individual or office that is still using earlier versions of AutoCAD.

The type of plot style table assigned to a new drawing depends on the settings in the Plot Style Table Settings dialog box, which you access through the Plot And Publish tab of the Options dialog.

**TIP**  You can change the type of plot style table assigned to a drawing. See the sidebar "Converting a Drawing from Color Plot Styles to Named Plot Styles," later in this chapter, for more information on plot style conversions.

Here's how to set up the plot style type for new files:

1. Open the Options dialog box, and click the Plot And Publish tab.

2. Click the Plot Style Table Settings button to open the Plot Style Table Settings dialog box.

3. In the Default Plot Style Behavior For New Drawings button group, click the Use Color Dependent Plot Styles radio button. In a later exercise, you'll use the Use Named Plot Styles option.

4. Click OK. Then, click OK again in the Options dialog box to return to the drawing.

After you've set up AutoCAD for color plot style tables, any new drawings you create are allowed to use only color plot style tables. You can change this setting at any time for new files, but after a file is saved, the type of plot style that is current when the file is created is the only type of plot style available to that file. If you need to change a color plot style to a named plot style drawing, see the sidebar "Converting a Drawing from Color Plot Styles to Named Plot Styles," later in this chapter.

Next, you'll set up a custom color plot style table. Plot style tables are stored as files with the .ctb or .stb filename extension. The table filenames that end with .ctb are color plot style tables. The table filenames that end with .stb are named plot style tables.

**TIP** You can also select between color and named plot styles when selecting a new drawing template. When you choose File ➢ New, you'll see that many of the template files in the Select Template dialog box have "Color Dependent Plot Styles" or "Named Plot Styles" as part of their name. If you have AutoCAD set up to use the Startup dialog box, you'll see the color and named plot style template files when you select the Use A Template option from the Create New Drawing dialog box.

## Creating a Color Plot Style Table

You can have several plot style table files on hand to quickly apply plot styles to any given plot or Layout tab. You can set up each plot style table to create a different look for your drawing. These files are stored in the `Plot Styles` folder of the `C:\Documents and Settings\`*Username*`\ Application Data\Autodesk\AutoCAD 2008\R17.1\enu\` folder. Follow these steps to create a new plot style table. You'll use an existing file that was created in Release 14 an example to demonstrate the plot style features:

**TIP** If you change your mind about a selection you make while using a wizard, you can move forward or backward by clicking the Next and Back buttons.

1. Open the sample file called `Plan-color`.dwg; then, click the Layout1 tab.

2. Right-click the Layout tab, and select Page Setup Manager. In the Page Setup Manager dialog box, click Modify.

3. The Page Setup dialog box is similar to the Plot dialog box. The main difference is that the Page Setup dialog box doesn't have the Apply To Layout button at the bottom.

**4.** In the Plot Style Table (Pen Assignments) group at upper right, open the drop-down list and select New to start the Add Color-Dependent Plot Style Table Wizard.

**5.** Click the Start From Scratch radio button, and then click Next. The next screen of the wizard asks for a filename.

**6.** Enter **Mystyle** for the filename, and click Next. The next screen of the wizard lets you edit your plot style and assign the plot style to your current, new, or old drawings. You'll learn about editing plot styles a bit later.

**7.** Click Finish to return to the Page Setup dialog box.

With the Add Color-Dependent Plot Style Table Wizard, you can create a new plot style table from scratch, or you can create one based on an AutoCAD R14 CFG, PCP, or PC2 file. You can also access the Add Color-Dependent Plot Style Table Wizard by choosing File ➢ Plot Style Manager and then double-clicking the Add-A-Plot Style Table Wizard icon.

The steps shown here are the same whether your drawing is set up for color plot styles or named plot styles.

## Editing and Using Plot Style Tables

You now have your own plot style table. In this exercise, you'll edit the plot style and see firsthand how plot styles affect your drawing:

**1.** In the Page Setup dialog box, the filename `Mystyle.ctb` should appear in the drop-down list of the Plot Style Table (Pen Assignments) group. If it doesn't, open the drop-down list to select it.

**2.** Click the Edit button to open the Plot Style Table Editor. The Edit button is the one just to the right of the Plot Style Table drop-down list. Click the Form View tab, which is shown at the top of Figure 9.1.

**TIP**    You can also open and edit existing plot style tables by choosing File ➢ Plot Style Manager to open the Plot Styles dialog box. You can then double-click the plot style you want to edit. A third option is to double-click the `Plot Style Table` file in `C:\Documents and Settings\`*Username*`\Application Data\Autodesk\AutoCAD 2008\R17.1\enu\Plot Styles`.

**FIGURE 9.1**

The Plot Style Table Editor dialog box, open at the Form View tab

The Plot Style Table Editor dialog box has three tabs that give you control over how each color in AutoCAD is plotted. The Form View tab lets you select a color from a list box and then set the properties of that color by using the options on the right side of the tab.

**TIP**   The Table View tab displays each color as a column of properties. Each column is called a plot style. The property names are listed in a column to the far left. Although the layout is different, both the Table View tab and the Form View tab offer the same functions.

Next, you'll continue by changing the line width property of the Color 3 (green) plot style. Remember that green is the color assigned to the Wall layer of your Plan drawing.

1. Click Color 3 in the Plot Styles list box.

2. Click the Lineweight drop-down list, and select 0.5000 mm.

3. Click Save & Close to return to the Page Setup dialog box.

4. Click the Display Plot Styles check box in the Plot Style Table (Pen Assignments) group. Then, click OK to close the Page Setup dialog box, and click Close to close the Page Setup Manager dialog box.

5. Zoom in to the plan to enlarge the view of a unit bathroom and entrance, as shown in Figure 9.2.

**FIGURE 9.2**
Adjust your view to look like this.

## Making Your Plot Styles Visible

You won't see any changes in your drawing yet. You need to make one more change to your drawing options:

1. Choose Format ➢ Lineweight to open the Lineweight Settings dialog box. The Lineweight Settings dialog box lets you control the appearances of lineweights in the drawing. If lineweights aren't showing up, this is the place to look to make them viewable. You can find out more about the Lineweight Settings dialog box in Chapter 16.

**TIP**    You can also click the User Preferences tab in the Options dialog box and then click the Line-weight Settings button to open the Lineweight Settings dialog box.

2. Click the Display Lineweight check box to turn on this option.

3. Just below the Display Lineweight option, click the Default drop-down list, and select 0.09 mm. This makes any unassigned or default lineweight a very fine line.

4. Click Apply & Close. The layout displays the drawing with the lineweight assignments you set up earlier (see Figure 9.3).

**FIGURE 9.3**
The drawing with new lineweight assignments

**WARNING**    If your view doesn't reflect the Plot Style settings, make sure you have the Display Plot Styles option selected in the Plot Style Table (Pen Assignments) group of the Page Setup dialog box.

## Making Changes to Multiple Plot Styles

Chances are, you'll want to plot your drawing in black and white for most of your work. You can edit your color plot style table to plot one or all of your AutoCAD colors as black instead of the AutoCAD colors.

You saw how you can open the Plot Style Table Editor from the Page Setup dialog box to edit your color plot style table. In this exercise, you'll try a different route:

1. Choose File ➤ Plot Style Manager to open the Plot Styles window. This is a view to the Plot Styles folder under the C:\Documents and Settings\*Username*\Application Data\ Autodesk\AutoCAD 2008\R17.1 \enu\ folder.

2. Locate the file Mystyle.ctb, and double-click it to open the Plot Style Table Editor dialog box.

3. Click the Form View tab.

4. Click Color 3 in the Plot Styles list box.

**5.** Click the Color drop-down list, and select Black.

**6.** Click Save & Close; then, close the Plot Styles window.

**7.** Choose View ➤ Regen All to view your drawing. The green objects appear black in the Layout tab.

**8.** Click the Model tab to view your drawing in Model Space. The objects are still their original colors. This shows that you haven't changed the colors of your objects or layers—you've only changed the color of the plotted output.

Next, try changing all the output colors to black:

**1.** Repeat steps 1 and 2 of the previous exercise to open the `Mystyle.ctb` file.

**2.** Click the Form View tab; then, click Color 1 in the Plot Styles list box.

**3.** Shift+click Color 9 in the Plot Styles list box to select all the plot styles from Color 1 to Color 9.

**4.** Click the Color drop-down list, and select Black.

**5.** Click Save & Close, and close the Plot Styles window.

**6.** Click the Layout1 tab, and then choose View ➤ Regen All. All the colors have changed to black.

Now, when you plot your drawing, you'll get a plot that is composed entirely of black lines.

These exercises have shown that the Plot Style Table Editor lets you set the color of your printed output to be different from the colors you see in Model Space. In the exercises, you set the pen colors to black, but if you look down the Color drop-down list, you'll see that you can choose from any number of colors. The Select Color option in the Color drop-down list lets you select colors from the Select Color dialog box.

**NOTE** To see the view shown here, make sure the True Color tab is selected and the HSL option is selected in the Color Model drop-down list. LT users won't see a Color Books tab.

In Chapter 5, you were introduced to the Select Color dialog box in the context of selecting colors for layers. Here, you can use it to assign colors to plot styles. The same three tabs are available: Index Color, True Color, and Color Books. (LT users won't see the Color Books tab.) The Index Color tab lets you select from the standard AutoCAD 255 index colors. The True Color tab lets you choose virtually any color you want. The Color Books tab lets you use PANTONE colors.

## Setting Up Line Corner Styles

You may notice that the corners of the wall lines appear to be rounded, as shown in Figure 9.4, instead of crisp and sharp.

**FIGURE 9.4**
The corners of thick lines may appear rounded.

You can adjust the way AutoCAD draws these corners at plot time through the Plot Style Table Editor:

1. Open the `Mystyle.ctb` plot style table, as you did in the previous exercise.

2. Click the Form View tab, and then click Color 3 in the Plot Styles list box.

**3.** Click the Line End Style drop-down list, and select Square.

**4.** Click Save & Close; then, click OK to close the Page Setup dialog box.

**5.** Choose View ➤ Regen All to view your changes. Now the corners meet in a sharp angle, as shown in Figure 9.5.

**FIGURE 9.5**
The Line End Style setting can alter the way corners are drawn.

**NOTE** The Line Join Style setting can have an adverse affect on AutoCAD fonts. If text appears distorted, check to see whether it's on a layer that uses a line join style other than the default Use Object End Style setting.

The Square option in the Line End Style drop-down list extends the endpoints of contiguous lines so that their corners meet in a clean corner instead of a notch. The Line Join Style drop-down list offers a similar set of settings for polylines. For example, you can round polyline corners by using the Round option in the Line Join Style drop-down list.

## Setting Up Screen Values for Solid Areas

The last option you'll look at is how to change a color into a screened area. Frequently, you'll want to add a gray or colored background to an area of your drawing to emphasize that area graphically, as in a focus area in a map, or to designate functions in a floor plan. The settings you're about to use enable you to create shaded backgrounds:

1. Open the Page Setup Manager, and click Modify to open the Page Setup dialog box again. Then, open the Plot Style Table Editor.

2. Select Color 3 from the Plot Styles list box.

3. In the Screening list box, click the number 100 to select it.

4. Type 50.⏎.

5. Click Save & Close. Click OK in the Page Setup dialog box, and click Close in the Page Setup Manager dialog box.

6. Choose View ➢ Regen All. The walls are a shade of gray instead of solid black.

In this exercise, you turned a wide black line into a gray one. The Screening option lets you tone down the chosen color from a solid color to a color that has 50 percent of its full intensity.

You can use the Screening option in combination with color to obtain a variety of tones. If you need to cover large areas with color, you can use the Solid hatch pattern to fill those areas and then use the Screening option in the Plot Style Table Editor to make fine adjustments to the area's color.

## Controlling the Visibility of Overlapping Objects

You should also know about the Draworder command in conjunction with solid filled areas. This command lets you control how objects hide or overlap when displayed or plotted. If your solid hatches are hiding text or other graphics, you need to learn about Draworder. See Chapter 14 for more information. Some output devices offer a Merge Control option that determines how overlapping graphics are plotted. For more information, see Appendix B.

## Other Options in the Plot Style Table Editor

You've seen a lot of the plot style options so far, but there are many others that you may want to use in the future. This section describes those options that weren't covered in the previous exercises.

**TIP**  The options in the Plot Style Table Editor are the same regardless of whether you're editing a color plot style table or a named plot style table.

### THE GENERAL TAB

You didn't really look at the General tab of the Plot Style Table Editor in the exercise presented earlier. The General tab offers information regarding the plot style you're currently editing. You can enter a description of the style in the Description box. This can be useful if you plan to include the plot style with a drawing you're sending to someone else for plotting.

The File Information group gives you the basic information about the file location and name, as well as the number of color styles included in the plot style table.

The Apply Global Scale Factor To Non-ISO Linetypes check box lets you specify whether ISO linetype scale factors are applied to all linetypes. When this item is selected, the Scale Factor input box becomes active, enabling you to enter a scale factor.

**NOTE** International Organization for Standardization (ISO) linetypes are special linetypes that conform to ISO standards for technical drawings.

### THE TABLE VIEW TAB

The Table View tab offers the same settings as the Form View tab, only in a different format. Each plot style is shown as a column, with the properties of the plot style listed along the left side of the tab. To change a property, click it in the column.

To apply the same setting to all plot styles at once, right-click a setting you want to use from a single plot style, and choose Copy from the shortcut menu. Right-click the setting again, and then choose Apply To All Styles from the shortcut menu.

Click the Edit Lineweights button to open the Edit Lineweights dialog box, which lets you adjust the lineweight settings for the plot styles.

### THE FORM VIEW TAB

You've already seen and worked with the Form View tab, shown in Figure 9.1 earlier in this chapter. This tab contains the same settings as the Table View tab but in a different format. Instead of displaying each color as a column of properties, the properties are listed as options along the right side, and the colors are listed in a list box.

To modify the properties of a color, you select the color from the list and then edit the values in the Properties group on the right side of the dialog box. For example, to change the screening value of the Color 3 style, you highlight Color 3 in the Plot Styles list, double-click the Screening input box, and enter a new value.

You've already seen what the Screening, Color, Lineweight, and Line Join Style options do. Here's a description of the other style properties:

**TIP** The names of the properties in the Table View tab are slightly different from those in the Form View tab. The Table View property names are enclosed in brackets in this listing.

**Description** This option enables you to enter a description for each color.

**Dither [Enable Dithering]** *Dithering* is a method that enables your plotter to simulate colors beyond the basic 255 colors available in AutoCAD. Although this option is desirable when you want to create a wider range of colors in your plots, it can also create distortions, including broken, fine lines and false colors. For this reason, dithering is usually turned off. This option isn't available in all plotters.

**[Convert To] Grayscale** This option converts colors to grayscale.

**[Use Assigned] Pen #** This option lets you specify which pen number is assigned to each color in your drawing. This option applies only to pen plotters.

**Virtual Pen #** Many ink-jet and laser plotters offer "virtual pens" to simulate the processes of the old-style pen plotters. Frequently, such plotters offer as many as 255 virtual pens. Plotters with virtual pens often let you assign AutoCAD colors to a virtual pen number. This is significant if the virtual pens of your plotter can be assigned screening, width, end style, and join styles. You can then use the virtual pen settings instead of using the settings in the Plot Style Table Editor. This option is most beneficial for users who already have a library of drawings that are set up for plotters with virtual-pen settings.

You can set up your ink-jet printer for virtual pens under the Vector Graphics listing of the Device And Documents Setting tab of the Plotter Configuration Editor. See Appendix B for more on setting up your printer or plotter configuration.

**Linetype** If you prefer, you can use this setting to control linetypes in AutoCAD based on the color of the object. By default, this option is set to Use Object Linetype. I recommend that you leave this option at its default.

**Adaptive [Adjustment]** This option controls how noncontinuous linetypes begin and end. It's on by default, which forces linetypes to begin and end in a line segment. With this option turned off, the same linetype is drawn without regard for its ending. In some cases, this can produce a line that appears incomplete.

**Line End Style** This option lets you specify the shape of the end of simple lines that have a lineweight greater than zero.

**Line Join Style** This option lets you determine the shape of the corners of polylines.

**Fill Style**   This option lets you set up a color to be drawn as a pattern when used in a solid filled area. The patterns appear as follows:

**Add Style**   Clicking this button lets you add more plot styles or colors. This option isn't available for color plot style tables.

**Delete Style**   Clicking this button deletes the selected style. This option isn't available for color plot style tables.

**Save As**   Clicking this button lets you save the current plot style table with a different filename.

# Assigning Named Plot Styles Directly to Layers and Objects

So far, you've learned that you can control how AutoCAD translates drawing colors into plotter output. You've been using a color plot style table, which assigns a plot style to each color in AutoCAD. You can also assign plot styles directly to objects or layers. To do this, you need to employ a named plot style table. As we said earlier, named plot style tables enable you to create plot styles that have names rather than being assigned directly to colors in AutoCAD. You can then assign a plot style by name to objects or layers in your drawing. In this section, you'll learn how to set up AutoCAD with a named plot style table to assign plot styles to objects; then, you'll create a new plot style table.

## Using Named Plot Style Tables

Out of the box, AutoCAD uses the color-dependent plot style table for all new drawings. You can create a new drawing that uses named plot style tables in two ways. The simpler way is to use any of the named plot style template files when you create a new drawing. You'll see these templates under the Use A Template option in the Create New Drawing dialog box or in the Select Template dialog box.

By offering both color and named plot style drawing templates, AutoCAD makes it easy to create and select the type of plot style for your drawing regardless of the current default style.

If you prefer, you can set up AutoCAD to use a named plot style by default when you create a drawing by using the Start From Scratch option in the Create New Drawing dialog box. To set up the default plot style table for new drawings, follow these steps:

1.  Choose Tools ➤ Options to open the Options dialog box, and click the Plot And Publish tab. This tab offers a variety of settings geared toward your plotter or printer.

2.  In the lower-right corner of the dialog box, click the Plot Style Table Settings button.

3.  In the Plot Style Table Settings dialog box, click the Use Named Plot Styles radio button. Notice that the Default Plot Style For Layer 0 and Default Plot Style For Objects options become available. Click OK.

4.  Click OK to close the Options dialog box.

To create and try out a new named plot style, you can open an existing file from an earlier version of AutoCAD. In the next few exercises, you'll use the Plan-named.dwg file. This is a Release 14 file that you'll assign the type of plot style table that is currently the default as determined by the Use Named Plot Styles option you set in the previous exercise. Follow these steps:

1.  Open the Plan-named.dwg file.

2.  Choose File ➤ Plot Style Manager to open a window to the Plot Styles folder.

3.  Double-click the Add-A-Plot Style Table Wizard icon to start the Plot Style Table Wizard.

4.  Click Next to open the Begin screen, choose Start From Scratch, and then click Next to open the Pick Plot Style Table screen.

5.  Click the Named Plot Style Table radio button, and then click Next to open the File Name screen.

6.  Enter **Mynamedstyle1** in the File Name input box, and click Next to open the Finish screen. Here you can exit, or you can edit the new plot style table. This time, you'll edit the table from the wizard.

**7.** Click the Plot Style Table Editor button to open the Plot Style Table Editor dialog box.

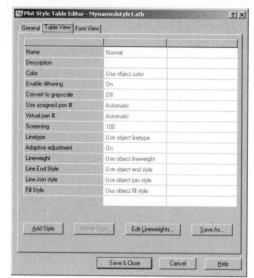

Notice that you have only one style named. Unlike the color plot style tables, you aren't assigning a style to each AutoCAD color; you don't need a style for each of the 255 colors. Instead, you can create a limited set of styles, giving each style the characteristics you want to apply to objects or layers. Continue by adding some plot styles:

**1.** Click the Add Style button to display a new Style 1 column. If you choose, you can give the style a different name at this point by clicking in the Name box and typing a new name.

**2.** Click the Form View tab, and then select Style 1 from the Plot Styles list.

**3.** Click the Lineweight drop-down list, and select 0.5000 mm.

4. Click the Add Style button, and then click OK in the Add Plot Style dialog box.

5. Select Style 2 from the Plot Styles list; then, click the Lineweight drop-down list, and select 0.7000 mm.

6. Click Save & Close to return to the Add Plot Style Table dialog box.

7. Click Finish to exit the wizard, and then close the Plot Styles window.

You may have noticed that the Add-A-Plot Style Table Wizard works in a slightly different way when you start it from the Plot Styles window. It adds an extra option (in step 5 of the exercise before the preceding one) that lets you choose between a color plot style table and a named plot style table.

You've just created a named plot style. Next, make `Mynamedstyle1.stb` the default plot style:

1. Open the Options dialog box, and click the Plot And Publish tab.

2. Click the Plot Style Table Settings button. Then, in the Default Plot Style Table drop-down list, select `Mynamedstyle1.stb`, the table you just created.

3. Click OK to exit the Plot Style Table Settings dialog box, and then click OK again to exit the Options dialog box.

Now, you're ready to start assigning plot styles to the objects in your drawing.

## Assigning Plot Styles to Objects

After you've set up AutoCAD to use named plot styles, you can begin to assign plot styles to objects through the Properties palette. Here are the steps to assign plot styles to objects:

1. Back in the `Plan-named.dwg` file, click the Layout1 tab.

2. Choose File ➢ Page Setup Manager; then, click the Modify button in the Page Setup Manager dialog box.

**WARNING**   If your plotter configuration is set up for a nonexistent printer, you'll see a warning message telling you that a driver for the plotter assigned to this drawing can't be found. This often occurs when you receive a file that has been set up to plot on a printer in another location. As the warning message explains, AutoCAD will set your plot device to None. You must then make sure your printer plotter is selected in the Printer/Plotter group of the Page Setup dialog box.

3. In the Page Setup dialog box, select `Mynamedstyle1.stb` from the drop-down list in the Plot Style Table (Pen Assignments) group.

4. Make sure the Display Plot Styles check box is selected; then, click OK.

5. Click Close to close the Page Setup Manager dialog box.

You've assigned a named plot style table to Layout1. Note that you can assign different named plot styles to different layouts.

Next, make sure the plot styles will be displayed in the drawing:

1. Choose Format ➢ Lineweight, make sure that the Display Lineweight check box is selected, and click OK.

2. Set up your view so you see a close-up of the lower-left corner unit.

3. Click the Model Or Paper Space button on the status bar so that the word *Model* shows in the button. This enables you to select objects in the drawing while in a Layout tab.

4. Select the line representing the outer wall of the unit at lower left in the plan, as shown in Figure 9.6; then, right-click, and choose Properties from the shortcut menu.

**FIGURE 9.6**
Select the line shown here.

5. In the Properties palette, click the Plot Style option. The option turns into a drop-down list with a downward-pointing arrow to the far right.

6. Click the downward-pointing arrow, and then select Other from the list to open the Select Plot Style dialog box.

**7.** Select Style 1, and click OK. Style 1 now appears as the value for the Plot Style in the Properties palette.

**8.** Close the Properties palette.

**9.** Choose View ➢ Regen All. If you have the lineweight visibility turned on, you see the results in the drawing editor. (Depending on how your display is set up, you may need to zoom in further.)

Another way to assign plot styles to individual objects is through the Plot Style Control drop-down list found in the Properties toolbar.

This enables you to select a plot style in a manner similar to the Layer & Linetype drop-down list. You can assign plot styles to individual objects by selecting the objects and then selecting a plot style from the Plot Style Control drop-down list. If you're using a color plot style table like the one you created in earlier exercises, the Plot Style Control drop-down list is unavailable.

## Assigning Plot Style Tables to Layers

You can also assign named plot style tables to layers. This has a similar effect to using the color plot style tables. The main difference is that with named plot style tables, you assign the plot style tables directly to the layer instead of assigning a plot style to the color of a layer. Here's how to assign a plot style table to a layer:

**1.** In the Layers toolbar, click the Layer Properties Manager button to open the Layer Properties Manager dialog box.

**2.** Select the Wall layer.

**3.** Click the Normal label in the Plot Style column of the Wall layer listing. You may have to scroll to the right to see the Plot Style column.

The Select Plot Style dialog box opens.

**4.** Select Style 1 from the Plot Styles list.

**5.** Click OK. You return to the Layer Properties Manager dialog box; this time, it shows the Plot Style property for the Wall layer listed as Style 1.

**6.** Click OK to close the Layer Properties Manager dialog box; then, choose View ➤ Regen All. Your view of the plan changes to reflect the new plot style assignment to the Wall layer.

---

**CONVERTING A DRAWING FROM COLOR PLOT STYLES TO NAMED PLOT STYLES**

If you need to convert a color plot style drawing to a named plot style drawing, you can use the Convertctb and Convertpstyles commands. The conversion is a two-part process. In the first stage, which is needed only the first time you perform the conversion, you convert a color plot style table file into a named plot style table file. Then, you convert the drawing file.

Here are the steps for the first part of the process:

**1.** Start AutoCAD, and, at the Command prompt, enter **Convertctb**↵. This command lets you convert a color plot style table file into a named plot style table file. A Select File dialog box opens to enable you to select a color plot style table file; these files have the filename extension .ctb. For this example, choose the Acad.ctb file.

**2.** Click Open to open the Create File dialog box, where you can provide a name for the converted file. If you opened the Acad.ctb file in step 1, you may want to give the new file the name AcadConvert so you know it's a converted .ctb file. AutoCAD automatically adds the .stb filename extension.

**3.** After you click Save, AutoCAD creates a new named plot style table file, with the .stb filename extension, from the .ctb file you selected in step 1.

The next part is to convert the drawing file:

**1.** Open the file you want to convert, and enter **Convertpstyles**↵ at the Command prompt. You'll see a warning message to make sure you've converted a .ctb file to a .stb file.

**2.** Click OK to open the Select File dialog box.

**3.** Select the converted .stb file you created using the Convertctb command. The current drawing is converted to use a named plot style table.

In the process shown here, I've suggested converting the Acad.ctb file; but if you've saved some custom settings in another .ctb file, you may want to convert your custom .ctb file instead.

To convert a drawing that uses a named plot style table to one that uses a color plot style table, open the file in question, and use the Convertpstyles command. You'll see a warning message telling you that all the named plot styles will be removed from the drawing. Click OK to convert the drawing.

---

## The Bottom Line

**Choosing between Color-Dependent and Named Plot Style Tables**    Plot styles let you control the way lines are printed on paper. You can control lineweights, shading of filled areas, corner treatment of thick lines, and more.

**Master It**    Describe some of the differences between named plot styles and color-dependent plot styles.

**Solution**   Color-dependent plot styles use the color of objects to control lineweights and other printed features. Named plot styles can be used to assign printed features to individual objects.

**Creating a Color Plot Style Table**   Both color and named plot styles are stored as files. You can create custom plot styles and apply them to any drawing.

**Master It**   In what dialog box do you select and edit plot styles?

**Solution**   Go to the Plot dialog box or the Page Setup dialog box; then, select New from the Plot Style Table drop-down list. You can also choose File ➢ Plot Style Manager and, in the Plot Styles window, double-click the Add-A-Plot Style Table Wizard.

**Editing and Using Plot Style Tables**   Plot styles give you a lot of control over the appearance of lines in your plotted output.

**Master It**   Name some of the settings offered in the Plot Style Table Editor.

**Solution**   Color, Screening, Lineweight, Line End Style, and Line Join Style are a few of the available options.

**Assigning Named Plot Styles Directly to Layers and Objects**   Named plots styles offer a bit more control over the way lines are plotted. If you choose, you can assign named plot styles to objects bypassing layer assignments.

**Master It**   Describe a method for assigning a plot style to an object.

**Solution**   You can assign a plot style to an object through the Plot Style setting in the Properties palette. You can also use the Plot Style Control drop-down list in the Properties toolbar.

# Chapter 10

# Adding Text to Drawings

One of the more tedious drafting tasks is applying notes to your drawing. Anyone who has had to manually draft a large drawing containing a lot of notes knows the true meaning of writer's cramp. AutoCAD not only makes this job go faster by enabling you to type your notes into the same document as the corresponding drawing, but it also helps you to create more professional-looking notes by using a variety of fonts, type sizes, and type styles.

In this chapter, you'll add notes to your apartment building plan. In the process, you'll explore some of AutoCAD's text-creation and -editing features. You'll learn how to control the size, slant, type style, and orientation of text and how to import text files. You'll start by working through some exercises that show you the process of preparing a drawing for text. You'll then add a few lines of text to the drawing and learn how text size and drawing scale interrelate. The rest of the chapter shows you the tools available for formatting text to fit your application.

Topics in this chapter include the following:

◆ Preparing a Drawing for Text

◆ Setting the Annotation Scale and Adding Text

◆ Understanding the Text Style Dialog Box Options

◆ Exploring Text Formatting in AutoCAD

◆ What Do the Fonts Look Like?

◆ Adding Simple Single-Line Text Objects

◆ Using the Check-Spelling Feature

◆ Substituting Fonts

◆ Finding and Replacing Text

## Preparing a Drawing for Text

In this first section, you'll go through the process of adding text to a drawing that currently has no text. By doing this, you'll gain firsthand experience in using all the tools you'll need for adding text to a drawing. Start by setting up a drawing to prepare it for the addition of text:

1. Start AutoCAD, and open the Unit file. If you haven't created the Unit file, you can use the file called 10a-unit.dwg. Metric users should use 10a-unit-metric.dwg. After it's open, choose File ➤ Save As to save the Unit drawing to a file called Unit.dwg.

2. Create a layer called Notes, and make it the current layer. Notes is the layer on which you'll keep all your text information.

**3.** Turn off the Flr-pat layer. Otherwise, the floor pattern you added previously will obscure the text you enter during the exercises in this chapter.

**TIP** It's a good idea to keep your notes on a separate layer, so you can plot drawings containing only the graphics information or freeze the Notes layer to save redraw/regeneration time.

**4.** Set up your view so it looks similar to the top image in Figure 10.1.

## Organizing Text by Styles

Before you begin to add text to your drawing, you should set up a text style or two. You can think of text styles as a tool to store your most common text formatting. Styles store text height and font information so you don't have to set these options every time you enter text. Generally, you'll only need a few text styles.

Even if you started to add text without creating your own text style, you would still be using a text style. That's because every text object must have a style, so AutoCAD includes the Standard text style in every new drawing. The Standard style uses an AutoCAD font called txt and includes numerous other settings that you'll learn about in this section. These other settings include width factor, oblique angle, and default height. In this next exercise, you'll create a text style called Note1, which you'll use to add notes to the Unit plan you've been working on:

**FIGURE 10.1**

The top image shows the points to pick to place the text boundary window. The bottom image shows the completed text.

Click here to start text boundary.

Text boundary window

Click here to finish.

Text flow direction indicated by arrow

**TIP**  If you don't like the way the AutoCAD default style is set up, open the Acad.dwt template file and change the Standard text style settings to your liking. You can also add other styles that you use frequently. Remember, AutoCAD files that use the .dwt filename extension are just AutoCAD .dwg files with a slightly different extension to set them apart.

1. Choose Format ➤ Text Style, or type **St⏎**. You can also click the Text Style tool in the Text control panel. This opens the Text Style dialog box.

2. Click the New to the right of the dialog box to open the New Text Style dialog box.

3. Enter **Note1 (Note one)** for the name of your new style; then, click OK.

4. Select a font for your style. In the Text Style dialog box again, click the Font Name drop-down list in the Font group.

5. Locate the Courier New TrueType font, and select it. A quick way to locate the font is to click in the list and start typing the font name.

6. Select the Annotative option in the Size group.

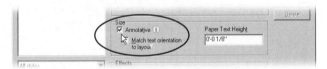

7. In the Paper Text Height input box, enter **0.1**. You'll see your input change to ⅛″. Metric users should enter **0.15**.

8. Click Apply, and then close the dialog box.

The Annotative option you turned on in step 7 is an important feature for keeping your text at the proper size for your drawing scale. You'll see how it works firsthand in the following section's exercises.

**NOTE**  Once you've created several styles, you can set the default current style by selecting it from the Text Style drop-down list in the Text control panel.

### Getting Familiar With the Text and Annotation Scale Control Panels

Before you get much further into AutoCAD's text features, take a moment to get familiar with the Text control panel and the Annotation Scale control panel (see Figure 10.2). You'll be using a few of these options in this chapter. If you need to, you can refer to this graphic as you work through the exercises.

**FIGURE 10.2**

The Annotation Scale control panel (left) and Text control Panel (right)

## Setting the Annotation Scale and Adding Text

You've got a text style set up and ready to use. Now, you'll add some text to your unit plan. Before you begin, you should determine a drawing scale. This is important because, with the annotative feature turned on, AutoCAD needs to know the drawing scale in order to set the size of the text.

**1.** In the lower-right corner of the AutoCAD window, click the arrow next to Annotation Scale.

**2.** Select ¼″=1′-0″. Metric users, select 1:100.

You've just set the drawing scale for the Model tab. This isn't a permanent setting; you can change it at any time, as you'll see later. The settings you used for the annotation scale are somewhat arbitrary for the purposes of demonstrating the annotative scale feature.

Finally, you can begin to add text:

**1.** Click the Multiline Text tool in the Text control panel. You can also choose Draw ➢ Text ➢ Multiline Text from the menu bar, or type **MT**↵. You see a prompt that tells you the current text style and height:

```
Current text style: "Note1" Text height: 1/8
Annotative: Yes
Specify first corner:
```

2. Click the first point indicated in the top image in Figure 10.1 to start the text boundary window. This boundary window indicates the area in which to place the text. Notice the arrow near the bottom of the window: It indicates the direction of the text flow.

**TIP**  You don't have to be too precise about where you select the points for the boundary because you can adjust the location and size later.

3. At the `Specify opposite corner of [Height/Justify/Line spacing/Rotation/Style/Width]:` prompt, click the second point indicated in the top image in Figure 10.1. The Text Formatting toolbar appears, with the Multiline Text Editor superimposed over the area you just selected.

4. Click the text panel, and type **Entry**. As you type, the word appears in the text panel, just as it will appear in your drawing.

5. Press ↵ to advance one line; then, enter **6′ by 7′**.

6. Press ↵ to advance another line, and enter **[182 cm by 213 cm]**.

7. Press ↵ again to advance another line, and enter **carpet floor**.

8. Click OK in the Text Formatting toolbar. The text appears in the drawing just as it did in the text editor. (See the bottom image in Figure 10.1.)

**NOTE**  After you've added text, if the text doesn't quite fit in the area you've indicated, you can make adjustments to the text boundary. Click the text to expose the text boundary, including the boundary grips. Then, click and drag the grips to resize the boundary. AutoCAD's word-wrap feature automatically adjusts the text formatting to fit the text boundary.

You may have noticed that the Text Formatting toolbar and text editor work like any text editor; if you make a typing error, you can highlight the error and retype the letter or word. You can also perform other word-processing functions such as search and replace, you can import text, and you can make font changes.

You also saw that the text editor shows how your text will appear in the location you selected using the text boundary. If your view of the drawing is such that the text is too small to be legible, the Text Formatting toolbar enlarges the text so you can read it clearly. Likewise, if you're zoomed in too close to see the entire text, the Text Formatting toolbar adjusts the text in its text editor to enable you to see all the text.

**TIP** If text is included in a selection where a hatch pattern is to be placed, AutoCAD automatically avoids hatching over the text. If you add text over a hatched area, you must rehatch the area to include the text in the hatch boundary.

## Exploring Text and Scale

Even though your text height is 0.1″ or 0.15 cm, it appears at the appropriate enlarged size for the current scale. If the text were drawn to the size of 0.1″, it would be very small and barely visible; but the Annotative scale feature makes the adjustment to your text size based on the Annotation Scale setting.

You can see firsthand how the Annotation Scale setting affects your text:

1. In the lower-right corner of the AutoCAD window, click the Annotation Scale setting, and select ¼″=1′-0″. Metric users should select 1:50.

2. Click the Add Current Scale tool in the Annotation Scale control panel, or enter **Objectscale**↵.

3. At the `Select annotative objects:` prompt, select the text, and press ↵.

4. At the `Enter an option [Add/Delete/?] <Add>:` prompt, press ↵.

5. At the `Enter named scale to add or [?] <1:50>:` prompt, press ↵.

6. At the prompt

   `1 object updated to support annotation scale <1:50>.`

   `Enter named scale to add or [?]:`

   press ↵.

The text changes to a smaller and more appropriate size for the new scale you selected in step 1. Now, test your settings by changing the Annotation Scale value back to the previous setting:

1. In the lower-right corner of the AutoCAD window, click the Annotation Scale setting, and select ⅛″=1′-0″. Metric users should select 1:100.

2. The text changes back to its original size.

In steps 2 through 6 of the first exercise in this section, you added a new annotation scale to the text. This is necessary in order for the text to be aware of the new annotation scale you want to use. Each time you include a new scale for your drawing, you need to add an annotation scale to the text in your drawing. Once it's added, you can quickly change between scales by selecting a scale from the Annotation Scale list.

So far, you've only used a single multiline text object; but if you have many notes distributed throughout a drawing, you'll need to add an annotation scale to all of them before they can automatically adjust themselves to the different scales you'll use with your drawing. This is easy to do, because you have the option to select as many objects as you need when adding annotation scales.

---

### TEXT AND SCALE IN LEGACY DRAWINGS

AutoCAD 2008 offers the Annotation Scale feature to automate the scaling of text and other objects to their proper sized based on the drawing's annotation scale. But there is a good chance that you'll encounter drawings that were created before the Annotation Scale feature was available. For that reason, you should have a basic understanding of scale factors as they apply to text.

As you know by now, AutoCAD lets you draw at full scale; that is, you can represent distances as values equivalent to the actual size of the object. When you later plot the drawing, you tell AutoCAD the scale at which you want to plot, and the program reduces the drawing accordingly. This gives you the freedom to enter measurements at full scale and not worry about converting them to various scales every time you enter a distance. Unfortunately, in earlier versions of AutoCAD, this feature created problems when users entered text and dimensions. You had to make the text height very large in order for it to be readable when scaled down.

To illustrate this point, imagine you're drawing the Unit plan at full size on a very large sheet of paper. When you're finished with this drawing, it will be reduced to a scale that enables it to fit on an 8.5″×11″ sheet of paper. So, you have to make your text large to keep it legible after it's reduced. If you want text to appear ⅛″ high when the drawing is plotted, you must convert it to a considerably larger size when you draw it. To do this, you multiply the desired height of the final plotted text by a scale-conversion factor (see Chapter 3 for more on scale-conversion factors).

For example, if your drawing is at a ⅛″=1′-0″ scale, you multiply the desired text height, ⅛″, by the scale-conversion factor of 96 to get a height of 12″. This is the height you must make your text to get ⅛″-high text in the final plot.

With AutoCAD 2008, you don't have to work through the math to get the right text size for your drawing. But if you encounter a drawing that was created in an earlier version of AutoCAD and you notice that the text size is very large, you'll know why.

## Understanding the Text Style Dialog Box Options

You've just taken nearly all the steps you'll need to know to add text to any drawing. Now, let's take a step back and look more closely at some of the finer points of adding text, starting with text styles. This section gives you more detailed information about the text style settings you saw in the early part of this chapter. The following is a list of those settings and their purposes. Some of them, such as Width Factor, can be quite useful. Others, such as the Backwards and Vertical options, are rarely used. Take a moment to study this list to become familiar with what is available and make a mental note of these items for future reference.

### Style

In the Style list box you'll see a list showing the current style. This list also contains other styles that may be present in the drawing. You can use the drop-down list to select a default style. In addition, there are the following buttons:

#### NEW/SET CURRENT/DELETE

*New* lets you create a new text style. *Set Current* makes the selected style the current one. *Delete* lets you delete the selected style. This option isn't available for the Standard style.

#### FONT

In the Font group, you have the following options:

**Font Name** Lets you select a font from a list of available fonts. The list is derived from the font resources available to Windows 2000 or Windows XP, plus the standard AutoCAD fonts.

**Font Style**    Offers variations of a font, such as italic or bold, when they're available.

**Height/Paper Text Height**    Lets you enter a font size. With the Annotative option turned off, this option is named *Height* and will set the absolute height of the text. With the Annotative option turned on, it shows *Paper Text Height* and will set the height of the text when printed. A 0 height has special meaning when you use the Dtext command to enter text, as described later in this chapter.

**Use Big Font**    Applicable to Asian fonts. This option is offered only with AutoCAD .shx fonts.

## EFFECTS

In the Effects group, you have the following options:

**Upside Down**    Prints text upside down.

**Backwards**    Prints text backward.

**Vertical**    Prints text in a vertical column.

**Width Factor**    Adjusts the width and spacing of the characters in the text. A value of 1 keeps the text at its normal width. Values greater than 1 expand the text, and values less than 1 compress the text.

> This is the Simplex font expanded by 1.4
> This is the simplex font using a width factor of 1
> This is the simplex font compressed by .6

**Oblique Angle**    Skews the text at an angle. When this option is set to a value greater than 0, the text appears italicized. A value of less than 0 (–12, for example) causes the text to lean to the left.

> *This is the simplex font*
> *using a 12-degree oblique angle*

**TIP**    You can also set the width factor and oblique angle directly for text using the Width Factor and Oblique Angle tools in the Text Formatting toolbar. These tools are located toward the lower-right end of the toolbar.

---

### RENAMING A TEXT STYLE OR OTHER NAMED OBJECT

If you need to rename a text style or other named object in AutoCAD, you can do so using the Rename command. Choose Format ➤ Rename, or enter **Ren**⏎ at the Command prompt to open the Rename dialog box. In the Named Objects list box to the left, choose Text Styles. Click the name of the style you want to change from the Items list on the right; the name appears in the Old Name input box below the list. In the input box next to the Rename To button, enter the new name. Click the Rename To button, and click OK.

# Exploring Text Formatting in AutoCAD

You've seen how you can set up a style and make scale adjustments. AutoCAD also offers a wide range of text-formatting options that are typical to most word-processing programs. You can control fonts, text height, justification, line spacing, and width. You can even include special characters such as degree symbols or stacked fractions. With these additional formatting tools, you can make adjustments to the text style you started with.

## Adjusting the Text Height and Font

To get some firsthand experience using the text-formatting tools in AutoCAD, try the following exercise. You'll use the Multiline Text tool again, but this time you'll get to try out some of its other features.

In this exercise, you'll see how you can adjust the size and font of text in the editor:

1. Pan your view so the kitchen is just at the top of the drawing, as shown in the first image in Figure 10.3.

2. Click the Multiline Text tool; then, select a text boundary window, as shown in the first image in Figure 10.3.

**FIGURE 10.3**
Placing the text-boundary window for the living-room label and the final label

Click here to start the text boundary.

Click here to finish.

Specify opposite corner or   8'-1 9/16"   < 306°

.carpet floor

Living Room
14'-0" by 16'-5"
[427 cm by 500 cm]

**3.** In the text editor, type the following:

```
Living Room
14'-0" by 16'-5" [427 cm by 500 cm]
```

Make sure you press ↵ after *Living Room*, but make the rest of the text a continuous string. As you type, the words wrap. AutoCAD uses word wrap to fit the text inside the text boundary area.

**4.** Highlight the text *14'-0" by 16'-5" [427 cm by 500 cm]* as you would in any word processor. For example, you can click the end of the line to place the cursor there; then, Shift+click the beginning of the line to highlight the whole line.

**5.** In the Text Formatting toolbar, click in the Text Height text box and enter **1/16**. Metric users, enter **0.08**. The highlighted text changes to a smaller size.

**6.** Highlight the words *Living Room*.

**7.** Click the Font drop-down list to display a list of font options.

**8.** Scroll up the list until you find Arial. The text in the text editor changes to reflect the new font.

**9.** With the words *Living Room* still highlighted, click the Underline button in the Text Formatting toolbar.

**10.** Click OK in the Text Formatting toolbar. The label appears in the area you indicated in step 2 (see the bottom image in Figure 10.3).

**11.** To see how you can go back to the Text Formatting toolbar, double-click the text. The Text Formatting toolbar and text editor appear, enabling you to change the text.

**12.** Click OK to exit the Text Formatting toolbar.

While using the Multiline Text tool, you may have noticed the [Height/Justify/Line spacing/Rotation/Style/Width/Columns]: prompt immediately after you picked the first point of the text boundary. You can use any of these options to make on-the-fly modifications to the height, justification, line spacing, rotation style, or width of the multiline text.

For example, after clicking the first point for the text boundary, you can type **R**↵ and then specify a rotation angle for the text window, either graphically with a rubber-banding line or by entering an angle value. After you've entered a rotation angle, you can resume selecting the text boundary.

## Understanding the Text Formatting Toolbar

You've just experimented with a few of the Text Formatting toolbar features. A variety of additional formatting tools are available. Figure 10.4 shows where these tools are, and Table 10.1 describes their uses. They're fairly straightforward, and if you've used other word-processing programs, you should find them easy to use. Most are common to the majority of word processors, although a few, such as Symbol, Oblique Angle, and Width Factor, are unique to AutoCAD. Look at Table 10.1, and see if there are any tools you think you'll find useful for future reference.

**FIGURE 10.4**

Additional features of the Text Formatting toolbar

**TABLE 10.1:** Text Formatting Tools

| TOOL | USE |
| --- | --- |
| Bold/Italic/Underline/Overline | Select text, and then select one of these options to add bold, italic, underline, or overline to the text. |
| Undo/Redo | Click to undo or redo current edits. |
| Stack/Unstack Fraction | Select a fraction, and then click this tool to either stack or unstack the fraction text. |
| Color | Select text, and then choose a color from this drop-down list. |
| Ruler | Click to turn the ruler at the top of the Text panel on or off. |
| Columns | Indicate the number of columns and how the columns are set up. |
| Paragraph | Set up paragraph formatting, including tabs, indents, and paragraph spacing. |
| Mtext Justification | Select the appropriate option to align the text to the top, middle, bottom, or other position within the text boundary. |
| Line Spacing | Set the line spacing in paragraphs. You can also set line spacing in the Properties palette for an mtext object, or by using the Paragraph dialog box (see "Setting Indents and Tabs" later in this chapter). |
| Left/Center/Right/Justify/ Distribute | Click the appropriate tool to align the text to the left, center, or right side of the text boundary. *Justify* adds space between words to force left and right alignment. *Distribute* adds space between letters to force left and right alignment. |
| Numbering | Select a list of text, click this tool, and then select Letter, Number, or Bullet to add letters, numbers, or bullets to the list. |
| Insert Field | Click to open the Fields dialog box, where you can add a field text. See "Adding Formulas to Cells," in Chapter 11, for more about fields. |
| Uppercase/Lowercase | Select a single letter or set of words, and then select the Uppercase or Lowercase tool to change the selection's case. |

**TABLE 10.1:**    Text Formatting Tools (CONTINUED)

| TOOL | USE |
| --- | --- |
| Symbol | Place the cursor at a location for the symbol, and then click the Symbol tool to find and add a symbol. (See Figure 10.5, later in this chapter, for the available symbols.) |
| Oblique Angle | Select text, and then enter an Oblique Angle value. The effect is to skew the text characters in a way similar to an italic formatting. |
| Tracking | Select text, and then enter a tracking value in the Tracking text box. A value greater than 1 increases the spacing between letters, and a value less than 1 decreases the spacing. |
| Width Factor | Select text, and enter a width value in the Width text box. A value greater than 1 stretches the text, including individual letters, horizontally. A value less than 1 compresses the text, including the letters. |

## Adding Symbols and Special Characters

The Text Formatting toolbar also offers a tool called Symbol. This tool lets you add special symbols common to technical drawing and drafting. Figure 10.5 shows the symbols that are offered in the Symbol tool in the form of a drop-down list.

At the bottom of the Symbol drop-down list is an option called Other. By clicking the Other option, you open the Windows Character Map dialog box. Characters such as the trademark (™) and copyright (©) symbols are often available in the fonts offered in the Character Map dialog box. The contents of the Symbol drop-down list depend on the font currently selected.

**WARNING**    The Character Map dialog box is a Windows accessory. If it doesn't appear when you choose Other from the Text Formatting Symbol tool menu, you may need to install the Character Map from your Windows installation CD.

Finally, if your application requires music, math, astronomy, Greek, or other symbols, AutoCAD offers a set of fonts with special symbols. Figure 10.10, later in the chapter, shows these fonts and the symbols they contain. You can set up text styles with these fonts or call them up directly from the Text Formatting toolbar's Font option.

## TEXT JUSTIFICATION AND OSNAPS

You may have noticed that the object-justification list offers three center options: Top Center, Middle Center, and Bottom Center. All three of these options have the same effect on the text's appearance, but they each have a different effect on how osnaps act on the text. Figure 10.6 shows where the osnap point occurs on a text boundary, depending on which justification option is selected. A multiline text object has only one insertion point on its boundary, which that you can access with the Insert osnap.

**FIGURE 10.5**
Symbols offered by the Symbol option. (See Symbol in Table 10.1 for information about how to use these symbols.)

| | | | |
|---|---|---|---|
| Degree | $x^{\circ}$ | Identity | $\equiv$ |
| Plus/Minus | $\pm$ | Initial Length | ⌒➘ |
| Diameter | $\phi$ | Monument Line | ℳℒ |
| Almost Equal | $\approx$ | Not Equal | $\neq$ |
| Angle | $\angle$ | Ohm | $\Omega$ |
| Boundary Line | ℬℒ | Omega | $\Omega$ |
| Center Line | ₵ℒ | Property Line | ℙℒ |
| Delta | $\Delta$ | Subscript 2 | $x_2$ |
| Electrical Phase | $\Phi$ | Squared | $x^2$ |
| Flow Line | ℱℒ | Cubed | $x^3$ |

**FIGURE 10.6**
The location of the Insert osnap point on a text boundary, based on its justification setting

Top Center grip

Living Room
14'-0" by 16'-5"
[427 cm by 500 cm]

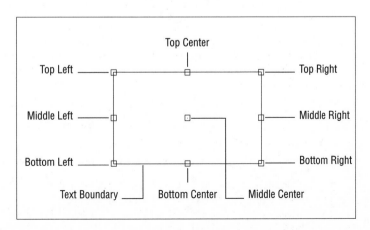

The Osnap point also appears as an extra grip point on the text boundary when you click the text. If you click the text you just entered, you'll see that a grip point now appears at the top center of the text boundary.

Knowing where the Osnap points occur can be helpful when you want to align the text with other objects in your drawing. In most cases, you can use the grips to align your text boundary, but the Top Center and Middle Center justification options enable you to use the center and middle portions of your text to align the text with other objects.

### CHANGING JUSTIFICATION OF MULTIPLE TEXT OBJECTS

You've seen how you can change the justification of an individual text object, but you'll often find that you need to change the justification of several text objects at one time. AutoCAD offers the Justifytext command for this purpose. To use it, choose Modify ➤ Object ➤ Text ➤ Justify, or type **Justifytext**↵ at the Command prompt. At the Select objects: prompt, select the text you want to change, and then press ↵ to confirm your selection. You'll see the following prompt in the command line:

```
[Left/Align/Fit/Center/Middle/Right/TL/TC/TR/ML/MC/MR/BL/BC/BR] <BC>:
```

Enter the letters corresponding to the type of justification you want to use for the text. (See the section "Justifying Single-Line Text Objects," later in this chapter, for a description of these options.) After you enter an option, the selected text changes to conform to the selected justification option.

## Setting Indents and Tabs

You should also know about the indent and tab features of the Text Formatting toolbar's text window. You may have noticed the ruler at the top of the text editor. Figure 10.7 shows that ruler, including tab and indent markers.

**FIGURE 10.7**
The ruler at the top of the text editor lets you quickly set tabs and indents for text.

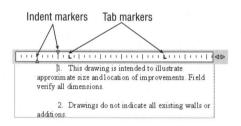

The indent markers let you control the indention of the first line and the rest of the paragraph. The tab markers give you control over tab spacing. For new text, the tab markers don't appear until you add them by clicking the ruler. The following exercises will demonstrate the use of these markers more clearly.

Start by practicing with the indent markers:

1. Save the Unit drawing, and then open the Indent.dwg file. This file contains some text that you'll experiment with.

2. Double-click the text at the top of the drawing to open the Text Formatting toolbar.

3. Press Ctrl+A to highlight all the text in the text editor. This is necessary to indicate the group of text to be affected by your indent settings.

**4.** Click and drag the top indent marker two spaces to the right. The indent of the first line moves with the marker. A note appears above the ruler, showing you how much indent you're applying. Also notice that the text at the first tab remains at its starting location.

**5.** Click and drag the bottom indent marker two spaces to the left. The rest of the paragraph moves with the marker. Again, you see a note by the ruler showing how much indent you're applying.

**6.** Click OK in the Text Formatting toolbar to exit.

Here you see how you can control the indents of the selected text with the indent markers. You can set paragraphs of a single Mtext object differently, giving you a wide range of indent-formatting possibilities. Just select the text you want to set, and then adjust the indent markers.

Now, try the tab markers. For this exercise, you'll try the text-import feature to import a tab-delimited text file:

**1.** Click the Multiline Text tool on the Draw toolbar.

**2.** For the first corner, click the upper-left corner of the large rectangle in the drawing, just below the paragraph.

**3.** For the opposite corner, click the lower-right corner of the rectangle.

**4.** Right-click in the text editor of the Text Formatting toolbar, and select Import Text.

**5.** In the Select File dialog box, locate and select the `tabtest.txt` file. The contents of the `tabtest.txt` file are displayed in the text editor.

The file you just imported was generated from the Attribute Extraction feature of AutoCAD. You'll learn more about this feature in Chapter 13. This file contains tabs to align the columns of information. You can adjust those tabs in the Text Formatting toolbar, as you'll see in the next set of steps.

Now, use the tab markers to adjust the tab spacing of the columns of text:

**1.** Press Ctrl+A to select all the text.

**2.** Click the ruler at a point that is at the twelfth mark from the left (that's three of the taller tick marks in the ruler). An L-shaped marker appears, and the first tab column of text moves to this position.

**3.** Click the ruler again at the twentieth mark. The second tab column aligns to this position.

**4.** Continue to click the ruler to add more tab markers so the text looks similar to Figure 10.8. Don't worry about being exact; this is just for practice. After you've placed a marker, you can click and drag it to make adjustments.

**5.** Click OK on the Text Formatting toolbar. The text appears in the drawing as a door schedule.

**FIGURE 10.8**

Add tab markers so your text looks similar to this figure.

Here you saw how you can create a table or a schedule from an imported text file. You can also create a schedule from scratch by composing it directly in the text editor of the Text Formatting toolbar. AutoCAD also offers the Table feature, which is specifically designed for creating tables (see Chapter 11). Still, this example offers a way to demonstrate the tab feature in the Multiline Text tool, and you may encounter a file in which a table is formatted in the way described here.

In addition to using the indent and tab markers on the ruler, you can control indents and tabs through the Paragraph dialog box. Do the following to get a firsthand look:

**1.** Double-click the text at the top of the Indent.dwg drawing (the one you edited in the first part of this section), and then press Ctrl+A to select all the text.

**2.** Right-click the ruler above the text editor, and select Paragraph to open the Paragraph dialog box.

**NOTE** The Paragraph dialog box also lets you set other paragraph settings such as alignment, spacing between paragraphs, and line spacing in the paragraph.

**3.** Change the value in the First Line input box to **1.5** and the Hanging input box to **2.2**.

4. Double-click the tab position input box in the upper-left corner, just below the row of tab symbols in the Tab group. Enter **2.2,** and click the Add button.

5. Click OK. The text now appears with the text indented from the numbers.

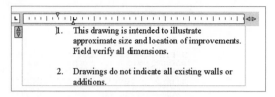

6. Close the Text Formatting toolbar. The text in the drawing is now formatted as it appeared in the text editor of the Text Formatting toolbar.

7. Exit the `Indent.dwg` file.

In this exercise, you used the Paragraph dialog box to set the paragraph indent and the first tab marker to be the same value. This causes the text portion of the list to be aligned at a distance of 2.2 drawing units from the left text boundary, leaving the list number extended farther to the left. This gives the list a more professional appearance.

The Paragraph dialog box gives you fine control over the formatting of your text. It lets you delete tabs by highlighting the tab in the list and clicking the Remove button. You can also add tabs at specific distances from the left margin of the text boundary by entering new tab locations in the Tab input box and clicking the Add button.

You specify distances in drawing units. If your drawing is set up to use Architectural units, for example, you can enter values in feet and inches or just inches. The First Line and Hanging input boxes you enter a numeric value for paragraph indents. As you've just seen, you can use the First Line and Hanging input boxes to create a numbered list by setting the Hanging input box value to be the same as the first tab stop position.

**TIP**    You may have noticed the Set Mtext Width and Set Mtext Height right-click shortcut menu options in step 2 of the preceding exercise. The Set Mtext Width option opens a dialog box that enables you to enter a width for the text boundary for situations where you need an exact width. You can also click and drag the right inside edge of the ruler to change the text-boundary width.

## What Do the Fonts Look Like?

You've already seen a few of the fonts available in AutoCAD. Chances are, you're familiar with the TrueType fonts available in Windows. You have some additional AutoCAD fonts from which to choose. You may want to stick with the AutoCAD fonts for all but your presentation drawings, because other fonts can consume more memory.

Figure 10.9 shows the basic AutoCAD text fonts. The Romans font is perhaps the most widely used because it offers a reasonable appearance while consuming little memory. Figure 10.10 lists some of the symbols and Greek fonts.

This section shows you samples of the AutoCAD fonts. You can see samples of all the fonts, including TrueType fonts, in the preview window of the Text Style dialog box. If you use a word processor, you're probably familiar with at least some of the TrueType fonts available in Windows and AutoCAD.

**FIGURE 10.9**

Some of the standard AutoCAD text fonts

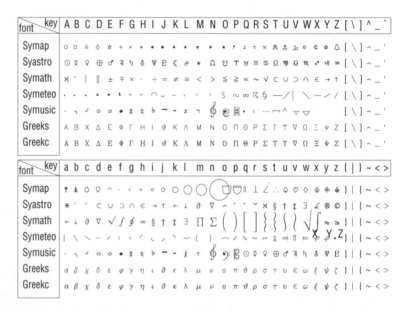

**FIGURE 10.10**

Some of the AutoCAD symbols and Greek fonts

**IMPORTING TEXT FILES**

With multiline text objects, AutoCAD enables you to import ASCII text or Rich Text Format (RTF) files. RTF files can be exported from Microsoft Word and most other word-processing programs and retain most of their formatting in AutoCAD. Here's how you import text files:

1. With the Text Formatting toolbar open, right-click in the text panel, and choose Import Text.

2. In the Select File dialog box, locate a valid text file. It must be a file in either a raw text (ASCII) format, such as a Notepad (.txt) file, or RTF (.rtf). RTF files can store formatting information, such as boldface and varying point sizes.

**3.** After you've highlighted the file you want, double-click it or click Open. The text appears in the Edit Mtext window.

**4.** Click OK, and the text appears in your drawing.

In addition, you can use the Windows Clipboard and the Cut and Paste functions to add text to a drawing. To do this, follow these steps:

**1.** Select some text, and then choose Cut or Copy in any Windows program to place text on the Windows Clipboard.

**2.** Open AutoCAD. Choose Edit ➢ Paste; the pasted text appears in your drawing. However, it isn't editable in AutoCAD.

If the text is from a text editor like Windows Notepad, the text is inserted as AutoCAD text. If the text contains formatting from a word processor like Microsoft Word, the text is an OLE object.

Because AutoCAD is an OLE client, you can also attach other types of documents to an AutoCAD drawing file. See Chapter 19 for more on AutoCAD's OLE support.

---

**THE TEXTFILL SYSTEM VARIABLE**

Unlike the standard sticklike AutoCAD fonts, TrueType and PostScript fonts have filled areas. These filled areas take more time to generate; so if you have a lot of text in these fonts, your redraw and regen times will increase. To help reduce redraw and regen times, you can set AutoCAD to display and plot these fonts as outline fonts, even though they're filled in their true appearance.

To change this setting, type **Textfill↵**, and then type **0↵**. Doing so turns off text fill for PostScript and TrueType fonts. (This is the same as setting the Textfill system variable to 0.)

---

## Adding Simple Single-Line Text Objects

You might find that you're entering a lot of single words or simple labels that don't require all the bells and whistles of the Multiline Text Editor. AutoCAD offers the *single-line text object*, which is simpler to use and can speed text entry if you're adding only small pieces of text.

Continue the tutorial on the Unit.dwg file by trying the following exercise:

**1.** Adjust your view so it looks like Figure 10.11.

**2.** Make sure Notes1 is the current text style; then, click the Single Line Text tool in the Text control panel.

**2.** You can also enter **Dt↵** or choose Draw ➢ Text ➢ Single Line Text to issue the Dtext command.

**3.** At the Specify start point of text or [Justify/Style]: prompt, pick the starting point for the text you're about to enter, just below the kitchen at coordinate 16´-2˝,21´-8˝ (490,664 for metric users). Note that the prompt offers the Justify and Style options.

**FIGURE 10.11**

Adding simple labels
to the kitchen and
bath by using the
Dtext command

4. At the `Specify rotation angle of text <0>:` prompt, press ↵ to accept the default, 0. You can specify any angle other than horizontal (for example, if you want your text aligned with a rotated object). You see a text I-beam cursor at the point you picked in step 3.

5. Type **Kitchenette**. As you type, the word appears directly in the drawing.

**TIP** If you make a typing error, use the Right and Left arrow keys to move the text cursor in the drawing area to the error; then, use the Backspace key to correct the error. You can also paste text from the Clipboard into the cursor location by using the Ctrl+V keyboard shortcut or by right-clicking in the drawing area to access the shortcut menu.

6. Press ↵ to move the cursor down to start a new line.

7. This time, you want to label the bathroom. Pick a point to the right of the door swing at coordinate 19′-11″,26′-5″ (610,805 for metric users). The text cursor moves to that point.

8. Type **Bathroom**↵. Figure 10.11 shows how your drawing should look now.

9. Press ↵ again to exit the Dtext command.

**TIP** If for some reason you need to stop entering single-line text objects to do something else in AutoCAD, you can continue the text where you left off by pressing ↵ at the `Specify start point of text or [Justify/Style]:` prompt of the Dtext command. The text continues immediately below the last line of text entered.

Here you were able to add two single lines of text in different parts of your drawing fairly quickly. Dtext uses the current default text style settings.

To edit single-line text, you can double-click the text. The text is highlighted, and you can begin typing to replace the entire text, or you can click a location in the text to make single word or character changes.

**NOTE** This is the end of the tutorial section of this chapter. The rest of this chapter offers additional information about text.

## Justifying Single-Line Text Objects

Justifying single-line text objects works in a slightly different way from justifying multiline text. For example, if you change the justification setting to Center, the text moves so the center of the text is placed at the text-insertion point. In other words, the insertion point stays in place while the text location adjusts to the new justification setting. Figure 10.12 shows the relationship between single-line text and the insertion point based on different justification settings.

**FIGURE 10.12**

Text inserted using the various justification options

To set the justification of text as you enter it, you must enter **J**↵ at the Specify start point of text or [Justify/Style]: prompt after issuing the Dtext command.

**TIP** You can also change the current default style by entering **S**↵ and then the name of the style at the Specify start point of text or [Justify/Style]: prompt.

After you've issued Dtext's Justify option, you get the following prompt:

```
Enter an option
[Align/Fit/Center/Middle/Right/TL/TC/TR/ML/MC/MR/BL/BC/BR]:
```

Here are descriptions of each of these options (I've left Fit and Align until last, because these options require more explanation):

**Center**   Centers the text on the start point, with the baseline on the start point.

**Middle**   Centers the text on the start point, with the baseline slightly below the start point.

**Right**   Justifies the text to the right of the start point, with the baseline on the start point.

**TL, TC, and TR**   TL, TC, and TR stand for Top Left, Top Center, and Top Right. Text using these justification styles appears entirely below the start point, justified left, center, or right, depending on which option you choose.

**ML, MC, and MR**   ML, MC, and MR stand for Middle Left, Middle Center, and Middle Right. These styles are similar to TL, TC, and TR, except that the start point determines a location midway between the baseline and the top of the lowercase letters of the text.

**BL, BC, and BR**   BL, BC, and BR stand for Bottom Left, Bottom Center, and Bottom Right. These styles, too, are similar to TL, TC, and TR, but here the start point determines the bottommost location of the letters of the text (the bottom of letters that have descenders, such as *p*, *q*, and *g*).

**Align and Fit**   With the Align and Fit justification options, you must specify a dimension in which the text is to fit. For example, suppose you want the word *Refrigerator* to fit in the 26″-wide box representing the refrigerator. You can use either the Fit or the Align option to accomplish this. With Fit, AutoCAD prompts you to select start and end points and then stretches or compresses the letters to fit within the two points you specify. You use this option when the text must be a consistent height throughout the drawing and you don't care about distorting the font. Align works like Fit, but instead of maintaining the current text style height, the Align option adjusts the text height to keep it proportional to the text width without distorting the font. Use this option when it's important to maintain the font's shape and proportion. Figure 10.13 demonstrates how Fit and Align work.

**FIGURE 10.13**

The word *Refrigerator* as it appears normally and with the Fit and Align options selected

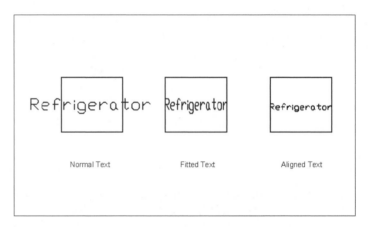

You can change the justification of single-line text by using the Properties palette, but the text moves from its original location while maintaining its insertion point. If you want to change the justification of text without moving the text, you can use the Justifytext command. Choose Modify ➢ Object ➢ Text ➢ Justify, or type **Justifytext** at the Command prompt; then, select the text you want to change. Justifytext works on both multiline and single-line text.

---

**KEEPING TEXT FROM MIRRORING**

At times, you'll want to mirror a group of objects that contain some text. This operation causes the mirrored text to appear backward. You can change a setting in AutoCAD to make the text read normally, even when it's mirrored:

1. At the Command prompt, enter **Mirrtext**↵.

2. At the `Enter new value for MIRRTEXT <1>:` prompt, enter **0**↵.

Now, any mirrored text that isn't in a block will read normally. The text's position, however, will still be mirrored, as shown in the following graphic. Mirrtext is set to 0 by default.

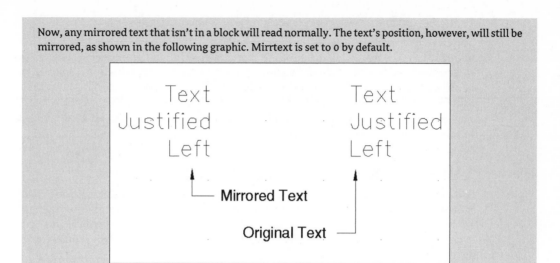

## Using Special Characters with Single-Line Text Objects

Just as with multiline text, you can add a limited set of special characters to single-line text objects. For example, you can place the degree symbol (°) after a number, or you can *underscore* (underline) text. To accomplish this, you use double percent (%%) signs in conjunction with a special code. For example, to underscore text, you enclose that text with %% followed by the letter *u,* which is the underscore code. So, to create this text, "This is underscored text." you enter the following at the prompt:

**This is %%uunderscored%%u text.**

*Overscoring* (putting a line above the text) operates in the same manner. To insert codes for symbols, you place the codes in the correct positions for the symbols they represent. For example, to enter 100.5°, you type **100.5%%d**. Table 10.2 shows some other examples of special character codes.

**TABLE 10.2:**     Here is a list of the codes you can use:

| CODE | WHAT IT DOES |
| --- | --- |
| %%o | Toggles overscore on and off. |
| %%u | Toggles underscore on and off. |
| %%c | Places a diameter symbol where the code occurs. |
| %%d | Places a degree sign (°) where the code occurs. |
| %%p | Places a plus/minus sign where the code occurs. |
| %%% | Forces a single percent sign. This is useful when you want a double percent sign to appear or when you want a percent sign in conjunction with another code. |
| %%nnn | Allows the use of extended characters when these characters are used in a text-definition file. *nnn* is the three-digit value representing the ASCII extended character code. |

**USING THE CHARACTER MAP DIALOG BOX TO ADD SPECIAL CHARACTERS**

You can add special characters to a single line of text in the same way you add special characters to multiline text. You may recall that to access special characters, you use the Character Map dialog box.

To open the Character Map dialog box, choose Start ≻ All Programs ≻ Accessories ≻ System Tools ≻ Character Map. You can then use the procedure discussed in the "Adding Symbols and Special Characters" section, earlier in this chapter, to cut and paste a character from the Character Map dialog box. If you use the Character Map dialog box often, create a shortcut for it, and place the shortcut in your Start menu or on your Desktop.

## Using the Check Spelling Feature

Although AutoCAD is primarily a drawing program, you'll find that some of your drawings contain more text than graphics. Autodesk recognizes this fact and has included a spelling checker since AutoCAD Release 14. If you've ever used the spelling checker in a typical word processor, such as Microsoft Word, the AutoCAD spelling checker's operation will be familiar to you. These steps show you how it works:

1. Click the Spell Check tool in the Text control panel. You can also choose Tools ≻ Spelling from the drop-down menu or type **Sp.↵**.

2. At the Select objects: prompt, select any text object you want to check. You can also enter **All↵** to select everything in the drawing. AutoCAD ignores nontext objects. You can select a mixture of multiline and single-line text. When the spelling checker finds a word it doesn't recognize, the Check Spelling dialog box opens.

In the Check Spelling dialog box, you see the word in question, along with the spelling checker's suggested alternate word in the Suggestions input box. If the spelling checker finds more than one suggestion, a list of suggested alternate words appears below the input box. You can then highlight the desired replacement and click the Change button to change the misspelled word, or you can click Change All to change all occurrences of the word in the selected text. If the suggested word is inappropriate, choose another word from the replacement list (if any), or enter your own spelling in the Suggestions input box. Then, click Change or Change All.

Here is a list of the options available in the Check Spelling dialog box:

**Ignore**   Skips the word.

**Ignore All**   Skips all occurrences of the word in the selected text.

**Change**   Changes the word in question to the word you've selected (or entered) from the Suggestions input box.

**Change All**   Changes all occurrences of the current word when there are multiple instances of the misspelling.

**Add To Dictionary**   Adds the word in question to the current dictionary.

**Dictionaries**   Lets you use a different dictionary to check spelling. This option opens the Change Dictionaries dialog box, described in the upcoming section.

The Check Spelling feature includes types of notation that are more likely to be found in technical drawings. It also checks the spelling of text that is included in block definitions.

## Choosing a Dictionary

Clicking the Dictionaries button in the Check Spelling dialog box opens the Dictionaries dialog box, where you can select a particular main dictionary for foreign languages or create or choose a custom dictionary. Main dictionary files have the `.dct` extension. The main dictionary for the U.S. version of AutoCAD is `Enu.dct`.

In the Change Dictionaries dialog box, you can also add or delete words from a custom dictionary. Custom dictionary files are ASCII files with the `.cus` extension. Because they're ASCII files, you can edit them outside AutoCAD. Click the Current custom dictionary drop-down list to view a list of existing custom dictionaries.

If you prefer, you can select a main or custom dictionary by using the Dctmain system variable. Click the Help button and search for Dctmain for more on the Dctmain system variable.

You can also select a dictionary from the Files tab of the Options dialog box (choose Tools ➢ Options). You can find the dictionary list under Text Editor, Dictionary, And Font File Names.

Click the plus sign next to this item, and then click the plus sign next to the Main Dictionary item to display the dictionary options.

From here, you can double-click the dictionary you prefer.

## Substituting Fonts

At times, you'll want to change all the fonts in a drawing quickly. For instance, you might want to convert TrueType fonts into a simple Txt.shx font to help shorten redraw times while you're editing. Or you might need to convert the font of a drawing received from another office to a font that conforms to your own office standards. The Fontmap system variable works in conjunction with a font-mapping table, enabling you to easily substitute fonts in a drawing.

The font-mapping table is an ASCII file called Acad.fmp. You can also use a file you create yourself. You can give this file any name you choose, as long as it has the .fmp extension.

This font-mapping table contains one line for each font substitution you want AutoCAD to make. A typical line in this file reads as follows:

```
romant; C:\Program Files\Acad 2008\Fonts\txt.shx
```

In this example, AutoCAD is directed to use the txt.shx font in place of the romant.shx font. To execute this substitution, you type **Fontmap.⏎ *Fontmap_filename*.**

*Fontmap_filename* is the font-mapping table you created. This tells AutoCAD where to look for the font-mapping information. Then, you issue the Regen command to view the font changes. To disable the font-mapping table, type

**Fontmap.⏎⏎**

You can also specify a font-mapping file in the Files tab of the Options dialog box. Look for the Text Editor, Dictionary, And Font File Names listing. Click the plus sign next to this listing, and then click the plus sign next to the Font Mapping File listing to display the current default font-mapping filename. If you hold the cursor over the name, AutoCAD displays the full location of the file.

You can double-click this filename to open the Select A File dialog box. From there, you can select a different font-mapping file.

---

### MAKING SUBSTITUTIONS FOR MISSING FONTS

When text styles are created, the associated fonts don't become part of the drawing file. Instead, AutoCAD loads the needed font file at the same time the drawing is loaded. If a text style in a drawing requires a particular font, AutoCAD looks for the font in the AutoCAD search path; if the font is there, it's loaded. Usually this isn't a problem if the drawing file uses the standard fonts that come with AutoCAD or Windows. But occasionally, you'll encounter a file that uses a custom font.

In earlier versions of AutoCAD, you saw an error message when you attempted to open such a file. This missing-font message often sent new AutoCAD users into a panic.

Fortunately, AutoCAD automatically substitutes an existing font for the missing font in a drawing. By default, AutoCAD substitutes the `simplex.shx` font, but you can specify another font by using the Fontalt system variable. Type **Fontalt↵** at the Command prompt, and then enter the name of the font you want to use as the substitute.

You can also select an alternate font through the Files tab of the Options dialog box. Locate the Text Editor, Dictionary, And Font File Names listing, and then click the plus sign at the left. Locate the Alternate Font File item, and click the plus sign at the left. The current alternate is listed. You can double-click the font name to select a different font through a standard file dialog box.

Be aware that the text in your drawing will change in appearance, sometimes radically, when you use a substitute font. If the text in the drawing must retain its appearance, substitute a font that is as similar in appearance to the original font as possible.

---

## Finding and Replacing Text

One of the most time-consuming tasks in drafting is replacing text that appears repeatedly through-out a drawing. Fortunately, you have a Find And Replace tool to help simplify this task. AutoCAD's Find And Replace works like any other find-and-replace tool in a word-processing program. A few options work specifically with AutoCAD. Here's how it works:

1. Click the Find tool in the Text control panel. You can also choose Edit ➤ Find from the menu bar or enter **Find**⏎ at the Command prompt to open the Find And Replace dialog box.

2. Enter the text you want to locate in the Find Text String input box.

3. Enter the replacement text in the Replace With input box.

4. Click Find. When AutoCAD finds the word, it appears in the Context window, along with any other text next to the word.

5. If you have any doubts, click the Zoom To button to display the text in the AutoCAD drawing area.

6. When you've made certain that this is the text you want to change, click Replace.

If you want to replace all occurrences of a word in the drawing, click Replace All. You can also limit your find-and-replace operation to a specific area of your drawing by clicking the Select Objects button in the upper-right corner of the Find And Replace dialog box.

When you click the Select Objects button, the Find And Replace dialog box closes temporarily to enable you to select a set of objects or a region of your drawing. Find And Replace then limits its search to those objects or the region you select.

You can further control the types of objects that Find And Replace looks for by clicking the Options button to open the Find And Replace Options dialog box.

With this dialog box, you can refine your search by limiting it to blocks, dimension text, standard text, or hyperlink text. You can also specify whether to match case or find whole words only.

**NOTE**   If you need to edit a large drawing that contains a lot of text, but you don't need to edit the text, you can use the Qtext command to help accelerate redraws and regenerations when you're working on the drawing. Qtext turns lines of text into rectangular boxes, saving AutoCAD from having to form every letter. This enables you to see the note locations so you don't accidentally draw over them. To use it, enter **qtext**⏎ at the command prompt, and enter **On** or select the On option from the dynamic input display.

---

### MANIPULATING TEXT BEYOND LABELS

This chapter concentrates on methods for adding labels to your drawing, but you also use text in other ways with AutoCAD. Many of the inquiry tools in AutoCAD, such as Dist and List, produce text data. You can use the Windows Clipboard to manipulate such data to your benefit.

For example, you can duplicate the exact length of a line by first using the List command to get a list of its properties. After you have the property list in the AutoCAD Text window, you can highlight its length listing and then press Ctrl+C to copy it to the Windows Clipboard. Next, start the Line command, and pick the start point for the new line. Click the Command window, and press Ctrl+V to paste the line-length data into the Command window; then, add the angle data, or use the Direct Distance method to draw the line.

You can copy any text data from dialog box input boxes or from the AutoCAD Text Window to the Clipboard by using the Ctrl+C keyboard shortcut. You can likewise import that data into any part of AutoCAD that accepts text.

Consider using the Clipboard the next time you need to transfer data in AutoCAD or even when you need to import text from some other application.

---

## The Bottom Line

**Preparing a Drawing for Text**   AutoCAD offers an extensive set of features for adding text to a drawing, but you need to do a little prep work before you dive in.

> **Master It**   Name two things you need to do to prepare a drawing for text.
>
> **Solution**   Set up a layer for your text. Create a text style for your drawing.

**Setting the Annotation Scale and Adding Text** Before you start to add text, you should set the annotation scale for your drawing. Once this is done, you can begin to add text.

**Master It** In a sentence or two, briefly describe the purpose of the Annotation Scale feature. Name the tool you use to add text to a drawing.

**Solution** The Annotation Scale feature converts your text size to the proper height for the scale of your drawing. To add text to a drawing, use the Mtext tool.

**Exploring Text Formatting in AutoCAD** Because text styles contain the font and text-size settings, you can usually set up a text style and then begin to add text to your drawing. For those special cases where you need to vary text height and font or other text features, you can use the Text Formatting toolbar.

**Master It** What Text Formatting tool can you use to change text to boldface type?

**Solution** The Bold button.

**Adding Simple Single-Line Text Objects** In many situations, you need only a single word or a short string of text. AutoCAD offers the Single Line Text object for these instances.

**Master It** Describe two of the three methods for starting the single-line text command.

**Solution** Click the Single Line Text tool in the Text control panel. Choose Draw ➢ Text ➢ Single Line Text. Enter **DT↵** at the command prompt.

**Using the Check Spelling Feature** It isn't uncommon for a drawing to contain the equivalent of several pages of text, and the likelihood of having misspelled words can be high. AutoCAD offers the Check Spelling feature to help you keep your spelling under control.

**Master It** What option do you select in the Check Spelling dialog box when it finds a misspelled word and you want to accept the suggestion it offers?

**Solution** Change.

**Finding and Replacing Text** A common activity when editing technical drawings is to have to find and replace a word throughout a drawing.

**Master It** True or false: The Find And Replace feature in AutoCAD works very differently than the find-and-replace feature in other programs.

**Solution** False.

# Chapter 11

# Using Fields and Tables

Adding text to a set of drawings can become a large part of your work. You'll find that you're editing notes and labels almost as frequently as you're editing the graphics in your drawings. To make some of those editing tasks easier, AutoCAD provides a few special text objects.

In this chapter, you'll look at fields and tables, two features that can help automate some of the more common tasks in AutoCAD. Fields are a special type of text that can automatically update to reflect changes in the drawing. Tables are a tool that helps to automate the process of creating and editing tables and schedules. Tables are a common part of technical drawings and are similar to spreadsheets. In fact, AutoCAD tables behave much like spreadsheets with the capability of adding formulas to cells.

You'll start this chapter with an introduction to fields and then go on to learn about tables. Toward the end, you'll revisit fields to see how they can be used to add formulas to tables.

- ◆ Topics in this chapter include the following:
- ◆ Using Fields to Associate Text with Drawing Properties
- ◆ Adding Tables to Your Drawing
- ◆ Editing the Table Line Work
- ◆ Adding Formulas to Cells
- ◆ Importing and Exporting Tables
- ◆ Creating Table Styles

## Using Fields to Associate Text with Drawing Properties

The text labels you worked with in Chapter 10 are static and don't change unless you edit them by using the tools described there. Another type of text object, called a *field*, behaves in a more dynamic way than the multiline text. A field can be linked to the properties of other objects and updates itself automatically as the associated properties change. For example, you can create a field that is associated with a block name. If the block name changes, the field text automatically changes as well.

Try the following exercise to see how this works:

1. Open the 11c-unit.dwg file. This file is similar to the drawing you worked on in Chapter 10.

2. Double-click the Kitchen text to highlight it and make it available for editing.

3. Right-click the highlighted Kitchen text, and then choose Insert Field to open the Field dialog box. A list to the left shows the types of fields available.

4. In the Field Category drop-down list, select Objects. This limits the display of field types to object fields.

5. In the Field Names list, select NamedObject.

6. Make sure that Block is selected in the Named Object Type drop-down list in the top of the dialog box; then, select Kitchen. This associates the field with the Kitchen block name.

7. In the Format list to the far right, select First Capital. This causes the field text to be lowercase with a capital first letter, regardless of how the block name is actually spelled.

8. Click OK to exit the Field dialog box; then, press ↵ twice to return to the Command prompt.

When you return to the drawing, the text appears in a gray background. This tells you that the text is a field rather than an Mtext or a Dtext object. The gray background is just a device to help you keep track of field text; it doesn't plot.

You've converted existing text into a field that is linked to a block name. Now, let's see how the field works:

1. Enter **Rename**↵ at the Command prompt to open the Rename dialog box.

2. Make sure Blocks is selected in the Named Objects list; then, select Kitchen from the Items list. The word *Kitchen* appears in the Old Name input box near the bottom of the dialog box.

3. Enter **Kitchenette** in the input box just below the Old Name box; then, click the Rename To button.

4. Click OK to close the Rename dialog box.

5. Choose View ➢ Regen. The field you created changes to reflect the new block name.

Fields can be associated with a wide variety of properties. You've just seen how a block name can be associated with a field. In this exercise, you'll use a field to display the area of an object:

1. Choose View ➢ Zoom ➢ Extents to view the entire plan.

2. Place a rectangle in the living room area so that it fills the area.

3. Double-click the Living Room text to open the Text Formatting toolbar.

4. Highlight the text that reads *230 square feet*. Right-click the selected text, and choose Insert Field from the shortcut menu.

5. In the Field dialog box, select Object from the Field Names list.

6. Click the Select Object button next to the Object Type input box at the top of the Field dialog box. The Field dialog box momentarily closes to enable you to select an object.

7. Select the rectangle you just added. The Field dialog box returns.

8. In the Property list just below the Object Type input box, select Area.

9. Select Architectural from the Format list to the far right.

10. Click OK. The field you just added appears in the drawing as the area of the rectangle.

11. Click OK to close the Text Formatting toolbar.

Next, you'll alter the rectangle to see how it affects the field:

1. Click the rectangle to expose its grips. Then, select the top two grips and move them upward so they align with the bathroom wall. Remember to Shift+click to select multiple grips.

2. Choose View ➢ Regen. The field you just added updates to reflect the new area of the rectangle.

3. After reviewing the results, close 11c-unit.dwg.

**TIP**    In previous exercises in this section, you changed existing text into fields. You can create new fields in either the Dtext or Mtext command by selecting Insert Field from the shortcut menu whenever you're typing the text content.

In this exercise, you used a rectangle, but you can use any closed polygon to create an area field. You've touched on just two of the many possible uses for fields. You can associate other types of properties including the current layer, the drawing name, linetypes, and more. You can include Diesel macros as part of fields. (You'll learn about Diesel macros in Chapter 26.) Fields can also be used in AutoCAD's Table feature, described in the next section, which enables you to quickly create tables and schedules. Fields are used to coordinate sheet labels with reference symbols in the AutoCAD Sheet Set feature described in Chapter 28.

For most of your work, the standard text objects will work just fine, but you may find fields useful when you know a label has to be associated with specific types of data in your drawing. In later chapters, you'll have more opportunities to work with fields.

# Adding Tables to Your Drawing

One of the more common text-related tasks you'll do for your drawings is to create schedules, such as door and window schedules or parts schedules. Such schedules are tables used to provide more detailed information regarding the elements in your design.

In the past, AutoCAD users used Mtext or Dtext to create the text for schedules and then used line-drawing tools to create the cells of the schedule. Since AutoCAD 2006, you can use tables to help you generate schedules more quickly. Tables allow you to automatically format the columns and rows of text in a way similar to spreadsheet programs.

## Creating a Table

The first step in creating a table is to determine the number of rows and columns you want. Don't worry if you aren't certain of the exact number of rows and columns; you can add or subtract them at any time. In this exercise, you'll create a table that contains 12 rows and 9 columns, as shown in Figure 11.1.

Start by creating the basic table layout:

1. Choose File ➢ New, and use the standard `Acad.dwt` drawing template.

**FIGURE 11.1**

A sample table created with the Table tool

| No. | Room | Finish | | | | Ceiling Ht. | Area | Remarks |
|-----|------|--------|--|--|--|-------------|------|---------|
| | | Floor | Base | Walls | Ceiling | | | |
| 110 | Lobby | B | 1 | A | 1 | 10'-0" | 200sf | |
| 111 | Office | A | 1 | B | 2 | 8'-0" | 96sf | |
| 112 | Office | A | 1 | B | 2 | 8'-0" | 96sf | |
| 113 | Office | A | 1 | B | 2 | 8'-0" | 96sf | |
| 114 | Meeting | C | 1 | B | 2 | 8'-0" | 150sf | |
| 115 | Breakout | C | 1 | B | 2 | 8'-0" | 150sf | |
| 116 | Womens | D | 2 | C | 3 | 8'-0" | 50sf | |
| 117 | Mens | D | 2 | C | 3 | 8'-0" | 50sf | |

Room Finish Schedule

2.  Click Table from the 2D Draw control panel, or choose Draw ➤ Table from the menu bar to open the Insert Table dialog box.

3.  In the Column & Row Settings group, enter **9** for Columns and **12** for Data Rows.

4.  Click OK. The dialog box closes, and the outline of a table follows your cursor.

5.  Position the table in the center of your drawing area, and click to place the table. The table appears with a cursor in the top cell of the table. You also see the Text Formatting toolbar above the table.

6.  Enter **Room Finish Schedule**, and press ↵. The cursor moves to the next cell.

7.  Click OK to exit the Text Formatting toolbar.

## Adding Cell Text

You've just created a table and added a title. Notice that the table actually contains 14 rows, including the title row at the top and an additional row for the headings of each column. You can delete these additional rows if you don't need them, but for now, you'll start to add some text to the table:

1.  Adjust your view so the table fills most of the drawing area.

2.  Double-click in the first cell at the top left, just below the Room Finish Schedule label. The cell turns gray, and the Text Formatting toolbar opens. You also see labels across the top and left side showing the row and column addresses.

3. Enter **Number** for the room number column at the far left, and then press the Tab key to advance to the next cell to the right.

4. Enter **Room**, and press the Tab key again.

5. Enter **Finish**, and press the Tab key four times to advance four columns. You do this because the Finish heading shown in Figure 11.1 has four columns under it: Floor, Base, Walls, and Ceiling. In the next exercise, you'll learn how to format those four columns under the single heading.

6. Enter **Ceiling Ht.**, and press the Tab key again.

7. Enter **Area**, press the Tab key, and enter **Remarks**.

8. Click OK in the Text Formatting toolbar to close it.

You have the column headings in place. Now, you need to do a little extra formatting. In step 5, you left four cells blank because four of the columns will be combined under one heading: The Finish heading covers the Floor, Base, Walls, and Ceiling columns. Next, you'll combine the blank headings with the Finish heading:

1. Click in the center of the cell with the Finish label to select it.

2. Shift+click in the third cell to the right of the Finish cell to select all four cells.

3. Right-click in the selected cells, and choose Merge ➢ All. The four selected cells merge into a single cell with the word *Finish*.

Now, you need to add the subheads under the Finish header:

1. Double-click in the leftmost cell below the Finish cell to open the Text Formatting toolbar.

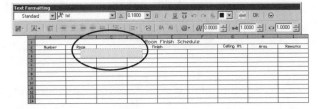

2. Enter **Floor**, and press the Tab key.

3. Enter **Base**, **Wall**, and **Ceiling** in each of the following columns as you've been doing. Remember that the Tab key advances you to the next cell to the right. Your table should look like Figure 11.2.

4. Click OK in the Text Formatting toolbar to close it.

**FIGURE 11.2**

The table so far

## Adjusting Table Text Orientation and Location

You now have the basic layout of the table, with one difference. The Floor, Base, Walls, and Ceiling labels you just added are oriented horizontally, but you want them oriented vertically, as in Figure 11.1. The following steps will show you how to rotate a set of labels in a table so they appear in the orientation you want:

1. Click in the cell labeled Floor to select it.

2. Shift+click in the cell labeled Ceiling to select all four of the cells below the Finish heading. The combined cells have four grips, one on each side of the group.

3. Click the grip at the bottom of the selected group, and move it down about four rows. The entire row becomes taller. This provides room for the text when you rotate it.

4. Right-click in the selected cells, and choose Properties from the shortcut menu to open the Properties palette.

5. In the Properties palette, click the Text Rotation input box under the Content group.

6. Enter 90↵ for a 90-degree rotation of the text. The text rotates into a vertical orientation.

7. Close the Properties palette.

With the text in this orientation, the columns are too wide, so you'll change the cell width for the selected cells.

8. Move the right grip to the left to decrease the width of the cells.

9. For the final touch, you'll center the text in the cells. With the cells still selected, right-click in the selected cells, and choose Alignment ➤ Bottom Center. The text becomes centered in the cells and aligned at the bottom of the cells.

**TIP** You can also control the margin between the text and the cell border by using the Cell Margin options in the Properties palette. Select the entire table, right-click, and choose Properties. In the Properties palette, click the Vertical Cell Margin option or the Horizontal Cell Margin option in the Table group.

In the last exercise, you learned how you can adjust the text orientation through the Properties palette. You can also adjust the width of multiple cells by adjusting the grip location. If you need to be more precise about the cell width, you can use the Cell Width option in the Properties palette for a set of cells.

Now, continue to add text to the cells and adjust their sizes:

1. Double-click in the cell in the Number column just below the row that contains the Floor, Base, Walls, and Ceiling cells. A text cursor appears in the cell, and the Text Formatting toolbar opens.

2. Enter **110**, and press ↵. Instead of advancing to the next cell to the right, you advance to the next cell below.

3. Enter **111**, and press ↵ again. Continue to enter each room number in this way. When you've finished entering the room numbers, click OK in the Text Formatting toolbar to close it.

   Next, you'll reduce the width of the column to fit the text a bit better.

4. Click in the cell with the Number text label. It's the first column heading in the table.

5. Shift+click in the bottom cell of the Number column to select the entire column.

6. Click the grip to the left of the column, and move the grip to the right so the column width is approximately half the width of the Room column. You can zoom in on the column to allow more control over the positioning of the grip.

**7.** Press Esc to exit the selection and view your table so far.

| Room Finish Schedule | | | | | | | | |
|---|---|---|---|---|---|---|---|---|
| Number | Room | Finish | | | | Celling Ht. | Area | Remarks |
| | | Floor | Base | Wall | Ceiling | | | |
| 110 | | | | | | | | |
| 111 | | | | | | | | |
| 112 | | | | | | | | |
| 113 | | | | | | | | |
| 114 | | | | | | | | |
| 115 | | | | | | | | |
| 116 | | | | | | | | |
| 117 | | | | | | | | |
| | | | | | | | | |
| | | | | | | | | |
| | | | | | | | | |

Now, suppose you want to delete one of the extra rows of cells at the bottom of the table or add a new row. Here's what to do:

**1.** Click the bottom-left cell of the table to select it.

**2.** Right-click, and choose Rows ➤ Delete from the shortcut menu. The row disappears.

**3.** To add a row, select a cell, right-click, and choose Rows ➤ Insert Above or Rows ➤ Insert Below, depending on where you want the new row.

You may notice the Delete Columns and Insert Columns options in the shortcut menu that let you add or delete columns. These options function in a similar way to the Delete Rows and Insert Rows options.

## Editing the Table Line Work

So far, you've concentrated on how you can format text and cells in a table, but you'll also want some control over the lines in the table. Typically, heavier lines are used around the border of the table and between the title and the rest of the table.

The Cell Borders shortcut menu option lets you modify the outline of the border. When you select this option, the Cell Border Properties dialog box opens.

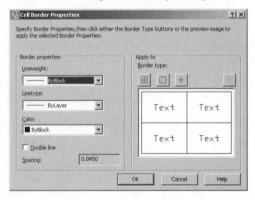

You can use this dialog box to fine-tune the appearance of the line work of the table. Try the following exercise to see firsthand how this dialog box works:

1. Turn on the display of lineweights by choosing Format ➢ Lineweight.

2. In the Lineweight Settings dialog box, turn on the Display Lineweight setting; then, click OK.

3. Click in the title cell at the top of the table to select the cell, and then right-click and choose Borders to open the Cell Border Properties dialog box.

4. Click the Lineweight drop-down list, and select 0.30 mm.

5. Click the Outside Borders button in the Apply To group to tell AutoCAD to change the borders of the cell to the selected lineweight.

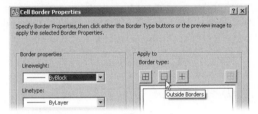

6. Click OK. The title cell is now outlined in a heavier line. To see it clearly, press the Esc key to close the Table toolbar.

You can also adjust the lineweights that encircle a group of cells, as in the following exercise:

1. Click the cell in the upper-left corner with the Number label.

2. Shift+click the cell in the lower-right corner of the table so that all the cells from the second-from-the-top row down are selected.

3. Right-click, and choose Borders.

4. Select 0.30 mm from the Lineweight drop-down list. Then, click the Outside Borders button as you did in step 5 of the previous exercise.

5. Click OK. The outlines of the selected cells are given the new lineweight setting.

6. Save this file for future reference.

| Number | Room | Finish | | | | Ceiling Ht. | Area | Remarks |
|---|---|---|---|---|---|---|---|---|
| | | Floor | Base | Wall | Ceiling | | | |
| 110 | | | | | | | | |
| 111 | | | | | | | | |
| 112 | | | | | | | | |
| 113 | | | | | | | | |
| 114 | | | | | | | | |
| 115 | | | | | | | | |
| 116 | | | | | | | | |
| 117 | | | | | | | | |
| | | | | | | | | |

*Room Finish Schedule*

**TIP** In addition to the table borders, you can change the background color for the cells of the table through the Background Fill option in the Properties palette. Select a group of cells in the table that you want to affect (but don't select the entire table), right-click, and choose Properties. In the Properties palette, click the Background Fill option in the Cell group.

The Cell Border Properties dialog box also lets you set the line colors by selecting a color from the Color drop-down list before selecting an Apply To option.

In addition, the Apply To group offers four buttons: All Borders, Outside Borders (which you've already tried), Inside Borders, and No Borders. The All Borders option applies the changes to all borders. The Inside borders option applies the changes to just the inside borders. This option works only if you've selected multiple cells. The No Borders option lets you clear your border selections if you change your mind.

If you want to select only the vertical or horizontal inside borders, you can use the graphic in the Cell Border Properties dialog box to select either the vertical or horizontal inside border. You can also use the graphic to select individual sides of the outside border by clicking the sample border in the graphic. The sample changes to show you which border lines are affected.

# Adding Formulas to Cells

In the beginning of this chapter, I mentioned that you can include formulas in cells of AutoCAD tables. This can be a great timesaver, because you can set up a table with quantities that automatically adjust to changes in values in the table. You don't have to manually calculate the changes.

You may recall that formulas are actually a type of field and that a field can be linked with objects in a drawing so that the field displays the linked object's properties. The formula field can be linked to several numeric text values.

Although fields are the tool you use for formulas, you don't have to consciously choose to add a field to a cell every time you want to add a formula. The following exercise will demonstrate how you can add a formula by typing directly in a cell. AutoCAD takes care of converting your input into a field.

## Using Formulas Directly in Cells

The simplest way to add a formula to a cell is to double-click the cell and then, when the Text Formatting toolbar appears, enter the formula directly in the cell with the addition of an = (equal sign) at the beginning. Try the following exercise to see how it works.

1. Open the FieldSample.dwg file.

2. Double-click in the cell, as shown in Figure 11.3, to select the location for your formula.

**FIGURE 11.3**

Selecting the cell for your formula

| Sample Table | | | | |
|---|---|---|---|---|
| 100 | 200 | 300 | 400 | |
| 150 | 250 | 350 | 450 | |
| 250 | 350 | 450 | 550 | |
| | | | | |

Double-click this cell.

3. Enter the following text in the cell to add the values in cell A2 and cell D4:

=A2+D4

**4.** Press ↵ after you enter the value. The value of A2 plus D4 appears in the cell.

| | A | B | C | D | E |
|---|---|---|---|---|---|
| 1 | | | Sample Table | | |
| 2 | 100 | 200 | 300 | 400 | |
| 3 | 150 | 250 | 350 | 450 | |
| 4 | 250 | 350 | 450 | 550 | |
| 5 | | | | | 650 |

In step 3, the equal sign tells AutoCAD to convert the text into a formula field. You may have noticed that when you start to edit a cell in a table, the row and column labels appear along the top and left side of the table. You can use these labels to determine the cell addresses for your formula.

In typical spreadsheet fashion, you can change the formula in a cell any time. Double-click the cell containing the formula, and then edit the formula values and operators.

You can also use the Formula drop-down list from the Table toolbar to select from a set of predefined math operations.

Click in the cell where you want to place the formula; then, in the Table toolbar, click the Formula drop-down list, and select the operation you want to use. Next, place a selection window around the cells you want to include in the formula. Click in the first cell that you want to include in the formula, and then click in the second cell. As you do this, a selection window appears. All the cells that are included in the selection window are included in the formula.

## Using Other Math Operations

In the previous exercise, you used the plus sign to add the value of two cells. You can string together several cells' addresses to add multiple cells, as follows:

```
=A2+A3+A4...
```

You can also subtract, multiply, or divide by using the – (subtract or minus), * (multiply or asterisk), or / (divide or hash) sign. To perform multiple operations on several cells, you can group operations with parentheses in a way similar to a typical spreadsheet formula. For example, if you want to add two cells together and then multiply their sum by another cell, use the following format:

```
=(A2+A3)*A4
```

The Average, Sum, and Count buttons that appear in the Formula drop-down list of the Table toolbar give you quick access to these frequently used functions. You can obtain the average value of a set of cells, quickly get the sum of a set of cells, or get a count of the number of cells you select. When you click one of these options, you're prompted to select several cells with a selection window. Once you've selected a set of cells, you see the appropriate formula in the selected cell. Clicking the Average button, for example, produces a formula similar to the following:

```
=Average(A1:B5)
```

Clicking the Sum button produces a formula like the following:

```
=Sum(A1:B5)
```

In both cases, a range of cells is indicated using a colon, as in A1:B5. You can use this format when entering formulas manually. You can also include a single cell with a range by using a comma:

```
=Sum(A1:B5,C6)
```

## Importing and Exporting Tables

Frequently, tables are created outside AutoCAD in a spreadsheet program such as Excel. You can import an Excel worksheet as an AutoCAD table by using the AutoCAD Entities option in the Paste Special feature. The ability to import tables lets non-AutoCAD users create the table data while you concentrate on the drawing.

Try the following exercise to see how you can import a table from a worksheet:

1. Open the Excel worksheet called 11a-plan.xls, and highlight the door data, as shown in Figure 11.4.

**FIGURE 11.4**

Selecting the door data in the 11a-plan.xls spreadsheet

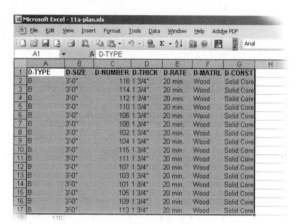

2. Choose Edit ➤ Copy to place a copy of the selected data into the Windows Clipboard; then, switch back to AutoCAD.

3. Choose Edit ➤ Paste Special to open the Paste Special dialog box.

4. With the Paste radio button selected, click AutoCAD Entities in the list, and then click OK.

5. At the Specify insertion point or [paste as Text]: prompt, click a point in the lower-right area of the drawing. The worksheet data appears in the drawing, although it's very small. You also see the Text Formatting toolbar.

6. Click OK in the Text Formatting toolbar to close it.

7. If needed, use the Scale tool to enlarge the table to a readable size.

In this exercise, you imported the worksheet by using the default standard table style. This gives you a simple-looking table using the AutoCAD Txt font. You can set up a custom table style, as described later in this chapter, with the fonts and borders you want, and then import the table for a more custom appearance. Make sure your custom table style is the current style before you import the worksheet.

## Exporting Tables

Some day, you might want to export your AutoCAD table to a spreadsheet program or database. You can do this through a somewhat hidden option in a shortcut menu. Follow these steps:

1. Select the entire table. You can do so by clicking in a spot above and to the right of the table. With the crossing selection window, completely enclose the table, and click.

2. Right-click anywhere in the table, and choose Export from the shortcut menu to open the Export Data dialog box.

3. Specify a name and location for your exported table data, and click Save.

The file is saved with a `.csv` filename extension. This type of file is a comma-delimited file and can be read by most spreadsheet programs, including Microsoft Excel. Unfortunately, the `.csv` file doesn't retain the AutoCAD table formatting.

To open the exported file from Excel, choose File ➤ Open in the Excel menu bar; then, in the Open dialog box, select Text File (*.prn, *.txt, *.csv) in the Files Of Type drop-down list. You can then locate the exported table and open it.

---

### ADDING GRAPHICS TO TABLE CELLS

One of the more interesting features of the Table tool is its ability to include blocks in a cell. This can be useful if you want to include graphic elements in your table. Adding a block to a cell is a simple process. Here are the steps:

1. Click in a cell to select it.

2. Right-click, and choose Insert ➤ Block from the shortcut menu to open the Insert A Block In A Table Cell dialog box.

3. Select a block name from the Name drop-down list. You can also click the button to the right of the list to open a file dialog box that enables you to select a drawing file for import to the cell.

4. After you've selected a block and specified the settings in the Properties group of the dialog box, click OK. The block appears in the cell you've selected.

The Properties group in the dialog box enables you to specify the alignment and size of the inserted block. By default, the AutoFit option is turned on. This option adjusts the size of the block to make it fit in the current cell size.

# Creating Table Styles

If you find that you're creating the same table layout over and over, you can set up predefined table styles. You can set up the properties of the title, column headings, and data in advance so you don't have to set them up each time you create a table. For example, if you prefer to use Arial bold at 0.25″ for the title and standard Arial at 0.125″ for the column headings, you can create a table style with those settings. The next time you need to create a table, you can select your custom table style and specify the number of columns and rows; then, you'll be ready to add the data without having to format the text.

To create a table style, follow these steps:

1. Choose Format ➤ Table Style from the menu bar to open the Table Style dialog box. You see the Standard table style in the list box. This is the one you used in the previous exercises.

2. Click the New button to open the Create New Table Style dialog box. This is where you give your new table style a name.

3. Enter **My Table Style**, and click Continue to open the New Table Style dialog box (see Figure 11.5).

**FIGURE 11.5**
The New Table Style
dialog box

4. You'll learn more about the options in this dialog box next. For now, click OK to close the dialog box.

5. Your new table style now appears in the Styles list of the Table Style dialog box. If you want to edit an existing table style, you can select the style from the list and click the Modify button. The Modify Table Style dialog box will appear, enabling you to edit the existing style. The Modify Table Style dialog box is identical to the New Table Style dialog box shown in Figure 11.5.

6. Click Close to exit the dialog box.

After you've created a style, you can select it from the Table Style Settings group of the Insert Table dialog box that you used to create the sample table (choose Draw ➤ Table).

You can also open the New Table Style dialog box by clicking the Table Style Dialog button just to the right of the Table Style Name drop-down list in the Insert Table dialog box.

## The Table Style Options

Let's take a closer look at the New Table Style dialog box shown earlier in Figure 11.5. It may seem a bit bewildering at first, but once you take the time to explore the parts of this dialog box, it's fairly straightforward. The following offers a description of the parts of the New Table Style dialog box by group:

**Starting Table**   Typically, you can set up a new table style using the settings in the other groups of this dialog box, but the Starting Table group gives you the ability to use an existing table in the drawing as the basis for your new table style. This can be helpful if you've already done some work formatting a table in your drawing. This group includes two buttons. The one on the left lets you select an existing table in the drawing for your new style. If you click this button, the dialog box closes temporarily to allow you to select a table in your drawing. The button on the right removes your in-drawing table selection and reverts to the settings in the dialog box.

**General**   The General group offers only one setting: the direction for the table. Typically, you'll use the Down option, which means the table reads from top to bottom. If for some reason you need a table with titles at the bottom, choose the Up option.

**Cell Styles**   You have a high degree of control over the appearance of individual cells through the cell styles. By default, your new table style will have three cell styles called Data, Header, and Title. You can select these cell styles from the drop-down list at the top of the Cell Styles group. You can then edit the selected style using the three tabs below the drop-down list. Here is a brief description of the function of each tab:

◆ General give you control over the background color, alignment, format, and type of information presented in the cell. The Margins options control the margins in the cell. The Merge Cells On Row/Column Creation option at the bottom of the General tab causes the cells to merge into a single cell for the selected cell style.

◆ Text gives you control over the default text style, height, and color, and the angle of the text in the cell.

◆ Borders lets you control the lineweight for the borders of the cell.

You can also create your own cell style using the two buttons to the right of the Cell Styles drop-down list. The left button lets you create a new cell style. The button on the right lets you create, rename, or delete a cell style through the Manage Cell Style dialog box.

**Cell Style Preview**   This window gives you a preview of what the cell style will look like with the settings you make in the tabs of the Cell Styles group. This preview changes in real time as you change the settings in the General, Text, or Borders tab.

## The Bottom Line

**Using Fields to Associate Text with Drawing Properties**   Fields are a special type of text object that can be linked to object properties. They can help to automate certain text-related tasks.

**Master It**   Name two uses for fields that you learned about in the first part of this chapter.

**Solution**   Fields can be used to update text that labels a block. They can also be used to update text and report the area enclosed by a polyline.

**Adding Tables to Your Drawing**   The Tables feature can help you make quick work of schedules and other tabular data that you want to include in a drawing.

**Master It**   What is the name of the dialog box that appears when you click the Table tool from the Tables control panel?

**Solution**   Insert Table.

**Editing the Table Line Work**   Because tables include line work to delineate their different cells, AutoCAD gives you control over table borders and lines.

**Master It**   How do you get to the Cell Border Properties dialog box?

**Solution**   Select the cell or cells in the table, right-click, and choose Borders.

**Adding Formulas to Cells**   Tables can also function like a spreadsheet by allowing you to add formulas to cells.

**Master It**   What type of text object lets you add formulas to cells?

**Solution**   Field.

**Importing and Exporting Tables**   The Table feature allows you to import Microsoft Excel spreadsheets into AutoCAD.

**Master It**   Describe how to import a spreadsheet from Excel into AutoCAD.

**Solution**   Open the spreadsheet, and select the cells you want to import. Choose Edit ➢ Copy to copy the spreadsheet data into the Clipboard. In AutoCAD, choose Edit ➢ Paste Special. In the Paste Special dialog box, select AutoCAD Entities, and click OK.

# Chapter 12

# Using Dimensions

Before you determine the dimensions of a project, your design is in flux, and many questions may be unanswered. After you begin dimensioning, you'll start to see whether things fit or work together. Dimensioning can be crucial to how well a design works and how quickly it develops. The dimensions answer questions about code conformance if you're an architect; they answer questions about tolerances, fit, and interference if you're involved in mechanical applications. After you and your design team reach a design on a schematic level, communicating even tentative dimensions to others on the team can accelerate design development. Dimensions represent a point from which you can further develop your ideas.

With AutoCAD, you can easily add tentative or final dimensions to any drawing. AutoCAD gives you an accurate dimension without your having to take measurements. You pick the two points to be dimensioned and the dimension line location, and AutoCAD does the rest. AutoCAD's *associative dimensioning* capability automatically updates dimensions whenever the size or shape of the dimensioned object changes. These dimensioning features can save you valuable time and reduce the number of dimensional errors in your drawings.

Topics in this chapter include the following:

◆ Understanding the Components of a Dimension

◆ Creating a Dimension Style

◆ Drawing Linear Dimensions

◆ Editing Dimensions

◆ Dimensioning Non-orthogonal Objects

◆ Adding a Note with a Leader Arrow

◆ Applying Ordinate Dimensions

◆ Adding Tolerance Notation

## Understanding the Components of a Dimension

Before you start the exercises in this chapter, it will help to know the names of the parts of a dimension. Figure 12.1 shows a sample of a dimension with the parts labeled. The *dimension line* is the line that represents the distance being dimensioned. It's the horizontal line with the diagonal tick marks on either end. The *extension lines* are the lines that originate from the object being dimensioned. They show you the exact location from which the dimension is taken. The *dimension text* is the dimension value, usually shown inside or above the dimension line.

**FIGURE 12.1**

The components of
a dimension

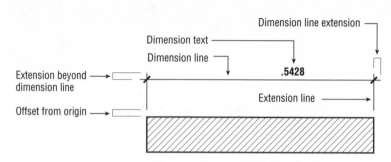

Another component of a dimension line is the *dimension line extension*. This is the part of the dimension line that extends beyond the extension line. Dimension line extensions are usually used only on architectural dimensions. The extension lines usually extend beyond the dimension lines in all types of dimensions. The extension line *offset from origin* is the distance from the beginning of the extension line to the object being dimensioned. The extension *beyond dimension line* is the distance the dimension line extends past the extension line and is most commonly used in architectural drawings.

You can control each of these components by creating or editing dimension styles. *Dimension styles* are the settings that determine the look of your dimensions. You can store multiple styles in a single drawing. The first exercise in this chapter will show you how to create a dimension style.

---

**DIMENSIONING STANDARDS**

In addition to the components of a dimension, you should know about the standards that govern the placement and style of dimensions in a drawing. Each industry has a different set of standards for text size, text style, arrow style, dimension placement, and general dimensioning methods. These issues are beyond the scope of this book; however, I urge you to become familiar with the standards associated with your industry. Many resources are available to you if you want to find out more about dimension standards. Here are a few resources on the subject:

◆ For mechanical drafting in the United States, check the American Society of Mechanical Engineers (ASME) website: http://www.asme.org.

◆ For European standards, see the International Organization for Standardization (ISO) website: http://www.iso.org.

◆ For architectural standards in the United States, see the American Institute of Architects (AIA) website: http://www.aia.org.

---

## Creating a Dimension Style

Dimension styles are similar to text styles. They determine the look of your dimensions as well as the size of dimensioning features, such as the dimension text and arrows. You can set up a dimension style to have special types of arrows, for instance, or to position the dimension text above or in line with the dimension line. Dimension styles also make your work easier by enabling you to store and duplicate your most common dimension settings.

AutoCAD gives you one of two default dimension styles, *ISO-25* or *Standard*, depending on whether you use the metric or Imperial (also called English) measurement system. You'll probably add many other styles to suit the types of drawings you're creating. You can also create variations of a general style for those situations that call for only minor changes in the dimension's appearance.

In this section, you'll learn how to set up your own dimension style based on the Standard dimension style (see Figure 12.2). For metric users, the settings are different, but the overall methods are the same.

**FIGURE 12.2**

AutoCAD's Standard dimension style compared with an architectural-style dimension

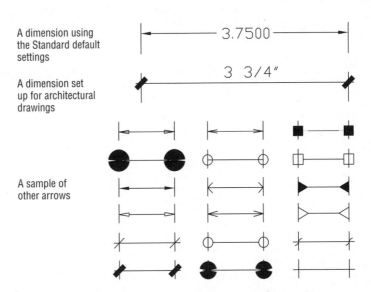

A dimension using the Standard default settings

A dimension set up for architectural drawings

A sample of other arrows

Follow these steps to create a dimension style:

1. Open the Unit file you edited in the preceding chapter. If you didn't create one, use the 12a-unit.dwg file and rename it Unit.dwg. Metric users should open 12a-unit-metric.dwg and rename it Unit.dwg.

2. Issue Zoom All to display the entire floor plan.

3. Click the Dimension Style tool in the Dimensions control panel. You can also choose Format ➢ Dimension Style or type **D**↵ at the Command prompt to open the Dimension Style Manager dialog box.

4. Select Standard from the Styles list box. Metric users should select ISO-25.

**5.** Click New to open the Create New Dimension Style dialog box.

**6.** With the Copy Of Standard or ISO-25 name highlighted in the New Style Name input box, enter **My Architectural**.

**7.** Click Continue to open the detailed New Dimension Style dialog box.

You've just created a dimension style called My Architectural, but at this point it's identical to the Standard style on which it's based. Nothing has happened to the Standard style; it's still available if you need to use it.

## Setting Up the Primary Unit Style

Now, you need to set up your new dimension style so that it conforms to the U.S. architectural style of dimensioning. Let's start by changing the unit style for the dimension text. Just as you changed the overall unit style of AutoCAD to a feet-and-inches style for your bath drawing in Chapter 3, you must do the same for your dimension styles. Setting the overall unit style doesn't automatically set the dimension unit style. Follow these steps:

**1.** In the New Dimension Style dialog box, click the Primary Units tab.

2. In the Linear Dimensions group, open the Unit Format drop-down list, and choose Architectural. Notice that this drop-down list contains the same unit styles as the main Drawing Units dialog box (choose Format ➤ Units). Metric users can skip this option.

**TIP**  The Decimal Separator option a few settings below the Unit Format option lets you choose between a period and a comma for decimal points. Metric users often use the comma for a decimal point, and U.S. users use a period. This option doesn't have any meaning for measurements other than decimal, so it's dimmed when the Architectural unit format is selected.

3. Select 0´-0¼˝ from the Precision drop-down list, just below the Unit Format list. Metric users should select 0.00. The Precision option enables you to set the level of precision that is displayed in the dimension text. It doesn't limit the precision of AutoCAD's drawing database. This value is used to limit only the display of dimension text values.

**TIP**  Every dimension style setting has an equivalent system variable. See Appendix C for more on system variables that are directly associated with dimensions.

4. Just below the Precision drop-down list, open the Fraction Format drop-down list, and select Diagonal. Notice what happens to the graphic: The fractional dimensions change to show how your dimension text will look. Metric users can skip this step, because it isn't available when the Decimal unit format is selected.

5. In the Zero Suppression group in the lower-left corner, click 0 Inches to deselect this check box. If you leave it turned on, indications of 0 inches will be omitted from the dimension text. (In architectural drawings, 0 inches are shown as in this dimension: 12´-0˝.) Metric users can ignore this option.

If you use the Imperial measurement system, you've set up My Architectural's dimension unit style to show dimensions in feet and inches, the standard method for U.S. construction documents. Metric users have changed the Precision value and kept the Decimal unit system.

## Setting the Height for Dimension Text

Along with the unit style, you should adjust the size of the dimension text. The Text tab of the New Dimension Style dialog box lets you set a variety of text options, including text location relative to the dimension line, style, and height.

Follow these steps to set the height of your dimension text:

1. Click the Text tab to display the text options.

2. Highlight the contents of the Text Height input box.

3. Type **1/8**↵ to make the text ⅛″ high. Metric users should enter **0.3**↵ for the text height.

Unlike the text you created in Chapter 10, you specify the text height by its final plot size. You then specify an overall dimension scale factor that affects the sizing of all dimensioning settings, such as text and arrows.

If you want to use a specific text style for your dimensions, select a text style in the Text Style drop-down list in the Text tab. If the style you select happens to have a height specification greater than 0, that height will override any text height settings you enter in the Text tab.

## Setting the Location and Orientation of Dimension Text

AutoCAD's default setting for the placement of dimension text puts the text in line with the dimension line, as shown in the example at the top of Figure 12.2, earlier in this chapter. However, you want the new Architectural style to put the text above the dimension line, as is done in the center of Figure 12.2. To do that, you'll use the Text Placement and Text Alignment options in the Text tab of the New Dimension Style dialog box:

1. In the Text Alignment group in the lower-right corner of the dialog box, click the Aligned With Dimension Line radio button.

2. In the Text Placement group, open the Vertical drop-down list, and select Above. The appearance of the sample image changes to show how your new settings will look.

3. Again in the Text Placement group, change the Offset From Dim Line value to ¹⁄₁₆. This setting controls the size of the gap between the dimension line and the dimension text.

Each time you change a setting, the graphic gives you immediate feedback about how your changes will affect your dimension style.

**TIP** Metric users may not need to change these settings, depending on your preference for dimension styles.

## Choosing an Arrow Style and Setting the Dimension Scale

Next, you'll specify a different type of arrow for your new dimension style. For linear dimensions in architectural drawings, a diagonal line, or *tick* mark, is typically used, rather than an arrow.

In addition, you want to set the scale for the graphical components of the dimension, such as the arrows and text. Recall from Chapter 10 that text must be scaled up in size in order to appear at the proper size in the final output of the drawing. Dimensions too must be scaled so they look correct when the drawing is plotted. The arrows are controlled by settings in the Symbols And Arrows tab, and the overall scale of the dimension style is set in the Fit tab.

Here are the steps for specifying the arrow type and scale:

1. Click the Symbols And Arrows tab to display the options for controlling the arrow style and dimension line extensions.

2. In the Arrowheads group, open the First drop-down list, and choose Architectural Tick. The graphic next to the arrowhead name shows you what the arrowhead looks like.

**TIP**   See Appendix C for details on how you can create your own arrowheads. AutoCAD also lets you set up a separate arrow style for leaders.

3. In the Arrowheads group, change the Arrow Size setting to ⅛. Metric users should enter .3.

Next, you need to set the behavior of the dimension line and extension lines:

1. Click the Lines tab to display the options for controlling the dimension and extension lines.

**2.** In the Dimension Lines group, highlight the value in the Extend Beyond Ticks input box, and enter **1/16**. (Metric users should enter **0.15**.) This causes the dimension lines to extend past the tick arrows. This is a standard graphic practice used for dimensioning linear dimensions in architectural plans.

**3.** In the Extension Lines group, change the Extend Beyond Dim Lines setting to ⅛. Metric users should change this to .3. This setting determines the distance the extension line extends past the dimension line.

**4.** Again in the Extension Lines group, change the Offset From Origin setting to ⅛. Metric users should change this to .3. This sets the distance from the point being dimensioned to the beginning of the dimension extension line.

**5.** Click the Fit tab of the New Dimension Style dialog box to display the options for overall dimension scale and miscellaneous settings.

**6.** Turn on the Annotative option in the Scale For Dimension Features group. You may recall from Chapter 10 that the Annotative option allows AutoCAD to automatically scale an object to the drawing's annotation scale.

**7.** Click OK to close the New Dimension Style dialog box. The Dimension Style Manager dialog box opens again.

---

#### SCALE FOR DIMENSIONS IN LEGACY DRAWINGS

Drawings created prior to AutoCAD 2008 relied on scale factors to determine the scaling of dimensions. Because it's likely that you'll run into legacy drawing files, here is some information about the settings used for those earlier dimensions.

Instead of using the Annotative option, the Use Overall Scale Of option is used in the Scale For Dimension Features group. You select the Use Overall Scale Of radio button and enter a drawing scale factor in the Use Overall Scale Of input box.

All the values you enter for the options in the New Dimension Style dialog box are multiplied by this Use Overall Scale Of value to obtain the final size of the dimension components. For example, the text height you entered earlier, ⅛″, is multiplied by 48 for a dimension text height of 6″. For metric users, the text height of 0.3 is multiplied by 50 for a text height of 15 cm. For more on the scaling of text and other object in AutoCAD, see Chapter 3.

---

**TIP**   If you use the Scale Dimensions To Layout option in the Scale For Dimension Features group of the Fit tab, AutoCAD uses the Layout viewport scale to size the dimension components. See Chapter 8 for more information about viewport scale settings. This can be useful if you have a drawing that you want to print at multiple scales.

## Setting Up Alternate Units

You can use the Alternate Units tab of the New Dimension Style dialog box to set up AutoCAD to display a second dimension in centimeters or millimeters. Likewise, if you're a metric user, you can set up a second dimension to display feet and inches. The following exercise shows you how to set up alternate dimensions. You don't have to do this exercise now; it's here for your information. If you like, come back later and try it to see how it affects your dimensions. You can pick up the tutorial in the next section, "Setting the Current Dimension Style."

**TIP**   If you decide later that you don't want the alternate units to be displayed, you can turn them off by returning to this dialog box and removing the check mark from the Display Alternate Units check box.

Here are the steps for setting up alternate dimensions:

1. In the Dimension Style Manager, select a style, and then click Modify. Or, if you want to create a new style, click New.

2. In the New Dimension Style dialog box, click the Alternate Units tab.

3. Click the Display Alternate Units check box. The options in the tab become available for your input.

4. Select the appropriate option from the Unit Format drop-down list. U.S. users should select Decimal to show metric alternate units. Metric users should select Architectural.

5. Select an appropriate precision value from the Precision drop-down list.

6. Enter a scale factor for your alternate dimension in the Multiplier For Alt Units input box. For U.S. users, the default value is **25.4**. This value converts feet-and-inch dimensions to millimeters. In our metric examples, you've been using centimeters, so change this setting to 2.54. Metric users should enter **0.3937** to convert centimeters to feet and inches.

7. In the Placement group, select where you want the alternate dimension to appear in relation to the main dimension.

8. Click OK to close the New Dimension Style dialog box. The Dimension Style Manager dialog box opens again.

## Setting the Current Dimension Style

Before you can begin to use your new dimension style, you must make it the current default:

1. Click My Architectural in the Styles list box in the Dimension Style Manager dialog box.

2. Click the Set Current button at far right in the dialog box.

3. Click Close to exit the Dimension Style Manager dialog box.

You can also select a dimension style from the Dim Style Control drop-down list in the Dimensions control panel. You're now ready to use your new dimension style.

---

### FITTING TEXT AND ARROWS IN TIGHT PLACES

Every now and then, you'll need to dimension a small gap or a small width of an object that won't allow dimension text to fit. The Fit tab includes a few other settings that control how dimensions act when the extension lines are too close. The Text Placement group contains three options to place the text in tight situations:

**Beside The Dimension Line**   Places text next to the extension line but close to the dimension line. You'll see how this affects your dimension later.

**Over Dimension Line, With Leader**   Places the dimension text farther from the dimension line, and includes an arrow or a leader from the dimension line to the text.

**Over Dimension Line, Without Leader**   Does the same as the previous setting, but doesn't include the leader.

The options in the Fit Options group let you control how text and arrows are placed when there isn't enough room for both between the extension lines.

---

In the next set of exercises, you'll use the My Architectural style you just created. To switch to another style, open the Dimension Style Manager dialog box again, select the style you want from the Styles list, and click Set Current, as you did in the previous exercise.

## Modifying a Dimension Style

To modify an existing dimension style, open the Dimension Style Manager dialog box, highlight the style you want to edit, and then click Modify to open the Modify Dimension Style dialog box. This is virtually identical to the New Dimension Style dialog box you've been working with. You can then make changes to the different components of the selected dimension style. When you've finished making changes and closed both dialog boxes, all the dimensions associated with the edited style update automatically in your drawing. For example, if you decide you need to change the dimension scale of a style, you can open the Modify Dimension Style dialog box and change the Scale value in the Fit tab.

This section introduces you to the various settings that let you determine the appearance of a dimension style. This section doesn't discuss every option; to learn more about the other dimension style options, consult Appendix B. There, you'll find descriptions of all the items in the New Dimension Style and Modify Dimension Style dialog boxes, plus reference material covering the system variables associated with each option.

**TIP** If your application is strictly architectural, you may want to make these same dimension style changes to the Acad.dwt template file or create a set of template files specifically for architectural drawings of different scales.

# Drawing Linear Dimensions

The most common type of dimension you'll be using is the *linear dimension*. The linear dimension is an orthogonal dimension measuring the width and length of an object. AutoCAD provides three dimensioning tools for this purpose: Linear (Dimlinear), Continue (Dimcont), and Baseline (Dimbase). These options are readily accessible from the Dimensions control panel's fly-out toolbar or the Dimension drop-down menu.

**WARNING** In the following set of exercises, you'll see figures displaying dimensions in both Imperial and metric units. I've included both measurements so that both Imperial and metric users can more easily follow the tutorial. But in your own drawing, you'll see only one dimension value displayed above the dimension line.

## Finding the Dimensions Control Panel

Before you apply any dimension, you should study the Dimensions control panel. This control panel contains nearly all the commands necessary to draw and edit your dimensions. It contains a toolbar fly-out to the right of the row of tools; this fly-out is similar to the one in the 2D Draw control panel. To open it, click the downward-pointing arrow to the far right of the row of tools.

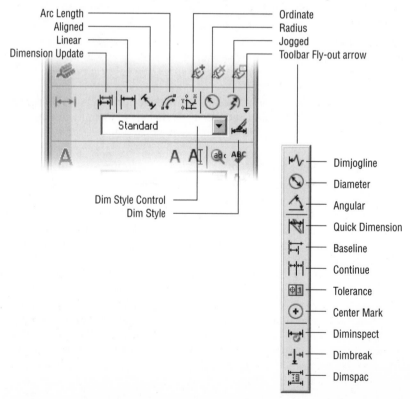

You can also open the Dimension toolbar, which contains many of the same tools as the Dimensions control panel. Right-click any toolbar, and choose Dimension from the shortcut menu. The Dimension commands are also available from the Dimension drop-down menu. Now, you're ready to begin dimensioning.

## Placing Horizontal and Vertical Dimensions

Let's start by looking at the basic dimensioning tool, Linear. The Linear button (the Dimlinear command) on the Dimensions control panel accommodates both the horizontal and vertical dimensions.

In this exercise, you'll add a vertical dimension to the right side of the Unit plan:

1. Before you start to dimension your drawing, you need to set the scale of your drawing. Select ¼″=1′-0″ from the Annotation Scale drop-down list. Metric users should select 1:50.

2. To start either a vertical or horizontal dimension, click Linear on the Dimensions control panel, or enter **Dli**↵ at the Command prompt. You can also choose Dimension ➢ Linear from the drop-down menu.

3. The `Specify first extension line origin or <select object>:` prompt asks you for the first point of the distance to be dimensioned. An extension line connects the object being dimensioned to the dimension line. Use the Endpoint Osnap override, and pick the upper-right corner of the entry, as shown in Figure 12.3.

**FIGURE 12.3**

The dimension line added to the Unit drawing

**TIP** The prompt in step 3 gives you the option of pressing ↵ to select an object. If you do this, you're prompted to pick the object you want to dimension, rather than the distance to be dimensioned. This method is discussed later in this chapter.

4. At the `Specify second extension line origin:` prompt, pick the lower-right corner of the living room, as shown in Figure 12.3.

5. In the next prompt, `Specify dimension line location or [Mtext/Text/Angle/ Horizontal/Vertical/Rotated]:`, the dimension line indicates the direction of the dimension and contains the arrows or tick marks. Move your cursor from left to right to display a temporary dimension. This enables you to visually select a dimension-line location.

**TIP**   In step 5, you can append information to the dimension's text or change the dimension text altogether. You'll see how later in this chapter.

6. Enter **@4´<0**↵ to tell AutoCAD you want the dimension line to be 4´ to the right of the last point you selected. Metric users should enter **@122<0**↵. (You could pick a point by using your cursor, but this doesn't let you place the dimension line as accurately.) After you've done this, the dimension is placed in the drawing, as shown in Figure 12.3.

## Continuing a Dimension

You'll often want to enter a group of dimensions strung together in a line. For example, you may want to continue dimensioning the balcony and align the continued dimension with the dimension you just entered.

To do this, use the Continue option found in both the toolbar fly-out of the Dimensions control panel and the Dimension drop-down menu:

1. Click the Continue option on the fly-out of the Dimensions control panel, or enter **Dco**↵. You can also choose Dimension ➢ Continue from the drop-down menu.

2. At the `Specify a second extension line origin or [Undo/Select] <Select>:` prompt, pick the upper-right corner of the balcony. (See the top image in Figure 12.4.)

**FIGURE 12.4**
The dimension string, continued and completed

3. Pick the right end of the rail on the balcony. See the bottom image in Figure 12.4 for the results.

4. Press ↵ twice to exit the command.

**TIP**   If you select the wrong location for a continued dimension, you can click the Undo tool or press **U**↵ to back up your dimension.

The Continue option adds a dimension from where you left off. The last drawn extension line is used as the first extension line for the continued dimension. AutoCAD keeps adding dimensions as you continue to pick points, until you press ↵.

You probably noticed that the 5″ dimension is placed away from the dimension line with a leader line pointing to it. This is the result of the 5″ dimension's text not having enough space to fit between the dimension extension lines. You'll learn about dimension style settings that can remedy this problem. For now, let's continue adding dimensions to the plan.

#### CONTINUING A DIMENSION FROM A PREVIOUS DIMENSION

If you need to continue a string of dimensions from an older linear dimension, instead of the most recently added one, press ↵ at the `Specify a second extension line origin or [Undo/Select]` `<Select>`: prompt you saw in step 2 of the previous exercise. Then, at the `Select continued` `dimension`: prompt, click the extension line from which you want to continue.

## Drawing Dimensions from a Common Base Extension Line

Another way to dimension objects is to have several dimensions originate from the same extension line. To accommodate this, AutoCAD provides the Baseline option on the Dimensions control panel or Dimension drop-down menu.

To see how this works, you'll start another dimension—this time a horizontal one—across the top of the plan:

1. Click Linear Dimension on the Dimensions control panel. Or, as you did for the vertical dimension, type **Dli**↵ to start the horizontal dimension. This option is also on the Dimension drop-down menu.

2. At the `Specify first extension line origin or <select object>`: prompt, use the Endpoint osnap to pick the upper-left corner of the bathroom, as shown in Figure 12.5.

3. At the `Specify second extension line origin`: prompt, pick the upper-right corner of the bathroom, as shown in Figure 12.5.

4. At the `Specify dimension line location or [Mtext/Text/Angle/ Horizontal/` `Vertical/Rotated]`: prompt, pick a point above the Unit plan, as shown in Figure 12.5. If you need to, pan your view downward to fit the dimension in.

**TIP**   Because you usually pick exact locations on your drawing as you dimension, you may want to turn on Running Osnaps to avoid the extra step of selecting osnaps from the Osnap shortcut menu.

5. You're set to draw another dimension continuing from the first extension line of the dimension you just drew. Click the Baseline option on the toolbar fly-out of the Dimensions control panel. Or, type **Dba**↵ at the Command prompt to start a baseline dimension.

6. At the `Specify a second extension line origin or [Undo/Select] <Select>`: prompt, click the upper-right corner of the entry, as shown in Figure 12.6.

**FIGURE 12.5**

The bathroom with horizontal dimensions

Start the dimension at this corner.

Select this corner for the second point.

**FIGURE 12.6**

The overall width dimension

Click here for the second extension line.

7. Press ↵ twice to exit the Baseline command.

8. Pan your view down so it looks similar to Figure 12.6.

In this example, you see that the Baseline option is similar to the Continue option, except that the Baseline option enables you to use the first extension line of the previous dimension as the base for a second dimension. The distance between the two horizontal dimension lines is controlled by the Baseline Spacing setting in the Lines tab of the New Dimension Style and Modify Dimension Style dialog boxes.

### CONTINUING FROM AN OLDER DIMENSION

You may have noticed in step 7 that you had to press ↵ twice to exit the command. As with Continue, you can draw the baseline dimension from an older dimension by pressing ↵ at the Specify a second extension line origin [Undo/Select] <Select>: prompt. You then get the Select base dimension: prompt, at which you can either select another dimension or press ↵ again to exit the command.

## Adjusting the Distance between Dimensions

As you work toward a deadline, you may find that you or someone else cut a few corners when adding dimensions, and a set of parallel dimension lines isn't accurately placed.

You can quickly adjust the spacing between dimension lines using the Dimspace tool in the Dimension control panel:

1. Click the Dimspace tool in the Dimensions control panel. You can also choose Dimension ➤ Dimension Space.

2. At the `Select base dimension:` prompt, click the dimension closest to the feature being dimensioned.

3. At the `Select dimensions to space:` prompt, click the next dimension.

4. Continue to select the other parallel dimensions. When you're finished with your selection, press ↵.

5. You see the prompt

```
Select dimensions to space:
Enter value or [Auto] <Auto>:
```

Enter a value for the distance between the dimension lines. This value should be in full-scale distances. You can also press ↵, and AutoCAD will adjust the distance between dimensions for you.

# Editing Dimensions

As you add more dimensions to your drawings, you'll find that AutoCAD occasionally places the dimension text or line in an inappropriate location, or you may need to modify the dimension text. In this section, you'll take an in-depth look at how you can modify dimensions to suit those special circumstances that always crop up.

## Appending Data to Dimension Text

So far in this chapter, you've been accepting the default dimension text. You can append information to the default dimension value or change it entirely if you need to. At the point when you see the temporary dimension dragging with your cursor, enter **T**↵. Then, using the less-than (<) and greater-than (>) symbols, you can add text either before or after the default dimension or replace the symbols entirely to replace the default text. The Properties button on the Properties toolbar lets you modify the existing dimension text in a similar way.

Let's see how this works by changing an existing dimension's text in your drawing:

1. Choose Modify ➢ Object ➢ Text ➢ Edit, or type **ED**↵.

2. Click the last horizontal dimension you added to the drawing at the top of the screen, to open the Text Formatting toolbar.

3. Press the End key to place the cursor at the end of the 14′-0″ text, and then type **to face of stud**.

4. Click OK on the Text Formatting toolbar, and then press ↵ to exit the Ddedit command. The dimension changes to read 14′-0″ to face of stud.

5. Because you don't need the new appended text for the tutorial, click the Undo button in the Standard toolbar to remove the appended text.

**TIP** In this exercise, you were able to edit only a single dimension. To append text to several dimensions at once, you need to use the Dimension Edit tool. See the "Making Changes to Multiple Dimensions" sidebar in this chapter for more on this command.

If you need to restore the original dimension text for a dimension whose value has been completely replaced, you can use the steps shown in the previous exercise, but in step 3, replace the text with the <> bracket symbols.

You can also have AutoCAD automatically add a dimension suffix or prefix to all dimensions, instead of just a chosen few, by using the Suffix or Prefix option in the Primary Units tab of the New Dimension Style or Modify Dimension Style dialog box. See Appendix C for more on this feature.

AutoCAD provides the associative dimensioning capability to automatically update dimension text when a drawing is edited. Objects called *definition points* determine how edited dimensions are updated.

The definition points are located at the same points you pick when you determine the dimension location. For example, the definition points for linear dimensions are the extension line origins. The definition points for a circle diameter are the points used to pick the circle and the opposite side of the circle. The definition points for a radius are the points used to pick the circle, plus the center of the circle.

Definition points are point objects. They're difficult to see because they're usually covered by the feature they define. You can, however, see them indirectly by using grips. The definition points of a dimension are the same as the dimension's grip points. You can see them by clicking a dimension. Try the following:

1. Make sure the Grips feature is turned on. (See Chapter 2 to refresh your memory on the Grips feature.)

2. Click the longest of the three vertical dimensions you drew in the earlier exercise. You'll see the grips of the dimension, as shown in Figure 12.7.

## MAKING CHANGES TO MULTIPLE DIMENSIONS

You can use the Dimension Edit tool to quickly edit existing dimensions. This tool gives you the ability to edit more than one dimension's text at one time. One common use for the Dimension Edit tool is to change a string of dimensions to read *Equal* instead of showing the actual dimensioned distance. The following example shows an alternative to using the Properties palette for appending text to a dimension:

1. Type **Ded**↵.

2. At this prompt

   ```
   Enter type of dimension editing [Home/New/Rotate/Oblique]<Home>:
   ```

   type **N**↵ to use the New option. The Multiline Text Editor opens, showing 0 in the text box.

3. Use the arrow keys to move the cursor behind or in front of the 0, and then enter the text you want to append to the dimension. Or, you can remove the 0 and replace the dimension with your text.

4. Click OK.

5. At the Select objects: prompt, pick the dimensions you want to edit. The Select objects: prompt remains, enabling you to select several dimensions.

6. Press ↵ to finish your selection. The dimension changes to include your new text or to replace the existing dimension text.

The Dimension Edit tool is useful in editing dimension text, but you can also use this tool to make graphical changes to the text. Here is a list of the other Dimension Edit tool options:

**Home**  Moves the dimension text to its standard default position and angle.

**Rotate**  Rotates the dimension text to a new angle.

**Oblique**  Skews the dimension extension lines to a new angle. (See the "Skewing Dimension Lines" section, later in this chapter.)

**FIGURE 12.7**
The grip points are the same as the definition points on a dimension.

## Using Grips to Make Minor Adjustments to Dimensions

The definition points, whose location you can see through their grips, are located on their own unique layer called *Defpoints*. Definition points are displayed regardless of whether the Defpoints layer is on or off. To give you an idea of how these definition points work, try the following exercises, which show you how to directly manipulate the definition points.

In this exercise, you'll use coordinates to move a dimension line:

**1.** With the grips visible, click the grip near the dimension text.

**TIP** Because the Defpoints layer has the unique feature of being visible even when turned off, you can use it as a layer for laying out your drawing. While Defpoints is turned off, you can still see objects assigned to it, but the objects won't plot.

**2.** Move the cursor around. When you move the cursor vertically, the text moves along the dimension line. When you move the cursor horizontally, the dimension line and text move together, keeping their parallel orientation to the dimensioned floor plan.

**TIP** Here the entire dimension line, including the text, moves. In a later exercise, you'll see how you can move the dimension text independently of the dimension line.

**3.** Enter @9´<0↵. Metric users should enter @275<0↵. The dimension line, text, and dimension extensions stretch to the new location to the right of the text (see Figure 12.8).

**FIGURE 12.8**
Moving the dimension line by using its grip

**TIP** If you need to move several dimension lines, select them all at the Command prompt; then, Shift+click one set of dimension-line grips from each dimension. After you've selected the grips, click one of the hot grips again. You can then move all the dimension lines at once.

In step 3 of the previous exercise, you saw that you can specify an exact distance for the dimension line's new location by entering a relative polar coordinate. Cartesian coordinates work just as well. You can even use object snaps to relocate dimension lines.

Next, try moving the dimension line back by using the Perpendicular osnap:

**1.** Click the grip at the bottom of the dimension line you just edited.

**2.** Shift+click the right mouse button, and choose Perpendicular from the Osnap shortcut menu.

**3.** Place the cursor on the vertical dimension line that dimensions the balcony and click it.

**4.** Choose View ➢ Zoom All, and then choose File ➢ Save to save this file in its current state.

The selected dimension line moves to align with the other vertical dimension, back to its original location.

## Changing Style Settings of Individual Dimensions

In some cases, you have to change an individual dimension's style settings in order to edit that dimension. For example, if you try to move the text of a typical linear dimension, you may find that the text and dimension lines are inseparable. You need to make a change to the dimension style setting that controls how AutoCAD locates dimension text in relation to the dimension line. This section describes how you can change the style settings of individual dimensions to facilitate changes in the dimension.

**TIP** If you need to change the dimension style of a dimension to match that of another, you can use the Match Properties tool. See Chapter 7 for details on how to use this tool.

### MOVING FIXED DIMENSION TEXT

You've seen how dimension text is attached to the dimension line so that when the text is moved, the dimension line follows. You may encounter situations in which you want to move the text independently of the dimension line. The following steps show how you can separate dimension text from its dimension line. These steps also show how you can change a single dimension's style settings:

**1.** Click the dimension you want to edit, to expose its grips.

**2.** Right-click, and choose Properties from the shortcut menu to open the Properties palette.

**3.** Scroll down the list of properties until you see the Fit category. If you don't see a list of options under Fit, click the downward-pointing arrow to the right to display a new set of options.

**4.** Scroll farther down the list until you see the Text Movement option to the right of the Text Movement listing, and then click this option.

**5.** Click the arrow that appears next to the Keep Dim Line With Text listing to open the drop-down list; then, select the Move Text, Add Leader option.

**6.** Close the Properties palette.

In the Properties palette, the Move Text, Add Leader option in the Fit category lets you move the dimension text independently of the dimension line. It also draws a leader from the dimension line to the text. Another option, Move Text, No Leader, does the same thing but doesn't include a leader. You can also set these options for a dimension style by using the Text Placement options in the Fit tab of the New Dimension Style or Modify Dimension Style dialog box.

As you can see from these steps, the Properties palette gives you access to many of the settings you saw for setting up dimension styles. The main difference here is that the Properties palette affects only the dimensions you've selected.

In a previous exercise, you changed the format setting of a single dimension *after* it was placed. These settings can be made a standard part of your Architectural dimension style by using the Modify button in the Dimension Style Manager dialog box.

**TIP**    If you have multiple dimension styles and you want to change an existing dimension to the current dimension style, use the Dimension Update tool. Choose Dimension Update on the Dimensions control panel, or choose Dimension ➤ _Update from the drop-down menu. Then, select the dimensions you want to change, and press ↵. The selected dimensions will be converted to the current style.

---

**ROTATING AND POSITIONING DIMENSION TEXT**

Once in a while, dimension text works better if it's kept in a horizontal orientation, even if the dimension itself isn't horizontal. To rotate dimension text, choose Dimension ➤ Align Text ➤ Angle, select the dimension text, and then enter an angle or select two points to graphically indicate an angle. You can also enter **0**↵ to return the dimension text to its default angle.

If you need to move the dimension text to the left, center, or right of the dimension line, you can use the Left, Center, or Right option under the Dimension ➤ Align Text menu options.

---

## Editing Dimensions and Other Objects Together

It's helpful to be able to edit a dimension directly by using its grips. But the key feature of AutoCAD's dimensions is their ability to *automatically* adjust themselves to changes in the drawing.

To see how this works, try moving the living room closer to the bathroom wall. You can move a group of lines and vertices by using the Stretch command and the Crossing option:

1. Click the Stretch tool in the Modify toolbar, or type **S**↵ and then **C**↵. You'll see the following prompts:

   ```
   At the Select objects to stretch by crossing-window or crossing-polygon...
   Select objects: C
   Specify first corner:
   ```

2. Pick a crossing window, as illustrated in Figure 12.9, and then press ↵ to confirm your selection.

**FIGURE 12.9**
The Stretch crossing window

Select this area with a crossing window.

3. At the `Specify base point or Displacement <Displacement>:` prompt, pick any point on the screen.

4. At the `Specify second point or <use first point as displacement>:` prompt, enter **@2´<90↵** to move the wall 2´ in a 90° direction. The wall moves, and the dimension text changes to reflect the new dimensions, as shown in Figure 12.10.

**FIGURE 12.10**
The moved wall, with the updated dimensions

5. After viewing the result of using the Stretch tool, click the Undo button in the toolbar or type **U↵** to change the drawing back to its previous state.

You can also use the Mirror, Rotate, and Stretch commands with dimensions. The polar arrays also work, and you can use Extend and Trim with linear dimensions.

When you're editing dimensioned objects, be sure to select the dimension associated with the object being edited. As you select objects, using the Crossing Window (C) or Crossing Polygon (CP) selection option helps you include the dimensions. For more on these selection options, see Chapter 2.

**TIP**   If a hatch pattern or solid fill completely covers a dimension, you can use the Draworder command to have AutoCAD draw the dimension over the hatch or solid fill. See Chapters 7, 14, and 18 for more on various uses of the Draworder command.

**MODIFYING THE DIMENSION STYLE SETTINGS BY USING OVERRIDE**

In the "Moving Fixed Dimension Text" section, you used the Properties palette to facilitate the moving of the dimension text. You can also choose Dimension ➢ Override (Dimoverride command) to accomplish the same thing. The Override option enables you to change an individual dimension's style settings. Here's an example that shows how you can use the Override option in place of the Properties palette in the first exercise of the "Moving Fixed Dimension Text" section:

1. Press the Esc key twice to make sure you aren't in the middle of a command. Then, choose Dimension ➢ Override from the drop-down menu.

2. At the next prompt

   ```
   Enter dimension variable name to override or [Clear overrides]:
   ```

   type **Dimfit↵**.

3. At the Enter new value for dimension variable <3>: prompt, enter **4↵**. This has the same effect as selecting Move Text, Add Leader from the Fit option of the Properties palette.

4. The Enter dimension variable name to override: prompt appears again, enabling you to enter another dimension variable. Press ↵ to move to the next step.

5. At the Select objects: prompt, select the dimension you want to change. You can select a group of dimensions if you want to change several dimensions at once. Press ↵ when you've finished with your selection. The dimension settings change for the selected dimensions.

As you can see from this example, the Dimoverride command requires that you know exactly which dimension variable to edit in order to make the desired modification. In this case, setting the Dimfit variable to 4 lets you move the dimension text independently of the dimension line. If you find the Dimoverride command useful, consult Appendix C to determine which system variable corresponds to the Dimension Style dialog box settings.

## Associating Dimensions with Objects

You've seen how dimensions and the objects they're associated with can move together so the dimension remains connected to the object. In the process of editing a drawing, dimensions may lose their association with objects; so, you may need to re-create an association between a dimension and an object. The following steps show you how this is done:

1. Choose Dimension ➢ Reassociate Dimensions. You can also type **Dimreassociate↵** at the Command prompt.

2. At the prompt

   ```
   Select dimension to reassociate
   Select Objects:
   ```

   select the dimension that you want to reassociate with an object, and then press ↵.

**3.** At the `Specify first extension line origin or [Select object] <next>`: prompt, an X appears at one of the dimension's definition points.

**4.** Use the Endpoint osnap, and click the end of the object you want to have connected to the definition point indicated in step 3.

**5.** An X appears at the dimension's other definition point. Use the Endpoint osnap again, and click the other endpoint of the object you want associated with the dimension. You now have the dimension associated with the endpoints of the object.

In step 3, you see an X at the location of a dimension definition point. If the definition point is already associated with an object, the X appears with a box around it. The box is a reminder that the definition point is already associated with an object and that you'll be changing its association. In this situation, you can press ↵ to switch to the dimension's other definition point.

Also in step 3, you have the option to select an object. This option enables you to associate the dimension with an entire object instead of with just one endpoint. If you type **S**↵ at that prompt in step 3, you can then select the object you want to associate with the dimension. The dimension changes so that its definition points coincide with the endpoints of the object. The dimension remains in its original orientation. For example, a vertical dimension remains vertical even if you associate the dimension with a horizontal line. In this situation, the dimension dutifully dimensions the endpoints of the line but shows a distance of zero.

**TIP** You can remove a dimension's association with an object by using the Dimdisassociate command. Type **Dimdisassociate.**↵ at the Command prompt, select the dimension(s), and then press ↵.

## Adding a String of Dimensions with a Single Operation

AutoCAD provides a method for creating a string of dimensions by using a single operation. The Qdim command lets you select a set of objects instead of having to select points. The following exercise demonstrates how the Qdim command works:

**1.** If you haven't done so already, zoom out so you have an overall view of the Unit floor plan.

**2.** Choose Dimension ➤ Quick Dimension, or click Quick Dimension on the fly-out of the Dimensions control panel.

3. At the `Select geometry to dimension:` prompt, place a selection window around the entire left-side wall of the unit.

4. Press ↵ to finish your selection. The following prompt appears:

```
Specify dimension line position, or
[Continuous/Staggered/Baseline/Ordinate/Radius/Diameter/
datumPoint/Edit/seTtings] <Continuous>:
```

5. Click a point to the left of the wall to place the dimension. A string of dimensions appears, displaying all the dimensions for the wall.

6. When you've finished reviewing the results of this exercise, exit the file without saving it.

The prompt in step 4 indicates several types of dimensions you can choose from. For example, if you want the dimensions to originate from a single baseline, you can enter **B**↵ in step 4 to select the Baseline option.

The Qdim command can be a time-saver when you want to dimension a wall quickly. It may not work in all situations, but if the object you're dimensioning is fairly simple, it can be all you need.

**TIP** In this exercise, you used a simple window to select the wall. For more complex shapes, try using a crossing polygon selection window. See Chapter 2 for more on crossing polygons.

## Adding or Removing the Alternate Dimensions

You may eventually encounter a drawing that contains alternate dimensions, as shown in some of the figures earlier in this chapter. You can remove those alternate dimensions by turning off the alternate dimension features. Here's how it's done:

1. Choose Dimension ➤ Dimension Style, or enter **D**↵ to open the Dimension Style Manager dialog box.

2. Select the style that uses the alternate units. In the Styles list box, choose Modify.

3. Click the Alternate Units tab.

4. Click the Display Alternate Units check box to remove the check mark.

5. Click OK, and then click Close to close the Dimension Style Manager dialog box.

The dimensions that use the style you just edited change to remove the alternate dimensions. You can also perform the reverse operation and add alternate dimensions to an existing set of dimensions. Follow the steps shown here, but instead of removing the check mark in step 4, add the check mark, and make the appropriate setting changes to the rest of the Alternate Units tab.

---

**USING OSNAP WHILE DIMENSIONING**

When you pick intersections and endpoints frequently, as you do during dimensioning, it can be inconvenient to use the Osnap shortcut menu. If you know you'll be using certain osnaps frequently, you can use Running Osnaps (See "The Osnap Options" in Chapter 3 for more on setting up Running Osnaps).

After you've designated your Running Osnaps, the next time you're prompted to select a point, the selected osnap modes are automatically activated. You can still override the default settings by using the Osnap shortcut menu (Shift+click the right mouse button).

There is a drawback to setting a Running Osnap mode: When your drawing gets crowded, you can end up picking the wrong point by accident. However, you can easily toggle Running Osnap mode off by clicking Osnap in the status bar or by pressing F3.

---

# Dimensioning Non-orthogonal Objects

So far, you've been reading about how to work with linear dimensions. You can also dimension non-orthogonal objects, such as circles, arcs, triangles, and trapezoids. In this section, you'll practice dimensioning a non-orthogonal object.

For the following exercises, you'll use a drawing of a hexagonal-shaped window. Open the 12a-wind.dwg file from the sample files; metric users should open the 12a-wind-metric.dwg file. You can use this file to follow along with the next set of exercises.

## Dimensioning Non-orthogonal Linear Distances

Now, you'll dimension the window. The unusual shape of the window prevents you from using the horizontal or vertical dimensions you've used already. However, choosing Dimension ➤ Aligned enables you to dimension at an angle:

1. Click the Aligned tool on the Dimensions control panel. You can also enter **Dal**↵ to start the aligned dimension, or choose Dimension ➤ Aligned.

2. At the Specify first extension line origin or <select object>: prompt, press ↵. You could pick extension-line origins as you did in earlier examples, but pressing ↵ shows you firsthand how the Select Object option works.

3. At the Select object to dimension: prompt, pick the upper-right face of the hexagon near coordinate 2´-5˝,1´-10˝ (75,55 for metric users). As the prompt indicates, you can also pick an arc or a circle for this type of dimension.

4. At the Specify dimension line location or [Mtext/Text/Angle]: prompt, pick a point near coordinate 2´-10˝,2´-2˝ (90,60 for metric users). The dimension appears in the drawing as shown in Figure 12.11.

**TIP**   Just as with linear dimensions, you can enter **T**↵ in step 4 to enter alternate text for the dimension.

**FIGURE 12.11**

The aligned dimension of a non-orthogonal line

Next, you'll dimension a face of the hexagon. Instead of its actual length, however, you'll dimension a distance at a specified angle—the distance from the center of the face:

1. Click the Linear tool on the Dimensions control panel.

2. At the `Specify first extension line origin or <select object>:` prompt, press ↵.

3. At the `Select object to dimension:` prompt, pick the lower-right face of the hexagon near coordinate 2′-6″,1′-4″ (77,33 for metric users).

4. At the `Specify dimension line location or [Mtext/Text/Angle/Horizontal/Vertical/Rotated]:` prompt, type **R**↵ to select the rotated option.

5. At the `Specify angle of dimension line <0>:` prompt, enter **30**↵.

6. At the `Specify dimension line location or [Mtext/Text/Angle/Horizontal/Vertical/Rotated]:` prompt, pick a point near coordinate 24′-11″,0′-8″ (88,12 for metric users). Your drawing will look like Figure 12.12.

**NOTE** The Dimrotate command accomplishes the same thing with a slight change in the sequence of steps.

**FIGURE 12.12**

A linear dimension using the Rotated option

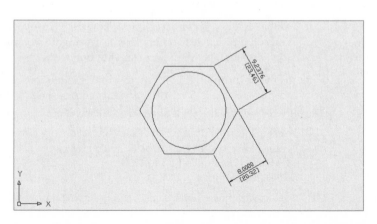

## Dimensioning Radii, Diameters, and Arcs

To dimension circular objects, you use another set of options from the Dimension menu:

1. Click the Angular tool on the Dimensions control panel. Or, enter **Dan**↵, or choose Dimension ➤ Angular from the drop-down menu to start the angular dimension.

2. At the Select arc, circle, line, or <specify vertex>: prompt, pick the upper-left face of the hexagon near coordinate 1´-3˝,1´-10˝ (44,57 for metric users).

3. At the Select second line: prompt, pick the top face at coordinate 1´-9˝,2´-2˝ (54,62 for metric users).

4. At the Specify dimension arc line location or [Mtext/Text/Angle]: prompt, notice that as you move the cursor around the upper-left corner of the hexagon, the dimension changes, as shown in the top images of Figure 12.13.

**FIGURE 12.13**
The angular dimension added to the window frame

5. Pick a point near coordinate 1´-9˝,1´-11˝(49,50 for metric users). The dimension is fixed in the drawing. (See the bottom image of Figure 12.13.)

**TIP** If you need to make subtle adjustments to the dimension line or text location, you can do so using grips after you place the angular dimension.

Now, try the Diameter option, which shows the diameter of a circle:

1. Click the Diameter tool on the Dimensions control panel. Or, enter **Ddi**↵ at the Command prompt.

2. At the Select arc or circle: prompt, pick the circle.

3. At the Specify dimension line location or [Mtext/Text/Angle]: prompt, you see the diameter dimension drag along the circle as you move the cursor. If you move the cursor outside the circle, the dimension changes to display the dimension on the outside. (See the top image in Figure 12.14.)

**FIGURE 12.14**
Dimension showing the diameter of a circle

**TIP** If the dimension text can't fit in the circle, AutoCAD gives you the option to place the dimension text outside the circle as you drag the temporary dimension to a horizontal position.

4. Place the cursor inside the circle so the dimension arrow points in a horizontal direction, as shown in the bottom image of Figure 12.14.

5. With the text centered, click the mouse.

The Radius tool on the Dimensions control panel gives you a radius dimension, just as the Diameter tool provides a circle's diameter.

Figure 12.15 shows a radius dimension on the outside of the circle, but you can place it inside in a manner similar to the diameter dimension. The Center Mark tool on the Dimensions control panel places a cross mark in the center of the selected arc or circle.

**TIP** You can alter the format of diameter dimensions by changing the Dimtix and Dimtofl dimension variable settings. For example, if you want two arrows to appear across the diameter of the circle, turn on both Dimtix and Dimtofl. See Appendix C for more details.

**FIGURE 12.15**
A radius dimension shown on the outside of the circle

If you need to dimension an arc or a circle whose center isn't in the drawing area, you can use the jogged dimension. Here are the steps:

1. Click the Jogged tool from the Dimensions control panel, choose Dimension ➤ Jogged, or enter **Dimjogged**↵.

2. At the Select arc or circle: prompt, select the object you want to dimension.

3. At the Specify center location override: prompt, select a point that indicates the general direction to the center of the arc or circle. A dimension line appears and follows the movement of your cursor.

4. Position the dimension line where you want it, and then click.

5. Position the dimension line jog where you want it, and then click. The jogged dimension is placed in the drawing.

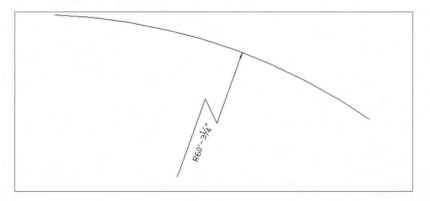

Arc lengths can also be given a dimension using the Arc Length tool. Choose the Arc Length tool from the Dimensions control panel, choose Dimension ➢ Arc Length, or enter **Dimarc**↵ at the Command prompt. At the `Select Arc or polyline arc segment:` prompt, select the arc you want to dimension. It can be either a plain arc or a polyline arc. Once you've selected the arc, the arc dimension appears and moves with the cursor. You can then select the location for the dimension.

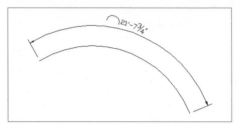

## Skewing Dimension Lines

At times, you may need to force the extension lines to take on an angle other than 90° to the dimension line. This is a common requirement of isometric drawings, in which most lines are at 30° or 60° angles instead of 90°. To facilitate non-orthogonal dimensions like these, AutoCAD offers the Oblique option:

1. Choose Dimension ➢ Oblique, or type **Ded**↵**O**↵.

2. At the `Select objects:` prompt, pick the aligned dimension at the upper-right of the drawing, and press ↵ to confirm your selection.

3. At the `Enter obliquing angle (Press ENTER for none):` prompt, enter **60** for 60°. The dimension will skew so that the extension lines are at 60°.

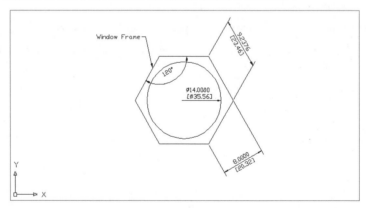

4. Save the drawing, and exit AutoCAD.

# Adding a Note with a Leader Arrow

One type of dimension is something like a text-dimension hybrid. The AutoCAD Multileader lets you add a text note combined with an arrow that points to an object in your drawing. Multileaders are easy to use and offer the same text-formatting tools as the Mtext tool. Try the following exercise to get familiar with multileaders:

1. Choose Dimension ➤ Multileader, click the Multileader tool in the Multileaders control panel (see Figure 12.16), or enter **Mld**↵.

**FIGURE 12.16**

The Multileader control panel

2. At the Specify leader arrowhead location or [leader Landing first/Content first/Options] <Options>: prompt, pick a point near the top-left edge of the hexagon at coordinate 1′-4″,2′-0″ (45,59 for metric users).

3. At the Specify leader landing location: prompt, enter **@6<110**↵. Metric users should enter **@15<110**↵. The Text Formatting toolbar appears, along with the text cursor at the note location.

4. Enter **Window Frame** for the note, and then click OK in the Text Formatting toolbar.

5. At the Specify text width <0.0000>: prompt, press ↵ or enter a width for your text. Your note appears with the leader arrow similar to the one in Figure 12.17.

The text in the note is in the current text style, unless you specify another style in the Text tab of the New Or Modify Dimension Style dialog box. (See the section "Setting the Appearance of Dimension Text," later in this chapter.)

**FIGURE 12.17**

The leader with a note added

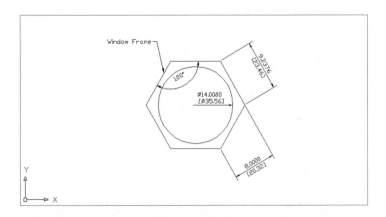

**NOTE** Multileaders have an annotative option that allows them to automatically adjust to the scale of the drawing. You can find the annotative option setting in the properties for the specific multileader in the drawing or in the multileader style setting. See the Scale option in Table 12.2, later in this chapter, under Leader Structure Tab.

The Leader tool offers a lot of options that aren't obvious when you're using it. In step 2 of the previous example, after choosing Dimension ➤ Multileader, you can press ↵ to modify the behavior of the Multileader tool. You'll see the following prompt:

```
Enter an option [Leader type/leader lAnding/Content type/Maxpoints/First angle/
Second angle/eXit options] <eXit options>:
```

Table 12.1 gives you a rundown of these options and their functions.

**TABLE 12.1:**   The Multileader Options

| OPTION | FUNCTION |
|---|---|
| Leader type | Allows you to choose between straight-line arrows and curved arrows. |
| Leader lAnding | Determines whether a leader landing is used. The *leader landing* is the short line that connects the arrow to the note. |
| Content type | Lets you select between text or a block for the leader note. You also have the option to choose None. |
| Maxpoints | Lets you set the number of points you select for the arrow. The default is 2. |
| First angle | Lets you constrain the angle of the leader arrow to a fixed value. |
| Second angle | Lets you constrain the angle of the arrow's second line segment, if you're using more than two points for the Maxpoints option. |
| eXit options | Lets you return to the main part of the Multileader command to draw the leader. |

## Creating Multileader Styles

Besides the options shown in Table 12.1, you can create multileader styles to control the appearance of multileaders. Multileader styles are similar in concept to text and dimension styles. They allow you to set up the appearance of the leader under a name that you can call up any time. For example, you may want to have one type of leader that uses a block instead of text for the note and another leader that uses a dot in place of an arrow. Or, you may want to set up a style that uses curved lines instead of straight ones for the leader line. You can create a multileader style for each of these types of leader features and then switch between the leader styles depending on the requirements of your leader note.

To set up or modify a multileader style, click the Multileader Style Manager tool in the Multileaders control panel. You can also enter **mleaderstyle**↵ at the command prompt. This opens the Multileader Style Manager dialog box shown in Figure 12.18. From here, you can select a style from the list to the right and click Modify to edit an existing style, or click New to create a new one. If you click New, you're asked to select an existing style as a basis for your new style.

**FIGURE 12.18**

The Multileader Style Manager

When you click Modify or New, the Modify Multileader Style dialog box opens (see Figure 12.19). Table 12.2 describes the options in each of the tabs of the Multileader Style dialog box. Some of these options are the same as those for the Multileader command.

**FIGURE 12.19**

The Modify Multi-leader Style dialog box

---

**TABLE 12.2:** The Multileader Style Dialog Box Options

| TAB AND PANEL | FUNCTION |
| --- | --- |
| **Leader Format Tab** | |
| General | Lets you set the leader line to straight or curved. You can also set the color, lineweight, and linetype for the leader line. |
| Arrowhead | Controls the arrowheads. |
| Leader Break | Controls the size of the gap in a leader line when the Leaderbreak command is applied. Leaderbreak places a break on a leader line where two leader lines cross. |

**TABLE 12.2:** The Multileader Style Dialog Box Options (CONTINUED)

| TAB AND PANEL | FUNCTION |
| --- | --- |
| **Leader Structure Tab** | |
| Constraints | Determines the number of line segments in the leader line. You can also apply angle constraints to the leader-line segments. |
| Landing Settings | Controls the leader-line landing segment. This is the last line segment that points to the note. |
| Scale | Lets you control the scale of the leader components. You can either apply a fixed scale or use the Annotative option to have the drawing annotation scale apply to the leader. |
| **Content Tab** | |
| Multileader Type | Lets you select the type of object that will be used for the leader note. The options are Mtext, block, and none. |
| Text Options | Gives you control over the way the leader note appears. You can control color, text style, size, justification, and orientation. |
| Leader Connection | Determines the position between the leader line and the note. |

Once you've set up a Multileader style, you can set it up as the default style by selecting the style from the Multileaders control panel drop-down list.

The selected style will be applied to any new multileader you add to your drawing. You can also change the style of an existing multileader. To do this, click the multileader to select it, and then select the multileader style you want from the Multileaders control panel drop-down list.

## Editing Multileader Notes

If you need to make changes to the note portion of a multileader, you can do so by double-clicking the note. This brings up the Text Formatting toolbar, allowing you to make changes as in a word processor.

At other times, you may want to change the leader line, arrows, or other graphic features of the multileader. For example, you may want to have all the notes aligned vertically for a neater appearance. Or, you may want to add more leader arrows so the note points to several objects in the drawing instead of just one.

The Multileaders control panel offers several tools that let you make these types of changes to your leader notes (see Figure 12.16). The Multileader Edit tool lets you add or remove leaders from a multileader; this is a handy tool if you want a single note to point to several objects. The Multileader Align tool lets you align the note portion of several multileaders. Finally, the Multiline Collect tool lets you collect several multileaders that use blocks for notes into a single note.

### Breaking a Dimension Line for a Leader

In a crowded drawing, your multileader arrow may have to cross over a dimension line. In many drafting conventions, when a leader line crosses over a dimension line, the dimension line must be shown with a gap.

You can apply a gap to a dimension line using the Dimbreak tool. Here's how it works:

1. Choose Dimension ➢ Dimension Break.

2. At the `Select a dimension or [Multiple]:` prompt, select a dimension line, or enter **M↵** and select multiple dimension lines.

3. When you're finished with your selection, press ↵.

4. At the `Select object to break dimension or [Auto/Restore/Manual] <Auto>:` prompt, press ↵. A gap appears wherever a leader line or other dimension line crosses over the selected dimension line.

If you prefer to manually indicate a break, enter **M↵** at the prompt in step 4. This allows you to select two points on the dimension, indicating where the gap is to occur. If additional dimension or leader lines are added that cross over the dimension line, repeat your use of the Dimbreak tool. To remove an existing break, use the Restore option in step 4 by entering **R↵**.

## Applying Ordinate Dimensions

In mechanical drafting, *ordinate dimensions* are used to maintain the accuracy of machined parts by establishing an origin on the part. All major dimensions are described as X coordinates or Y coordinates of that origin. The origin is usually an easily locatable feature of the part, such as a machined bore or two machined surfaces.

Figure 12.21 shows a typical application of ordinate dimensions. In the lower-left corner, note the two dimensions whose leaders are jogged. Also note the origin location in the upper-right corner.

To use AutoCAD's Ordinate command, perform the following steps:

1. Choose Tools ➢ New UCS ➢ Origin, or type **UCS↵Or↵**.

2. At the `Specify new origin point <0,0,0>:` prompt, click the exact location of the origin of your part.

**FIGURE 12.20**
A drawing using ordi-
nate dimensions

3. Toggle Ortho mode on.

4. Click the Ordinate tool on the Dimensions control panel. You can also enter **Dor.↵** to start the ordinate dimension.

5. At the `Specify feature location:` prompt, click the item you want to dimension.

**TIP** The direction of the leader determines whether the dimension will be of the Xdatum or the Ydatum.

6. At the `Specify leader endpoint or [Xdatum/Ydatum/Mtext/Text/Angle]:` prompt, indicate the length and direction of the leader. Do this by positioning the rubber-banding leader perpendicular to the coordinate direction you want to dimension and then clicking that point.

In steps 1 and 2, you used the UCS feature to establish a second origin in the drawing. The Ordinate Dimension tool then uses that origin to determine the ordinate dimensions. You'll get a chance to work with the UCS feature in Chapter 21.

You may have noticed options in the Command window for the Ordinate Dimension tool. The Xdatum and Ydatum options force the dimension to be of the X or Y coordinate no matter what direction the leader takes. The Mtext option opens the Text Formatting toolbar, enabling you to append or replace the ordinate dimension text. The Text option lets you enter replacement text directly through the Command window.

**TIP** As with all other dimensions, you can use grips to adjust the location of ordinate dimensions.

If you turn off Ortho mode, the dimension leader is drawn with a jog to maintain the orthogonal (look back at Figure 12.21).

## Adding Tolerance Notation

In mechanical drafting, *tolerances* are a key part of a drawing's notation. They specify the allowable variation in size and shape that a mechanical part can have. To help facilitate tolerance notation, AutoCAD provides the Tolerance command, which offers common ISO tolerance symbols together with a quick way to build a standard feature-control symbol. *Feature-control symbols* are industry-standard symbols used to specify tolerances. If you're a mechanical engineer or drafter, AutoCAD's tolerance notation options will be a valuable tool. However, a full discussion of tolerances requires a basic understanding of mechanical design and drafting and is beyond the scope of this book.

To use the Tolerance command, choose Tolerance from the Dimensions control panel, type **Tol**↵ at the Command prompt, or choose Dimension ➤ Tolerance from the drop-down menu to open the Geometric Tolerance dialog box.

This is where you enter tolerance and datum values for the feature-control symbol. You can enter two tolerance values and three datum values. In addition, you can stack values in a two-tiered fashion.

Click a box in the Sym group to open the Symbol dialog box.

The top image in Figure 12.22 shows what each symbol in the Symbol dialog box represents. The bottom image shows a sample drawing with a feature symbol used on a cylindrical object. The symbols in the sample drawing show that the upper cylinder needs to be concentric within 0.0003″ of the lower cylinder.

In the Geometric Tolerance dialog box, you can click a box in any of the Datum groups or a box in the right side of the Tolerance groups to open the Material Condition dialog box. This dialog box contains standard symbols relating to the maximum and minimum material conditions of a feature on the part being dimensioned.

## Adding Inspection Dimensions

Another type of dimension related to tolerances is the inspection dimension. This is a type of dimension notation that indicates how often the tolerances of a dimension should be checked.

To add an inspection dimension, first add a regular linear dimension as described in the early part of this chapter. Next, follow these steps:

1. Choose Diminspect from the Dimensions control panel. You can also choose Dimension ➤ Inspection. The Inspection Dimension dialog box appears.

**FIGURE 12.21**
The tolerance symbols

| | |
|---|---|
| Position (true) | ⊕ |
| Concentricity | ◎ |
| Symmetry | ⩦ |
| Parallelism | // |
| Perpendicularity | ⊥ |
| Angularity | ∠ |
| Cylindricity | ⌭ |

| | |
|---|---|
| Flatness | ▱ |
| Circularity | ○ |
| Straightness | — |
| Profile of a surface | ⌓ |
| Profile of a line | ⌒ |
| Circular runout | ↗ |
| Total runout | ⌰ |

Datum reference by feature symbol

Parallel symbol

Tolerance

Datum

2. Click the Select Dimension tool. The dialog box temporarily closes to allow you to select a dimension.

3. Select a shape option from the Shape group.

4. Enter a value for the Label and Inspection rate input boxes, and then click OK.

The dimension appears with the additional changes from the dialog box.

A 2.2500 100%

# The Bottom Line

**Understanding the Components of a Dimension**   Before you start to dimension with AutoCAD, it helps to become familiar with the different parts of a dimension. This will help you set up your dimensions to fit the style of dimensions that you need.

**Master It**   Name a few of the dimension components.

**Solution**   Dimension line, dimension text, extension line, arrow.

**Creating a Dimension Style**   As you become more familiar with technical drawing and drafting, you'll learn that there are standard formats for drawing dimensions. Arrows, text size, and even the way dimension lines are drawn are all subject to a standard format. Fortunately, AutoCAD offers dimension styles that let you set up your dimension format once and then call up that format whenever you need it.

**Master It**   What is the name of the dialog box that lets you manage dimension styles, and how do you open it?

**Solution**   The Dimension Style Manager is the name of the dialog box. You can open it by clicking the Dim Style tool in the Dimensions control panel. You can also choose Dimension ➢ Dimension Style.

**Drawing Linear Dimensions**   The most common dimension that you'll use is the linear dimension. Knowing how to place a linear dimension is a big first step in learning how to dimension in AutoCAD.

**Master It**   Name the three locations you're asked for when placing a linear dimension.

**Solution**   First extension line origin, second extension line origin, and dimension line location.

**Editing Dimensions**   Dimensions often change in the course of a project, so you should know how to make changes to dimension text or other parts of a dimension.

**Master It**   How do you start the command to edit dimension text?

**Solution**   Choose Modify ➢ Object ➢ Text ➢ Edit, or enter ed↵ at the Command prompt.

**Dimensioning Non-orthogonal Objects**   Not everything you dimension will use linear dimensions. AutoCAD offers a set of dimension tools for dimensioning objects that aren't made up of straight lines.

**Master It**   Name some of the types of objects for which a linear dimension isn't appropriate.

**Solution**   Arc and angle between two lines. Linear dimensions can be used for circles in certain situations.

**Adding a Note**   In addition to dimensions, you'll probably add lots of notes with arrows pointing to features in a design. AutoCAD offers the multileader for this purpose.

**Master It**   What two types of objects does the multileader combine?

**Solution**   Lines with arrows and text.

**Applying Ordinate Dimensions**   When accuracy counts, ordinate dimensions are often used because they measure distances that are similar to coordinates from a single feature.

**Master It**   What AutoCAD feature do you use for ordinate dimensions that isn't strictly associated with dimensions?

**Solution**   UCS.

**Adding Tolerance Notation**    Mechanical drafting often requires the use of special notation to describe tolerances. AutoCAD offers some predefined symbols that address the need to include tolerance notation in a drawing.

**Master It**    How do you open the Geometry Tolerance dialog box?

**Solution**    Choose Dimension ➢ Tolerance, or enter **tol**↵. You can also click the Tolerance tool in the Dimensions control panel.

# Part 3

# Mastering Advanced Skills

**In this part:**

# Chapter 13

# Using Attributes

Early in this book, you learned how to create blocks, which are assemblies of AutoCAD objects. Blocks enable you to form parts or symbols that can be easily reproduced. Furniture, bolts, doors, and windows are a few common items that you can create with blocks. And as you saw in later chapters, whole rooms and appliances can be made into blocks. There is no limit to a block's size.

AutoCAD also offers a feature called *attributes* that allows you to store text information as a part of a block. For example, you can store the material specifications for a bolt or other mechanical part that you've converted into a block. If your application is architecture, you can store the material, hardware, and dimensional information for a door or window that has been converted into a block. By storing this information in a block, you can quickly gather information about that block that may not be obvious from the graphics.

Attribute text can be set up to be invisible, or it can be displayed as text in the drawing. If it's invisible, you can easily view the attribute information by double-clicking the block that contains the attribute. The attribute information is displayed in a dialog box. This information can also be extracted to a database or spreadsheet, giving you the ability to keep an inventory of the blocks in your drawing. You can even convert attribute information into tables in an AutoCAD drawing. This can help you make quick work of parts lists or door and window schedules. By using attributes, you can keep track of virtually any object in a drawing or maintain textual information in the drawing that can be queried.

Keeping track of objects is just one way to use attributes. You can also use them in place of text objects when you must keep text and graphic items together. One common example is the reference symbol in an architectural drawing. Reference symbols are used to indicate the location of more detailed information in a drawing set, such as the elevation views of a room or a cross-section of a wall or other part of a building. In this chapter, you'll use attributes for one of their common functions: maintaining lists of parts. In this case, the parts are doors. This chapter also describes how to import these attributes into a database-management program. As you go through the exercises, think about the ways attributes can help you in your particular application.

This chapter covers the following topics:

◆   Creating Attributes

◆   Editing Attributes

◆   Extracting and Exporting Attribute Information

## Creating Attributes

Attributes depend on blocks. You might think of an attribute as text information attached to a block. The information can be a description of the block or some other pertinent text. For example, you can include an attribute definition with the door block you created in Chapter 3. Then, every time you subsequently insert the door block, you're be prompted for a value associated with that door. The value can be a number, a height or width value, a name, or any type of text information you want. After you enter a value, it's stored as part of the door block in the drawing database. This value can be displayed as text attached to the door block, or it can be invisible. You can change the value at any time. You can even specify the prompts for the attribute value.

However, suppose you don't have the attribute information when you design the door block. As an alternative, you can add the attribute to a *symbol* that is later placed by the door when you know enough about the design to specify what type of door goes where. Figure 13.1 shows a sample door symbol and a table to which the symbol refers. The standard door-type symbol suits this purpose nicely because it's an object that you can set up and use as a block independent of the door block.

**FIGURE 13.1**

A door symbol tells you what type of door goes in the location shown. Usually, the symbol contains a number or a letter that is keyed to a table that shows more information about the door.

A door symbol placed by a door in a floor plan refers to a specification in a table in another drawing.

DOOR AND WINDOW SCHEDULE

**TIP**    A *door-type symbol* is a graphic code that indicates special characteristics of the associated door. The code refers to a note or detailed drawing on another drawing, or it can refer to a detailed description in a set of written specifications.

## Adding Attributes to Blocks

In the following exercise, you'll create a door-type symbol, which is commonly used to describe the size, thickness, and other characteristics of any given door in an architectural drawing. The symbol is usually a circle, a hexagon, or a diamond with a number in it. The number is generally cross-referenced to a schedule that lists all the door types and their characteristics.

You'll create a new block containing attribute definitions, in the file for which the block is intended: the Plan file. You may also use the 13a-plan file. You'll create the block in the file so you can easily insert it where it belongs in the plan.

First, you open the Plan file and set up a view appropriate for creating the block with the attribute:

1. Open the 13a-plan.dwg file. Metric users can use the file 13a-plan-metric.dwg. These are the same as the Plan.dwg file you've created on your own, with a few additions to facilitate the exercises in this chapter.

2. Choose View ➢ Zoom ➢ Window. You'll use the Window Zoom option to specify an area in the drawing.

3. At the Specify first corner: prompt, enter **0,0**↵.

4. At the Specify opposite corner: prompt, enter **12,9**. This causes your view to zoom in to a location near the origin of the drawing in a 12-by-9-inch area.

You zoom in to this small area because you'll draw the block at its paper size of ¼″. Now, you're ready to create the block and attribute. You'll start by drawing the graphics of the block, and then you'll add the attribute definition:

1. Draw a circle with its center at coordinate 7,5 and a diameter of 0.25 (0.6 for metric users).

**TIP**   Because this is a new drawing, the circle is automatically placed on Layer 0. Remember that objects in a block that are on Layer 0 take on the color and linetype assignment of the layer on which the block is inserted.

2. Zoom in to the circle so it's about the same size as that shown in Figure 13.2.

3. If the circle looks like an octagon, choose View ➢ Regen or type **Re**↵ to regenerate your drawing.

**FIGURE 13.2**
The attribute definition inserted in the circle

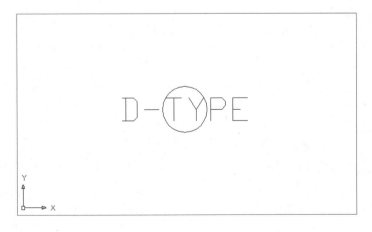

**4.** Choose Draw ➢ Block ➢ Define Attributes or type **Att.**⏎ to open the Attribute Definition dialog box.

**5.** In the Attribute group, click the Tag input box, and enter **D-TYPE**.

**TIP** The attribute tag is equivalent to a field name in a database. You can also think of the tag as the attribute's name or ID. It can help to identify the purpose of the attribute. The tag can be a maximum of 255 characters but can't contain spaces. If you plan to use the attribute data in a database program, check that program's documentation for other restrictions on field names.

**6.** Press the Tab key or click the Prompt input box, and enter **Door type**. This is the text for the prompt that will appear when you insert the block containing this attribute. Often the prompt is the same as the tag, but it can be anything you like. Unlike the tag, the prompt can include spaces and other special characters.

**TIP** Use a prompt that gives explicit instructions so the user will know exactly what is expected. Consider including an example in the prompt. (Enclose the example in square brackets to imitate the way AutoCAD prompts often display defaults.)

**7.** Click the Value input box, and enter a hyphen (-). This is the default value for the door-type prompt.

**TIP** If an attribute is to contain a number that will later be used for sorting in a database, use a default value such as 000 to indicate the number of digits required. The zeros can also serve to remind the user that values less than 100 must be preceded by a leading zero, as in 099.

**8.** Click the Justification drop-down list, and select Middle. This enables you to center the attribute on the circle's center. The Text Options group includes several other options. Because attributes appear as text, you can apply the same settings to them as you would to single-line text.

**9.** In the input box next to the Height < button, change the value to **0.125**. (Metric users should enter **0.3**.) This makes the attribute text 0.125″ (0.3 cm) high.

**10.** In the Insertion Point group, make sure that the Specify On-Screen check box is selected.

11.  Select the Annotative option. This allows the attribute to automatically adjust in size according to the annotation scale of the drawing.

12.  Click OK to close the dialog box.

13.  Using the Center osnap, pick the center of the circle. You need to place the cursor on the circle's circumference, not in the circle's center, to obtain the center by using the osnap. The attribute definition appears at the center of the circle (see Figure 13.2).

You've just created your first attribute definition. The attribute definition displays its tag in all uppercase letters to help you identify it. When you later insert this file into another drawing, the tag turns into the value you assign to it when it's inserted. If you want only one attribute, you can stop here and save the file. The next section shows how you can quickly add several more attributes to your drawing.

## Copying and Editing Attribute Definitions

Next, you'll add a few more attribute definitions; but instead of using the Attribute Definition dialog box, you'll make an arrayed copy of the first attribute and then edit the attribute definition copies. This method can save you time when you want to create several attribute definitions that have similar characteristics. By making copies and editing them, you'll also get a chance to see firsthand how to change an attribute definition.

Follow these steps to make copies of the attribute:

1.  Click Array on the Modify toolbar or type **Ar↵** to open the Array dialog box.

2.  Click the Rectangular Array radio button in the upper-left corner.

3.  Click the Select Objects button, and select the attribute definition you just created. Press ↵ to confirm your selection.

4.  In the Rows input box, enter **7**; in the Columns input box, enter **1**.

5.  Enter **–0.18** in the Row Offset input box (**–0.432** for metric users) and **0** in the Column Offset input box. The Row Offset value is approximately 1.5 times the height of the attribute text height. The minus sign in the Row Offset value causes the array to be drawn downward.

6.  Click OK.

7.  Issue a Zoom Extents command or click the Zoom Realtime tool to view all the attributes.

Now, you're ready to modify the copies of the attribute definitions:

1.  Press Esc to clear any selections or commands, and click the attribute definition just below the original.

2.  Right-click, and choose Properties from the shortcut menu to open the Properties palette.

**TIP**    You can double-click an attribute definition to change its Tag, Prompt, or Default value in the Edit Attribute Definition dialog box. However, this dialog box doesn't let you change an attribute definition's visibility mode.

3. Scroll down the list of properties until you see the Invisible option in the Misc category.

4. Select Yes from the Invisible option drop-down list.

5. Scroll back up the list of properties, and locate the Tag option in the Text category.

6. Highlight the Tag value to the right, and type **D-SIZE**↵. The attribute changes to reflect the change in the Tag value.

7. While still in the Text category, highlight the Prompt value, and type **Door size**↵.

8. In the Value field, type **3´-0˝**↵. Metric users should type **90**↵.

**TIP**    Make sure you press ↵ after entering a new value for the properties in the Properties palette. Pressing ↵ confirms your new entry.

You've just learned how to edit an attribute definition. Now, you'll make changes to the other attribute definitions:

1. Press Esc twice so that no attribute is selected, and then click the next attribute down so you can display its properties in the Properties palette.

2. Continue to edit this and the rest of the attribute definition properties by using the attribute settings listed in Table 13.1. To do this, repeat steps 5 through 8 of the preceding exercise for each attribute definition, replacing the Tag, Prompt, and Default values with those shown in Table 13.1. Also, make sure all but the original attributes have the Invisible option selected.

3. When you've finished editing the attribute definition properties, close the Properties palette.

When you later insert a file or a block containing attributes, the attribute prompts will appear in the order that their associated definitions were created. If the order of the prompts at insertion time is important, you can control it by editing the attribute definitions so their creation order corresponds to the desired prompt order. You can also control the order by using the Block Attribute Manager, which you'll look at later in this chapter.

**TABLE 13.1:** Attributes for the Door-Type Symbol

| TAG | PROMPT | DEFAULT VALUE |
| --- | --- | --- |
| D-NUMBER | Door number | – |
| D-THICK | Door thickness | – |
| D-RATE | Fire rating | – |
| D-MATRL | Door material | – |
| D-CONST | Door construction | – |

*Make sure the invisible option is selected for the attributes in this table.*

---

### UNDERSTANDING ATTRIBUTE DEFINITION MODES

The Attribute Definition dialog box includes several choices in the Mode group; you've used one of these modes to see what it does. You won't use any of the other modes in this tutorial, so here is a list describing all the modes for your reference:

**Invisible** Controls whether the attribute is shown as part of the drawing.

**Constant** Creates an attribute that doesn't prompt you to enter a value. Instead, the attribute has a constant, or fixed, value you give it during creation. Constant mode is used when you know you'll assign a fixed value to an object. After constant values are set in a block, you can't change them by using the standard set of attribute-editing commands.

**Verify** Causes AutoCAD to review the attribute values you enter at insertion time and ask you whether they're correct. This option appears only when the Attribute dialog box is turned off (the Attdia system variable is set to 0).

**Preset** Causes AutoCAD to automatically assign the default value to an attribute when its block is inserted. This saves time because a preset attribute won't prompt you for a value. Unlike Constant mode, a preset attribute can be edited.

**Lock Position** Prevents the attribute from being moved from its original location in the block when you're grip editing.

**Multiple Lines** Allows the attribute to contain multiple lines of text, similar to Mtext objects. When this option is turned on, you can specify a text boundary width.

With the exception of Invisible mode, none of these modes can be altered after the attribute becomes part of a block. Later in this chapter, I'll show you how to make an invisible attribute visible.

## Turning the Attribute Definitions into a Block

You need to perform one more crucial step before these attribute definitions can be of any use. You need to turn the attribute definitions into a block, along with the circle:

1. Click the Make Block tool in the 2D Draw control panel, or enter **B**↵.

2. In the Block Definition dialog box, enter **S-DOOR** for the name.

3. In the Base Point group, click the Pick Point tool, and then use the Center osnap to select the center of the circle.

4. In the Objects group, click the Select Objects tool, and select the circle and all the attributes. Press ↵ when you've completed your selection.

5. In the Behavior group, select the Annotative option. This ensures that the block is scaled to the appropriate size for the scale of the drawing into which it's inserted.

6. Click OK.

7. The attributes and the circle are now a block called S-DOOR. You can delete the S-DOOR block on your screen.

Once you've created the block, you can place it anywhere in the drawing using the Insert command or the Insert Block tool in the 2D Draw control panel. You'll insert this block in another location in the drawing. If you want to use the block in other drawings, you can use the Wblock command to save the block as a drawing file, or you can use the DesignCenter palette to drag and drop blocks from a drawing file. (See Chapter 27 for more on the DesignCenter.)

## Inserting Blocks Containing Attributes

In the preceding section, you created a door-type symbol at the desired size for the plotted symbol. This size is known as the *paper size*. Because you turned on the Annotative property for the attribute and block, you can use the Annotation Scale setting to have the block insert at the appropriate size for the scale of the drawing. The following steps demonstrate the process of inserting a block that contains attributes. First, set up your view and annotation scale in preparation to insert the blocks:

1. Turn on Attribute Dialog mode by entering **Attdia.↵1↵** at the Command prompt. This enables you to enter attribute values through a dialog box in the next exercise. Otherwise, you'd be prompted for the attribute values in the command window.

2. Select ⅛″=1′-0″ from the Annotation Scale drop-down list in the lower-right corner of the AutoCAD window. This ensures that the block appears at the proper size for the drawing scale.

3. In the 2D Navigate control panel, click the drop-down list, and select First. This is a view that has been saved in this drawing. (See "Taking Control of the AutoCAD Display" in Chapter 7 for more on saving views.)

4. Be sure the Ceiling and Flr-pat layers are off. Normally, in a floor plan, the door headers aren't visible, and they will interfere with the placement of the door-reference symbol.

5. Finally, you can begin to place the blocks in the drawing:

6. Click the Insert Block tool from the 2D Draw control panel or type I↵ to open the Insert dialog box.

7. Select S-DOOR from the Name drop-down list.

8. In the Insertion Point group, make sure the Specify On-Screen option is turned on.

9. In the Scale group, make sure the Uniform Scale check box is selected.

10. In the Rotation group, make sure the Specify On-Screen option is turned off; then, click OK.

   Now you're ready to place the block in your drawing in the appropriate locations and enter the attribute values.

**11.** AutoCAD is waiting for you to select a location for the symbol. To place the symbol, click in the doorway of the lower-left unit, near coordinate 41′-3″,72′-4″. Metric users should use coordinate 1256,2202. When you click the location, the Enter Attributes dialog box opens.

**12.** In the Door Type input box, enter **A**⏎. Note that this is the prompt you created. Note also that the default value is the hyphen you specified.

**TIP**   Attribute data is case sensitive, so any text you enter in all capital letters is stored in all capital letters.

**13.** In the Door Number input box, change the hyphen to **116**. Continue to change the values for each input box, as shown in Table 13.2.

**TABLE 13.2:**   Attribute Values for the Typical Studio Entry Door

| PROMPT | VALUE |
| --- | --- |
| Door Type | A |
| Door Size | 3′-0″ |
| Door Number | (Same as room number; see Figure 13.5) |
| Door Thickness | 1¾″ |
| Fire Rating | 20 min. |
| Door Material | Wood |
| Door Construction | Solid core |

**1.** When you're finished changing values, click OK, and the symbol appears. The only attribute you can see is the one you selected to be visible: the door type.

**2.** Add the rest of the door-type symbols for the apartment entry doors by copying or arraying the door symbol you just inserted. You can use the previously saved views found in the 2D Navigate control panel drop-down list to help you get around the drawing quickly.

Don't worry that the attribute values aren't appropriate for each unit; you'll see how to edit the attributes in the next section.

In addition to the S-DOOR block, you'll need another block for the room number. To save some time, I've included a block called S-APART that contains a rectangle and a single attribute definition for the room number (see Figure 13.3).

**FIGURE 13.3**

The apartment-number symbol

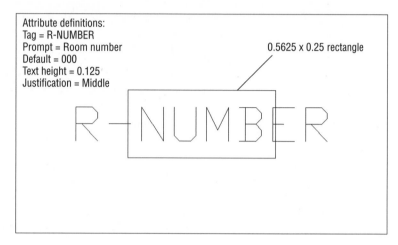

Do the following to insert the room-number block:

1. Choose Insert Block from the 2D Draw control panel, and select S-APART from the Name drop-down list.

2. Make sure the Specify On-Screen setting is turned on only for the Insertion point, and then click OK.

3. Insert the S-APART block into the lower-left unit. Give the attribute of this block the value **116**.

4. Copy or array the S-APART block so there is one S-APART block in each unit. You'll learn how to modify the attributes to reflect their proper values in the following section, "Editing Attributes." Figure 13.4 shows what the view should look like after you've entered the door symbols and the apartment numbers.

**FIGURE 13.4**

An overall view of the plan with door symbols and apartment numbers added

# Editing Attributes

Because drawings are usually in flux even after construction or manufacturing begins, you'll eventually have to edit previously entered attributes. In the example of the apartment building, many things can change before the final set of drawings is completed.

Attributes can be edited individually or *globally*—you can edit several occurrences of a particular attribute tag all at one time. In this section, you'll make changes to the attributes you've entered so far, using both individual and global editing techniques, and you'll practice editing invisible attributes.

**TIP**  If you prefer to start commands by using a toolbar, the Modify II toolbar in AutoCAD contains tools for the Enhanced Attribute Editor and the Block Attribute Manager discussed in this section.

## Editing Attribute Values One at a Time

AutoCAD offers an easy way to edit attributes one at a time through a dialog box. The following exercise demonstrates this feature:

1. Restore the First view by selecting First from the 2D Navigate control panel drop-down list.

2. Double-click the apartment number attribute in the unit just to the right of the first unit in the lower-left corner to open the Enhanced Attribute Editor. You can also choose Modify ➢ Object ➢ Attribute ➢ Single and then select the attribute.

**TIP**  LT users will see the Edit Attributes dialog box, which lists the attributes in a single column.

3. Change the value in the Value input box to **112**, and click OK to make the change.

4. Do this for each room, using Figure 13.5 as a reference for assigning room numbers.

**FIGURE 13.5**
Apartment numbers for one floor of the studio apartment building

**5.** Go back and edit the door-number attribute for the S-DOOR block. Give each door the same number as the room number it's associated with. See Figure 13.5 for the room numbers.

**TIP** If you're a veteran AutoCAD user, you can still use the Ddatte command (**Ate.⏎** shortcut) to open the Edit Attributes dialog box. This dialog box is useful for reviewing attributes as well as editing them because both visible and invisible attributes are displayed in the dialog box.

## Editing Attribute Text Formats and Properties

You may have noticed that the Enhanced Attribute Editor in the preceding exercise has three tabs: Attribute, Text Options, and Properties. When you double-click a block containing an attribute, the Enhanced Attribute Editor dialog box opens at the Attribute tab. You can use the other two tabs to control the size, font, color, and other properties of the selected attribute.

The Text Options tab lets you alter the attribute text style, justification, height, rotation, width factor, and oblique angle. (See Chapter 10 for more on these text options.)

The Properties tab lets you alter the attribute's layer, linetype, color, lineweight (effective only on AutoCAD fonts), and plot-style assignments.

In the previous exercise, you edited a block containing a single attribute. Double-clicking a block that contains multiple attributes, such as the S-door block, opens the Enhanced Attribute Editor dialog box at the Attribute tab. This tab displays all the attributes, regardless of whether they're visible, as shown in Figure 13.6. You can then edit the value, formats, and properties of the individual attributes by highlighting the attribute in the Attribute tab and using the other tabs to make changes. The changes you make affect only the attribute you've highlighted in the Attribute tab.

**TIP** If you want to change the location of individual attributes in a block, you can move attributes by using grips. Click the block to expose the grips, and then click the grip connected to the attribute. Or, if you've selected several blocks, Shift+click the attribute grips; then, move the attributes to their new location. They are still attached to their associated blocks.

**FIGURE 13.6**

The Enhanced Attribute Editor showing the contents of a block that contains several attributes

The Enhanced Attribute Editor lets you change attribute values, formats, and properties one block at a time; but, as you'll see in the next section, you can also make changes to several attributes at once.

## Making Global Changes to Attribute Values

At times, you'll want to change the value of several attributes in a file to be the same value. You can use the Edit Attribute Globally option to make global changes to attribute values.

Suppose you decide you want to change all the entry doors to a type designated as B, rather than A. Perhaps door-type A was an input error, or type B happens to be better suited for an entry door. The following exercise demonstrates how this is done:

1. Choose View ➢ Named Views to open the View Manager dialog box, and then restore the view named Fourth. Pan your view down so you can see the door-reference symbol for all the rooms in this view of the drawing.

2. Choose Modify ➢ Object ➢ Attribute ➢ Global, or type **–Attedit**↵ at the Command prompt. Make sure you include the dash at the beginning of –Attedit.

3. At the `Edit Attributes one at a time? [Yes/No] <Y>:` prompt, enter **N**↵ for No. You see the message `Performing global editing of attribute values`. This tells you that you're in Global Edit mode.

4. At the `Edit only attributes visible on screen? [Yes/No] <Y>:` prompt, press ↵. As you can see from this prompt, you have the option to edit all attributes, including those out of the view area. You'll get a chance to work with this option later in the chapter.

5. At the `Enter block name specification <*>:` prompt, press ↵. Optionally, you can enter a block name to narrow the selection to specific blocks.

6. At the `Enter attribute tag specification <*>:` prompt, press ↵. Optionally, you can enter an attribute tag name to narrow your selection to specific tags.

7. At the `Enter attribute value specification <*>:` prompt, press ↵. Optionally, you can narrow your selection to attributes containing specific values.

8. At the `Select Attributes:` prompt, select the door-type symbols for units 103 to 115. You can use a window to select the attributes if you prefer.

9. At the `Enter string to change:` prompt, enter **A**↵.

10. At the `Enter new string:` prompt, enter **B**↵. The door-type symbols all change to the new value.

In step 8, you were asked to select the attributes to be edited. AutoCAD limits the changes to those attributes you select. If you know you need to change every attribute in your drawing, you can do so by answering the series of prompts in a slightly different way, as in the following exercise:

1. Try the same procedure again, but this time enter **N** at the Edit only attributes visible on screen? [Yes/No] <Y>: prompt (step 4 in the previous exercise). The message Drawing must be regenerated afterwards appears. The AutoCAD Text Window appears.

2. Once again, you're prompted for the block name, the tag, and the value (steps 5, 6, and 7 in the previous exercise). Respond to these prompts as you did before. You then get the message 128 attributes selected. This tells you the number of attributes that fit the specifications you just entered.

3. At the Enter string to change: prompt, enter **A↵** to indicate you want to change the rest of the A attribute values.

4. At the Enter new string: prompt, enter **B↵**. A series of Bs appears, indicating the number of strings that were replaced.

**WARNING**  If the Regenauto command is off, you must regenerate the drawing to see the change.

In the previous exercise, AutoCAD skipped the Select Attribute: prompt and went directly to the String to change: prompt. AutoCAD assumes that you want it to edit every attribute in the drawing, so it doesn't bother asking you to select specific attributes.

## Making Invisible Attributes Visible

You can globally edit invisible attributes, such as those in the door-reference symbol, by using the tools just described. You may, however, want to be more selective about which invisible attribute you want to modify. Or, you may want to make invisible attributes temporarily visible for other editing purposes.

This exercise shows how you can make invisible attributes visible:

1. Enter **Attdisp↵**.

**TIP**  You can also use the View menu to change the display characteristics of attributes. Choose View ➤ Display ➤ Attribute Display, and then click the desired option on the cascading menu.

2. At the Enter attribute visibility setting [Normal/ON/OFF] <Normal>: prompt, enter **ON↵**. Your drawing looks like Figure 13.7. If Regenauto is turned off, you may have to issue the Regen command.

3. At this point, you could edit the invisible attributes individually, as in the first attribute-editing exercise. For now, set the attribute display back to Normal. Enter **Attdisp↵** again; then, at the Enter attribute visibility setting [Normal/ON/OFF] <ON>: prompt, enter **N↵** for Normal.

**TIP**  You've seen the results of the On and Normal options. The Off option makes all attributes invisible, regardless of the mode used when they were created.

**FIGURE 13.7**

The drawing with all the attributes visible. (Door-type symbols are so close together that they overlap.)

Because the attributes weren't intended to be visible, they appear to overlap and cover other parts of the drawing when they're made visible. Remember to turn them back off when you're done reviewing them.

---

### USING SPACES IN ATTRIBUTE VALUES

At times, you may want the default value to begin with a blank space. This enables you to specify text strings more easily when you edit the attribute. For example, suppose you have an attribute value that reads 3334333. If you want to change the first 3 in this string of numbers, you have to specify 3334 when prompted for the string to change; then, for the new string, you enter the same set of numbers again with the first 3 changed to the new number. If you only specify 3 for the string to change, AutoCAD will change all the 3s in the value. If you start with a space, as in _3334333 (I'm using an underline here only to represent the space; it doesn't mean you type an underline character), you can isolate the first 3 from the rest by specifying _3 as the string to change (again, type a space instead of the underline).

You must enter a backslash character (\) before the space in the default value to tell AutoCAD to interpret the space literally, rather than as a press of the spacebar (which is equivalent to pressing ↵).

---

## Making Global Format and Property Changes to Attributes

While we're on the subject of global editing, you should know how to make global changes to the format and properties of attributes. Earlier in this section, you saw how to make format changes to individual attributes by using the Enhanced Attribute Editor dialog box. You can also use the Edit Attribute dialog box to make global changes, as the following exercise demonstrates.

**TIP** Although LT doesn't support the Edit Attribute dialog box, you can use the command-line version of the Attedit command to edit some of the format and property values of attributes. Enter **–Attedit**↵ at the command line, and follow the prompts.

Follow these steps to make the global changes:

1. Choose Modify ➤ Object ➤ Attribute ➤ Block Attribute Manager to open the Block Attribute Manager dialog box. You can also enter **battman**↵.

**2.** Select S-APART from the Block drop-down list at the top of the dialog box. This list displays all the blocks that contain attributes. The only attribute you've defined for the selected block is displayed in the list box below it.

**3.** Click the attribute value in the list, and click the Edit button to open the Edit Attribute dialog box. The Edit Attribute dialog box is nearly identical to the Enhanced Attribute Editor you saw earlier.

**TIP** If there is only one attribute in the attribute list box, you don't have to select it before clicking the Edit button.

**4.** Click the Properties tab, select Red from the Color drop-down list, and click OK.

**5.** Click OK to exit the dialog box.

The Edit Attribute dialog box you saw in this exercise offers a slightly different set of options from those in the Enhanced Attribute Editor dialog box. In the Attribute tab of the Edit Attribute dialog box, you can change some of the mode settings for the attribute, such as visibility and the Verify and Preset modes. You can also change the Tag, Prompt, and Default values. In contrast, the Attribute tab in the Enhanced Attribute Editor dialog box enables you to change the attribute value but none of the other attribute properties.

### OTHER BLOCK ATTRIBUTE MANAGER OPTIONS

The Block Attribute Manager dialog box includes a few other options that weren't covered in the exercises. Here's a rundown of the Settings, Move Up, Move Down, and Remove and Sync buttons:

**Settings**   Click this button to open the Settings dialog box, which lets you control which attribute properties are displayed in the list box of the Block Attribute Manager dialog box.

You can then select the properties to be displayed. The Emphasize Duplicate Tags option high-lights duplicate tag names by showing them in red. The Apply Changes To Existing References option forces any changes you make to the attribute properties to be applied to existing attributes. If this setting is turned off, you have to use the Sync button in the Block Attribute Manager dialog box to update existing attributes, and the changes you make to attribute properties are applied only to new attributes added after the change. You can also enter **Attsync↵** at the Command prompt to synchronize older attributes.

**Move Up and Move Down**   Clicking these buttons moves a selected attribute up or down the list of attributes in the list box. If you move an item down the list, the item changes its position when viewed using the Ddatte command or when viewing the attribute's properties in the Enhanced Attribute Editor dialog box. Of course, this has an effect only on blocks containing multiple attributes.

**Remove**   Clicking this button removes the selected attribute from the block, so make sure you mean it before you click.

**Sync**   This option updates the attribute properties such as the attribute order, text formatting, mode, and so on. It can also be used to globally update blocks that have had new attribute definitions added or deleted. It doesn't affect the individual attribute values.

## Redefining Blocks Containing Attributes

Attributes act differently from other objects when they're included in redefined blocks. Normally, blocks that have been redefined change their configuration to reflect the new block definition. But if a redefined block contains attributes, the attributes maintain their old properties, including their position in relation to other objects in the block. This means the old attribute position, style, and so on don't change even though you may have changed them in the new definition.

Fortunately, AutoCAD offers a tool that's specifically designed to let you update blocks with attributes. The following steps describe how to update attribute blocks:

1. Before you use the command to redefine an attribute block, you must create the objects and attribute definitions that will make up the replacement attribute block. The simplest way to do this is to explode a copy of the attribute block you want to update. This ensures that you have the same attribute definitions in the updated block.

2. Make your changes to the exploded attribute block.

**WARNING**   Before you explode the attribute block copy, be sure it's at a 1-to-1 scale. This is important, because if you don't use the original size of the block, you could end up with all your new attribute blocks at the wrong size. Also be sure you use a marker device, such as a line, to locate the insertion point of the attribute block before you explode it. This will help you locate and maintain the original insertion point for the redefined block.

3. Type **Attredef**↵.

4. At the `Enter name of block you wish to redefine:` prompt, enter the appropriate name.

5. At the `Select objects:` prompt, select all the objects, including the attribute definitions, that you want to include in the revised attribute block.

6. At the `Specify insertion base point of new Block:` prompt, pick the same location used for the original block.

After you pick the insertion point, AutoCAD takes a few seconds to update the blocks. The amount of time depends on the complexity of the block and the number of times the block occurs in the drawing. If you include a new attribute definition with your new block, it too is added to all the updated blocks, with its default value. Attribute definitions that are deleted from your new definition are removed from all the updated blocks.

**TIP**   You can also use the Refedit command (choose Tools ➢ Xref And Block In-Place Editing ➢ Edit Reference In-Place) to modify attribute definitions. After editing, you must use the Sync option in the Block Attribute Manager to update all instances of the modified block.

## Extracting and Exporting Attribute Information

After you enter the attributes in your drawing, you can extract the information contained in the attributes and use it to generate reports or to analyze the attribute data in other programs. You might, for example, want to keep track of the number and type of doors in your drawing through a database manager. This is especially useful if you have a project such as a large hotel that contains thousands of doors.

When you extract attribute data, AutoCAD creates a text file. You can choose to export the file in either comma-delimited or tab-delimited format. If you have Microsoft Excel or Access installed, you can also export the attribute data in a format compatible with these programs.

### Performing the Extraction

In the past, extracting the attribute data from a drawing was an error-prone task requiring the creation of a template file. This template file had to contain a series of codes that described the data you wanted to extract. AutoCAD 2008 has a greatly improved system for attribute data extraction, in the form of the Attribute Extraction Wizard. The following exercises will walk you through a sample extraction.

**NOTE**   LT doesn't offer the Attribute Extraction Wizard. Instead, you see the more simplified Attribute Extraction dialog box, which offers the file-format options (comma- or space-delimited or DXF output), the output filename, and template file options. For LT, the template file is used as an option to filter the attributes.

### USING THE DATA EXTRACTION WIZARD

In this first exercise, you'll explore the Data Extraction Wizard: You can use the `13c-plan.dwg` sample file if you haven't done the tutorials from the beginning of the chapter.

1. Go back to the `Plan` file, and choose Tools ➤ Data Extraction to start the Data Extraction Wizard. In the Begin screen, you can choose to start an extraction from scratch or use an existing data-extraction setup that you've created from previous extractions.

2. Click Next to open the Save Data Extraction As dialog box. This dialog box lets you save the data-extraction settings you're about to set up in a file with the `.dxe` filename extension. Enter a name, and click Save. The Define Data Source dialog box opens.

3. Click Settings to view other options. These options let you further refine the content of your extraction.

4. Click Cancel to close the Additional Settings dialog box; then, click Next to open the Select Objects screen.

Take a moment to study the Select Objects screen. It's the heart of the extraction process. Here, you select the blocks that contain attributes as well as the specific attributes you want to extract. The list shows all the object types in the drawing. You'll pare down this list to show only the blocks with attributes.

### SELECTING WHAT TO EXTRACT

Let's continue by selecting specific information for the extraction:

1. Select the Display All Object Types option in the lower-left corner of the dialog box, and make sure the Display Blocks Only radio button is selected.

2. Select the Display Blocks With Attributes Only option.

3. In the Object list, click the S-DOOR item to select it.

**4.** Click Next to open the Select Properties screen, which displays a list of the different types of data available for extraction

**5.** In the Category Filter panel, deselect all the options except Attribute. Now you see only the attribute data listed in the Properties panel.

**6.** Select each item in the Properties panel. A check mark appears by each item.

**7.** Click Next. The Refine Data window appears. Here, you can continue to filter out data. For example, you can deselect the Show Count Column and Show Name Column options, because they may be unnecessary for your purpose. You can also get a preview of your extracted data by clicking the Full Preview button.

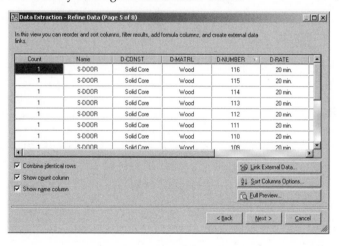

**NOTE** If you want to sort your data by column, you can do so by clicking the column title. To change the order of the columns, click and drag the column titles horizontally.

### SAVING THE ATTRIBUTE DATA TO A FILE

Now, let's complete the extraction process.

1. Click Next. The Choose Output screen appears. This window lets you determine whether to convert the data into a table in the drawing, extract the data as an external data file, or both.

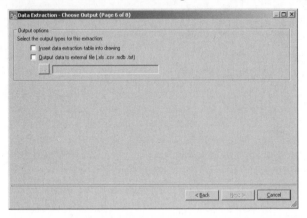

2. Select the Output Data To External File option. The input box just below the option becomes available for input. You can type a location for the external file input box, or you can click the browse button to browse to a location.

Browse button

3. You have the option to extract an .xls, .csv, .mdb, or .txt file. You can select the type of file to use when you click the browse button to show where you want the file to go. The browse button opens a Save As dialog box, where you can select the type of file to save from the File Of Type drop-down list. The default filename is the current drawing filename with an .xls extension.

4. Click Next to open the Finish screen. It gives you a brief message explaining what to do next.

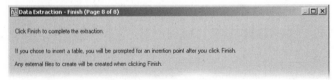

5. Click Finish. A file with the current drawing name and the .xls filename extension is created. By default, the file is placed in the My Documents folder unless you specify a different location in step 2.

You now have a file called plan.xls (13a-plan.xls if you used the sample file) that contains the data you saw earlier in the Full Preview window of the Attribute Extraction Wizard. You can open this file with Microsoft Excel.

## Extracting Attribute Data to an AutoCAD Table

You may have noticed the option to extract the attribute data to an AutoCAD table in the Choose Output screen of the Data Extraction Wizard. This option lets you convert the attribute data directly into a table in the current drawing. Besides making it easy to create parts lists or other types of tables in your drawing, you get the added benefit of having tables update automatically whenever attribute data changes.

If you turn on this option and click Next, you'll see the Table Style screen instead of the Finish screen.

From here, you can follow these steps:

1. Select a table style for the extracted data, enter a title, and click Next. The Finish screen opens.

2. Click Finish. You see a warning message saying that changes made to the table will be lost if the table is refreshed.

3. Click OK; you're prompted to select a point. Click in the drawing to place the table.

The table may appear at a small size depending on the scale of your drawing. Zoom in to the location where you clicked, and you'll see the table.

| Quantity | D-CONST | D-MATRL | D-NUMBER | D-RATE | D-SIZE | D-THICK | D-TYPE | Name |
|---|---|---|---|---|---|---|---|---|
| 1 | Solid Core | Wood | 103 | 20 min. | 3'-0" | 1 3/4" | B | S-DOOR |
| 1 | Solid Core | Wood | 111 | 20 min. | 3'-0" | 1 3/4" | B | S-DOOR |
| 1 | Solid Core | Wood | 108 | 20 min. | 3'-0" | 1 3/4" | B | S-DOOR |
| 1 | Solid Core | Wood | 107 | 20 min. | 3'-0" | 1 3/4" | B | S-DOOR |
| 1 | Solid Core | Wood | 115 | 20 min. | 3'-0" | 1 3/4" | B | S-DOOR |
| 1 | Solid Core | Wood | 102 | 20 min. | 3'-0" | 1 3/4" | B | S-DOOR |
| 1 | Solid Core | Wood | 101 | 20 min. | 3'-0" | 1 3/4" | B | S-DOOR |
| 1 | Solid Core | Wood | 105 | 20 min. | 3'-0" | 1 3/4" | B | S-DOOR |
| 1 | Solid Core | Wood | 113 | 20 min. | 3'-0" | 1 3/4" | B | S-DOOR |
| 1 | Solid Core | Wood | 109 | 20 min. | 3'-0" | 1 3/4" | B | S-DOOR |
| 1 | Solid Core | Wood | 112 | 20 min. | 3'-0" | 1 3/4" | B | S-DOOR |
| 1 | Solid Core | Wood | 116 | 20 min. | 3'-0" | 1 3/4" | B | S-DOOR |
| 1 | Solid Core | Wood | 106 | 20 min. | 3'-0" | 1 3/4" | B | S-DOOR |
| 1 | Solid Core | Wood | 104 | 20 min. | 3'-0" | 1 3/4" | B | S-DOOR |
| 1 | Solid Core | Wood | 110 | 20 min. | 3'-0" | 1 3/4" | B | S-DOOR |
| 1 | Solid Core | Wood | 114 | 20 min. | 3'-0" | 1 3/4" | B | S-DOOR |

You also see the Data Link icon in the lower-right corner of the AutoCAD window.

One unique characteristic of a table created from attributes is that you have the option to be notified whenever the table needs to be updated. For example, the first time an attribute value for the doors in the plan is changed in any way, you'll see a balloon warning message in the lower-right corner of the AutoCAD window.

You can then click the Update Tables Using The Data Link item in the balloon to update the table to the new attribute values. You can also dismiss the balloon warning and update the table later. When you're ready to update the table, right-click the Data Extraction icon in the lower-right corner of the AutoCAD window, and select Update All Data Links. The table will be updated to reflect the latest attribute values.

## The Bottom Line

**Creating Attributes**   Attributes are a great tool for storing data with drawn objects. You can include as little or as much data as you like in an AutoCAD block.

**Master It**   What is the name of the object you must include in a block to store data?

**Solution**   Attribute definition.

**Editing Attributes**   The data you include in a block is easily changed. You may have several copies of a block, each of which must contain its own unique sets of data.

**Master It**   What is the simplest way to gain access to a block's attribute data?

**Solution**   Double-click the block to open the Enhanced Attribute Editor.

**Extracting and Exporting Attribute Information**   Attribute data can be extracted in a number of ways so that you can keep track of the data in a drawing.

**Master It**   How do you start the data-extraction process?

**Solution**   Choose Tools ➤ Data Extraction to open the Data Extraction Wizard.

# Chapter 14

# Copying Existing Drawings into AutoCAD

At times, you'll want to turn a hand-drafted drawing into an AutoCAD drawing file. You may be modifying a design you created before you started using AutoCAD or converting your entire library of drawings for future AutoCAD use. Or perhaps you want to convert a sketch into a formal drawing. This chapter discusses ways to enter a hand-drafted drawing: tracing, scaling, and scanning. Each method has its advantages and disadvantages.

Topics in this chapter include the following:

◆ Methods for Converting Paper Drawings to AutoCAD Files

◆ Importing a Raster Image

◆ Work with a Raster Image

## Methods for Converting Paper Drawings to AutoCAD Files

*Tracing* with a digitizing tablet used to be the only way to enter a hand-drafted drawing into AutoCAD, but a traced drawing usually requires some cleanup and reorganization.

*Scaling* a drawing is the most flexible method because you don't need a tablet to do it, and, generally, you're faced with less cleanup afterward. Scaling also facilitates the most accurate input of orthogonal lines because you can read dimensions directly from the drawing and enter them into AutoCAD. The main drawback with scaling is that if the drawing doesn't contain complete dimensional information, you must constantly look at the hand-drafted drawing and measure distances with a scale. Also, irregular curves are difficult to scale accurately.

Programs are available that automatically convert an image file into an AutoCAD drawing file consisting of lines and arcs. These programs may offer some help, but they require the most cleanup of the options presented here. Like tracing, scanning is best used for drawings that are difficult to scale, such as complex topographical maps containing more contours than are practical to trace on a digitizer, or nontechnical line art, such as letterhead and logos.

The simplest method for converting paper drawings, and the method I show you in this chapter, is to scan your drawings as image files to be used as a background in AutoCAD. You can import your image files into AutoCAD and then trace directly over them. This technique allows you to see the original drawing in the AutoCAD window, saving you the effort of diverting your attention to other areas of your workstation.

---

**WORKING WITH A DIGITIZER**

If you're working with AutoCAD LT, you may find that your only option is to use a digitizing table to trace existing paper drawings. AutoCAD's Help window offers an excellent description of how to use a digitizer.

Use AutoCAD's Help window to find information on the Tablet command. Choose Help ➢ Help; then, in the AutoCAD Help window, select the Contents tab. Expand the Command Reference listing, and then select Commands. Open the T Commands option, and select Tablet. If you haven't configured your table yet, look at the description of the CFG (configure) option for the Tablet command. Once you've configured your tablet, read the instructions for the CAL (calibration) option.

---

## Importing a Raster Image

If you have a scanner and you'd like to use it to import drawings and other images into AutoCAD, you can use AutoCAD's ability to import raster images. There are many reasons you may want to import a scanned image. In architectural plans, a vicinity map is frequently used to show the location of a project. With the permission of its creator, you can scan a map into AutoCAD and incorporate it into a cover sheet. That cover sheet can also contain other images, such as photographs of the site, computer renderings and elevations of the project, and company logos.

**NOTE**    LT users can't import raster images. However, images placed in drawings can be viewed, moved, and scaled in LT, and you can turn their frames on or off.

Another reason for importing a scanned image is to use the image as a reference to trace over. You can trace a drawing with greater accuracy by using a scanned image as opposed to a digitizing tablet. Now that the price of a scanner has fallen to less than $100, a scanner is a cost-effective tool for tracing a wide variety of graphic material. In this section, you'll learn firsthand how you can import an image as a background for tracing.

Choose Insert ➢ External References to open the External References palette, which lets you import a full range of raster image files.

If you've read Chapter 7, this palette should look familiar. It's the same palette you use to manage external references. Just like external references (Xrefs), raster images are loaded when the current file is open, but they aren't stored as part of the current file when the file is saved. This helps keep file sizes down, but it also means that you need to keep track of inserted raster files. You must make sure they're kept together with the AutoCAD files in which they're inserted. For example, you might want to keep image files in the same folder as the drawing file to which they're attached.

**NOTE**   AutoCAD has a utility called eTransmit that collects AutoCAD files and their related support files, such as raster images, external references, and fonts, into any folder or drive you specify. See Chapter 27 for details.

Another similarity between Xrefs and imported raster images is that you can clip a raster image so that only a portion of the image is displayed in your drawing. Portions of a raster file that are clipped aren't stored in memory, so your system won't get bogged down, even if the raster file is huge.

The following exercise gives you step-by-step instructions for importing a raster file. It also lets you see how scanned resolution translates into an image in AutoCAD. This is important if you're interested in scanning drawings for the purpose of tracing over them. Here are the steps:

1. Create a new file called `Rastertrace`.

2. Set up the file as an architectural drawing with a ¼"=1´ scale on an 8½" × 11" sheet (Limits set to 0,0 for the lower-left corner and 528,408 for the upper-right corner). Make sure the drawing units type is set to Architectural. Metric users should set up their drawing at a 1:50 scale on an A4 size sheet. (Limits for metric users should be 0,0 for the lower-left corner and 1480,1050 for the upper-right corner.)

3. Choose View ➢ Zoom ➢ All to make sure the entire drawing limits are displayed on the screen.

4. Draw a line across the screen from coordinates 0,20´ to 64´,20´. Metric users should draw the line from 0,600 to 1820,600. You'll use this line in a later exercise.

5. Click the line you just drew, and then select Red from the Color Control drop-down list in the Properties toolbar. This helps make the line more visible.

6. Choose Insert ➢ Raster Image Reference, or type **iat.↵** to open the Select Image File dialog box. This is a typical AutoCAD file dialog box complete with a preview window.

   Locate and select the `raster1.jpg` project file. You can see a preview of the file on the right side of the dialog box.

7. Click Open to open the Image dialog box. Click OK.

8. Press ↵ at the Specify insertion point: prompt to accept the 0,0 coordinates.

9. At the Specify scale factor <1>: prompt, use the cursor to scale the image so it fills about half the screen, as shown in Figure 14.1. The raster1.jpg filename appears in the External References palette.

**FIGURE 14.1**
Manually scaling the raster image

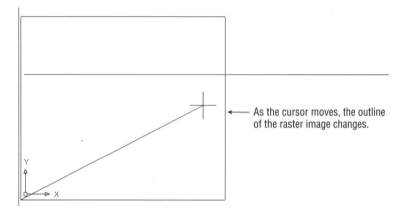

As the cursor moves, the outline of the raster image changes.

---

**TIPS FOR IMPORTING RASTER IMAGES**

When you scan a document into your computer, you get a raster image file. Unlike AutoCAD files, *raster image files* are made up of a matrix of colored pixels that form a picture, which is why raster images are also sometimes called *bitmaps*. *Vector files*, like those produced by AutoCAD, are made up of instructions to draw lines, arcs, curves, and circles. The two formats, raster and vector, are so different that it's difficult to accurately convert one format to the other. It's easier to trace a raster file in AutoCAD than it is to try to have a computer program make the conversion for you.

But even tracing a raster image file can be difficult if the image is of poor quality. Here are a few points you should consider if you plan to use raster imports for tracing drawings:

♦ Scan in your drawing by using a grayscale or color scanner, or convert your black-and-white scanned image to grayscale by using your scanner software.

♦ Use a paint program or your scanner software to clean up unwanted gray or spotted areas in the file before importing it into AutoCAD.

♦ If your scanner software or paint program has a "de-speckle" or "de-spot" feature, use it. It can help clean up your image and ultimately reduce the raster image's file size.

♦ Scan at a reasonable resolution. Remember that the human hand usually is no more accurate than a few thousandths of an inch, so scanning at 150dpi to 200dpi may be more than adequate.

♦ If you plan to make heavy use of raster imports, upgrade your computer to the fastest processor you can afford, and don't spare the memory.

The raster-import commands can incorporate paper maps or plans into 3D AutoCAD drawings for presentations. I know of one architectural firm that produces impressive presentations with little effort by combining 2D scanned images with 3D massing models for urban-design studies. (A *massing model* is a model that shows only the rough outline of buildings without giving too much detail. Massing models show the general scale of a project without being too fussy.) Raster images don't, however, appear in perspective views.

# Working with a Raster Image

Once you've imported a raster image, you can begin to work with it in a variety of ways. You can resize the image to suit your needs and even adjust its size to a particular scale. Raster images can be made to overlap AutoCAD objects, or you can have raster images appear in the background. There are also rudimentary controls for brightness, contrast, and transparency. In this section, you'll continue to use the image you attached to your drawing to explore some of these options.

## Scaling a Raster Image

The `raster1.jpg` file was scanned as a grayscale image at 100dpi. This shows that you can get a reasonable amount of detail at a fairly low scan resolution.

Now, suppose you want to trace over this image to start an AutoCAD drawing. The first thing you should do is scale the image to the appropriate size. You can scale an image file to full size. Try the following steps to see how you can begin the process:

1. Choose View ➢ Zoom ➢ Extents.

2. Click Scale on the Modify toolbar.

3. Click the edge of the raster image to select it.

4. Press ↵ to finish your selection.

5. At the `Specify base point:` prompt, click the X in the lower-left corner of the image—the one you used in the first exercise to calibrate your digitizing tablet.

6. At the `Specify scale factor or [Copy/Reference]:` prompt, enter **R↵** to use the Reference option.

7. At the `Specify reference length <1>:` prompt, type **@↵**. This tells AutoCAD that you want to use the last point selected as one end of the reference length. After you enter the @ symbol, you'll see a rubber-banding line emanating from the X.

8. At the `Specify second point:` prompt, click the X at the lower-right corner of the image.

9. At the `Specify new length or [Points]:` prompt, enter **44´↵**. Metric users should enter **1341↵**. The image enlarges. Remember that this reference line is 44´ or 1341 cm in length.

The image is now scaled properly for the plan it portrays. You can proceed to trace over the image. You can also place the image on its own layer and turn it off from time to time to check your trace work. Even if you don't trace the scanned floor plan line for line, you can read the dimensions of the plan from your computer monitor, instead of having to go back and forth between measuring the paper image and drawing the plan on the computer.

## Controlling Object Visibility and Overlap with Raster Images

With the introduction of raster-image support, AutoCAD inherited a problem that's fairly common to programs that use such images: Raster images obscure other objects that were placed before they were. The image you imported in the previous exercise, for example, obscures the line you drew when you first opened the file. In most cases, this overlap isn't a problem; but in some situations you'll want AutoCAD vector objects to overlap an imported raster image. An example is a civil-engineering drawing showing an AutoCAD drawing of a new road superimposed over an aerial view of the location for the road.

Paint and page-layout programs usually offer a "to front/to back" tool to control the overlap of objects and images. AutoCAD offers the Draworder command. Here's how it works:

1. Choose View ➢ Zoom ➢ Extents to get an overall view of the image.

2. Choose Tools ➢ Draw Order ➢ Bring Above Objects.

3. At the `Select objects:` prompt, select the horizontal line you drew when you first opened the file.

4. You can select other objects if you wish. Press ↵ to finish your selection.

5. At the `Select reference objects:` prompt, click the edge of the raster image of the utility room, and then press ↵.

The drawing regenerates, and the entire line appears, no longer obscured by the raster image.

**TIP**  You can mask out areas of an imported raster image by creating a solid hatch area and using the Draworder command to place the solid hatch on top of the raster image. Such masks can be helpful as backgrounds for text that must be placed over a raster image. You can also use the Wipeout command (Draw ➢ Wipeout) to mask areas of a drawing.

The Draworder command you just used has four options:

**Tools ➢ Draw Order ➢ Bring To Front**   Places an object or a set of objects at the top of the draw order for the entire drawing. The effect is that the objects are completely visible.

**Tools ➢ Draw Order ➢ Send To Back**   Places an object or a set of objects at the bottom of the draw order for the entire drawing. The effect is that other objects in the drawing may obscure those objects.

**Tools ➢ Draw Order ➢ Bring Above Objects**   Places an object or a set of objects above another object in the draw order. This has the effect of making the first set of objects appear above the second selected object.

**Tools ➢ Draw Order ➢ Bring Under Objects**   Places an object or a set of objects below another object in the draw order. This has the effect of making the first set of objects appear underneath the second selected object.

You can also use the **Dr** keyboard shortcut to issue the Draworder command. If you do this, you see these prompts:

```
Select objects:
Enter object ordering option [Above objects/Under objects/Front/Back]<Back>:
```

You must then select the option by typing the capitalized letter of the option.

Although this section discussed the Draw Order tools in relation to raster images, they can also be invaluable in controlling visibility of line work in conjunction with hatch patterns and solid fills. See Chapter 7 for a detailed discussion of the Draw Order tools and hatch patterns.

## Clipping a Raster Image

In Chapter 7, you saw how you can clip an external-reference object so that only a portion of it appears in the drawing. You can also clip imported raster images in the same way. Just as with Xrefs, you can create a closed outline of the area you want to clip, or you can specify a simple rect-angular area.

---

**IMAGES AND THE EXTERNAL REFERENCE PALETTE**

The External Reference Palette you saw in Chapter 7 helps you manage your imported image files. It's especially helpful when you have a large number of images in your drawing. You can control imported images in a way similar to xrefs; you can temporarily unload images (to help speed up the editing of AutoCAD objects), reload, detach, and relocate raster image files. See Chapter 7 for a detailed description of these options.

---

In the following exercise, you'll try the Imageclip command to control the display of the raster image:

1. Choose Modify ➢ Clip ➢ Image, or type **Icl**↵.

2. At the `Select image to clip:` prompt, click the edge of the raster image.

3. At the `Enter image clipping option [ON/OFF/Delete/New boundary]<New>:` prompt, press ↵ to create a new boundary.

4. At the `Enter clipping type [Polygonal/Rectangular]<Rectangular>:` prompt, enter **P**↵ to draw a polygonal boundary.

5. Select the points shown in the top image in Figure 14. 2 and then press ↵. The raster image is clipped to the boundary you created, as shown in the second image in Figure 14. 2.

As the prompt in step 3 indicates, you can turn the clipping off or on, or you can delete an existing clipping boundary through the Clip Image option.

After you clip a raster image, you can adjust the clipping boundary by using its grips:

1. Click the boundary edge of the raster image to expose its grips.

2. Click a grip in the upper-right corner, as shown in the final image in Figure 14. 2.

3. Drag the grip up and to the right, and then click a point. The image adjusts to the new boundary.

In addition to hiding portions of a raster image that are unimportant to you, clipping an image file reduces the amount of RAM the raster image uses during your editing session. AutoCAD loads only the visible portion of the image into RAM and ignores the rest.

## Adjusting Brightness, Contrast, and Strength

AutoCAD offers a tool that enables you to adjust the brightness, contrast, and strength of a raster image. Try making some adjustments to the raster image of the utility room in the following exercise:

1. Choose Modify ➢ Object ➢ Image ➢ Adjust, or type **Iad**↵.

2. At the `Select image(s):` prompt, click the edge of the raster image, and press ↵ to open the Image Adjust dialog box.

**FIGURE 14.2**

Adjusting the boundary of a clipped image

3. Click and drag the Fade slider to the right so it's near the middle of the slider scale, or enter **50** in the Fade input box to the right of the slider. The sample image fades to the AutoCAD background color as you move the slider.

4. Click OK. The raster image appears faded.

5. Save the file as `Rasterimport.dwg`.

You can adjust the brightness and contrast by using the other two sliders in the Image Adjust dialog box. Clicking the Reset button resets all the settings to their default values.

By using the Image Adjust option in conjunction with image clipping, you can create special effects. Figure 14.3 shows an aerial view with labels of downtown San Francisco. This view consists of two copies of the same raster image. One copy serves as a background, which was lightened using the method demonstrated in the previous exercise. The second copy is the darker area of the image with a roughly triangular clip boundary applied. You might use this technique to bring focus to a particular area of a drawing you're preparing for a presentation.

**FIGURE 14.3**
Two copies of the same image can be combined to emphasize a portion of the drawing.

If the draw order of objects is incorrect after you open a file or perform a Pan or Zoom, issue a Regen to recover the correct draw-order view.

## Turning Off the Frame, Adjusting Overall Quality, and Controlling Transparency

You can make three other adjustments to your raster image: frame visibility, image quality, and image transparency.

By default, a raster image displays an outline, or a *frame*. In many instances, this frame can detract from your drawing. You can globally turn off image frames by choosing Modify ➤ Object ➤ Image ➤ Frame (LT users should choose Modify ➤ Object ➤ Image Frame) and then entering **1** (on) or **0** (off), depending on whether you want the frame visible or invisible (see Figure 14.4). You can also type **Imageframe⤶0⤶**. A third option, 2, leaves the frame visible but doesn't plot the frame.

**TIP**  If you turn off a raster image's frame, you can't select the image for editing. You can use this to your advantage if you don't want a raster image to be moved or otherwise edited. To make a raster image selectable, turn on the image frame setting.

If your drawing doesn't require the highest-quality image, you can set the image quality to Draft mode. You may use Draft mode when you're tracing an image or when the image is already of a high quality. To set the image quality, choose Modify ➤ Object ➤ Image ➤ Quality, and then enter **H** for High mode (high quality) or **D** for Draft mode. In Draft mode, your drawing will regenerate faster.

High mode softens the pixels of the raster image, giving the image a smoother appearance. Draft mode displays the image in a raw, pixelated state. If you look carefully at the regions between the motorcycle and the background in the second image in Figure 14.5, you'll see that it appears a bit jagged. The first image in Figure 14.5 uses the High setting to soften the edges of the motorcycle. You may need to look closely to see the difference.

**FIGURE 14.4**
A raster image with the frame on (top) and off (bottom)

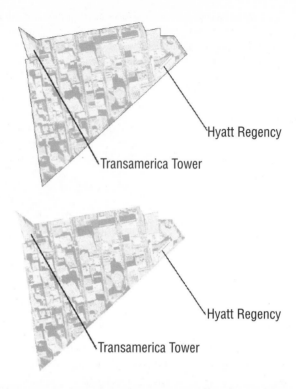

**FIGURE 14.5**
A close-up of a raster image with quality set to High (top) and Draft (bottom)

Finally, you can control the transparency of raster-image files that allow transparent pixels. Some file formats, such as the CompuServe GIF 89a format, enable you to set a color in the image to be transparent (usually the background color). Most image-editing programs support this format because it's a popular one used on web pages.

When you turn on the Transparency setting, objects normally obscured by the background of a raster image may show through. Choose Modify ➤ Object ➤ Image ➤ Transparency, and then select the raster image you want to make transparent. Press ↵, and then enter **On** or **Off**, depending on whether you want the image to be transparent. Unlike the Frame and Quality options, Transparency works on individual objects rather than globally.

**NOTE**   The Properties palette offers many of the same adjustments described in this section, and you can use it for quick access to the Transparency setting and other raster-image settings. You can access the Image Adjust dialog box, hide or display clipped areas, or hide the entire raster image.

**NOTE**   In earlier versions of AutoCAD, you could import PostScript files. AutoCAD no longer support this function. If you need to import a PostScript file, you must convert the file into a format that AutoCAD will accept. Most programs that generate PostScript files also produce DXF files or Windows Metafile files (WMF). WMF files can be imported into AutoCAD by using the Insert menu, and DXF files can be opened using the standard File ➤ Open menu option.

## The Bottom Line

**Turning Paper Drawings into AutoCAD Drawings**   AutoCAD gives you some great tools that let you convert your paper drawings into AutoCAD files. Several options are available; depending on your needs, you'll find at least one solution that will allow you to quickly convert your drawings.

**Master It**   Describe the different methods available in AutoCAD for converting paper drawings into CAD files.

**Solution**   The methods are tracing with a digitizer, scaling directly from a drawing, scanning and converting with a third-party program, and scanning to a raster file that can then be imported into AutoCAD to be traced over.

**Importing a Raster Image**   You can use bitmap raster images as backgrounds for your CAD drawings or as underlay drawings that you can trace over.

**Master It**   Import a raster image of your choice, and use the AutoCAD drawing tools to trace over your image.

**Solution**   Choose Insert ➤ Raster Image Reference, or type **iat**↵ to open the Select Image File dialog box. Locate and select the raster image file you want to import. Click Open to open the Image dialog box, and then click OK. Specify an insertion point and scale factor.

**Working with a Raster Image in AutoCAD**   Once imported, raster images can be adjusted for size, brightness, contrast, and transparency.

**Master It**   Import a raster image of your choice, and fade the image so it appears lighter and with less contrast.

**Solution**   Import your raster image, and then choose Modify ➤ Object ➤ Image ➤ Adjust or type **Iad**↵. Click the border of the raster image, and press ↵ to open the Image Adjust dialog box. Click and drag the Fade slider to the right so it's near the middle of the slider scale, or enter **50** in the Fade input box to the right of the slider. Click OK. The raster image appears faded.

# Chapter 15

# Advanced Editing and Organizing

Because you may not know all of a project's requirements when it begins, you usually base the first draft of a design on anticipated needs. As the plan goes forward, you adjust for new requirements as they arise. As more people enter the project, additional design restrictions come into play, and the design is further modified. This process continues throughout the project, from the first draft to the end product.

In this chapter, you'll gain experience with some tools that will help you edit your drawings more efficiently. You'll take a closer look at Xrefs and how they may be used to help streamline changes in a drawing project. You'll also be introduced to tools and techniques you can use to minimize duplication of work, such as the Quick Select tool and the QuickCalc feature. AutoCAD can be a powerful time-saving tool if used properly. This chapter examines ways to harness that power.

Topics in this chapter include the following:

◆ Using External References (Xrefs)

◆ Managing Layers

◆ Using Advanced Tools: Filter, Quick Select, and QuickCalc

◆ Using the QuickCalc Calculator

## Using External References (Xrefs)

Chapter 7 mentioned that careful use of blocks, external references (Xrefs), and layers can help improve your productivity. In this section, you'll see firsthand how to use these features to help reduce design errors and speed up delivery of an accurate set of drawings. You do this by controlling layers in conjunction with blocks and Xrefs to create a common drawing database for several drawings.

**TIP**   You can also use AutoCAD DWF files as Xrefs. See Chapter 27 for more on DWF files.

In the next section, you'll start to use Xrefs to create different floor plans for the building you worked on earlier in this book. To save some time, I've created a second one-bedroom unit plan called Unit2 that you'll use in these exercises (see Figure 15.1). You can find this new unit plan in the Chapter 15 sample files.

**FIGURE 15.1**

The one-bedroom unit

## Preparing Existing Drawings for Cross-Referencing

Chapter 7 discussed how you can use Xrefs to assemble one floor of the apartment. In this section, you'll explore the creation and use of Xrefs to build multiple floors, each containing slightly different sets of drawing information. By doing so, you'll learn how Xrefs enable you to use a single file in multiple drawings to save time and reduce redundancy. You'll see that by sharing common data in multiple files, you can reduce your work and keep the drawing information consistent.

You'll start by creating the files that you'll use later as Xrefs:

1. Open the Plan file. If you didn't create the Plan file, you can use the 15a-plan.dwg file (see Figure 15.2).

**FIGURE 15.2**

The overall plan

2. Turn off the Ceiling, Notes, and Flr-pat layers to get a clear, uncluttered view of the individual unit plans.

3. Use the Wblock command (enter **W**↵ at the Command prompt), and write the eight units in the corners of your plan to a file called Floor1.dwg (see Figure 15.3). When you select objects

for the Wblock, be sure to include the door symbols and apartment number symbols for those units. Use 0,0 for the Wblock insertion base point. Also make sure the Delete From Drawing check box is selected in the Write Block dialog box before you click OK.

**FIGURE 15.3**

Units to be exported to the Floor1 file

Select these units for the Wblock command.

4. Using Figure 15.4 as a guide, insert the Unit2.dwg file into the corners where the other eight units were previously. Metric users should use Unit2-metric.dwg. These files can be found in the Chapter 15 sample files.

**FIGURE 15.4**

Insertion information for Unit2. Metric coordinates are shown in brackets.

Insert Unit2 at coordinate 31'-5", 104'-6" [957,3184]; x-scale factor = 1; y-scale factor = −1 (minus one).

Insert Unit2 at coordinate 31'-5", 43'-8" [957,1330]; x and y scale factor = 1.

Mirror inserted Unit2 blocks to this side.

**TIP** If you didn't create the Unit2 file earlier in this chapter, use the 15a-unit2.dwg file.

5. After you've accurately placed the corner units, use the Wblock command to write these corner units to a file called Floor2.dwg. Again, use the 0,0 coordinate as the insertion base point for the Wblock, and make sure the Delete From Drawing check box is selected.

6. Choose File ➢ Save As to turn the remaining set of unit plans into a file called Common.dwg.

You've just created three files: Floor1, Floor2, and Common. Each of these files contains unique information about the building. Next, you'll use the Xref command to recombine these files for the different floor plans in your building.

## Assembling Xrefs to Build a Drawing

You'll now create composite files for each floor, using Xrefs of only the files needed for the individual floors. You'll use the Attach option of the Xref command to insert all the files you exported from the Plan file.

Follow these steps to create a file representing the first floor:

1. Close the Common.dwg file, open a new file, and call it Xref-1.

2. Set up this file as an architectural drawing 8½″ × 11″ with a scale of ¹⁄₁₆″ = 1′. The upper-right corner limits for such a drawing are 2112,1632. Metric users should set up a drawing at 1:200 scale on an A4 sheet size. Your drawing area should be 4200 cm × 5940 cm. Choose View ➤ Zoom ➤ All so your drawing area is adjusted to the window.

**TIP**  In this exercise, you're asked to use a small paper size because it's the most common size available. Normally, you would specify a larger size and scale for architectural drawings.

3. Set the Ltscale value to 192. Metric users should set it to 200.

4. Open the Reference toolbar by right-clicking a toolbar and choosing Reference from the shortcut menu.

5. Click Attach Xref on the Reference toolbar or type **Xa↵** to open the Select Reference File dialog box.

6. Locate and select the Common.dwg file.

7. In the External Reference dialog box, make sure the Specify On-Screen check box in the Insertion Point group isn't selected. Then, make sure the X, Y, and Z values in the Insertion Point group are all 0.

**TIP**  Because the insertion points of all the files are the same (0,0), they will fit together perfectly when they're inserted into the new files.

8. Click OK. The `Common.dwg` file appears in the drawing.

9. Click the Attach Xref tool on the Reference toolbar again, and then click the Browse button to locate, select, and insert the `Floor1` file.

10. Repeat step 9 to insert the `Col-grid.dwg` file as an Xref. You now have the plan for the first floor.

11. Save this file.

Next, use the current file to create another file representing a different floor:

1. Choose File ➢ Save As to save this file as `Xref-2.dwg`.

2. Click the External Reference tool in the Reference toolbar, or type **Xr**↵.

3. In the External References palette, highlight Floor1 in the list of Xrefs, and then right-click and select Detach from the shortcut menu.

4. Right-click in the blank portion of the list in the External References palette, and select Attach DWG from the shortcut menu.

5. Locate and select `Floor2.dwg`.

6. In the External Reference palette, make sure the X, Y, and Z values in the Insertion Point group are all set to 0.

7. Click OK. The Floor2 drawing appears in place of Floor1. Turn off the Notes layer to see the plan clearly.

Now, when you need to make changes to `Xref-1` or `Xref-2`, you can edit their individual Xref files. The next time you open `Xref-1` or `Xref-2`, the updated Xrefs will automatically appear in their most recent forms.

### LOCATING XREF FILES

If you move an Xref file after you insert it into a drawing, AutoCAD may not be able to find it later when you attempt to open the drawing. If this happens, you can click the Browse button of the Found At option at the bottom of the External References palette to tell AutoCAD the new location of the Xref file. The Browse button appears at the far right of the Found At text box when you click in the text box.

If you know that you'll be keeping your project files in one place, you can use the Projectname system variable in conjunction with the Options dialog box to direct AutoCAD to look in a specific location for Xref files. Here's what to do:

1. Choose Tools ➢ Options.

2. Click the File tab, and then locate and select the Project File Search Path option.

3. Click Add, and either enter a name for your project or accept the default name of Project1.

4. Click Browse, and locate and select the folder where you plan to keep your Xref files.

5. Close the Options dialog box, and then enter **Projectname**↵ at the command prompt.

6. Enter the project name you used in step 3. Save your file so it remembers this setting.

Xrefs don't need to be permanent. As you saw in the previous exercise, you can attach and detach them easily at any time. This means that if you need to get information from another file—to see how well an elevator core aligns, for example—you can temporarily attach the other file as an Xref to quickly check alignments, and then detach it when you're finished.

Think of these composite files as final plot files that are used only for plotting and reviewing. You can then edit the smaller, more manageable Xref files. Figure 15.5 illustrates the relationship of these files.

**FIGURE 15.5**
A diagram of Xref file relationships

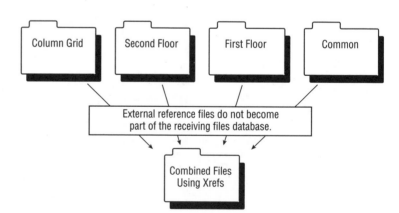

The combinations of Xrefs are limited only by your imagination, but you should avoid multiple Xrefs of the same file in one drawing.

**TIP** Because Xref files don't become part of the file they're referenced into, you must take care to keep Xref files in a location where AutoCAD can find them when the referencing file is opened. This can be a minor annoyance when you need to send files to others outside your office. To help keep track of Xrefs, choose File ➢ eTransmit. See Chapter 27 for details.

### UPDATING BLOCKS IN XREFS

Several advantages are associated with using Xref files. Because the Xrefs don't become part of the drawing file's database, the referencing files remain small. Also, because Xref files are easily updated, work can be split up among several people in a workgroup environment or on a network. For example, in your hypothetical apartment building, one person can be editing the Common file while another works on Floor1, and so on. The next time the composite Xref-1.dwg or Xref-2.dwg file is opened, it automatically reflects any new changes made in the Xref files. If the Xref is updated while you still have the receiving file open, you receive a balloon message telling you that an Xref requires a reload.

Let's see how to set this up:

1. Save and close the Xref-2 file, and then open the Common.dwg file.

2. Update the Unit plan you edited earlier in this chapter. Click Insert Block on the Draw toolbar.

3. In the Insert dialog box, click the Browse button, and then locate and select Unit.dwg. Click Open, and then click OK in the Insert dialog box.

4. At the warning message, click Yes.

5. At the Insertion point: prompt, press the Esc key.

6. Enter RE↵ to regenerate the drawing. You see the new Unit plan in place of the old one (see Figure 15.6). You may also see all the dimensions and notes for each unit.

**FIGURE 15.6**
The Common file with the revised Unit plan

7. If the Notes layer is on, use the Layer drop-down list to turn it off.

8. Using the Insert Block tool on the Draw toolbar again, replace the empty room across the hall from the lobby with the utility room you created in Chapter 14 (see Figure 15.7). If you didn't create the utility room drawing, use the utility.dwg file.

9. Save the Common file.

10. Open the Xref-1 file, right-click Common in the External References palette, and select Reload from the shortcut menu. You can also right-click the Manage Xrefs icon in the lower-right corner of the AutoCAD Window and select Reload DWG Xrefs. You see the utility room and the typical units in their new form. Your drawing should look like the top image in Figure 15.8.

**FIGURE 15.7**
The utility room installed

Add the Utility file.

**FIGURE 15.8**
The Xref-1 file with the units updated

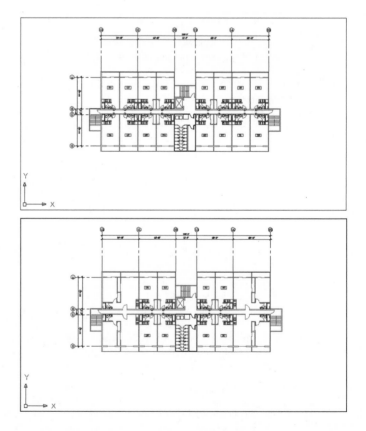

**11.** Open Xref-2, and reload the Common Xref as you did in step 10. You see that the utility room and typical units are updated in this file as well (see the bottom image in Figure 15.8).

## Importing Named Elements from Xrefs

Chapter 5 discussed how layers, blocks, linetypes, and text styles—called *named elements*—are imported along with a file that is inserted into another file. Xref files don't import named elements. You can, however, review their names and use a special command to import the ones you want to use in the current file.

**TIP**   You can set the Visretain system variable to 1 to force AutoCAD to remember layer settings of Xref files. Or, turn on the Retain Changes To Xref Layers option in the Open And Save tab of the Options dialog box. You can also use the Layer States Manager in the Layer Properties Manager dialog box to save layer settings for later recall. The Layer States Manager is described in detail later in this chapter.

AutoCAD renames named elements from Xref files by giving them the prefix of the filename from which they come. For example, the Wall layer in the Floor1 file is called Floor1 | WALL in the Xref-1 file; the Toilet block is called Floor1 | TOILET. You can't draw on the layer Floor1 | WALL, nor can you insert Floor1 | TOILET; but you can view Xref layers in the Layer Properties Manager dialog box, and you can view Xref blocks by using the Insert dialog box.

Next, you'll look at how AutoCAD identifies layers and blocks in Xref files, and you'll get a chance to import a layer from an Xref:

1. With the Xref-1 file open, open the Layer Properties Manager dialog box. Notice that the names of the layers from the Xref files are all prefixed with the filename and the vertical bar ( | ) character. Exit the Layer Manager Properties dialog box.

**TIP**   You can also open the Layer Control shortcut menu to view the layer names.

2. Click the Xbind tool on the Reference toolbar or enter **Xb**↵ to open the Xbind dialog box. You see a listing of the current Xrefs. Each item shows a plus sign to the left. This list box follows the Microsoft Windows format for expandable lists, much like the tree view in Windows Explorer.

3. Click the plus sign next to the Floor1 Xref item. The list expands to show the types of elements available to bind.

4. Click the plus sign next to the Layer item. The list expands further to show the layers available for binding.

5. Locate Floor1 | WALL in the list, click it, and then click the Add button. Floor1 | WALL is added to the list to the right: Definitions To Bind.

6. Click OK to bind the Floor1 | WALL layer.

7. Open the Layer Properties Manager dialog box.

8. Scroll down the list, and look for the Floor1 | WALL layer. You won't find it. In its place is a layer called Floor1$0$WALL.

**TIP** The AutoCAD DesignCenter lets you import settings and other drawing components from any drawing, not just Xref drawings. You'll learn more about the AutoCAD DesignCenter in Chapter 27.

As you can see, when you use Xbind to import a named item, such as the Floor1 | WALL layer, the vertical bar ( | ) is replaced by two dollar signs surrounding a number, which is usually zero. (If for some reason the imported layer name Floor1$0$WALL already exists, the zero in that name is changed to 1, as in Floor1$1$WALL.) Other named items are renamed in the same way, using the $0$ replacement for the vertical bar.

You can also use the Xbind dialog box to bind multiple layers, as well as other items from Xrefs attached to the current drawing.

**TIP** You can bind an entire Xref to a drawing, converting it to a simple block. By doing so, you have the opportunity to maintain unique layer names of the Xref being bound or to merge the Xref's similarly named layers with those of the current file. See Chapter 7 for details.

## Controlling the Xref Search Path

One problem AutoCAD users have encountered in the past is lost or broken links to an Xref. This occurs when an Xref file is moved from its original location or when you receive a set of drawings that includes Xrefs. The Xref links are broken because AutoCAD doesn't know where to look. Since AutoCAD 2005, you have better control over how AutoCAD looks for Xref files.

When you insert an Xref, the External Reference dialog box opens, offering you options for insertion point, scale, and rotation. This dialog box also provides the Path Type option, which enables you to select a method for locating Xrefs. You can choose from three path type options:

**Full Path** Lets you specify the exact filename and path for an Xref, including the disk drive or network location. Use this option when you want AutoCAD to look in a specific location for the Xref.

## NESTING XREFS AND USING OVERLAYS

Xrefs can be nested. For example, if the Common.dwg file created in this chapter used the Unit.dwg file as an Xref rather than an inserted block, you would still get the same result in the Xref-1.dwg file. That is, you would see the entire floor plan, including the unit plans, when you opened Xref-1.dwg. In this situation, Unit.dwg would be nested in the Common.dwg file, which is in turn externally referenced in the Xref-1.dwg file.

Although nested Xrefs can be helpful, take care in using Xrefs this way. For example, you might create an Xref by using the Common.dwg file in the Floor1.dwg file as a means of referencing walls and other features of the Common.dwg file. You might also reference the Common.dwg file into the Floor2.dwg file for the same reason. After you did this, however, you'd have three versions of the Common plan in the Xref-1.dwg file, because each Xref would have Common.dwg attached to it. And because AutoCAD would dutifully load Common.dwg three times, Xref-1.dwg would occupy substantial computer memory, slowing your computer when you edited the Xref-1.dwg file.

To avoid this problem, use the Overlay option in the External Reference dialog box. An overlaid Xref can't be nested. For example, if you use the Overlay option when inserting the Common.dwg file into the Floor1.dwg and Floor2.dwg files, the nested Common.dwg files are ignored when you open the Xref-1.dwg file, thereby eliminating the redundant occurrence of Common.dwg. In another example, if you use the Overlay option to import the Unit.dwg file into the Common.dwg file and then attach the Common.dwg into Xref-1.dwg as an Xref, you don't see the Unit plan in Xref-1.dwg. The nested Unit.dwg drawing is ignored.

**Relative Path**    Lets you specify a file location relative to the location of the current or host drawing. For example, if the host drawing is in a folder called C:\mycadfiles and the Xrefs are in a folder called C:\mycadfiles\xrefs, you can specify .\xrefs for the location of the Xref file. This option is useful when you know you'll maintain the folder structure of the host and Xref files when moving or exchanging these files. Note that because this is a relative path, this option is valid only for files that reside on the same local hard disk.

**No Path**    Perhaps the most flexible option; tells AutoCAD to use its own search criteria to find Xrefs. When No Path is selected, AutoCAD first looks in the same folder of the host drawing; then it looks in the project search path defined in the Files tab of the Options dialog box. (See Appendix A for more on the Options dialog box.) Last, AutoCAD looks in the Support File Search Path, also defined in the Files tab of the Options dialog box. If you plan to send your files to a client or a consultant, you may want to use this option.

# Managing Layers

In a survey of AutoCAD users, Autodesk discovered that one of the most frequently used features in AutoCAD is the Layer command. You'll find that you turn layers on and off to display and edit the many levels of information contained in your AutoCAD files. As your files become more complex, controlling layer visibility becomes more difficult. Fortunately, AutoCAD offers the Layer States Manager to make your work a little easier.

## Saving and Recalling Layer Settings

The Layer States Manager lets you save layer settings. This can be crucial when you're editing a file that serves multiple uses, such as a floor plan and reflected ceiling plan. You can, for example, turn layers on and off to set up the drawing for a reflected ceiling plan view, and then save the layer settings. Later, when you need to modify the ceiling information, you can recall the layer setting to view the ceiling data.

The following steps show you how the Layer States Manager works:

1. In AutoCAD, open the 15b-unit.dwg file. Click the Layer Properties Manager tool in the Layers control panel to open the Layer Properties Manager dialog box, and turn on all the layers except Notes and Flr-pat. Your drawing should look similar to the top image in Figure 15.9.

2. Click the Layer States Manager tool in the Layers control panel to open the Layer States Manager dialog box. Take a moment to look at the options in this dialog box. This is where you can specify which layer settings you want saved with this layer state.

3. You're ready to save the current layer state. Click the New button in the Layer States Manager dialog box. The New Layer State To Save dialog box opens.

4. Enter **blank floor plan** in the New Layer State Name input box. Note that you can also enter a brief description of your layer state. Click OK to return to the Layer States Manager dialog box.

5. Click the More Restore Options button in the lower-right corner of the Layer States Manager dialog box to expand the list of options.

**FIGURE 15.9**

The view of the
`15b-unit.dwg` file
before and after
changing layer
settings

6. Make sure the On/Off check box is selected; then, click Close. Several other options are available, but you can leave them as they are.

7. Back in the Layer Properties Manager dialog box, turn on the Flr-pat and Notes layers and turn off the Ceiling layer.

8. Click OK. Your drawing looks like the bottom image in Figure 15.9.

You've just saved a layer state and then changed the layer settings to something different from the saved state. The following steps demonstrate how you can restore the saved layer state:

1. Click the Layer States Manager tool in the Layers control panel to reopen the Layer States Manager dialog box.

2. Select Blank Floor Plan from the list, and click Restore. Your drawing reverts to the previous view with the Notes and Flr-pat layers turned off and the Ceiling layer on.

3. This brings you to the end of the Xref tutorial. Save the file and close it.

The layer states are saved with the file so you can retrieve them at a later date. As you can see in the Layer States Manager dialog box, you have a few other options, as shown in Table 15.1.

**TABLE 15.1:**    Layer States Manager Dialog Box Options

| OPTION | PURPOSE |
| --- | --- |
| New | Creates a new layer state. |
| Save | Saves the selected layer state after edits. |
| Edit | Lets you edit the layer settings for the selected layer state. |
| Rename | Renames a selected layer state. |
| Delete | Deletes a layer state from the list. |
| Import | Imports a set of layer states that have been exported using the Export option of this dialog box. |
| Export | Saves a set of layer states as a file. By default, the file is given the name of the current file with the .las filename extension. You can import the layer-state file into other files. |
| Layer Properties to Restore (in the expanded dialog box) | Lets you select the layer properties to be controlled by the Layer States Manager. |

In addition to saving layer states by name, you can quickly revert to a previous layer state by clicking the Layer Previous tool on the right side of the Layers toolbar. This tool enables you to revert to the previous layer settings without affecting other settings in AutoCAD. Note that Layer Previous mode doesn't restore renamed or deleted layers, nor does it remove new layers.

After you become familiar with these layer-state tools, you'll find yourself using them frequently in your editing sessions.

**TIP**    The Layerpmode command controls the tracking of layer states. It's normally turned on; but if it's turned off, the Layer Previous tool won't work. To turn it on, enter **Layerpmode↵On↵**.

## Using Advanced Tools: Filter, Quick Select, and QuickCalc

Two other tools are extremely useful in your day-to-day work with AutoCAD: selection filters and QuickCalc. I've saved the discussion of these tools until this part of the chapter because you don't need them until you've become accustomed to the way AutoCAD works. Chances are, you've already experimented with some of the AutoCAD menu options not yet discussed in the tutorial. Many of the drop-down menu options and their functions are self-explanatory. Selection filters and QuickCalc, however, don't appear in any of the menus and require further explanation.

Let's start with selection filters. AutoCAD includes two selection-filtering tools: The *Quick Select tool* offers a quick way to locate objects based on their properties. The *Filter tool* lets you select objects based on a more complex set of criteria.

### Filtering Selections

Suppose you need to isolate just the walls of your drawing in a separate file. One way to do this is to turn off all the layers except the Wall layer. You can then use the Wblock command and select the remaining walls, using a window to write the wall information to a file. Filters can simplify this operation by enabling you to select groups of objects based on their properties.

Follow these steps to select objects based on their layer assignment:

1. Open the Unit file.

2. Type **w↵** to start the Wblock command. Then, in the Write Block dialog box, enter **Unitwall** in the File Name And Path input box.

3. Make sure the Objects and Retain radio buttons are selected in the dialog box, and then click the Select Objects button in the Objects group. The dialog box closes so that you can select objects.

4. At the Select Objects: prompt, type **'Filter↵** to open the Object Selection Filters dialog box.

5. Open the drop-down list in the Select Filter group.

6. Scroll down the list, and find and highlight the Layer option.

7. Click the Select button next to the drop-down list to display a list of layers. Highlight Wall, and click OK.

8. Click the Add To List button toward the bottom of the Select Filter group to add Layer = Wall to the list box.

9. Click Apply to close the Object Selection Filters dialog box.

10. Type **all↵** to select everything in the drawing. Only the objects assigned to the Wall layer are selected. You see a message in the Command window indicating how many objects were found.

11. Press ↵. You see the message Exiting Filtered selection Resuming WBLOCK command - Select objects: 29 found.

12. Press ↵ again to complete the selection, and then click OK to complete the Wblock command. All the walls are written out to a file called Unitwall.

13. After reviewing the results of the exercise, type **U↵** or click the Undo button in the Standard toolbar to undo the Wblock command.

In this exercise, you filtered out a layer by using the Wblock command. After you designate a filter, you then select the group of objects you want AutoCAD to filter through. AutoCAD finds the objects that match the filter requirements and passes those objects to the current command.

As you've seen from the previous exercise, you can choose from many options in this utility. Let's take a closer look.

### WORKING WITH THE OBJECT SELECTION FILTERS DIALOG BOX

To use the Object Selection Filters dialog box, first select the criterion for filtering from the drop-down list. If the criterion you select is a named item (layer, linetype, color, or block), you can then click the Select button to choose specific items from a list. If there is only one choice, the Select button is dimmed.

After you've determined what to filter, you must add it to the list by clicking the Add To List button. The filter criterion then appears in the list box at the top of the Object Selection Filters dialog box, and you can apply that criterion to your current command or to a later command. AutoCAD remembers your filter settings, so if you need to reselect a filtered selection set, you don't have to redefine your filter criteria.

### SAVING FILTER CRITERIA

If you prefer, you can preselect filter criteria. Then, at any `Select objects:` prompt, you can type **'Filter.⏎**, highlight the appropriate filter criteria in the list box, and click Apply. The specifications in the Object Selection Filters dialog box remain in place for the duration of the current editing session.

You can also save a set of criteria by entering a name in the input box next to the Save As button and then clicking the button. The criteria list data is saved in a file called `Filter.nfl` in the current drawing's folder. You can access the criteria list at any time by opening the Current drop-down list and choosing the name of the saved criteria list.

### FILTERING OBJECTS BY LOCATION

Notice the X, Y, and Z drop-down lists just below the main Select Filter drop-down list in the Object Selection Filters dialog box. These lists become accessible when you select a criterion that describes a geometric property or a coordinate (such as an arc's radius or center point). You can use these lists to define filter selections even more specifically, using greater than (>), less than (<), equal to or greater than (>=), equal to or less than (<=), equal to (=), or not equal to (!=) comparisons (called *relational operators*).

For example, suppose you want to grab all the circles whose radii are greater than 4.0 units. To do this, choose Circle Radius from the Select Filter drop-down list. Then, in the X list, select >. Enter **4.0** in the input box to the right of the X list, and click Add To List. The items

```
Circle Radius > 4.0000
Object = Circle
```

are added to the list box at the top of the dialog box. You used the > operator to indicate a circle radius greater than 4.0 units.

### CREATING COMPLEX SELECTION SETS

At times, you'll want to create a specific filter list. For instance, say you need to filter out all the Door blocks on the layer Floor2 *and* all arcs with a radius equal to 1. To do this, you use the *grouping operators* found at the bottom of the Select Filter drop-down list. You'll need to build a list as follows:

```
** Begin OR
** Begin AND
Block Name = Door
```

```
Layer = Floor2
** End AND
** Begin AND
Entity = Arc
Arc Radius = 1.0000
** End AND
** End OR
```

Notice that the `Begin` and `End` operators are balanced; that is, for every `Begin OR` or `Begin AND`, there is an `End OR` or `End AND`.

This list may look simple, but it can get confusing. If criteria are bounded by the AND grouping operators, objects must fulfill *both* criteria before they're selected. If criteria are bounded by the OR grouping operators, objects fulfilling *either* criteria will be selected.

Here are the steps to build the previous list.

**TIP**  If you add the wrong option accidentally, select it from the list and click the Delete button. If you need to insert an option in the middle of the list, select the item in the list that comes after the item you want to insert, and then select and add the item:

1. In the Select Filter drop-down list, choose **Begin OR, and then click Add To List. Do the same for **Begin AND.

2. Click Block Name in the Select Filter drop-down list, click the Select button, and select Door from the list that appears. Click Add To List.

3. For the layer, click Layer in the Select Filter drop-down list. Click Select, choose the layer name, and click Add To List.

4. In the Select Filter drop-down list, choose **End AND, and then click Add To List. Do the same for **Begin AND.

5. Select Arc from the Select Filter drop-down list and click Add To List.

6. Select Arc Radius from the Select Filter list, and enter **1.0** in the input box next to the X drop-down list. Be sure the equal sign (=) shows in the X drop-down list, and then click Add To List.

7. Choose **End AND, and click Add To List. Do the same for **End OR.

If you make an error in any step, highlight the item, select an item to replace it, and click the Substitute button instead of the Add To List button. If you need to only change a value, click the Edit Item button near the center of the dialog box.

---

### QUICK ACCESS TO YOUR FAVORITE COMMANDS

As you continue to work with AutoCAD, you'll find that you use a handful of commands 90 percent of the time. You can collect your favorite commands into a single toolbar by using AutoCAD's toolbar customization feature. This way, you can have ready access to your most frequently used commands. Chapter 26 gives you all the information you need to create your own custom toolbars.

## Using Quick Select

The Filter command offers a lot of power in isolating specific types of objects, but in many situations, you may not need such an elaborate tool. The Qselect command can filter your selection based on the object properties, which are more common filter criteria. To access the Qselect command, choose Tools ➣ Quick Select, or right-click the drawing area when no command is active and choose Quick Select from the shortcut menu to open the Quick Select dialog box.

Quick Select is also offered as an option in a few dialog boxes. Try using the Wblock command again, this time using the Quick Select option offered in its dialog box:

1. With the Unit file open, type **W**↵ to start the Wblock command. Then, in the Write Block dialog box, enter **Unitwall2** in the File Name And Path input box.

2. Make sure the Objects radio button is selected at the top of the dialog box. Then, click the Quick Select button to the right of the Select Objects button in the Objects group to open the Quick Select dialog box.

3. Select Layer from the Properties list.

4. Select Wall from the Value drop-down list near the bottom of the dialog box.

5. Click the Select Objects button in the upper-right corner of the dialog box. The dialog boxes close so you can select objects.

6. Select the entire drawing by using a window; press ↵ to finish your selection. The Quick Select dialog box returns.

7. Click OK, and then click OK in the Write Block dialog box. The walls disappear, indicating that they have been written to a file.

8. Click the Undo button to undo the deletion.

The Qselect command selects objects based on the object's properties, as shown in the Properties list box. You can apply the selection criteria based on the entire drawing, or you can use the Select Objects button in the upper-right corner of the dialog box to isolate a set of objects to which you want to apply the selection criteria.

In the previous exercise, you used Quick Select from within another dialog box. As mentioned earlier, you can also use Quick Select by choosing Tools ➢ Quick Select or by right-clicking the drawing area when no command is active and choosing Quick Select from the shortcut menu. Quick Select then uses the Noun/Verb selection method: You select objects using Quick Select first, and then you apply editing commands to the selected objects.

**TIP**   If you want to use Quick Select with a command that doesn't allow the Noun/Verb selection method, you can select objects by using Quick Select, start the command you want to use, and then use the Previous Selection option.

Here is a description of the Quick Select dialog box options:

**Apply To**   Lets you determine the set of objects to which you want to apply the Quick Select filters. The default is the entire drawing, but you can use the Select Objects button to select a set of objects. If you select a set of objects before issuing the Quick Select command, you also see the Current Selection option in the Apply To drop-down list.

**Object Type**   Lets you limit the filter to specific types of objects such as lines, arcs, circles, and so on. The Multiple option lets you filter your selection from all the objects in the drawing regardless of type.

**Properties**   Lets you select the property of the object type you want to filter, after you select an object type. The Properties list changes to reflect the properties that are available to be filtered.

**Operator**   Offers a set of criteria to apply to the property you select in the Properties list to make your selection. You can select objects that are *equal to* or *not equal to* the criteria you select in the Object Type and Properties lists. Depending on the property you select, you also may have the option to select objects that are *greater than* or *less than* a given property value. For example, you can select all lines whose X coordinate is less than 5 by choosing Line from the Object Type drop-down list and Start X from the Properties list. You then select < Less Than from the Operator drop-down list and enter **5** in the Value input box.

**Value**   Displays the values of the property you select in the Properties list. For example, if you select Layer from the Properties list, the Value option lists all the layers available.

**How To Apply**   Lets you specify whether to include or exclude the filtered objects in a new selection set.

**Append To Current Selection Set**   Lets you append the filtered objects to an existing selection set or create an entirely new selection set.

## Using the QuickCalc Calculator

You may have noticed a calculator icon in the Standard toolbar. This is the QuickCalc tool. If you click it, you'll see the QuickCalc calculator shown in Figure 15.10. At first glance, it looks like a typical calculator. It has both the standard math functions as well as scientific functions that are available when you click the More button. If your view of QuickCalc doesn't look like Figure 15.10, click the More/Less button, and then expand the Number Pad or Scientific section by clicking the arrow in the section title. You'll also see a section for converting units, which comes in handy when you want to find the metric equivalent of an Imperial measurement.

At the bottom is a section for variables. This area lets you store custom formulas and values that you want to refer to frequently.

**FIGURE 15.10**

QuickCalc and
its parts

Toolbar

Display area

Input box

More/Less button
Open/Close arrow in title bar

Number pad

Near the top is the display area. This is where QuickCalc keeps a running record of your calculation results. It also allows you to recall both the results and formulas you've used. Just below the display area is the input box. As you type or as you click the keys of QuickCalc, your input appears in this box. Pressing Enter displays the resulting value both in the input box and in the display area.

Above the display area is a set of tools in a toolbar. These tools let you obtain other types of data from the drawing, such as the coordinate of a point or the intersection of two lines (see Figure 15.11).

**FIGURE 15.11**

The QuickCalc toolbar

Clear
Clear History
Paste value to
command line

Intersection of two lines
defined by four points
Angle of line defined by two points
Distance between two points
Get coordinate

The function of these tools will become clearer as you become familiar with QuickCalc. Table 15.2 describes each tool. Next, you'll get a chance to try out QuickCalc on some typical AutoCAD tasks.

**TABLE 15.2:** QuickCalc Tools

| TOOL | PURPOSE |
|---|---|
| Clear | Clears the value from the input box. |
| Clear History | Clears the display area. |
| Paste Value To Command Line | Pastes data from the input box to the command line. |

**TABLE 15.2:** QuickCalc Tools (CONTINUED)

| TOOL | PURPOSE |
| --- | --- |
| Get Coordinates | Temporarily closes QuickCalc, and prompts you to pick a point or points. Coordinates of the point or the angle value are placed in the input area. |
| Distance Between Two Points | Temporarily closes QuickCalc, and prompts you to enter a point. Select two points; the distance between the points is placed in the input area of QuickCalc. |
| Angle Of Line Defined By Two Points | Returns the angle of two points. |
| Intersection Of Two Lines Defined By Two Points | Returns the coordinate of the intersection of four points. |

## Adding Foot and Inch Lengths and Finding the Sum of Angles

Although QuickCalc may look simple, it provides a powerful aid in your work in AutoCAD. Besides offering the typical calculator functions, QuickCalc also enables you to quickly add and subtract angle values, feet-and-inches lengths, and much more. You can paste the results from calculations into the command line so you easily include results as part of command-line responses.

To get a full appreciation of what QuickCalc can do for you, try the following exercises.

Imagine that you have a renovation project for which someone has taken dimensions in the field. You may be asked to draw a section of wall for which the overall dimension isn't given, but portions of the wall are dimensioned in a sketch as shown in Figure 15.12.

**FIGURE 15.12**
A sketch of measurements taken from an existing building

You can use QuickCalc to add a series of feet-and-inches dimensions:

1. Open the QuickCalc.dwg sample file, which contains some lines you can work with. It's set up to use architectural units.

2. Click the QuickCalc tool in the Standard toolbar.

**3.** Double-click in the QuickCalc input box, and then enter **4′+36+5′6**. As you type, your entry appears in the input box.

**4.** Press ↵. The sum of the lengths, 12′-6″, appears in the input box and in the display area.

Notice that you only had to enter the foot (′) sign. QuickCalc assumes that a value is in inches unless you specify otherwise. You can also enter distances in the more traditional way using dashes and zeros, as in 4′-0″ or 5′-6″. QuickCalc ignores the dashes.

Now, suppose you want to use your new-found length to draw a line. You can quickly add the results from the input box to the command line, as shown in the following exercise.

**1.** Click the Line tool, click a point in the left portion of the drawing area, and then enter @ in preparation for the inclusion of a coordinate.

**2.** In the QuickCalc toolbar, click the Paste Value To Command Line tool. Notice that the value in the input box appears in the command line after the @ symbol.

**3.** Click in the drawing area or command line to continue drawing the line.

**4.** With Polar mode turned on in the status bar, press ↵ while pointing the rubber-banding line directly to the right. A horizontal line is drawn to the length of 12′-6″.

In this example, you used of the Paste Value To Command Line tool in the QuickCalc toolbar. If you want to use a value that has scrolled up in the display area, you can select that value, right-click, and choose Paste To Command Line.

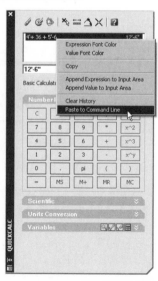

This is especially useful when you've used QuickCalc to add several strings of dimensions and you need to recall them individually from the display area. In addition to adding feet and inches, you can also perform other math functions, such as dividing a length by two or multiplying a length. If the input value is in feet and inches, the resulting value is returned in feet and inches. For example, if you divide 25´ by 6, the result is 4´-2″.

Another useful QuickCalc tool is Angle Of Line Defined By Two Points, which allows you to obtain the angle defined by two points:

1. In QuickCalc, click the Angle Of Line Defined By Two Points tool. QuickCalc temporarily closes to allow you to select points.

2. With osnaps turned on, select the endpoints of the lower line, starting with the bottom endpoint, as shown in Figure 15.13.

**FIGURE 15.13**
Select these endpoints using the Angle Of Line Defined By Two Points option.

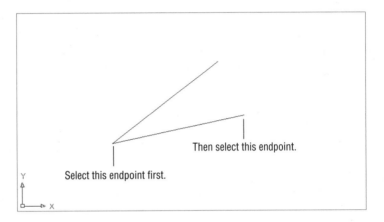

3. Back in QuickCalc, click the plus button in the number pad or enter +; then, click the Angle Of Line Defined By Two Points tool again.

4. Select the endpoints of the upper line, starting with the bottom end of the line.

5. Back in QuickCalc, you see the angle value of the second line added to the input box. Press ↵ to get the total angle value.

Here you added the angle of two lines, but you could just as easily have subtracted one angle from another or multiplied the value of a single angle. This can be useful if you need to find a fraction or a multiple of an angle. For example, you might need to find one-quarter of the angle described by a line, or you might want to find the angle that bisects two lines. You can do so by adding the value of two angles, as described in the exercise, and then dividing by 2 using the number pad or including /2 in the input box. Once you've obtained a value, you can paste it into the command line while specifying angles for drawing input.

## Using the Display Area and Units Conversion

In addition to performing math functions on distances and angles, you can also do some basic unit conversions. QuickCalc performs length, area, volume, and angle conversions in its Units Conversion group. Try the following exercise to learn how to convert a length from centimeters to feet and inches. In the process, you'll also learn how you can move a value from the Units Conversion area to the QuickCalc input box.

Suppose you have a paper drawing that was done in metric, and you need to turn it into an AutoCAD drawing in feet and inches. Here's an example of how you can convert centimeters to feet and inches:

1. In QuickCalc, expand the Units Conversion group by clicking the arrow to the right of the Units Conversion title bar.

2. Select Length from the Units Type drop-down list.

3. Select Centimeters from the Convert From drop-down list.

4. Select Feet from the Convert To drop-down list.

5. In the Value To Convert input box, enter **450**↵ for 450 cm. The equivalent value in feet appears in the Converted Value box.

6. Click the Converted Value option, and you also see QuickCalc icon to the far right. Click this icon to display the value in the input box at the top of QuickCalc.

The value is in feet and decimal feet. You can convert the value to feet and inches by doing the following.

1. Edit the value in the input box to read as follows: **14′ +(.763779527559*12)**.

2. Press ↵. The value converts to a feet-and-inches value of 14′-9$\frac{9}{16}$″.

One limitation to the unit-conversion feature is that it won't take feet-and-inches input when converting from feet. For example, if you want to convert 12′-4″ to centimeters, you have to enter 12.334. In other words, you have to convert the inches to decimal feet. Because the Unit Conversion area is part of QuickCalc, this just means an extra step. You can quickly calculate the decimal feet equivalent of feet and inch values and then transfer them to the Units Conversion area.

Try the following to see how this works:

1. Click the Clear button in the QuickCalc toolbar (it looks like an eraser), and then double-click in the QuickCalc input box.

2. Enter **12 + (4 / 12)**↵ in QuickCalc's input box. The first 12 is the 12 feet. The 4/12 is for the 4 inches converted to decimal feet. Once you press ↵, the value of 12.333333 appears.

3. Click anywhere in the Units Conversion group. The value from the input box is automatically transferred to the Value To Convert input box.

4. Select Feet from the Convert From drop-down list, and select Centimeters from the Convert To drop-down list. The centimeter equivalent of 12.333333 feet appears in the Converted Value input box.

Here you saw how values from the input box automatically transfer to the Units Conversion area. You can also cut and paste values from other sources into either the main calculator input box or the Units Conversion input box.

## Using QuickCalc to Find Points

You've seen how QuickCalc will let you add values of distances and angles and how it can perform unit conversions. You can also use it to calculate coordinate locations. To work with coordinates, you need to use a few special functions built into QuickCalc that let you select points and manipulate their value.

Before AutoCAD added the Midpoint Between Two Points osnap, the AutoCAD Cal command was the only way to find the midpoint between two points without drawing a temporary line. In the following example, you'll use QuickCalc to perform the same function as an example of how you can acquire point data and manipulate it to derive other coordinate locations.

1. Click the Clear button on the QuickCalc toolbar; then, double-click in the QuickCalc input box.

2. In the QuickCalc input box, enter **(end + end)/2**↵. QuickCalc closes temporarily to allow you to select points.

3. Select the endpoints of the two lines, as shown in Figure 15.14.

**FIGURE 15.14**

The endpoints of the two lines

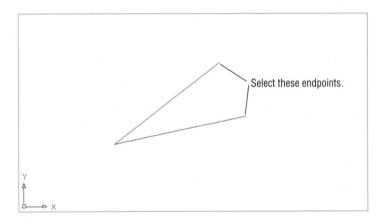

Select these endpoints.

4. QuickCalc returns and displays the coordinates of a point exactly between the two endpoints of the lines you selected in step 3.

In step 2, you used the *end* function that is built into QuickCalc. As you saw, the end function lets you select the endpoint of an object. The end + end in the formula tells QuickCalc to add the two coordinates you selected in step 2. The /2 in the formula divides the sum of the coordinates to find their average, which happens to be the midpoint between the two points.

If you were to perform this calculation using pencil and paper, you would add the X, Y, and Z coordinate values of each point separately and then divide each coordinate by 2. Finally, you would combine the resulting X, Y, and Z coordinates back into a single point location.

### USING OSNAP MODES IN QUICKCALC EXPRESSIONS

In the previous exercise, you used osnap modes as part of arithmetic formulas (or *expressions*, as they're called in AutoCAD). QuickCalc treats osnap modes as temporary placeholders for point coordinates until you pick the points (at the prompts shown in steps 2 and 3 of the previous exercise).

The expression

```
(end + end)/2
```

finds the average of two values. In this case, the values are coordinates, so the average is the midpoint between the two coordinates. You can take this one step further and find the centroid of a triangle by using this expression:

```
(end + end + end)/3
```

Note that you enter only the first three letters of the Osnap mode in calculator expressions. Table 15.3 shows what to enter in an expression for Osnap modes. Table 15.3 includes two items that aren't really osnap modes, although they work similarly when they're used in an expression. The first is Rad. When you include Rad in an expression, you get the following prompt:

```
Select circle, arc or polyline segment for RAD function:
```

You can then select an arc, a polyline arc segment, or a circle, and its radius is used in place of Rad in the expression.

The other item, Cur, prompts you for a point. Instead of looking for specific geometry on an object, it just locates a point. You could have used Cur in the previous exercise in place of the End and Cen modes to create a more general-purpose midpoint locator, as in the following formula:

```
(cur + cur)/2
```

**TABLE 15.3:**     The Geometry Calculator's Osnap Modes

| CALCULATOR OSNAP | MEANING |
| --- | --- |
| End | Endpoint |
| Ins | Insert |
| Int | Intersection |
| Mid | Midpoint |
| Cen | Center |
| Nea | Nearest |
| Nod | Node |
| Qua | Quadrant |
| Per | Perpendicular |
| Tan | Tangent |
| Rad | Radius of object |
| Cur | Cursor pick |

## Pasting to the Command Line

Now that you have the coordinate for the midpoint, try the next exercise to apply that coordinate to a command. In this example, you'll use the coordinate found in step 3 as the starting point for a line:

1. Click the Line tool on the Draw toolbar.

2. In QuickCalc, right-click the (end + end)/2 listing in the display area, and then select Paste To Command Line.

3. The coordinate value from the display area is pasted into the command line at the Line command's `Specify first point:` prompt. Press ↵ to accept the input from QuickCalc. You see a rubber-banding line beginning at a point midway between the two endpoints of the lines you selected in the previous exercise.

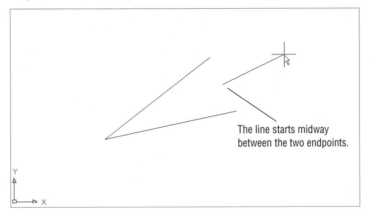

The line starts midway between the two endpoints.

4. Click another point to place the line in the drawing, and then press ↵ to exit the Line command.

## Finding Fractional Distances between Two Points

Another common need of AutoCAD users is the ability to find a location that is a fractional distance along a line. For example, users frequently need to find a point that is one-third the distance from the endpoint of a line. Here's how that can be accomplished using QuickCalc:

1. Enter **plt (end, end, 0.333)**↵ in the QuickCalc input box. QuickCalc closes temporarily to allow you to select points.

2. Click the endpoints of the line shown in Figure 15.15. QuickCalc returns with the coordinates of a point that is 33.33 percent of the length of the line from the first endpoint you selected.

**FIGURE 15.15**
Select these points to find a point that is one-third the distance from an endpoint.

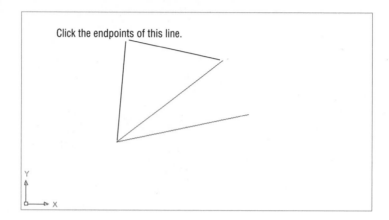

Click the endpoints of this line.

3. Click the Line tool.

4. Click in the QuickCalc display area on the last entry, right-click, and choose Paste To Command Line.

5. Press ↵, and you see a line start at a point that is one-third the distance from the endpoint.

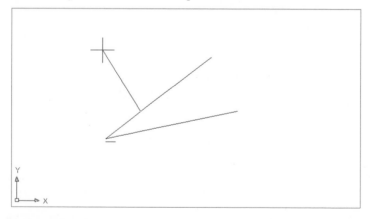

6. Press Esc to exit the Line command. You don't need to draw the line, because this exercise is only intended to show you how the formula in step 1 works.

In step 1, you used a formula that contained the Plt function. This function finds a point that is a particular percentage between two points. You specify the two points first, using the now-familiar end function, and then you specify the percentage between the two endpoints as a decimal value. The (end, end, 0.333) indicates the two endpoints you selected in step 2 and the percentage as a decimal value of 0.333.

**TIP** In the formulas you've seen so far, you've used the end function to select endpoints. If you prefer to select your own osnaps during the point-selection process, you can use the cur function. Cur lets you use any osnap you want when selecting points. In the first example, you could use (cur + cur)/2 instead of (end + end)/2.

The Plt function is just one of several special functions you can use with QuickCalc. Table 15.4 lists other functions you can use to find points in your drawing and gather other data. In the table, 2D points are represented as pt1, pt2, and so on. 3D points or points describing a plane are indicated by ptp1, ptp3, and so on. The center of an arc or a circle is indicated with apex for a 2D location or apex1 and apex2 for a 3D axis.

**TABLE 15.4:**    Functions in QuickCalc and the Format for Their Use

| FUNCTION AND FORMAT | DESCRIPTION |
| --- | --- |
| Getvar (*system variable name*) | Gets the value of a system variable |
| Vec(*pt1,pt2*) | Returns the vector described by the distance between the two points |
| Vec1(*pt1,pt2*) | Returns the vector described by 1 unit length |
| Abs(*vector*) | Returns the absolute value of the length of a vector |
| Cur (no arguments required) | Gets a point |
| @ (no arguments required) | Returns the last point |
| w2u(*point*) and u2w(*point*) | Converts world coordinates to current user coordinates (w2u) or user coordinates to world |
| Pld(*pt1,pt2,distance*) | Returns the point on a line at a specified distance |
| Plt(*pt1,pt2,percent*) | Returns the point on a line at a percentage (decimal) of the line length |
| Rot(*pt1,apex,angle*) or Rot(*pt1,apex1,apex2,angle*) | Returns the rotation angle of a point pt1 about an apex |
| Ill(*pt1,pt2,pt3,pt4*) | Returns the intersection between two lines |
| Ilp(*pt1,pt2,ptp1,ptp2,ptp3*) | Returns the intersection between a line and a plane; five points required |
| Dist (*pt1,pt2*) | Returns the distance between two points |
| Dpl (*point,pt1,pt2*) | Returns the shortest distance between a point and a line |
| Dpp(*point,ptp1,ptp2,ptp3*) | Returns the shortest distance between a point and a plane |
| Rad (no arguments required) | Returns a radius |
| Ang (*vector* or *pt1,pt2* or *apex,pt1,pt2* or *apex1,pt1,pt2,apex2*) | Returns an angle; can use up to four parameters when working in 3D |
| Nor (*vector* or *pt1,pt2* or *ptp1,ptp2,ptp3*) | Finds the normal of a vector or plane |

## Using QuickCalc While in the Middle of a Command

In all the previous examples, you've used QuickCalc as a stand-alone calculator. You've also seen how you can insert a calculation into the command line while a command is in progress. A third way to work with QuickCalc is to open it while in the middle of a command.

In a previous exercise, you used the (end + end)/2 formula to find the midpoint between two points, and then you inserted the resulting value into the Line command. Suppose you start the Line command before you open QuickCalc. Try the following to see how you can use QuickCalc once a command has been initiated:

1. Close QuickCalc.

2. Start the Line command.

3. Click the QuickCalc tool on the Standard toolbar.

4. In the QuickCalc input box, enter **(end + end)/2** but don't press ↵. Instead, click the Apply button at the bottom of the QuickCalc window.

5. Select the endpoints of two lines. A line starts at the midpoint between the two points.

6. Click another point to draw the line, and then press ↵ to end the Line command.

In this exercise, you saw that an Apply option appears at the bottom of the QuickCalc window, along with Close and Help buttons. These buttons aren't present when you open QuickCalc with no command active. The Apply button executes the formula and then immediately returns the resulting value to the command. Using QuickCalc this way eliminates a few steps.

### FINDING A POINT RELATIVE TO ANOTHER POINT

Now, suppose you want to start a line at a relative distance from another line. The following steps describe how to use the calculator to start a line from a point that is 2.5″ in the X axis and 5.0″ in the Y axis from the endpoint of another line:

1. Make sure QuickCalc is closed, and start the Line command.

2. Click the QuickCalc tool on the Standard toolbar, and enter **end + [2.5,5.0]**↵ in the input box.

3. Click the Apply button at the bottom of the QuickCalc window.

4. Click the endpoint of the line you just drew. Another line starts at a location that is at a distance of 2.5 in the X axis and 5.0 in the Y axis from the endpoint you selected.

In this example, you used the Endpoint osnap mode to indicate a point of reference. This is added to Cartesian coordinates in square brackets, describing the distance and direction from the reference point. You could enter any coordinate value within the square brackets. You also could enter a polar coordinate in place of the Cartesian coordinate, as in the following: **end + [5.59<63]**.

You can replace the end in the expression with the at sign (@) to continue from the last point you selected. Also, it's not necessary to include every coordinate in the square brackets. For example, to indicate a displacement in only one axis, you can leave out a value for the other two coordinates while leaving in the commas, as in the following examples:

```
[4,5] = [4,5,0]
[,1] = [0,1,0]
[,,2] = [0,0,2]
```

### COMBINING COORDINATES AND EXPRESSIONS

In the previous two examples, you saw that you can use an expression or enter coordinates; but what if you want to combine an expression within a coordinate? For example, in the beginning of this section, you added feet and inches and then transferred the result to the command line. In that example, you had to switch back and forth between QuickCalc and the command line to create the response for the Command prompt. If you prefer, you can create an expression that supplies the entire command input. Here are the steps to do this:

1. Close QuickCalc, and then start the Line command.

2. Click the QuickCalc tool on the Standard toolbar.

3. Enter the following in the input box:

   ```
   End + [(4´+36+5´6)<45]
   ```

4. Click Apply.

5. In the drawing area, click the endpoint of a line. AutoCAD draws a line that begins at 12´-6″ from and at a 45° angle to the endpoint you select.

In this exercise, you used the expression (4´+36+5´6) right in the middle of a coordinate value. As described earlier, the coordinate is within square brackets. By using this method, you can more easily calculate measurements and apply them to commands. The trick is to become familiar with the syntax QuickCalc requires so you can write these expressions without errors.

## Storing Expressions and Values

The ability to create expressions to manipulate coordinates can be useful, but you may find it difficult to remember an expression once you've created it. Fortunately, QuickCalc offers the Variables group, which allows you to store frequently used expressions and values.

At the bottom of the QuickCalc window is the Variables group, which has its set of tools in its title bar (see Figure 15.16).

**FIGURE 15.16**

The Variables group

These tools let you add items to the list, edit items, or delete items from the list. A fourth option lets you send a variable to the main calculator input box.

**TIP** You can also right-click in the Variables group list box and select the same options from a shortcut menu. The shortcut menu also lets you create a new category and rename an existing one.

The Variables group also contains a list of currently stored variables. Some sample variables are shown in the list. If you select a variable, you see a description of that variable's function at the bottom of the group. You may need to click the bottom edge of the QuickCalc window and drag downward to see the description.

To use an existing variable, select it from the list and click the Return Variable To Input Area button; it looks like a calculator. To add a variable to the list, click the New Variable button, which opens the Variable Definition dialog box.

This dialog box lets you enter the properties of the variable and choose the type. In the Variable Properties group, you enter the name of the variable in the Name text box. In the Group With drop-down list, you select a category under which your formula will appear in the Variables list. You can also create a new category. The Value Or Expression input box is where you put your formula; it can also be a single value, such as a number or a coordinate. At the bottom is a space to enter a description for the variable. This description will appear in the Variables group's detail box at the bottom of QuickCalc.

At the top, you see two options: Constant and Function. If you choose Function, your variable will behave as it normally does when you enter it in the input box. If you choose Constant and your variable is a formula, your variable will be executed when you close the Variable Definition dialog box. The resulting value will become the value for the variable.

To edit an existing variable, highlight it in the Variables group list, and then click the Edit Variable button to open the Variable Definition dialog box.

## Guidelines for Working with QuickCalc

You may notice some patterns in the way expressions are formatted for the calculator. Here are some guidelines to remember:

◆ Coordinates are enclosed in square brackets.

◆ Nested or grouped expressions are enclosed in parentheses.

- ◆ Operators are placed between values, as in simple math equations.

- ◆ Object snaps can be used in place of coordinate values.

Table 15.5 lists all the operators and functions available in QuickCalc. You may want to experiment with these functions on your own. You can enter many of these operators using the keys on the number pad or in the scientific group.

**TABLE 15.5:**    The QuickCalc Functions

| OPERATOR/FUNCTION | WHAT IT DOES | EXAMPLE |
|---|---|---|
| + or − | Adds or subtracts numbers or vectors | 2 − 1 = 1<br>[a,b,c] + [x,y,z] = [a+x, b+y, c+z] |
| * or / | Multiplies or divides numbers or vectors | 2 * 4.2 = 8.4<br>a*[x,y,z] = [a*x, a*y, a*z] |
| ^ | Returns the exponent of a number | 3^2 = 9 |
| sin | Returns the sine of an angle | sin (45) = 0.707107 |
| cos | Returns the cosine of an angle | cos (30) = 0.866025 |
| tang | Returns the tangent of an angle | tang (30) = 0.57735 |
| asin | Returns the arcsine of a real number | asin (0.707107) = 45.0 |
| acos | Returns the arccosine of a real number | acos (0.866025) = 30.0 |
| atan | Returns the arctangent of a real number | atan (0.57735) = 30.0 |
| ln | Returns the natural log | ln (2) = 0.693147 |
| log | Returns the base-10 log | log (2) = 0.30103 |
| exp | Returns the natural exponent | exp (2) = 7.38906 |
| exp10 | Returns the base-10 exponent | exp10 (2) = 100 |
| sqr | Squares a number | sqr (9) = 81.0 |
| abs | Returns the absolute value | abs (−3.4) = 3.4 |
| round | Rounds to the nearest integer | round (3.6) = 4 |
| trunc | Drops the decimal portion of a real number | trunc (3.6) = 3 |
| r2d | Converts radians to degrees | r2d (1.5708) = 90.0002 |
| d2r | Converts degrees to radians | d2r (90) = 1.5708 |
| pi | Provides the constant pi | 3.14159 |

QuickCalc is capable of much more than the typical uses you've seen here. A description of its full capabilities extends beyond the scope of this text. However, the processes described in this section will be helpful as you use AutoCAD. If you want to know more about QuickCalc, consult the AutoCAD Help User Documentation (choose Help ➢ Help).

---

**SINGLING OUT PROXIMATE OBJECTS**

You'll sometimes need to select an object that overlaps or is very close to another object. Often, in this situation, you end up selecting the wrong object. To select the exact object you want, you can use the Selection Cycling tool and the Draworder command.

*Selection cycling* lets you cycle through objects that overlap until you select the one you want. To use this feature, first enter **Legacyctrlpick.⏎1.⏎**. This changes the way Ctrl-click functions in AutoCAD. Next, hold down the Ctrl key, and click the object you want to select. If the first object highlighted isn't the one you want, click again, but this time don't hold down the Ctrl key. When several objects overlap, keep clicking until the correct object is highlighted and selected. When the object you want is highlighted, press ⏎, and then select other objects or press ⏎ to finish the selection process. If you do a lot of work in 3D, make sure you set Legacyctrlpick back to 0 by entering **Legacyctrlpick.⏎0.⏎**.

Another way to gain access to an overlapped object is to use the Draworder command. You can select the overlapping object and then choose Tools ➢ Draw Order ➢ Send To Back. This has the effect of "moving" the overlapping object underneath the overlapped object. You can then click the previously overlapped object to select it. You can also use the Draw Order toolbar to access the Draworder command.

---

# The Bottom Line

**Using External References (Xrefs)**   You've seen how you can use Xrefs to quickly build variations of a floor plan that contains repetitive elements. This isn't necessarily the only way to use Xrefs, but the basic idea of how to use Xrefs is presented in the early exercises.

**Master It**   Try putting together another floor plan that contains nothing but the Unit2 plan.

**Solution**   Replace the eight studio units in the Common.dwg file with four of the Unit2 plans.

**Managing Layers**   Once you start to edit complex drawings, you'll find that you'll want to save the on/off or freeze/thaw layer states so you can more easily access parts of a drawing. The Layer States Manager offers the ability to save as many layer conditions as you may need in the course of a project.

**Master It**   What part of the Layer States Manager dialog box lets you control the layer properties that are affected by a saved layer state?

**Solution**   The Layer Properties To Restore group in the expanded view of the Layer States Manager.

**Using Advanced Tools: Filter, Quick Select**   The filter and Quick Select tools are great for isolating objects in a crowded drawing. You can select objects by their color or layer assignment. You can select all instances of a specific block.

**Master It**   True or false: The Quick Select tool lets you select a set of objects to limit your selections.

**Solution**   True.

**Using the QuickCalc Calculator**   The QuickCalc calculator offers many standard calculator tools plus a few that you may not see in other calculators.

**Master It**   Name a few of the more unusual features offered by the QuickCalc calculator.

**Solution**   Add feet and inch lengths; find percentages of lengths; obtain coordinates, lengths, and angles graphically from a drawing.

# Chapter 16

# Laying Out Your Printer Output

Your set of drawings for this studio apartment building would probably include a larger-scale, more detailed drawing of the typical unit plan. You already have the beginnings of this drawing in the form of the Unit file.

As you've seen, the notes and dimensions you entered into the Unit file can be turned off or frozen in the Plan file so they don't interfere with the graphics of the drawing. The Unit file can be part of another drawing file that contains more detailed information on the typical unit plan at a larger scale. To this new drawing, you can add notes, symbols, and dimensions. Whenever the Unit file is altered, you update its occurrence in the large-scale drawing of the typical unit as well as in the Plan file. The units are thus quickly updated, and good correspondence is ensured among all the drawings for your project.

Now, suppose you want to combine drawings having different scales in the same drawing file—for example, the overall plan of one floor plus an enlarged view of one typical unit. You can do so using the Layout tabs and a feature called Paper Space.

Topics in this chapter include the following:

◆ Understanding Model Space and Paper Space

◆ Working with Paper Space Viewports

◆ Creating Odd-Shaped Viewports

◆ Understanding Lineweights, Linetypes, and Dimensions in Paper Space

## Understanding Model Space and Paper Space

So far, you've looked at ways to help you get around in your drawing while using a single view. This single-view representation of your AutoCAD drawing is called *Model Space* display mode. You can also set up multiple views of your drawing, called *floating viewports*. You create floating viewports by using the Layout tabs to work in *Paper Space* display mode.

To get a clear understanding of the Model Space and Paper Space modes, imagine that your drawing is actually a full-size replica or model of the object you're drawing. Your computer screen is your window into a "room" where this model is being constructed, and the keyboard and mouse are your means of access to this room. You can control your window's position in relation to the object through the use of Pan, Zoom, View, and other display-related commands. You can also construct or modify the model by using drawing and editing commands. Think of this room as your Model Space.

You've been working on your drawings by looking through a single window into Model Space. Now, suppose you have the ability to step back and add windows with different views looking into your Model Space. The effect is as if you have several video cameras in your Model Space room, each connected to a different monitor. You can view all your windows at once on your computer screen or enlarge a single window to fill the entire screen. Further, you can control the shape of your windows and easily switch from one window to another. This is what Paper Space is like.

Paper Space lets you create and display multiple views of Model Space. Each view window, called a *viewport,* acts like an individual virtual screen. One viewport can have an overall view of your drawing, while another can be a close-up. You can also control layer visibility individually for each viewport and display different versions of the same area of your drawing. You can move, copy, and stretch viewports and even overlap them.

**TIP** You can set up another type of viewport, called the *Tiled viewport,* in Model Space. Chapter 21 discusses this type of viewport.

One of the more powerful features of Paper Space is the ability to plot several views of the same drawing on one sheet of paper. You can also include graphic objects such as borders and notes that appear only in Paper Space. In this function, Paper Space acts much like a page-layout program such as QuarkXPress or Adobe InDesign. You can paste up different views of your drawing and then add borders, title blocks, general notes, and other types of graphic and textural data. Figure 16.1 shows the Plan drawing set up in Paper Space mode to display several views.

**FIGURE 16.1**
Different views of the same drawing in Paper Space

## Creating a Paper Space Layout

Your gateway to Paper Space is the Layout tabs at the bottom of the AutoCAD Window. When the Model tab is selected, you're in Model Space. When you select a Layout tab, you're in Paper Space.
Let's start with the basics of entering Paper Space:

1. Open the Xref-1 file you saved from the last chapter, and ensure that your display shows the entire drawing. You can also use 16-xref1.dwg.

2. Click the Layout1 tab, and choose File ➤ Page Setup Manager to open the Page Setup Manager dialog box.

---

**SWITCHING BETWEEN TABS AND THE MODEL AND LAYOUT1 TOOLS**

In this chapter, you'll see references to the Model and Layout tabs. AutoCAD offers the option to hide the tabs to increase the size of the drawing area. If you don't see the tabs, you can switch back to the tab view of Model Space and Paper Space. To turn on the tabs, locate the Model and Layout1 tools in the status bar at the bottom of the AutoCAD Window.

Right-click the Model or Layout1 tool, and select Display Layout And Model Tabs. The tabs appear just below the drawing area. To hide the tabs, right-click any tab and select Hide Layout And Model Tabs. Note that the Paper/Model button in the status bar doesn't appear unless the tabs are visible.

If you prefer, you can use the Model and Layout1 tools in place of the tabs to gain a little extra space in the drawing area. If you turn off the tabs, and you have multiple layouts, you can use the Additional Layouts drop-down list to switch to a different layout in your drawing.

To create new layouts while using the Model and Layout1 tools, choose Insert ➤ Layout ➤ New Layout, and follow the command prompts.

---

**3.** Click the Modify button to open the Page Setup dialog box.

**4.** Select the Letter paper-size option from the Paper Size drop-down list. Metric users should select A4 (210 mm × 297 mm). The paper size you select here determines the shape and margin of the Paper Space layout area.

**5.** Select a printer from the Printer/Plotter name drop-down list.

**6.** Click OK to close the Page Setup dialog box, and then click Close to close the Page Setup Manager dialog box. Note that the word *PAPER* appears in the status bar; this tells you at a glance that you're in Paper Space.

AutoCAD bases the Paper Space work area on the paper size you specify. The area shown in Paper Space reflects the area of the paper size you selected in step 4. If for some reason you need to change the paper size, repeat steps 2 through 5. You can also store the way you've set up your Paper Space layout using the Page Setup Manager you saw in step 2. See Chapter 8 for more on this feature.

## Creating New Paper Space Viewports

As you saw in Chapter 8, the different look of the Layout tab tells you that you're in Paper Space. You also learned that a viewport is automatically created when you first open a Layout tab. The viewport displays an overall view of your drawing to no particular scale.

In this section, you'll work with multiple viewports in Paper Space, instead of just the default single viewport you get when you open the Layout tab.

This first exercise shows you how to create three new viewports at once:

1. Right-click the Standard Annotation toolbar above the drawing area, and choose Viewports to open the Viewports toolbar. You'll use this toolbar a bit later in this exercise.

2. Click the viewport border to select it. The viewport border is the solid rectangle surrounding your drawing, just inside the dashed rectangle.

3. Click the Erase tool to erase the viewport. Your drawing disappears. Don't panic; remember that the viewport is like a window to Model Space. The objects in Model Space are still there.

4. Click Display Viewports Dialog in the Viewports toolbar to open the Viewports dialog box. You can also choose View ➢ Viewports ➢ New Viewports. This dialog box contains a set of predefined viewport layouts.

**TIP**  You'll learn more about the Viewports dialog box and its options in Chapter 21.

5. Click the Three: Above option in the Standard Viewports list box. The box to the right shows a sample view of the Three: Above layout you selected.

6. Click OK. The `Specify first corner or [Fit] <Fit>:` prompt appears.

7. Press ↵ to accept the default Fit option. The Fit option fits the viewport layout to the maximum area allowed in your Paper Space view. Three rectangles appear in the formation, as shown in Figure 16.2. Each of these is a viewport to your Model Space. The viewport at the top fills the whole width of the drawing area; the bottom half of the screen is divided into two viewports.

When you create new viewports, AutoCAD automatically fills the viewport with the extents of your Model Space drawing. You can specify an exact scale for each viewport, as you'll see later.

Notice that the dashed line representing your paper margin has disappeared. That's because the viewports are pushed to the margin limits, thereby covering the dashed line.

You could have kept the original viewport that appeared when you first opened the Layout1 tab and then added two new viewports. Completely replacing the single viewport is a bit simpler because the Viewports dialog box fits the viewports in the allowed space for you.

**FIGURE 16.2**
The newly created
viewports

## Reaching Inside Viewports

Now, suppose you need access to the objects in the viewports in order to adjust their display and edit your drawing. Try these steps:

1. Click Paper on the status bar. This gives you control over Model Space even though you're in Paper Space. (You can also enter **MS.↵** as a keyboard shortcut to enter Model Space mode.)

   The first thing you notice is that the UCS icon changes back to its L-shaped arrow form. It also appears in each viewport, as if you had three AutoCAD windows instead of just one.

2. Move your cursor over each viewport. In one of the viewports, the cursor appears as the AutoCAD crosshair cursor, whereas in the other viewports it appears as an arrow pointer. The viewport that shows the AutoCAD cursor is the active one; you can pan, zoom, and edit objects in the active viewport.

**TIP** If your drawing disappears from a viewport, you can usually retrieve it by choosing View ➢ Zoom ➢ Extents (type **Zoom.↵E.↵**).

3. Click in the lower-left viewport to activate it.

4. Choose View ➢ Zoom ➢ Window, and place a window selection around the elevator area.

5. Click the lower-right viewport, and choose View ➢ Zoom ➢ Window to enlarge your view of a typical unit. You can also use the Pan Realtime and Zoom Realtime tools.

**TIP** If you don't see the UCS icon, it has been turned off. Type **UCSicon.↵On.↵** to turn it on. See Chapter 21 for more on the UCS icon.

When you click the Paper button on the status bar, the UCS icon again changes shape—instead of one triangular-shaped icon, you have three arrow-shaped ones, one for each viewport on the screen. Also, as you move your cursor into the currently active viewport, the cursor changes from an arrow into the usual crosshair. Another way to tell which viewport is active is by its bold border.

**TIP** You can also switch between Model Space and Paper Space by double-clicking an area in either region. For example, to go to Model Space from Paper Space, double-click inside a viewport. To get back to Paper Space, double-click the area outside the viewport. If you have an enlarged view of a viewport, and no portion of the Paper Space area is available to click, click the Paper button on the status bar.

You can move from viewport to viewport even while you're in the middle of most commands. For example, you can issue the Line command, pick the start point in one viewport, go to a different viewport to pick the next point, and so on. To activate a different viewport, you click inside the viewport (see Figure 16.3).

**FIGURE 16.3**

The three viewports, each with a different view of the plan

**TIP** You may find it difficult to access the contents of overlapping viewports, especially if the viewports are the same size or if one is enclosed by another. In this situation, you can move between viewports by pressing Ctrl+R repeatedly until you get to the viewport you want.

You've seen how you can zoom into a viewport view, but what happens when you use the Zoom command while in Paper Space? Try the following exercise to find out:

1. Click the Model button on the status bar or double-click an area outside the viewports to return to Paper Space.

2. Click the Zoom Realtime tool in the 2D Navigate control panel and then zoom in to the Paper Space view. The entire view enlarges, including the views in the viewports.

3. Right-click, and select Exit. Choose View ➢ Zoom ➢ All or enter Z↵A↵ to return to the overall view of Paper Space.

This brief exercise showed that you can use the Zoom tool in Paper Space just as you would in Model Space. All the display-related commands are available, including the Pan Realtime command.

### Getting Back to Full-Screen Model Space

After you've created viewports, you can reenter Model Space through the viewport by clicking the Model/Paper button on the status bar. This button performs two functions: It shows you which space you're in, and it enables you to switch between the two spaces. But what if you want to quickly get back into the old, familiar, full-screen Model Space you were in before you entered Paper Space?

The following exercise demonstrates how this is done:

1.  Click the Model tab at the bottom of the drawing area, or enter **Tm↵1↵**. Your drawing returns to the original full-screen Model Space view—everything is back to normal.

2.  Click the Layout1 tab, or enter **Tm↵0↵**. You're back in Paper Space.

    All the viewports are still there when you return to Paper Space. After you've set up Paper Space, it remains part of the drawing until you delete all the viewports. Also notice that you didn't see the Page Setup dialog box this time. After you've chosen a sheet size, AutoCAD assumes that you'll continue to use that sheet size and other page setup information until you tell it otherwise.

You may prefer using Model Space for doing most of your drawing and using Paper Space for setting up views for printing. Because viewport layouts are retained, you won't lose anything when you go back to Model Space to edit your drawing.

## Working with Paper Space Viewports

Paper Space is intended as a page-layout or composition tool. You can manipulate viewports' sizes, scale their views independently of one another, and even set layering and linetype scales independently.

Let's try manipulating the shape and location of viewports by using the Modify toolbar options:

1.  Turn off Running Osnaps if it's on.

2.  Make sure you're in Paper Space. (The Paper button should appear to the right of the status bar buttons.) Then, click the bottom edge of the lower-left viewport to expose its grips (see the top image in Figure 16.4).

3.  Click the upper-right grip, and drag it to the location shown in the top image in Figure 16.4.

4.  Press the Esc key, and erase the lower-right viewport by selecting it and clicking Erase in the Modify toolbar. Then, click the bottom edge of the viewport.

5.  Move the lower-left viewport so it's centered in the bottom half of the window, as shown in the bottom image in Figure 16.4.

In this exercise, you clicked the viewport edge to select it for editing. If, while in Paper Space, you attempt to click the image in the viewport, you won't select anything. Later, you'll see that you can use the Osnap modes to snap to parts of the drawing image in a viewport.

Because viewports are recognized as AutoCAD objects, you can manipulate them by using all the editing commands, just as you would manipulate any other object. In the previous exercise, you moved, stretched, and erased viewports.

**FIGURE 16.4**
Stretching, erasing, and moving viewports

Next, you'll see how layers affect viewports:

1. Create a new layer called Vport.

2. In the Properties palette, change the viewport borders to the Vport layer.

3. Turn off the Vport layer. You see a warning message telling you that the members of the selected objects are on a layer that is off or frozen. Click OK; the viewport borders disappear.

4. After reviewing the results of step 3, turn the Vport layer back on.

You can assign a viewport's border a layer, a color, a linetype, and even a lineweight. If you put the viewport's border on a layer that has been turned off or frozen, that border becomes invisible, just like any other object on such a layer. Making the borders invisible is helpful when you want to compose a final sheet for printing. Even when turned off, the active viewport has a heavy border around it when you switch to Floating Model Space, and all the viewports still display their views.

## Scaling Views in Paper Space

Paper Space has its own unit of measure. You've already seen how you're required to specify a paper size when opening a Layout tab to a Paper Space view. When you first enter Paper Space, regardless of the area your drawing occupies in Model Space, you're given limits that are set by the paper size you specify in the Page Setup dialog box. If you keep in mind that Paper Space is like a paste-up area that is dependent on the printer you configured for AutoCAD, this difference of scale becomes easier to comprehend. Just as you might paste up photographs and maps representing several square miles onto an 11″ × 17″ board, so can you use Paper Space to paste up views of scale drawings representing city blocks or houses on an 8½″ × 11″ sheet of paper. But in AutoCAD, you have the freedom to change the scale and size of the objects you're pasting up.

**TIP** While in Paper Space, you can edit objects in a Model Space viewport; but to do so, you must use Floating Model Space. You can then click a viewport and edit in that viewport. In this mode, objects that were created in Paper Space can't be edited. Choosing View ➢ Paper Space brings you back to the Paper Space environment.

If you want to be able to print your drawing at a specific scale, you must indicate a scale for each viewport. Viewport scales are set in a way similar to the annotation scale in the Model tab. Let's see how to put together a sheet in Paper Space and still maintain accuracy of scale:

1. Make sure you're in Paper Space. Check to see whether the Paper button appears on the status bar. If Model appears there, click that button to change it to Paper.

2. Click the topmost viewport's border to select it.

3. In the lower-right corner of the AutoCAD Window, click the VP Scale drop-down list, and select ¹⁄₃₂″ = 1′-0″. Notice how the view in the top viewport changes.

4. Press the Esc key twice to clear the selection in the viewport.

5. Click the lower viewport border.

6. Click the VP Scale drop-down list again, and select ³⁄₁₆″ = 1′-0″ from the list. The view in the viewport changes to reflect the new scale (see Figure 16.5).

**FIGURE 16.5**
Paper Space viewport views scaled to ¹⁄₃₂″ = 1′-0″ and ³⁄₁₆″ = 1′-0″

It's easy to adjust the width, height, and location of the viewports so they display only the parts of the unit you want to see. While in Paper Space, use the Stretch, Move, or Scale command to edit any viewport border, or use the viewport's grips to edit its size. The view in the viewport remains at the same scale and location, while the viewport changes in size. You can move and stretch viewports with no effect on the size and location of the objects in the view.

If you need to overlay one drawing on top of another, you can overlap viewports. Use the osnap overrides to select geometry in each viewport, even while in Paper Space. This enables you to align one viewport on top of another at exact locations.

You can also add a title block in Paper Space at a 1:1 scale to frame your viewports and then plot this drawing from Paper Space at a scale of 1:1. Your plot appears just as it does in Paper Space, at the appropriate scale. Paper Space displays a dashed line to show you where the nonprintable areas occur near the edge of the paper.

While you're working in Paper Space, pay close attention to whether you're in Paper Space or Floating Model Space mode. It's easy to accidentally pan or zoom in a Floating Model Space viewport when you intend to pan or zoom your Paper Space view. This can cause you to lose your viewport scaling or alignment with other parts of the drawing. It's a good idea to save viewport views by choosing View ➤ Named Views in case you happen to accidentally change a viewport view.

Another way to prevent your viewport view from being accidentally altered is to turn on View Lock. To do this, while in Paper Space, click a viewport border. Right-click to open the shortcut menu, and then choose Display Locked ➤ Yes. After the view is locked, you can't pan or zoom a viewport view. You also can't change the size of the viewport. This setting is also available in the viewport's Properties palette.

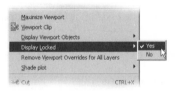

**TIP** If your viewport views are automatically zooming to extents when you enter them, the Ucsfollow system variable has been changed from its default setting of 0 (zero). Change Ucsfollow back to 0 by typing **Ucsfollow**↵**0**↵. You can also use the UCS dialog box to change this setting. Choose Tools ➤ Named UCS. In the UCS dialog box, click the Settings tab, and then make sure the Update View To Plan When UCS Is Changed option is turned off.

## Setting Layers in Individual Viewports

Another unique feature of Paper Space viewports is their ability to freeze layers independently. You can, for example, display the usual plan information in the overall view of a floor but show only the walls in the enlarged view of one unit.

You control viewport layer visibility through the Layer Properties Manager dialog box. You may have noticed that there are three sun icons for each layer listing.

**TIP** You may need to widen the Layer Properties Manager dialog box to view all the columns. To do so, click and drag the right border of the dialog box to the right.

You're already familiar with the sun icon farthest to the left: This is the Freeze/Thaw icon that controls the freezing and thawing of layers globally. Several columns to the right of that icon are two sun icons with transparent rectangles. These icons control the freezing and thawing of layers in individual viewports. Of this pair, the one on the left controls existing viewports and the one on the right controls settings for newly created viewports.

This exercise shows you firsthand how the sun icon for existing viewports works:

1. Click the Paper button on the status bar to go to Floating Model Space.

2. Activate the lower viewport.

3. Open the Layer Properties Manager dialog box.

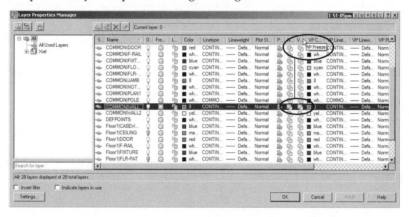

4. Locate the COMMON | WALL layer; then, click its name to help you isolate this layer.

**WARNING** You can't use the VP Freeze and New VP Freeze options in the Layer Properties Manager dialog box while you're in the Model tab.

5. Click the column labeled VP Freeze for the selected layer. You may need to widen the Layer Properties Manager dialog box to do this; the column title may only show V until you widen the column. The Current VP Freeze column is the sixth column from the right side of the dialog box. Click the icon, which looks like a transparent rectangle under a sun. The sun changes to a snowflake, telling you that the layer is now frozen for the current viewport.

6. Click OK. The active viewport regenerates, with the Wall layer of the Common Xref becomes invisible in the current viewport. However, the walls remain visible in the other viewport (see Figure 16.6).

7. After reviewing the effects of the Current VP Freeze setting, go back to the Layer Properties Manager dialog box and thaw the COMMON | WALL layer by clicking its Current VP Freeze icon again so it turns back into a sun.

8. Click OK to exit the dialog box.

9. Take a moment to study the drawing, and then save the Xref-1 file.

**FIGURE 16.6**

The drawing with the COMMON|WALL layer turned off in the active viewport

You may have noticed another, identical sun icon next to the one you used in the previous exercise. This icon controls layer visibility in any new viewports you create next, rather than controlling existing viewports.

If you prefer, you can use the Layer drop-down list in the Layers toolbar to freeze layers in individual viewports. Double-click in the viewport you want to modify, select the layer from the list, and then click the same sun icon with the small rectangle beneath it.

In addition to setting the visibility of layers, you can also set the other layer properties such as color, linetype, and lineweight for each viewport. First, make sure you're in Floating Model Space for the viewport whose layers you want to set up, and then open the Layer Properties Manager. You can set the properties for the current viewport using the VP Freeze, VP Color, VP Linetype, VP Lineweight, and VP Plot settings for each layer.

This section concludes the apartment building tutorial. Although you haven't drawn the complete building, you've learned all the commands and techniques you need to do so. Figure 16.7 shows you a completed plan of the first floor; to complete your floor plans and get some practice using AutoCAD, you may want to add the symbols shown in this figure to your Plan file.

Because buildings like this one often have the same plans for several floors, the plan for the second floor can also represent the third floor. Combined with the first floor, this gives you a three-level apartment building. This project might also have a ground-level garage, which would be a separate file. You can use the Col-grid.dwg file in the garage file as a reference for dimensions. The other symbols can be blocks stored as files that you can retrieve in other files.

**FIGURE 16.7**
A completed floor
of the apartment
building

**FIGURE 16.7**
A completed floor
of the apartment
building

---

**MASKING OUT PARTS OF A DRAWING**

Chapter 7 described a method for using AutoCAD's Draw Order feature to hide floor patterns under equipment or furniture in a floor layout. You can use a similar method to hide irregularly shaped areas in a Paper Space viewport. This is desirable for plotting site plans, civil plans, or floor plans that require portions of the drawing to be masked out. Or you may want to mask part of a plan that is overlapped by another to expose dimension or text data.

---

## Creating and Using Multiple Paper Space Layouts

You're not limited to just one or two Paper Space layouts. You can have as many Paper Space layouts as you want, with each layout set up for a different sheet size containing different views of your drawing. You can use this feature to set up multiple drawing sheets based on a single AutoCAD drawing file. For example, suppose a client requires full sets of plans in both ⅛″ = 1′ scale and 1/16″ = 1″ scale. You can set up two Layout tabs, each with a different sheet size and viewport scale.

You can also set up different Paper Space layouts for the different types of drawings. In the San Francisco Main Library project, a single drawing contained the data for mechanical layout, equipment and furnishing, floor plans, and reflected ceiling plans. Although that project used multiple files to set the layers for each plan, a single file with multiple Layout tabs can serve the same purpose in AutoCAD 2008.

To create new Layout tabs, do the following:

1. Right-click any tab.

2. Choose New Layout from the shortcut menu to add a new tab to those that already exist.

3. Click the new Layout tab. The layout appears with a single default viewport.

In step 1, the Layout tab shortcut menu included the From Template option. The From Template option lets you create a Paper Space layout based on an AutoCAD template file. AutoCAD provides several standard layouts that include title blocks based on common sheet sizes.

The Layout tab shortcut menu also includes options that enable you to delete, rename, move, copy, or select all the tabs. If there are more tabs than can fit in the space provided, you can navigate the tabs by using the arrows just to the left of the tabs.

## Creating Odd-Shaped Viewports

In many situations, a rectangular viewport doesn't provide a view appropriate for what you want to accomplish. For example, you might want to isolate part of a floor plan that is L-shaped or circular. You can create viewports for virtually any shape you need, as the following exercise demonstrates.

**WARNING**   This feature isn't available in AutoCAD LT.

Follow these steps to set up a Layout tab that shows only the lower apartment units and the elevators and stairs:

1. Click the Clip Existing Viewport tool in the Viewports toolbar. You can also choose Modify ➤ Clip ➤ Viewport.

2. At the `Select viewport to clip:` prompt, click the viewport border.

3. At the `Select clipping object or [Polygonal] <Polygonal>:` prompt, press ↵.

4. Turn off Running Osnaps, and draw the outline shown in the top portion of Figure 16.8.

5. After you finish selecting points, press ↵. The viewport changes to conform to the new shape.

6. Click the viewport border to expose its grips.

7. Click a grip, and move it to a new location. The viewport view conforms to the new shape.

The new viewport shape gives you more flexibility in isolating portions of a drawing. This can be especially useful if you have a large project that is divided into smaller sheets. You can set up several Layout tabs, each displaying a different portion of the plan.

What if you want a viewport that isn't rectilinear? This exercise shows you how to create a circular viewport:

1. Erase the viewport you just modified.

2. Draw a circle that roughly fills the Paper Space area.

3. Click the Convert Object To Viewport option on the Viewports toolbar, or choose View ➤ Viewports ➤ Object.

4. Click the circle. The plan appears inside the circle, as shown in Figure 16.9.

**FIGURE 16.8**
Drawing a polygon
outline for a viewport

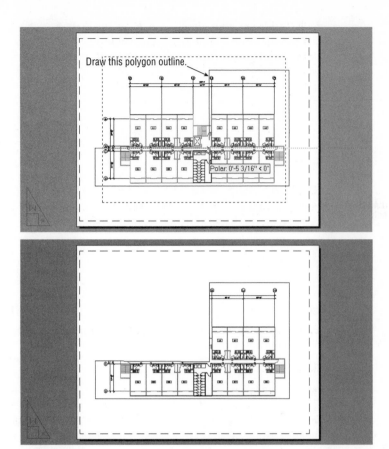

**FIGURE 16.9**
A circular viewpoint

To simplify this exercise, you were asked to draw a circle as the basis for a new viewport. However, you aren't limited to circles; you can use a closed polyline or spline of any shape. (See Chapter 18 for a detailed discussion of polylines and splines.) You can also use the Polygon tool on the Draw toolbar to create a shape and then turn it into a viewport.

If you look carefully at the series of prompts for the previous exercise, you'll notice that the Convert Object To Viewport option invokes a command-line version of the Vports command (-vports). This command-line version offers some options that the standard Vports command doesn't. The following options are available with the command-line version of Vports:

```
-vports
[ON/OFF/Fit/Shadeplot/Lock/Object/Polygonal/Restore/2/3/4] <Fit>:
```

You used two of the options in the two previous exercises: Polygonal and Object. If you're an experienced AutoCAD user, you may notice that this command-line version of Vports is the same as the Mview command of earlier releases. You can still use the Mview command if you prefer.

# Understanding Lineweights, Linetypes, and Dimensions in Paper Space

The behavior of several AutoCAD features depends on whether you're in Paper Space or Model Space. The most visible of these features are lineweights, linetypes, and dimensions. In this section, you'll take a closer look at these features and see how to use them in conjunction with Paper Space.

## Controlling and Viewing Lineweights in Paper Space

Lineweights can greatly improve the readability of technical drawings. You can make important features stand out with bold lineweights while keeping the noise of smaller details from overpowering a drawing. In architectural floor plans, walls are traditionally drawn with heavier lines so the outline of a plan can be easily read. Other features exist in a drawing for reference only, so they're drawn in a lighter weight than normal.

In Chapter 9, you saw how to control lineweights in AutoCAD by using plot-style tables. You can apply either a named plot-style table or a color plot-style table to a drawing. If you already have a library of AutoCAD drawings, you may want to use color plot-style tables for backward compatibility. AutoCAD also enables you to assign lineweights directly to layers or objects and to view the results of your lineweight settings in Paper Space.

Here's an exercise that demonstrates how to set lineweights directly:

1. Click the Layout1 tab; then, open the Layer Properties Manager dialog box.

2. Right-click the Layer list, and choose Select All.

3. Click the Lineweight column to open the Lineweight dialog box.

**4.** Select 0.13 mm from the list, and click OK. You've just assigned the 0.13 mm lineweight to all layers.

**5.** Right-click the Layer list again, and choose Clear All.

**6.** Click the Common | WALL layer, and Ctrl+click the Floor1 | WALL layer to select these two layers.

**7.** Click the Lineweight column for either of the two selected layers to open the Lineweight dialog box again.

**8.** Select 0.40 mm from the dialog box, and click OK. You've just assigned the 0.4 mm lineweight to the two selected layers.

**9.** Click OK in the Layer Properties Manager dialog box.

Although you set the lineweights for the layers in the drawing, you need to make a few more changes to the file settings before they're visible in Paper Space:

**1.** Choose Format ➢ Lineweight to open the Lineweight Settings dialog box.

**2.** Select the Display Lineweight check box, and then click OK.

**3.** Make sure you're in Paper Space, and then zoom in to the drawing.

**4.** Choose View ➢ Regen All. The lines representing the walls are now thicker, as shown in Figure 16.10.

**5.** After reviewing the results of this exercise, close the file.

**FIGURE 16.10**
An enlarged view of the plan with line-weights displayed

With the ability to display lineweights in Paper Space, you have better control over your output. Instead of using a trial-and-error method to print your drawing and then checking your printout to see whether the lineweights are correct, AutoCAD 2008 lets you see the lineweights on your screen.

This exercise showed you how to set lineweights so they appear in Paper Space as they will when you plot your drawing. If you normally plot your drawings in black, you can go one step further and set all your layer colors to black to really see how your plots will look. But you'll need to save your layer settings so you can restore the layers to their original colors. You'll learn more about saving and restoring layer settings later in this chapter. Another way to view your drawing in black and white without affecting your layer settings is to use the color plot-style table described in Chapter 9.

**TIP** When lineweight display is turned on, you see lineweights in Model Space as well as in Paper Space. Lineweights can be distracting while you work on your drawing in Model Space, but you can quickly turn them off by entering **Lwdisplay.⏎Off.⏎** at the Command prompt. Entering **Lwdisplay.⏎On.⏎** turns the lineweight display back on.

### The Lineweight Settings Dialog Box

The Lineweight Settings dialog box includes a few other settings that you didn't use in the previous exercise. Here is a description of those settings for your reference:

**Units For Listing** You can choose between millimeters and inches for the unit of measure for lineweights. The default is millimeters.

**Adjust Display Scale** This setting lets you control just how thick lineweights appear in the drawing. Move the slider to the right for thicker lines and to the left for thinner lines. This setting affects only the display on your monitor. As you move the slider, you can see a sample of the results in the Lineweights list box.

**Default drop-down list** This drop-down list lets you select the default lineweight you see in the Layer Properties Manager dialog box. It's set to 0.01″ (0.25 mm) by default. You may want to lower the default lineweight to .005″ (.13 mm) as a matter of course, because most printers these days can print lines that size and even smaller.

### Linetype Scales and Paper Space

As you've seen in previous exercises, you must carefully control drawing scales when creating viewports. Fortunately, this is easily done through the Properties palette. Although Paper Space offers the flexibility of combining images of different scale in one display, it also adds to the complexity of your task in controlling that display. Your drawing's linetype scale, in particular, needs careful attention.

In Chapter 5, you saw that you had to set the linetype scale to the scale factor of the drawing in order to make the linetype visible. If you intend to plot that same drawing from Paper Space, you have to set the linetype scale back to 1 to get the linetypes to appear correctly. This is because AutoCAD faithfully scales linetypes to the current unit system. Remember that Paper Space units are different from Model Space units. When you scale a Model Space image down to fit in the smaller Paper Space area, the linetypes remain scaled to the increased linetype scale settings. In the Chapter 5 example, linetypes are scaled up by a factor of 48. This causes noncontinuous lines to appear as continuous in Paper Space because you see only a small portion of a greatly enlarged noncontinuous linetype.

The Psltscale system variable enables you to determine how linetype scales are applied to Paper Space views. You can set Psltscale so the linetypes appear the same, regardless of whether you view them directly in tiled Model Space or through a viewport in Paper Space. By default, this system variable is set to 1. This causes AutoCAD to scale all the linetypes uniformly across all the viewports in Paper Space. You can set Psltscale to 0 to force the viewports to display linetypes exactly as they appear in Model Space.

You can also control this setting in the Linetype Manager dialog box (choose Format ➢ Linetype). When you click the Show Details button, you see a setting called Use Paper Space Units For Scaling in the lower-left corner. When this check box is selected, Psltscale is set to 1. When it isn't selected, Psltscale is set to 0.

## Dimensioning in Paper Space Layouts

At times, you may find it more convenient to add dimensions to your drawing in Paper Space rather than directly on your objects in Model Space. This can be helpful when you're using Layout tabs to produce views of the same Model Space drawing at different scales. Or you may want to combine several drawings at different scales in one Layout tab as in a detail sheet.

You have two basic options when dimensioning Model Space objects in Paper Space. The Associative Dimensioning feature can make quick work of dimensions for Layout tabs containing drawings of differing scales. Or, if you prefer not to use Associative Dimensioning, you can adjust settings for individual dimension styles.

### USING ASSOCIATIVE DIMENSIONING IN PAPER SPACE

Perhaps the simplest way to dimension in Paper Space is to use the Associative Dimensioning feature. With this feature turned on, you can dimension Model Space objects while in a Paper Space layout. Furthermore, Paper Space dimensions of Model Space objects are automatically updated if the Model Space object is edited.

Try the following exercise to see how Associative Dimensioning works:

1. Choose File ➢ New, and use the Start From Scratch option to create a new blank file. If you're using a template for new files, use the Acad.dwt template.

2. Draw a rectangle 12 units wide by 4 units high. If you're using a metric file, make the rectangle 480 units wide by 160 units high.

3. Click the Layout1 tab, right-click the tab, and select Page Setup Manager.

4. In the Page Setup Manager dialog box, click Modify. Then, in the Page Setup dialog box, choose the Letter paper size in the Printer/Plotter section.

5. Click OK, and then close the Page Setup Manager dialog box.

6. Right-click in the drawing area, and choose Options from the shortcut menu.

7. In the Options dialog box, click the User Preferences tab, and make sure the Make New Dimensions Associative option in the Associative Dimensioning group is turned on. Click OK to exit the dialog box.

Next, you'll use the rectangle you drew in Model Space to test the Associative Dimensioning feature in the Layout1 tab:

1. Choose Dimension ➢ Linear. Using the Endpoint osnap, dimension the bottom edge of the rectangle you drew in Model Space. The dimension shows 12.0000 (480 for metric drawings), the actual size of the rectangle.

2. Double-click inside the viewport, and use the Zoom Realtime tool to zoom out a bit so the rectangle appears smaller in the viewport. After you exit the Zoom Realtime tool, the dimension follows the new view of the rectangle.

3. While you're in Floating Model Space, click the rectangle, and then click the grip in the lower-left corner and drag it upward and to the right.

4. Click again to place the corner of the rectangle in a new location. The dimension changes to conform to the new shape.

**5.** Close the rectangle file without saving it. You won't need it in the future.

You've just seen how you can dimension an object in Model Space while in Paper Space. You can also dimension Model Space Xrefs in Paper Space in much the same way. The only difference is that changes to the Xref file don't automatically update dimensions made in Paper Space. You need to employ the Dimregen command to refresh Paper Space dimensions of Xref objects.

### UPDATING ASSOCIATIVE DIMENSIONS

If you use a wheel mouse to pan and zoom in a Floating Model Space viewport, you may need to use the Dimregen command to refresh an associative dimension. To do so, type **Dimregen**⏎ at the Command prompt. You can also use Dimregen to refresh dimensions from drawings that have been edited in earlier versions of AutoCAD or, as mentioned already, to refresh dimensions of objects contained in external references.

### PAPER SPACE DIMENSIONING WITHOUT ASSOCIATIVE DIMENSIONING

In some situations, you may not want to use Associative Dimensioning, although you still want to dimension Model Space objects in Paper Space. For example, you might be in an office that has different versions of AutoCAD, or you might be sharing your drawings with other offices that aren't using AutoCAD 2008, and the use of Associative Dimensioning creates confusion.

To dimension Model Space objects in Paper Space without Associative Dimensioning, you need to have AutoCAD adjust the dimension text to the scale of the viewport from which you're dimensioning. You can have AutoCAD scale dimension values in Paper Space so they correspond to a viewport zoom-scale factor. The following steps show you how this setting is made:

**1.** Open the Dimension Style Manager dialog box.

**2.** Select the dimension style you want to edit, and click Modify.

**3.** Click the Primary Units tab.

**4.** In the Measurement Scale group, enter the scale factor of the viewport you intend to dimension in the Scale Factor input box. For example, if the viewport is scaled to a ½″ = 1′-0″ scale, enter **24**.

**5.** Click the Apply To Layout Dimensions Only check box.

**6.** Click OK, and then click Close in the Dimension Style Manager dialog box. You're ready to dimension in Paper Space.

Remember that you can snap to objects in a floating viewport so you can add dimensions as you normally would in Model Space. If you're dimensioning objects in viewports of different scales, you need to set up multiple dimension styles, one for each viewport scale.

## Other Uses for Paper Space

The exercises in this section should give you a sense of how you work in Paper Space. I've given examples that reflect common uses of Paper Space. Remember that Paper Space is like a page-layout portion of AutoCAD—separate yet connected to Model Space through viewports.

You needn't limit your applications to floor plans. Interior and exterior elevations, 3D models, and detail sheets can all take advantage of Paper Space. When used in conjunction with AutoCAD's raster-import capabilities, Paper Space can be a powerful tool for creating large-format presentations.

# The Bottom Line

**Understanding Model Space and Paper Space**   AutoCAD offers two viewing modes for viewing and printing your drawings. Model Space is where you do most of your work; it's the view you see when you create a new file. Layouts, also called Paper Space, are views that let you arrange the layout of your drawing similar to a page-layout program.

**Master It**   What are the two ways of moving from Model Space to Paper Space?

**Solution**   You can use the Model and Layout1 tools in the status bar, or you can switch to showing the Model and Layout tabs in the AutoCAD window and use the tabs.

**Working with Paper Space Viewports**   While in Paper Space, you can create views into your drawing using viewports. You can have several viewports, each showing a different part of your drawing.

**Master It**   Name some of the ways you can enlarge a view in a viewport.

**Solution**   You can double-click inside a viewport and then use the Zoom tool to enlarge the view. You can also use the VP scale setting in the status bar to set the scale of the view.

**Creating Odd-Shaped Viewports**   Most of the time, you'll probably use rectangular viewports, but you have the option to create a viewport of any shape.

**Master It**   Describe the process for creating a circular viewport.

**Solution**   In Paper Space, draw a circle. Next, choose Modify ➢ Object ➢ Viewport, and then follow the prompts.

**Understanding Lineweights, Linetypes, and Dimensions in Paper Space**   You can get an accurate view of how you drawing will look on paper by making a few adjustments to AutoCAD. Your layout view will reflect how your drawing will look when plotted.

**Master It**   Name the two dialog boxes you must use to display lineweights in a layout view.

**Solution**   Layer Properties Manager to set up lineweights, and the Lineweight Settings dialog box.

# Chapter 17

# Using Dynamic Blocks

Blocks are a great way to create and store ready-made symbols. They can be a real time-saver, especially when you have assemblies that you use often. Earlier in this book, you learned how to create a basic, no-frills block. Once you've understood the basics of block creation, you can begin to work with *dynamic blocks*.

Dynamic blocks have properties that you can modify using grips. For example, you can create a dynamic block of a door and then easily grip-edit its size and orientation. In another example, a single block can be used to represent several versions of a similar object. You can have a single block of a bed that can be modified to show a single-, twin-, queen-, or king-sized shape.

In this chapter, you'll explore the use of dynamic blocks through a series of tutorials. Each tutorial will show you an example of how dynamic blocks can be used in different ways. This will help you become familiar with the methods involved in creating dynamic blocks. You'll start by looking at the Block Editor, which in itself makes editing blocks much easier. Then you'll be introduced to the tools used to create dynamic blocks.

- ◆ Topics in this chapter include the following:

- ◆ Exploring the Block Editor

- ◆ Creating a Dynamic Block

- ◆ Keeping an Object Centered

- ◆ Adding Scale and Stretch Actions to a Parameter

- ◆ Adding More Than One Parameter for Multiple Grip Functions

- ◆ Creating Multiple Shapes in One Block

- ◆ Rotating Objects in Unison

- ◆ Filling in a Space Automatically with Objects

## Exploring the Block Editor

Before you start to add dynamic block features to blocks, you'll want to get familiar with the Block Editor. The Block Editor offers an easy way to make changes to existing blocks, and as you'll see a bit later, it's also the tool you'll use to give your blocks some additional capabilities.

As an introduction to the Block Editor, you'll make changes to the now-familiar unit plan from earlier tutorials. Start by editing the kitchen block in the unit:

1. Open the Unit.dwg file you've saved from earlier exercises. You can also use the 17-unit.dwg file.

2. Double-click the kitchenette in the plan to open the Edit Block Definition dialog box. Notice that all the blocks in the drawing are listed in the dialog box and that the kitchen block is highlighted. You also see a preview of the block in the Preview panel.

3. With the KITCHEN block name selected, click OK.

4. You see a message asking if you want a demonstration of dynamic blocks in the New Features Workshop. Click No. You may also want to select the Do Not Display This Alert Again option. You can always get to the New Features Workshop through the Help menu bar option. Once you've clicked No, you see an enlarged view of the kitchenette in the drawing area with a yellow background (see Figure 17.1).

The yellow background tells you that you're in the Block Editor. You'll also see the Block Editor toolbar along the top of the drawing area, and the Block Authoring palettes, as shown in Figure 17.1.

**FIGURE 17.1**
The Block Editor and its components

Take a moment to look over the Block Editor. The toolbar across the top offers several house-keeping tools that let you open, save, and exit the Block Editor. You can point to each tool to see a description of it. Figure 17.2 shows the toolbar and each tool's description.

**FIGURE 17.2**

The Block Editor toolbar

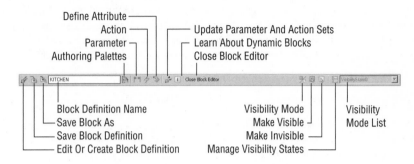

Both the toolbar and the Block Authoring palettes offer tools for adding dynamic block features that you'll explore later in this chapter. For now, let's continue our look at the basic features of the Block Editor.

## Editing a Block and Creating New Blocks

The Block Editor lets you edit a block using all the standard AutoCAD editing tools. In the following exercise, you'll modify the kitchen sink and save your changes to the drawing:

1. Delete the rectangle that represents the sink in the kitchen block.

2. Click the Close Block Editor button on the Block Editor toolbar.

3. A message appears, asking if you want to save your changes to the kitchen block. Click Yes. Your view returns to the standard AutoCAD drawing area, and you can see the changes you made to the kitchen, as shown in Figure 17.3.

**FIGURE 17.3**

The unit plan with the edited kitchen block

As you can see, editing blocks with the Block Editor is simple and straightforward. In this example, you deleted part of the block, but you can perform any type of drawing or editing to modify the block. The Block Editor also offers other block-saving options in its toolbar. You can save the block as you work by clicking the Save Block Definition button. If you need to create a variation on the block you're currently editing, you can click the Save Block As button (see Figure 17.2, earlier in this chapter) to create a new block or overwrite an existing one with the drawing that is currently in the Block Editor.

If you want to edit a different block after editing the current one, you can click the Save Block Definition button to save your current block and then click the Edit Or Create Block Definition button.

This button opens the Edit Block Definition dialog box that you saw earlier. You can then select another block to edit or create a new block by entering a name for your block in the Block To Create Or Edit input box.

## Creating a Dynamic Block

Now that you've seen how the Block Editor works, you can begin to explore the creation of dynamic blocks. As an introduction, you'll create a rectangle that you'll use to replace the sink in the kitchen. You'll add a dynamic block feature that will allow you to adjust the width of the sink using grips. In addition, you'll add a control that limits the size to 1-unit increments.

Start by creating a block from scratch using the Block Editor:

1. Click the Block Editor tool on the Standard toolbar.

2. In the Edit Block Definition dialog box, enter **Sink** in the Block To Create Or Edit input box, and then click OK. If a message asks if you want to see a demonstration, click No. The Block Editor opens with a blank screen.

3. Use the Rectangle tool on the Draw toolbar to draw a rectangle that is 12 units in the X axis and 15 units in the Y axis.

4. Zoom in to the rectangle so your view looks similar to Figure 17.4.

**FIGURE 17.4**
The rectangle for
the Sink block

You could save this block now, and you'd have a simple, nondynamic block. Next, you'll add a couple of features called *parameters* and *actions*. As their names imply, parameters define the parameters or limits of what the dynamic block will do, and actions describe the particular action taken when the grips of the dynamic block are edited. For example, in the next section, you'll add a Linear parameter that tells AutoCAD that you want to restrain the grip editing to a linear direction. You'll also add a Stretch action that tells AutoCAD that you want the grip edit to behave like a Stretch command that pulls a set of vertices in one direction or another.

## Adding a Parameter

The first parameter you'll add establishes the base point for the block. This will let you determine the point used when inserting the block in your drawing:

1. In the Block Authoring palettes, select the Parameters tab.

2. Click the Base Point Parameter tool, Shift+right-click, select the Endpoint osnap, and then click the lower-left corner of the rectangle. This is how you determine the base point or insertion point of a block while using the Block Editor.

**TIP**    You can also click the Parameter tool on the Block Editor toolbar and then enter **B.↵** to insert a base point parameter.

Next, you'll add a parameter that will determine the type of editing you want to add to the block. In this case, you want to be able to grip edit the width of the block. For that you'll use the Linear Parameter tool.

1. Click the Linear Parameter tool on the Parameters tab, or click the Parameter tool on the Block Editor toolbar and enter **L.↵**.

2. At the prompt

```
Specify start point or [Name/Label/Chain/Description/Base/Palette/Value set]:
```

Shift+right-click and select the Midpoint osnap; then, select the left side of the rectangle.

3. Shift+right-click again, select Midpoint from the Osnap menu, and select the right side of the rectangle.

4. At the `Specify label location:` prompt, the parameter name appears with the parameter label at the cursor. Click below the rectangle to place the label as shown in Figure 17.5.

**FIGURE 17.5**
Placing the Linear parameter

**NOTE**   If you use the Parameter tool, you see an additional prompt asking if you want 0, 1, or 2 grips. Press ↵ to accept the default of 2.

The parameter you just added lets you modify the block in a linear fashion. In this case, it will allow you to change the width of the rectangle. As you'll see, the locations of the parameter's arrows later become the grip locations for the dynamic block.

But just adding the parameter doesn't make the block dynamic. You need to include an action before a parameter can be used. You may have noticed the warning symbol in the parameter you just added: It tells you that you need to take some further steps to make the parameter useful.

**TIP**   When you see the warning symbol in a parameter, you can double-click the symbol to display a list of options.

## Adding an Action

Next, you'll add a Stretch action that will enable you to use the Linear parameter you just added. The Stretch action will let you stretch the block horizontally using grips. As you add the action, notice that it's similar to using the Stretch command. The only difference is that you don't stretch the object—you only specify the vertices to stretch and the object you want to stretch.

Follow these steps:

1. Click the Actions tab in the Block Authoring palettes, and select Stretch Action.

2. At the `Select parameter:` prompt, click the left-pointing parameter arrow at the middle of the rectangle on the left side. You see a circle with an X through it showing the location of a parameter point.

3. At the `Specify parameter point to associate with action or enter [sTart point/ Second point] <Second>:` prompt, point to the left-pointing arrow again.

4. Click the circle with the arrow.

5. At the `Specify first corner of stretch frame or [CPolygon]:` prompt, place a window selection around the entire left side of the rectangle. This selects the portion of the rectangle that is to be stretched when you grip-edit the block.

6. At the `Specify objects to stretch:` prompt, select the rectangle and the base point you added earlier; then, press ↵ to complete your selection.

7. At the `Specify action location [Multiplier/Offset]:` prompt, place the Action icon to the left of the rectangle.

You've just added an action to the Linear parameter you added earlier. Notice that the warning symbol is still showing. You need to add another action to the right side of the parameter, because the parameter expects that you'll want to be able to grip-edit both sides:

1. Repeat the previous set of steps, but instead of clicking the left arrow of the Linear parameter in step 2, click the right arrow.

2. In steps 3 and 4, point to and click the Linear parameter's right arrow.

3. In step 5, place a window selection around the right side of the rectangle; then, at step 6, select the rectangle again.

4. At the `Specify action location:` prompt, place the Action icon to the right of the rectangle.

This time the warning symbol disappears, telling you that you've completed the steps you need for the parameter. You're ready to save the block and try it out:

1. Click the Close Block Editor button on the Block Editor toolbar.

2. At the message asking if you want to save changes to the Sink block, click Yes.

Next, insert the sink to see how it works:

1. Click the Insert Block tool on the Draw toolbar.

2. In the Insert dialog box, enter **Sink** in the Name input box, and then click OK. The sink appears at the cursor.

3. Place the block at the location shown in Figure 17.6.

**FIGURE 17.6**
The Sink block in place

Place the block in this location.

4. Make sure the Dynamic Input display is turned on by clicking the DYN button on the status bar; then, click the newly inserted sink. You see two arrows at the vertical midpoints of the block.

5. Turn on Ortho mode, and click and drag the arrow on the right side of the block. The width of the block follows the arrow as you drag it. You also see the dimension of the sink as you drag the arrow.

6. Enter **3↵**. The width of the block changes to 15 inches from the original 12.

Although you entered a value in step 6 to change the width of the sink, you could have clicked the mouse to visually change the width. The rectangle is still a block. You didn't have to explode it to change its width. If you hover the cursor over the dynamic block grip, you see the block's width dimension.

## Adding an Increment Value

You can grip-edit your dynamic Sink block to modify its width; and as you saw in the last exercise, you can enter a specific value for the width as well. But suppose you'd like to limit grip movement so that the sink only changes in 1-inch increments. Or you might have a dynamic block representing a bolt, and you want the bolt length to increment in $\frac{1}{16}$-inch steps.

You can set parameters to have an increment value so that grip-edits are limited to a specific distance. The following steps show how you can set up the Linear parameter of the Sink block so the sink width can be grip-edited to 1-inch increments:

1. Double-click the Sink block; then, in the Edit Block Definition dialog box, make sure Sink is selected, and click OK.

2. Click the Linear parameter's Distance label, right-click, and choose Properties.

3. In the Properties palette, scroll down to the Value Set group and click the Dist Type listing. The Dist Type option changes to a drop-down list.

4. Expand the list, and select Increment.

5. Click in the Dist Increment input box just below the Dist Type options, and enter **1** for an increment distance of 1 inch.

6. Close the Properties palette, and then click Close Block Editor on the Block Editor toolbar.

7. Save the Sink block.

8. Click the Sink block to expose its grips.

9. Click and drag the right arrow grip to the left. As soon as you click the grip, you see a set of increment marks appear indicating the increment steps for the grip. As you move the grip, the sink width jumps to the increment marks, which are 1 inch apart, as shown in Figure 17.7.

10. Set the width of the sink back to 12 inches.

**TIP** You can set the increment value of a Linear parameter at the time you add it to your block. Click the parameter from the Parameters tab of the Block Authoring palettes; then, before you click a location, enter **V↵**. You see a prompt asking for a distance value. Type **I↵** to use the Increment option, and then enter an increment value. Once you've done this, you're also prompted for a minimum and maximum value.

**FIGURE 17.7**
Grip-editing the Sink
block with the Linear
parameter's incre-
ment value set to 1

The width changes in
1-inch increments.

In addition to an increment distance, you can also set a range of movement for the Linear parameter. You may have noticed the minimum and maximum input boxes in the Properties palette in steps 4 and 5. You can enter values for these settings that define the range of movement allowed for the grip edits.

**TIP**    You can turn on the Cycling option in the Misc group of the Properties palette of any parameter grip. Cycling allows you to use the parameter grip as an insertion point. With this option turned on, you can press the Alt key to cycle between the standard insertion point and the cycle-enabled grip of a parameter while inserting the block.

The sink exercise is a simple demonstration of how you can create and use dynamic blocks. But as you can see from the Block Authoring palettes, you can add many other parameters and actions to a block.

## Editing Parameters and Actions

In the previous exercises, you inserted parameters and actions using the default settings. These settings give you default names and labels for the parameters and actions, but you can always change these settings later. To change the label that appears for a parameter, double-click the label. The label will then appear in a rectangular box, showing you that you can change its text. To edit an action's label, choose Modify ➤ Object ➤ Text ➤ Edit, and then select the action's label. The label will show a gray background, and you can type changes.

If you want to include additional objects for an action, double-click the action. You'll see the prompt

```
Specify first corner of stretch frame or [Cpolygon]:
```

Press ↵ to skip this prompt. You then see the next prompt:

```
Select object to add to action set or [Remove]:
```

You can select additional objects or enter **R**↵ and select objects to remove from the selection set of the action.

---

**SETTING PARAMETER OPTIONS WHILE INSERTING PARAMETERS**

The values discussed in this section—increment, minimum, and maximum—can all be set at the time you insert the Linear parameter. When you first click the parameter in the Block Authoring palettes, you'll see this prompt:

```
Specify start point or
  [Name/Label/Chain/Description/Base/Palette/Value set]:
```

If you enter **V**↵ at this prompt for Value Set, you'll be prompted to select from three options: None, List, or Increment. If you select Increment, you'll be prompted for the increment value and for the minimum and maximum values. You can modify all these options through the Properties palette.

As you may guess from the prompt, you can also enter the name, label, and description of the parameter. The Chain option lets you determine whether to link the action of the parameter so that it affects another parameter. (See the section "Adding Scale and Stretch Actions to a Parameter," later in this chapter.) The Base option lets you select a base point from which the parameter operates. The Palette option determines whether the parameter's label appears in the Properties palette when a block is selected.

---

# Keeping an Object Centered

Now, suppose you want to add a drain to the sink; but to make things a little more complicated, you want to make sure the drain remains centered if the sink is widened or made narrower. You can add a Move action to the existing Linear parameter and then use an option of the Move action to keep the drain centered. Here's how it works.

1. Double-click the Sink block to open the Edit Block Definition dialog box; make sure Sink is selected, and click OK.

2. Add a 3″ diameter circle in the center of the rectangle. This circle will represent the drain.

3. On the Actions tab of the Block Authoring palettes, click Move Action.

4. At the Select parameter: prompt, click the right Linear parameter arrow shown in Figure 17.8.

**FIGURE 17.8**
Adding the Move action to the sink drain

5. At the `Specify parameter point to associate with action or enter [sTart point/ Second point] <Second>:` prompt, click the parameter point on the right arrow, as shown in Figure 17.8.

6. At the `Select objects:` prompt, select the circle and press ↵.

7. At the `Specify action location or [Multiplier/Offset]:` prompt, enter **M**↵ to use the Multiplier option.

8. At the `Enter distance multiplier <1.0000>:` prompt, enter **0.5**↵. This indicates that you want the move to occur at half the rate (0.5) of the Linear parameter motion.

9. At the `Specify action location or [Multiplier/Offset]:` prompt, click the location shown in Figure 17.8.

10. Click the Close Block Editor button, and save the sink block.

Now, try grip-editing the block to see how the Move action affects the sink drain:

1. Click the sink to select it.

2. Click and drag the right arrow grip to the right. The drain stays centered in the sink.

You could have entered any value for the multiplier in step 8 of the previous exercise to alter the degree of motion that the sink drain would follow. For example, if you entered **2**, the drain would move twice the distance of the grip motion.

## Adding Scale and Stretch Actions to a Parameter

In the sink example, you added two Stretch actions to a Linear parameter. This enabled the block to be stretched in both the left and right directions. But you aren't restricted to assigning one type of action to a parameter. In the next section, you'll turn a simple door block into a dynamic block. In the process, you'll learn how to add two different actions to a single Linear parameter.

At first, you may think that changing the scale of a door would be all you need for editing a door. But when you scale the door, all its features, including the door width, are scaled proportionally. You only want to stretch the door width and scale the door swing, leaving the door thickness at the same dimension. This can be accomplished by adding a Linear parameter with a Scale action and a Stretch action.

Start by opening the door block in the Block Editor and adding the Linear parameter:

1. Click the Block Editor tool on the Standard toolbar.

2. In the Edit Block Definition dialog box, select DOOR, and then click OK.

3. Click the Linear Parameter tool on the Parameters tab of the Block Authoring palettes, and then click the endpoints of the door block, as shown in Figure 17.9, starting with the hinge side. The order of selection is important as you'll see a bit later. Use the Endpoint osnaps to select the exact endpoints of the door.

4. Place the parameter label as shown in Figure 17.9.

**FIGURE 17.9**
Placing the Linear
parameter for the
Door block

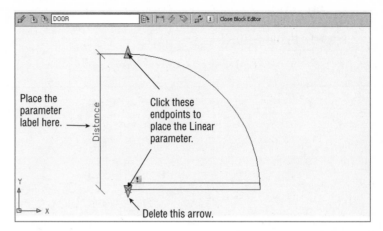

Most likely, you'll only need to scale the door based on the door opening, which is represented by the location and orientation of the Linear parameter you just added. In addition, you'll probably only stretch the door from the end of the door swing arc, so you can remove the parameter arrow from the hinge side of the door:

1. Click the blue arrow on the hinge side of the door, as shown in Figure 17.9.

2. Press the Delete key to delete the arrow. You now have only one end of the parameter that needs an action. Earlier, when you placed the Linear parameter, you selected the hinge side first. This allows you to delete a single arrow. If you attempt to delete the arrow on the opening side of the door, both arrows are deleted.

Just as with the sink, you have a Linear parameter for the door that describes the direction of the grip edit. Now, you need to add the actions associated with the parameter. You'll add the Stretch action first. You used the Stretch action before for the sink, but this time, you'll need to modify the way the Stretch action works.

First, you'll add the action, and then you'll make a change to the action to better suit the Door block:

1. Click the Actions tab in the Block Authoring palettes, and select Stretch Action.

2. At the `Select parameter:` prompt, click the blue parameter arrow at the end of the arc.

3. At the `Specify parameter point to associate with action or enter [sTart point/ Second point] <Second>:` prompt, click the red marker on the same arrow.

4. At the `Specify first corner of stretch frame or [CPolygon]:` prompt, place a window selection around the right end of the door, as shown in Figure 17.10.

5. At the `Specify objects to stretch:` prompt, select the lines that represent the length of the door and the door edge, as shown in Figure 17.11. These are the parts of the door that you want to stretch.

6. At the `Specify action location or [Multiplier/Offset]:` prompt, type **O**↵. This lets you specify an angle for the Stretch action.

7. At the `Enter angle offset <0>:` prompt, enter **–90**↵.

8. At the `Specify action location or [Multiplier/Offset]:` prompt, click a location near the parameter arrow to place the action icon.

**FIGURE 17.10**
Selecting the
parameter and the
stretch frame

**FIGURE 17.11**
Selecting the lines of
the door

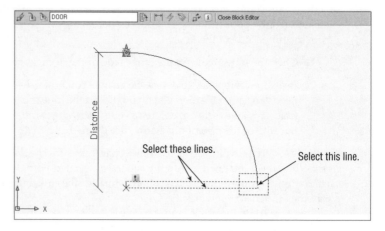

Normally, you'd want the Stretch action to move in the same direction as the arrow in the Linear parameter. But in this case, you want the door to stretch in a direction that is –90° from Linear parameter. Figure 17.12 shows how the Stretch action needs to work. The Offset option you used in steps 6 and 7 allows you to do just that. By using the Offset option, you told AutoCAD that the Stretch action should work in a direction that is –90° from the direction of the grip-edit motion. This will become clearer once you've used the door block's grip to change its size.

In addition to stretching the door, you'll want to scale the door arc in size as the door width is grip-edited. For this, you need to add a Scale action:

1. Click Scale Action on the Actions tab of the Block Authoring palettes.

2. At the `Select parameter:` prompt, click the blue arrow of the Linear parameter, the same arrow you selected for the scale parameter earlier.

3. At the

   ```
   Specify selection set for action
   Select objects:
   ```

   prompt, select the arc. Press ↵ to finish your selection.

**FIGURE 17.12**

The Stretch action works in a negative 90° direction to the grip movement direction.

Pull the grip in this direction…

…minus 90°.

The stretch frame is pulled in this direction.

**4.** At the `Specify action location or [Base type]:` prompt, click a location near the midpoint of the arc to place the action icon.

**5.** Click the Close Block Editor tool on the Block Editor toolbar, and save the door block.

Now, you're ready to try the new Door block:

**1.** Pan your view so you can see the entry door clearly, as shown in Figure 17.13.

**FIGURE 17.13**

The Door block with its grips exposed

**2.** Click the door to select it. The added Linear parameter arrow appears as a grip on the right end of the Door block.

**3.** Click the arrow grip. The length dimension becomes available for your input; and as you move the mouse, the door changes in size. Note that the thickness of the door doesn't change as you alter its width.

**4.** Enter **24↵** to change the door width to 24″.

Notice that although you were able to enter a door dimension directly to the block, you didn't change the door thickness when the door size changed. Only the door swing and width changed to accommodate the new door size.

## Adding More Than One Parameter for Multiple Grip Functions

In addition to adding more than one action to a parameter, you can add multiple parameters to a block. In the door example, you added only the single Linear parameter. Suppose you'd also like a quick way to mirror, or *flip*, the door so it changes from a left-hand door to a right-hand door and vice versa.

### Including a Mirror Capability

In the next exercise, you'll add the Flip parameter to the door, which does exactly that: It enables you to mirror the door at the click of a mouse. Follow these steps:

1. Click the Block Editor tool on the Standard toolbar.

2. In the Edit Block Definition dialog box, select DOOR, and then click OK.

3. In the Block Authoring palettes, select the Parameters tab, and then select Flip Parameter.

4. At the Specify base point of reflection line or [Name/Label/Description/Palette]: prompt, use the Midpoint osnap, and select the midpoint of the door, as shown in Figure 17.14.

**FIGURE 17.14**
Adding a Flip parameter

5. At the Specify endpoint of reflection line: prompt, use the Endpoint osnap, and select the lower-right corner of the door, as shown in Figure 17.14.

6. At the Specify label location: prompt, place the label as shown in Figure 17.14.

As you did with the Linear parameter, you need to assign an action to the newly placed parameter. In this case, you'll add the Flip action:

1. In the Block Authoring palettes, select the Actions tab, and select Flip Action.

2. At the Select parameter: prompt, click the blue arrow of the Flip parameter, as shown in Figure 17.15.

**FIGURE 17.15**
Adding the Flip action

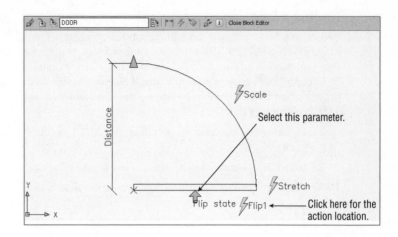

3. At the `Select objects:` prompt, select the entire block, including all the parameters and actions. Press ↵ when you've selected everything.

4. At the `Specify action location:` prompt, place the action icon as shown in Figure 17.15.

The Flip parameter and action are complete. Now, you can try to use them:

1. Click the Save Block Definition tool in the Block Editor. A warning message appears, telling you that changes to blocks containing parameters may not be obvious. Click Yes, and then click the Close Block Editor tool.

2. Click the entry door.

3. Click the arrow pointing to the door, as shown in Figure 17.16. The door mirrors to point toward the bathroom.

4. Click the arrow again to return the door to its original position

**FIGURE 17.16**
Click the arrow grip to
flip the door.

## Adding a Selectable List

Earlier, you saw how you can add an increment value set to make a dynamic block stay in a set range of sizes. You can also set up a dynamic block to offer a range of sizes in a pop-up list. To do this, you need to employ two parameters: the Visibility parameter and the Lookup parameter.

In the following exercise, you'll add these parameters to the Door block to allow the door size to be selected from a list. Start by adding the List parameter, which offers a way to define and name a set of parameter criteria:

1. Double-click the door to open the Edit Block Definition dialog box, select DOOR, and then click OK.

2. In the Block Authoring palettes, select Lookup Parameter from the Parameters tab.

3. Place the Lookup parameter in the location shown in Figure 17.17.

**FIGURE 17.17**

Adding the Lookup parameter and action

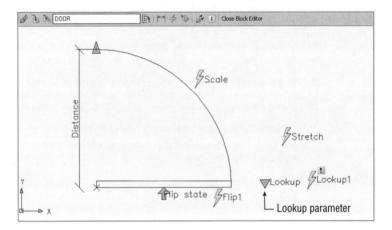

4. On the Actions tab, select Lookup Action.

5. At the `Select parameter` prompt, select the Lookup Parameter arrow that you just added in step 3.

6. At the `Specify location` prompt, place the Lookup action in the location shown in Figure 17.17. The Property Lookup Table dialog box opens.

7. You'll need to make some changes to this dialog box, but for now, click OK to close it.

The Lookup action in the drawing shows the exclamation-point icon telling you that you need to make some changes before the action is complete. If you hover over the icon, you see a message that says Empty Lookup Table. In the next set of steps, you'll start to add items to the Property Lookup Table dialog box to make the action functional:

1. Double-click the warning exclamation on the Lookup action to open the Property Lookup Table dialog box.

2. Click the Add Properties button at the top of the dialog box to open the Add Parameter Properties dialog box.

3. Select Linear, and then click OK. The Distance column appears.

4. In the first input box, just below the Distance column heading, enter **24**, and then press the Tab key. The cursor advances to the next input box under the Distance column.

5. Enter **36**.

6. Click the input box just under the Lookup column, and then enter **24″ wide door.↵**. Once you press ↵, the cursor advances to the next input box below the one you just edited.

7. Enter **36″ wide door.↵**.

You've added the Linear parameter to the property lookup table. You need to make one last setting change in order for the whole thing to work:

**1.** Click the Read Only item at the bottom of the Lookup column, and select Allow Reverse Lookup.

**2.** Click OK. The warning message is gone, telling you that you've completed the Lookup action.

**3.** Click the Close Block Editor button on the Block Editor toolbar, and save the Door block.

Now you can select from two door sizes in a pop-up list:

**1.** Click the door to select it.

**2.** Click the downward-pointing grip closest to the door, as shown at the left side of Figure 17.18.

**3.** Select 36″ Door from the list that appears. The door changes to a 36″-wide door. (See the view to the right in Figure 17.18.)

**FIGURE 17.18**
Selecting a door size from a list

Click this grip.

Select a door size from the pop-up list.

## Including Block Information with Data Extraction

In Chapter 13, you learned how you can attach data to blocks through attributes and then extract that data to spreadsheets or AutoCAD tables. You can also include dynamic block information that has been included in a property lookup table. This can be extremely useful for generating data for a bill of material or in other situations if you need to track the numbers and types of items in your drawing.

To see how this works, you'll continue to edit the Door block to include the flip state of the door. You can then use the flip state to determine if the door is a left- or right-hand door. You can extract this information as part of the attribute-extraction process.

First, you'll add the flip state to the property lookup table. By adding the flip state, you can track whether doors are left- or right-handed:

1. Double-click the door to open the Edit Block Definition dialog box, select DOOR, and click OK.

2. In the Block Editor, double-click the Lookup action to open the Property Lookup Table dialog box.

3. Click the Add Properties button to open the Add Parameter Properties dialog box.

4. Select Flip, and click OK.

5. Back in the Property Lookup Table dialog box, you see the Flip State column added in the Input Properties list. Double-click the top input box, just below the Flip State column, and select Not Flipped from the drop-down list. Not Flipped is now a property that is included for a 24″-wide door.

6. In the top input box of the Lookup column, add the text **RH** (for right-hand) so that it reads *24″ wide door RH* (see Figure 17.19).

**FIGURE 17.19**

Adding items to the Property Lookup Table dialog box

7. Repeat steps 5 and 6 for the 36″ door input box, but change the lookup text to read *36″ wide door RH* (see Figure 17.19).

8. Add two more rows as shown in Figure 17.19 to include the flipped condition for each door size. Note that the Lookup column includes the text *LH* for left-hand for the flipped state.

9. At the bottom of the Lookup column, make sure Allow Reverse Lookup is selected, and then click OK.

10. Click Close Block Editor on the Block Editor toolbar, and save the Door block.

You've added a property to the Property Lookup Table dialog box. Now, let's see how this has affected the block:

**1.** Copy the entry door upward so it appears above the existing door. You may need to pan your view to make room for the copy. This gives you an additional door to experiment with.

**2.** Click the copy of the door to select it.

**3.** Click the downward-pointing grip closest to the door, as shown in Figure 17.20.

**FIGURE 17.20**
Click the lookup grip, and select 24″ Wide Door LH from the list.

Click this grip.

Select an option from the pop-up menu.

**4.** Select 24″ Wide Door LH from the list that appears. The door changes to a 24″-wide door that is flipped.

Next, you'll use the Attribute Extraction command to see how the data you added appears as an exported table or a spreadsheet:

**1.** Choose Tools ➢ Data Extraction to start the Attribute Extraction Wizard.

**2.** On the Begin screen, click Next.

**3.** In the Save Data Extraction As dialog box, enter **Test** for the name, and Save.

**4.** On the Define Data Source screen, click Next.

**5.** On the Select Objects screen, remove the check mark from all but DOOR in the left column, and then click Next.

**6.** On the Select Properties screen, remove the check mark from all but the Dynamic Block option in the right column, and make sure the Distance and Lookup options in the left column are the only ones selected (see Figure 17.21).

**7.** Click Next. On the Refine Data page, you see the data that will be exported to a spreadsheet file or table (see Figure 17.22).

**8.** You don't really want to extract this data, so once you've taken a good look at this screen, click Cancel.

This is the end of the door example, so you can exit this file. Save it for future reference if you like.

**FIGURE 17.21**
Set up the Select Properties screen to look like this.

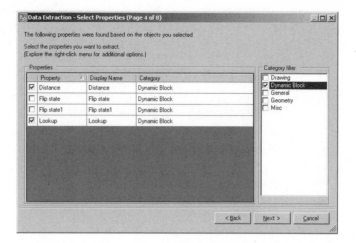

**FIGURE 17.22**
The resulting table to be extracted, as shown on the Refine Data screen of the Attribute Extraction Wizard

Notice that Figure 17.22 shows the two doors: one 24″ wide LH and one 36″ wide RH. If you had more doors, they would also appear on this screen. You can edit the bathroom block to gain access to its door, and it will also show the lookup data.

**WARNING**    If you use the Mirror command to mirror a block that contains a Flip action in a property lookup table, the Attribute Extraction command still reports the nonmirrored flip state of the door. Therefore, be sure that if you set up a block with parameters and actions, you use those actions to edit the door, and don't rely on standard editing tools. That way, you'll ensure the accuracy of your extracted data.

## Creating Multiple Shapes in One Block

Depending on circumstances, you may need a block to display a completely different form. For example, you might want a single generic bath that can morph into a standard bath, a corner bath, or a large spa-style bath with jets.

Using dynamic blocks, you can hide or display elements of a block by selecting a *visibility state* from a list. For example, you can draw the three different bath sizes and then set up a visibility state for each size. Each visibility state displays only one bath size at a time. You can then select a visibility state depending on the bath size you want.

Try the following exercise to see how this works first hand:

1. Open the `visibilitysample.dwg` file, and then click the Block Editor tool on the Standard toolbar.

2. In the Edit Block Definition dialog box, select Bathtub from the list, and click OK. Click No if you're asked if you want to see how dynamic blocks are made.

   You see the contents of the Bathtub block. It's just the three existing blocks—Standard, Jetted, and Corner—inserted at the same origin.

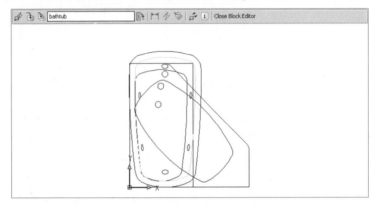

If you were to insert this block in a drawing, it would appear just as you currently see it with each bathtub type overlaid on another. Next, you'll see how you can add control over the visibility of each bathtub type so that only one is displayed at a time.

The first thing you need to do is add a Visibility parameter:

1. On the Parameters tab of the Block Authoring palettes, click Visibility Parameter.

2. Click below the blocks to place the Visibility parameter as shown in Figure 17.23.

**FIGURE 17.23**
Adding the Visibility parameter

3. Double-click the Visibility parameter you just added to open the Visibility States dialog box. One visibility state, VisibilityState0, is already provided.

You'll need three visibility states: one for each type of bathtub whose visibility you want to control. You've already got one, but you want a name that is more appropriate to the application:

1. Click the Rename button. The existing visibility state in the list to the left becomes editable.

2. Enter **Standard.⏎**. This is the visibility state for your standard bathtub.

3. Click the New button to open the New Visibility State dialog box.

4. Enter **Jetted** in the Visibility State Name input box.

5. Make sure the Leave Visibility Of Existing Objects Unchanged In New State radio button is selected, and then click OK.

6. Click the New button again.

7. In the New Visibility State dialog box, enter **Corner** in the Visibility State Name input box.

8. Make sure Leave Visibility Of Existing Objects Unchanged In New State is selected, and click OK.

You've just created all the visibility states you need.

9. Select Standard from the list, and click the Set Current button. (You can also double-click the Standard item.) A check mark appears to the left of Standard, showing you that it's now the current state.

10. Click OK to exit the Visibility States dialog box.

You have the visibility states you need, and you have the objects whose visibility you want to control. Now you need to determine which block is visible for each state.

Remember that in step 9 of the previous exercise, you made Standard the current visibility state. You'll want only the standard Bathtub block visible for this state. Do the following to turn off the other two Bathtub blocks for the current state:

**1.** Select the Jetted and Corner blocks (see Figure 17.24).

**FIGURE 17.24**

Locating the blocks

**2.** Right-click, and choose Object Visibility ➤ Hide For Current State. You can also click the Make Invisible tool on the right side of the Block Editor toolbar.

The selected blocks disappear. They didn't go anywhere; they were just made invisible.

**3.** Click the drop-down list at far right on the Block Editor toolbar, and select Jetted. The hidden blocks appear.

The current visibility state is now Jetted, so you want only the Jetted block to be visible. Select the Standard and Corner blocks, and then click the Make Invisible tool. You can also right-click and then choose Object Visibility ➤ Hide For Current State. Now, only the Jetted block is visible.

**4.** On the Block Editor toolbar, click the drop-down list again, and select Corner. All the blocks appear.

**5.** Select the Standard and Jetted blocks, and click the Make Invisible tool. Now, only the Corner block is visible.

You've created visibility states and set up the blocks so they appear only when the appropriate visibility state is current. Next, you'll test the blocks:

**1.** Click Close Block Editor, and save the changes you've made.

**2.** Click the Insert Block tool on the Draw toolbar. In the Insert dialog box, select Bathtub from the Name drop-down list.

**3.** In the Insertion Point group, make sure Specify On Screen is checked, click OK, and then place the block to the right of the other three blocks.

**4.** Click the Bathtub block you just inserted, and then click the Visibility grip (see Figure 17.25).

**Figure 17.25**

Using the Visibility
grip to change the
bathtub

5. Select Jetted from the list. The Jetted bathtub appears.

6. Click the Bathtub block again, click the Visibility grip, and select Corner. The Corner tub appears.

**TIP**   You can set up AutoCAD to display objects whose visibility has been turned off while editing them in the Block Editor. If you set the bvmode system variable to 1, objects appear gray when their visibility has been turned off.

In this example, you used a set of bathtubs, but you can use the Visibility parameter for anything that requires a different appearance. AutoCAD comes with an example of a weldment symbol that can be changed using visibility states. As mentioned at the beginning of this chapter, another use might be a block of a bed that contains a double-, queen-, and king-sized bed.

You can also combine the Visibility parameter with the property lookup table to produce preset variations of each type of bathtub. The possibilities are limited only by your imagination.

## Rotating Objects in Unison

You've seen how actions and parameters can control the behavior of a single object in a block. You can also apply actions to multiple objects so they move or change in unison. The following example shows how you can apply more than one Rotate action to a single Rotation parameter to control two objects:

1. Open the gatesample.dwg file.

2. Double-click the object in the drawing to open the Edit Block Definition dialog box, and then click OK. The Gate block opens for editing.

3. In the Block Authoring palettes, select Rotation Parameter from the Parameters tab.

4. At the Specify base point or [Name/Label/Chain/Description/Palette/Value set]: prompt, use the Center osnap, and select the center of the arc, as shown in Figure 17.26.

5. At the Specify radius of parameter: prompt, click a point to the right of the center, as shown in Figure 17.26. You don't have to be exact about the radius dimension as long as it's directly to the right of the center.

6. At the Specify default rotation angle or [Base angle] <0>: prompt, press ↵ to accept the default of 0° for the rotation angle.

**FIGURE 17.26**
Adding the Rotation
parameter to the
gatesample.dwg
drawing

You have the Rotation parameter. Now, you need to add an action. You'll add an action for each of the two gate objects in the drawing:

1. On the Actions tab of the Block Authoring palettes, click Rotate Action.

2. At the Select parameter: prompt, click the blue dot of the Rotate parameter, as shown in Figure 17.27.

**FIGURE 17.27**
Setting up the
Rotate action

3. At the Select objects: prompt, select the gate on the left, as shown in Figure 17.27, and then press ↵.

4. At the Specify action location or [Base type]: prompt, click below the block you selected in step 3.

You have enough now to rotate the block to the left with a rotation grip. Add another Rotate action to rotate the block to the right in unison with the one on the left:

1. On the Actions tab of the Block Authoring palettes, click Rotate Action.

2. At the Select parameter: prompt, click the same blue dot of the Rotate parameter that you selected for the first Rotate action (see Figure 17.28).

**FIGURE 17.28**
Adding the second
Rotate action

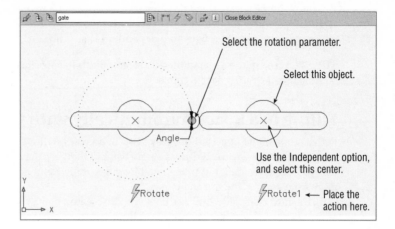

3. At the Select objects: prompt, select the gate on the right.

4. At the Specify action location or [Base type]: prompt, type **B↵** for the Base type option.

5. At the Enter base point type [Dependent/Independent] <Dependent>: prompt, enter **I↵** for the Independent option.

6. At the Specify base point location <xx.xxxx,yy.yyyy>: prompt, click the center of the block to the right, as shown in Figure 17.28.

7. At the Specify action location or [Base type]: prompt, click below the block to the right to place the action icon.

Now, you're ready to save the block and try it out:

1. Click the Close Block Editor button on the Block Editor toolbar, and save the block.

2. Click the block to expose its grips.

3. Click and drag the blue dot grip downward. Both sides of the block rotate about their own centers (see Figure 17.29).

**FIGURE 17.29**
The two parts rotate
independently
because the action for
the right side uses the
Independent base type.

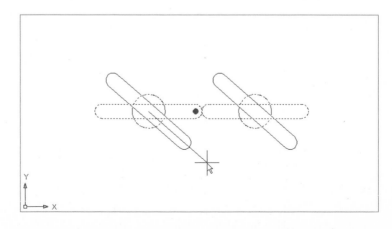

This example shows that you can specify a different base point for an action. You saw that you can use the same parameter for two different actions; one action uses the base point of the original parameter, and the other uses an independent base point.

**TIP**   You can set up a dynamic block to rotate objects in opposite directions using a lookup action similar to the earlier door example.

## Filling in a Space Automatically with Objects

Perhaps one of the more tedious tasks you'll face is drawing the vertical bars of a hand railing for an elevation view. You can draw a single bar and then use the Array command to repeat the bar as many times as needed; but when you have to edit the railing, you may find that you're spending more time adding and erasing bars.

In the next example, you'll see how you can create a block that automatically fills in vertical bars as the width of the railing changes. You'll start with an existing drawing of a single vertical bar and an outline of the railing opening around the bar:

1. Open the `railsample.dwg` file.

2. Double-click the object in the drawing to open the Edit Block Definition dialog box, and then click OK. This opens the Railvertical block for editing.

   When the Block Editor opens, notice that the block already has a Linear parameter and a Stretch action added. Recall from the sink example at the beginning of this chapter that the Linear parameter and Stretch action let you vary the width of an object. In this case, the outermost rectangle is being stretched.

3. On the Actions tab of the Block Authoring palettes, click Array Action.

4. At the `Select parameter:` prompt, click the blue arrow for the Linear parameter, as shown in Figure 17.30.

5. At the `Select objects:` prompt, select the dark vertical rectangle representing the vertical bar of the railing, as shown in Figure 17.30, and then press ↵.

**FIGURE 17.30**
Adding the Array action to the Railvertical block

6. At the `Enter the distance between columns (|||):` prompt, enter **4.**↵.

7. At the `Specify action location:` prompt, make sure Ortho mode is turned off, and place the action next to the arrow, as shown in Figure 17.30.

8. Click the Close Block Editor button on the Block Editor toolbar, and save the block.

9. Click the block to expose its grips.

10. Click and drag the blue arrow grip to the right. As the rail expands, additional vertical bars are added at 4″ intervals (see Figure 17.31).

**FIGURE 17.31**
The Railvertical block adds vertical bars as its width expands.

You can now use this block wherever you need to draw a simple railing with vertical bars. Another example of how the Array action might be used is in a side view of a bolt. You could show the threads of the bolt and use the Array action to increase the number of threads as the bolt was lengthened.

---

**USING PARAMETER SETS**

You probably noticed the Parameter Sets tab in the Block Authoring palettes. The options in this tab are predefined combinations of parameters and actions that are commonly used together. For example, the Polar Array set inserts a Polar parameter with an Array action. You only need to supply the object. The Polar Array set causes the associated object to rotate about a center point with a grip. You can also array the object by stretching the grip away from the rotation center.

To associate an object with a parameter set, double-click the action included in the set, and then select an object. If a stretch is employed, select the parameter point, and then select a stretch frame and an object to stretch.

---

## The Bottom Line

**Exploring the Block Editor**  To create dynamic blocks, you need to become familiar with the Block Editor. You can use the Block Editor to modify existing block in your drawing.

**Master It**  What does the Edit Block Definition dialog box allow you to do?

**Solution**  The Edit Block Definition dialog box lets you select the block you want to edit from a list of blocks in the drawing.

**Creating a Dynamic Block**   Dynamic blocks allow you to add grips to a block that let you modify the block in a number of different ways.

**Master It**   Name the two main features of the Block Editor that let you add additional grip-editing functions to a block.

**Solution**   Parameters and actions.

**Adding Scale and Stretch Actions to a Parameter**   You can set up a dynamic block to perform multiple operations with a single grip.

**Master It**   What do you need to do to have one grip perform two functions?

**Solution**   Use a single parameter to control two actions.

**Adding More Than One Parameter for Multiple Grip Functions**   In addition to having one grip perform multiple operations, you can add as many grips as you need to make your block even more customizable.

**Master It**   What parameter do you use to set up a list of options for a block?

**Solution**   The Lookup parameter.

**Creating Multiple Shapes in One Block**   Many of the dynamic-block functions let you adjust the shape of the original block. Another feature lets you choose completely different shapes for the block.

**Master It**   When a block uses the Visibility parameter to set up different shapes, how do you select a different block shape in the drawing?

**Solution**   Click the block, and then click the Visibility grip. A list appears, showing the different shapes that are available.

**Rotating Objects in Unison**   Blocks can be set up so the action of one set of objects affects another set. This chapter gives the example of rotating objects in unison.

**Master It**   How many parameters were needed in the example of rotating objects in unison?

**Solution**   One.

**Filling in a Space Automatically with Objects**   A dynamic block can help you automate the addition of repetitive elements to your drawing.

**Master It**   What is the name of the action used to produce an array of an object in a block when the block is stretched?

**Solution**   The Array action.

# Chapter 18

# Drawing Curves

So far in this book, you've been using basic lines, arcs, and circles to create your drawings. Now it's time to add polylines and spline curves to your repertoire. Polylines offer many options for creating forms, including solid fills and free-form curved lines. Spline curves are perfect for drawing accurate, smooth, nonlinear objects.

Topics in this chapter include the following:

◆ Creating and Editing Polylines

◆ Creating a Polyline Spline Curve

◆ Using True Spline Curves

◆ Marking Divisions on Curves

## Introducing Polylines

*Polylines* are like composite line segments and arcs. A polyline may look like a series of line segments, but it acts like a single object. This characteristic makes polylines useful for a variety of applications, as you'll see in the upcoming exercises.

### Drawing a Polyline

First, to introduce you to the polyline, you'll begin a drawing of the top view of the joint shown in Figure 18.1.

**FIGURE 18.1**
A sketch of a
metal joint

Follow these steps to draw the joint:

1. Open a new file, and save it as Joint2d. Don't bother to make special setting changes, because you'll create this drawing with the default settings.

2. Set the limits to 0,0 for the lower-left corner and 12,9 for the upper-right corner, and then choose View ➤ Zoom ➤ All or type Z↵A↵.

3. Click the Polyline tool on the Draw toolbar, or type Pl↵.

4. At the Specify start point: prompt, enter a point at coordinate 3,3 to start your polyline.

5. At the Specify next point or [Arc/Halfwidth/Length/Undo/Width]: prompt, enter @3<0↵ to draw a horizontal line of the joint.

**TIP** You can draw polylines just as you do with the Line command. Or you can use the other Pline options to enter a polyline arc, specify the polyline thickness, or add a polyline segment in the same direction as the previously drawn line.

6. At the Specify next point or [Arc/Close/Halfwidth/Length/Undo/Width]: prompt, enter A↵ to continue your polyline with an arc.

**NOTE** The Arc option enables you to draw an arc that starts from the last point you selected and then select additional options. Select the Arc option; as you move your cursor, an arc follows it in a tangential direction from the first line segment you drew. You can return to drawing line segments by entering L↵.

7. At the prompt

    Specify endpoint of arc or
    [Angle/CEnter/CLose/Direction/Halfwidth/Line/Radius/Second pt/Undo/Width]:

    enter @4<90↵ to draw a 180° arc from the last point you entered. Your drawing should now look similar to Figure 18.2.

**FIGURE 18.2**
A polyline line and arc

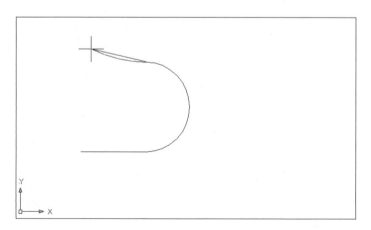

8. To continue the polyline with another line segment, enter **L**↵.

9. At the Specify next point or [Arc/Close/Halfwidth/Length/Undo/Width]: prompt, enter **@3<180**↵. Another line segment continues from the end of the arc.

10. Press ↵ to exit Pline.

You now have a sideways, U-shaped polyline that you'll use in the next exercise to complete the top view of your joint.

## Setting Polyline Options

Let's take a break from the tutorial to look at some of the options in the Polyline prompt that you didn't use:

**Close**   Draws a line segment from the last endpoint of a sequence of lines to the first point picked in that sequence. This works exactly like the Close option for the Line command.

**Length**   Enables you to specify the length of a line that will be drawn at the same angle as the last line entered.

**Halfwidth**   Creates a tapered line segment or an arc by specifying half its beginning and ending widths (see Figure 18.3).

**FIGURE 18.3**
A tapered line segment and an arc created with Halfwidth

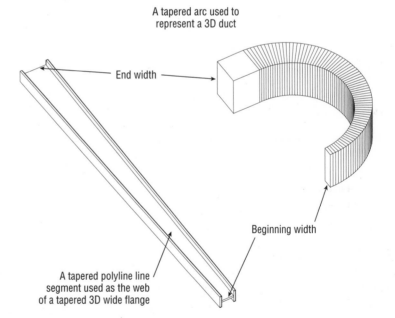

A tapered arc used to represent a 3D duct

End width

Beginning width

A tapered polyline line segment used as the web of a tapered 3D wide flange

**Width**   Creates a tapered line segment or an arc by specifying the full width of the segment's beginning and ending points.

**Undo**   Deletes the last line segment drawn.

If you want to break a polyline into simple lines and arcs, you can use the Explode option on the Modify toolbar, just as you would with blocks. After a polyline is exploded, it becomes a set of individual line segments or arcs.

To turn off the filling of solid polylines, open the Options dialog box and click the Display tab. Clear the Apply Solid Fill check box in the Display Performance group.

**NOTE**   You can use the Fillet tool on the Modify toolbar to fillet all the vertices of a polyline composed of straight-line segments. Click Fillet, set your fillet radius, type **P**↵ to select the Polyline option, and then pick the polyline you want to fillet.

## Editing Polylines

You can edit polylines with many of the standard editing commands. To change the properties of a polyline, double-click the polyline to open the Properties palette. You can use the Stretch command on the Modify toolbar to move vertices of a polyline; the Trim, Extend, and Break commands on the Modify toolbar also work with polylines.

In addition, many editing capabilities are offered only for polylines. For instance, later in this section you'll see how to smooth out a polyline by using the Fit option in the Pedit command.

In this exercise, you'll use the Offset command on the Modify toolbar to add the inside portion of the joint:

1.  Click the Offset tool in the Modify toolbar, or type **O**↵.

2.  At the Specify offset distance or [Through/Erase/Layer] <THROUGH>: prompt, enter **1**.

3.  At the Select object to offset or [Exit/Undo]<exit>: prompt, pick the U-shaped polyline you just drew.

4.  At the Specify point on side to offset or [Exit/Multiple/Undo] <Exit>: prompt, pick a point toward the inside of the U. A concentric copy of the polyline appears (see Figure 18.4).

5.  Press ↵ to exit the Offset command.

The concentric copy of a polyline made by choosing Modify ➢ Offset can be useful when you need to draw complex parallel curves like the ones in Figure 18.5.

Next, complete the top view of the joint:

1.  Connect the ends of the polylines with two short line segments (see Figure 18.6).

**FIGURE 18.4**
The offset polyline

**FIGURE 18.5**

Sample complex
curves drawn by using
offset polylines

The outside profile was
drawn first; then the Offset
command was used to draw
the inside profile.

120°

2.7500

1.1250

←—1.6250—→

←——————— 4.7500 ———————→

**FIGURE 18.6**

The drawing polyline

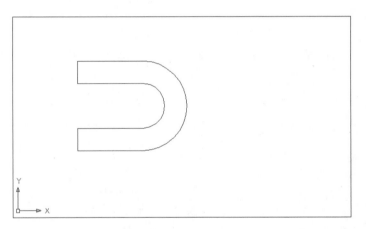

**NOTE**   If the objects to be joined don't touch, you can use the *fuzz* join feature. Type **Pe↵M↵** to
start the Pedit command with the Multiple option; then, select all the objects you want to join. If
you see a convert message, enter **Y↵**. At the `Enter fuzz distance or [Jointype]:` prompt,
enter a distance that approximates the size of the gap between objects. By default, AutoCAD
extends the lines so they join end to end. You can use the Jointype option if you want Pedit to join
segments with an additional segment.

**2.**  Choose Modify ➢ Object ➢ Polyline, type **Pe↵**, or choose Edit Polyline from the Modify II
toolbar.

**3.**  At the `Select polyline or [Multiple]:` prompt, pick the outermost polyline.

**4.**  At the prompt

`Enter an option [Close/Join/Width/Edit vertex/Fit/Spline/Decurve/Ltypegen/Undo]:`

enter **J↵** for the Join option.

5. At the `Select objects:` prompt, select all the objects you've drawn so far.

6. Press ↵ to join all the objects into one polyline. It appears that nothing has happened, although you see the message `5 segments added to polyline` in the Command window.

7. Press ↵ again to exit the Pedit command.

8. Click the drawing to expose its grips. The entire object is highlighted, indicating that all the lines have been joined into a single polyline.

By using the Width option under Edit Polyline, you can change the thickness of a polyline. Let's change the width of your polyline, to give some thickness to the outline of the joint:

1. Type **Pe**↵, or click the Edit Polyline tool on the Modify II toolbar.

2. Click the polyline.

3. At the `Enter an option [Open/Join/Width/Edit vertex/Fit/Spline/Decurve/ Ltypegen/Undo]:` prompt, enter **W**↵ for the Width option.

4. At the `Specify new width for all segments:` prompt, enter **.03**↵ for the new width of the polyline. The line changes to the new width (see Figure 18.7), and you now have a top view of your joint.

**FIGURE 18.7**
The polyline with a new thickness

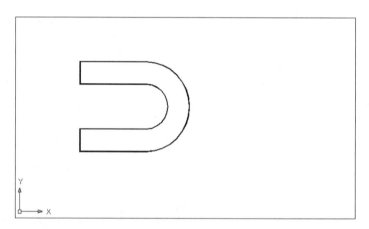

5. Press ↵ to exit the Pedit command.

6. Save this file.

## Setting Pedit Options

Here's a brief look at a few of the Pedit options you didn't try firsthand:

**Close** Connects the two endpoints of a polyline with a line segment. If the polyline you selected to be edited is already closed, this option changes to Open.

**Open** Removes the last segment added to a closed polyline.

**Spline/Decurve** Smoothes a polyline into a spline curve (discussed in detail later in this chapter).

**Edit Vertex** Lets you edit each vertex of a polyline individually (discussed in detail later in this section).

**Fit**   Turns polyline segments into a series of arcs.

**Ltype Gen**   Controls the way noncontinuous linetypes pass through the vertices of a polyline. If you have a fitted or spline curve with a noncontinuous linetype, turn on this option.

**TIP**   You can change the thickness of regular lines and arcs by using Pedit to change them into polylines and then using the Width option to change their width.

## Smoothing Polylines

You can create a curve in AutoCAD in many ways. If you don't need the representation of a curve to be accurate, you can use a polyline curve. In the following exercise, you'll draw a polyline curve to represent a contour on a topographical map:

1. Open the topo.dwg drawing. The first image in Figure 18.8 contains the drawing of survey data. Some of the contours have already been drawn in between the data points.

2. Zoom in to the upper-right corner of the drawing, so your screen displays the area shown in the second image in Figure 18.8.

**FIGURE 18.8**
The topo.dwg drawing shows survey data portrayed in an AutoCAD drawing. Notice the dots indicating where elevations were taken. The actual elevation value is shown with a diagonal line from the point.

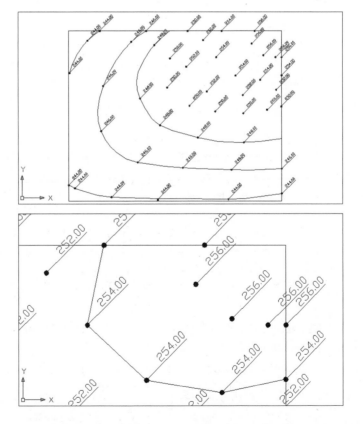

**3.** Click the Polyline tool on the Draw toolbar. Using the Center osnap, draw a polyline that connects the points labeled 254.00. Your drawing should look like the second image in Figure 18.8.

**4.** Press ↵.

**NOTE** If Running Osnaps aren't set, you can choose Tools ➤ Drafting Settings or type **Os.**↵ to open the Drafting Settings dialog box. From there, select the Object Snap tab, and turn on the Center option. See Chapter 3 for more on this dialog box.

**5.** Next, you'll convert the polyline you just drew into a smooth contour line. Choose Modify ➤ Object ➤ Polyline, or type **Pe.**↵.

**6.** At the `Select polyline or [Multiple]:` prompt, pick the contour line you just drew.

**7.** At the prompt

`Enter an option [close/Join/Width/Edit vertex/Fit/Spline/Decurve/Ltype gen/Undo]:`

type **F**↵ to select the Fit option. The polyline smooths out into a series of connected arcs that pass through the data points.

**8.** Press ↵ to end the Pedit command.

Your contour is now complete. The Fit option under the Pedit command causes AutoCAD to convert the straight-line segments of the polyline into arcs. The endpoints of the arcs pass through the endpoints of the line segments, and the curve of each arc depends on the direction of the adjacent arc. This gives the effect of a smooth curve. Next, you'll use this polyline curve to experiment with some of the editing options unique to the Pedit command.

---

**TURNING OBJECTS INTO POLYLINES AND POLYLINES INTO SPLINES**

At times, you'll want to convert regular lines, arcs, or even circles into polylines. You might want to change the width of lines or join lines to form a single object such as a boundary. Here are the steps to convert lines, arcs, and circles into polylines:

**1.** Choose Modify ➤ Object ➤ Polyline, or type **Pe.**↵ at the Command prompt.

**2.** At the `Select polyline or [Multiple]:` prompt, pick the object you want to convert. If you want to convert a circle to a polyline, first break the circle (using the Break option on the Modify toolbar) so it becomes an arc of approximately 359°.

**3.** At the prompt

`Object selected is not a polyline. Do you want to turn it into one? <Y>:`

press ↵. The object is converted into a polyline.

If you want to convert several objects to polylines, type **M.**↵ at the `Select polyline or [Multiple]:` prompt; then, select the objects you want to convert. You see the `Convert Lines and Arcs to polylines [Yes/No]?:` prompt. Type **Y.**↵, and all the selected objects are converted to polylines. You can then go on to use other Pedit options on the selected objects.

To turn a polyline into a true spline curve, do the following:

1. Choose Modify ➤ Object ➤ Polyline, or type **Pe**↵. Select the polyline you want to convert.

2. Type **S**↵ to turn it into a polyline spline; then, press ↵ twice to exit the Pedit command.

3. Click the Spline tool on the Draw toolbar, type **Spl**↵, or choose Draw ➤ Spline from the drop-down menu.

4. At the Specify first point or [Object]: prompt, type **O**↵ for the Object option.

5. At the Select objects: prompt, click the polyline spline. Although it may not be apparent at first, the polyline is converted into a true spline.

You can also use the Spline Edit tool (choose Modify ➤ Object ➤ Spline, or enter **Spe**↵) on a polyline spline. If you do, the polyline spline is automatically converted into a true spline.

If you know you'll always want to convert an object into a polyline when using Pedit, you can turn on the Peditaccept system variable. Enter **peditaccept**↵ at the Command prompt, and then enter **1**↵.

## Editing Vertices

One of the Pedit options that I haven't yet discussed, Edit Vertex, is almost like a command in a command. Edit Vertex has numerous suboptions that enable you to fine-tune your polyline by giving you control over individual vertices.

To access the Edit Vertex options, follow these steps:

1. Turn off the Data and Border layers to hide the data points and border.

2. Issue the Pedit command, and then select the polyline you just drew.

3. Type **E**↵ to enter Edit Vertex mode. An X appears at the beginning of the polyline, indicating the vertex that will be affected by the Edit Vertex options.

**NOTE** When using Edit Vertex, you must be careful about selecting the vertex to be edited. Edit Vertex has six options, and you often have to exit the Edit Vertex operation and use Pedit's Fit option to see the effect of Edit Vertex's options on a curved polyline.

### EDIT VERTEX SUBOPTIONS

After you enter the Edit Vertex mode of the Pedit command, you have the option to perform the following functions:

◆ Break the polyline between two vertices.

◆ Insert a new vertex.

◆ Move an existing vertex.

◆ Regen the drawing to view the current shape of the polyline.

◆ Straighten a polyline between two vertices.

◆ Change the tangential direction of a vertex.

◆ Change the width of the polyline at a vertex.

These functions are presented in the form of the following prompt:

```
[Next/Previous/Break/Insert/Move/Regen/Straighten/Tangent/Width/eXit] <N>:
```

This section examines each of the options in this prompt, starting with Next and Previous.

### The Next and Previous Options

These options let you select a vertex for editing. When you start the Edit Vertex option, an X appears on the selected polyline to designate its beginning. As you select Next or Previous, the X moves from vertex to vertex to show which one is being edited. Let's try this:

1. Press ↵ a couple of times to move the X along the polyline. (Because Next is the default option, you only need to press ↵ to move the X.)

2. Type **P**↵ for Previous. The X moves in the opposite direction. The default option becomes P.

**TIP**  To determine the direction of a polyline, note in which direction the X moves when you use the Next option. Knowing the direction of a polyline is important for some of the other Edit Vertex options.

### The Break Option

The Break option breaks the polyline between two vertices:

1. Position the X on one end of the segment you want to break.

2. Enter **B**↵ at the Command prompt.

3. At the `Enter an option [Next/Previous/Go/eXit] <N>:` prompt, use Next or Previous to move the X to the other end of the segment to be broken.

4. When the X is in the proper position, enter **G**↵ to break the polyline (see Figure 18.9).

**TIP**  You can also use the Break and Trim options on the Modify toolbar to break a polyline anywhere, as you did when you drew the toilet seat in Chapter 3.

**FIGURE 18.9**
How the Break option works

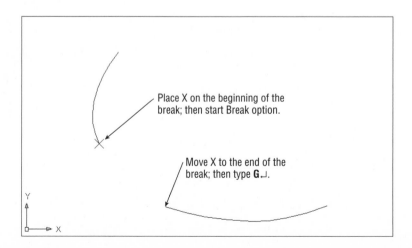

Place X on the beginning of the break; then start Break option.

Move X to the end of the break; then type **G**↵.

### The Insert Option

Next, try the Insert option, which inserts a new vertex:

1. Type **X**↵ to temporarily exit the Edit Vertex option. Then, type **U**↵ to undo the break.

2. Type **E**↵ to return to the Edit Vertex option.

3. Press ↵ to advance the X marker to the next point.

4. Enter **I**↵ to select the Insert option.

5. When the prompt Specify location for new vertex: appears, along with a rubber-banding line originating from the current X position (see Figure 18.10), pick a point indicating the new vertex location. The polyline is redrawn with the new vertex.

**FIGURE 18.10**

The new vertex location

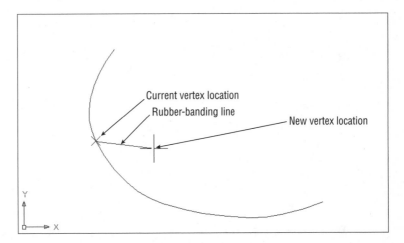

Notice that the inserted vertex appears between the currently marked vertex and the *next* vertex, so the Insert option is sensitive to the direction of the polyline. If the polyline is curved, the new vertex won't immediately be shown as curved. (See the first image in Figure 18.11.) You must smooth it out by exiting the Edit Vertex option and then using the Fit option, as you did to edit the site plan. (See the second image in Figure 18.11.) You can also use the Stretch command (on the Modify toolbar) to move a polyline vertex.

### The Move Option

In this brief exercise, you'll use the Move option to move a vertex:

1. Undo the inserted vertex by exiting the Edit Vertex option (enter **X**↵) and typing **U**↵.

2. Restart the Edit Vertex option, and use the Next or Previous option to place the X on the vertex you want to move.

3. Enter **M**↵ for the Move option.

4. When the Specify new location for marked vertex: prompt appears, along with a rubber-banding line originating from the X (see the first image in Figure 18.12), pick the new vertex. The polyline is redrawn (see the second image in Figure 18.12). Again, if the line is curved, the new vertex appears as a sharp angle until you use the Fit option (see the final image in Figure 18.12).

**TIP** You can also move a polyline vertex by using its grip.

**FIGURE 18.11**
The polyline before
and after the curve
is fitted

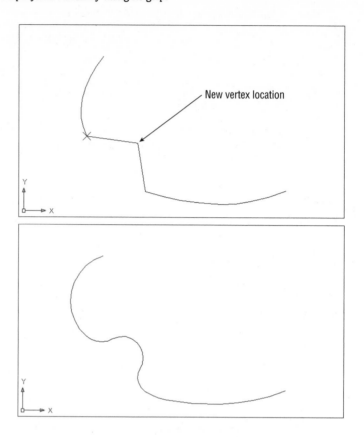

### The Regen Option

In some cases, the effect of the option does not appear in the drawing immediately. You can use the Regen option to update the display of the polyline and see any changes you've made so far.

### The Straighten Option

The Straighten option straightens all the vertices between two selected vertices, as shown in the following exercise:

1. Undo the moved vertex (from the previous exercise).

2. Start the Edit Vertex option again, and select the starting vertex for the straight line.

3. Enter S.↵ for the Straighten option.

4. At the Enter an option [Next/Previous/Go/eXit] <N>: prompt, move the X to the location for the other end of the straight-line segment.

**5.** After the X is in the proper position, enter **G**↵ for the Go option. The polyline straightens between the two selected vertices (see Figure 18.13).

**TIP**   Using the Straighten option is a quick way to delete vertices from a polyline.

**FIGURE 18.12**

Picking a new location for a vertex, with the polyline before and after the curve is fitted

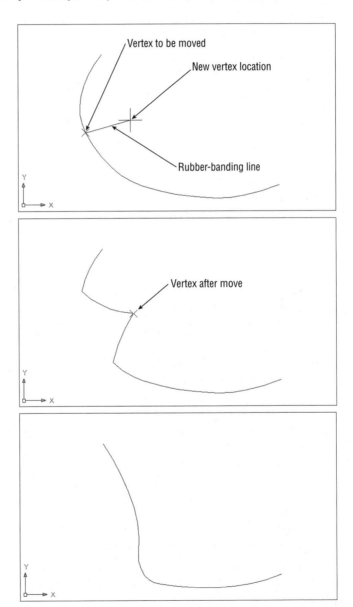

**FIGURE 18.13**
A polyline after
straightening

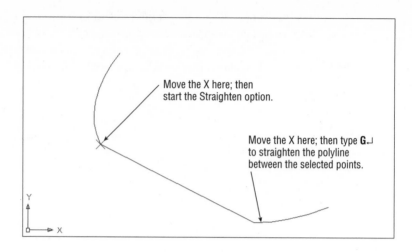

Move the X here; then
start the Straighten option.

Move the X here; then type **G.⏎**
to straighten the polyline
between the selected points.

### The Tangent Option

The Tangent option alters the direction of a curve on a curve-fitted polyline:

1. Undo the straightened segment from the previous exercise.

2. Restart the Edit Vertex option, and position the X on the vertex you want to alter.

3. Enter **T.⏎** for the Tangent option. A rubber-banding line appears. (See the top image in Figure 18.14.)

4. Point the rubber-banding line in the direction for the new tangent, and click the mouse. An arrow appears, indicating the new tangent direction. (See the second image in Figure 18.14.)

Don't worry if the polyline shape doesn't change. You must use Fit to see the effect of Tangent. (See the final image in Figure 18.14.)

### The Width Option

Finally, you'll try the Width option. Unlike the Pedit command's Width option, the Edit Vertex/ Width option enables you to alter the width of the polyline at any vertex. Thus, you can taper or otherwise vary polyline thicknesses. Try these steps:

1. Undo the tangent arc from the previous exercise.

2. Return to the Edit Vertex option, and place the X at the beginning vertex of a polyline segment you want to change.

3. Type **W.⏎** to issue the Width option.

4. At the `Specify starting width for next segment <0.0000>:` prompt, enter a value— **12**, for example—indicating the polyline width desired at this vertex.

5. At the `Specify ending width for next segment <12.0000>:` prompt, enter the width— **24**, for example—for the next vertex.

The width of the polyline changes to your specifications. (See Figure 18.15.)

**FIGURE 18.14**
Picking a new tangent
direction

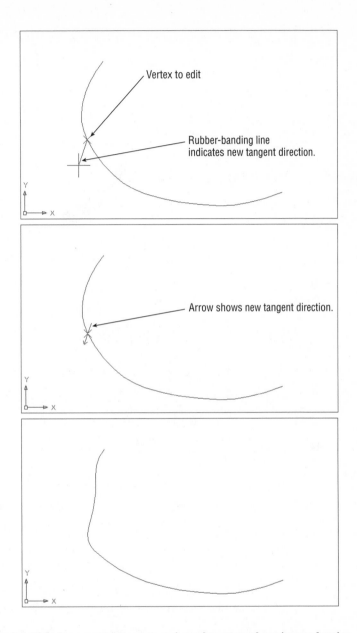

**NOTE**   The Width option is useful when you want to create an irregular or curved area in your drawing that is to be filled in solid. This is another option that is sensitive to the polyline direction.

As you've seen throughout these exercises, you can use the Undo option to reverse the last Edit Vertex option used. And you can use the Exit option to leave Edit Vertex at any time. Enter **X**↵ to display the Pedit prompt:

```
Enter an option [Close/Join/Width/Edit vertex/Fit/Spline/Decurve/Ltypegen/Undo]:
```

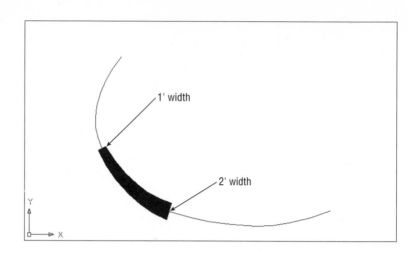

**FIGURE 18.15**
A polyline with the width of one segment increased

---

**FILLING IN SOLID AREAS**

You've learned how to create a solid area by increasing the width of a polyline segment. But suppose you want to create a solid shape or a thick line. AutoCAD provides the Solid, Trace, and Donut commands to help you draw simple filled areas. The Trace command acts just like the Line command (with the added feature of drawing wide line segments). Trace lets you create solid filled areas with straight sides, and Donut draws circles with a solid width.

You can create free-form, solid-filled areas by using the solid hatch pattern. Create an enclosed area by using any set of objects, and then use the Hatch tool to apply a solid hatch pattern to the area. See Chapter 7 for details on using the Hatch tool.

---

## Creating a Polyline Spline Curve

The Pedit command's Spline option (named after the spline tool used in manual drafting) offers you a way to draw smoother and more controllable curves than those produced by the Fit option. A polyline spline doesn't pass through the vertex points as a fitted curve does. Instead, the vertex points act as weights pulling the curve in their direction. The polyline spline touches only its beginning and end vertices. Figure 18.16 illustrates this concept.

**NOTE** A polyline spline curve doesn't represent a mathematically true curve. See the next section, "Using True Spline Curves," to learn how to draw a more accurate spline curve.

Let's see how using a polyline spline curve may influence the way you edit a curve:

1. Undo the width changes you made in the previous exercise.

2. To change the contour into a polyline spline curve, choose Modify ➤ Object ➤ Polyline.

**3.** Pick the polyline to be curved.

**4.** At the prompt

```
Enter an option [Close/Join/Width/Edit vertex/Fit/Spline/Decurve/Ltypegen/Undo]:
```

enter **S**↵. Your curve changes to look like Figure 18.17.

**FIGURE 18.16**

The polyline spline curve pulled toward · its vertices

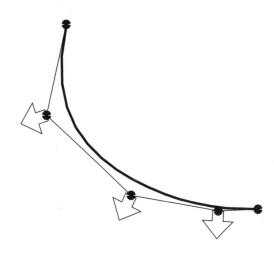

**FIGURE 18.17**

A spline curve

**5.** Press ↵ to exit Edit Polyline.

The curve takes on a smoother, more graceful appearance. It no longer passes through the points you used to define it. To see where the points went and to find out how spline curves act, do the following:

**1.** Make sure Noun/Verb Selection mode and the Enable Grips feature are turned on.

**2.** Click the curve. The original vertices appear as grips. (See the first image in Figure 18.18.)

**FIGURE 18.18**

The fitted curve changed to a spline curve, with the location of the second vertex and the new curve

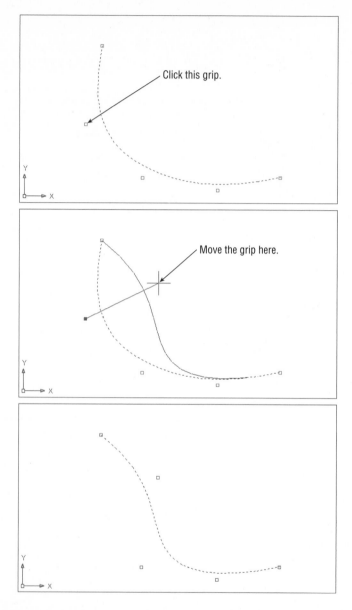

3. Click the grip that is second from the top of the curve, as shown in the first image in Figure 18.18, and move the grip around. The curve follows, giving you immediate feedback on how the curve will look.

4. Pick a point as shown in the second image in Figure 18.18. The curve is fixed in its new position.

**NOTE** You can set up AutoCAD to display both the curved and the straight segments defining the curve by turning on the Splframe system variable. Enter **splframe↵1↵**, and then issue a Regen command. You see a frame that connects the grips of the curve. To turn off the display of the straight segments, enter **splframe↵0↵**.

# Using True Spline Curves

So far, you've been working with polylines to generate spline curves. The advantage of using polylines for curves is that they can be enhanced in other ways. You can modify their width, for instance, or join several curves. But at times, you'll need a more exact representation of a curve. The spline object, created by choosing Draw ➤ Spline, produces a more accurate model of a spline curve, as well as giving you more control over its shape.

The splines are true *Non-Uniform Rational B-Splines (NURBS)* curves. A full description of NURBS is beyond the scope of this book; but basically, NURBS are a standard mathematical form used to represent shapes.

## Drawing a True Spline

To create a spline curve, follow the steps described here. You don't have to do them now. Make a note of this section, and refer to it when you need to draw and edit a spline:

1. Choose Draw ➤ Spline, or type **Spl↵**.

2. At the `Specify first point or [Object]:` prompt, select a point to start the curve. (See Figure 18.19.) The prompt changes to `Specify next point:`.

**FIGURE 18.19**
Starting the spline curve at the first data point

3. Continue to select points until you've entered all the points you need. As you pick points, a curve appears, and it bends and flows as you move your cursor.

4. After you've selected the last point, press ↵. The prompt changes to `Specify start tangent:`. Also, a rubber-banding line appears from the first point of the curve to the cursor. As you move the cursor, the curve adjusts to the direction of the rubber-banding line. Here, you can set the tangency of the first point of the curve. (See the first image in Figure 18.20.)

5. If you press ↵, AutoCAD determines the first point's tangency based on the current shape of the curve. Next, a rubber-banding line appears from the last point of the curve. As with the first point, you can indicate a tangent direction for the last point of the curve. (See the second image in Figure 18.20.)

6. Press ↵ to exit the Spline command without changing the endpoint tangent direction.

**FIGURE 18.20**

The last two prompts of the Spline command let you determine the tangent direction of the spline.

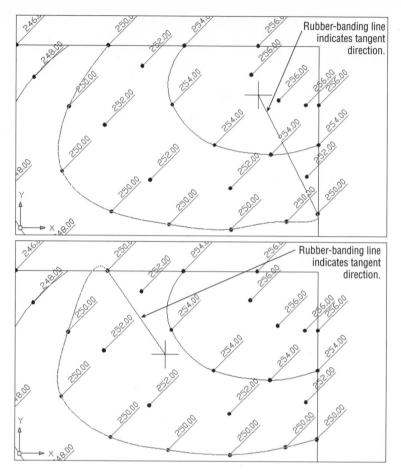

You now have a smooth curve that passes through the points you selected. These points are called the *control points*. If you click the curve, you'll see the grips appear at the location of these control points, and you can adjust the curve by clicking the grip points and moving them. (You may need to turn off the Data layer to see the grips clearly.)

You may have noticed two other options—Fit Tolerance and Close—as you were selecting points for the spline in the previous exercise. Here is a description of these options:

**Fit Tolerance**   Lets you change the curve so it doesn't pass through the points you pick. When you select this option, you get the prompt `Specify fit tolerance <0.0000>`. Any value greater than 0 causes the curve to pass close to, but not through, the points. A value of 0 causes the curve to pass through the points.

**Close**   Lets you close the curve into a loop. If you choose this option, you're prompted to indicate a tangent direction for the closing point.

## Fine-Tuning Spline Curves

Spline curves are different from other types of objects, and many of the standard editing commands won't work on splines. AutoCAD offers the Modify ➤ Object ➤ Spline option (Splinedit command) for making changes to splines.

### CONTROLLING THE FIT DATA OF A SPLINE

The Fit Data option of the Splinedit command lets you adjust the tangency of the beginning and end points, add new control points, and adjust spline tolerance settings. To get to these options, follow these steps:

1. Choose Modify ➤ Object ➤ Spline, or type **Spe↵** at the Command prompt.

2. At the `Select spline:` prompt, select the spline you drew in the previous exercise.

3. At the prompt

   ```
   Enter an option [Fit data/Close/Move vertex/Refine/rEverse/Undo]:
   ```

   type **F↵** to select the Fit Data option.

4. At the prompt

   ```
   [Add/Close/Delete/Move/Purge/Tangents/toLerance/eXit] <eXit>:
   ```

   enter the option you want to use. For example, to change the tangency of the first and last points of your spline, type **t↵**. You're prompted to select the tangent point of the first and last points. Table 18.1 lists the Splinedit Fit Data options and what they're for.

**TABLE 18.1:**     The Fit Data options of the Splinedit Command

| OPTION | FUNCTION |
| --- | --- |
| Add | Lets you add more control points |
| Close | Lets you close the spline into a loop |
| Delete | Removes a control point from the spline |
| Move | Lets you move a control point |
| Purge | Deletes the fit data of the spline, thereby eliminating the Fit Data option for the purged spline |
| Tangents | Lets you change the tangency of the first and last points |
| toLerance | Controls the distance between the spline and a control point |

**TIP**     The Refine option of the Spline Edit command lets you control the pull exerted on a spline by an individual control point.

### WHEN CAN'T YOU USE FIT DATA?

The Fit Data option of the Splinedit command offers many ways to edit a spline; however, this option isn't available to all spline curves. When you invoke certain other Splinedit options, a spline curve loses its fit data, thereby disabling the Fit Data option. These operations are as follows:

- Fitting a spline to a tolerance (Spline/Fit Tolerance), and moving its control vertices.

- Fitting a spline to a tolerance (Spline/Fit Tolerance), and opening or closing it.

- Refining the spline.

- Purging the spline of its fit data by using the Purge option of the Splinedit command. (Choose Modify ➤ Object ➤ Spline; or enter **Splinedit**↵, and then select the spline and enter **F↵P↵**.)

Also, note that the Fit Data option isn't available when you edit spline curves that were created from polyline splines. See the "Turning Objects into Polylines and Polylines into Splines" sidebar, earlier in this chapter.

If you'd like to learn more about the Splinedit options, check the AutoCAD help window. It offers a detailed description of how these options work.

## Marking Divisions on Curves

Perhaps one of the most difficult things to do in manual drafting is to mark regular intervals on a curve. AutoCAD offers the Divide and Measure commands to help you perform this task with speed and accuracy.

**NOTE**  The Divide and Measure commands are discussed here in conjunction with polylines, but you can use these commands on any object except blocks and text.

### Dividing Objects into Segments of Equal Length

You use the Divide command to divide an object into a specific number of equal segments. For example, suppose you need to mark off the contour you've been working on in this chapter into nine equal segments. One way to do this is to first find the length of the contour by using the List command and then sit down with a pencil and paper to figure out the exact distances between the marks. But there is another, easier way.

The Divide command places a set of point objects on a line, an arc, a circle, or a polyline, marking off exact divisions. The following exercise shows how it works:

1. Open the 18a-divd.dwg file. This file is similar to the one you've been working with in the previous exercises.

2. Choose Draw ➤ Point ➤ Divide, or type **Div↵↵**.

3. At the Select object to divide: prompt, pick the spline contour line that shows Xs in Figure 18.21.

4. The Enter the number of segments or [Block]: prompt that appears next is asking for the number of divisions you want on the selected object. Enter **9↵**.

   The Command prompt returns, and it appears that nothing has happened. But AutoCAD has placed several points on the contour that indicate the locations of the nine divisions you requested. To see these points more clearly, continue with the exercise.

**FIGURE 18.21**

Using the Divide command on a polyline

5. Choose Format ➤ Point Style to open the Point Style dialog box.

6. Click the X point style at upper-right in the dialog box, click the Set Size Relative To Screen radio button, and then click OK.

7. If the Xs don't appear, choose View ➤ Regen or enter **Re.**⏎. A set of Xs appears, showing the nine divisions (see Figure 18.21).

**TIP** You can also change the point style by changing the Pdmode system variable. When Pdmode is set to 3, the point appears as an X. See Appendix C for information on Pdmode.

The Divide command uses *point* objects to indicate the division points. You create point objects by using the Point command; they usually appear as dots. Unfortunately, such points are nearly invisible when placed on top of other objects. But as you've seen, you can alter their shape by using the Point Style dialog box. You can use these X points to place objects or references to break the object being divided. (The Divide command doesn't cut the object into smaller divisions.)

**TIP** If you're in a hurry, and you don't want to bother changing the shape of the point objects, you can do the following: Set Running Osnaps to Node. Then, when you're in Point Selection mode, move the cursor over the divided curve. When the cursor gets close to a point object, the Node osnap marker appears.

## Dividing Objects into Specified Lengths

The Measure command acts just like Divide; however, instead of dividing an object into segments of equal length, the Measure command marks intervals of a specified distance along an object. For example, suppose you need to mark some segments exactly 5´ apart along the contour. Try the following exercise to see how the Measure command is used to accomplish this task:

1. Erase the X-shaped point objects.

2. Choose Draw ➤ Point ➤ Measure, or type **Me.**⏎.

3. At the Select object to measure: prompt, pick the contour at a point closest to its lower endpoint. I'll explain shortly why this is important.

4. At the Specify length of segment or [Block]: prompt, enter 60.⏎. The X points appear at the specified distance.

5. Exit this file.

**NOTE** The Measure command is AutoCAD's equivalent of the divider tool in manual drafting. A divider is a V-shaped instrument, similar to a compass, used to mark off regular intervals along a curve or line.

Bear in mind that the point you pick on the object to be measured determines where the Measure command begins measuring. In the previous exercise, for example, you picked the contour near its bottom endpoint. If you picked the top of the contour, the results would be different because the measurement would start at the top, not the bottom.

---

### MARKING OFF INTERVALS BY USING BLOCKS INSTEAD OF POINTS

You can also use the Block option under the Divide and Measure commands to place blocks at regular intervals along a line, a polyline, or an arc. Here's how to use blocks as markers:

1. Be sure the block you want to use is part of the current drawing file.

2. Start either the Divide or Measure command.

3. At the Specify length of segment or [Block]: prompt, enter **B.**⏎.

4. At the Enter name of block to insert: prompt, enter the name of a block.

5. At the Align Block with Object? [Yes/No]: prompt, press ⏎ if you want the blocks to follow the alignment of the selected object. (Entering **N**⏎ inserts each block at a 0 angle.)

6. At the Enter the number of Segments: prompt or the Specify length of segment: prompt, enter the number or length of the segments. The blocks appear at regular intervals on the selected object.

One example of using the Block option of Divide or Measure is to place a row of sinks equally spaced along a wall. Or you might use this technique to make multiple copies of an object along an irregular path defined by a polyline. In civil-engineering projects, you can indicate a fence line by using Divide or Measure to place Xs along a polyline.

## Sketching with AutoCAD

AutoCAD offers the Sketch command that lets you do freehand drawing. Lines created with the Sketch command become polylines. If you'd like to know more about Sketch, the AutoCAD Help window offers an excellent description of how it works. Choose Help ➢ Help, open the Contents tab, and then expand the Command Reference listing to Command ➢ S Commands ➢ Sketch.

## The Bottom Line

**Creating and Editing Polylines**  Polylines are extremely versatile. You can use them in just about any situation where you need to draw linework that is continuous. For this reason, you'll want to master polylines early in your AutoCAD training.

**Master It**  Draw the part shown in Figure 18.22.

**Solution**

1. Open a new file called PART14. Set the Snap spacing to 0.25, and be sure Snap mode is on. Use the Pline command to draw the object shown in step 1 of Figure 18.22. Start at the upper-left corner, and draw in the direction indicated by the arrows. Use the Close option to add the last line segment.

2. Start the Pedit command, select the polyline, and then type **E**⏎ to issue the Edit Vertex option. Press ⏎ until the X mark moves to the first corner, shown in step 2 of Figure 18.22. Enter **S**⏎ for the Straighten option.

**Figure 18.22**
Drawing a simple plate with curved edges

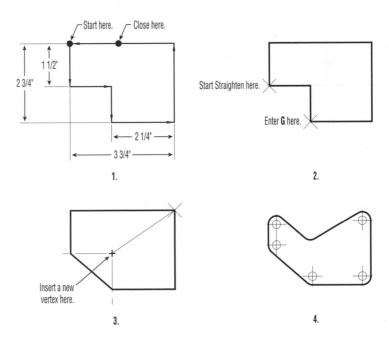

3. At the `Enter an option` prompt, press ↵ twice to move the X to the other corner shown in step 2 of Figure 18.22. Press **G**↵ for Go to straighten the polyline between the two selected corners.

4. Press ↵ twice to move the X to the upper-right corner, and then enter **I**↵ for Insert. Pick a point as shown in step 3 of Figure 18.22. The polyline changes to reflect the new vertex. Enter **X**↵ to exit the Edit Vertex option, and then press ↵ to exit the Pedit command.

5. Start the Fillet command, use the Radius option to set the fillet radius to .30, and then use the Polyline option and pick the polyline you just edited. All the corners fillet to the .30 radius. Add the .15 radius circles as shown in step 4 of Figure 18.22, and exit the file with the End command.

### Creating a Polyline Spline Curve

**Master It**   Try drawing the outline of an object that has no or few straight lines in it, like the sample file `Lowerfairing.jpg` that is included in the Chapter 18 sample files. You can use the methods described in Chapter 14 to import a raster image of your object, and then trace over the image using polyline splines.

**Solution**   Import a raster image using Insert ➤ Raster Image Reference. Use the Polyline tool to trace over the image. Use short, straight polyline segments while you trace. After you place each polyline, double-click it and select the Spline option. Once you change the line to a spline curve, it may shift away from the original line you traced over. Click the polyline, and then adjust the grips so the line fits over the raster image.

### Creating and Editing True Spline Curves

**Master It**   Try tracing over the same image from the previous "Master It" section, but this time use the Spline tool.

**Solution**   Import a raster image using Insert ➤ Raster Image Reference. Use the Spline tool to trace over the image. As you draw the spline, select control points that are closer together for tighter curves. The closer the control points are, the tighter you can make the curve. Notice that, unlike with a polyline spline, you don't have to readjust the curve after it's been placed.

### Marking Divisions on Curves

**Master It**   Mark off 12 equal divisions of the spline curves you drew in the previous "Master It" exercise.

**Solution**   Choose Draw ➤ Point ➤ Divide, click the spline, and then enter **12**↵. If you don't see the points that mark off the divisions, choose Format Point Style, select the X point style, and click OK.

# Chapter 19

# Getting and Exchanging Data from Drawings

AutoCAD drawings contain a wealth of data—graphic information such as distances and angles between objects, as well as precise areas and the properties of objects. But as you become more experienced with AutoCAD, you'll also need data of a different nature. For example, as you begin to work in groups, the various settings in a drawing become important. You'll need statistics on the amount of time you spend on a drawing when you're billing computer time. As your projects become more complex, file maintenance requires a greater degree of attention. To take full advantage of AutoCAD, you'll want to exchange much of this data with other people and other programs.

In this chapter, you'll explore the ways in which all types of data can be extracted from AutoCAD and made available to you, your coworkers, and other programs. First, you'll learn how to obtain specific data about your drawings. Then, you'll look at ways to exchange data with other programs—such as word processors, desktop-publishing software, and even other CAD programs.

Topics in this chapter include the following:

◆ Finding the Area of Closed Boundaries

◆ Getting General Information

◆ Using the DXF File Format to Exchange CAD Data with Other Programs

◆ Using AutoCAD Drawings in Desktop Publishing

◆ Using OLE to Import Data

## Finding the Area of Closed Boundaries

One of the most frequently sought pieces of data you can extract from an AutoCAD drawing is the area of a closed boundary. In architecture, you want to find the area of a room or the footprint of a building. In civil engineering, you want to determine the area covered by the boundary of a property line or the area of cut for a roadway. In this section, you'll learn how to use AutoCAD to obtain exact area information from your drawings.

**TIP** To find absolute coordinates in a drawing, use the ID command. Choose Tools ➤ Inquiry ➤ ID Point, or type **ID**↵. At the ID Point: prompt, use the Osnap overrides to pick a point; its X, Y, and Z coordinates are displayed on the prompt line.

## Finding the Area of an Object

Architects, engineers, and facilities planners often need to know the square footage of a room or a section of a building. A structural engineer might want to find the cross-sectional area of a beam. In this section, you'll practice determining the areas of regular objects.

First, you'll determine the square-foot area of the living room and entry of your studio unit plan:

1. Start AutoCAD. Open the Unit file you created earlier, or use the 19a-unit.dwg file.

2. Enter **Blipmode.⏎on.⏎**. This turns on a marking feature that displays a tiny cross called a *blip* whenever you click in the drawing area. Blips don't print and can be cleared from the screen with a redraw. You'll use them to help keep track of your point selections in this exercise.

3. Zoom in to the living room and entry area so you have a view similar to Figure 19.1.

4. Choose Tools ➢ Inquiry ➢ Area, or type **Area.⏎** at the Command prompt.

**TIP** You can also select the Area command from the Inquiry toolbar. Right-click any toolbar, and choose Inquiry from the shortcut menu.

**FIGURE 19.1**
Selecting the points to determine the area of the living room and entry

5. Using the Endpoint osnap, start with the lower-left corner of the living room and select the points shown in Figure 19.1. You're indicating the boundary.

6. When you've come full circle to the eighth point shown in Figure 19.1, press ↵. You get the following message:

```
Area = 39570.00 square in. (274.7917 square ft), Perimeter = 76'-0"
```

7. Turn off Blipmode by typing **Blipmode.↵off.↵**. Then, choose View ➤ Redraw to clear the blips from the screen.

The number of points you can pick to define an area is limitless, so you can obtain the areas of complex shapes. Use the Blipmode feature to keep track of the points you select so you know when you come to the beginning of the point selections.

## Using Hatch Patterns to Find Areas

Hatch patterns are used primarily to add graphics to your drawing, but they can also serve as a means to finding areas. You can use any hatch pattern you want because you're only interested in the area it reports back to you. You can also set up a special layer devoted to area calculations and then assign the hatch patterns you use to find areas to this layer. That way, you can turn off the hatch patterns so they don't plot, or you can turn off the Plot setting for that layer to ensure that it doesn't appear in your final output.

To practice using hatch patterns to find an area, do the following:

1. Set the current layer to Floor.

2. Turn off the Door and Fixture layers. Also make sure the Ceiling layer is turned on. You want the hatch pattern to follow the interior wall outline, so you need to turn off any objects that will affect the outline, such as the door and kitchen.

3. Choose Draw ➤ Hatch, or type **h↵** to open the Hatch And Gradient dialog box.

**WARNING**   If the area you're trying to measure has gaps, set the Gap Tolerance setting in the Hatch And Gradient dialog box to a value higher than the size of the gaps. If you don't see the Gap Tolerance setting, click the More Options button in the lower-right corner of the Hatch And Gradient dialog box.

4. Click the Add Pick Points button to close the dialog box.

5. At the `Pick internal point or [Select objects/remove Boundaries]:` prompt, click in the interior of the Unit plan. The outline of the interior is highlighted (see Figure 19.2).

6. Press ↵; then, in the Hatch And Gradient dialog box, click OK.

7. Choose Tools ➤ Inquiry ➤ Area again, or type **Area.↵** at the Command prompt. Then, enter **O.↵** for the Object option.

8. Click the hatch pattern you just created; when it's highlighted, press ↵. Again, you get the following message:

```
Area = 39570.00 square in. (274.7917 square ft), Perimeter = 76'-0"
```

**TIP**   If you need to recall the last area calculation value you received, enter ´**Setvar.↵Area.↵**. The area is displayed in the prompt. Enter ´**Perimeter.↵** to get the last perimeter calculated.

**FIGURE 19.2**
After you select a point on the interior of the plan by using the hatch pattern, an outline of the area is highlighted by a dotted line.

The Hatch command creates a hatch pattern that conforms to the boundary of an area. This feature, combined with the ability of the Area command to find the area of a hatch pattern, makes short work of area calculations. Another advantage of using hatch patterns is that, by default, hatch patterns avoid islands within the boundary whose area you're trying to find.

The area of a hatch pattern is also reported by the Properties palette. Select the hatch pattern whose area you want to find, and then click the Properties tool in the Standard toolbar. Scroll down to the bottom of the Geometry group, and you'll see the Area listing for the hatch pattern you selected. You can select more than one hatch pattern and find the cumulative area of the selected hatch patterns in the Properties palette.

## Adding and Subtracting Areas with the Area Command

Hatch patterns work extremely well for finding areas, but if you find that, for some reason, you can't use hatch patterns, you have another alternative. You can still use a command called Boundary to generate polyline outlines of enclosed boundaries and then obtain the area of the outline using the Area command. If islands are present within the boundary, you have to use the Subtract feature of the Area command to remove the area of the island from the overall boundary area. In this section, you'll use the example of the flange part, which contains two islands in the form of the two circles at the lower end (see Figure 19.3).

**FIGURE 19.3**
A flange to a mechanical device

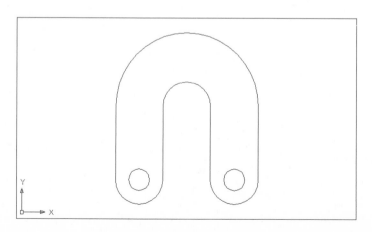

By using the Add and Subtract options of the Area command, you can maintain a running total of several separate areas being calculated. This gives you flexibility in finding areas of complex shapes. This section guides you through the use of these options.

For the following exercise, you'll use a flange shape that contains circles. This shape is composed of simple arcs, lines, and circles. Use these steps to see how you can keep a running tally of areas:

1. Exit the Unit file, and open the file Flange.dwg (see Figure 19.3). Don't bother to save changes in the Unit file.

2. Choose Draw ➤ Boundary to open the Boundary Creation dialog box.

3. Click Pick Points.

4. Click in the interior of the flange shape. The entire shape is highlighted, including the circle islands.

5. Press ↵. You now have a polyline outline of the shape, although it won't be obvious that polylines have been created because they're drawn over the boundary objects.

6. Continue by using the Area command's Add and Subtract options. Choose Tools ➤ Inquiry ➤ Area.

7. Type A↵ to enter Add mode, and then type O↵ to select an object.

8. Click a vertical edge of the flange outline. You see the following message:

```
Area = 27.7080, Perimeter = 30.8496
Total area = 27.7080
```

9. Press ↵ to exit Add mode.

10. Type S↵ to enter Subtract mode, and then type O↵ to select an object.

11. Click one of the circles. You see the following message:

```
Area = 0.6070, Perimeter = 2.7618
Total area = 27.1010
```

This shows you the area and perimeter of the selected object and a running count of the total area of the flange outline minus the circle.

**12.** Click the other circle. You see the following message:

```
Area = 0.6070, Perimeter = 2.7618
Total area = 26.4940
```

Again, you see a listing of the area and perimeter of the selected object along with a running count of the total area, which now shows a value of 26.4940. This last value is the true area of the flange.

**13.** Press ↵ twice to exit the Area command.

In this exercise, you first selected the main object outline and then subtracted the island objects. You don't have to follow this order; you can start by subtracting areas to get negative area values and then add other areas to come up with a total. You can also alternate between Add and Subtract modes, in case you forget to add or subtract areas.

You may have noticed that the Area Command prompt offered Specify first corner point or [Object/Add/Subtract]: as the default option for both Add and Subtract modes. Instead of using the Object option to pick the circles, you can start selecting points to indicate a rectangular area, as you did in the first exercise in this chapter.

Whenever you press ↵ while selecting points for an area calculation, AutoCAD automatically connects the first and last points and returns the calculated area. If you're in Add or Subtract mode, you can then continue to select points, but the additional areas are calculated from the *next* point you pick.

As you can see from these exercises, it's simpler to first outline an area with a polyline, wherever possible, and then use the Object option to add and subtract area values of polylines.

In this example, you obtained the area of a mechanical object. However, the same process works for any type of area you want to calculate. It can be the area of a piece of property on a topographical map or the area of a floor plan. For example, you can use the Object option to find an irregular area such as the one shown in Figure 19.4, as long as it's a polyline.

**FIGURE 19.4**

The site plan with an area to be calculated

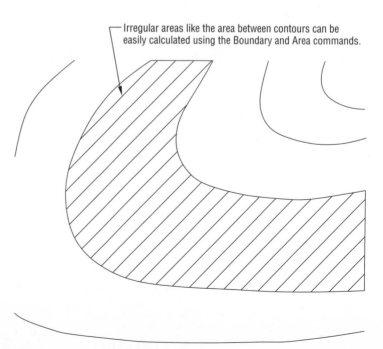

Irregular areas like the area between contours can be easily calculated using the Boundary and Area commands.

> ### RECORDING AREA DATA IN A DRAWING FILE
>
> After you find the area of an object, you'll often need to record it somewhere. You can write it down in a project logbook, but this is easy to overlook. A more dependable way to store area information is to use *attributes*.
>
> Consider the following example: In a building project, you can create a block that contains attributes for the room number, the room area, and the date when the room area was last measured. You might make the area and date attributes invisible, so only the room number appears. You can then insert this block into every room. After you find the area, you can easily add it to your block attribute with the Ddatte command. You can use such a block with any drawing in which you want to store area data. See Chapter 13 for more on attributes.

# Getting General Information

So far in this book, you've seen how to get data about the geometry of your drawings. AutoCAD also includes a set of tools that you can use to access the general state of your drawings. You can gather information about the status of current settings in a file or the time at which a drawing was created and last edited.

In this section, you'll practice extracting this type of information from your drawing, using the tools found in the Tools ➤ Inquiry option's cascading menu.

## Determining the Drawing's Status

When you work with a group of people on a large project, keeping track of a drawing's setup becomes crucial. You can use the Status command to obtain general information about the drawing you're working on, such as the base point, current mode settings, and workspace or computer memory use. The Status command is especially helpful when you're editing a drawing someone else has worked on, because you may want to identify and change settings for your own style of working. Choosing Tools ➤ Inquiry ➤ Status displays a list like the one shown in Figure 19.5.

**FIGURE 19.5**

The Status screen of the AutoCAD Text Window

```
AutoCAD Text Window - C:\Mastering AutoCAD 2008\Projects\Chapter 19\19a-unit.dwg
Edit

Command: status
374 objects in C:\Mastering AutoCAD 2008\Projects\Chapter 19\19a-unit.dwg
Model space limits are X:     0'-0"    Y:      0'-0"   (Off)
                       X:    44'-0"    Y:     34'-0"
Model space uses       X:    14'-7"    Y:  2'-3 1/2"
                       X:    33'-9"    Y: 35'-2 3/4" **Over
Display shows          X: -10'-8 5/8"  Y: -0'-3 1/4"
                       X:  54'-8 5/8"  Y: 49'-7 7/8"
Insertion base is      X:    15'-0"    Y:     2'-5"   Z:     0'-0"
Snap resolution is     X:     0'-1"    Y:     0'-1"
Grid spacing is        X:     4'-0"    Y:     4'-0"

Current space:          Model space
Current layout:         Model
Current layer:          "WALL"
Current color:          BYLAYER -- 83
Current linetype:       BYLAYER -- "CONTINUOUS"
Current material:       BYLAYER -- "Global"
Current lineweight:     BYLAYER
Current elevation:       0'-0"  thickness:       0'-0"
Fill on  Grid on  Ortho off  Qtext off  Snap off  Tablet off
Object snap modes:   Center, Endpoint, Intersection, Extension,
Free dwg disk (C:) space: 168747.4 MBytes
Press ENTER to continue:
Free temp disk (C:) space: 168747.4 MBytes
Free physical memory: 1539.6 Mbytes (out of 2047.2M).
Free swap file space: 3543.2 Mbytes (out of 3941.2M).

Command:
```

**TIP**    If you have problems editing a file created by someone else, the difficulty can often be attributed to a new or different setting you aren't used to working with. If AutoCAD is acting in an unusual way, use the Status command to get a quick glimpse of the file settings before you start calling for help.

Here is a brief description of each item on the Status screen. Note that some of the items you see on the screen will vary somewhat from what I've shown here, but the information applies to virtually all situations except where noted:

**(*Number*) Objects In *Drive:\Folder\Subfolder\Name.dwg***    The number of entities or objects in the drawing.

**Model Space Limits Are**    The coordinates of the Model Space limits. Also indicates whether limits are turned off or on. (See Chapter 3 for more details on limits.)

**Model Space Uses**    The area the drawing occupies; equivalent to the extents of the drawing.

**\*\*Over**    If present, means that part of the drawing is outside the limit boundary.

**Display Shows**    The area covered by the current view.

**Insertion Base Is, Snap Resolution Is, and Grid Spacing Is**    The current default values for these mode settings.

**Current Space**    Model Space or Paper Space.

**Current Layout**    The current tab.

**Current Layer**    The current layer.

**Current Color**    The color assigned to new objects.

**Current Linetype**    The linetype assigned to new objects.

**Current Material**    The material assigned to new objects.

**Current Lineweight**    The current default lineweight setting.

**Current Elevation/Thickness**    The current default Z coordinate for new objects, plus the default thickness of objects; these are both 3D-related settings. (See Chapter 20 for details.)

**Fill, Grid, Ortho, Qtext, Snap, and Tablet**    The status of these options.

**Object Snap Modes**    The current active Osnap setting.

**Free Dwg Disk (*Drive:*) Space**    The amount of space available to store drawing-specific temporary files.

**Free Temp Disk (*Drive:*) Space**    The amount of space left on your hard drive for AutoCAD's resource temporary files.

**Free Physical Memory**    The amount of free RAM available.

**Free Swap File Space**    The amount of Windows swap-file space available.

**TIP**    When you're in Paper Space, the Status command displays information regarding the Paper Space limits. See Chapter 16 for more on Model Space and Paper Space.

In addition to being useful in understanding a drawing file, the Status command is an invaluable tool for troubleshooting. Frequently, a technical support person can isolate problems by using the information provided by the Status command.

**TIP**    For more information on memory use, see Appendix B.

## Keeping Track of Time

The Time command enables you to keep track of the time spent on a drawing, for billing or analysis purposes. You can also use the Time command to check the current time and find out when the drawing was created and most recently edited. Because the AutoCAD timer uses your computer's time, be sure the time is set correctly in Windows.

To access the Time command, enter **Time.┘** at the Command prompt or choose Tools ➤ Inquiry ➤ Time. You get a message like the one in Figure 19.6.

**FIGURE 19.6**

The Time screen in the AutoCAD Text Window

The first four lines of this message tell you the current date and time, the date and time the drawing was created, and the last time the drawing was saved or ended.

The fifth line shows the total time spent on the drawing from the point at which the file was opened. This elapsed timer lets you time a particular activity, such as changing the width of all the walls in a floor plan or redesigning a piece of machinery. The last line tells you when the next automatic save will be.

You can turn the elapsed timer on or off or reset it by entering **ON**, **OFF**, or **Reset** at the prompt shown at the bottom of the message. Or press ┘ to exit the Time command.

## Getting Information from System Variables

If you've been working through this book's ongoing studio apartment building tutorial, you'll have noticed occasional mentions of a *system variable* in conjunction with a command. You can check the status or change the setting of any system variable while you're in the middle of another command. To do this, you type an apostrophe (´), followed by the name of the system variable, at the Command prompt.

For example, if you start to draw a line and suddenly decide you need to rotate your cursor 45°, you can do the following:

1. At the Specify next point or [Undo]: prompt, enter **´snapang**.

2. At the Enter new value for SNAPANG <0>: prompt, enter a new cursor angle. You're returned to the Line command with the cursor in its new orientation.

You can also recall information such as the last area or distance calculated by AutoCAD. Because the Area system variable duplicates the name of the Area command, you need to choose Tools ➤ Inquiry ➤ Set Variable, and then type **Area┘** to read the last area calculation. You can also type **´Setvar┘Area┘**. The Tools ➤ Inquiry ➤ Set Variable option also lets you list all the system variables and their status, as well as access each system variable individually by entering a question mark (**?**). You can then indicate which variables to list using wildcard characters such as the asterisk or question mark. For example, you can enter **g\*** to list all the system variables that start with the letter *G*.

Many system variables give you direct access to detailed information about your drawing. They also let you fine-tune your drawing and editing activities. In Appendix C, you'll find all the information you need to familiarize yourself with the system variables. Don't feel that you have to memorize them all at once; just be aware that they're available.

**TIP** Many of the dialog box options you've been using throughout this book, such as those in the Options dialog box, are actually system-variable settings.

## Keeping a Log of Your Activity

At times, you may find it helpful to keep a log of your activity in an AutoCAD session. A *log* is a text file containing a record of your activities. It can also contain notes to yourself or others about how a drawing is set up. Such a log can help you determine how frequently you use a particular command, or it can help you construct a macro for a commonly used sequence of commands.

The following exercise demonstrates how to save and view a detailed record of an AutoCAD session by using the Log feature:

1. Choose Tools ➢ Options to open the Options dialog box. Click the Open And Save tab. A new set of options appears.

**TIP** As a shortcut, you can quickly turn the Maintain A Log File feature on and off by typing **Logfileon**↵ and **Logfileoff**↵, respectively, at the Command prompt.

2. In the File Safety Precautions group, click the Maintain A Log File check box, and then click OK.

3. Choose Tools ➢ Inquiry ➢ Status.

4. Return to the Open And Save tab of the Options dialog box, and turn off the Maintain A Log File option.

5. Click OK to exit the dialog box.

6. Switch to Windows, and start the Notepad application or any text editor.

7. With the text editor, open the log file whose name starts with Flange in the folder listed here:

```
C:\Documents and Settings\User Name\Local Settings\Application
Data\Autodesk\AutoCAD 2008\R17.1\enu\
```

This file stores the text data from the Command prompt whenever the Log File option is turned on. You must turn off the Log File option before you can view this file. When you're attempting to view the log file using Windows Notepad, make sure you set File Of Type in the Notepad Open dialog box to All Files.

As you can see in step 7, the log file is given the name of the drawing file from which the log is derived, with some additional numeric values. Because the Flange log file is a standard text file, you can easily send it to other members of your workgroup or print it for a permanent record.

**TIP** If you can't find the log file for the current drawing, you can enter **logfilename**↵ at the Command prompt, and AutoCAD will display the filename including the full path. If you want to change the default location for the log file, open the Options dialog box and click the Files tab. Click the plus sign to the left of the Log File Location option in the list box. A listing appears, showing you where the drawing log file is stored. You can then modify this setting to indicate a new location. LT users, enter **Modemacro**↵ and then **$(getvar, logfilepath)**.

## Capturing and Saving Text Data from the AutoCAD Text Window

If you're working in groups, it's often helpful to have a record of the status, editing time, and system variables for particular files readily available to other group members. It's also convenient to keep records of block and layer information, so you can see whether a specific block is included in a drawing or what layers are normally on or off.

You can use the Windows Clipboard to capture and save such data from the AutoCAD Text Window. The following steps show you how it's done:

1. Move the arrow cursor to the Command prompt at the bottom of the AutoCAD Text Window.

2. Right-click, and choose Copy History from the shortcut menu to copy the contents of the AutoCAD Text Window to the Clipboard.

If you want to copy only a portion of the AutoCAD Text Window to the Clipboard, perform the following steps:

1. Press the F2 function key to open the AutoCAD Text Window.

2. Using the I-beam text cursor, highlight the text you want to copy to the Clipboard.

3. Right-click, and choose Copy from the shortcut menu. You can also choose Edit ≻ Copy from the AutoCAD Text Window's menu bar. The highlighted text is copied to the Clipboard.

4. Open Notepad or another text-editing application, and paste the information.

Although you used the AutoCAD Text Window to copy text in this exercise, you can also copy from the docked command line at the bottom of the AutoCAD window.

You may notice four other options on the shortcut menu: Recent Commands, Paste, Paste To CmdLine, and Options. Choosing Recent Commands displays a list of the most recent commands. For most activities, you'll use a handful of commands repeatedly; the Recent Commands option can save you time by giving you a shortcut to those commands you use the most. The Paste options paste the first line of the contents of the Clipboard into the command line or input box of a dialog box. This can be useful for entering repetitive text or for storing and retrieving a frequently used command. Choosing Options opens the Options dialog box.

**TIP** Items copied to the Clipboard from the AutoCAD Text Window can be pasted into dialog box input boxes. This can be a quick way to transfer layers, linetypes, or other named items from the AutoCAD Text Window into dialog boxes. You can even paste text into the drawing area.

## Storing Searchable Information in AutoCAD Files

As you start to build a library of AutoCAD files, you'll have to start thinking about how to manage those files. Keeping track of AutoCAD files can be a daunting task. Most AutoCAD users start to name files by their job number to keep things organized. But even the best organization schemes don't help if you need to find that one special file among thousands of files in your library. In this section, you'll learn how to include information in an AutoCAD file that you can use later to locate the file by using the Windows Search utility.

**TIP** AutoCAD includes the DesignCenter, a tool that can help you locate a file more easily based on a keyword or description. Chapter 27 contains a complete discussion of the DesignCenter.

To add general, searchable information about your drawing file, use the drawing Properties dialog box (choose File ➢ Drawing Properties).

Here's a description of the four tabs in this dialog box:

**General**   The General tab gives you general information about the file. This information is similar to what you see if you use the Properties options in Windows Explorer to view the properties of a file.

**Summary**   In the Summary tab, enter any text in the Title, Subject, Author, and Keywords fields that is appropriate to the drawing. The information you enter here is stored with the drawing and can be used to locate the file through the AutoCAD DesignCenter or the Windows Search utility (choose Start ➢ Search).

In addition, you can enter a base location for hyperlinks that are applied to objects in your drawing. This base location can be a folder on your computer or network or an Internet web address. See Chapter 27 for more information on hyperlinks.

**Statistics**   The Statistics tab contains the Windows username of the person who last saved the drawing, as well as the time spent on the file. This is the login name at the beginning of the Windows session.

**Custom**   The Custom tab contains two columns of input boxes. This tab lets you store additional custom data with the drawing that is also searchable. For example, you might enter **Job Number** in the Name column and then enter **9901** in the Value column. You might also include information such as project manager names, consultants, or revision numbers. You can then locate the file by using the AutoCAD DesignCenter or the Windows Search utility and doing a search for those keywords from the Name and Value columns.

## Searching for AutoCAD Files

After you've included information in a file's Properties dialog box, you can use the AutoCAD DesignCenter, the File dialog box, or the Windows Search function to locate your file.

A Find option is also located in the Tools menu in the upper-right corner of the AutoCAD Select File dialog box. To access it, choose File ➢ Open; then, in the Select File dialog box, choose Tools ➢ Find.

This option opens a Find dialog box that works just like the Windows XP Search Results window.

### Recovering Corrupted Files

No system is perfect. Eventually, you'll encounter a file that is corrupted in some way. Two AutoCAD tools can frequently salvage a corrupted file:

**Audit**   Enables you to check a file that you can open but suspect has some problem. Audit checks the currently opened file for errors and displays the results in the AutoCAD Text Window.

**Recover**   Enables you to open a file that is so badly corrupted that AutoCAD is unable to open it in a normal way. A Select File dialog box appears, in which you select a file for recovery. After you select a file, it's opened and checked for errors.

You can access these tools from the File ➢ Drawing Utilities cascading menu. More often than not, these tools will do the job, although they aren't a panacea for all file-corruption problems. In the event that you can't recover a file even with these tools, make sure your computer is running smoothly and that other systems aren't faulty.

If for some reason your computer shuts down while you're in the middle of editing a file, you'll see the Drawing Recovery Manager the next time you start AutoCAD. The Drawing Recovery Manager lets you recover the file you were working on when AutoCAD unexpectedly shut down. This feature works just like the file-recovery feature in Microsoft Office: A panel appears to the left of the AutoCAD Text Window, showing you a list of recoverable files. You can then select the filename from the panel to open it. You can always get to the File Recovery Manager by choosing File ➢ Drawing Utilities ➢ Drawing Recovery Manager.

## Using the DXF File Format to Exchange CAD Data with Other Programs

AutoCAD offers many ways to share data with other programs. Perhaps the most common type of data exchange is to share drawing data with other CAD programs. In this section, you'll see how to export and import CAD drawings using the DXF file format.

A *Drawing Exchange Format (DXF) file* is a plain-text file that contains all the information needed to reconstruct a drawing. It's often used to exchange drawings created with other programs. Many CAD and technical drawing programs, including some 3D perspective programs, can generate or read files in DXF format. You might want to use a 3D program to view your drawing in a Perspective view, or you might have a consultant who uses a different CAD program that accepts DXF files.

Be aware that not all programs that read DXF files accept all the data stored therein. Many programs that claim to read DXF files throw away much of the DXF files' information. Attributes are perhaps the most commonly ignored objects, followed by many of the 3D objects, such as meshes and 3D faces.

**TIP**   AutoCAD no longer supports the Initial Graphics Exchange Specification (IGES) standard for CAD data translation.

## Exporting DXF Files

To export your current drawing as a DXF file, follow these steps:

1. Choose File ➤ Save As to open the Save Drawing As dialog box.

2. Click the Files Of Type drop-down list. You can export your drawing under a number of formats, including four DXF formats.

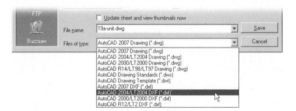

3. Select the appropriate DXF format, and then enter a name for your file. You don't have to include the `.dxf` filename extension.

4. Select a folder for the file, and click Save.

In step 2, you can select from the following DXF file formats:

◆ AutoCAD 2007 DXF (AutoCAD 2007 and 2008 share file formats)

◆ AutoCAD 2004/LT 2004 DXF

◆ AutoCAD 2000/LT 2000 DXF

◆ AutoCAD R12/LT2 DXF

Choose the format appropriate to the program you're exporting to. In most cases, the safest choice is AutoCAD R12/LT2 DXF if you're exporting to another CAD program, although AutoCAD won't maintain the complete functionality of AutoCAD 2008 for such files.

After you've selected a DXF format from the Files Of Type drop-down list, you can set more detailed specifications by choosing Tools ➤ Options in the upper-right corner of the Save Drawing As dialog box. Doing so opens the Saveas Options dialog box. For DXF files, select the DXF Options tab.

The DXF Options tab contains the following options:

**Format**   Lets you choose between ASCII (plain text) or binary file formats. Most other programs accept ASCII, so it's the safest choice. Some programs accept binary DXF files, which have the advantage of being more compact than the ASCII format.

**Select Objects**   Lets you select specific objects in the drawing for export. You can select objects after you close the Saveas Options dialog box and choose Save from the Save Drawing As dialog box.

**Decimal Places Of Accuracy (0–16)**   Enables you to determine the accuracy of the exported file. Keeping this value low helps reduce the size of the export file, particularly if it's to be in ASCII format. Some CAD programs don't support AutoCAD's high accuracy, so using a high value here may have no significance.

**TIP**   You can also type **Dxfout.**↵ at the Command prompt to open the Create DXF File dialog box. This is a standard Windows file dialog box that includes the Options button described here.

## Opening or Importing DXF Files

Some offices have made the DXF file format their standard for CAD drawings. This is most commonly seen in offices that use a variety of CAD software besides AutoCAD.

AutoCAD can be set up to read and write DXF files by default, instead of the standard DWG file format. Here's how it's done:

1. Choose Tools ➢ Options to open the Options dialog box.

2. Select the Open And Save tab.

3. In the File Save group, select any of the DXF formats from the Save As drop-down list.

4. Click OK.

After you do this, all your drawings are automatically saved in the DXF format of your choice. You can also set the default AutoCAD file type by clicking the Options button in the Save Drawing As dialog box. As you saw in an earlier section, the Saveas Options dialog box includes the DWG Options tab. You can select a default file type from the Save All Drawings As drop-down list.

If you need to open a DXF file only once in a while, you can do so by selecting DXF from the Files Of Type drop-down list in the Select File dialog box. This is the dialog box you see when you choose File ➢ Open. You can also use the Dxfin command:

1. Type **Dxfin.**↵ at the Command prompt to open the Select File dialog box.

2. Locate and select the DXF file you want to import.

3. Double-click the filename. If the drawing is large, the imported file may take several minutes to open.

If you want to import a DXF file into the current drawing, you can use the Insert dialog box (choose Insert ➢ Block). Click the Browse button to locate and select a file. Make sure the Files Of Type option is set to DXF.

# Using AutoCAD Drawings in Desktop Publishing

As you probably know, AutoCAD is a natural for creating line art; and because of its popularity, most desktop-publishing programs are designed to import AutoCAD drawings in one form or another. Those of you who employ desktop-publishing software to generate user manuals or other technical documents will probably want to use AutoCAD drawings in your work. In this section, you'll examine ways to output AutoCAD drawings to formats that most desktop-publishing programs can accept.

You can export AutoCAD files to desktop-publishing formats in two ways: by using raster export and by using vector file export.

## Exporting Raster Files

In some cases, you may need only a rough image of your AutoCAD drawing. You can export your drawing as a raster file that can be read in virtually any desktop-publishing and word-processing program. To do this, you must create a new plotter configuration that plots to an image file instead of an output device. (Chapter 8 describes how to use the Add-A-Plotter Wizard to add a plotter configuration to AutoCAD.)

Here is some additional information on how to use that wizard to set up AutoCAD for raster file output:

1. Start the Add-A-Plotter Wizard, and choose Next on the Introduction screen.

2. On the Begin screen of the Add-A-Plotter Wizard, choose My Computer.

3. On the Plotter Model screen, select Raster File Formats from the Manufacturers list, and then select the type of raster file you want to use from the Models list. For example, you can choose Independent JPEG Group JFIF (JPEG Compression). This is one of the more universal file types. Click Next when you've made your selection.

4. Skip the Import PCP or PC2 screen and the Ports screen.

5. Enter a name for your raster output settings on the Plotter Name screen.

6. On the Finish screen, click the Edit Plotter Configuration button to open the Plotter Configuration Editor dialog box.

7. Click the Source And Size item that appears in the large list box in the top of the dialog box. A list of options appears in the Size list box in the lower-right corner of the dialog box.

8. Click Custom Paper Sizes in the large list box at the top of the dialog box. The options change in the lower half of the dialog box.

9. Click the Add button to start the Custom Paper Size Wizard.

10. Click the Start From Scratch radio button, and then click Next to open the Media Bounds screen.

11. Enter a height and width in pixels for your image file, and then click Next to open the Paper Size Name screen. Enter a name that best describes the size of the image file, and click Next to open the File Name screen.

12. Enter a name for the Plotter Model Parameters file. This file stores specific setting information about the plotter. Click Next when you're finished.

13. On the Finish screen, click Finish. The Plotter Configuration Editor dialog box reappears. Click OK, and then click Finish in the Add-A-Plotter Wizard.

After you've finished creating a plotter configuration, it appears as a file in the `Application Data\Autodesk\AutoCAD 2008\R17.1\enu\Plotters` subfolder of your profile folder. You can access this file through Windows Explorer or from AutoCAD by choosing File ➤ Plotter Manager.

**NOTE** The `Application Data` folder is typically a hidden folder. To get to it, you have to turn off the "hide hidden folders" feature of Windows Explorer. See "Finding Hidden Folders That Contain AutoCAD Files" in Appendix A for more information.

To create a raster-file version of your drawing, choose File ➤ Plot; then, in the Plot dialog box, select your raster-file plotter configuration from the Name drop-down list of the Printer/Plotter group. You can then proceed to plot your drawing, but instead of paper output, you'll get a raster file. You can specify the filename and location when you click the OK button to plot the file.

If you need to make changes to your raster-file configuration, choose File ➤ Plotter Manager; then, in the Plotters window, double-click your raster-file configuration file. You'll see the same Plotter Configuration Editor you used to set up the raster plotter configuration.

You can set up a different plotter configuration for each type of raster file you use. You can also set up plotter configurations for different resolutions, if you choose. To learn more about plotting in general, see Chapter 8. Appendix B provides detailed information on the Plotter Configuration Editor.

---

### EXCHANGING FILES WITH EARLIER RELEASES

One persistent dilemma that has plagued AutoCAD users is how to exchange files between earlier versions of the program. In the past, if you upgraded AutoCAD, you were locked out from exchanging your drawings with people using earlier versions. Release 12 alleviated this difficulty by making Release 12 files compatible with Release 11 files.

With Release 13, the file structure was radically different from earlier versions of AutoCAD. Then, AutoCAD 14 made it possible to freely exchange files between Release 13 and 14.

AutoCAD 2002 uses the AutoCAD 2000 file format, which has some features, such as multiple layouts and searchable properties, that don't translate to earlier versions. AutoCAD 2006 shares the same file format with AutoCAD 2004, but it has new features that make it incompatible with AutoCAD 2000 and 2002. AutoCAD 2007 and 2008 share the same file format, and they also use a unique file format that isn't compatible with earlier versions.

If compatibility with earlier versions is more important than the new features of AutoCAD 2008, you can set up AutoCAD 2008 to read and write to AutoCAD 2006 or earlier. Or, if you're willing to work with DXF files, you can set up AutoCAD 2008 to automatically write AutoCAD 2006 DXF files.

To set up AutoCAD to automatically write earlier versions, use the Options dialog box to set the default file type, as described earlier in the "Opening or Importing DXF Files" section; but instead of selecting a DXF file type, select the DWG file type you want to use.

## Exporting Vector Files

If you need to preserve the accuracy of your drawing, or if you want to take advantage of TrueType or PostScript fonts, you can use the DXF, Windows Metafile (WMF), or PostScript vector format. You can also export to DGN and SAT file formats. Intergraph's DGN format is popular in civil engineering, mapping, and other CAD applications. The SAT format is associated with ACIS and is a 3D modeling format.

For vector-format files, DXF is the easiest to work with; and with TrueType support, DXF can preserve font information between AutoCAD and desktop-publishing programs that support the DXF format. The WMF format is also a commonly accepted file format for vector information, and it preserves TrueType fonts and lineweights used in your drawings.

PostScript is a raster/vector hybrid file format that AutoCAD supports; unfortunately, AutoCAD dropped direct PostScript font support with Release 14. However, you can still use substitute fonts to stand in for PostScript fonts. These substitute fonts are converted to true PostScript fonts when AutoCAD exports the drawing. You don't see the true results of your PostScript output until you print your drawing on a PostScript printer.

The DXF file export was covered in the previous section of this chapter, so this section will concentrate on the WMF and PostScript file formats.

### WMF OUTPUT

The WMF file type is one of the more popular vector file formats in Windows. It can be opened and edited by most illustration programs, including CorelDRAW and Adobe Illustrator. Most word-processing, database, and worksheet programs can also import WMF files. It's a great option for AutoCAD file export because it preserves TrueType fonts and lineweight settings; you can export WMF files that preserve lineweights as well.

To export WMF files, do the following:

1. Choose File ➢ Export to open the Export Data dialog box.

2. Enter a name and location for your WMF file, select Metafile (*.wmf) from the File Of Type drop-down list, and then click OK. The dialog box closes, and you're prompted to select objects.

3. Select the objects you want to export to the WMF file, and press ↵. The objects are saved to your WMF file.

### POSTSCRIPT OUTPUT

AutoCAD can export to the Encapsulated PostScript (EPS) file format. If you're using AutoCAD 2008, you can obtain PostScript output in two ways: You can choose File ➢ Export, or you can enter **Psout.**↵ at the Command prompt. Another method is to install a PostScript printer driver and plot your drawing to an EPS file. LT users can't export to EPS by choosing File ➢ Export; you must set up a PostScript plotter and use it to plot to a file.

To set up AutoCAD to plot your drawing to an EPS file, follow the steps described in the "Exporting Raster Files" section earlier in this chapter; but in step 2, select Adobe from the Manufacturers list, and then select the appropriate PostScript level from the Models list.

AutoCAD doesn't preserve font information when creating EPS files from the printer option. It also produces larger files, especially if your drawing contains a lot of area fills and filled fonts. As an alternative to EPS, you can "plot" to an Adobe PDF file. EPS files can often be substituted with PDF files. You'll need to install the Autodesk-provided PDF plotter driver using the Add-A-Plotter Wizard described in the previous section. When you get to the Plotter Model screen, select the Autodesk ePlot (PDF) option from the Manufacturers list. You can also use the full version of Adobe Acrobat or Acrobat Pro to produce PDF files from AutoCAD.

**TIP** The HPGL plot-file format is another vector format you can use to export your AutoCAD drawings. Use the method described earlier in the section "Exporting Raster Files" to add the HPGL plotter driver to your printer/plotter configuration.

---

**USING AUTOCAD DWF FILES**

The Autodesk DWF file format is another format you can use to exchange drawing data with others. It offers features that are geared toward AutoCAD users. You can import DWF files as external references; and using a free DWF viewer, you can gather information about a drawing such as block information, attribute data, and distance measurements. See Chapter 27 for more on DWF.

---

## Using OLE to Import Data

To import data from other applications, you use the Cut and Paste features found in virtually all Windows programs. You cut the data from the source document and then paste it into AutoCAD. Typically, you'll want to paste data into AutoCAD in AutoCAD's native object format; but if you prefer, you can use a Windows feature called Object Linking and Embedding (OLE) to import files.

When you paste data into your AutoCAD file using OLE, you can link it to the source file or you can embed it. If you *link* it to the source file, the pasted data is updated whenever the source file is modified. This is similar to an AutoCAD cross-referenced file. (See Chapter 15 for more on cross-referenced files.) If you *embed* data, you're pasting it into AutoCAD without linking it. You can still open the application associated with the data by double-clicking it, but the data is no longer associated with the source file. Importing files using OLE is similar to other cut-and-paste operations. First, cut the data from the source application. This could be Microsoft Excel or Word. In AutoCAD, choose Edit ➤ Paste Special to open the Paste Special dialog box.

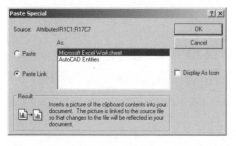

Click the Paste Link radio button to tell AutoCAD that you want this paste to be a link. Notice that the list of source types changes to show only one option: Microsoft Office Excel Worksheet. Click OK. You're prompted to select an insertion point. Place the cursor in the location for the paste, and click. The imported data appears within a bounding box. You can adjust the size of the bounding box to fit the scale of the drawing.

In addition to using the Edit ➤ Paste Special option, you can also import an OLE object by choosing Insert ➤ OLE Object to open the Insert Object dialog box.

You can then select the type of object you want to import from the Object Type list box. Two radio buttons to the left of the list box let you import an existing object or create a new object of the type listed in the list box. If you choose the Create New radio button, the application associated with the object type will start and open a new file. If you choose the Create From File radio button, the dialog box changes to show a filename and a Browse button.

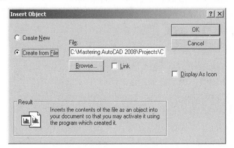

You can then browse for an existing file to import. The Link check box lets you specify whether the imported file is to be linked. If you choose Insert ➤ OLE Object to import an Excel worksheet, the entire worksheet is imported.

## Editing OLE Links

After you've pasted an object with links, you can control the links by choosing Edit ➤ OLE Links. If there are no linked objects in the drawing, this option is grayed out; otherwise it opens the Links dialog box.

The options available in the Links dialog box are as follows:

**Cancel**   Cancels the link between a pasted object and its source file. After you use this option, changes in the source file have no effect on the pasted object. This is similar to using the Bind option in the Xref command.

**Update Now**   Updates an object's link when the Manual option is selected.

**Open Source**   Opens the linked file in the application associated with the object, and lets you edit it.

**Change Source**   Lets you change the object's link to a different file. When you select this option, AutoCAD opens the Change Link dialog box, where you can select another file of the same type. For example, if you're editing the link to a sound file, the Change Link dialog box displays files with the .wav file extension.

**Automatic and Manual**   Radio buttons that control whether linked objects are updated automatically or manually.

**Break Link**   Disconnects the link between the inserted data and the source document. The inserted data then becomes embedded, rather than linked.

## Importing Worksheets as AutoCAD Tables

Although it can be beneficial to import worksheets as linked OLE objects, you may prefer to import worksheets as AutoCAD entities. You may not need the direct link to the source material that OLE linking offers. The ability to edit the imported worksheet directly in AutoCAD may have a higher priority for you.

In Chapter 10, you saw how you could create tables in AutoCAD by using the Table tool. You can import an Excel worksheet as an AutoCAD table by using the AutoCAD Entities option in the Paste Special dialog box. By importing worksheets as tables, you have more control over the layout and appearance of the worksheet data.

Try the following exercise to see how you can create a table from a worksheet:

1. Open the Excel worksheet called 19a-plan.xls, and highlight the door data, as shown in Figure 19.7.

**FIGURE 19.7**

The Excel worksheet

2. Choose Edit ➢ Copy to place a copy of the selected data into the Windows Clipboard; then, switch back to AutoCAD.

3. Choose Edit ➢ Paste Special to open the Paste Special dialog box.

4. With the Paste radio button selected, select AutoCAD Entities from the list, and then click OK.

5. At the `Specify insertion point or [paste as Text]:` prompt, click a point in the lower-right area of the drawing. The worksheet data appears in the drawing, although it's very small. You also see the Text Formatting dialog box.

6. Click OK in the Text Formatting toolbar to close it.

7. Use the Scale tool to enlarge the table to a readable size, and use the corner grips to adjust the width.

| D-TYPE | D-SIZE | D-NUMBER | D-THICK | D-RATE | D-MATRL | D-CONST |
|--------|--------|----------|---------|--------|---------|---------|
| B | 3'-0" | 116 | 1 3/4" | no rating | Wood | Solid Core |
| B | 3'-0" | 114 | 1 3/4" | 20 min | Wood | Solid Core |
| B | 3'-0" | 112 | 1 3/4" | 20 min | Wood | Solid Core |
| B | 3'-0" | 110 | 1 3/4" | 20 min | Wood | Solid Core |
| B | 3'-0" | 106 | 1 3/4" | 20 min | Wood | Solid Core |
| B | 3'-0" | 108 | 1 3/4" | 20 min | Wood | Solid Core |
| B | 3'-0" | 102 | 1 3/4" | 20 min | Wood | Solid Core |
| B | 3'-0" | 104 | 1 3/4" | 20 min | Wood | Solid Core |
| B | 3'-0" | 115 | 1 3/4" | 20 min | Wood | Solid Core |
| B | 3'-0" | 111 | 1 3/4" | 20 min | Wood | Solid Core |
| B | 3'-0" | 107 | 1 3/4" | 20 min | Wood | Solid Core |
| B | 3'-0" | 103 | 1 3/4" | 20 min | Wood | Solid Core |
| B | 3'-0" | 101 | 1 3/4" | 20 min | Wood | Solid Core |
| B | 3'-0" | 105 | 1 3/4" | 20 min | Wood | Solid Core |
| B | 3'-0" | 109 | 1 3/4" | 20 min | Wood | Solid Core |
| B | 3'-0" | 113 | 1 3/4" | 20 min | Wood | Solid Core |

8. Close the Excel file.

You can edit this imported worksheet using the editing methods for AutoCAD tables described in Chapter 10. In that chapter, you learned that you can edit the text format, the border lineweight and color, and the background of cells. You can add rows and columns and rotate text so that it fits more uniformly in a vertical column.

In this exercise, the worksheet was imported using the default standard table style. This gives you a simple-looking table using the AutoCAD Txt font. You can set up a custom table style with the fonts and borders you want and then import the table for a more custom appearance. Make sure your custom table style is the current style before you import the worksheet.

## Understanding Options for Embedding Data

The Paste Special dialog box offers several other options that may better suit your needs. Here is a brief description of each format that is available:

**Picture (Metafile)**  Imports the data as vector or bitmap graphics, whichever is appropriate. If applicable, text is also maintained as text, although you can't edit it in AutoCAD.

**Bitmap**  Imports the data as a bitmap image, closely reflecting the appearance of the data as it appears on your computer screen in the source application.

**Picture (Enhanced Metafile)**  Similar to the Picture (Metafile) option, with support for more features.

**AutoCAD Entities**  Converts the data into AutoCAD objects such as lines, arcs, and circles. Text is converted into AutoCAD single-line text objects. Worksheets are converted into AutoCAD tables.

**Image Entity**    Converts the data into an AutoCAD raster image. You can then edit it by using the raster image–related tools found in the Modify ➢ Object ➢ Image cascading menu of the menu bar. See Chapter 14 for more on how to use raster images.

**Text**    Converts the data into AutoCAD multiline text objects. Formatting isn't imported with text.

**Unicode Text**    Imports text data in the Unicode format. Unicode is an international standard for encoding text. If the Text option doesn't work, try Unicode Text.

The options you see in the Paste Special dialog box depend on the type of data being imported. You saw how the Microsoft Excel Worksheet option maintains the imported data as an Excel worksheet. If the contents of the Clipboard come from another program, you're offered that program as a choice in place of Excel.

**TIP**    Choosing Edit ➢ Paste embeds OLE data objects into AutoCAD, as does the Paste From Clipboard tool in the Standard toolbar.

## Using the Clipboard to Export AutoCAD Drawings

Just as you can cut and paste data into AutoCAD from applications that support OLE, you can also cut and paste AutoCAD images to other applications. This can be useful as a way of including AutoCAD images in word-processing documents, worksheets, or desktop-publishing documents. It can also be useful in creating background images for visualization programs such as Autodesk's 3ds Max or VIZ, or paint programs such as Corel Painter.

**TIP**    If you cut and paste an AutoCAD drawing to another file by using OLE and then send the file to someone using another computer, they must also have AutoCAD installed before they can edit the pasted AutoCAD drawing.

The receiving application doesn't need to support OLE, but if it does, the exported drawing can be edited with AutoCAD and will maintain its accuracy as a CAD drawing. Otherwise, the AutoCAD image will be converted to a bitmap graphic.

To use the Clipboard to export an object or a set of objects from an AutoCAD drawing, choose Edit ➢ Copy. You're then prompted to select the objects you want to export. If you want to simultaneously export and erase objects from AutoCAD, choose Edit ➢ Cut.

If you want the AutoCAD image to be linked to AutoCAD, choose Edit ➢ Copy Link. You won't be prompted to select objects. The current visible portion of your drawing will be exported. To export the entire drawing, choose View ➢ Zoom ➢ Extents before using the Copy Link option. Otherwise, before using Copy Link, set up AutoCAD to display the portion of your drawing that you want to export,

In the receiving application, choose Edit ➢ Paste Special. You'll see a dialog box similar to AutoCAD's Paste Special dialog box. Select the method for pasting your AutoCAD image, and then click OK. If the receiving application doesn't have a Paste Special option, choose Edit ➢ Paste. The receiving application converts the image into a format it can accept.

**TIP**    You can copy multiple viewport views from Paper Space into the Clipboard by choosing Edit ➢ Copy Link.

## The Bottom Line

**Finding the Area of Closed Boundaries**   There are a number of ways to find the area of a closed boundary. The easiest way is also perhaps the least obvious.

**Master It**   What AutoCAD feature would you use to quickly find the area of an irregular shape like a pond or lake?

**Solution**   Hatch.

**Getting General Information**   A lot of information is stored in AutoCAD drawings that can tell you about the files. You can find out how much memory a file uses as well as the amount of time spent editing the file.

**Master It**   What feature lets you store your own searchable information about a drawing file, and how to you get to this feature?

**Solution**   You can open the Properties dialog box by choosing File ➢ Drawing Properties.

**Using the DXF File Format to Exchange CAD Data with Other Programs**   Autodesk created the DXF file format as a means of sharing vector drawings with other programs.

**Master It**   Name some of the versions of AutoCAD you can export to using the File ➢ Save As option.

**Solution**   2007, 2004, 2002, and R12.

**Using AutoCAD Drawings in Desktop Publishing**   AutoCAD drawings find their way into all types of documents, including brochures and technical manuals. Users are often asked to convert their CAD drawings into formats that can be read by desktop-publishing software.

**Master It**   Name some file formats, by file extension or type, that desktop-publishing programs can accept.

**Solution**   PDF, WMF, EPS, and a wide variety of bitmap-image files.

**Using OLE to Import Data**   You can import data into AutoCAD from a variety of sources. Most sources, such as bitmap images and text, can be imported as native AutoCAD objects. Other sources may need to be imported as OLE objects.

**Master It**   To link imported data to a source program through OLE, what dialog box would you use?

**Solution**   Paste Special.

# Part 4

# 3D Modeling and Imaging

**In this part:**

# Chapter 20

# Creating 3D Drawings

Viewing an object in three dimensions gives you a sense of its true shape and form. It also helps you conceptualize your design, which results in better design decisions. In addition, using three-dimensional objects helps you communicate your ideas to those who may not be familiar with the plans, sections, and side views of your design.

A further advantage to drawing in three dimensions is that you can derive 2D drawings from your 3D models, which may otherwise take considerably more time with standard 2D drawing methods. For example, you can model a mechanical part in 3D and then quickly derive its 2D top, front, and right-side views by using the techniques discussed in this chapter.

Topics in this chapter include the following:

- ◆ Getting to Know the 3D Modeling Workspace
- ◆ Drawing in 3D Using Solids
- ◆ Creating 3D Forms from 2D Shapes
- ◆ Isolating Coordinates with Point Filters
- ◆ Moving Around Your Model
- ◆ Getting a Visual Effect
- ◆ Turning a 3D View into a 2D AutoCAD Drawing

## Getting to Know the 3D Modeling Workspace

Most of this book is devoted to showing you how to work in what is called the *AutoCAD Classic* workspace. This classic workspace is basically a 2D drawing environment, although you can certainly work in 3D as well.

AutoCAD 2008 offers something called the *3D Modeling* workspace, which gives you a set of tools to help ease your way into 3D modeling. This 3D Modeling workspace gives AutoCAD a different appearance, but don't worry. AutoCAD behaves in the same basic way, and the AutoCAD files produced are the same regardless of whether they're 2D or 3D drawings.

You can get to the 3D Modeling workspace in two ways. The first is to select 3D Modeling from the Workspace toolbar that you see when you start AutoCAD (see Figure 20.1).

Second, if you start AutoCAD in the 2D Drafting and Annotation or AutoCAD Classic workspace, you can do the following to get to the 3D Modeling workspace:

1. Start AutoCAD, and then choose 3D Modeling from the Workspace toolbar. You see a new palette to the right of the AutoCAD Window.

2. To start a new 3D model, choose File ➤ New to open the Select Template dialog box. Select the acad3D.dwt template file, and click Open. Your screen will look similar to Figure 20.2.

**FIGURE 20.1**

The Workspace toolbar

**FIGURE 20.2**

The AutoCAD 3D Modeling workspace

The drawing area displays the workspace as a perspective view with a gray background and a grid. This is really just a typical AutoCAD drawing file with a couple of setting changes. The view has been set up to be a perspective view by default, and a new feature called *Visual Styles* has been set to show 3D objects as solid objects. You'll learn more about the tools that let you adjust the appearance of your workspace later in this chapter. For now, let's look at the tool palette to the right of the AutoCAD window.

Two palettes appear in the 3D Modeling workspace. To the far right is the AutoCAD Tool Palettes window that you've already seen; it contains shortcuts to various AutoCAD tools. To the left of the Tool Palettes window is the *Dashboard*. Like the 2D Drafting & Annotation Dashboard, the 3D workspace Dashboard offers all the tools you'll need to create 3D models. The Dashboard is divided into seven control panels, each marked by an icon in the far-left border (see Figure 20.3). The familiar Layers control panel sits at the top of the Dashboard. The following list describes the function of the other six control panels:

**TIP**  You can open the Dashboard at any time in any workspace by choosing Tools ➢ Palettes ➢ Dashboard or by entering **dashboard.**↵ at the Command prompt.

**FIGURE 20.3**

The Dashboard and its components

Layers — 3D Make — Visual Style — Light — Materials — Render — 3D Navigate

**3D Make**    Contains tools you'll use to create 3D objects. You'll also find tools that are specifically designed to edit 3D objects in this control panel.

**Visual Style**    Gives you tools that change the way AutoCAD displays your 3D model. I mentioned earlier that the reason your drawing in the workspace looks different from what you're used to is that a different visual style is applied to the drawing. You can select from five visual styles in this control panel. You can even create your own visual style, although that is an advanced topic not discussed in this book.

**Light**    Lets you add lights to create presentation views of your model. You can set up point lights, which are like lightbulbs, or spotlights, which point a light in a specific direction. If your application is architecture, you can set up an accurate representation of sunlight to perform shadow studies for any location and time of day.

**Materials**    Lets you create and apply textures to your 3D objects. Textures can be anything from a shiny metallic surface to a brick pattern. The pattern emerges when you use the Render control panel to create a rendered view of your model. A crude representation of the material also appears when you use the default Realistic visual style in your workspace.

**Render**    Lets you generate a high-quality rendering of your model based on the lighting and materials you've used. The rendering appears in a separate window that opens when you start the render process. You can save a rendered view as an image file such as a TIFF or JPEG file.

**3D Navigate**    Contains tools to help you get around in your 3D model. You'll find tools to change your view angle as well as your field of view when using a perspective view. You can switch between perspective views and isometric-style views called *parallel projections*. With the tools in this control panel, you can even create an animation known as a *walkthrough*, which allows you to move around as if you're walking through your model.

In addition to the Dashboard, the bottom of the AutoCAD window contains a few extra tools, as shown in Figure 20.4. Using these tools is just a different way to get to the layout tabs. You'll also notice that the cursor and UCS icon are different. You'll learn more about these features in the "Rotating Objects in 3D Using Dynamic UCS" section, later in this chapter.

**FIGURE 20.4**

Tools to switch from
Model Space to layouts

Model    Layout1    Additional layouts

In the next section, you'll gain firsthand experience creating and editing some 3D shapes using the 3D Make, 3D Navigate, and Visual Style control panels. This way, you'll get a feel for how things work in the 3D Modeling workspace.

## Drawing in 3D Using Solids

You can work with two types of 3D objects in AutoCAD: solids and surfaces. You can treat solid objects as if they're solid material. For example, you can create a box and then remove shapes from the box as if you're carving it, as shown in Figure 20.5.

**FIGURE 20.5**

Solid modeling
lets you remove or
add shapes.

With surfaces, you create complex surfaces shapes by building on lines, arcs, or polylines. For example, you can quickly turn a series of curved polylines, arcs, or lines into a warped surface, as shown in Figure 20.6.

Next, you'll learn how to create a solid box and then make simple changes to it, as an introduction to 3D modeling.

**FIGURE 20.6**

Using the Loft tool,
you can use a set of
2D objects (left) to
define a complex
surface (right).

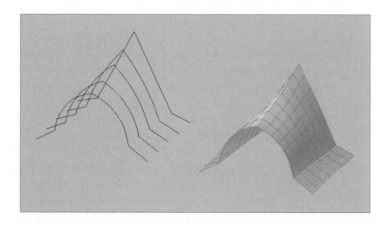

**TIP**    If you have some experience with AutoCAD 3D, note that the new surface-modeling features aren't the same as the surface objects you may have created in the older version of AutoCAD. The new surface objects can interact with solid primitive objects and can be converted into 3D solids. You can still create the old-style 3D surface objects, but be aware that they aren't the same type of object as the 3D surfaces in AutoCAD 2008. You can convert the old-style surfaces into the new 3D surfaces using the Convtosurface command described in the sidebar "Converting Objects with Thickness into 3D Solids," later in this chapter.

## Creating a 3D Box

Start by creating a box using the Box tool in the 3D Make control panel:

1. Close the Tool Palettes window. You won't need it for this chapter.

2. Click the Box tool in the 3D Make control panel.

3. Click a point near the origin of the drawing shown in Figure 20.7. You can use the coordinate readout to select a point near 0,0. Once you click, you see a rectangle follow the cursor.

4. Click another point near coordinate 20,15, as shown in Figure 20.7. As you move the cursor, the rectangle is fixed, and the height of the 3D box appears.

5. Enter 4↵ for a height of 4 units for the box. You can also click to fix the height of the box.

**FIGURE 20.7**
Drawing a
3D solid box

Selection a location near coordinate 20,15 for the other corner.

Start the box at coordinate 0,0.

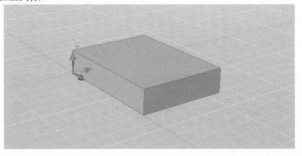

**TIP** When you start a 3D model using the acad3D.dwt template, the default layer 0 is set to a color that is a light gray instead of the white or black that is used in the standard acad.dwt template. The gray color is used so you can see the 3D shapes clearly when the model is displayed using a shaded visual style. If you happen to start a 3D model using the acad.dwt template, you may want to change the default color to something other than white or black.

You used three basic steps in creating the box. You first clicked one corner to establish a location for the box; then, you clicked another corner to establish the base size. Finally, you selected a height. You use a similar set of steps to create any of the other 3D solid primitives found in the 3D Make control panel. For example, for a cylinder, you select the center, then the radius, and then the height. For a wedge, you select two corners as you did with the box, and then you select the height. You'll learn more about these 3D solid primitives in Chapter 23.

## Editing 3D Solids with Grips

Once you've created a solid, you can fine-tune its shape by using grips:

1. Click the solid to select it. You may see a message alerting you to the new editing options. Dismiss the message, and grips appear on the 3D solid, as shown in Figure 20.8.

   The square grips at the base of the solid allow you to adjust the location of those grips in a way that is similar to adjusting the grips on 2D objects. The arrow grips let you adjust the length of the site to which the arrows are attached. If you click an arrow grip and you have Dynamic Input turned on, a dimension appears at the cursor, as shown in Figure 20.8. You can enter a new dimension for the length associated with the selected grip, or you can drag and click the arrow to adjust the length. Remember that you can press the Tab key to shift between dimensions shown in the Dynamic input display.

**FIGURE 20.8**
Grips appear on 3D solid.

Click this arrow grip.

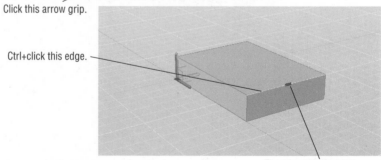

Ctrl+click this edge.

The edge grip appears.

**NOTE** If your Ctrl+click doesn't work as described, you may need to change the setting for the Legacyctrlpick system variable. At the command prompt, enter **legacyctrlpick**↵, and then enter **0**↵.

2. Click the arrow grip toward the front of the box, as shown at upper left in Figure 20.8. Now, as you move the cursor, the box changes in length.

3. Press Escape to clear the grip selection.

You can also move individual edges by using a Ctrl+click:

1. Ctrl+click the top-front edge, as shown at lower right in Figure 20.8. The edge is highlighted, and a grip appears at its midpoint.

2. Click the edge's grip, and move the cursor. The edge follows the grip.

3. Hold down the Shift key, and pull the grip forward, away from the box's center. The Shift key constrains the motion in the X, Y, or Z axis.

4. Click a point to fix the edge's new position.

5. Click the Undo button to return the box to its original shape.

As you can see, you have a great deal of flexibility in controlling the shape of the box. Using the Shift key lets you constrain the motion of the grip.

## Constraining Motion with the Grip Tool

Another handy tool for grip-editing 3D objects is the *grip tool*. This is an icon that looks like the UCS icon and that appears whenever you hover over a grip. Try the next exercise to see how the grip tool works:

1. Ctrl+click the top-front edge of the box again to expose the edge's grip.

2. Place the cursor on the grip, but don't click. The grip tool appears, as shown in Figure 20.9.

**FIGURE 20.9**
Using the grip tool to constrain motion

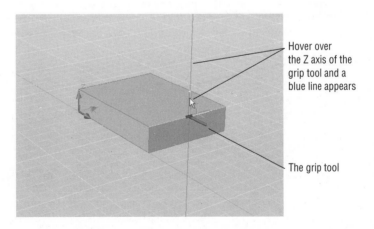

Hover over the Z axis of the grip tool and a blue line appears

The grip tool

3. Place the cursor on the blue Z axis of the grip tool, but don't click. A blue line appears that extends across the drawing area, and the Z axis of the grip tool changes color as shown in Figure 20.9.

4. Click the Z axis. Now, as you move the cursor, the grip motion is constrained in the Z axis.

5. Click again to fix the location of the grip.

6. Press the Escape key to clear your grip selection.

7. Click the Undo tool to undo the grip edit.

Here you used the grip tool to easily change the Z location of a grip. You can use the grip tool to modify the location of a single grip or the entire object.

## Rotating Objects in 3D Using Dynamic UCS

Typically, you work in what is known as the *World Coordinate System* (WCS). This is the default coordinate system that AutoCAD uses in new drawings, but you can also create your own coordinate systems that are subsets of the WCS. A coordinate system that you create is known as a *User Coordinate System* (UCS).

UCSs are significant in 3D modeling because they can help you orient your work in 3D space. For example, you could set up a UCS on a vertical face of the 3D box you created earlier. You could then draw on that vertical face just as you would on the drawing's WCS. Figure 20.10 shows a cylinder drawn on the side of a box. The vertical grid shows the orientation of the UCS. Also notice the orientation of the UCS at the center of the cylinder.

The UCS has always been an important tool for 3D modeling in AutoCAD. AutoCAD 2007 introduced the Dynamic UCS, which automatically changes the orientation of the X, Y, and Z axes to conform to the flat surface of a 3D object.

You may have noticed that when you created the new 3D file using the acad3D.dwt template, the cursor looked different. Instead of the usual cross, you saw three intersecting lines. If you look carefully, you'll see that each line of the cursor is a different color. In its default configuration, AutoCAD shows a red line for the X axis, a green line for the Y axis, and a blue line for the Z axis. This mimics the color scheme of the UCS icon, as shown in Figure 20.11.

**FIGURE 20.10**
Drawing on the side of a box

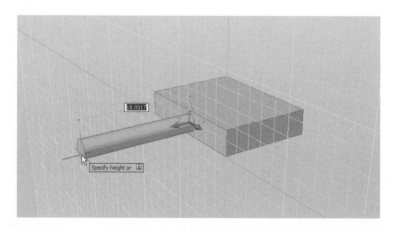

**FIGURE 20.11**

The UCS icon at the left and the cursor in 3D to the right are color matched.

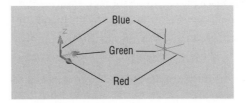

As you work with the Dynamic UCS, you'll see that the orientation of these lines changes when you point at a surface on a 3D object. The following exercise shows you how to use the Dynamic UCS to help you rotate the box about the X axis:

1. Be sure the Osnap and Dynamic UCS features are turned on. Be sure the DUCS button at the bottom of the AutoCAD Window is in the down, or on, position. If it isn't, click it to turn it on.

2. Choose Modify ➤ Rotate.

3. At the `Select objects:` prompt, click the box, and then press ↵ to finish your selection.

4. At the `Specify base point:` prompt, don't click anything, but move the cursor from one surface of the box to a side of the box. As you do this, pay attention to the orientation of the cursor. It changes depending on which surface you're pointing to.

5. Place the cursor on the left side, as shown in Figure 20.12.

**FIGURE 20.12**

Selecting a base point, and the resulting box orientation

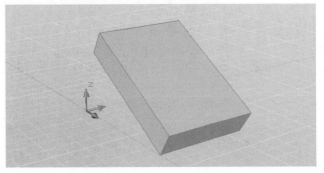

6. Place the osnap cursor on the lower-front corner of the box, as shown in the left image in Figure 20.12. Click this corner. As you move the cursor, the box rotates about the Y axis.

7. Enter **–30** for the rotation angle. Your box should look like the image at lower right in Figure 20.12.

Here you saw that you can hover over a surface to indicate the plane about which the rotation is to occur. Now, suppose you want to add an object to one of the sides of the rotated box. The next section will show you another essential tool you can use to do just that.

---

**USING OBJECT SNAPS AND OSNAP TRACKING IN 3D SPACE**

If you need to place objects in precise locations in 3D, such as endpoints or midpoints of other objects, you can do so using object snaps, just as you would in 2D. But you must take care when using osnaps where the Dynamic UCS is concerned.

In the exercise in the "Rotating Objects in 3D Using Dynamic UCS" section, you were asked to make sure you placed the cursor on the side of the box that coincided with the rotational plane *before* you selected the Endpoint osnap. This ensures that the Dynamic UCS feature has selected the proper rotational plane; otherwise, the box may rotate in the wrong direction.

In some operations, you can't use osnaps in perspective mode. Osnap Tracking also doesn't work in perspective mode. Switch to a parallel projection view if you know you'll want to use osnaps. (See the section "Changing from Perspective to Parallel Projection," later in this chapter.) If you need to snap to points that are in the back of an object, switch to 2D or 3D wireframe visual style. See the section "Getting a Visual Effect," later in this chapter, for more on visual styles.

---

## Drawing on a 3D Object's Surface

In the rotation exercise, you saw that you can hover over a surface to indicate the plane of rotation. You can use the same method to indicate the plane on which you want to place an object. Try the following exercise to see how it's done:

1. Choose Draw ➢ Circle ➢ Center, Radius.

2. Place the cursor on the top surface of the rectangle, as indicated in Figure 20.13, and hold it there for a moment. The cursor aligns with the angle of the top surface.

3. With the cursor aligned with the top surface of the box, click a point roughly at the center of the box. The circle appears on the surface, and as you move the cursor, the circle's radius follows.

4. Adjust the circle so it's roughly the same 6-unit radius as the one shown on the right in Figure 20.13, and then click to set the radius. You can also enter **6↵**.

5. Choose Modify ➢ Offset, and offset the circle 2 units inward, as shown in the second panel of Figure 20.13.

This demonstrates that you can use Dynamic UCS to align objects with the surface of an object. Note that the Dynamic UCS only works on flat surfaces. For example, you can't use Dynamic UCS to place an object on the curved side of a cylinder.

**FIGURE 20.13**

Drawing circles on the surface of a 3D solid

Align the cursor with the top surface, and select a point at the center of the box.

Offset the circle toward the center.

---

**USING A FIXED UCS**

If you're working in a crowded area of a drawing, or if you know you need to do a lot of work on one particular surface of an object, you can create a UCS that remains in a fixed orientation until you change it, instead of relying on the Dynamic UCS feature. Choose Tools ➤ New UCS ➤ Face, click the surface that defines the plane on which you want to work, and press ↵. The UCS aligns with the selected surface, and you won't have to worry about accidentally drawing in the wrong orientation. To return to the WCS, choose Tools ➤ New UCS ➤ World. You'll learn more about the UCS in Chapter 21.

---

## Pushing and Pulling Shapes from a Solid

You've just added a 2D circle to the top surface of the 3D box. AutoCAD offers a tool that lets you use that 2D circle or any closed 2D shape to modify the shape of your 3D object. The Presspull tool in the 3D Make control panel lets you "press" or "pull" a 3D shape from the surface of a 3D object. The following exercise shows how this works:

1. Make sure the Polar button in the status bar is in turned on, and then click the Presspull tool in the 3D Make control panel. You can also enter **Presspull**↵ at the Command prompt.

2. Place the cursor over the center of the inner circle, but don't click yet. The circle is high-lighted. (See the top-left panel of Figure 20.14.)

3. Move the cursor to the top surface of the box between both circles. The area between the circles is highlighted. (See the right panel of Figure 20.14.)

4. With the cursor between the two circles, click the mouse. As you move the mouse, the circular area defined by the two circles moves.

5. Adjust the cursor location so the polar coordinate readout shows a minus Z (−Z), as shown in the top panel of Figure 20.15. Enter **3**↵ to create a 3-unit indentation, as shown in the second panel of Figure 20.15.

**FIGURE 20.14**
Move the cursor over different areas of the box, and notice how the areas are highlighted.

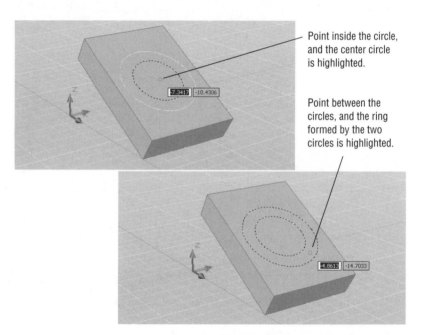

Point inside the circle, and the center circle is highlighted.

Point between the circles, and the ring formed by the two circles is highlighted.

You've created a circular indentation in the box by pressing the circular area defined by the two circles. You could have pulled the area upward to form a circular ridge on the box. Pressing the circle into the solid is essentially the same as subtracting one solid from another. When you press the shape into the solid, AutoCAD assumes you want to subtract the shape.

**TIP** Presspull works with any closed 2D shape, such as a circle, closed polyline, or other com-pletely enclosed area. An existing 3D solid isn't needed. For example, you can draw two concen-tric circles without the 3D box and then use Presspull to convert the circles into a 3D solid ring. In the previous exercise, the solid box showed that you can use Presspull to subtract a shape from an existing solid.

As you saw in this exercise, the Presspull tool can help you quickly subtract a shape from an exist-ing 3D solid. Figure 20.16 shows some other examples of how you can use Presspull. For example, you can draw a line from one edge to another and then use Presspull to extrude the resulting trian-gular shape. You can also draw concentric shapes and extrude them; you can even use offset spline curves to add a trough to a solid.

**FIGURE 20.15**
Creating an indentation in the box using Presspull

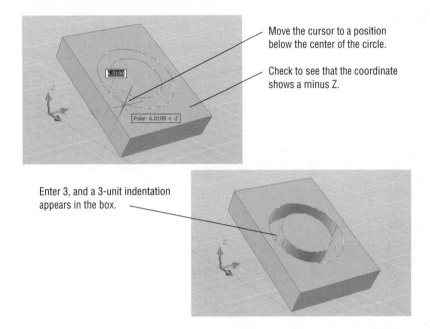

Move the cursor to a position below the center of the circle.

Check to see that the coordinate shows a minus Z.

Enter 3, and a 3-unit indentation appears in the box.

**FIGURE 20.16**
Adding complex shapes using the Presspull tool

**WARNING**    If you use an open 2D object on a 3D surface, such as a curved spline or line, the endpoints must touch exactly on the edge of the surface before Presspull will work.

## Making Changes to Your Solid

When you're creating a 3D model, you'll hardly ever get the shape right the first time. Suppose you decide that you need to modify the shape you've created so far by moving the hole from the center of the box to a corner. The next exercise will show you how you can gain access to the individual components of a 3D solid to make changes.

The model you've been working with is composed of two objects: a box and a cylinder. These two components of the solid are referred to as *subobjects* of the main solid object. Faces and edges of 3D solids are also considered subobjects. When you use the Union, Subtract, or Intersect tool on a set of objects, the objects merge into a single solid—or at least that is how it seems at first. You can gain access to and modify the shape of the subobjects from which the shape is constructed by using the Ctrl key while clicking the solid. Try the following:

1. Place the cursor on the solid you've made so far. The entire object is highlighted as if it were one object. If you were to click it (don't do it yet), the entire object would be selected.

2. Hold down the Ctrl key, and move the cursor over the circular indentation. As you do this, the indentation is highlighted (see the left image in Figure 20.17).

**FIGURE 20.17**
You can select sub-objects of a 3D solid when you hold down the Ctrl key.

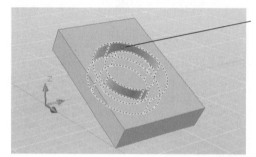

Hold down the Ctrl key, and hover over the circular indentation. Click the mouse when the indentation is highlighted.

Click the center square grip. The indentation will move with the mouse.

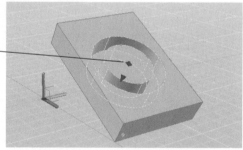

3. While still holding down the Ctrl key, click the indentation. The grips for the indentation appear, as shown on the right in Figure 20.17. As you may guess, you can use these grips to change the shape and location of a feature of the selected solid.

4. Click the center square grip of the indentation, and move your cursor around. If you find it a bit uncontrollable, turn off Polar mode. As you move the cursor, the indentation moves with it.

5. Place the indentation in the location shown in Figure 20.18, and click. You've just moved the indentation from the center to the edge of the cylinder.

6. Press the Escape key to clear the selection.

This example showed that the Ctrl key can be an extremely useful tool when you have to edit a solid; it allows you to select the subobjects that form your model. Once the subobjects are selected, you can move them, or you can use the arrow grips to change their size.

**FIGURE 20.18**
You can move the indentation to a new location using its grip.

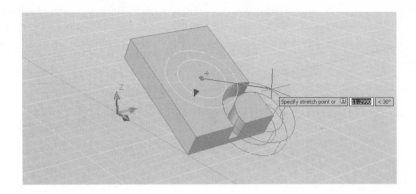

# Creating 3D Forms from 2D Shapes

The 3D solid primitives are great for creating basic shapes, but in many situations, you'll want to create a 3D form from a more complex shape. Fortunately, you can extrude 2D objects into a variety of shapes using additional tools found in the 3D Make control panel. For example, you can draw a shape like a star and then extrude it into a third dimension, as shown in Figure 20.19. Or you can use several strategically placed 2D objects to form a flowing surface like the wing of an airplane.

## Extruding a Polyline

You can create a 3D solid by extruding a 2D closed polyline. This is a more flexible way to create shapes, because you can create a polyline of any shape and extrude it to a fairly complex form.

**FIGURE 20.19**
The closed polyline on the left can be used to construct the 3D shape on the right.

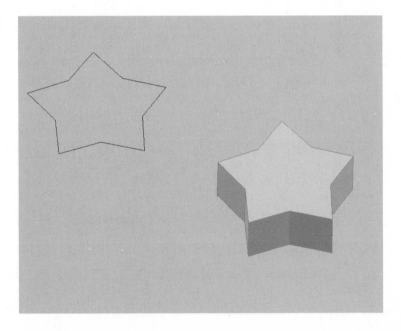

In the following set of exercises, you'll turn the apartment room from previous chapters into a 3D model. I've created a version of the apartment floor plan that has a few additions to make things a little easier for you. Figure 20.20 shows the file you'll use in the exercise. It's the same floor plan you've been working with in earlier chapters, but with the addition of closed polylines outlining the walls.

**FIGURE 20.20**
The Unit plan with closed polylines outlining the walls

Polyline outlines of the walls

The plan isn't shaded as in the previous examples in this chapter. You can work in 3D in this display mode just as easily as in a shaded mode:

1. Open the 20-unit.dwg file. Metric users should open 20-unit-metric.dwg.

2. Choose Southwest Isometric from the 3D Navigate control panel drop-down list.

You can also choose View ➤ 3D Views ➤ SW Isometric. Your view now looks as if you're standing above and to the left of your drawing, rather than directly above it (see Figure 20.21). The UCS icon helps you get a sense of your new orientation.

**FIGURE 20.21**

A 3D view of the floor plan

3. Click the Extrude tool in the 3D Make control panel.

You can also choose Draw ➤ Modeling ➤ Extrude or enter **Extrude** at the Command prompt. You see the message `Current wire frame density: ISOLINES=4` in the Command window, followed by the `Select objects to extrude:` prompt.

4. Select the wall outlines shown in Figure 20.21, and then press ↵.

5. At the `Specify height of extrusion or [Direction/Path/Taper angle] <0.0000>:` prompt, enter **8′**↵. Metric users should enter **224**↵. The walls extrude to the height you entered, as shown in Figure 20.22.

Unlike the earlier exercise with the box, you can see through the walls because this is a Wireframe view. A *Wireframe view* shows the volume of a 3D objects by displaying the lines representing the edges of surfaces. Later in this chapter, I'll discuss how to make an object's surfaces appear opaque like the box earlier in this chapter.

Next, you'll add door headers to define the wall openings:

1. Adjust your view so you get a close look at the door shown in Figure 20.23. You can use the Pan and Zoom tools in this 3D view as you would in a 2D view.

**FIGURE 20.22**

The extruded walls

**FIGURE 20.23**

Adding the door header to the opening at the balcony of the unit plan

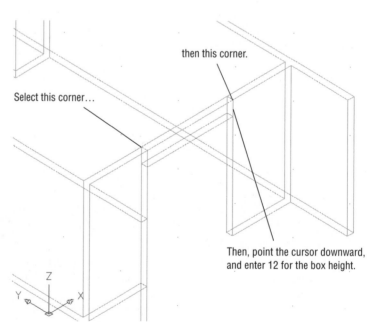

Select this corner…

then this corner.

Then, point the cursor downward, and enter 12 for the box height.

2. Turn off Dynamic UCS mode by clicking the DUCS button in the status bar so it's in the up position. This helps you avoid accidentally orienting your cursor to the wall behind the door header.

3. Click the Box tool in the 3D Make control panel.

4. Use the Endpoint osnaps, and click the two points shown in Figure 20.23.

5. At the Specify height or [2Point] <8'-0">: prompt, point the cursor downward from the points you just selected, and enter **12.**↵. Metric users should enter **30.**↵. The door header appears.

6. Repeat steps 4 and 5 to draw the other door headers shown in Figure 20.24.

**FIGURE 20.24**

Adding the remaining door headers

Add these three door headers.

The walls and door headers give you a better sense of the space in the Unit plan. To further enhance the appearance of the 3D model, you can join the walls and door headers so they appear as seamless walls and openings:

1. Zoom out so you can see the entire unit, and then click the Union tool in the 3D Make control panel.

You can also choose Modify ➤ Solid Editing ➤ Union.

**2.** At the Select objects: prompt, select all the walls and headers, and then press ↵.

Now the walls and headers appear as one seamless surface without any distracting joint lines. You can really get a sense of the space of the Unit plan. You'll want to explore ways of viewing the unit in 3D; but before you do that, you need to know about one more 3D modeling feature: *point filters*.

---

### CONVERTING OBJECTS WITH THICKNESS INTO 3D SOLIDS

If you've worked with 3D in AutoCAD before, you probably know that you can give an object a thickness property greater than 0 to make it a 3D object. For example, a line with a thickness property greater than 0 looks like a vertical surface.

Lines with thickness

In the Unit plan exercise, you can do the same for the polylines used to draw the walls. Click the wall polylines, and then right-click and choose Properties. In the Properties palette, change the Thickness value to 8´ or 224 cm.

---

Close the Properties palette. The walls appear in three dimensions. But be aware that these walls aren't 3D solids. If you zoom in to a detail of the walls, they appear hollow.

Fortunately, AutoCAD supplies a tool that converts a closed polyline with thickness into a solid. Expand the 3D Make control panel by clicking the downward-pointing arrow in the 3D Make title bar, and then click the Convert To Solid tool in the 3D Make toolbar. You can also enter **convtosolid**↵.

Click the downward-pointing arrow in the title bar to expand the 3D Make control panel.

Click the Convert To Solid tool.

Select the polyline walls; press ↵ when you've finished your selection. Once you do this, the walls become 3D solids. This operation works with any closed polyline, providing an alternate way of creating a 3D solid. If you have existing 3D models that have been produced using the Thickness property, you can use the Convert To Solid tool to bring your 3D models up to date. The Convert To Solid tool can also convert open polylines that have a width and thickness greater than 0. (See Chapter 18 for more on polylines.)

Another tool called Convert To Surface converts objects with thickness into 3D surface objects. You can use 3D surfaces to slice or thicken 3D solids into full 3D solids. You'll learn more about 3D surfaces in Chapter 23.

## Isolating Coordinates with Point Filters

AutoCAD offers a method for 3D point selection, called *point filters*, that can help you isolate the X, Y, or Z coordinate of a location in 3D. Point filters enable you to enter an *x*, *y*, or *z* value by picking a point on the screen and telling AutoCAD to use only the *x*, *y*, or *z* value of that point or any combination of those values. For example, suppose you want to start the corner of a 3D box at the X and Y coordinates of the corner of the Unit plan, but you want the Z location at 3′ instead of at ground level. You can use point filters to select only the X and Y coordinates of a point and then specify the Z coordinate as a separate value. The following exercise demonstrates how this works:

1. Zoom in to the balcony door, and turn on the F-Rail layer.

2. Click the Box tool on the 3D Make control panel.

3. At the `Specify first corner or [Center]:` prompt, Shift+right-click to display the Osnap menu; then, choose Point Filters ➢ .XY. As an alternative, you can enter **.xy↵**. By doing this, you tell AutoCAD that you're going to first specify the X and Y coordinates for this beginning point and then later indicate the Z coordinate.

**TIP** You may have noticed the .X, .Y, and .Z options on the Object Snap menu (Shift+right-click) in step 3. These are the 3D point filters. By choosing one of these options as you select points in a 3D command, you can filter an *x*, *y*, or *z* value, or any combination of values, from that selected point. You can also enter filters through the keyboard.

4. At the `Specify first corner or [Center]: .XY of:` prompt, pick the corner of the Unit plan, as shown in Figure 20.25.

5. At the `(need Z):` prompt, enter **36↵** (the Z coordinate). Metric users, enter **92↵**. The outline of the box appears at the 36″ (or 92 cm) elevation and at the corner you selected in step 4.

6. At the `Specify other corner or [Cube/Length]:` prompt, Shift+right-click to display the Osnap menu again, and choose Point Filters ➢ .XY. Select the other endpoint indicated in Figure 20.25.

7. At the `(need Z):` prompt, a temporary outline of the box appears at the 36″ height. Click the mouse to fix the base outline of the box.

8. Enter **4↵** (**10↵** for metric users) for the height of the box. The box appears as the balcony rail.

In step 4, you selected the corner of the unit, but the box didn't appear right away. You had to enter a Z value in step 5 before the outline of the box appeared. Then, in step 6, you saw the box begin at the 36″ elevation. Using point filters allowed you to accurately place the box in the drawing even though there were no features that you could snap to directly.

Now that you've gotten most of the unit modeled in 3D, you'll want to be able to look at it from different angles. The next section shows you some of the tools available to control your views in 3D.

**TIP** In my own work in 3D, point filters are a real lifesaver. Understanding this tool will greatly improve your ability to work in 3D.

**FIGURE 20.25**
Constructing the rail
using point filters

Select the .XY filter, and
then select this corner.

The box outline appears.

Select this endpoint for
the other corner.

The rail in place at the
specified height

## Moving Around Your Model

AutoCAD offers a number of tools to help you view your 3D model. You've already used one to get the current 3D view. Choosing Southwest Isometric from the 3D Navigate control panel's drop-down list displays an isometric view from a southwest direction. You may have noticed several other isometric view options in that list. This section introduces you to some of the ways you can move around in your 3D model.

### Finding Isometric and Orthogonal Views

Figure 20.26 illustrates the isometric view options you saw earlier in the 3D Navigate control panel drop-down list: Southeast Isometric, Northeast Isometric, and Northwest Isometric. The cameras represent the different viewpoint locations. You can get an idea of their location in reference to the grid and UCS icon.

The 3D Navigate control panel's drop-down list also offers another set of options: Top, Bottom, Left, Right, Front, and Back. These are orthogonal views that show the sides, top, and bottom of the model, as illustrated in Figure 20.27. In this figure, the cameras once again show the points of view.

When you use any of the view options described here, AutoCAD attempts to display the extents of the drawing. You can then use the Pan and Zoom tools to adjust your view.

**FIGURE 20.26**
The isometric viewpoints for the four isometric views available from the 3D Navigate control panel drop-down list.

**FIGURE 20.27**
This diagram shows the six viewpoints of the Orthogonal view options on the View 3D Views cascading menu.

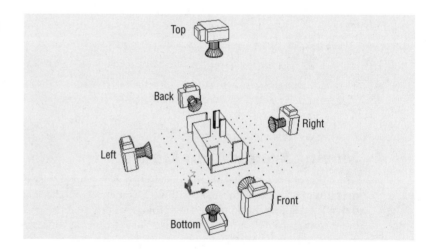

**TIP** If you don't have the Dashboard open, you can get to the isometric and orthogonal views by choosing View ➢ 3D Views.

## Rotating Freely Around Your Model

You may find the isometric and orthogonal views a bit restrictive. The Constrained Orbit tool lets you move around your model in real time. You can fine-tune your view by clicking and dragging the mouse using this tool. Try the following to see how it works:

1. Zoom out so you see an overall view of your model.

2. Click the Constrained Orbit tool in the 3D Navigate control panel. If you don't see the Constrained Orbit tool, click and hold the mouse and select Constrained Orbit from the button fly-out.

3. You can also choose View ➤ Orbit ➤ Constrained Orbit.

4. Click and drag in the drawing area. As you drag the mouse, the view revolves around your model. The cursor changes to an orbit icon to let you know you're in the middle of using the Constrained Orbit tool.

If you have several objects in your model, you can select an object that you want to revolve around, and then click the Constrained Orbit tool. It also helps to pan your view so the object you select is in the center of the view.

When you've reached the view you want, right-click and choose Exit. You're then ready to make more changes or use another tool.

**TIP**   If you have a mouse with a scroll wheel, you can hold down the Shift key while clicking and dragging the wheel to get the same effect as using the Constrained Orbit tool.

## Changing Your View Direction

AutoCAD uses a camera analogy for views in 3D models. With a camera, you have a camera location and a target, and both can be fined-tuned in AutoCAD. The Constrained Orbit tool is a bit like moving a camera around an object. Using the Swivel tool is like keeping the camera stationary while pointing in a different direction.

At first, the Swivel tool may seem just like the Pan tool. But in the 3D world, Pan moves both the camera and target in unison. Pan is like pointing a camera out the side of a moving car. If you don't keep the view in the camera fixed on an object, you're panning across the scenery. The Swivel tool is like standing in one spot and swiveling the camera to take in a panoramic view.

To use Swivel, click the Swivel tool, and then click and drag the mouse across the view.

The icon changes to a camera with a swivel arrow. When you've adjusted your view to your liking, right-click and choose Exit.

## Flying through Your View

Another tool for getting around in your model is the Walk/Fly tool. If you're familiar with computer games, this tool is for you. When you click the Walk tool in the 3D Navigate control panel, you may see a message asking if you want to change to perspective mode. Click Yes to proceed. You may then see a message box telling you how to use Walk and Fly.

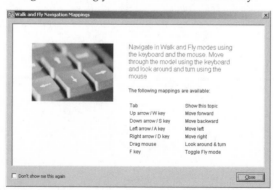

This message tells you all you need to know about the Walk and Fly tools. Click the Close button, and you can use the arrow keys to move through your model. Click and drag the mouse to change the direction in which you're looking.

If you press the F key, Walk changes to Fly mode. The main difference between Walk and Fly is that in Walk, both your position in the model and the point at which you're looking move with the Up and Down arrow keys. Walk is a bit like Pan. When you're in Fly mode, the arrow keys move you toward the center of your view, which is indicated by a crosshair.

In addition to the crosshair, you'll see a palette that shows your position in the model from a top-down view.

You can use the palette to control your view by clicking and dragging the camera or the view target graphic. If you prefer, you can close the palette and continue to "walk" through your model. When you're finished using Walk, right-click and choose Exit.

### Changing from Perspective to Parallel Projection

When you create a new drawing using the acad3D.dwt template, you're automatically given a perspective view of the file. If you need a more schematic parallel projection style of view, you can get one by selecting the Parallel Projection tool in the 3D Navigate control panel (see Figure 20.28).

You can return to a perspective view by clicking the Perspective Projection tool next to the Parallel Projection tool as shown in Figure 20.28.

## Getting a Visual Effect

3D models are extremely useful in communicating your ideas to others, but sometimes you find that the default appearance of your model isn't exactly what you want. If you're only in a schematic design stage, you may want your model to look more like a sketch instead of a finished product. Conversely, if you're trying to sell someone on a concept, you may want a realistic look that includes materials and even special lighting.

AutoCAD provides a variety of tools to help you get a visual style, from a simple wireframe to a fully rendered image complete with chrome and wood. In this section, you'll get a preview of what is available to control the appearance of your model. Later, in Chapter 22, you'll get an in-depth look at rendering and camera tools that allow you to produce views from hand-sketched "napkin" designs to finished renderings.

**FIGURE 20.28**
The Perspective Projection and Parallel Projection tools

## Using Visual Styles

In the earlier tutorials in this chapter, you drew a box that appeared to be solid. When you then opened an existing file to extrude the Unit plan into the third dimension, you worked in a Wireframe view. These views are known as *visual styles* in AutoCAD. You used the default 3D visual style called Realistic when you drew the box. The Unit plan used the default 2D Wireframe view that is used in the AutoCAD Classic style of drawing.

Sometimes, it helps to use a different visual style depending on your task. For example, the 2D Wireframe view in your Unit plan model can help you visualize and select things that are behind a solid. AutoCAD includes several shaded view options that can bring out various features of your model. Try the following exercises to explore some of the other visual styles:

1. Click the Visual Styles drop-down list in the Visual Style control panel. A set of graphic images appear that give you an idea of what each visual style shows you.

2. Select 3D Wireframe. You can also choose View ➢ Visual Styles ➢ Wireframe. Your model appears as a transparent wireframe object with a gray background.

3. To get to the shaded view of your model, choose Realistic from the Visual Styles drop-down list or choose View ➤ Visual Styles ➤ Realistic.

You may have noticed a few other Visual Styles options. Figure 20.29 shows those options as they're applied to a sphere. 2D Wireframe and 3D Wireframe may appear the same, but 3D Wireframe uses a perspective view and a background color, whereas 2D Wireframe uses a parallel projection view and no background color.

**FIGURE 20.29**
Visual styles applied to a sphere

| 2D Wireframe | Hidden | 3D Wireframe | Conceptual | Realistic |

## Creating a Sketched Look with Visual Styles

You may notice a blank in the visual styles options in the Visual Style control panel. This is a space to allow you to create a custom visual style. This is significant for designers because it gives you an opportunity to create a visual style that mimics a hand-drawn sketch. The following exercise will step you through the process:

1. Click the Visual Styles Manager tool in the Visual Style control panel.

The Visual Styles Manager palette appears. This palette looks similar to the Properties palette, with the addition of thumbnail examples of the visual styles at the top of the palette.

2. Click the Create New Visual Style tool in the Visual Styles Manager palette toolbar.

The Create New Visual Style dialog box opens.

3. Enter **Sketch**↵ in the Name input box.

4. Enter **Hand Drawn Appearance** in the Description input box, and then click OK. You see a new thumbnail in the bottom-right corner of the samples at the top of the palette.

You've just created a new visual style. This new style uses the default settings that are similar to the Realistic visual style but without the Material Display option turned on. The material setting causes objects in your drawing to display any material assignments that have been given to objects. You'll learn more about materials in Chapter 22.

Now that you have a new visual style, you can begin to customize it. But before you start your customization, make your new visual style the current one so you can see the effects of your changes as you make them:

1. Click the Apply Selected Visual Style To Current Viewport tool in the Visual Styles Manager toolbar.

The display changes slightly, and you see the name Sketch appear in the Visual Style control panel drop-down list.

Next, you'll turn on the two features that will give your new visual style a sketch-like appearance.

**2.** Use the scroll bar to the left of the Visual Styles Manager toolbar to scroll down to the bottom of the list of options.

**3.** Locate the Edge Modifiers option group, and click the Overhanging Edges tool in the Edge Modifiers title bar.

Edges of your model now appear to be drawn with lines extending beyond the corners (see Figure 20.30).

**FIGURE 20.30**
The 3D unit plan with the Sketch visual style

**4.** Click the Jitter Edges tool in the Edge Modifiers title bar.

**5.** The edges take on a sketched look, as shown in Figure 20.30.

**6.** Close the Visual Styles Manager toolbar.

**7.** Save the Unit plan file.

The 3D view has taken on a hand-drawn appearance. Notice that the lines overhang the corners in a typical architectural sketch style. This is the effect of the Overhanging Edges option in step 3. The lines are made rough and broken by the Jitter Edges setting. You can control the amount of overhang and jitter in the Edge Modifiers group of the Visual Styles Manager to exaggerate or soften these effects.

You can also turn on the Jitter and Edges settings for an existing visual style by using the Edge Overhand and Edge Jitter tools in the expanded Visual Style control panel. The sliders to the right of these tools control the amount of overhang and jitter applied to the style.

# Turning a 3D View into a 2D AutoCAD Drawing

Many architectural firms use AutoCAD 3D models to study their designs. After a specific part of a design is modeled and approved, they convert the model into 2D elevations, ready to plug in to their elevation drawing.

If you need to convert your 3D models into 2D line drawings, you can use the Flatshot tool in the 3D Make toolbar.

Set up your drawing view, and then click the Flatshot tool or enter **Flatshot↵** at the Command prompt to open the Flatshot dialog box:

---

**PRINTING YOUR MODEL USING VISUAL STYLES**

You can print a drawing that uses visual styles either from the Model tab or from a Layout tab. If you're printing from the Model tab, choose File ➢ Plot. Then, in the Plot dialog box, select the visual style from the Shade Plot drop-down list in the Shaded Viewport Options group. If you're plotting from a Layout tab, select the layout viewport border, right-click, and choose Shade Plot from the shortcut menu. You can select from a list of visual styles from a cascading menu. Once you've done this, plot your layout as you normally would.

---

Select the options you want to use for the 2D line drawing, and then click Create. Depending on the options you select, you'll be prompted to select an insertion point or indicate a location for an exported drawing file.

Flatshot offers the ability to place the 2D version of your model in the current drawing as a block, to replace an existing block in the current drawing, or to save the 2D version as a DWG file. Table 20.1 describes the Flatshot options in more detail.

**TABLE 20.1:**     Flatshot Options

| OPTION | WHAT IT DOES |
|---|---|
| **Destination** | |
| Insert As New Block | Inserts the 2D view in the current drawing as a block. You're prompted for an insertion point, a scale, and a rotation. |
| Replace Existing Block | Replaces an existing block with a block of the 2D view. You're prompted to select an existing block. |

**TABLE 20.1:**     Flatshot Options *(CONTINUED)*

| OPTION | WHAT IT DOES |
|---|---|
| **Destination** | |
| Select Block | If Replace Existing Block is selected, lets you select a block to be replaced. A warning is shown if no block is selected. |
| Export To A File | Exports the 2D view as a drawing file. |
| File Name And Path | Displays the location for the export file. Click the Browse button to specify a location. |
| **Foreground Lines** | |
| Color | Sets the overall color for the 2D view. |
| Linetype | Sets the overall linetype for the 2D view. |
| **Obscured Lines** | |
| Show | Displays hidden lines. |
| Color | If Show is turned on, sets the color for hidden lines. |
| Linetype | If Show is turned on, sets the linetype for hidden lines. The Current Linetype Scale setting is used for linetypes other than continuous. |

One very useful feature of Flatshot is that it can create a 2D drawing that displays the hidden lines of a 3D mechanical drawing. Turn on the Show option, and then select a line type such as Hidden for obscured lines to produce a 2D drawing like the one shown in Figure 20.31.

**FIGURE 20.31**
A sample of a 2D drawing generated from a 3D model using Flatshot. Note the dashed lines showing the hidden lines of the view.

**THINGS TO WATCH OUT FOR WHEN EDITING 3D OBJECTS**

You've seen how you can use the Copy command on 3D objects. You can also use the Move and Stretch commands on 3D objects to modify their Z coordinate values—but you have to be careful with these commands when editing in 3D. Here are a few tips:

◆ If you want to move a 3D solid using grips, you need to select the square grip at the bottom center of the solid. The other grips only move the feature associated with the grip, like a corner or edge. Once that bottom grip is selected, you can switch to another grip as the base point for the move by doing the following: After selecting the base grip, right-click, select Base Point from the shortcut menu, and click the grip you want to use.

◆ The Scale command will scale an object's Z coordinate value as well as the standard X coordinate and Y coordinate. Suppose you have an object with an elevation of 2 units. If you use the Scale command to enlarge that object by a factor of 4, the object will have a new elevation of 2 units times 4, or 8 units. If, on the other hand, that object has an elevation of 0, its elevation won't change, because 0 times 4 is still 0.

◆ You can also use Array, Mirror, and Rotate (on the Modify toolbar) on 3D solid objects, but these commands don't affect their Z coordinate values. Z coordinates can be specified for base and insertion points, so take care when using these commands with 3D models.

◆ Using the Move, Stretch, and Copy commands (on the Modify toolbar) with osnaps can produce unpredictable and unwanted results. As a rule, it's best to use point filters when selecting points with osnap overrides. For example, to move an object from the endpoint of one object to the endpoint of another on the same Z coordinate, invoke the .XY point filter at the Specify base point : and Specify second point : prompts before you issue the Endpoint override. Proceed to pick the endpoint of the object you want; then, enter the Z coordinate, or pick any point to use the current default Z coordinate.

◆ When you create a block, it uses the currently active UCS to determine its own local coordinate system. When that block is later inserted, it orients its own coordinate system with the current UCS. (The UCS is discussed in more detail in Chapter 21.)

# The Bottom Line

**Getting to Know the 3D Modeling Workspace**   When you work in 3D, you need a different set of tools from those for 2D drafting. AutoCAD offers the 3D Modeling workspace, which provides the tools you need to create 3D models.

**Master It**   Name the Dashboard control panels in the 3D Workspace.

**Solution**   3D Make, 3D Navigate, Visual Styles, Light, Materials, Render.

**Drawing in 3D Using Solids**   AutoCAD offers a type of object called a 3D solid that lets you quickly create and edit shapes.

**Master It**   What does the Presspull command do?

**Solution**   Presspull lets you press or pull a 3D solid shape from another 3D solid.

**Creating 3D Forms from 2D Shapes**   The 3D Make control panel offers a set of basic 3D shapes, but you can create virtually any shape you want from 2D drawings.

**Master It**   Name the command that lets you change a closed 2D polyline into a 3D solid.

**Solution**   Extrude.

**Isolating Coordinates with Point Filters**  When you're working in 3D, selecting points can be a complicated task. AutoCAD offers point filters to let you specify the individual X, Y, and Z coordinates of a location in space.

**Master It**  What does the .XY point filter do?

**Solution**  The .XY point filter lets you select an X,Y coordinate, after which you can specify a Z coordinate as a separate value.

**Moving Around Your Model**  Getting the view you want in a 3D model can be tricky.

**Master It**  What tool in the 3D Navigate control panel lets you select a view from a list of predefined views?

**Solution**  The 3D Navigate drop-down list. You can also choose View ➢ Named Views and select views from the View Manager dialog box.

**Getting a Visual Effect**  At certain points in your model making, you'll want to view your 3D model with surface colors and even material assignments. AutoCAD offers several ways to do this.

**Master It**  What are the steps to take to change the view from wireframe to conceptual?

**Solution**  Click the Visual Styles drop-down list, and select Conceptual.

**Turning a 3D View into a 2D AutoCAD Drawing**  Sometimes, it's helpful to convert a 3D model view into a 2D AutoCAD drawing. AutoCAD offers the Flatshot tool, which quickly converts a 3D view into a 2D line drawing.

**Master It**  What type of object does Flatshot create?

**Solution**  A block or drawing file.

# Chapter 21

# Using Advanced 3D Features

AutoCAD 2008's extended set of tools for working with 3D drawings lets you create 3D objects with few limitations on shape and orientation. This chapter focuses on the use of these tools, which help you easily generate 3D forms and view them in both Perspective and Orthogonal modes.

**WARNING**   AutoCAD LT doesn't support any of the features described in this chapter.

Topics in this chapter include the following:

◆ Setting Up AutoCAD for This Chapter

◆ Mastering the User Coordinate System

◆ Understanding the UCS Options

◆ Using Viewports to Aid in 3D Drawing

◆ Creating Complex 3D Surfaces

◆ Creating Spiral Forms

◆ Creating Surface Models

◆ Moving Objects in 3D Space

## Setting Up AutoCAD for This Chapter

Before you start, I'd like you to set up AutoCAD in a way that will make your work a little easier. You'll use the AutoCAD Classic workspace, but you'll also open the Dashboard, which is the 3D palette you were introduced to in Chapter 20. To do so, follow these steps:

1. Open AutoCAD. When you see the Workspaces dialog box, select AutoCAD Classic. If for some reason the Workspaces dialog box doesn't appear, choose AutoCAD Classic from the Workspaces toolbar.

2. Close the Tool Palettes window and the Sheet Set Manager palette to get a clear view of the drawing area.

3. Choose Tools ➢ Palettes ➢ Dashboard to open the Dashboard palette. Your screen should look similar to Figure 21.1.

With this setup, you can quickly select items from the Draw and Modify toolbars. You also have access to the Properties and Layers toolbars. Now you're ready to get to work.

FIGURE 21.1

The AutoCAD window set up for this chapter

# Mastering the User Coordinate System

The User Coordinate System (UCS) enables you to define a custom coordinate system in 2D and 3D space. You've been using a default UCS, called the *World Coordinate System (WCS)*, all along. By now, you're familiar with the L-shaped icon in the lower-left corner of the AutoCAD screen, containing a small square and the letters X and Y. The square indicates that you're currently in the WCS; the X and Y indicate the positive directions of the X and Y axes. WCS is a global system of reference from which you can define other UCSs.

It may help to think of these AutoCAD UCSs as different drawing surfaces, or two-dimensional planes. You can have several UCSs at any given time. By setting up these different UCSs, you can draw as you would in the WCS in 2D, yet draw a 3D image.

Suppose you want to draw a house in 3D with doors and windows on each of its sides. You can set up a UCS for each of the sides; then, you can move from UCS to UCS to add your doors and windows (see Figure 21.2). In each UCS, you draw your doors and windows as you would in a typical 2D drawing. You can even insert elevation views of doors and windows that you created in other drawings.

In this chapter, you'll experiment with several views and UCSs. All the commands you'll use are available both at the command line and via the menu bar. In addition, you can access a number of the UCS commands from the UCS toolbar.

## Defining a UCS

In the first set of exercises, you'll draw a chair that you can later add to your 3D unit drawing. In drawing this chair, you'll be exposed to the use of the UCS, as well as to some of the other 3D capabilities available in AutoCAD:

1. Open the `barcelona1.dwg` file. Metric users should open `barcelona1_metric.dwg`. This file contains two rectangles that you'll use to create a chair.

**2.** Select Southwest Isometric from the 3D Navigate control panel, or choose View ➤ 3D Views ➤ SW Isometric. This gives you a 3D view from the lower left of the rectangles, as shown in the bottom image in Figure 21.3. Zoom out a bit to give yourself some room to work.

**FIGURE 21.2**
Different UCSs in a
3D drawing

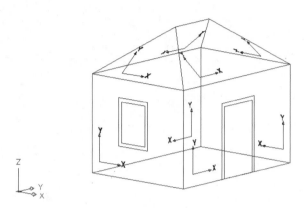

**FIGURE 21.3**
The chair seat and
back in the Plan (top)
and Isometric (bottom) views

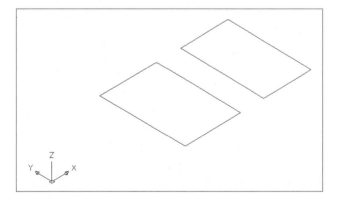

**3.** Select the two rectangles, and then click the Properties tool on the Standard toolbar.

**4.** In the Properties palette, enter **3** in the Thickness setting, and press ↵. This gives the seat and back a thickness of 3″. Metric users should make the thickness 7.6 cm.

**5.** Press the Escape key, and close the Properties palette. Click the Convert To Solid tool in the expanded 3D Make control panel. To expand the 3D Make control panel, point to the 3D Make title bar, and then click the downward-pointing arrow that appears.

Click here to expand the
3D Make control panel.

**6.** Select the two rectangles, and then press ↵.

Notice that the UCS icon appears in the same plane as the current coordinate system. The icon will help you keep track of which coordinate system you're in. Now you can see the chair components as 3D objects.

Next, you'll define a UCS that is aligned with one side of the seat:

**1.** Right-click any toolbar, and choose UCS from the shortcut menu to open the UCS toolbar.

Choose Tools ➢ Named UCS to open the UCS dialog box.

**2.** Select the Orthographic UCSs tab to view a set of predefined UCSs.

**3.** Select Front in the list box. Figure 21.4 shows the orientation of the Front UCS.

**FIGURE 21.4**
The six predefined
UCS orientations

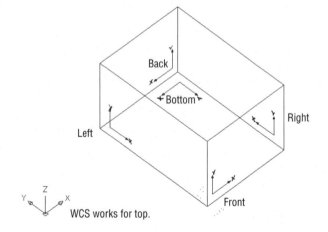

**4.** Click the Set Current button to make the Front UCS current.

**5.** Click OK to close the dialog box.

The Orthographic UCSs tab offers a set of predefined UCSs for each of the six standard orthographic projection planes. Figure 21.4 shows these UCSs in relation to the WCS.

Because a good part of 3D work involves drawing in these orthographic planes, AutoCAD supplies the ready-made UCS orientations for quick access. But you aren't limited to these six orientations. If you're familiar with mechanical drafting, you'll see that the orthographic UCSs correspond to the typical orthographic projections used in mechanical drafting. If you're an architect, the Front, Left, Back, and Right UCSs correspond to the south, west, north, and east elevations of a building.

Before you continue building the chair model, you'll move the UCS to the surface on which you'll be working. Right now, the UCS has its origin located in the same place as the WCS origin.

You can move a UCS so that its origin is anywhere in the drawing where it's needed:

1. Click the Origin UCS tool in the UCS toolbar, or choose Tools ➤ New UCS ➤ Origin.

2. Use the Endpoint osnap, and click the bottom-front corner of the chair seat, as shown in Figure 21.5. The UCS icon moves to indicate its new origin's location.

**FIGURE 21.5**
Setting up a UCS

Click this corner for the new UCS origin.

You just created a new UCS based on the Front UCS you selected from the UCS dialog box. Now, as you move your cursor, the origin of the UCS icon corresponds to a 0,0 coordinate. Although you have a new UCS, the WCS still exists; you can always return to it when you need to.

## Saving a UCS

After you've gone through the work of creating a UCS, you may want to save it, especially if you think you'll come back to it later. Here's how to save a UCS:

1. Choose Tools ➤ Named UCS to open the UCS dialog box.

2. Make sure the Named UCSs tab is selected, and then highlight the Unnamed option in the Current UCS list box.

3. Right-click Unnamed, and choose Rename from the shortcut menu. The item changes to allow editing.

4. Type **3DSW↵** for the name of your new UCS.

5. Click OK to exit the dialog box.

Your UCS is now saved with the name 3DSW. You can recall it from the UCS dialog box or by using other methods that you'll learn about later in this chapter.

## Working in a UCS

Next, you'll arrange the seat and back, and draw the legs of the chair. Your UCS is oriented so that you can easily adjust the orientation of the chair components. As you work through the next exercise, notice that although you're manipulating 3D objects, you're really using the same tools you've used to edit 2D objects.

Follow these steps to adjust the seat and back and to draw legs:

1. Click the seat back to expose its grips.

2. Click the bottom grip, as shown in the first image in Figure 21.6.

**FIGURE 21.6**
Moving the components of the chair into place

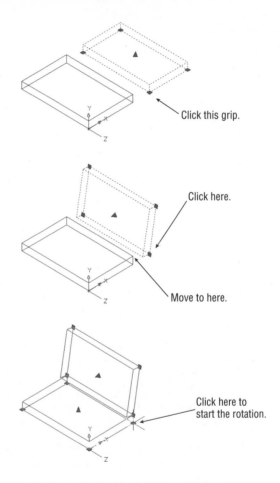

Click this grip.

Click here.

Move to here.

Click here to start the rotation.

3. Right-click the mouse to open the Grip Edit shortcut menu.

4. Choose Rotate from the menu. The seat back now rotates with the movement of the cursor. It rotates in the plane of the new UCS you created earlier.

5. Type **80**↵ to rotate the seat back 80°. Your view looks like the second image in Figure 21.6.

6. Click the bottom grip, as shown in the second image in Figure 21.6.

7. Right-click the mouse again, and choose Move.

8. Using the Endpoint osnap, click the top corner of the chair seat to join the chair back to the seat, as shown in the second image in Figure 21.6.

9. Click both the chair seat and back; then, click the bottom-corner grip of the seat, as shown in the third image in Figure 21.6.

10. Right-click, and choose Rotate from the Grip Edit shortcut menu.

11. Enter –10↵ to rotate both the seat and back minus 10 degrees. Press the Esc key to clear the grips. Your chair looks like Figure 21.7.

**FIGURE 21.7**

The chair after rotating and moving the components

The new UCS orientation enabled you to use the grips to adjust the chair seat and back. All the grip rotation in the previous exercise was confined to the plane of the new UCS. Mirroring and scaling will also occur in relation to the current UCS.

## Building 3D Parts in Separate Files

As you work in 3D, your models will become fairly complex. When your model becomes too crowded to see things clearly, it helps to build parts of the model and then import them instead of building everything in one file. In the next set of exercises, you'll draw the legs of the chair and then import them to the main chair file to give you some practice in the procedure.

I've prepared a drawing called `legs.dwg`, which consists of two polylines that describe the shape of the legs. I did this to save you some tedious work that isn't related to 3D modeling. You'll use this file as a starting point for the legs, and then you'll import the legs into the `barcelona1.dwg` file:

1. Open the `legs.dwg` file. The file consists of two polyline splines that are in the shape of one set of legs. You'll turn these simple lines into 3D solids.

2. Choose Modify ➢ Object ➢ Polyline.

3. At the `Select polyline or [Multiple]:` prompt, enter **M**↵ to select multiple polylines. Then, select the two polylines, and press ↵.

4. At the `Enter an option [Close/Open/Join/Width/Fit/Spline/Decurve/Ltype gen/ Undo]:` prompt, enter **W**↵↵.

5. At the `Specify new width for all segments:` prompt, enter **0.5**↲ to give the polylines a width of 0.5″. Metric users should enter **1.27**↲.

6. Press ↲↲ to exit the Pedit command.

Next, you need to change the Thickness property of the two polylines to make them 2″ or 5 cm wide:

1. With the two polylines selected, open the Properties palette, and set their Thickness to 2″. Metric users should make the thickness 5 cm.

2. Close the Properties palette.

3. Click the Convert To Solid tool in the 3D Make control panel, choose Modify ➢ 3D Operations ➢ Convert To Solid, or enter **convtosolid**↲ at the Command prompt.

4. Select the two polylines, and then press ↲. The lines become 3D solids, as shown in Figure 21.8.

**FIGURE 21.8**
Move the legs so they meet the chair seat at the corner indicated.

5. Click the Union tool in the 3D Make control panel, select the two legs, and press ↲. The two legs are now a single 3D solid.

As you've just seen, you can convert polylines that have both a width and a thickness into 3D solids. Now you're ready to add the legs to the rest of the chair:

**TIP** Polylines are the best objects to use for 3D, because you can generate complex shapes easily by giving the polylines thickness and width. But when you convert a polyline into a solid, you must be in the same UCS as the one in which the object was created. You can use the Object option of the UCS command to orient the UCS to the polyline before you use the Convert To Solid tool.

1. Choose Window ➢ Tile Vertically. You see the legs drawing on the left and the rest of the chair on the right.

2. Click in the Barcelona1 drawing, and choose View ➢ Zoom ➢ Extents to get an overall view of the chair so far.

**3.** Click in the Legs drawing, and then click the legs 3D solid to select it.

**4.** Click and hold the cursor on the legs until you see the arrow cursor with a small rectangle.

**5.** When you see the rectangle, drag the mouse into the Barcelona1 drawing. The legs appear in the proper orientation.

**6.** Release the mouse to place the legs in the Barcelona1 drawing. You don't need to be precise about placing the legs; you can move them into position next.

**7.** Use the Move tool to move the legs so the endpoint of the upper leg joins the chair seat, as shown in Figure 21.8.

**8.** Save and close the `legs.dwg` file, and expand the `barcelona1.dwg` file to fill the AutoCAD window.

In these last few exercises, you worked on the legs of the chair in a separate file and then imported them into the main chair file with a click-and-drag motion. By working on parts in separate files, you can keep your model organized and more manageable. You may have also noticed that although the legs were drawn in the WCS, they were inserted in the 3DSW UCS that you created earlier. This shows you that imported objects are placed in the current UCS. The same would have happened if you inserted an Xref or another file.

## Understanding the UCS Options

You've seen how to select a UCS from a set of predefined UCSs. You can frequently use these preset UCSs and make minor adjustments to them to get the exact UCS you want.

---

### CONTROLLING THE UCS ICON

If the UCS icon isn't behaving as described in this chapter's exercises, chances are that its settings have been altered. You can control the behavior of the UCS icon through the UCS dialog box. To open the UCS dialog box, choose Tools ➢ Named UCS or click the Named UCS tool on the UCS II toolbar; then, click the Settings tab.

The settings in the UCS Icon Settings group affect the way the UCS icon behaves. Normally, the On and Display At UCS Origin Point check boxes are selected. If On isn't selected, you won't see the UCS icon. If the Display At UCS Origin Point check box isn't selected, the UCS icon remains in the lower-left corner of the drawing window, no matter where its origin is placed in the drawing.

If you have multiple viewports set up in a drawing, you can set these two options independently for each viewport. The third option, Apply To All Active Viewports, forces the first two settings to apply in all viewports.

Two more options appear in the UCS Settings group. If you have multiple viewports open, the Save UCS With Viewport option enables AutoCAD to maintain a separate UCS for each viewport. The Update View To Plan When UCS Is Changed option forces the display to show a plan view of the current UCS. This means that if you change a UCS orientation, AutoCAD automatically shows a plan view of the new UCS orientation. This option also forces viewport views to show the extents of plan views; if you find that your views are automatically zooming to extents when you don't want them to, turn off this setting.

Another tool for controlling the UCS icon is the UCS Icon dialog box. To open it, enter **Ucsicon P↲**.

By using this dialog box, you can fine-tune the appearance of the UCS icon, including its size and color. The 2D radio button in the UCS Icon Style group changes the UCS icon to the old-style UCS icon used in earlier versions of AutoCAD.

You can define a UCS in other ways. You can, for example, use the surface of your chair seat to define the orientation of a UCS. In the following section, you'll be shown the different ways you can set up a UCS. Learning how to move effortlessly between UCSs is crucial to mastering the creation of 3D models, so you'll want to pay special attention to the command options shown in these examples.

Note that these examples are for your reference. You can try them out on your own model. These options are accessible from either the Tools ➢ New UCS cascading menu or the UCS toolbar.

## UCS Based on Object Orientation

You can define a UCS based on the orientation of an object. This is helpful when you want to work on a predefined object to fill in details on its surface plane. Follow these steps to define a UCS this way:

**NOTE**    These steps are for information only and aren't part of the tutorial. You can try this at another time when you aren't working through an exercise.

1. Click the Object UCS tool on the UCS toolbar, choose Tools ➢ New UCS ➢ Object, or type **UCS↲OB↲**.

2. At the Select object to align UCS: prompt, pick the object that you want to use to define the UCS. For example, you could click a polyline that you want to edit in 3D. The UCS icon shifts to reflect the new coordinate system's orientation. Figure 21.9 shows an example of using the OB option to select the edge of the chair seat.

**FIGURE 21.9**

Using the Object option of the UCS command to locate a UCS

Click this edge.

The UCS will align to the selected object using the Object option.

When you create a UCS using the Object option, the location of the UCS origin and its orientation depend on how the selected object was created. Table 21.1 describes how an object can determine the orientation of a UCS.

**TABLE 21.1:**     Effects of Objects on the Orientation of a UCS

| OBJECT TYPE | UCS ORIENTATION |
| --- | --- |
| Arc | The center of the arc establishes the UCS origin. The X axis of the UCS passes through the pick point on the arc. |
| Circle | The center of the circle establishes the UCS origin. The X axis of the UCS passes through the pick point on the circle. |
| Dimension | The midpoint of the dimension text establishes the origin of the UCS origin. The X axis of the UCS is parallel to the X axis that was active when the dimension was drawn. |
| Face (of a 3D solid) | The origin of the UCS is placed on a quadrant of a circular surface or on the corner of a polygonal surface. |
| Line | The endpoint nearest the pick point establishes the origin of the UCS, and the X-Z plane of the UCS contains the line. |
| Point | The point location establishes the UCS origin. The UCS orientation is arbitrary. |
| 2D polyline | The starting point of the polyline establishes the UCS origin. The X axis is determined by the direction from the first point to the next vertex. |
| Solid | The first point of the solid establishes the origin of the UCS. The second point of the solid establishes the X axis. |
| Trace | The direction of the trace establishes the X axis of the UCS, and the beginning point sets the origin. |

**TABLE 21.1:** Effects of Objects on the Orientation of a UCS (CONTINUED)

| OBJECT TYPE | UCS ORIENTATION |
| --- | --- |
| 3D Face | The first point of the 3D Face establishes the origin. The first and second points establish the X axis. The plane defined by the 3D Face determines the orientation of the UCS. |
| Shapes, text, blocks, attributes, and attribute definitions | The insertion point establishes the origin of the UCS. The object's rotation angle establishes the X axis. |

## UCS Based on Offset Orientation

At times, you may want to work in a UCS that has the same orientation as the current UCS but is offset. For example, you might be drawing a building that has several parallel walls offset with a sawtooth effect (see Figure 21.10).

**FIGURE 21.10**
Using the Origin option to shift the UCS

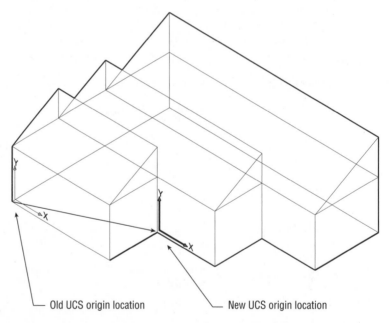

Old UCS origin location          New UCS origin location

You can easily hop from one UCS to a parallel UCS by using the Origin option. Click the Origin UCS tool on the UCS toolbar, choose Tools ➢ New UCS ➢ Origin, or type **UCS**⤶**O**⤶. At the Specify new origin point <0,0,0>: prompt, pick the new origin for your UCS.

## Moving vs. Creating a UCS Origin

The Origin UCS tool creates a new UCS that you can save under its own name. A similar option is Move UCS on the Tools drop-down menu. At first glance, these tools seem to do the same thing; that is, they create a new UCS by moving an existing UCS's origin. There is a subtle difference between the two, however. Choosing Tools ➤ Move UCS moves an existing named UCS to a new location—it doesn't create a new one. For example, if you use Move UCS to move the 3DSW UCS you created earlier in this chapter, 3DSW will appear in its new location when you recall it. On the other hand, if you use the Origin UCS tool to change the origin of the 3DSW UCS, AutoCAD creates an entirely different UCS and maintains the original location of 3DSW.

You can also find the Tools ➤ Move UCS option on the UCS II toolbar. You'll get a chance to work with the UCS II toolbar in the next section.

**NOTE**   The steps in this section are for information only and aren't part of the tutorial. You can try this at another time when you aren't working through an exercise.

## UCS Rotated Around an Axis

Suppose you want to change the orientation of the X, Y, or Z axis of a UCS. You can do so by using the X, Y, or Z Axis Rotate UCS options on the UCS toolbar. This is perhaps one of the most frequently used UCS options:

1. Click the Z tool on the UCS toolbar, choose Tools ➤ New UCS ➤ Z, or type **UCS↵Z↵**. This enables you to rotate the current UCS around the Z axis.

2. At the Specify rotation angle about Z axis <90>: prompt, press ↵ to accept the default of 90°. The UCS icon rotates about the Z axis to reflect the new orientation of the current UCS (see Figure 21.11).

Similarly, the X and Y Axis Rotate UCS options enable you to rotate the UCS about the current X and Y axis, respectively, just as you did for the Z axis earlier. The X and Y Axis Rotate UCS tools are helpful in orienting a UCS to an inclined plane. For example, if you want to work on the plane of a sloped roof of a building, you can first use the Origin UCS tool to align the UCS to the edge of a roof and then use the X Axis Rotate UCS tool to rotate the UCS to the angle of the roof slope, as shown in Figure 21.12. Note that the default is 90°, so you only have to press ↵ to rotate the UCS 90°; but you can also enter a value at the Specify another rotation angle: prompt.

**FIGURE 21.11**
Rotating the UCS about the Z axis

The UCS rotates 90 degrees from this orientation…          to this orientation.

**FIGURE 21.12**
Moving a UCS to the
plane of a sloping roof

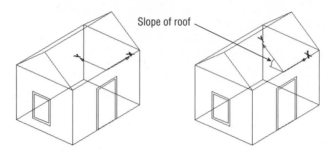

Finally, you align the Z axis between two points using the Z Axis Vector option. This is useful when you have objects in the drawing that you can use to align the Z axis. Here are the steps:

1. Click the Z Axis Vector tool on the UCS toolbar, choose Tools ➤ New UCS ➤ Z Axis Vector, or type **UCS**↵**ZA**↵.

2. At the `Specify new origin point or [Object]<0,0,0>:` prompt, press ↵ to accept the default, which is the current UCS origin; or you can select a new origin.

3. At the next prompt

   `Specify point on positive portion of Z-axis <0'-0", 0'- 0", 0'-1">:`

   select another point to indicate the Z axis orientation. Figure 21.13 shows the resulting UCS if you use the bottom of the Barcelona1 chair leg to define the Z axis.

**WARNING**  Because your cursor location is in the plane of the current UCS, it's best to pick a point on an object by using either the Osnap overrides or the coordinate filters.

**FIGURE 21.13**
Picking points for the
Z Axis Vector option

### Orienting a UCS in the View Plane

Finally, you can define a UCS in the current view plane. This is useful if you want to switch quickly to the current view plane for editing or for adding text to a 3D view.

Click the View UCS tool on the UCS toolbar, choose Tools ➢ New UCS ➢ View, or type **UCS↲V↲**. The UCS icon changes to show that the UCS is aligned with the current view.

AutoCAD uses the current UCS origin point for the origin of the new UCS. By defining a view as a UCS, you can enter text to label your drawing, just as you would in a technical illustration. Text entered in a plane created this way appears normal.

You've finished your tour of the UCS command. Set the UCS back to the WCS, and save the Barcelona1.dwg file.

You've explored nearly every option in creating a UCS, except one. Later on in this chapter, you'll learn about the 3 Point option for creating a UCS. This is the most versatile method for creating a UCS, but it's more involved than some of the other UCS options.

### Saving a UCS with a View

AutoCAD has the ability to save a UCS with a view. Choose View ➢ Named Views to open the Views dialog box, and then click the Named Views tab. Click the New button to open the New View dialog box. Enter a name for your new view; then, make sure the Save UCS With View check box is selected. By default, AutoCAD saves the current UCS with the view. You can also choose a UCS to save with a new view by using the UCS Name drop-down list.

## Using Viewports to Aid in 3D Drawing

In Chapter 15, you worked extensively with AutoCAD's floating viewports in Paper Space. In this section, you'll use *tiled* viewports to see your 3D model from several sides at the same time. This is helpful in both creating and editing 3D drawings because it enables you to refer to different portions of the drawing without having to change views.

Tiled viewports are created directly in Model Space, as you'll see in the following exercise:

**1.** Choose View ➢ Viewports ➢ Named Viewports to open the Viewports dialog box.

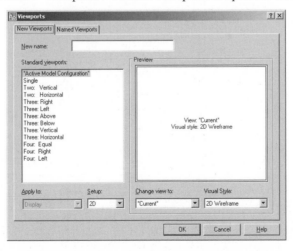

2. Make sure the New Viewports tab is selected, and then select Three: Right from the Standard Viewports list on the left. The window on the right changes to display a sample of the viewport configuration. It shows three rectangles, which represent the viewports, arranged with two on the left and one larger one to the right. Each rectangle is labeled as Current; this tells you that the current view will be placed in each viewport.

3. Open the Setup drop-down list at the bottom of the dialog box, and select 3D. The labels in the viewport sample change to indicate Top, Front, and SE Isometric. This is close to the arrangement you want, but you need to make one more adjustment. The viewport to the right, SE Isometric, shows the back side of the chair. You want an SW Isometric view in this window.

4. Click the SE Isometric viewport sample. The sample viewport border changes to a double border to indicate that it's selected.

5. Open the Change View To drop-down list just below the sample viewports, and select SW Isometric. The label in the selected viewport changes to let you know that the view will now contain the SW Isometric view. The Change View To list contains the standard four isometric views and the six orthogonal views. By clicking a sample viewport and selecting an option from the Change View To drop-down list, you can arrange your viewport views nearly any way you want.

6. To keep this viewport arrangement, enter **My Viewport Setup** in the New Name input box.

7. Click OK. Your display changes to show three viewports arranged as they were indicated in the Viewports dialog box (see Figure 21.14).

You've set up your viewports. Let's check to see that your viewport arrangement was saved:

1. Choose View ➢ Viewports ➢ Named Viewports to open the Viewports dialog box again.

2. Click the Named Viewports tab. My Viewport Setup is listed in the Named Viewports list box. If you click it, a sample view of your viewport arrangement appears on the right.

3. After you've reviewed the addition to the Named Viewports list, close the dialog box.

**FIGURE 21.14**
Three viewports, each displaying a different view

Now, take a close look at your viewport setup. The UCS icon in each of the two orthogonal views in the two left viewports is oriented to the plane of the view. AutoCAD enables you to set up a different UCS for each viewport. The top view uses the WCS because it's in the same plane as the WCS. The side view has its own UCS, which is parallel to its view. The isometric view to the right retains the UCS you saved—namely, the 3DSW UCS.

Another Viewports dialog box option you haven't tried yet is the Apply To drop-down list in the New Viewports tab.

This list shows two options: Display and Current Viewport. When Display is selected, the option you choose from the Standard Viewports list applies to the overall display. When Current Viewport is selected, the option you select applies to the selected viewport in the sample view in the right side of the dialog box. You can use the Current Viewport option to build multiple viewports in custom arrangements.

You have the legs for one side. The next step is to mirror those legs for the other side:

1. Click the top view of the chair in the upper-left viewport.

2. Turn on Polar mode, and then click the Mirror tool on the Modify toolbar.

3. In the upper-left viewport, click the 3D solid representing the chair legs, and then press ↵.

4. At the `Specify first point of mirror line:` prompt, use the Midpoint osnap and select the midpoint of the chair seat, as shown in Figure 21.15.

**FIGURE 21.15**
Mirroring the legs from one side to another

Click the midpoint of this edge.

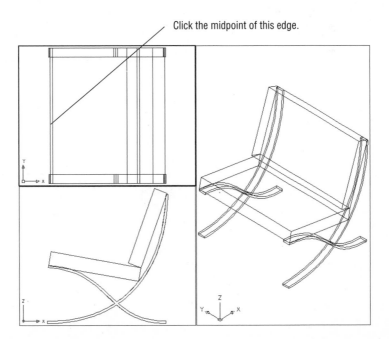

5. At the `Specify second point of mirror line:` prompt, pick any location to the right of the point you selected so the rubber-banding line is exactly horizontal.

6. Press ↵ at the `Erase source objects? [Yes/No]:` prompt. The legs are mirrored to the opposite side of the chair. Your screen should look similar to Figure 21.15.

Your chair is complete. Let's finish by getting a better look at it:

1. Click the viewport to the right, showing the Isometric view.

2. Choose View ➢ Viewports ➢ 1 Viewport.

3. Use the Zoom tool to adjust your view so that it looks similar to Figure 21.16.

**FIGURE 21.16**
The chair in 3D with hidden lines removed

4. Click the drop-down list in the Visual Styles control panel, and select 3D Hidden to get a view similar to Figure 21.16.

# Creating Complex 3D Surfaces

In the previous example, you drew a chair composed of objects that were mostly straight lines or curves with a thickness. All the forms in that chair were defined in planes perpendicular to one another. For a 3D model such as this, you can get by using the orthographic UCSs. At times, however, you'll want to draw objects that don't fit so easily into perpendicular or parallel planes. In this section, you'll create more-complex forms by using some of AutoCAD's other 3D commands.

## Laying Out a 3D Form

In this next group of exercises, you'll draw a butterfly chair. This chair has no perpendicular or parallel planes to work with, so you'll start by setting up some points that you'll use for reference only. This is similar in concept to laying out a 2D drawing. As you progress through the drawing construction, notice how the reference points are established to help create the chair. You'll also construct some temporary 3D lines to use for reference. These temporary lines will be your layout. These points will define the major UCSs needed to construct the drawing. The main point is to show you some of the options for creating and saving UCSs.

To save time, I've created the 2D drawing that you'll use to build your 3D layout. This drawing consists of two rectangles that are offset by 4″ (10 mm for metric users). To make it more interesting, they're also off center from each other (see Figure 21.17). The first thing you'll need to do is set up the drawing for the layout.

**FIGURE 21.17**

Setting up a layout for a butterfly chair

1. Open the Butterfly1.dwg file.

2. Choose View ➤ 3D Views ➤ SW Isometric. This gives you a view from the lower-left side of the rectangles.

3. Zoom out so the rectangles occupy about a third of the drawing area window.

Now, you need to move the outer rectangle in the Z axis so its elevation is 30″ (76 cm for metric users):

1. Click the outer rectangle, and then click one of its grips.

2. Right-click to open the Grip Edit shortcut menu.

3. Choose Move, and then enter **@0,0,30**↵; metric users should enter **@0,0,76**↵. This tells AutoCAD to move the rectangle a 0 distance in both the X and Y axes and 30″ (or 76 cm) in the Z axis.

**TIP**   As an alternate method in step 3, after choosing Move from the Grip Edit shortcut menu, you can turn on Ortho mode and point the cursor vertically so it shows −Z in the coordinate readout; then, enter **30**↵ or **76**↵ for metric users.

4. Pan your view downward so it looks similar to Figure 21.18.

**FIGURE 21.18**
The finished
chair layout

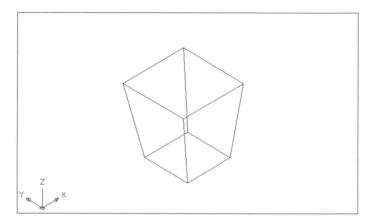

5. Use the Line tool to draw lines from the corners of the outer square to the corners of the inner square. Use the Endpoint osnap to select the exact corners of the squares. This is the layout for your chair—not the finished product.

## Spherical and Cylindrical Coordinate Formats

In the previous exercise, you used relative Cartesian coordinates to locate the second point for the Move command. For commands that accept 3D input, you can also specify displacements by using the Spherical and Cylindrical Coordinate formats.

The *Spherical Coordinate format* lets you specify a distance in 3D space while specifying the angle in terms of degrees from the X axis of the current UCS and degrees from the X-Y plane of the current UCS (see the top image in Figure 21.19). For example, to specify a distance of 4.5″ (11.43 cm) at a 30° angle from the X axis and 45° from the X-Y plane, enter **@4.5<30<45** (or **@11.43<30<45** for metric users). This refers to the direct distance, followed by a < symbol; then the angle from the X axis of the current UCS followed by another < symbol; and then the angle from the X-Y plane of the current UCS. To use the Spherical Coordinate format to move the rectangle in the exercise, enter **@30<0<90** at the Second point: prompt, or **@76<0<90** for metric users.

The *Cylindrical Coordinate format*, on the other hand, lets you specify a location in terms of a distance in the plane of the current UCS and a distance in the Z axis. You also specify an angle from the X axis of the current UCS (see the bottom image in Figure 21.19). For example, to locate a point that is a distance of 4.5″ (11.43 cm) in the plane of the current UCS, at an angle of 30° from the X axis and a distance of 3.3″ (8.38 cm) in the Z axis, enter **@4.5<30,3.3** (or **@11.43<30,8.38** for metric users). This refers to the distance of the displacement from the plane of the current UCS, followed by the < symbol; then the angle from the X axis, followed by a comma; and then the distance in the Z axis. Using the Cylindrical Coordinate format to move the rectangle, you enter **@0<0,30** at the Second point: prompt, or **@0<0,76** for metric users.

**FIGURE 21.19**
The Spherical and Cylindrical Coordinate formats

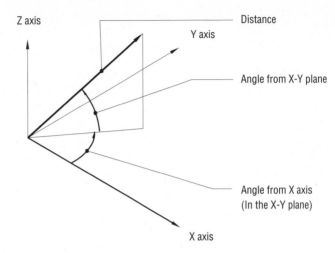

[Distance] < [Angle from X axis] < [Angle from X-Y plane]

The Spherical Coordinate Format

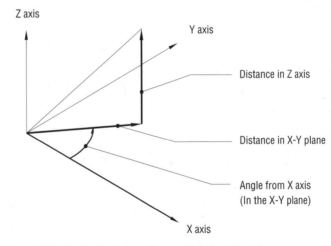

[Distance in X-Y plane] < [Angle from X axis] , [Distance in Z axis]

The Cylindrical Coordinate Format

## Using a 3D Polyline

Now, you'll draw the legs for the butterfly chair by using a 3D polyline. This is a polyline that can be drawn in 3D space. Here are the steps:

1. Choose Draw ➢ 3D Polyline, or type **3p**↵.

2. At the `Specify start point of polyline:` prompt, pick a series of points, as shown in Figure 21.20 (top), by using the Endpoint and Midpoint osnaps.

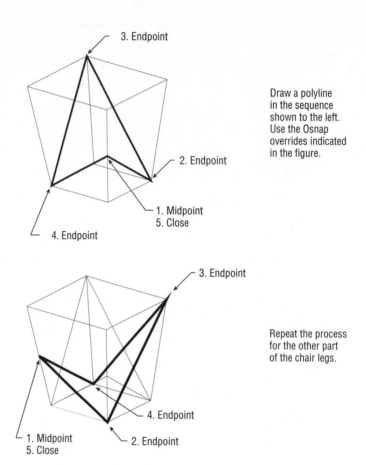

3. Endpoint

Draw a polyline
in the sequence
shown to the left.
Use the Osnap
overrides indicated
in the figure.

2. Endpoint

1. Midpoint
5. Close

4. Endpoint

3. Endpoint

Repeat the process
for the other part
of the chair legs.

4. Endpoint

1. Midpoint
5. Close

2. Endpoint

**TIP**    This would be a good place to use the Running Osnaps feature.

**3.** Draw another 3D polyline in the mirror image of the first (see the lower image in Figure 21.20).

**4.** Erase the connecting vertical lines that make up the frame, but keep the rectangles. You'll use them later.

All objects, with the exception of lines and 3D polylines, are restricted to the plane of your current UCS. Two other legacy 3D objects, 3D faces and 3D meshes, are also restricted. You can use the Pline command to draw polylines in only one plane, but you can use the 3DPoly command to create a polyline in three dimensions. 3DPoly objects can't, however, be given thickness or width.

## Creating a Curved 3D Surface

Next, you'll draw the seat of the chair. The seat of a butterfly chair is usually made of canvas and drapes from the four corners of the chair legs. You'll first define the perimeter of the seat by using arcs, and then you'll use the Edge Surface tool on the Surfaces toolbar to form the shape of the draped canvas. The Edge Surface tool creates a surface based on four objects defining the edges of that surface. In this example, you'll use arcs to define the edges of the seat.

To draw the arcs defining the seat edge, you must first establish the UCSs in the planes of those edges. In the previous example, you created a UCS for the side of the chair before you could draw the legs. In the same way, you must create a UCS defining the planes that contain the edges of the seat.

Because the UCS you want to define isn't orthogonal, you'll need to use the three-point method. This lets you define the plane of the UCS based on three points:

1. Click the 3 Point UCS tool on the UCS toolbar, choose Tools ➢ New UCS ➢ 3 Point, or type **UCS⏎3⏎**. This option enables you to define a UCS based on three points that you select.

**TIP** Remember, it helps to think of a UCS as a drawing surface situated on the surface of the object you want to draw or edit.

2. At the `Specify new origin point <0,0,0>:` prompt, use the Endpoint osnap to pick the bottom of the chair leg to the far left, as shown in the left image of Figure 21.21. This is the origin point of your new UCS.

**FIGURE 21.21**
Defining and saving three UCSs

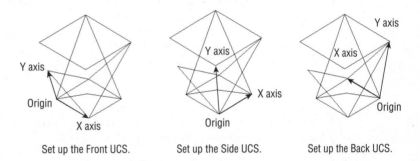

Set up the Front UCS.     Set up the Side UCS.     Set up the Back UCS.

3. At the `Specify point on positive portion of X-axis:` prompt, use the Endpoint osnap to pick the bottom of the next leg to the right of the first one, as shown in the left image in Figure 21.21.

4. At the `Specify point on positive-Y portion of the UCS XY plane:` prompt, pick the top corner of the butterfly chair seat, as shown in the left image in Figure 21.21. The UCS icon changes to indicate your new UCS.

5. Now that you've defined a UCS, you need to save it so that you can return to it later. Choose Tools ➢ Named UCS, or type **UC⏎** to open the UCS dialog box.

6. With the Named UCSs tab selected, right-click the Unnamed item in the list box, and choose Rename from the shortcut menu.

7. Enter **Front⏎**.

8. Click OK to exit the UCS dialog box.

You've defined and saved a UCS for the front side of the chair. As you can see from the UCS icon, this UCS is at a non-orthogonal angle to the WCS. Continue by creating UCSs for two more sides of the butterfly chair:

1. Define a UCS for the side of the chair, as shown in the middle image in Figure 21.21. Use the UCS Control dialog box to rename this UCS **Side**, just as you did for Front in the previous steps 5 through 8. Remember that you renamed the Unnamed UCS.

**2.** Repeat these steps for a UCS for the back of the chair, named Back. Use the right image in Figure 21.21 for reference.

**3.** Open the UCS dialog box again; in the Named UCSs tab, highlight Front.

**4.** Click the Set Current button, and then click OK. This activates Front as the current UCS.

**5.** Choose Draw ➤ Arc ➤ Start, End, Direction.

**6.** Draw the arc defining the front edge of the chair (see Figure 21.22). Use the Endpoint Osnap override to pick the top endpoints of the chair legs as the endpoints of the arc. (If you need help with the Arc command, refer to Chapter 3.)

**FIGURE 21.22**
Drawing the front and back seat edge using arcs and a polyline spline

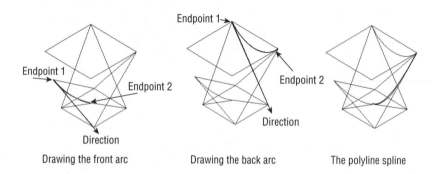

Drawing the front arc          Drawing the back arc          The polyline spline

**7.** Repeat steps 3 through 6 for the UCS named Back—each time using the top endpoints of the legs for the endpoints of the arc.

**8.** Restore the UCS for the side; but instead of drawing an arc, use the Polyline tool and draw a polyline spline similar to the one in Figure 21.22. If you need help with polyline splines, see Chapter 14.

Next, you'll mirror the side-edge spline to the opposite side. This will save you from having to define a UCS for that side:

**1.** Click the World UCS tool on the UCS toolbar to restore the WCS. You do this because you want to mirror the arc along an axis that is parallel to the plane of the WCS. Remember that you must use the coordinate system that defines the plane in which you want to work.

**2.** Click the polyline you drew for the side of the chair (the one drawn on the Side UCS).

**3.** Click the midpoint grip of the arc in the Side UCS; then, right-click, and choose Mirror from the shortcut menu.

**4.** Enter C↵ to select the Copy option.

**5.** Enter B↵ to select a new base point for the mirror axis.

**6.** At the Specify base point: prompt, use the Midpoint override to pick the midpoints of the rectangle at the bottom of the model. Refer to Figure 21.23 for help. The polyline should mirror to the opposite side, and your chair should look like Figure 21.24.

**7.** Press the Esc key twice to clear the grips.

**FIGURE 21.23**
Set your UCS to World, and then mirror the arc that defines the side of the chair seat.

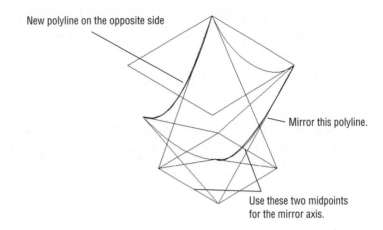

New polyline on the opposite side

Mirror this polyline.

Use these two midpoints for the mirror axis.

**FIGURE 21.24**
Your butterfly chair so far

ACAD
only

## QUICK HOPS TO YOUR UCSS

If you find you're jumping from one saved UCS to another, you'll want to know about the UCS II toolbar. The UCS II toolbar has a drop-down list that contains the World and Previous UCS options as well as all the saved UCSs in a drawing. You can use this list as a quick way to move between UCSs that you've set up or between the predefined orthogonal UCSs.

Two other tools on the UCS II toolbar give you access to the UCS dialog box and the Move UCS tool, which moves an existing UCS to another location. As with all toolbars, you can open the UCS II toolbar by right-clicking any toolbar and then choosing UCS II from the shortcut menu.

Another great way to jump quickly between UCSs is to use the UCS Face option. The Face option requires a 3D solid; but once you have one in place, you can choose Tools ➢ New UCS ➢ Face and then click the face of the solid to which you want to align your UCS. For example, you can use the Loft command (see the section "Shaping the Solid," later in this chapter) to create a solid similar to the solid shown later in Figure 21.27 that connects the top and bottom rectangles of the butterfly chair. You can then use the UCS Face option to align to the sides of that solid to draw the arcs and polylines for the seat outline. This way, you're using the 3D solid as a layout tool.

Finally, let's finish this chair by adding the mesh representing the chair seat:

1. Click the Loft tool in the 3D Make control panel, choose Draw ➢ Modeling ➢ Loft, or enter **Loft.↵** at the Command prompt.

2. At the Select cross-sections in lofting order: prompt, click the arc at the front of the layout.

3. At the Select cross-sections in lofting order: prompt, click the arc at the back of the layout, and then press ↵ to finish your selection of cross-sections.

4. At the Enter an option [Guides/Path/Cross-sections only] <Cross-sections only>: prompt, enter **G.↵** for the Guides option. You'll use the other two arcs as guides.

5. At the Select guide curves: prompt, select the two polylines on the sides of the layout, and then press ↵ to complete your selection. Your chair begins to take form, as shown in Figure 21.25.

6. Choose File ➢ Save to save the chair so far.

You've got the beginnings of a butterfly chair with the legs drawn in schematically and the seat as a 3D surface. You can add some detail by using a few other tools, as you'll see in the next set of exercise.

**FIGURE 21.25**
The butterfly chair
so far

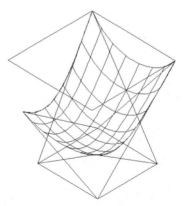

## Converting the Surface into a Solid

In the previous example, you used the Loft tool to create a 3D surface. Once you have a surface, you can convert it to a solid to perform other modifications.

You'll want to round the corners of the seat surface to simulate the way a butterfly chair hangs off its frame. You'll also round the corners of the frame and turn the frame into a tubular form. Start by rounding the seat surface. This will involve turning the surface into a solid so you can use solid editing tools to get the shape you want:

1. Click the Thicken Surface tool in the 3D Make control panel.

You can also choose Modify ➤ 3D Operations ➤ Thicken or enter **Thicken⏎** at the Command prompt.

2. Select the seat surface, and press ⏎ to finish your selection.

3. At the `Specify thickness <0'-0">:` prompt, enter **0.01⏎**, or **0.025⏎** for metric users.

The seat surface appears to loose its webbing, but it has just been converted to a very thin 3D solid.

## Shaping the Solid

The butterfly chair is in a fairly schematic state. The corners of the chair are sharply pointed, whereas a real butterfly chair would have rounded corners. In this section, you'll round the corners of the seat with a little help from the original rectangles you used to form the layout frame.

First, you'll use the Fillet command to round the corners of rectangles. Then, you'll use the rounded rectangles to create a solid from which you'll form a new seat:

1. Choose the Fillet tool from the Modify toolbar, choose Modify ➤ Fillet, or enter **F⏎** at the Command prompt.

2. At the `Select first object or [Undo/Polyline/Radius/Trim/Multiple]:` prompt, enter **R⏎**.

3. At the `Specify fillet radius <0'-0">:` prompt, enter **3⏎**.

4. At the `Select first object or [Undo/Polyline/Radius/Trim/Multiple]:` prompt, enter **P⏎** for the Polyline option.

5. At the `Select 2D polyline:` prompt, select the top rectangle, as shown in Figure 21.26. The polyline corners become rounded.

6. Press ⏎ to repeat the Fillet command.

7. Enter **P⏎** to use the Polyline option, and then click the bottom rectangle as shown in Figure 21.26. Now both polylines have rounded corners.

**FIGURE 21.26**
Round the corners
of the rectangles with
the Fillet command.

Start the Fillet command and
select the top rectangle to
round its corners.

Repeat the Fillet command to round
the corners of the bottom rectangle.

Next, create a 3D solid from the two rectangles using the Loft tool:

1. Click the Loft tool in the 3D Make control panel, or choose Draw ➢ Modeling ➢ Loft.

2. At the `Select cross-sections in lofting order:` prompt, select the two rectangles, and then press ↵ to finish your selection.

3. At the `Enter an option [Guides/Path/Cross-sections only] <Cross-sections only>:` prompt, press ↵. The Loft Settings dialog box appears.

4. Click the Ruled option, and click OK. The rectangles join to form a 3D solid (see Figure 21.27).

## Finding the Interference between Two Solids

In this next exercise, you'll use a tool that is intended to find the interference between two solids. This is useful if you're working with crowded 3D models and you need to check whether objects may be interfering with each other. For example, a mechanical designer might want to check to make sure duct locations aren't passing through a structural beam.

**FIGURE 21.27**
The lofted rectangles
form a 3D solid.

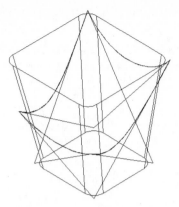

You'll use Interfere as a modeling tool to obtain a shape that is a combination of two solids: the seat and the rectangular solid you just created. Here are the steps:

1. Click the Interference Checking tool in the 3D Make control panel.

You can also choose Modify ➤ 3D Operations ➤ Interference or enter **interfere**↵ at the Command prompt.

2. At the `Select first set of objects or [Nested selection/Settings]:` prompt, select the chair seat solid, and then press ↵.

3. At the `Select second set of objects or [Nested selection/checK first set] <checK>:` prompt, click the rectangular solid you created in the previous exercise, and then press ↵. The Interference Checking dialog box appears, and the drawing temporarily changes to a view similar to the Realistic visual style.

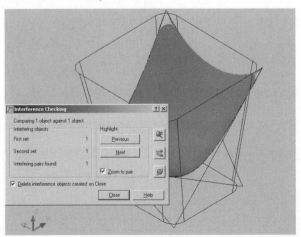

The view shows the interference of the two solids in red. Notice that the corners are rounded on the red interference.

4. In the Interference Checking dialog box, turn off the Delete Interference Objects Created On Close option, and then click Close. The display returns to the Wireframe view. If you look carefully at the seat corners, you see a new solid overlaid on the seat (see Figure 21.28).

**FIGURE 21.28**
The Interference solid appears on top of the original seat.

Delete the rectangular solid.

Delete the original seat.

5. Delete the rectangular solid and the original seat, as shown in Figure 21.28.

As mentioned earlier, the Interference Checking tool is intended to help you find out whether objects are colliding in a 3D model; but as you've just seen, it can be an excellent modeling tool that can help you derive a form that you may otherwise not have the ability to create.

A number of other options are available when using the Interference Checking tool. Table 21.2 lists the options in the Interference Checking dialog box.

**TABLE 21.2:**   Interference Checking Dialog Box Options

| OPTION | WHAT IT DOES |
| --- | --- |
| First Set | Specifies the number of objects in the first set of selected objects |
| Second Set | Specifies the number of objects in the second set of selected objects |
| Interfering Pairs Found | Indicates the number of interferences found |
| Previous | Highlights the previous interference object |
| Next | Highlights the next interference object if multiple objects are present |
| Zoom To Pair | Zooms to the interference object while using the Previous and Next options |
| Zoom Realtime | Closes the dialog box to allow you to use Zoom Realtime |
| Pan Realtime | Closes the dialog box to allow you to use Pan |
| 3D Orbit | Closes the dialog box to allow you to use 3D Orbit |
| Delete Interference Objects Created On Close | Deletes the interference object after the dialog box is closed |

The prompt for the Interference Checking command also showed some options. The prompt in step 2 shows `Nested selection/Settings`. The `Nested selection` option lets you select objects that are nested in a block or an Xref. The `Settings` option opens the Interference Settings dialog box.

This dialog box offers settings for the temporary display of interference objects while in the Interference command. Table 21.3 lists the options for this dialog box.

**TABLE 21.3:**    Interference Settings Dialog Box Options

| OPTION | WHAT IT DOES |
| --- | --- |
| Visual Style | Controls the visual style for interference objects |
| Color | Controls the color for interference objects |
| Highlight Interfering Pair | Highlights the interfering objects |
| Highlight Interference | Highlights the resulting interference objects |
| Visual Style | Controls the visual style for the drawing while displaying the interference objects |

## Creating Tubes with the Sweep Tool

One more element needs to be taken care of before your chair is complete. The legs are currently simple lines with sharp corners. In this section, you'll learn how you can convert lines into 3D tubes. To make it more interesting, you'll add rounded corners to the legs.

Start by rounding the corners on the lines you've created for the legs:

1. Use the Explode tool to explode the 3D polyline legs into simple lines.

2. Choose the Fillet tool from the Modify toolbar, choose Modify ➢ Fillet, or enter **F⏎** at the Command prompt.

3. At the `Select first object or [Undo/Polyline/Radius/Trim/Multiple]:` prompt, enter **R⏎**.

4. At the `Specify fillet radius <0'-0">:` prompt, enter **2⏎**.

5. At the `Select first object or [Undo/Polyline/Radius/Trim/Multiple]:` prompt, enter **M↵**, and then select pairs of lines to fillet their corners.

6. When all the corners are rounded, press ↵ to exit the Fillet command.

7. Delete the two polyline splines you used to form the sides of the seat. Your drawing should look like Figure 21.29.

**FIGURE 21.29**

Drawing the circles for the tubes

Draw a circle here, and make 15 copies for a total of 16 circles.

The chair is almost complete, but the legs are just wireframes. Next, you'll give them some thickness by turning them into tubes. Start by creating a set of circles. You'll use the circles to define the diameter of the tubes:

1. Draw a ¾″ (19 mm) diameter circle in the location shown in Figure 21.29. Don't worry if your location is a little off; the placement of the circle isn't important.

2. Use the Array command to make 15 copies of the circle. In Figure 21.29, a 4 × 4 array is used with the default 1″ spacing. Metric users should use a spacing of about 30 mm.

Now you're ready to form the tubes:

1. Click the Sweep tool in the 3D Make toolbar. You can also choose Draw ➤ Modeling ➤ Sweep or enter **sweep↵** at the Command prompt.

2. At the `Select objects to sweep:` prompt, click one of the circles you just created. It doesn't matter which circle you use, because they're identical. Press ↵ when you're finished.

3. At the `Select sweep path or [Alignment/Base point/Scale/Twist]:` prompt, select one of the lines or fillet arcs that make up the legs.

4. Press ↵ to repeat the Sweep command, and then repeat steps 2 and 3 for each part of the leg segments, including the fillet arcs.

5. Continue with step 4 until all the lines in the legs have been converted into tubes.

6. Change the color of the solid representing the seat to cyan, and then select the Realistic visual style from the Visual Style control panel. Your drawing will look similar to the image on the left of Figure 21.30, which shows a Perspective view. The image on the right is the chair with some materials assigned to the parts of the chair and a slight adjustment to the seat location.

## Using Sweep to Create Complex Forms

Although you used circles with the Sweep command to create tubes, you can use any closed polyline shape. Figure 21.31 gives some examples of other shapes you can use with the Sweep command.

**FIGURE 21.30**
A Perspective view of the butterfly chair with tubes for legs

**FIGURE 21.31**
You can use any closed shape with the Sweep command.

In step 3 of the previous exercise, you may have noticed some command-line options. These options offer additional control over the way Sweep works. Here is a rundown on these options and their function:

**Alignment** This option lets you determine whether the object to sweep is automatically set perpendicular to the sweep path. By default, this option is set to Yes, which means the object to sweep is set perpendicular to the path. If set to no, Sweep assumes the current angle of the object, as shown in Figure 21.32.

**FIGURE 21.32**
Alignment lets you set the angle between the object to sweep and the sweep path.

By default, the object to sweep is aligned perpendicular to the sweep path.

Rotate the object to sweep to an angle away from the WCS, and then turn off the Alignment option.

You can skew the object to sweep in relation to the sweep path using the Alignment option.

**Base Point** By default, Sweep uses the center of the object to sweep as the location to align with the path, as shown in Figure 21.33. Base Point lets you set a specific location on the object.

**Scale** You can have Sweep scale the sweep object from one end of the path to the other to create a tapered shape, as shown in Figure 21.34. This option requires a numeric scale value.

**Twist** You can have the object to sweep twist along the path to form a spiral shape, as shown in Figure 21.35. This option requires a numeric value in the form of degrees of rotation.

These options are available as soon as you select the sweep object and before you select the path object. You can use any combination of options you need. For example, you can apply the Twist and Scale options together, as shown in Figure 21.36.

**FIGURE 21.33**
Base Point lets you set a point on the object to sweep that is aligned with the sweep path.

By default, the center of the object to sweep is aligned with the sweep path.

With the Base Point option, you can select a location on the object to sweep that will align with the sweep path.

Center        Sweep path                    Base point        Sweep path

**FIGURE 21.34**
Scale lets you scale the object to sweep as it's swept along the path.

**FIGURE 21.35**
You can have the object to sweep twist along the path to create a spiral effect.

**FIGURE 21.36**
The Scale and
Twist options
applied together

## Creating Spiral Forms

You can use the Sweep tool in conjunction with the Helix tool to create a spiral form, such as a spring or the threads of a screw. You've already seen how the Sweep tool works. Try the following to learn how the Helix tool works firsthand.

In this exercise, you'll draw a helicoil thread insert. This is a device used to repair stripped threads; it's basically a coiled steel strip that forms internal and external threads. Here are the steps:

1. Open the `Helicoil.dwg` file. This is a standard AutoCAD drawing containing a closed polyline in a stretched octagon shape.

This is the cross-section of the helicoil thread, and you'll use it as an object to sweep after you've created a helix.

2. Click the Helix tool in the expanded 3D Make control panel.

You see the following prompt:

```
Number of turns = 3.0000    Twist=CCW
Specify center point of base:
```

3. Pick a point roughly in the center of the view. A rubber-banding line appears along with a circle.

4. At the `Specify base radius or [Diameter] <1.0000>:` prompt, enter **.375**↵.

5. At the `Specify top radius or [Diameter] <0.3750>:` prompt, press ↵ to accept the default, which is the same as the value you entered in step 4.

6. At the `Specify helix height or [Axis endpoint/Turns/turn Height/tWist]` `<1.0000>:` prompt, enter **T**↵ to use the Turns option.

7. At the `Enter number of turns <3.0000>:` prompt, enter **15**↵ to create a helix with 15 turns total.

8. At the `Specify helix height or [Axis endpoint/Turns/turn Height/tWist]` `<1.0000>:` prompt, press ↵ to accept the default height of 1. The helix appears as a spiral drawn to the dimensions you've just specified for diameter, turns, and height (see Figure 21.37).

In step 6, you used the Turns option to specify the total number of turns in the helix. You also have other options that give you control over the shape of the helix. Figures 21.38 shows you the effects of the Helix command options. You may want to experiment with them on your own to get familiar with Helix.

**FIGURE 21.37**
The helix and
the helicoil after
using Sweep

**TIP**   If you find that you've created a helix with the wrong settings, you don't have to erase and re-create it. You can use the Properties palette to make adjustments to any of the helix options presented in Figure 21.38 even after a helix has been created. Select the helix, right-click, and then choose Properties. Look in the Geometry section of the Properties palette for the helix settings.

**FIGURE 21.38**
The Helix command options

Axis Endpoint lets you select the endpoint of the helix to adjust the helix direction.

The Turns option determines the number of turns in the helix.

Turn Height lets you specify the height between coils.

Center of base

The tWist option lets you determine whether the helix twists clockwise or counterclockwise.

Now, use the Sweep tool to complete the helicoil:

1. Click the Sweep tool in the 3D Make control panel, choose Draw ➢ Modeling ➢ Sweep, or enter **Sweep** at the Command prompt.

2. At the `Select objects to sweep:` prompt, select the thread cross section in the lower-left corner of the drawing, and then press ↵.

3. At the `Select sweep path or [Alignment/Base point/Scale/Twist]:` prompt, select the helix. After a moment, the helicoil appears.

4. To see the helicoil more clearly, choose the Realistic option from the Visual Styles drop-down list, and then change the helicoil to the helicoil layer.

**WARNING**   If the space between the coils is too small for the cross section, you may get an error message. If you get an error message at step 3, make sure you created the helix exactly as specified in the previous exercise. You may also try increasing the helix height.

In step 3, instead of selecting the sweep path, you can select an option to apply to the object to sweep. For example, by default, Sweep aligns the object to sweep at an angle that is perpendicular to the path and centers the object to sweep. See "Using Sweep to Create Complex Forms," earlier in this chapter.

## Creating Surface Models

In an earlier exercise, you used the Loft command to create the seat of a butterfly chair. In this section, you'll return to the Loft command to explore some of its other uses. This time, you'll use it to create a 3D model of a hillside based on a set of site-contour lines. You'll also see how you can use a surface created from the Loft command to slice a solid into two pieces, imprinting the solid with the surface shape.

**WARNING** If you've used earlier versions of AutoCAD to create 3D models, be aware that the surfaces created with the Loft command aren't the same as those created with the Surfaces toolbar. You can convert those older mesh objects into the new surface objects using the Convert To Surface tool, which is next to the Convert To Solid tool in the 3D Make control panel.

1. Open the contour.dwg file.

2. Click the Loft tool on the 3D Make control panel.

3. Select each brown contour in consecutive order from right to left or left to right. It doesn't matter whether you start at the left end or the right end, but you must select the contours in order.

4. When you're finished selecting all the contours, press ↵.

5. At the Enter an option [Guides/Path/Cross-sections only] <Cross-sections only>: prompt, press ↵ and wait a moment. AutoCAD requires a bit of time to calculate the surface. Once it does, you see the Loft Settings dialog box and the surface.

6. Click the Ruled radio button, and then click OK. You can now see the surface clearly, as shown in Figure 21.39.

**FIGURE 21.39**
Creating a 3D surface
from contour lines

In the butterfly chair exercise, you used the Guides option in the Loft command prompt. This allowed you to use the polyline curves to guide the loft shape from the front arc to the back arc. In this exercise, you didn't use the command options and went straight to the Loft Settings dialog box. The Ruled setting that you used in step 6 generates a surface that connects the cross sections in a straight line. You'll learn more about the options in this dialog box later in this section.

## Slicing a Solid with a Surface

In the Barcelona chair example, you converted a surface into a solid using the Thicken command. Next, you'll use a surface to create a solid in a slightly different way. This time, you'll use the surface to slice a solid into two pieces. This will give you a form that is more easily read and understood as a terrain model:

1. Click the Extrude tool in the 3D Make control panel.

2. At the `Select objects to extrude:` prompt, select the large rectangle below the contours, and press ↵. The rectangle turns into a box whose height follows your cursor.

3. At the Specify `height of extrusion or [Direction/Path/Taper angle] <0´-0″>:` prompt, move the cursor upward so the box looks similar to the one in Figure 21.40. Then, click the mouse to fix the box's height.

**FIGURE 21.40**
The box extruded through the contours

You may have noticed that as you raised the box height, you could see how it intersected the contour surface. Next, you'll slice the box into two pieces:

1. Click the Slice tool in the expanded 3D Make control panel.

2. At the `Select objects to slice:` prompt, select the box and press ↵.

3. At the `Specify start point of slicing plane or [planar Object/Surface/Zaxis/ View/XY/YZ/ZX/3points] <3points>:` prompt, enter **S↵**.

4. At the `Select a surface:` prompt, select the contour surface.

5. At the `Select solid to keep or [keep Both sides] <Both>:` prompt, click the part of the box that is below the surface. The top part of the box disappears, and you see the surface once again.

6. Delete the contour surface. The box remains with an imprint of the surface, as shown in Figure 21.41.

**FIGURE 21.41**

The box with the contour surface imprinted

In step 3, you saw a prompt that offered a variety of methods for slicing the box. The Surface option allowed you to slice the box using an irregular shape, but most of the other options let you slice a solid by defining a plane or a series of planar objects.

## Finding the Volume of a Cut

A question I hear frequently from civil engineers is, "How can I find the volume of earth from an excavated area?" This is often referred to as a *cut* from a *cut and fill* operation. To do this, you have to first create the cut shape. Next, you use the Interfere command to find the intersection between the cut shape and the contour surface. You can then find the volume of the cut shape using one of AutoCAD's inquiry commands. The following exercise demonstrates how this is done.

Suppose that the contour model you've just created represents a site where you'll excavate a rectangular area for a structure. You want to find the amount of earth involved in the excavation. A rectangle has been placed in the contour drawing representing such an area:

1. Select the 3D Wireframe option from the Visual Styles drop-down list. This allows you to see the excavation rectangle more clearly.

2. Click the Extrude tool in the 3D Make control panel.

3. Select the rectangle shown in Figure 21.42, and then press ↵.

**FIGURE 21.42**
Selecting the rectangle representing the excavation area

4. Extrude the rectangle to the height of 10′.

With the excavation rectangle in place, you can use the Interfere command to find the volume of the excavation:

1. Click the Interference Checking tool in the 3D Make control panel.

2. At the `Select first set of objects or [Nested selection/Settings]:` prompt, click the contour and press ↵.

3. At the `Select second set of objects or [Nested selection/checK first set]` `<checK>:` prompt, select the box and press ↵. The Interference Checking dialog box appears.

4. In the Interference Checking dialog box, turn off the Delete Interference Objects Created On Close option, and click Close.

5. Delete the box you used to represent the excavation area. The remaining shape contains the volume of the excavation.

6. Choose Tools ➢ Inquiry ➢ Region/Mass Properties.

7. At the `Select Objects:` prompt, select the excavation solid, as shown in Figure 21.43, and then press ↵. The AutoCAD Text Window appears, and it displays the properties of the excavation area. At the top, you see the volume of the selected solid in cubic inches.

**FIGURE 21.43**
The 3D solid representing the excavation

8. At the Write analysis to a file? [Yes/No] <N>: prompt, you can press ↵ to exit the command or enter **Y**↵ to save the information to a text file.

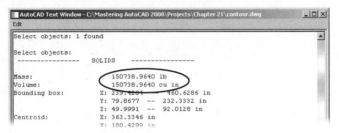

## Understanding the Loft Command

As you've seen from the exercises in this chapter, the Loft command lets you create just about any shape you can imagine, from a simple sling to the complex curves of a contour map. If your loft cross sections are a set of closed objects like circles or closed polygons, the resulting object is a 3D solid instead of a surface.

The order in which you select the cross sections is important, because Loft will follow your selection order to create the surface or solid. For example, Figure 21.44 shows a series of circles used for a lofted solid. The circles are identical in size and placement, but the order of selection is different. The solid on the left was created by selecting the circles in consecutive order from bottom to top, creating an hourglass shape. The solid on the right was created by selecting the two larger circles first from bottom to top; the smaller, intermediate circle was selected last. This selection order created a hollowed out shape with more vertical sides.

In addition to the selection order, several other settings affect the shape of a solid created by the Loft command. In the contour-map example, you selected a setting in the Loft Settings dialog box. This dialog box appears when you select the Cross Section Only option after you've selected a set of cross sections.

You can radically affect the way the Loft command forms a surface or a solid through the options in this dialog box, so it pays to understand what those settings do. Take a moment to study the following sections that describe the Loft Settings dialog box options.

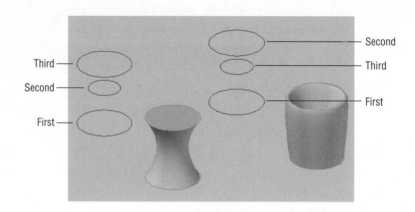

### RULED AND SMOOTH FIT

The Ruled option connects the cross sections with straight surfaces, as shown in the sample to the left in Figure 21.45.

**FIGURE 21.45**
Samples of a Ruled loft
at left and a Smooth
Fit loft on the right

The Smooth Fit option connects the cross sections with a smooth surface. It attempts to make the best smooth transitions between the cross sections, as shown in the right image in Figure 21.45.

### NORMAL TO

Normal To is a set of four options presented in a drop-down list. To understand what this option does, you need to know that *normal* is a mathematical term referring to a direction that is perpendicular to a plane, as shown in Figure 21.46. In these options, Normal refers to the direction the surface takes as it emerges from a cross section.

If you use the All Cross Sections option, the surfaces emerge in a perpendicular direction from all the cross sections, as shown in the first image in Figure 21.47. If you use the End Cross Section option, the surface emerges in a direction that is perpendicular to just the end cross section, as shown in the second image in Figure 21.47. The Start Cross Section option causes the surface to emerge in a direction perpendicular to the start cross section. The Start And End Cross Sections option combines the effect of the Start Cross Section and End Cross Section options.

### DRAFT ANGLES

The Draft Angles option affects only the first and last cross sections. This option generates a smooth surface with added control over the start and end angle. Unlike the Normal To option, which forces a perpendicular direction to the cross sections, Draft Angles allows you to set an angle for the surface direction. For example, if you set Start Angle to a value of 0, the surface will bulge outward from the start cross section, as shown in the first image of Figure 21.48.

**FIGURE 21.46**
A normal is a direction perpendicular to a plane.

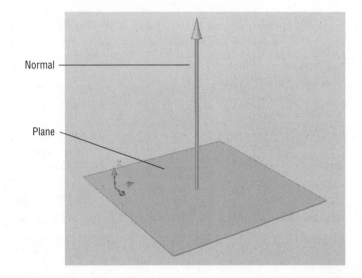

**FIGURE 21.47**
Samples of the Normal To options applied to the same set of cross sections

**FIGURE 21.48**
The Draft Angle options

Likewise, an End Angle setting of 0 will cause the surface to bulge at the end cross section (see the second image in Figure 21.48).

The Start and End Magnitude settings let you determine a relative strength of the bulge. The right image in Figure 21.48 shows a Draft Angle of 0 and magnitude of 50 for the last cross section.

### CLOSE SURFACE OR CLOSE SOLID AND PREVIEW CHANGES

The Close Surface or Close Solid option is available only when the Smooth Fit option is selected; it causes the first and last cross section objects to be connected so the surface or solid loops back from the last to the first cross section. Figure 21.49 shows the cross sections at the left, a smooth version in the middle, and a smooth version with the Close Surface or Close Solid option turned on. The Close Surface option causes the solid to become a tube.

**FIGURE 21.49**
The Close Surface or Close Solid option connects the end and the beginning cross sections.

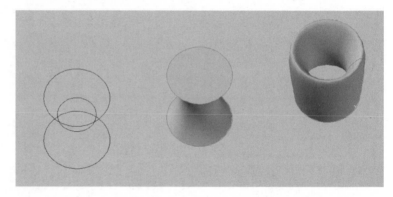

The Preview Changes option lets you see in real time the effects of the Loft Settings dialog box options.

## Moving Objects in 3D Space

AutoCAD provides three tools specifically designed for moving objects in 3D space: Align, 3D Move, and 3D Rotate. You can find all three commands by choosing Modify ➤ 3D Operations. These tools help you perform some of the more common moves associated with 3D editing.

### Aligning Objects in 3D Space

In mechanical drawing, you often create the parts in 3D and then show an assembly of the parts. The Align command can greatly simplify the assembly process. The following steps show how to use Align to line up two objects at specific points:

1. Open the Align drawing from the Chapter 21 folder of the sample files.

2. Choose Modify ➤ 3D Operations ➤ Align, or type Al↵.

3. At the Select objects: prompt, select the 3D wedge-shaped object. (The *source object* is the object you want to move.)

4. At the Specify base point or [Copy]: prompt, pick a point on the source object that is the first point of an alignment axis, such as the center of a hole or the corner of a surface. For the Align drawing, use the upper-left corner of the wedge.

**5.** At the `Specify second point or [Continue] <C>:` prompt, pick a point on the source object that is the second point of an alignment axis, such as another center point or other corner of a surface. For this example, select the other top corner of the wedge.

**6.** At the `Specify third source point or [continue] <C>:` prompt, you can press ↵ if two points are adequate to describe the alignment. Otherwise, pick a third point on the source object that, along with the first two points, best describes the surface plane you want aligned with the destination object. Pick the lower-right corner of the wedge shown in Figure 21.50.

**FIGURE 21.50**
Aligning two
3D objects

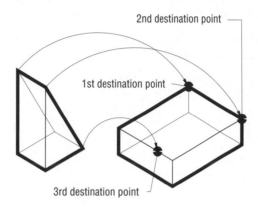

2nd destination point

1st destination point

3rd destination point

Result

**7.** At the `Specify first destination point:` prompt, pick a point on the destination object to which you want the first source point to move. (The *destination object* is the object with which you want the source object to align.) This is the top corner of the rectangular shape. (See the first destination point in Figure 21.50.)

**8.** At the `Specify second destination point or [eXit]:` prompt, pick a point on the destination object indicating how the first and second source points are to align in relation to the destination object. (See the second destination point in Figure 21.50.)

**9.** If you picked a third source point in step 6, you're prompted for a third destination point. Pick a point on the destination object that, along with the previous two destination points, describes the plane with which you want the source object to be aligned. (See the third destination point in Figure 21.50.) The source object will move into alignment with the destination object.

**10.** If you pressed ↵ at step 6, you see the Scale objects based on alignment points? [Yes/No] <N>: prompt. If you press ↵ to accept the default, the selected object(s) move into alignment with the destination points without changing size. If you enter **Y**↵, the selected object(s) are scaled up or down to align exactly with the two destination points.

## Moving an Object in 3D

In Chapter 20, you saw how you can use the Grip tool to help restrain the motion of an object in the X, Y, or Z axis. AutoCAD offers a Move command specifically designed for 3D editing that includes a Grip tool to restrain motion. Here's how it works:

**TIP** You don't need to perform these steps as an exercise. You can try the command on your own when you need to use it.

**1.** Click the 3D Move tool in the 3D Make control panel.

You can also choose Modify ➤ 3D Operations ➤ 3D Move. The Visual Style temporarily changes to Realistic.

**2.** Select the object or set of objects you want to move, and press ↵. The grip tool appears at the cursor.

The grip tool

**3.** Select a base point for the move. The grip tool remains fixed at the base point.

**4.** Point to the X, Y, or Z axis of the grip tool and click it. As you move the cursor, the motion of your selected objects is restrained to the selected axis.

**5.** Enter a distance along the axis, or click a point to complete the move.

## Rotating an Object in 3D

The 3D Rotate command is another command that is like an extension of its 2D counterpart. With 3D Rotate, a Rotate Grip tool appears that restrains the rotation about the X, Y, or Z axis. Here's how it works.

**TIP**  You don't need to perform these steps as an exercise. You can try the command on your own when you need to use it.

1. Click the 3D Rotate tool in the 3D Make toolbar. You can also choose Modify ➤ 3D Operations ➤ 3D Rotate.

2. Select the object or objects you want to rotate and then press ↵. The rotate grip tool appears at the cursor.

The rotate grip tool

3. At the Specify a base point: prompt, select a point about which the selected objects are to be rotated.

4. Point to the colored circle that represents the axis of rotation for your objects. A line appears, representing the axis of rotation. When you're happy with the selected axis, click the mouse.

5. At the Specify angle start point: prompt, you can enter an angle value or click a point. You can use the Shift key or Ortho mode to restrain the direction to 90°.

6. At the Specify angle end point: prompt, enter an angle value or click another point for the rotation angle.

### USING 3DMIRROR AND 3DARRAY

Two other commands, 3Dmirror and 3Darray, are available in the Modify ➤ 3D Operations menu. These are 3D Versions of the Mirror and Array commands. They work in a way similar to the standard Mirror and Array commands, with a slight difference.

3Dmirror begins by asking you to select objects; then, you're asked to specify a mirror plane instead of a mirror axis. You can define a plane using the default three points, or you can use one of the seven other options: Object/Last/Zaxis/View/XY/YZ/ZX. By using a plane instead of an axis, you can mirror an object or set of objects anywhere in 3D space. One way to visualize this is to imagine holding a mirror up to your 3D model. The mirror is your 3D plane, and the reflected image is the mirrored version of the object. Imagine tilting the mirror to various angles to get a different mirror image. In the same way, you can tilt the plane in the 3Dmirror command to mirror an object in any number of ways.

3Darray works like the command-line version of the Array command and offers the same prompts with a couple of additions. If you choose to do a rectangular array, you're prompted for the usual row and column numbers, along with the number of levels for the third dimension. You're also prompted for the distance between rows, columns, and levels.

For polar arrays, you're prompted for the number of items to array and the angle to fill, just as with the standard Array command; but instead of a point to indicate the center of the array, you're prompted to select two points to indicate an axis. The axis can be defined in any direction in 3D space, so your array can be tilted from the current UCS. One way to visualize this is to think of a bicycle wheel with the axle of the wheel as the array axis and the array objects as the spokes. You can align the axle in any direction, and the array of spokes will be perpendicular to the axle.

## The Bottom Line

**Mastering the User Coordinate System**   The User Coordinate System (UCS) is a vital key to editing in 3D space. If you want to master 3D modeling, you should become familiar with this tool.

**Master It**   Name some of the predefined UCS planes.

**Solution**   Front, Back, Left, Right, Top, Bottom.

**Understanding the UCS Options**   You can set up the UCS orientation for any situation. It isn't limited to the predefined settings.

**Master It**   Give a brief description of some of the ways you can set up a UCS.

**Solution**   Object orientation, select three points, about an axis, Z axis direction, the view plane.

**Using Viewports to Aid in 3D Drawing**   In some 3D modeling operations, it helps to have several different views of the model through the Viewport feature.

**Master It**   Name some of the predefined standard viewports offered in the Viewports dialog box.

**Solution**   Two: Vertical, Two: Horizontal, Three Right, Three Left, Three Above, Three: Below, Three: Vertical, Three: Horizontal, Four: Equal, Four: Right, Four: Left.

**Creating Complex 3D Surfaces**    You aren't limited to straight, flat surfaces in AutoCAD. You can create just about any shape you want, including curved surfaces.

>   **Master It**    What tool did you use in this chapter's chair exercise to convert a surface into a solid?
>
>   **Solution**    The Thicken tool.

**Creating Spiral Forms**    Spiral forms frequently occur in nature, so it's no wonder that we often use spirals in our own designs. Spirals are seen in screws, stairs, and ramps, as well as other manmade forms.

>   **Master It**    Name the commands used in the "Creating Spiral Forms" example, and name two elements that are needed to create a spiral.
>
>   **Solution**    The commands are Helix and Sweep. A helix and a profile are needed.

**Creating Surface Models**    You can create a 3D surface by connecting a series of lines that define a surface contour. You can create anything from 3D landscape to a car fender using this method.

>   **Master It**    What is the tool used to convert a series of lines into a 3D surface?
>
>   **Solution**    Loft.

**Moving Objects in 3D Space**    You can move objects in 3D space using tools that are similar to those for 2D drafting. But when it comes to editing objects, 3D modeling is much more complex than 2D drafting.

>   **Master It**    What does the rotate grip tool do?
>
>   **Solution**    It lets you graphically determine the axis of rotation for an object being rotated.

# Chapter 22

# Rendering 3D Drawings

In this chapter, you'll learn how to use rendering tools in AutoCAD to produce rendered still images of your 3D models. With these tools, you can add materials, control lighting, and even add landscaping and people to your models. You also have control over the reflectance and transparency of objects, and you can add bitmap backgrounds to help set the mood.

 **WARNING** AutoCAD 2008 LT doesn't support any of the features described in this chapter.

Topics in this chapter include the following:

◆ Creating a Quick-Study Rendering

◆ Simulating the Sun

◆ Using Materials

◆ Creating Effects Using Materials and Lights

◆ Applying and Adjusting Texture Maps

◆ Understanding the Rendering Options

◆ Adding Cameras for Better View Control

◆ Printing Your Renderings

◆ Simulating Natural Light

## Creating a Quick-Study Rendering

Throughout this chapter, you'll work with a 3D model that was created using AutoCAD's 3D modeling tools. The model is of two buildings on a street corner. You'll start by using the default rendering settings to get a quick view of what you have to start with:

1. Open the facade.dwg file.

2. Click the Render tool in the Render control panel.

3. The Render window appears, and you see the rendering generated in the Render window display (see Figure 22.1).

FIGURE 22.1
The Render Window
with your first
rendered view

The Render window displays the render settings in a column to the right. At the bottom of the window, you see the name that AutoCAD gives to the rendering as well as the rendering resolution in pixels, the time it took, and the preset that was used for the rendering. You'll learn more about these options later in this chapter.

## Simulating the Sun

AutoCAD allows you to create several types of light sources. If you don't add a light source, AutoCAD uses a default lighting source that has no particular direction or characteristic. The rendering you just did uses the default lighting to show your model.

You can add a point light that behaves like a lightbulb, a spot light, or a directed light that behaves like a distant light source such as the Sun. AutoCAD also offers a sunlight option that can be set for the time of the year and the hour of the day. This sunlight option is especially important for shadow studies in architectural models.

### Setting Up the Sun

Let's add the Sun to the model to give a better sense of the building's form and relationship to its site. Start by making sure the Sun is set for your location:

1. Close the Render window; then, expand the Lights control panel by clicking the downward-pointing arrows in the Lights control panel title bar (see Figure 22.2).

2. Turn on the Sun Status tool by clicking the Sun icon in the Lights control panel.

You see a message box warning you that the default lighting must be turned off when using other lights. Click Yes.

**FIGURE 22.2**

The Lights control panel title bar arrows and the Geographic Location tool

Click here to expand the control panel.

Geographic Location tool

3. Click the Geographic Location tool in the expanded portion of the Lights control panel, as shown in Figure 22.2. The Geographic Location dialog box appears.

4. For the sake of this tutorial, suppose the Facade model is a building in San Francisco, California, USA. Select North America from the Region drop-down list below the map.

5. Locate and select San Francisco, CA in the Nearest City drop-down list. The Latitude and Longitude input boxes at upper left in the dialog box change to reflect the location of San Francisco. For locations not listed, you can enter values manually in those input boxes.

6. Click OK. Next, you need to set the date and time of day for the rendering.

7. Click the Edit The Sun tool in the Lights control panel.

**8.** In the Date input box of the Sun Properties palette, enter **9/21/2007**.

**9.** Click in the Time input box of the Sun Properties palette, and select 2:00 PM from the drop-down list.

**10.** Click the Render tool in the Render control panel. The Render window appears and begins to create a new rendering with the sunlight option turned on, as shown in Figure 22.3.

**FIGURE 22.3**
The rendering with the Sun turned on

Now that you've added the Sun, you can see the shadows that the sunlight casts. You can turn off the shadows for the Sun if you prefer, but they're on by default.

## Setting Polar North

If you're including the Sun as a light source in a drawing in order to run shade studies, it's essential to orient your drawing accurately. To set the direction of polar north in your drawing, you use the North Direction setting in the Geographic Location dialog box (see Figure 22.4).

**FIGURE 22.4**
The North Direction setting in the Geographic Location dialog box

To change the north direction, click and drag the north arrow or…

enter a value.

By using this setting, you can set true north in either of the following ways:

- Click and drag the north arrow in the graphic to point to the north direction.
- Enter a value directly in the input box.

### IMPROVING THE SMOOTHNESS OF CIRCLES AND ARCS

You may notice that at times, when you're using the Render, Hide, or Shade tool, solid or region arcs appear segmented rather than curved. This may be fine for producing layouts or backgrounds for hand-rendered drawings, but for final plots, you want arcs and circles to appear as smooth curves. You can adjust the accuracy of arcs in your hidden, rendered, or shaded views through a setting in the Options dialog box.

You can modify the Rendered Object Smoothness setting in the Display tab of the Options dialog box to improve the smoothness of arcs. Its default value is 0.5, but you can increase this to as high as 10 to smooth out faceted curves. In the Facade.dwg model, you can set Rendered Object Smoothness to 1.5 to render the arch in the entry as a smooth arc instead of a series of flat segments. You can also adjust this setting by using the Facetres system variable.

## Adding a Distant Light

The rendering gives you a fairly accurate idea of how the shadows will fall. This may be all you need if you're doing a shadow study. For example, you can render a plan view of a 3D model to see where the shadow will fall on a street or a neighboring building, as shown in Figure 22.5.

**FIGURE 22.5**
A series of simple renderings showing the way shadows fall from a set of buildings

8:00 am   10:00 am   noon   2:00 pm   4:00 pm

Isometric

But the current rendering needs more attention in order to show the building detail. One problem is that the shadows are too dark and hide some of the building's features. To bring out those features, you'll add ambient light.

In the real world, a good deal of light is reflected from the ground. You can simulate that reflected light by adding a distant light that shines from below the model. A distant light is like a cross between a point light and a spotlight. Like the Sun, distant light is a point source of light, but one so far away that its rays are essentially parallel (see Figure 22.6).

A distant light pointing straight up can simulate reflected light from the ground; in the following
set of exercises, you'll add a directed light to do just that. In the process, you'll see how you can
quickly switch from a single view to a multi-viewport view using tools in the Navigate control panel.

First, change your single view into a four-viewport view:

1. Expand the 3D Navigate control panel by clicking the downward-pointing arrow in the 3D
   Navigate control panel title bar.

2. Click the Multiple Viewports tool in the expanded 3D Navigate control panel shown in
   Figure 22.7.

**FIGURE 22.7**

Expanding the 3D
Navigate control pan-
el to display the Multi-
ple Viewports tool

Click this arrow to expand the
3D Navigate control panel.

3. Expand the Lights control panel as you did the 3D Navigate control panel; then, click the
   Create A Distant Light tool in the Lights control panel to start the Distantlight command.

4. At the Specify light direction FROM <0,0,0> or [Vector]: prompt, click in the
   lower-left viewport; then, click below the model, as shown in Figure 22.8.

**FIGURE 22.8**
Add the directed light as shown in the lower-left viewport.

First, click a point below the model.          Then, click a point directly above the first point.

5. At the `Specify light direction TO <1,1,1>:` prompt, click a point to indicate an upward direction for the directed light, as shown in Figure 22.8.

6. At the `Enter an option to change [Name/Intensity/Status/shadoW/Color/eXit] <eXit>:` prompt, press ↵ to exit the directed light command.

7. Click the perspective view in the upper-right corner of the AutoCAD Window to make it active; then, open the 3D Navigate control panel, and click the Single Viewport tool to return to a single view of the model.

You've just added a directed light, although nothing in the drawing tells you it's there. Even though it isn't visible, you can access the distant light you just added through the Light List tool. In the next exercise, you'll see how you can control the intensity of the directed light through the Light list:

1. Click the Light List tool in the Lights control panel, or enter **Lightlist**↵.

The Lights In Model palette appears.

2. Double-click Distantlight1 in the list. The Properties palette appears, displaying the properties of the distant light you just added.

3. Locate the Intensity Factor setting in the General group of the Properties palette, and change the value to **0.3**.

4. Locate the Shadows setting, and turn it off.

5. Close the Properties palette and the Lights In Model palette.

6. Click the Render tool in the Render control panel. Your rendering now shows more natural-looking shadows on the building to the left, as shown in Figure 22.9.

**FIGURE 22.9**
The model rendered with the distant light added

## Using Materials

The rendering methods you've learned so far can be of enormous help in your design effort. Simply being able to see how the Sun affects your design can help sell your ideas or move plans through a tough planning-board review. But the look of the building is still somewhat cartoonish. You can further enhance the rendering by adding materials to the objects in your model.

### Adjusting the Global Material

AutoCAD uses a default material, called the *global material*, for objects in a drawing that don't have a specific material assigned to them. The global material is just like other materials you could use in your drawing, but it's set up in a way that is as generic as possible to produce simple renderings. For example, the global material uses the object's color to determine the rendered color.

As an introduction to materials, try the following exercise. You'll change the global material so that it applies a specific color to objects when they're rendered, rather than rely on the object's color:

1. Click the Materials tool in the Materials control panel.

The Materials palette appears, as shown in Figure 22.10. At the top, you see the Available Materials In Drawing panel, which currently shows only the global material. This is a default material that is applied to everything in the drawing that doesn't already have a material assignment.

**FIGURE 22.10**

The Materials palette

**2.** Turn off the By Object color option that appears in the Material Editor - Global panel.

**3.** Click the Diffuse Color swatch that appears next to the By Object check box. The Select Color dialog box appears.

**4.** Move the Luminance slider up until the Luminance value is set to 93, and then click OK to close the Select Color dialog box.

**5.** Click the Render tool in the Render control panel. This time, you see a monochrome image in the Render window.

You've just changed the color of the global material to off-white. Everything in the model now appears in shades of gray.

## Creating a New Material and Changing Its Properties

Two of the most glaring problems in the rendering are the black background and the white glass in the building. You'll learn how to add a background later, but first you'll tackle the glass. To do this, you need to become familiar with the Materials dialog box:

**1.** Click the Create New Material button on the Materials palette toolbar.

**2.** In the Create New Material dialog box, enter **Glass1** for the name. You can leave the Description blank. Click OK to close the dialog box.

You've just created a new material, but it isn't assigned to anything, nor is it much different from the global material already in the drawing. To make this new Glass1 material appear as glass, you need to make some adjustments. You can make a material translucent or transparent, give it color, and even have it glow with self-illumination. You'll start by giving your new material a set of pre-defined values that will provide the basis for your glass:

1. In the Materials palette, select Glass - Clear from the Template drop-down list. The settings and options for your new material change to the default values you just selected.

2. The sample image in the Materials Available In Drawing panel looks like a blank. To see the glass more clearly, click the Checkered Underlay On button just below the samples. This provides a background in the sample so you can see transparent materials clearly.

3. To add the glass to the building on the right, click the Apply Material To Objects tool on the Materials palette toolbar.

4. Select the blue box in the drawing that represents the glass, as shown in Figure 22.11, and then press ↵ to finish your selection.

5. Click the Render tool in the Render control panel. The building on the right now has the glass exterior.

**FIGURE 22.11**
Selecting the glass

Click the blue box in the drawing.

The glass is too dark and ominous looking. You can lighten the glass and even add a fake reflection to give it a bit more life:

1. Back in the Materials palette, look in the Diffuse Map group of the Map - Glass1 panel, and click the Select Image button.

2. Browse to the sample files folder for Chapter 22, and select sky.jpg. This is a copy of a file from an earlier version of AutoCAD.

3. Notice that the Diffuse Map slider is all the way to the right to give the glass bitmap full strength. In the Material Editor panel, click and drag the Opacity slider to the right. As you do this, you see a numeric readout at the cursor. Set the slider so it reads 12 or 13. You'll begin to see the clouds appear in the sample image at the top of the Materials palette.

You've added a diffuse map to your glass, which is like adding a surface pattern to your material. More on that a bit later; right now, you need to do one more thing to make the sky reflection work. The material has to be set up to fit the box representing the glass in the model. The Material Scaling and Tiling panel helps you do this:

1. In the Materials palette, use the scroll bar to scroll down the set of panels. Click the arrows to the left of the Material Scaling & Tiling title bar to open the panel (see Figure 22.12).

**FIGURE 22.12**
The Material Scaling &Tiling panel in the Materials palette

Click and drag the scroll bar to get to the Material Scaling & Tiling panel.

Click these arrows to expand the panel.

2. Select Feet from the Scale Units drop-down list.

3. Enter **80** for the Width and Height values. This tells AutoCAD to make the image size 80 feet in width and height. This causes the image to fit the glass area in the model.

4. Click the Render tool in the Render control panel. Now the building to the right looks like it's reflecting a cloud-filled sky, as shown in Figure 22.13.

**FIGURE 22.13**
The rendering after adding glass

With the Opacity slider set to 12 or 13, the glass is able to display the sky.jpg diffuse map you added earlier and still be transparent enough to show some of the interior of the building.

## Adding a Background

You've got the glass looking a bit more real. Next, you'll add a background to your view so it doesn't render as black. Backgrounds are added through the View Manager dialog box:

1. In the 3D Navigate control panel, select Manage Views from the drop-down list. The View Manager dialog box appears.

2. Click the New button. The New View dialog box appears.

3. Enter the name **My 3D View** in the View Name input box.

4. In the Background group toward the bottom of the dialog box, select Image from the drop-down list. The Background dialog box appears.

5. In the Image Options group, click the Browse button.

6. Make sure the File Of Type setting is set to .JPG, browse to the Chapter 22 sample file folder, and select and open the sky.jpg file. This is the same file you used for the glass earlier.

**7.** Click the Adjust Image button to open the Adjust Background Image dialog box.

**8.** The sky.jpg file appears in the sample panel. Select Stretch from the Image Position drop-down list. The image expands to fill the sample panel area.

**9.** Click OK in all the dialog boxes until you get to the View Manager dialog box.

**10.** In the View Manager dialog box, select My 3D View from the list to the left, and then click the Set Current button.

**11.** Click OK to exit the View Manager dialog box. The background appears in the drawing area.

**12.** Render the view to see the results. You should have something that looks similar to Figure 22.14.

**FIGURE 22.14**
The rendered model with a background added

## Creating Effects Using Materials and Lights

Up to now, you've used only two light sources: a distant light and the Sun. Two other light sources are available to help simulate light: point-light sources and spotlights. This section will show you some examples of how to use these types of light sources, along with some imagination, to perform any number of visual tricks.

The office building on the right half of the rendering is still a bit cold looking. It's missing a sense of activity. You may notice that when you look at glass office buildings, you can frequently see the ceiling lights from the exterior of the building—provided the glass isn't too dark. In a subtle way, those lights lend a sense of life to a building.

### Adding a Self-Illuminated Material

To help improve the image, you'll add some ceiling lights to the office building. I've already supplied the lights in the form of square 3D Faces arrayed just at the ceiling level of each floor, as shown in Figure 22.15. In this section, you'll learn how to make the ceiling lights appear illuminated.

**FIGURE 22.15**
The 3D Face squares representing ceiling light fixtures

Follow these steps to assign a reflective white material to the ceiling fixtures:

1. In the Materials control panel, click the Materials tool.

   Click the Create New Material tool in the Materials palette, enter **Ceiling Light** in the Name input box of the Create New Material dialog box, and click OK.

2. Back in the Materials palette, move the Self-Illumination slider all the way to the right. The sample image at the top of the palette brightens and appears lighted.

3. Click the Diffuse Color swatch just under the Template setting.

The Select Color dialog box appears.

**4.** Move the Luminance slider to the top to set the diffuse color to white, and then click OK.

## USING PROCEDURAL MAPS

*Procedural maps* are texture maps that are derived mathematically rather than from a bitmap image. The advantage of a procedural map is that it gives a more natural representation of a material. For example, if you cut a notch out of a box that uses a wood procedural map, the notch appears correctly with the appropriate wood grain. Do the same for a box that uses a bitmap texture map, and the grain doesn't appear correctly. With a bitmap texture map, the same image is placed on all four sides of the box, so cuts don't show the grain properly.

The procedural map shows the grain properly in the notch.

The bitmap texture map uses the same image for all sides.

AutoCAD offers several types of procedural maps. You can select them from the Map Type drop-down list.

If you select a procedural map, you can click the button to the right of the drop-down list to open a Materials palette panel that lets you control the map's properties. You can set the color and grain thickness of wood or the vein spacing and width of marble. These options let you customize a texture to your specifications. You may want to experiment with these settings on your own to see how they affect the appearance of an object.

Procedural maps aren't affected by the material map of an object (see "Applying and Adjusting Texture Maps," later in this chapter). Also, they don't appear in the Realistic visual style like other texture maps. You must render your view to see the results of a procedural map.

## Assigning Materials by Layer

You've just created a self-illuminated material. The next step is to assign the material to the ceiling lights in the model. So far, you've used the Apply Material To Objects tool in the Materials palette toolbar, but it would be too time-consuming to have to select each light individually. You can assign materials to layers, which can save time as long as you've organized your model into layers that represent materials.

In the Facade drawing, I've already set up some layers for you. The ceiling lights are on a layer called Clglite. The next exercise shows you how to apply a material to a layer:

1. Click the Attach By Layer tool in the Materials control panel.

   The Material Attachment Options dialog box appears. You see a list of materials on the left and a list of layers on the right.

2. Click and drag Ceiling Light from the left panel to the Clglite item in the right panel. The name Ceiling Light appears next to the Clglite layer name along with an X.

3. While you're here, click and drag Glass1 from the left panel to the Dkglass and Glass layers in the right panel.

4. Click OK to exit the dialog box.

5. Render your view. The lights appear in the ceiling of each of the floors (see Figure 22.16).

**FIGURE 22.16**
The lights appear in the ceilings of the building to the right.

In the previous exercise, you created a self-illuminated material that, when assigned to an object, appears to glow. You then added this material to the ceiling lights in the model. This self-illuminated material doesn't actually produce light in the model, however. To do that, you'll have to add light objects such as a distant lights or spotlights.

## Simulating a Night Scene with Spotlights

*Spotlights* are lights that can be directed and focused on a specific area. They're frequently used to provide emphasis and are usually used for interior views or product presentations. In this exercise, you'll set up a night view of the Facade model by using spotlights to illuminate the facade.

You'll start by setting up a view to help place the spotlights. You'll save this view because you'll be going back to it several times:

1. Select Southeast Isometric from the 3D Navigate control panel's drop-down list.

2. Select Parallel Projection from the 3D Navigate control panel.

3. Adjust your view so it looks similar to Figure 22.17.

4. In the 3D Navigate control panel, select New View from the bottom of the drop-down list.

**FIGURE 22.17**
Set up your view to look
similar to this, and then
add the spotlight.

Place the spotlight here...        and the spotlight target here.

**5.** In the New View dialog box, enter **SE Isometric Wireframe** for the name, and then click OK.

**6.** Select SE Isometric Wireframe from the 3D Navigate control panel's drop-down list. Because you didn't select a background for your new view, selecting SE Isometric Wireframe clears the background from the view.

Now, you're ready to add the lights:

**1.** Expand the Lights control panel by clicking the downward-pointing arrow in the Lights control panel's title bar.

**2.** Click the Create A Spotlight tool, or enter **spotlight.↵** at the Command prompt.

3. At the `Specify source location <0,0,0>:` prompt, click the point shown in Figure 22.17. Don't use osnaps, because you don't want the light to be accidentally placed below the ground plane. You don't have to be exact, but the idea is to place the spotlight in front of the windows on the right side of the entrance to the building.

4. At the `Specify target location <0,0,-10>:` prompt, use the Midpoint osnap, and select the bottom of the window sill of the upper window as shown in Figure 22.17. You see the prompt

```
Enter an option to change
[Name/Intensity/Status/Hotspot/Falloff/shadoW/Attenuation/Color/eXit] <eXit>:
```

5. Press ↵ to accept the default settings. You can always change the optional settings for the light through the Properties dialog box.

6. Copy the spotlight you just created to the location shown in Figure 22.18. You can use the spotlight target to copy from the midpoint of one window sill to the other.

7. You're trying to produce a night-time rendering, so turn off the Sun by clicking the Sun Status tool in the Lights control panel. The Sun Status tool looks like the Light Glyphs tool lower in the same control panel, so make sure you click the right tool near the top of the Lights control panel.

8. Return to the original view by choosing My 3D View from the 3D Navigate control panel.

9. Click the Render tool in the Render control panel to see the results of your spotlight addition. Your rendering will look similar to Figure 22.19.

**FIGURE 22.18**
Copy the spotlight to this location.

Copy the spotlight to this location.

**FIGURE 22.19**
The rendered view
of the model with
the spotlights

## Adding a Point Light

A few things still need to be added to improve this rendering. You can adjust the spotlight so it casts light over a wider area. You can also add a light in the entrance so it isn't quite so dark. The next section will show you how to make adjustments to your spotlight. First, you'll add a point light to obtain a different lighting effect:

1. Return to the view you used to add the spotlights by choosing SE Isometric Wireframe from the 3D Navigate control panel drop-down list.

2. Click the Create A Point Light tool in the Lights control panel, or enter **Pointlight**.↵.

3. At the `Specify source location <0,0,0>:` prompt, Shift+right-click and select Center. Then, select the arch over the entrance, as shown in Figure 22.20 to place the point light.

**FIGURE 22.20**
Select the center of
the arch.

Select the center of the archway for the point light.

4. At the prompt

```
Enter an option to change [Name/Intensity/Status/shadoW/Attenuation/Color/eXit]
<eXit>:
```

press ↵ to accept the default settings for the point light.

5. The point light appears as a spherical glyph in the archway of the building.

## Editing Lights

You've added the point light. Before you see the results in a rendering, you'll also change the spread of the spotlights. In this exercise, you'll edit the properties of the spotlight. Not all lights have the same properties, but the basic process for editing all lights is the same:

1. Click the two spotlights, and then right-click and choose Properties. The Properties palette appears.

**TIP** You can also access the properties of lights by clicking the Light List tool in the Lights control panel and then, from the Lights In Model palette, selecting the lights whose properties you want to adjust. Right-click, and select Properties. This method is useful if your light glyphs are turned off.

2. Look for the Falloff Angle setting in the General section of the palette, and change the value from 50 to 90. Notice how the falloff cone changes in the drawing (see Figure 22.21).

3. Close the Properties palette.

4. Return to the original view by choosing My 3D View from the 3D Navigate control panel drop-down list.

5. Click the Render tool in the Render control panel to see the results of your spotlight addition. Your rendering will look similar to Figure 22.22.

**FIGURE 22.21**
Adjust the falloff of the spotlight.

The falloff cones enlarge in the drawing when the Falloff Angle value is increased to 90.

**FIGURE 22.22**
The rendered view of the model with the spotlights modified and the point light added

In step 2, you saw a list of options for the spotlight. Many of these options are available when you first insert the light; they appear as command-line options. Often, it's easier to place the light first and then play with the settings.

In this example, you adjusted the spotlight's falloff. By increasing the falloff angle, you broadened the spread of the light cast by the spotlight and also made the transition from light to dark appear smoother, as shown in Figure 22.23. The hotspot can also be adjusted to a narrow beam or a wide swath.

**FIGURE 22.23**
The hotspot and falloff of a spotlight at top produce the lighting shown at the bottom.

Many other light properties are available to you in the Properties dialog box. Table 22.1 describes them.

**TABLE 22.1:**   Properties Available for Lights

| GENERAL | |
| --- | --- |
| Name | Name of light |
| Type | Type of light |
| On/Off Status | On or Off |
| Hotspot Angle | Spotlight hotspot angle |
| Falloff Angle | Spotlight falloff angle |
| Intensity Factor | Light intensity |
| Color | Light color |
| Plot Glyph | Allows the light glyph to be plotted |
| **Attenuation** | |
| Type | Type of attenuation: inverse linear, inverse square, or none |
| Use Limits | Lets you turn on attenuation limits |
| Start Limit Offset | If Use Limits is on, sets the distance to the beginning of attenuation |
| End Limit Offset | If Use Limits is on, sets the distance to the end of attenuation |
| **Render Shadow Details** | |
| Type | Lets you select between Sharp and Soft shadow edges |
| Map Size | When shadow maps are used, lets you determine the size of the shadow map |
| Softness | When shadow maps are used, determines the softness of shadows |

## Applying and Adjusting Texture Maps

You've already seen how to assign a material to an object by adding the glass material to the building in the `facade.dwg` file. You used a sky bitmap image to simulate a reflection on the glass. You can create other surface textures by using bitmaps in other ways to help enhance your rendering. For example, you can include a photograph of existing buildings that may exist in the scene you're rendering.

## Creating a Building from a Box

Figure 22.24 shows a bitmap image that was scanned into the computer and edited using a popular paint program.

**FIGURE 22.24**
A bitmap image of a building you'll use in the model

I've added some blank white space to the bitmap image of the building so you can get some practice fitting an image to an object. Imagine that this building is across the street from the Facade model, and you want to include it in the scene to show its relationship to your building. The following exercise will show you how it's done:

1. Return to the view you used to add the spotlights by choosing SE Isometric Wireframe from the 3D Navigate control panel drop-down list, and then choose Southwest Isometric from the list. The Southwest view offers a clear view to your work.

2. Adjust your view so it looks similar to Figure 22.25, and then draw a box that is approximately 130´ square by 80 ´ tall (see Figure 22.25).

**FIGURE 22.25**
Drawing the box representing the building on the next block

The box you just added represents the building on the next block. Now, create the material that you'll use to give this building some detail:

1. Click the Materials tool in the Materials control panel to open the Materials palette.

2. Click the Create New Material tool on the Materials palette toolbar, and enter **Build1** for the material name.

3. In the Diffuse Map group of the Materials Palette, click the Select button.

4. Locate and select the MARKET1.tif file in the Chapter 22 sample files.

5. Click Open to exit this dialog box.

6. In the Materials palette, go to the Material Scaling & Tiling panel, and make sure the Fit To Gizmo option is selected in the Bitmap Scale group. You'll see first hand what the gizmo looks like in the next exercise.

7. While in the Material Scaling & Tiling panel, change the U Tile and V Tile values to 1.0000. Click Close when you're finished.

8. In the Materials palette, make sure Build1 is selected in the Materials list, and then click the Apply Material To Objects button.

9. Select the box you added in step 2 of the previous exercise, and then press ↵.

10. To see how the bitmap fits on the box, choose Realistic from the Visual Styles drop-down list.

## Adjusting a Material to Fit an Object

The entire image, including the blank white space, is placed on the box. You even see the image on the rooftop, although you won't see the rooftop in any of the renderings. (You can hide it with another box or 3D surface if you want an aerial view.) You can adjust the position and scale of the bitmap by using the mapping tools in the Materials control panel. The mapping tools make the mapping gizmo visible:

1. Click and hold the Planar Mapping tool in the Materials control panel. The mapping fly-out appears.

2. Select the Box Mapping tool from the fly-out. You can also enter **Materialmap**↵, and then enter **B**↵ for the Box option.

3. At the Select faces or objects: prompt, click the box you just created, and press ↵. The box is outlined in yellow, and a set of arrows appears around the box, as shown in Figure 22.26. This yellow outline is the mapping gizmo.

**FIGURE 22.26**
The material mapping appears as a yellow outline around the selected box.

Top arrow          East arrow

4. Hover on the arrow at the top of the box (see Figure 22.26); when it turns green, click it. Now, as you move the cursor, the arrow follows, and the image stretches or compresses.

5. Stretch the image upward until the white space at the top of the building is gone and the building image fills the upper portion of the box. When you're satisfied, click the mouse.

6. Hover over the arrow pointing to the east (see Figure 22.26); when it turns green, click it.

7. Drag the arrow to the right until the white space of the image is gone and the image of the building fills the box.

8. Repeat steps 6 and 7 for the north side. Your box should look like Figure 22.27.

9. Press ↵ to exit the Materialmap command.

**FIGURE 22.27**
The box after adjusting the map

You just added a mapping gizmo to the box and then adjusted the gizmo so the material fit the box. If you need to make further adjustments to the gizmo, click the Box Mapping tool again and click the object you need to adjust.

Now, look at the rendered version. First you'll turn off the spotlight and point light and turn on the Sun to return to a daylight setting:

1. Click the Light List tool in the Lights control panel.

2. Select the two spotlights and the point light from the list box of the Lights In Model palette.

3. Right-click, and select Properties.

4. Select Off in the On/Off Status setting of the Properties palette.

5. Close the Properties palette and the Lights In Model palette.

6. Click the Sun Status tool in the Lights control panel to turn the Sun back on.

You've set the lighting for a daylight rendering. Notice that you were able to select several lights to turn them off all at once.

Next, render your view:

1. Choose My 3D View from the 3D Navigate control panel.

2. Click the Render tool in the Render control panel. The building appears to the left of the image (see Figure 22.28).

**FIGURE 22.28**
The rendering with
the new building

The building is too dark in the shadow. You can lighten it by increasing the Self-Illumination setting in the Materials palette:

1. Open the Materials palette by clicking the Materials button in the Materials control panel.

2. Make sure the Building1 material is selected, and then move the Self-Illumination slider to the right. As you do this, a numeric value appears at the cursor. Set this value to 24 or 25.

3. Render the view again. This time, the building on the next block shows up more clearly.

Another option is to use a paint program to refine the bitmap image before you use it in AutoCAD. AutoCAD attempts to place the bitmap accurately on a surface, so if the bitmap is fairly clean and doesn't have any extra blank space around the edges, you can usually place it on an object without having to make any adjustments other than its orientation. I purposely made the spaces in the image so you can practice using the Materialmap feature.

NOTE   You briefly encountered the Template drop-down list in the Materials palette when you created a material. The settings of these templates depend on the kind of material you're trying to model.

## Other Material-Mapping Options

You may have noticed several material-mapping options in the previous exercise. You used the Box option because it was a natural fit for the box you created. But other options are offered for a planar surface, a cylinder, and a sphere. Figure 22.29 shows how these other options may be applied to the shapes for which they're intended.

**FIGURE 22.29**

The planar, box, cylinder, and sphere material maps

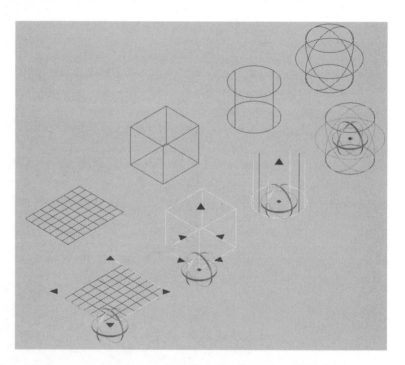

You don't have to apply the maps to the shapes they describe. Later, you'll see how you can apply a planar map to a box. You can apply a cylinder map to a thin box to achieve an interesting effect. Or a spherical map can be applied to a cube (see Figure 22.30).

## Specifying the Size of a Bitmap

As you've just seen, the Material Map feature gives you a quick and intuitive way to set the location of a material map onto an object. There are several other ways to control the appearance of a material on an object. If you have a surface pattern that repeats over the surface, such as a tile pattern, you can set the frequency and size of the pattern. For example, you might have a brick pattern that repeats over a 12′ square area, and you want that pattern reproduced accurately on a surface.

**FIGURE 22.30**
A material map
applied to a
different shape

Imagine you need to apply a brick pattern to a wall that is 8′ wide by 4′ tall. The blocks are the standard 8″ by 16″ split-face concrete masonry units, and you have an image that shows 4 courses of blocks 2 blocks wide, as shown in Figure 22.31. This is the `Masonry.Unit Masonry.CMU.Split-Face.Running.jpg` file in the Textures folder that is installed with AutoCAD 2008.

The following exercise shows you how you can control the size of a material map.

**FIGURE 22.31**
The bitmap image of a
set of blocks

1. Open the `CMUwall.dwg` sample file. This file contains a simple box representing the 4′ by 8′ wall.

2. Click the Materials tool in the Materials control panel to open the Materials palette.

3. Click the Create New Material tool in the toolbar, and give your new material the name **CMU**.

4. Click the Select Image button in the Diffuse Map group of the Maps - CMU panel, and then locate and select the `Masonry.Unit Masonry.CMU.Split-Face.Running.jpg` file in the AutoCAD Textures folder. This is typically found at `C:\Documents and Settings\All Users\Application Data\Autodesk\AutoCAD 2008\R17.1\enu\`. You may also use `CMU.Split-Face.Running.jpg` in the sample project files for Chapter 22.

**5.** Click the Apply Material To Objects tool in the Materials palette toolbar, and then click the wall object and press ↵. The wall displays the material you just created, as shown in the left panel of Figure 22.32.

**FIGURE 22.32**
The wall with the material applied

The wall has a concrete block texture. You see the results of a material with the default settings. Although it looks OK, the blocks are too large for the scale of the wall. You need to adjust the bitmap options so the texture appears to the proper scale on the wall object:

**1.** In the Materials palette, scroll down to the Material Scaling & Tiling panel.

**2.** In the Material Scaling & Tiling panel, select Inches from the Units drop-down list.

**3.** Change the Width and Height values to 32 inches. You use 32 inches because that is the actual width and height of the set of blocks shown in the bitmap image used for the CMU (See Figure 22.31). As you enter these values, the block wall changes to reveal the blocks at the proper size, as shown in the image at right in Figure 22.32.

**4.** Close the Materials palette, and then close and save the CMUwall.dwg file.

Now, suppose you want the blocks to appear 4″ high instead of 8″ high. You can go back to the Adjust Bitmap dialog box and change the Height setting to 16 (half the height you specified originally). The block wall changes to show a 4″ high block, as shown in Figure 22.33.

**FIGURE 22.33**
Change the Height setting in the Adjust Bitmap dialog box, and the wall also changes.

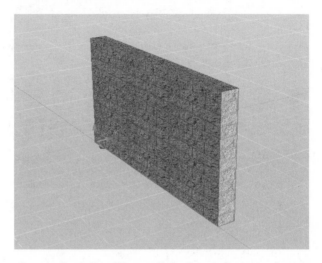

You can use many other settings in the Adjust Bitmap dialog box to fine-tune the appearance of a material over an object. You've used the major settings in these exercises.

## Simulating Trees and People with Opacity Maps

There's nothing like adding landscaping and people to a rendering to add a sense of life and scale. Computer images, in particular, need landscape props because they tend to appear cold and lifeless.

In the following set of exercises, you'll create a tree material and apply it to a 3D solid to simulate a tree. In doing so, you'll get a chance to explore some of the other features of the Materials palette. You'll use the same Diffuse Map texture-map option you've been using so far to create the tree material, but you'll also add something called an *opacity map*. An opacity map lets you control the transparency of a texture map through a black-and-white image file. For example, in the tree you'll be creating, you'll apply a tree material to a simple rectangular 3D solid. You'll want the area around the tree to be transparent, creating an illusion of a complex, tree-shaped outline.

The opacity map lets you determine transparency through black-and-white areas of an image. White areas are transparent, and black areas are opaque. You can use shades of gray to vary transparency. Figure 22.34 shows an example of how an opacity map works.

**FIGURE 22.34**

A material using an opacity map can be applied to a 3D solid to create the illusion of a complex outline such as a tree.

In the model, the tree is a flat, opaque surface.

With a material that uses an opacity map, the opaque surface becomes a complex shape.

To start your tree, create a new material in the Materials palette:

1. Open the Materials palette by clicking the Materials tool in the Materials control panel.

2. Click the Create New Material tool in the Materials palette toolbar.

3. Give the new material the name **Tree1**.

Next, add a texture map of a tree:

1. In the Diffuse Map group of the Maps - Tree1 panel, click the Select Image button.

2. Use the Select Image File dialog box to browse to the Chapter 22 project folder and locate and open the file CamphorAM.tif.

3. In the Material Scaling & Tiling panel, select Feet from the Scale Units drop-down list, and change the Width and Height values to **30.0000**.

Finally, add an opacity map for the tree. The process is basically the same as adding a texture map:

1. In the Opacity Map group of the Maps - Tree1 panel, click the Select Image button.

2. Use the Select Image File dialog box to browse to the Chapter 22 project folder and locate and open the file CamphorOP.tif.

3. In the Material Scaling & Tiling panel, make sure Feet is selected in the Scale Units drop-down list and the Width and Height values are set to 30.0000.

The sample image at the top of the Materials palette shows the tree. If you look carefully, you can see that the tree includes only its outline. Areas outside the tree appear transparent. Create an object representing a tree in the drawing, and then apply the Tree1 material to the object:

1. Adjust your view so it looks similar to Figure 22.35.

2. Set up a UCS that is vertical to the ground plane. Choose Tools ➤ New UCS ➤ Face, click the location shown in Figure 22.35, and then press ↵ to accept the new UCS.

**FIGURE 22.35**
Adding a tree

Select the edge of the sidewalk
for the UCS Face option.

Draw this planar surface.

**3.** Click the Planar Surface tool in the 3D Make control panel.

**4.** Draw a planar surface that is 30′ by 30′ to match the Tree1 Material Scaling & Tiling unit settings.

**5.** Open the Materials palette, select the Tree1 material from the sample panel at the top, and click the Apply Material To Objects tool.

**6.** Click the surface you just created, and press ↵.

**7.** Select My 3D View in the 3D Navigate control panel, and then click Render in the Render control panel to see the results of your work (see Figure 22.36).

**FIGURE 22.36**
The tree added to your
rendering

The process of adding people is just the same. You create a material that includes a texture map and an opacity map and then apply the material to a flat box. Make sure you turn on the Fit To Object option in the Adjust Bitmap dialog box for both the texture and the opacity map. Figure 22.37 shows a rendering that includes some additional trees and people.

**FIGURE 22.37**
A rendering with more trees and people

## Understanding the Rendering Options

Quite a few settings are available to control the quality of your renderings. If you expand the Render control panel, several other options appear, as shown in Figure 22.38.

**FIGURE 22.38**
The expanded Render control panel

The Save Rendering To File option lets you set up a file to which the renderings will be saved. If you turn on this option, then each time you render your model, the rendering will be saved automatically to the file you designate.

The Output Size option lets you set the vertical and horizontal resolution of the rendering in pixels. The default is 640 × 480. You can choose from a set of predetermined standard sizes or set a custom size.

The Render Environment option lets you add a fog effect to your rendering (see Figure 22.39). Click this option to open the Render Environment dialog box. This dialog box offers a set of options to control how the fog appears in the rendering. For example, Enable Fog lets you turn the fog effect

---

## WHAT IS A BUMP MAP?

You may have noticed the Bump Map group just below the Opacity Map group in the Map - Global panel of the Material palette. The Bump Map option lets you insert another image to add texture to a surface. For example, you can include a series of dots on a material to simulate a bumpy surface.

You can adjust the depth of the bump using the Bump Map slider in the Bump Map group. Move the slider to the right for a deeper bump.

---

on or off. Fog Color lets you select a color for the fog. You can experiment with the Render Environment dialog box on your own: When you click an option name in the left column, you see a description of the option at the bottom of the dialog box.

**FIGURE 22.39**
The Render Environment option lets you add fog to a rendering.

 Select Render Preset is a drop-down list that gives you a set of options you can use to select the quality of the rendering. The default is Medium, which is the setting you've been using. This offers a decent quality rendering without taking a lot of time. When you want to produce a final, high-quality rendering, select Presentation from this list. The rendering will take longer, but more detail will be brought out.

 Clicking Advanced Render Settings opens the Advanced Render Settings palette. These settings are for the advanced user, and most users won't need to work with them. Rendering presets are predetermined sets of the Advanced Render Settings. You can make adjustments to these settings if you need to (see "Rendering Interior Views" later in this chapter for more on the Advanced Render Settings).

The Sampling Limit slider controls the level at which AutoCAD samples each pixel of the rendering. Move the slider to the left, and the rendering appears blocky, as if it were a low-resolution image. Move the slider to the right, and the rendering becomes sharper and more detailed.

The Adjust Exposure tool opens the Adjust Rendering Exposure dialog box. Note that a system variable called Lightingunits must be set to 1 or 2 before this option works. The Adjust Rendering Exposure dialog box lets you set the brightness, contrast, and midtones of renderings that use photometric lighting. You'll see how this works later in this chapter.

### Checking and Saving Renderings in the Render Window

All your renderings appear in the Render window, which has a few options you'll want to know about. At the bottom of the window is a list of all the renderings you've done in the current AutoCAD session. If you've done several renderings, you can go back to an earlier rendering by clicking it in the list. Right-click an item in the list to display a list of options that you can apply to the selected item. Table 22.2 describes these options.

**TABLE 22.2:**     Right-Click Options for Image Filenames in the Render Window

| OPTION | WHAT IT DOES |
| --- | --- |
| Render Again | Renders the selected image again. |
| Save | Saves the selected image to a file. AutoCAD offers a choice of monochrome, 8-bit grayscale, 8-bit color, and 24-bit color. You can save your image as a BMP, PCX, TGA, TIFF JPEG, or PNG file. |
| Save Copy | If you've already saved a file once, lets you save it again under a different name. |
| Make Render Settings Current | If you've rendered several views and you want to return to the setting of a previous rendering, select the view whose settings you want to restore, and select this option. |
| Remove From The List | Removes the selected rendering from the list. |
| Delete Output File | If you've saved a rendered view as a file, deletes the file. |

Perhaps the most important of these options are Save and Save Copy. These enable you to keep copies of your rendered views as bitmap images.

If you want to check a detail in the rendering, you can use the Tools menu to zoom in or zoom out of the image. When you zoom in, horizontal and vertical scroll bars are displayed to allow you to pan over the image.

To the right of the window is a listing of the rendering's statistics. You can make adjustments to many of these settings through system variables and the Advanced Render Settings palette.

## Adding Cameras for Better View Control

Throughout this chapter, you've seen how you can save and recall views. Views can be a real time-saver, especially if you have several views that you save and recall. Views will also save background and visual styles. Typically, you set up a view using the tools you've learned so far; but another tool can give you that extra level of control you may need for special circumstances.

---

## USING THE RENDER CROPPED REGION TOOL FOR A QUICK CHECK

At times, you may want to just check a part of your model see if it will render correctly without having to do a full-blown rendering. You can use the Render Cropped Region tool in the Render control panel to do just that.

Click the Render Cropped Region tool, and then place a selection window around the area you want to check. AutoCAD renders just the selected area directly in the drawing area. Choose View ➢ Redraw to clear the screen of the rendered region.

---

What isn't obvious is that your views are also represented as cameras. Right now, you can't see the cameras because a setting called *Camera Glyph* is turned off. Try the following to visualize your My 3D View as a camera:

1. Return to the SE Isometric Wireframe view using the 3D Navigate control panel drop-down list.

2. Adjust your view so it looks similar to Figure 22.40.

3. Expand the 3D Navigate control panel, and then click the Display Cameras tool. You see two cameras in the lower half of the drawing.

**FIGURE 22.40**
Adding a new camera

These cameras appear when you click Display Cameras.

Click here for the camera location.

**4.** Click one of the cameras. A window appears that shows you what the camera sees.

**5.** Press the Escape key, and then click the other camera. The camera preview changes to show you samples of the other view.

When you select a camera, not only do you see the camera preview, but you also see a set of grips for the camera. You'll get a chance to work with some of those grips a little later. Next, try to create a view using the Camera tool.

The following exercise shows an example of adding a camera to the Facade model. You'll add a camera, and you'll apply one of the options available for the camera:

**1.** Enter **UCS↵W↵** to go to the WCS. Click the Create Camera tool in the 3D Navigate control panel.

You see this prompt:

```
Current camera settings: Height=0' Lens Length=50.0000 mm
Specify camera location:
```

**2.** Click the point shown in Figure 22.40 to set the camera location.

**3.** At the `Specify target location:` prompt, use the Center osnap, and select the center of the arch. You see this prompt:

```
Enter an option [?/Name/LOcation/Height/Target/LEns/Clipping/View/eXit]<eXit>:
```

**4.** To set the height of the camera at eye level, type **H↵** for the Height option.

**5.** At the `Specify camera height <0">:` prompt, enter **5'↵**. The options prompt returns, to allow you to enter more options.

**6.** Press ↵ to complete the camera insertion. The camera appears at the location you selected in step 2.

You were able to set the height of the camera independent of the location you selected in step 2 by using one of the options in the prompt. Table 22.3 describes the other options that are available.

**TIP**  AutoCAD gives your camera the default name Camera1. You can rename it at any time in the Properties palette or in the View Manager dialog box.

**TABLE 22.3:**  Camera Prompt Options

| OPTION | WHAT IT DOES |
| --- | --- |
| ? | Displays a list of cameras in the current drawing |
| Name | Lets you provide a name for your camera (no spaces allowed) |
| LOcation | Lets you change the location of the camera |
| Height | Lets you specify the height of the camera |
| Target | Lets you select a target location |
| LEns | Lets you specify a lens focal length in mm |
| Clipping | Lets you include front and back clipping planes |
| View | Lets you go to the camera's view |
| eXit | Exits the command |

## Making Adjustments to Your Camera

Now that you've got the camera in place, you can see what the view looks like. You can use the 3D Navigate drop-down list to display the view from your new camera, or you can click the camera to open the Camera Preview window. Before you do any of that, try making some adjustments to the camera:

1. Click the camera you just created. The Camera Preview dialog box shows a sample of the view from your camera (see Figure 22.41). You also see the camera view frame and target.

**FIGURE 22.41**
The Camera Preview dialog box

**2.** Click the camera grip, and move the camera around. You can see the changes you make in real time in the Camera Preview dialog box.

**3.** Adjust the camera location back to its original location so your preview looks similar to the one in Figure 22.41.

Now, turn on the clipping planes to see how they work:

**1.** With the camera still selected, right-click, and select Properties.

**2.** At the bottom of the Properties palette, click the Clipping option, and select Front And Back On.

The sample view changes.

**3.** Change the Front Plane value to 20′ and the Back Plane value to –20′ (minus 20 feet). The Camera Preview view now shows the view of just the entry.

The clipping planes hide objects either behind or in front of the target location. As you've just seen, you can indicate the clipping-plane distance from the target in the Properties palette. You can also make adjustments to the clipping plane directly in the drawing using the camera's grips:

**1.** Hover over the Front Clip Plane grip shown in Figure 22.42 so you can see the ToolTip describing the grip.

**2.** Click the grip, drag it back and forth, and watch the camera preview. You can see how the clipping plane hides more or less of the foreground as you move the grip.

**3.** Click the original location of the grip (the red grip) to keep it at 20′.

**FIGURE 22.42**
Selecting the camera grips

Move the left grip to the side.

Click the front clip plane, and watch the camera preview.

You can adjust the back grip the same way so you can get direct feedback on how much of your view is being clipped.

Next, try adjusting one of the other grips:

1. Click the Lens Length grip on the left side, as shown in Figure 22.42, and drag it to the left. This has the effect of shortening the lens length. The shorter the lens length, the more of the view the camera is able to take in. But past a certain point, the view begins to distort.

2. Click a point to the left, as shown in Figure 22.42, to fix the view at a lower lens length. The Lens Length value changes in the Properties palette.

3. In the Properties palette, change the Lens Length value back to the default of 50.

As you can see in the Properties palette for the camera, you have a number of controls to affect the view. Because cameras and user-created views are basically the same thing, the properties you see for cameras are the same as those you would see for views in the View Manager. (Open the 3D Navigate drop-down list, and select Manage Views at the bottom of the list.) Obviously, the options presented here apply to other views as well.

Let's see the results of your work:

1. In the 3D Navigate control panel, select Camera1 from the drop-down list. You see the camera view you just set up.

2. Expand the Visual Style control panel, and click the Edge Overhang option.

Your view now has a sketched appearance.

## Creating an Animated Walk-Through

Another feature that is related to the camera is the *motion path animation*. This is a feature that allows you to create an animated walk-through of your design. Such animations can be a great aid in helping others to visualize your ideas more clearly. Try this exercise:

1. Choose SE Isometric Wireframe from the 3D Navigate control panel drop-down list, and then adjust your view so it looks similar to Figure 22.43.

**FIGURE 22.43**
Draw the polyline for the motion path.

Select the arch center for the animation target.

Create this polyline at a 5′ elevation.

Select the line for the animation path.

2. Draw the polyline shown in Figure 22.43, and then move the polyline in the Z axis so it's at the 5′ level.

3. Choose View ➤ Motion Path Animations. The Motion Path Animation dialog box appears.

4. In the Camera group, select the Path option, and then click the Select Path button.

5. Select the polyline you just drew, and then click OK to accept the default path name.

6. Back in the Motion Path Animation dialog box, select Point in the Target group, and then click the Pick Point button.

7. Pick the center of the arch in the building entrance, as shown in Figure 22.43, and then click OK in the Point Name dialog box to accept the default name.

8. Make sure As Displayed is selected in the Visual Style drop-down list, and then click the Preview button. A preview window appears, and you see a sample of your animation. The animation is a bit fast, but you can make adjustments later.

9. Close the Animation Preview window, and then click OK.

10. In the Save As dialog box, save your animation with the default filename. AutoCAD takes a moment to generate the animation, and then you see a camera at the end of your animation path.

You were asked to save the animation, even though it was in a fairly crude state and was too fast. The advantage of saving the animation right away is that you then have access to the animation camera.

AutoCAD creates a new camera with default settings when an animation is created. You can then make adjustments to the camera and other animation settings to refine your animation.

## Fine-Tuning the Animation

Once you've created and saved an animation, no matter how crude, you can edit the camera settings for that animation, as well as the animation's speed, resolution, and visual style. To get a feel for how to edit an animation, try the following:

1. Click the camera at the end of the animation path, right-click, and select Properties.

2. In the Properties palette, change the Lens Length setting to **35** to get a wider field of view. Close the Properties palette.

3. Choose View ➢ Motion Path Animation.

4. Change the Duration setting to 8 seconds.

5. Change the visual style to 3D Hidden.

6. Click OK, and save the animation again. You can save it under a different name if you like, so you have a record of the original animation.

This time, AutoCAD takes more time to process the animation, because you've increased the duration. When it's done, locate your animation file using Windows Explorer, and double-click it to view the results.

As you saw in step 5, you can use any visual style that is in the drawing. You can even create a fully rendered version of the animation—but be aware that the more complex the animation, the longer AutoCAD will take to process it.

You can also modify the polyline path by adding more segments or changing the location of the path's vertices.

You've seen how a few of the options in the Motion Path Animation dialog box work. If you think you may find this tool useful, you'll want to experiment with some of the other settings. Table 22.4 describes these options.

**TABLE 22.4:** Motion Path Animation, Camera, and Target Options

| OPTION | WHAT IT DOES |
| --- | --- |
| **Camera and Target Options** | |
| Point/Path | Selects between a point or a path for the camera or target. |
| Select Path/Pick Point | Temporarily closes the dialog box to allow you to select a path or a point. |
| Drop-down list | Lets you choose from a point or a path that has already been selected. |
| **Animation Settings Options** | |
| Frame Rate (FPS) | Sets the frame rate in frames per second. 16 is the lowest you can go for a smooth animation. TV is usually around 30 fps. |
| Number Of Frames | Sets the total number of frames in the animation. The lower the number, the faster the animation. This setting is dependent on the Duration and Frame Rate settings. |
| Duration | Sets the duration of the animation. 10 seconds is a typical duration. |
| Visual Style | Sets the visual style for the animation. You can also select Rendered for a fully rendered animation. |
| Format | Lets you choose an animation file format. If you plan to use the Windows Movie Maker application to edit your animation, use WMV. Other options are AVI (Windows), MOV (QuickTime), and MPG (Mpeg 1 or 2). |
| Resolution | Sets the resolution of the animation. 320 × 240 is typical for computer video and VCD. 640 × 480 is typical for DVD quality. |
| **Other Options** | |
| Corner Deceleration | Automatically decelerates the animation motion at corners for smoother transitions. |
| Reverse | Reverses the animation. |
| When Previewing Show Camera Preview | Displays the preview in a window; otherwise, the camera motion is shown along the animation path. |
| Preview | Shows a preview of your animation. |

# Printing Your Renderings

When you've decided that your rendering is perfect, you can print a copy directly from AutoCAD. Through a Layout tab, you can also put together presentations that include 2D floor plans and elevations with your rendering on a single sheet. Or you can have several renderings on one sheet.

Try the following to set up a Layout tab to render the 3D model in both a rendered view and a hidden-line view:

1. Click the Layout1 tab.

2. Click the viewport border to expose its grips, and then use a grip to make the viewport smaller so it's about half the height of the Paper Space layout. Keep the height-to-width proportions of the viewport as close to the original as possible.

3. Double-click inside the viewport, and enter **V**↵ to open the View Manager dialog box.

4. Select My 3D View from the Views list, and then click Set Current. Click OK to exit the View Manager dialog box.

5. Turn on the Sun Status in the Lights control panel.

6. Double-click outside the viewport, and then copy the viewport down so you have an identical viewport just below the original.

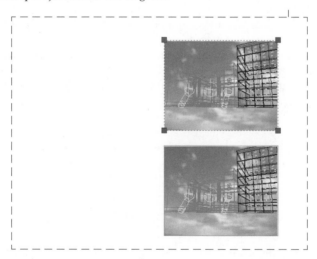

Now you're ready to set up the viewport to render the views in specific ways. For example, you can set one viewport to render as a fully rendered view while rendering another viewport as a hidden-line view:

1. Click the border of the top viewport, right-click, and choose Shade Plot ➤ Rendered.

2. Click the border of the lower viewport, right-click, and choose Shade Plot ➤ Hidden.

3. Right-click the Layout1 tab, and select Plot.

4. Choose a printer name for the Printer/Plotter group, and then click Preview. After a moment, you see a preview of your plot showing a fully rendered view in the top viewport and a hidden-line view in the lower viewport.

You can add viewports to include floor plans and elevations if needed. Or you can add isometric views with labels that point out drawing features.

You also have control over the quality of the rendered viewport. If you right-click the Layout tab and choose Page Setup Manager, the Page Setup Manager dialog box opens. Click the Modify button to open the Page Setup dialog box. You can use the Shaded Viewport Options group to select from a set of viewport-quality settings.

You can choose from Draft, Preview, Normal, Presentation, Maximum, and Custom. These options are described in detail in Chapter 8, so I won't go into detail here. Just remember that the options are available to help you get the most from your rendered printer output.

## Simulating Natural Light

Most of the rendering you've done so far relies on fairly simple lighting methods. These methods can give you a decent rendering in a short amount of time, and you'll probably do 90 percent of your rendering work using these methods. But you may eventually want to see the way your model looks under more realistic lighting conditions.

AutoCAD offers advanced lighting tools that can add impressive realism to your renderings. These tools simulate the way light behaves in the real world by taking into account the effects of light bouncing off nearby surfaces. In this section, you'll get a glimpse of some of the AutoCAD tools that will give your renderings an added level of realism.

**GETTING A SKETCH PRESENTATION WITH VISUAL STYLES**

This chapter has focused on getting a realistic rendering of your model, but frequently, you'll want to show your model in a less realistic view. This is especially true in the early stages when you don't want to give the impression that you've created a finished design.

In Chapter 21, you saw how you can create a custom visual style. You may find that for most of your work, a custom visual style is all you need to get your ideas across. You can plot visual styles from either the Model tab or the Layout tab. If you choose a Layout tab to plot a visual style, select the viewport border, right-click, and select the Shadeplot option. You'll see a cascading menu that contains a list of the visual styles available. Select the visual style you want to use for your plot.

In addition, if you need to get a bitmap version of your plot file for use in Photoshop or another image-editing program, you can add a raster plotter to AutoCAD. Use the Add-A-Plotter Wizard as described in Chapter 8; when you get to the part that asks for the plotter model, select Raster File Format and continue with the wizard. Once you've installed the raster plotter, you can select it as a plot device in the Plot Or Page Setup dialog box. The raster plotter will produce a bitmap image file. See Chapter 8 for more on plotting your drawing.

## Rendering Interior Views

If you're more interested in rendering interior architectural views, you should know about some of the advanced rendering settings that are available in AutoCAD 2008. Two groups of settings are particularly important to understand when you're rendering interior views.

Figure 22.44 is a rendering of a simple model using the material techniques described in this chapter. It also includes a sunlight source. As you can see, the rendering is fairly dark and not interesting.

Figure 22.45 is the same model rendered using two advanced rendering features: Global Illumination and Final Gathering. Global Illumination simulates the way light bounces off objects in a scene. When you turn on this option, AutoCAD calculates the reflection of light off the various surfaces in the model and applies that reflected light to neighboring objects. For example, the orange hue from the floor is reflected on the walls. The Final Gathering feature has the effect of refining the rendering by increasing the amount of detail that Global Illumination produces.

**FIGURE 22.44**
An interior rendering using just the Sun

**FIGURE 22.45**
The same interior rendering with Global Illumination and Final Gathering turned on

**TIP** It helps to add a background to simulate a view out the window. After you've rendered your view using Global Illumination, go back to the image you used for a background and adjust its brightness to match the rendering's brightness.

You can turn on and edit these two features using the Advanced Render Settings tool in the Render control panel. This tool opens the Advanced Render Settings palette, shown in Figure 22.46.

Select the Render preset you want to use from the Select Render Preset drop-down list at the top. You can then turn on the Global Illumination feature by clicking the lightbulb icon in the Global Illumination title bar (see Figure 22.46). To turn on the Final Gathering feature, click the lightbulb icon in the Final Gather title bar.

**FIGURE 22.46**
The Advanced Render Settings palette

Select the presets you want to work with from this drop-down list.

Click the lightbulb icon to turn on Global Illumination.

Turn on the Use Radius setting.

Set the Radius value to around 36″ or 900 mm.

Click the lightbulb icon to turn on Final Gathering.

Set Energy Multiplier to 0.008, and adjust to suit the conditions.

Just turning on these features won't give you great results right away, however. You'll need to make some careful setting adjustments. First, you must set up your drawing units using the Drawing Units dialog box (choose Format ➢ Units). Once you've done this, you must stick to that unit style. If you choose architectural, for example, you don't want to change to decimal.

After you've set your units, turn on the Use Radius setting in the Global Illumination group (see Figure 22.46), and then set Radius to 36″. If you're working in metric, set Radius to a value similar to 36″. If this value is too small, the rendering will appear splotchy.

Next, scroll down to the Light Properties group, and change the Energy Multiplier setting to a value around 0.008.

Once you've made these settings, you can render your interior view and see the results. If the direct sunlight is too bright, reduce the Sun's intensity factor by clicking the Edit The Sun tool in the Lights control panel and adjusting the intensity factor in the Sun Properties palette. If the interior appears too dark or too light, adjust the Energy Multiplier value in the Light Properties group of the Advanced Render Settings palette.

You can adjust the Sun angle by setting the date and time in the Sun Properties palette. To do quick study renderings, you can turn off Final Gathering and increase the Global Lighting Radius setting to 100 inches or 2000 mm. You can also reduce the Global Illuminations Photons/Sample setting and the Light Properties Photons/Light setting while making your study rendering. You'll probably end up making several renderings before you arrive at one that you like.

Although it isn't perfect, Global Illumination can greatly improve your interior views. You can save time by getting a rendering close to what you want and then using an image-editing program to fine-tune the image.

**TIP**   If you'd like to see how the file used in Figure 22.45 is set up, you can find it as `22-setting` `.dwg` in the projects folder for this chapter.

---

### MAKING YOUR OWN RENDERING PRESETS

If you want to create your own custom rendering presets so you have the default ones available, follow these steps:

1. In the Advanced Render Settings palette (see Figure 22.46), select Manage Render Presets from the drop-down list at the top of the palette. The Render Presets Manager dialog box opens.

2. Select a preset that you'd like as your prototype from the list to the left, and then click the Create Copy button.

3. In the Copy Render Presets dialog box, enter a name for your presets and a description if you like. Click OK.

4. Your copy appears at the bottom of the list to the right, under Custom Render Presets.

You can also edit the render presets from the Render Presets Manager using the settings in the middle column. Once you've created a set of custom render presets, you can select it from the Render control panel drop-down list.

## Using the Sun And Sky Simulation

Just like the interior view discussed in the last section, you can set up AutoCAD to simulate realistic lighting effects in exterior views. Earlier in this chapter, you added a distant light to approximate the light bouncing off the ground. AutoCAD's Sun And Sky Simulation feature offers a more accurate rendition of reflected light that takes into account the light bouncing off neighboring buildings and surfaces. To see how this feature works, try the following exercise:

1. Open the Facade With Landscape.dwg file. This is the same file you've been working on in this chapter, but it was created with an earlier version of AutoCAD.

2. At the command prompt, enter **Lightingunits**↵.

3. At the Enter new value for LIGHTINGUNITS <0>: prompt, enter **2**.

By changing the Lightingunits setting, you turn on the Photometric Lighting feature in AutoCAD. The Photometric Lighting feature give you finer control over the intensity of the lights you add to your model. The Lightingunits system variable can be set to 0 (off), 1(international units), or 2 (American units). It also turns on the Sun And Sky Simulation feature.

This next exercise demonstrates how the Sun And Sky Simulation feature works:

1. In the Lighting control panel, click and hold the Sky Off tool.

2. A fly-out appear. Select the Sky Background And Illumination tool from it.

3. The background of your main view changes. This sky background replaces the bitmap image of the sky.

4. Click the Render tool. After a minute or two, you get a finished rendering. Your model renders using the current Sun setting. The shadows on the center building are more realistic and show more detail of the building (see Figure 22.47).

**FIGURE 22.47**
The rendering with the Sky Background And Illumination feature turned on.

You can further refine your image by adjusting the brightness and contrast. To do this, you use the Adjust Rendered Exposure dialog box:

1. Click the Adjust Exposure tool in the expanded Render control panel.

2. The Adjust Rendered Exposure dialog box appears and generates a thumbnail rendering.

3. Click in the Brightness input box. A pair of arrows appears to the right.

4. Click and drag the arrows upward. The value in the input box changes, and the image brightens. Adjust the Brightness value to 65 using the click-and-drag motion on the arrows.

5. Click in the Contrast input box, and click and drag the input-box arrows to adjust the value upward to 80.

6. Click OK, and render the view again.

This time, the rendering is brighter and has more contrast. If you prefer, you can also set the brightness, contrast, and midtone settings in the expanded Lights control panel.

The Sun And Sky Simulation feature causes AutoCAD to take more time to render a view, so you should use it only when you really need the lighting effects it offers.

As mentioned earlier, when the Lightingunits system variable is set to 1 or 2, the Photometric Lighting feature is turned on. Photometric lighting offers additional settings for the Sun in the Sun Properties palette. For example, you can set the appearance of the Sun disk, the horizon, and the ground color through the Sun Properties palette. You can open the Sun Properties palette by clicking the Edit The Sun tool in the expanded Lights control panel.

With photometric lighting turned on, you see additional settings in the Properties palette for other types of lights as well. You have finer control over lighting intensity through the Photometric Properties panel (see Figure 22.48). If you change the Type setting in the General panel to Web, you can import IES web files that control the way a fixture spreads its light. Once a web file is selected, its Goniometric diagram is displayed in the Properties palette, as shown in Figure 22.48. A *Goniometric diagram* is a graphic that shows the distribution of light intensity from a light fixture.

**FIGURE 22.48**
Photometric lighting offers additional options in the Properties palette for lights.

Change the Type setting to Web to import IES web files.

Use the Web File input box to import IES web files.

Once the file is imported, its Goniometric diagram appears.

Click the dialog box icon in the Lamp Intensity input box to open the Lamp Intensity dialog box.

**NOTE** AutoCAD offers some sample IES web files in the `C:\Documents and Settings\All Users\Application Data\Autodesk\AutoCAD 2008\R17.1\enu\WebFiles` folder. To use these web files, you'll need to add this location to the Web File Search Path setting in the Files tab of the Options dialog box. See Appendix A for more on the Options dialog box.

This brings us to the end of the chapter. I've just scratched the surface of AutoCAD's rendering capabilities. You'll want to explore many more features once you get the basics down. To find out more about the Photometric Lighting feature, look up Photometric and Sky in the index of the AutoCAD Help window.

## The Bottom Line

**Simulating the Sun** One of the more practical uses of AutoCAD's rendering feature is to simulate the Sun's location and resulting shadows. You can generate shadow studies for any time of the year in any location on the Earth.

**Master It** Name three items that can be set to position the Sun in relation to your model.

**Solution** Date, time, and geographic location.

**Using Materials** AutoCAD lets you create materials that you can apply to the objects in your model to simulate a realistic appearance.

**Master It** Name the palette that is used to create materials, and describe some of that palette's features.

**Solution** The Materials palette lets you create materials that you can then apply to objects in your model. You use a bitmap image to simulate a texture. You can also control a material's transparency. Other features allow you to set the size of the material over the surface of an object.

**Creating Effects Using Materials and Lights** You can use materials and lights together to control the appearance of your model.

**Master It** Name the part of the example model in this chapter that was used to show how a material can appear to glow.

**Solution** Ceiling lights.

**Applying and Adjusting Texture Maps** Texture maps can be used to create a number of effects in your model. You can use a brick texture map that repeats over a surface to simulate a brick wall, or you can use a photograph of a building to turn a box into a building.

**Master It** What is the name of the feature that lets you graphically adjust a texture map on an object?

**Solution** Gizmo.

**Understanding the Rendering Options** In addition to adjusting the materials and lighting to control the look of your rendering, you can make other adjustments to your rendering through the Render control panel and the Render window.

**Master It** Name some of the right-click menu options that appear for image filenames in the Render window.

**Solution** Render Again, Save, Save Copy, Make Render Settings Current, Remove From The List, and Delete Output File.

**Adding Cameras for Better View Control**   When you create a view, you're actually creating a camera. Cameras are objects that let you control the orientation and view target for a view, among other things.

**Master It**   Name some of the options you can set to control a camera.

**Solution**   Name, camera location, height, target location, focal length, and front and back clipping.

**Printing Your Renderings**   You can save your rendered views as bitmap files using the Render window. If you prefer, you can also have AutoCAD include a rendering in a layout. You can include different renderings of the same file in a single layout.

**Master It**   Give a general description of the process for setting up a rendered viewport in a layout.

**Solution**   Create a viewport, and then set up the view you want for the viewport using the View Manager dialog box. Select the viewport's border, right-click, and select a Shade Plot menu option.

**Simulating Natural Light**   When you want to get a more accurate rendition of the lighting effects on your model, you can use some of the advanced rendering features that simulate natural light.

**Master It**   Name the two setting groups you need to use to accurately render an interior view.

**Solution**   The Global Illumination and Final Gather groups of the Advanced Render Settings palette.

# Chapter 23

# Editing and Visualizing 3D Solids

In the previous 3D chapters, you spent some time becoming familiar with the AutoCAD 3D modeling features. In this chapter, you'll focus on 3D solids and how they're created and edited. You'll also learn how you can use some special visualization tools to show your 3D solid in a variety of ways.

You'll create a fictitious mechanical part to explore some of the ways you can shape 3D solids. This will also give you a chance to see how you can turn your 3D model into a standard 2D mechanical drawing. In addition, you'll learn about the 3D solid editing tools that are available through the Solid Editing toolbar.

**TIP**   LT users don't have solid-modeling capabilities. However, you can take advantage of the region objects and their related editing commands described in the sidebar "Using 3D Solid Operations on 2D Drawings" in this chapter.

Topics in this chapter include the following:

◆   Understanding Solid Modeling

◆   Creating Solid Forms

◆   Creating Complex Solids

◆   Editing Solids

◆   Streamlining the 2D Drawing Process

◆   Visualizing Solids

## Understanding Solid Modeling

Solid modeling is a way of defining 3D objects as solid forms. When you create a 3D model by using solid modeling, you start with the basic forms of your model—cubes, cones, and cylinders, for instance. These basic solids are called *primitives*. Then, using more of these primitives, you begin to add to or subtract from your basic forms.

For example, to create a model of a tube, you first create two solid cylinders, one smaller in diameter than the other. You then align the two cylinders so they're concentric and tell AutoCAD to subtract the smaller cylinder from the larger one. The larger of the two cylinders becomes a tube whose inside diameter is that of the smaller cylinder, as shown in Figure 23.1. Several primitives are available for modeling solids in AutoCAD (see Figure 23.2).

You can join these shapes—box, wedge, cone, cylinder, sphere, pyramid, polysolid, and donut (or *torus*)—in one of four ways to produce secondary shapes. The first three, demonstrated in Figure 23.3 using a cube and a cylinder as examples, are called *Boolean operations*. (The name comes from the 19th-century mathematician George Boole.)

**FIGURE 23.1**
Creating a tube by
using solid modeling

Create two cylinder primitives,
one for the outside diameter
and one for the inside diameter.

Cylinder for
inside diameter

Cylinder for
outside diameter

Superimpose the cylinder
for the inside diameter onto
the cylinder for the outside
diameter.

Use the Subtract command
to subtract the inside
diameter cylinder from
the outside diameter cylinder.

**FIGURE 23.2**
The solid primitives

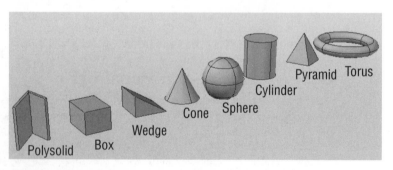

The three Boolean operations are as follows:

**Intersection**   Uses only the intersecting region of two objects to define a solid shape.

**Subtraction**   Uses one object to cut out a shape in another.

**Union**   Joins two primitives so they act as one object.

**FIGURE 23.3**

The intersection, subtraction, and union of a cube and a cylinder

A solid box and a solid cylinder are superimposed.

The intersection of the primitives creates a solid cylinder with the ends skewed.

The cylinder subtracted from the box creates a hole in the box.

The union of the two primitives creates a box with two round pegs.

The fourth option, *interference*, lets you find exactly where two or more solids coincide in space—similar to the results of a union. The main difference between interference and union is that interference enables you to keep the original solid shapes, whereas union discards the original solids, leaving only their combined form. With interference, you can have AutoCAD either show you the shape of the coincident space or create a solid based on the coincident space's shape.

Joined primitives are called *composite solids*. You can join primitives to primitives, composite solids to primitives, and composite solids to other composite solids.

Now, let's look at how you can use these concepts to create models in AutoCAD.

**TIP** To simplify the exercises in this chapter, the instructions don't specify inches or centimeters. This way, users of both the metric and Imperial measurement systems can use the exercises without having to read through duplicate information.

## Creating Solid Forms

In this section, you'll begin to draw the object shown later in the chapter in Figure 23.20. In the process, you'll explore the creation of solid models by creating primitives and then setting up special relationships between them.

Primitives are the basic building blocks of solid modeling. At first, it may seem limiting to have only eight primitives to work with, but consider the varied forms you can create with just a few two-dimensional objects. Let's begin by creating the basic mass of your steel bracket.

First, prepare your drawing for the exercise:

1. Open the file called Bracket.dwg. This file contains some objects that you'll use in the first half of this chapter to build a 3D solid shape.

2. If you aren't already in the 3D Modeling workspace, select 3D Modeling from the Work-space toolbar.

## Joining Primitives

In this section, you'll merge the two box objects. First, you'll move the new box into place, and then you'll join the two boxes to form a single solid:

1. Start the Move command, pick the smaller of the two boxes, and then press ↵.

2. At the Specify base point or [Displacement] <Displacement>: prompt, use the Mid-point osnap override, and pick the middle of the front edge of the smaller box, as shown in the top image in Figure 23.4.

**FIGURE 23.4**
Moving the
smaller box

3. At the Specify second point or <use first point as displacement>: prompt, use the Midpoint osnap to pick the middle of the bottom edge of the larger box, as shown in the bottom image in Figure 23.4.

4. Click the Union tool in the 3D Make control panel, choose Modify ➤ Solid Editing ➤ Union, or type **Uni**↵.

5. At the Select objects: prompt, pick both boxes and press ↵. Your drawing now looks like Figure 23.5.

**FIGURE 23.5**

The two boxes joined

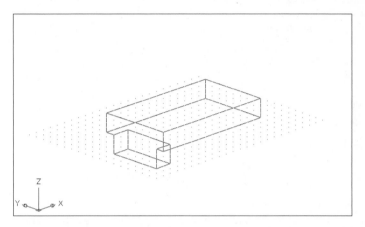

As you can see in Figure 23.5, the form has joined to appear as one object. It also acts like one object when you select it. You now have a composite solid made up of two box primitives.

Now, let's place some holes in the bracket. In this next exercise, you'll discover how to create negative forms to cut portions out of a solid:

1. Turn on the layer called Cylinder. Two cylinder solids appear in the model, as shown in Figure 23.6. These cylinders are 1.5 units tall.

2. Choose Modify ➤ Solid Editing ➤ Subtract, type **Su**↵, or click the Subtract tool in the 3D Make control panel.

**FIGURE 23.6**

The cylinders appear when the Cylinder layer is turned on.

**3.** At the Select solids and regions to subtract from.. Select objects: prompt, pick the composite solid of the two boxes and press ⏎.

**4.** At the Select solids and regions to subtract.. Select objects: prompt, pick the two cylinders and press ⏎. The cylinders are subtracted from the bracket.

**5.** To view the solid, choose View ➤ Hide. You see a hidden-line view of the solid, as shown in Figure 23.7.

**FIGURE 23.7**
The bracket so far, with hidden lines removed

As you learned in the earlier chapters in Part 4, Wireframe views, such as the one in step 3, are somewhat difficult to decipher. Until you use the Hide command (step 5), you can't be sure that the subtracted cylinders are in fact holes. Using the Hide command frequently will help you keep track of what's going on with your solid model.

You may also have noticed in step 4 that the cylinders changed shape to conform to the depth of the bracket. The cylinders were 1.5 units tall, not 1 unit, which is the thickness of the bracket. Having drawn the cylinders taller than needed, you saw that when AutoCAD performed the subtraction, it ignored the portion of the cylinders that didn't affect the bracket. AutoCAD always discards the portion of a primitive that isn't used in a subtract operation.

---

**USING 3D SOLID OPERATIONS ON 2D DRAWINGS**

You can apply some of the features described in this chapter to 2D drafting by taking advantage of AutoCAD's region object. *Regions* are two-dimensional objects to which you can apply Boolean operations.

Figure 23.8 shows how a set of closed polyline shapes can be quickly turned into a drawing of a wrench using regions. The shapes at the top of the figure are first converted into regions using the Region tool on the 2D Draw control panel. Next, the shapes are aligned, as shown in the middle of Figure 23.8. Finally, the circles and rectangle are joined with the Union command (choose Modify ➤ Solid Editing ➤ Union or, if you're using LT, choose Modify ➤ Region ➤ Union); then, subtract the hexagonal shapes from the shape (choose Modify ➤ Solid Editing ➤ Subtract or, if you're using LT, Modify ➤ Region ➤ Subtract). You can use the Region.dwg sample file if you'd like to experiment.

**FIGURE 23.8**
Working with regions
in the Region.dwg file

Create closed polyline
shapes, and convert
them to regions.

Move the shapes into
position to lay out
the object.

Use the Union and
Subtract commands
to create the final object.

**FIGURE 23.9**
You can use the
regional model to
create complex
2D surfaces for use in
3D surface modeling.

**NOTE** You can use regions to generate complex surfaces that may include holes or unusual bends (see Figure 23.9).

Keep in mind the following:

◆ Regions act like surfaces; when you remove hidden lines, objects behind the regions are hidden.

◆ You can explode regions to edit them. However, exploding a region causes the region to lose its surface-like quality, and objects longer hide behind its surface(s).

## Creating Complex Solids

As you learned earlier, you can convert a polyline into a solid by using the Extrude option in the 3D Make control panel. This process lets you create more-complex shapes than the built-in primitives. In addition to the simple straight extrusion you've already tried, you can also extrude shapes into curved paths, or you can taper an extrusion.

### Tapering an Extrusion

Let's look at how you can taper an extrusion to create a fairly complex solid with little effort:

1. Turn on the Taper layer. A rectangular polyline appears. This rectangle has its corners rounded to a radius of 0.5 using the Fillet command.

2. Click the Extrude button in the 3D Make control panel, or enter **Ext↵** at the Command prompt.

3. At the Select objects to extrude: prompt, pick the polyline you just drew, and press ↵.

4. At the Specify height of extrusion or [Direction/Path/Taper angle] <3.0000>: prompt, enter **t↵**.

5. At the Specify angle of taper for extrusion <0>: prompt, enter **4↵**.

6. At the Specify height of extrusion or [Direction/Path/Taper angle] <1.0000>: prompt, enter **3↵**. The extruded polyline looks like Figure 23.10.

**FIGURE 23.10**
The extruded polyline

7. Join the part you just created with the original solid. Choose Modify ➢ Solid Editing ➢ Union, and then select the extruded part and the composite solid just below it. Press ↵ to complete your selection.

**TIP**    In step 5, you can indicate a taper for the extrusion. Specify a taper in terms of degrees from the Z axis, or enter a negative value to taper the extrusion outward. Or press ↵ to accept the default of 0°, to extrude the polyline without a taper.

---

### WHAT ARE ISOLINES?

You may have noticed the message that reads as follows:

```
Current wire frame density: ISOLINES=4
```

This message tells you the current setting for the Isolines system variable, which controls the way curved objects, such as cylinders and holes, are displayed. A setting of 4 causes a cylinder to be represented by four lines with a circle at each end. You can see this in the holes that you created for the Bracket model in the previous exercise. You can change the Isolines setting by entering **Isolines**↵ at the Command prompt. You then enter a value for the number of lines to use to represent surfaces. This setting is also controlled by the Contour Lines Per Surface option in the Display tab of the Options dialog box.

---

## Extruding on a Curved Path

As you'll see in the following exercise, the Extrude command lets you extrude virtually any polyline shape along a path defined by a polyline, an arc, or a 3D polyline. At this point, you've created the components needed to do the extrusion. Next, you'll finish the extruded shape:

1. Turn on the Path layer. This layer contains the circle you'll extrude and the path, which looks like an S, as shown in Figure 23.11.

2. Click the Sweep button in the 3D Make control panel, click the circle, and then press ↵.

3. At the `Select sweep path or [Alignment/Base point/Scale/Twist]:` prompt, click the polyline curve. AutoCAD pauses a moment and then generates a solid tube that follows the path. The tube may not look like a tube because AutoCAD draws extruded solids such as this with four lines showing its profile.

**FIGURE 23.11**
Hidden-line view showing parts of the drawing you'll use to create a curved extrusion

The polyline path                    The circle you'll extrude

4. Click the Subtract tool in the 3D Make control panel or choose Modify ➢ Solid Editing ➢ Subtract, and then select the composite solid.

5. Press ↵. At the `Select objects:` prompt, click the curved solid and press ↵. The curved solid is subtracted from the square solid. Your drawing looks like Figure 23.12.

**FIGURE 23.12**
The solid after subtracting the curve

In this exercise, you used a curved polyline for the extrusion path, but you can use any type of 2D or 3D polyline, as well as a line or arc, for an extrusion path.

## Revolving a Polyline

When your goal is to draw a circular object, you can use the Revolve command on the 3D Make control panel to create a solid that is *revolved*, or swept in a circular path. Think of Revolve's action as similar to a lathe that lets you carve a shape from a spinning shaft. In this case, the spinning shaft is a polyline, and rather than carving it, you define the profile and then revolve the profile around an axis.

In the following exercise, you'll draw a solid that will form a slot in the tapered solid. I've already created a 2D polyline that is the profile of the slot. You'll use a simple cut and paste to bring the polyline into the bracket drawing:

1. Zoom in to the top of the tapered box, so you have a view similar to Figure 23.13.

**FIGURE 23.13**
An enlarged view
of the top of the
tapered box and
pasted polyline

2. Turn on the Revolve layer. This layer contains a closed polyline that you'll use to create a cylindrical shape.

3. Click the Revolve tool in the 3D Make control panel, or type **Rev**↵ at the Command prompt.

4. At the `Select objects to revolve:` prompt, pick the polyline you just drew, and press ↵.

5. When you see the next prompt

   ```
   Specify axis start point or define axis by [Object/X/Y/Z] <Object>:
   ```

   use the Endpoint osnap override, and pick the beginning corner endpoint of the polyline you just added, as shown in Figure 23.13.

6. At the `Specify axis endpoint:` prompt, turn on Ortho mode (press F8). Then, pick a point at far left on the screen so the rubber-banding line is parallel with the X axis.

7. At the `Specify angle of revolution or [STart angle] <360>:` prompt, press ↵ to sweep the polyline a full 360°. The revolved form appears, as shown in Figure 23.14.

**FIGURE 23.14**

The revolved polyline

You just created a revolved solid that will be subtracted from the tapered box to form a slot in the bracket. But before you subtract it, you need to make a slight change in the orientation of the revolved solid:

1. Choose Modify ➢ 3D Operations ➢ 3D Rotate. You see the prompt

   ```
   Current positive angle in UCS:  ANGDIR=counterclockwise  ANGBASE=0
   Select objects:
   ```

2. Select the revolved solid, and press ↵.

3. At the `Specify base point:` prompt, use the Midpoint osnap, and click the right side edge of the top surface, as shown in Figure 23.15.

Select this edge of the top surface for the 3D Rotate base point.

Point to the green circle for the rotation axis.

When you see the axis line, click the circle.

Point the cursor along the X axis for the angle start point.

4. At the `Pick a rotation axis:` prompt, point to the green rotation grip tool. When you see a green line appear along the Y axis, click the mouse.

5. At the `Specify angle start point:` prompt, point the cursor in the direction of the X axis, and click the mouse.

6. At the `Specify angle end point:` prompt, enter –5↵ for a minus 5 degrees rotation. The solid rotates 5° about the Y axis.

7. Click the Subtract tool in the 3D Make control panel, or choose Modify ➢ Solid Editing ➢ Subtract. Click the tapered box, and then press ↵.

8. At the `Select objects:` prompt, click the revolved solid, and press ↵↵. Your drawing looks like Figure 23.16.

## Editing Solids

Basic solid forms are fairly easy to create. Refining those forms requires some special tools. In this section, you'll learn how to use familiar 2D editing tools, as well as some new tools, to edit a solid. You'll also be introduced to the Slice tool, which lets you cut a solid into two pieces.

**FIGURE 23.16**

The composite solid

## Splitting a Solid into Two Pieces

One of the more common solid-editing tools you'll use is the Slice tool. As you may guess from its name, Slice enables you to cut a solid into two pieces. The following exercise demonstrates how it works:

1. Zoom to the previous view.

2. Click the Slice tool in the 3D Make control panel, or type **Slice**↵. You may have to expand the 3D Make control panel to find the Slice tool.

3. At the `Select objects to slice:` prompt, click the part you've been working on, and press ↵.

**TIP** In step 3, you could select more than one solid. The Slice command would then slice all the solids through the plane indicated in steps 4 and 5.

4. At the prompt

   ```
   Specify start point of slicing plane or [planar Object/Surface/Zaxis/View/XY/
   YZ/ZX/3points] <3points>:
   ```

   type **XY**↵. This lets you indicate a slice plane parallel to the XY plane.

5. At the `Specify a point on the XY-plane <0,0,0>:` prompt, type **0,0,0.5**↵. This places the slice plane at the Z coordinate of 0.5 units. You can also use the Midpoint osnap and pick any vertical edge of the rectangular base of the solid.

**TIP** If you want to delete one side of the sliced solid, you can indicate the side you want to keep by clicking it in step 6, instead of entering **B**↵.

6. At the `Specify a point on desired side or [keep Both sides]:` prompt, type **B**↵ to keep both sides of the solid. AutoCAD divides the solid horizontally, one-half unit above the base of the part, as shown in Figure 23.17.

In step 4, you saw a number of options for the Slice command. You may want to make note of those options for future reference. Table 23.1 provides a list of the options and their purpose.

**FIGURE 23.17**
The solid sliced through the base

**TABLE 23.1:**    Slice Command Options

| OPTION | PURPOSE |
| --- | --- |
| Planar Object | Lets you select an object to define the slice plane. |
| Surface | Lets you select a surface object to define the shape of a slice (see Chapter 21). |
| Zaxis | Lets you select two points defining the Z axis of the slice plane. The two points you pick are perpendicular to the slice plane. |
| View | Generates a slice plane that is perpendicular to your current view. You're prompted for the coordinate through which the slice plane must pass—usually a point on the object. |
| XY/YZ/ZX | Pick one of these to determine the slice plane based on the X, Y, or Z axis. You're prompted to pick a point through which the slice plane must pass. |
| 3points | The default; lets you select three points defining the slice plane. Normally, you pick points on the solid. |

## Rounding Corners with the Fillet Tool

Your bracket has a few sharp corners that you may want to round in order to give the bracket a more realistic appearance. You can use the Modify menu's Fillet and Chamfer commands to add these rounded corners to your solid model:

1. Adjust your view of the model so it looks similar to the first image in Figure 23.18.

**FIGURE 23.18**
Filleting solids

2. Click the Fillet tool on the Modify toolbar.

3. At the `Select first object or [Polyline/Radius/Trim/Multiple]:` prompt, pick the edge indicated in the first image in Figure 23.19.

4. At the `Enter fillet radius:` prompt, type **0.2**↵.

5. At the `Select an edge or [Chain/Radius]:` prompt, type **C**↵ for the Chain option. Chain lets you select a series of solid edges to be filleted.

6. Select one of the other seven edges at the base of the tapered form, and press ↵.

7. Choose View ➤ Hide or type **Hide**↵ to get a better look at your model, as shown in the second image in Figure 23.18.

As you saw in step 5, Fillet acts a bit differently when you use it on solids. The Chain option lets you select a set of edges instead of just two adjoining objects.

## Chamfering Corners with the Chamfer Tool

Now, let's try chamfering a corner. To practice using Chamfer, you'll add a countersink to the cylindrical hole you created in the first solid:

1. Type **Regen**↵ to return to a Wireframe view of your model.

2. Click the Chamfer tool on the Modify toolbar, or type **Cha**↵.

3. At this prompt

   `Select first line or [Undo/Polyline/Distance/Angle/Trim/mEthod/Multiple]:`

   pick the edge of the hole, as shown in Figure 23.19. Notice that the top surface of the solid is highlighted and that the prompt changes to `Enter surface selection option [Next/OK (current)] <OK>:`. The highlighting indicates the base surface, which will be used as a reference in step 5. (You could also type **N**↵ to choose the other adjoining surface, the inside of the hole, as the base surface.)

4. Press ↵ to accept the current highlighted face.

5. At the `Specify base surface chamfer distance:` prompt, type **0.125**↵. This indicates that you want the chamfer to have a width of 0.125 across the highlighted surface.

6. At the `Specify other surface chamfer distance <0.1250>:` prompt, type **0.2**↵.

7. At the `Select an edge or [Loop]:` prompt, click the edges of both holes, and then press ↵. When the Chamfer command has completed its work, your drawing looks like Figure 23.20.

8. After reviewing the work you've done here, save the `Bracket.dwg` file.

**TIP**  The Loop option in step 7 lets you chamfer the entire circumference of an object. You don't need to use it here because the edge forms a circle. The Loop option is used when you have a rectangular or other polygonal edge you want to chamfer.

**FIGURE 23.19**
Picking the edge
to chamfer

**FIGURE 23.20**
The chamfered edges

## Using the Solid-Editing Tools

You've added some refinements to the Bracket model by using standard AutoCAD editing tools. A set of tools is specifically geared toward editing solids. You already used the Union and Subtract tools found in the 3D Make control panel. In this section, you'll explore some of the other tools in that control panel as well as the tools available in the Solid Editing toolbar.

You don't have to perform the exercises described in this section, but reviewing it will show you what's available. When you're more comfortable working in 3D, you may want to come back and experiment with the file called solidedit.dwg shown in the figures in this section.

**WARNING**    Many of the features discussed in this section work only in a parallel-projection view. You can switch to a parallel-projection view by choosing the 2D Wireframe visual style or by clicking the Parallel Projection tool in the 3D Navigate control panel.

### MOVING A SURFACE

You can move any flat surface of a 3D solid using the Move Faces tool in the Solid Editing toolbar. When you click this tool, you're prompted to select faces. Because you can only select the edge of two joining faces, you must select an edge and then use the Remove option to remove one of the two selected faces from the selection set (see Figure 23.21). Once you've made your selection, press ⏎. You can then specify a distance for the move.

After you've selected the surface you want to move, the Move Faces tool acts just like the Move command: You select a base point and a displacement. Notice how the curved side of the model extends its curve to meet the new location of the surface. This shows you that AutoCAD attempts to maintain the geometry of the model when you make changes to the faces.

Move Faces also lets you move entire features, such as the hole in the model. In Figure 23.22, one of the holes has been moved so that it's no longer in line with the other three. This was done by selecting the countersink and the hole while using the Move Faces tool.

**FIGURE 23.21**

To select the vertical surface to the far right of the model, click the edge, and then use the Remove option to remove the top surface from the selection.

**FIGURE 23.22**

Selecting a surface to offset

### OFFSETTING A SURFACE

Suppose you want to decrease the radius of the arc in the right corner of the model, and you also want to thicken the model by the same amount as the decrease in the arc radius. To do this, you can use the Offset Faces tool. The Offset Faces tool performs a similar function to the Offset command you used earlier in this book. The difference is that the Offset Faces tool on the Solid Editing toolbar affects 3D solids.

When you click the Offset Faces tool on the Solid Editing toolbar, you're prompted to select faces. As with the Move tool, you must select an edge that will select two faces. If you want to offset only one face, you must use the Remove option to remove one of the faces. In Figure 23.22, an edge is selected. Figure 23.23 shows the effect of the Offset Faces tool when both faces are offset.

**FIGURE 23.23**
The model after off-setting the curved and bottom surfaces

### DELETING A SURFACE

Now, suppose you've decided to eliminate the curved part of the model. You can delete a surface by using the Delete Faces tool. Once again, you're prompted to select faces. Typically, you'll want to delete only one face, as in the curved surface in the example model; you use the Remove option to remove the adjoining face that you don't want to delete before finishing your selection of faces to remove.

When you attempt to delete surfaces, keep in mind that the surface you delete must be recoverable by other surfaces in the model. For example, you can't remove the top surface of a cube, expecting it to turn into a pyramid. That would require the sides to change their orientation, which isn't allowed in this operation. You can, on the other hand, remove the top of a box with tapered sides. Then, when you remove the top, the sides converge to form a pyramid.

### ROTATING A SURFACE

All the surfaces of the model are parallel or perpendicular to each other. Imagine that your design requires two sides to be at an angle. You can change the angle of a surface by using the Rotate Faces tool:

As with the prior solid-editing tools, you're prompted to select faces. You must then specify an axis of rotation. You can either select a point or use the default of selecting two points to define an axis of rotation, as shown in Figure 23.24. Once the axis is determined, you can specify a rotation angle. Figure 23.25 shows the result of rotating the two front-facing surfaces 4°.

**FIGURE 23.24**
Defining the axis
of rotation

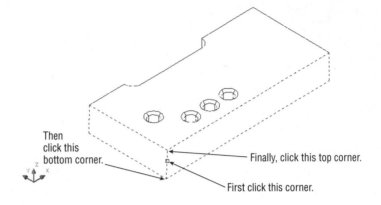

Then
click this
bottom corner.

Finally, click this top corner.

First click this corner.

**FIGURE 23.25**
The model after rotat-
ing two surfaces

### TAPERING A SURFACE

In an earlier exercise, you saw how to create a new tapered solid by using the Extrude command. But what if you want to taper an existing solid? Here's what you can do to taper an existing 3D solid.

The Taper Faces tool on the Solid Editing toolbar prompts you to select faces. You can select faces as described for the previously discussed solid-editing tools using the Remove or Add option to select different faces (see Figure 23.26). Press ↵ when you finish your selection, and then indicate the axis from which the taper is to occur. In the model example in Figure 23.26, select two corners defining a vertical axis. Finally, enter the taper angle. Figure 23.27 shows the model tapered at a 4° angle.

### EXTRUDING A SURFACE

You've used the Extrude command to create two of the solids in the Bracket model. The Extrude command requires a closed polyline as a basis for the extrusion. As an alternative, the Solid Editing toolbar offers the Extrude Faces tool, which extrudes a surface of an existing solid.

**FIGURE 23.26**

Selecting the surfaces to taper and indicating the direction of the taper

**FIGURE 23.27**

The model after tapering the sides

When you click the Extrude Faces tool on the Solid Editing toolbar, you see the Select faces or [Undo/Remove]: prompt. Select an edge or a set of edges, or use the Remove or Add option to select the faces you want to extrude. Press ↵ when you've finished your selection, and then specify a height and taper angle. Figure 23.28 shows the sample model with the front surface extruded and tapered at a 45° angle. You can extrude multiple surfaces at one time if you need to by selecting multiple surfaces.

Aside from those features, the Extrude Faces tool works just like the Extrude command.

### TURNING A SOLID INTO A SHELL

In many situations, you'll want your 3D model to be a hollow, rather than solid, mass. The Shell tool lets you convert a solid into a shell.

When you click the Shell tool on the Solid Editing toolbar, you're prompted to select a 3D solid. You're then prompted to remove faces. At this point, you can select an edge of the solid to indicate the surface you want removed. The surface you select is completely removed from the model, exposing the interior of the shell. For example, if you select the front edge of the sample model shown in Figure 23.29, the top and front surfaces are removed from the model, revealing the interior of the solid as shown in Figure 23.30. After selecting the surfaces to remove, you can enter a shell thickness.

**FIGURE 23.28**
The model with a
surface extruded
and tapered

**FIGURE 23.29**
Selecting the edge to
be removed

Select this edge.

**FIGURE 23.30**
The solid model after
using the Shell tool

The shell thickness is added to the outside surface of the solid. When you're constructing your solid with the intention of creating a shell, you need to take this into account.

### COPYING FACES AND EDGES

At times, you may want to create a copy of a surface of a solid to analyze its area or to produce another part that mates to that surface. The Copy Faces tool creates a copy of any surface on your model. The copy it produces is a type of object called a *region*. You'll learn more about regions later in this chapter.

The copies of the surfaces are opaque and can hide objects behind them when you perform a hidden-line removal (choose View ➤ Hide).

Another tool that is similar to Copy Faces is Copy Edges. Instead of selecting surfaces, as in the Copy Faces tool, you select all the edges you want to copy. The result is a series of simple lines representing the edges of your model. This tool can be useful if you want to convert a solid into a set of 3D Faces. The Copy Edges tool creates a framework onto which you can add 3D Faces.

### ADDING SURFACE FEATURES

If you need to add a feature to a flat surface, you can do so with the Imprint tool. An added surface feature can then be colored or extruded. This feature is a little more complicated than some of the other solid-editing tools, so you may want to try the following exercise to see firsthand how it works.

You'll start by inserting an object that will be the source of the imprint. You'll then imprint the main solid model with the object's profile:

1. Choose Insert ➤ Block to open the Insert dialog box.

2. Click Browse; then, locate the `imprint.dwg` sample file and select it.

3. In the Insert dialog box, make sure the Explode check box is selected, and remove the check mark from the Specify On-Screen check box in the Insertion Point group.

4. Click OK. The block appears in the middle of the solid.

5. Click the Imprint tool.

6. Click the main solid model.

7. Click the inserted solid.

8. At the `Delete the source object [Yes/No]<N>:` prompt, enter **Y**↵.

You now have an outline of the intersection between the two solids imprinted on the top surface of your model. To help the imprint stand out, try the following steps to change its color:

1. Click the Color Faces tool on the Solid Editing toolbar.

2. Click the imprint from the previous exercise. The imprint and the entire top surface are highlighted.

3. At the `Select faces or [Undo/Remove/ALL]:` prompt, type **R**↵; then, click the outer edge of the top surface to remove it from the selection set.

4. Press ↵ to open the Select Color dialog box.

5. Click the red color sample in the dialog box; then, click OK. The imprint is now red.

6. Press ↵ twice to exit the command.

7. To see the full effect of the Color Faces tool, choose the Conceptual or Realistic visual style in the Visual Style control panel. You can also find the visual styles in the View ➤ Visual Styles menu.

If you want to remove an imprint from a surface, use the Clean tool on the Solid Editing toolbar. Click the Clean tool, and then click the imprint you want to remove.

---

### USING THE COMMAND LINE FOR SOLID EDITING

The solid-editing tools are options of a single AutoCAD command called Solidedit. If you prefer to use the keyboard, here are some tips on using the Solidedit command. When you first enter **Solidedit.⏎** at the Command prompt, you see the following prompt:

```
Enter a solids editing option [Face/Edge/Body/Undo/eXit] <eXit>:
```

You can select the Face, Edge, or Body option to edit the various parts of a solid. If you select Face, you see the following prompt:

```
[Extrude/Move/Rotate/Offset/Taper/Delete/Copy/coLor/mAterial/Undo/eXit] <eXit>:
```

The options from this prompt produce the same results as their counterparts on the Solid Editing toolbar.

If you select Edge at the first prompt, you see the following prompt:

```
Enter an edge editing option [Copy/coLor/Undo/eXit] <eXit>:
```

The Copy option lets you copy a surface, and the Color option lets you add color to a surface.

If you select Body from the first prompt, you see the following prompt:

```
[Imprint/sePaarate solids/Shell/cLean/Check/Undo/eXit] <eXit>:
```

These options also perform the same functions as their counterparts on the Solid Editing toolbar. As you work with this command, you can use the Undo option to undo the last Solidedit option you used without exiting the command.

---

### SEPARATING A DIVIDED SOLID

While editing solids, you can end up with two separate solid forms that were created from one solid, as shown in Figure 23.31. Even though the two solids appear separated, they act like a single object. In these situations, AutoCAD offers the Separate tool on the Solid Editing toolbar. To use it, click the Separate tool, and select the solid that has been separated into two forms.

**FIGURE 23.31**
When the tall, thin solid is subtracted from the larger solid, the result is two separate forms, yet they still behave as a single object.

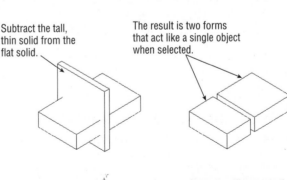

Subtract the tall, thin solid from the flat solid.

The result is two forms that act like a single object when selected.

Separate will separate the two forms into two distinct solids.

Through some simple examples, you've seen how each of the solid-editing tools works. You aren't limited to using these tools in the way shown in this section, and this book can't anticipate every situation you may encounter as you create your solid models. These examples are intended as an introduction to these tools, so feel free to experiment with them. You can always use the Undo option to backtrack in case you don't get the results you expect.

**TIP**   Figure 23.31 is included in the sample figures under the name of `Separate example.dwg`. You can try the Separate tool in this file on your own.

This concludes your tour of the Solid Editing toolbar. Next, you'll learn how to use your 3D solid models to quickly generate 2D working drawings.

### FINDING THE PROPERTIES OF A SOLID

All this effort to create a solid model isn't just to create a pretty picture. After your model is drawn and built, you can obtain information about its physical properties. In this section, you'll look at a command that lets you gather such information.

You can find the volume, the moment of inertia, and other physical properties of your model by using the Massprop command. These properties can also be recorded as a file on disk so you can modify your model without worrying about losing track of its original properties.

To find the mass properties of a solid, choose Tools ➤ Inquiry ➤ Region/Mass Properties, or enter **Massprop.↵**, and then follow the prompts.

**TIP**   LT users can use the Massprop command described here to find the properties of solids that are part of an existing drawing.

## Streamlining the 2D Drawing Process

Using solids to model a part—such as the Bracket and the Solidedit examples used in this chapter—may seem a bit exotic, but there are definite advantages to modeling in 3D, even if you want to draw the part only in 2D as a page in a set of manufacturing specs.

The exercises in this section show you how to quickly generate a typical mechanical drawing from your 3D model by using Paper Space and the 3D Make control panel. You'll also examine techniques for dimensioning and including hidden lines.

**TIP**   If your application is architecture, and you've created a 3D model of a building by using solids, you can use the tools described in this section to generate 2D elevation drawings from your 3D solid model.

### Drawing Standard Top, Front, and Right-Side Views

One of the more common types of mechanical drawings is the *orthogonal projection*. This style of drawing shows separate top, front, and right-side views of an object. Sometimes a 3D image is added for clarity. You can derive such a drawing in a few minutes using the Flatshot tool described in Chapter 20 (see "Turning a 3D View into a 2D AutoCAD Drawing" in Chapter 20).

With Flatshot, you can generate the standard top, front, and right-side orthogonal projection views, which you can further enhance with dimensions, hatch patterns, and other 2D drawing features. Follow these steps:

1. Choose an orthogonal projection view from the 3D Navigate control panel.

2. Click the Flatshot tool on the 3D Make control panel.

3. In the Flatshot dialog box, select the options you want, and click Create. (See Table 20.1 for the Flatshot options.)

If you select Insert As New Block in the Flatshot dialog box, you're prompted to select an insertion point to insert the block that is the 2D orthogonal view of your model. By default, the view is placed in the same plane as your current view, as shown in Figure 23.32. Once you've created all your views, you can move them to a different location in your drawing so you can create a set of layout views to your 2D orthogonal views, as shown in Figure 32.33. You can also place the orthogonal view blocks on a separate layer and then, for each layout viewport, freeze the layer of the 3D model so only the 2D views are displayed.

**FIGURE 23.32**
The 2D orthogonal views shown in relation to the 3D model

**FIGURE 23.33**
You can use a layout to arrange a set of views created by Flatshot. Dimensions, notes, and a title block can be added to complete the layout.

If your model changes and you need to update the orthogonal views, you can repeat the steps listed here; but instead of selecting Insert As New Block in the Flatshot dialog box, select Replace Existing Block to update the original orthogonal view blocks. If you want, you can include an isometric view to help communicate your design more clearly.

**TIP**   To set up a viewport to display a view, like a top or right-side view of a 3D model, select a view from the 3D Navigate control panel drop-down list, and then click the viewport whose view you want to set up. To set the scale of a viewport, click the viewport border, and then select a scale from the VP Scale drop-down list on the status bar. If you'd like to refresh your memory on layouts in general, refer to Chapter 16.

## Adding Dimensions and Notes in a Layout

Although I don't recommend adding dimensions in Paper Space for architectural drawings, it may be a good idea for mechanical drawings such as the one in this chapter. By maintaining the dimensions and notes separate from the actual model, you keep these elements from getting in the way of your work on the solid model. You also avoid the confusion of having to scale the text and dimension features properly to ensure that they will plot at the correct size.

**TIP**   See Chapters 10 and 12 for a more detailed discussion of notes and dimensions.

As long as you set up your Paper Space work area to be equivalent to the final plot size, you can set dimension and text to the sizes you want at plot time. If you want text ¼″ high, you set your text styles to be ¼″ high.

To include dimensions, make sure you're in a Layout tab, and then use the dimension commands in the normal way. However, you need to make sure full associative dimensioning is turned on. Choose Tools ≻ Options to open the Options dialog box, and then click the User Preferences tab. In the Associative Dimensioning group, make sure the New Dimensions Associative check box is selected. With associative dimensioning turned on, dimensions in a Layout tab display the true dimension of the object being dimensioned, regardless of the image scale in the viewport.

If you don't have the associative dimensioning option turned on and your viewports are set to a scale other than 1 to 1, you have another option: You can set the Annotation Units option in the Dimension Style dialog box to a proper value. The following steps show you how:

1. Select the Model tab at the bottom of the AutoCAD Window, and then choose Dimension ≻ Dimension Style to open the Dimension Style Manager dialog box.

2. Make sure you've selected the style you want to use, and then click Modify to open the Modify Dimension Style dialog box.

3. Click the Primary Units tab.

4. In the Scale Factor input box in the Measurement Scale group, enter the value by which you want your Paper Space dimensions multiplied. For example, if your Paper Space views are scaled at one-half the actual size of your model, enter **2** in this box to multiply your dimensions' values by two.

**TIP**   To make sure the value in step 4 is correct, determine which scale factor you need for your Paper Space drawing to get its actual size. That's the value you need to enter.

5. Click the Apply To Layout Dimensions Only check box. This ensures that your dimension is scaled only while you're adding dimensions in Paper Space. Dimensions added in Model Space aren't affected.

6. Click OK to close the Modify Dimension Style dialog box; then, click Close in the Dimension Style Manager dialog box.

You've had to complete a lot of steps to get the final drawing, but compared with drawing these views by hand, you undoubtedly saved a great deal of time. In addition, as you'll see later in this chapter, what you have is more than just a 2D drafted image. With what you created, further refinements are now easy.

## Using Visual Styles with a Viewport

In Chapter 20, you saw how you can view your 3D model using visual styles in Model Space. A visual style can give you a more realistic representation of your 3D model, and it can show off more of the details, especially on rounded surfaces. You can also view and plot a visual style in a Layout tab. To do this, you make a viewport active and then turn on the visual style you want to use for that viewport. The following exercise gives you a firsthand look at how this is done:

1. Click the ANSI D title block tab in the lower portion of the AutoCAD Window.

2. Double-click inside the viewport with the isometric view of the model to switch to Floating Model Space.

3. Select Conceptual from the Visual Styles drop-down list.

**NOTE** The view may appear a bit dark because of the black color setting for the object. You can change the color to a lighter one such as cyan or blue to get a better look.

4. Double-click outside the isometric viewport to return to Paper Space.

You changed the visual style of one viewport without affecting the other viewports. This can help others visualize your 3D model more clearly.

You'll also want to know how to control the hard-copy output of a shaded view. For this, you use the shortcut menu:

1. Click the isometric view's viewport border to select it.

**2.** Right-click to open the shortcut menu, and select the Shade Plot option to display a set of Shade Plot options.

**3.** Take a moment to study the menu, and then click As Displayed.

The As Displayed option plots the viewport as it appears in the AutoCAD window. You use this option to plot the currently displayed visual style. Wireframe plots the viewport as a Wireframe view. Hidden plots the viewport as a Hidden-line view similar to the view you see when you use the Hide command. Below the As Displayed option in the shortcut menu is a list of the available visual styles. At the bottom of the menu, the Rendered option plots the view by using AutoCAD's Render feature, described in Chapter 22. You can use the Rendered option to plot ray-traced renderings of your 3D models.

Remember these options on the shortcut menu as you work on your drawings and when you plot. They can be helpful in communicating your ideas, but they can also get lost in the array of tools that AutoCAD offers.

## Visualizing Solids

If you're designing a complex object, sometimes it helps to be able to see it in ways that you couldn't in the real world. AutoCAD offers two visualization tools that can help others understand your design ideas.

If you want to show off the internal workings of a part or an assembly, you can use X-ray mode, which can be found in the Visual Styles control panel.

Figure 23.34 shows an isometric view of the bracket using the Realistic visual style and X-ray mode turned on. You can see the internal elements as if the object were semi-transparent. X-ray mode works with any visual style, although it works best with a style that shows some of the surface features (such as the Conceptual or Realistic visual style).

Another tool to help you visualize the internal workings of a design is the sectionplane command. This command creates a plane that defines the location of a cross-section. A sectionplane can also do more than just show a cross-section. Try the following exercise to see how it works:

1. Go to the Bracket.dwg file if it isn't already the current file.

2. Click the Model tab, and then change the color of Layer0 to a light gray so you can see the bracket more clearly when using the Realistic visual style.

3. Select Realistic from the Visual Styles control panel.

4. Enter **sectionplane**↵ at the Command prompt. You'll see the prompt

   ```
   Select face or any point to locate section line or [Draw section/Orthographic]:
   ```

5. Click the front plane of the bracket, as shown in Figure 23.35. A plane appears on that surface.

You can move the section plane object along the solid to get a real-time view of the section it traverses. To do this, you need to turn on the Live Section feature. To check whether Live Section is turned on, do the following:

1. Click the section plane, and then right-click. If you see a check mark by the Activate Live Sectioning option, then you know it's on. If you don't see a check mark, then choose Activate Live Sectioning to turn it on.

2. Click the triangular grip at the center of the section plane, as shown in Figure 23.36.

**3.** Move the cursor slowly toward the back of the bracket. As you do this, the bracket becomes invisible in the foreground while remaining solid in the background. You also see the section of the bracket at the location of the cursor (see Figure 23.37).

**4.** When your view looks similar to Figure 23.37, click the mouse.

**FIGURE 23.35**
Adding the surface plane to your bracket

**FIGURE 23.36**
Moving the surface plane across the bracket

Click this arrow.

**FIGURE 23.37**
The surface plane fixed at a location

Now you see only the portion of the bracket behind the section plane plus the cross-section of the plane, as shown in Figure 23.37. You can have the section plan display the front portion as a ghosted image by doing the following:

1. With the section plane selected (you should still see its blue grips), right-click, and choose Show Cut-Away Geometry. After a moment, the front portion of the bracket appears (see Figure 23.38).

2. Press the Escape key to remove the section plane from the current selection. You can see the entire bracket, including the geometry at the section plane.

You can keep the Show Cut-Away Geometry setting on as you work on your section views or turn it off to help speed things up.

You can also add a jog in the section plane to create a more complex section cut. Here's how it's done:

1. Click the section plane, right-click, and choose Add Jog To Section.

2. At the `Specify a point on the section line to add jog:` prompt, click the arrow grip at the center of the section plane (the same one you used to move the section plane). After a moment, a jog appears in the section plane.

3. To see the section plane more clearly, press Escape, and then click the section plane (see Figure 23.39).

4. Click the arrow grip on the back portion of the section plane, as shown in Figure 23.39, and drag it toward the right so the jog looks similar to the second panel in Figure 23.39.

5. Press the Escape key to get a clear view of the new section.

As you can see from this example, you can adjust the section using the arrow grips. You can click either the center arrow grip or the endpoint grips to add a jog.

You may have also noticed two other arrows in the section plane. The arrow next to the center arrow grip reverses the side that appears solid; if you need a view from the opposite side, you can reverse the slice with this arrow (see Figure 23.40).

When you click the other downward-pointing arrow, you see three options for visualizing the section boundary: Section Plane, Section Boundary, and Section Volume.

**FIGURE 23.38**
The entire bracket is displayed with the Show Cut-Away Geometry option turned on

**FIGURE 23.39**
Moving the jog in the
section plane

Click this arrow grip, and move it
to the right to get this view.

**FIGURE 23.40**
One arrow reverses
the side of the section
plane that appears
solid. The other
arrow presents addi-
tional options for the
section plane.

Click this arrow, and the
hidden side of the slice
is reversed.

By using these other settings, you can start to include sections through the sides, back, top, or bottom of the solid. For example, if you click the Section Boundary option, another boundary line appears with grips. To see it clearly, you may have to press Escape and then select the section plane again.

You can then manipulate these grips to show section cuts along those boundaries.

The Section Volume option displays the boundary of a volume along with grips at the top and bottom of the volume. These grips allow you to create a cut plane from the top or bottom of the solid.

Finally, you can get a copy of the solid that is behind or in front of the section plane. Right-click the section plane, and choose Generate 2D/3D Section to open the Generate Section/Elevation dialog box. Click the Show Details button to expand the dialog box and display more options.

Click this arrow, and the hidden side of the slice is reversed.

If you select 2D Section/Elevation, a 2D image of the section plane is inserted in the drawing in a manner similar to the insertion of a block. You're asked for an insertion point, an X and Y scale, and a rotation angle.

**TIP** If your application is architectural, you can use a section plane and the 2D Section/Elevation option to get an accurate elevation drawing. Instead of placing the section plane inside the solid, move it away from the solid model and use the 2D Section/Elevation shortcut menu option.

The 3D Section option creates a copy of the portion of the solid that is bounded by the section plane or planes, as shown in Figure 23.41.

You can access more detailed settings for the 2D Section/Elevation, 3D Section, and Live Section Settings by clicking the Section Settings button at the bottom of the Generate Section/Elevation dialog box. This button opens the Section Settings dialog box, which lists the settings for the section feature.

If you create a set of orthogonal views in a layout, the work you do to find a section is also reflected in the layout views.

**FIGURE 23.41**
A copy of the solid minus the section area is created using the 3D Section option of the Generate Section/Elevation dialog box.

### TAKING ADVANTAGE OF STEREOLITHOGRAPHY

A discussion of solid modeling wouldn't be complete without mentioning stereolithography. This is one of the more interesting technological wonders that has appeared as a by-product of 3D computer modeling. *Stereolithography* is a process that generates resin reproductions of 3D computer solid models. It offers the mechanical designer a method for rapidly prototyping designs directly from AutoCAD drawings. The process requires special equipment that reads computer files in a particular format.

AutoCAD supports stereolithography through the Stlout command. This command generates a .stl file, which can be used with a *Stereolithograph Apparatus* (*SLA*) to generate a model. You must first create a 3D solid model in AutoCAD; then, you can use the Export Data dialog box to export your drawing in the STL format. Choose File ➢ Export, and make sure the File Of Type drop-down list shows Lithography (*.stl) before you click the Save button.

The AutoCAD 3D solids are translated into a set of triangular-faceted meshes in the .stl file. You can use the Facetres system variable to control the fineness of these meshes. See Chapter 22 for more information on Facetres.

## The Bottom Line

**Understanding Solid Modeling**   Solid modeling lets you build 3D models by creating and joining 3D shapes called solids. There are several built-in solid shapes, called primitives, and you can create others using the Extrude tool.

   **Master It**   Name some of the built-in solid primitives available in AutoCAD.

   **Solution**   Box, wedge, cone, sphere, cylinder, pyramid, torus, polysolid.

**Creating Solid Forms**   You can use Boolean operations to sculpt 3D solids into the shape you want. Two solids can be joined to form a more complex one, or you can remove one solid from another.

   **Master It**   Name the three Boolean operations you can use on solids.

   **Solution**   Intersection, subtraction, union.

**Creating Complex Solids** Besides the primitives, you can create your own shapes based on 2D polylines.

**Master It** Name three tools that let you convert closed polylines and circles into 3D solids.

**Solution** Extrude, Revolve, Sweep.

**Editing Solids** Once you've created a solid, you can make changes to it using the solid-editing tools offered on the Solid Editing toolbar.

**Master It** Name at least four of the tools found on the Solid Editing toolbar.

**Solution** Union, Subtract, Intersect, Extrude, Move, Offset, Rotate, Delete, Taper, Copy, Color.

**Streamlining the 2D Drawing Process** You can create 3D orthogonal views of your 3D model to create standard 2D mechanical drawings.

**Master It** What is the name of the tool in the 3D Make control panel that lets you create a 2D drawing of a 3D model?

**Solution** Flatshot.

**Visualizing Solids** In addition to viewing your 3D model in a number of different orientations, you can view it as if it were transparent or cut in half.

**Master It** What is the name of the command that lets you create a cut view of your 3D model?

**Solution** Sectionplane.

# Part 5

# Customization and Integration

**In this part:**

- ◆ **Chapter 24: Using the Express Tools**
- ◆ **Chapter 25: Introducing AutoLISP**
- ◆ **Chapter 26: Customizing Toolbars, Menus, Linetypes, and Hatch Patterns**
- ◆ **Chapter 27: Managing and Sharing Your Drawings**
- ◆ **Chapter 28: Keeping a Project Organized with Sheet Sets**

# Chapter 24

# Using the Express Tools

You can use a wealth of AutoCAD features to improve your productivity. But even with these aids to efficiency, you can always further automate in certain situations. In this chapter, I'll introduce you to some ways you can enhance AutoCAD with add-on utilities. You'll also learn how to adapt AutoCAD to fit your particular needs by customizing its menus and toolbars.

First, you'll learn how to load and run the AutoCAD Express tools that are supplied on the AutoCAD distribution CD. By doing so, you'll be prepared to take advantage of the many utilities available from user groups and online services. You'll also see how third-party tools can enhance AutoCAD's role in your workplace. Then, you'll learn how you can create keyboard macros and incorporate them into custom menus and toolbars. And, finally, you'll learn how to create custom linetypes and hatch patterns.

Topics in this chapter include the following:

◆ Using Enhancements Straight from the Source

◆ Putting AutoLISP to Work

## Using Enhancements Straight from the Source

If you've followed the tutorial in this book, you've already used a few add-on programs that come with AutoCAD, perhaps without even being aware that they were not part of the core AutoCAD program. In this section, I'll introduce you to the AutoCAD Express tools: a set of AutoLISP, ARX, and VBA tools that showcase these powerful customization environments. The best part about the Express tools is that you don't have to know a thing about programming to take advantage of them.

**NOTE** If you're using LT, you can skip this chapter.

There are so many Express tools that I can't provide step-by-step instructions for all of them. Instead, I'll give you details about some of the more complicated tools and provide shorter descriptions of others.

## Opening the Express Toolbars

Although you may have the Express menu in the AutoCAD menu bar, you may also want to use the Express toolbars. Here are the steps to open them:

1. Locate a blank area to the right of the toolbars at the top of the AutoCAD Window. If you don't see a blank area, move the Layers toolbar into the drawing area so you can gain access to some blank space.

Layers toolbar moved to gain access to a blank area

Right-click in a blank area by the toolbars.

2. Right-click in the blank area, and select Express ➤ ET:Text.

3. Right-click in the blank area again, and select Express ➤ ET:Blocks.

4. Right-click in the blank area again, and select Express ➤ ET:Standard.

5. You should have all three Express toolbars on your screen. If you need to, move the Layers toolbar back to its docked position at the top of the AutoCAD Window.

You can close the Express toolbars and later reopen them by right-clicking any blank area of the toolbar region and selecting a toolbar from the shortcut menu.

## Tools for Managing Layers

In a survey of AutoCAD users, Autodesk discovered that one of the most frequently used AutoCAD features was the Layer command. As a result, the layer controls in AutoCAD have been greatly improved. Still, there is room for more improvement. The Layers II toolbar discussed in this section isn't really a part of the Express tools, but it's a former set of Express tools that has migrated to the main AutoCAD program.

**TIP** All the tools discussed in this section have keyboard command equivalents. Check the status bar for the keyboard command name when you select one of these tools from the toolbar or drop-down menu.

**LOADING THE EXPRESS TOOLS**

If you installed AutoCAD by using the Typical Installation option, you may not have installed the AutoCAD Express tools. Fortunately, you can install these utilities separately without having to reinstall the entire program.

Place the AutoCAD 2008 installation CD in your CD drive. When you see the AutoCAD 2008 installation window, make sure the Install option is selected. You'll see a set of numbered steps on the left side of the window. In step 5, Install Supplemental Tools, click the AutoCAD Express Tools option. Follow the installation instructions from there. After you've installed the Express tools, they will appear the next time you open AutoCAD.

### USING LAYER WALK TO EXPLORE LAYERS

When you work with a file that was produced by someone else, you usually have to spend some time becoming familiar with the way layers are set up in that file. This can be a tedious process, but the Layer Walk Express tool can help.

As the name implies, the Layer Walk tool lets you "walk through" the layers of a file, visually isolating each layer as you select its name from a list. You can use Layer Walk to select the layers that you want visible, or you can turn layers on and off to explore a drawing without affecting the current layer settings. To open the LayerWalk dialog box, do the following:

1. Right click any toolbar, and select Layer II from the shortcut menu.

2. Click the Layer Walk tool on the Layer II toolbar, or enter **Laywalk**↵.

You can click and drag the bottom edge of the dialog box to expand the list so you can see all the layers in the drawing. When you first open the LayerWalk dialog box, you see the current visible layers selected. Layers that are off aren't selected. Click a single layer, and AutoCAD displays just that layer.

You can use this dialog box to set up layer settings visually by Ctrl+clicking layer names to make them visible. Turn off Restore On Exit to maintain the layer settings you set up in the LayerWalk dialog box, or turn it on if you want the drawing to revert to the layer settings that were in place before you opened the LayerWalk dialog box. Right-click the list of layers to display a set of other options that let you save the layer state and invert the selection.

### CHANGING THE LAYER ASSIGNMENT OF OBJECTS

In addition to the Layer Walk tool, the Layers II toolbar includes two tools that change the layer assignments of objects: the Layer Match tool and the Change To Current Layer tool.

The Layer Match tool is similar to the Match Properties tool, but it's streamlined to operate only on layer assignments. After clicking this tool, select the object or objects you want to change, press ↵, and then select an object whose layer you want to match.

The Change To Current Layer tool changes an object's layer assignment to the current layer. This tool has long existed as an AutoLISP utility, and you'll find that you'll get a lot of use from it.

### CONTROLLING LAYER SETTINGS THROUGH OBJECTS

The remaining Express Layer tools let you make layer settings by selecting objects in the drawing. These tools are easy to use: Click a tool, and then select an object. These tools are so helpful that you may want to consider docking them permanently in your AutoCAD window.

The following list describes each tool:

**Layer Isolate/Layer Unisolate**   Layer Isolate turns off all the layers except for the layer of the selected object. Layer Unisolate restores the layer settings to the way the drawing was set before you used Layer Isolate.

**Layer Freeze**   Freezes the layer of the selected object.

**Layer Off**   Turns off the layer of the selected object.

**Layer Lock**   Locks the layer of the selected object. A locked layer is visible but can't be edited.

**Layer Unlock**   Unlocks the layer of the selected object.

**Layer Walk**   Lets you dynamically change layer visibility.

**Copy Objects To New Layer**   Copies an object or set of objects to a different layer.

## Tools for Editing Text

It seems that we can never have enough text-editing features. Even in the realm of word processors, numerous tools let you configure fonts, paragraphs, tabs, and tables. Some programs even check your grammar. Although you may not be trying to write the great American novel in AutoCAD, you're interested in getting your text in the right location, at the right size, and with some degree of style. This often means using a mixture of text- and graphics-editing tools. The following describes some additional tools that will help ease your way through otherwise difficult editing tasks.

### MASKING TEXT BACKGROUNDS

One problem AutoCAD users frequently face is how to get text to read clearly when it's placed over a hatch pattern or other graphic. The Hatch command hatches around existing text, leaving a clear space behind it. But what about those situations in which you must add text *after* a hatch pattern has been created? Or what about instances when you need to mask behind text that is placed over a nonhatch object, such as dimension leaders or raster images?

The Text Mask tool addresses this problem by masking the area behind text with a special masking object called a Wipeout.

**TIP**   The AutoCAD Mtext command offers a Background Mask option that performs a similar function to the Text Mask tool. While editing text with the Text Formatting toolbar, select the text, right-click, and select Background Mask. You can also turn on the Background Mask through the Properties palette of an Mtext object.

**TIP** If you want to remove the effects of the Express Text Mask tool, choose Express ➢ Text ➢ Unmask Text. This option prompts you to select an object. Select the masked text, and press ⏎ to delete the mask background.

### ADDING LINKED TEXT DOCUMENTS

One of the more frustrating and time-consuming aspects of drafting is editing lengthy notes. General notes and specifications change frequently in the life of a project, so editing notes can be a large part of what you do in AutoCAD. Frequently, notes are written by someone else, perhaps a specifications writer who doesn't work directly with the drawings.

To help make note-editing easier, AutoCAD supplies the Remote Text object. This special object is linked to an external text document. Remote Text objects automatically update their contents when the source document changes.

Using Remote Text is fairly straightforward. Choose Express ➢ Text ➢ Remote Text, or type **Rtext**⏎ at the Command prompt. Press ⏎⏎ when you see the `Enter an option[Style/Height/ Rotation/File/Diesel] <File>:` prompt, and then locate and select a text file to import.

## Express Blocks Tools

Every now and then, you'll want to use objects in a block to trim or extend to, or perhaps you'll want to copy a part of a block to another part of your drawing. In these situations, you can use the following tools. They're fairly simple to use, so the descriptions in this section should be enough to get you started.

You'll find these tools on the Express Blocks toolbar:

**Copy Nested Objects** Lets you copy single objects within a block. You're allowed to select objects only individually—one click at a time.

**Trim To Nested Objects** Trims to objects in a block. This tool works just like the standard Trim command with the exception that you must select the cutting-edge objects individually.

**Extend To Nested Objects** Extends to objects in a block. This tool also works like its standard counterpart with the exception that you must select the boundary-edge objects you want to extend to individually.

**List Xref/Block Properties** Displays basic information about an Xref or a block.

**Extended Clip** In Chapter 7, you saw how to limit the display of an Xref to an L-shaped, rectilinear area. Extended Clip adds the ability to use arcs, circles, and polylines to clip the view of an Xref.

**Explode Attributes To Text** Explodes blocks containing attributes so that the attribute values are converted into plain single-line text.

In addition to the tools on the Express Blocks toolbar, you can access the following tools by choosing Express ➢ Blocks:

**Convert Shape To Block** Converts a shape object into a block. You can then explode the block to its component objects if needed.

**Export Attribute Information** Offers a quick way to extract attribute information from a block to a simple text file. You're prompted to select a file location and name and then select the attributes you want to export. The text file is formatted as a tab-delimited file. You can then edit the exported text file and use the Import Attribute Information tool (described next) to update the drawing with the modifications you made to the text file.

**Import Attribute Information** Enables you to import changes to the attribute information that has been exported using the Export Attribute Information tool.

**Convert Block To Xref** Lets you replace block references in your drawing with Xrefs. For example, you can replace the tub blocks in the apartment plan from earlier tutorials with an Xref of a different tub. When you select this option, the BLOCKTOXREF dialog box opens.

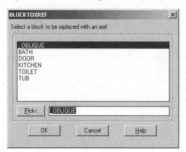

From here, you can select the block you want to replace. You're then asked to select a file that will be the replacing Xref.

**Replace Block With Another Block** Replaces one set of block references with another. For example, you can replace the tub block in the apartment plan with the door block, turning all the bathtubs into doors. This tool works in a way similar to the Convert Block To Xref tool.

## Express Standard Tools

The Express Standard toolbar seems to be the answer to most AutoCAD users' wish lists. As with many of the Express tools discussed so far, these tools have been floating around in the AutoCAD user community as AutoLISP utilities. Multiple Object Stretch lets you use the crossing polygon selection option to select endpoints and vertexes for stretching. The Move/Copy/Rotate tool combines these three functions into one command. The Break Line Symbol adds the standard break line to your drawing. The Super Hatch tool offers an easy way to create custom hatch patterns. Super Hatch is fairly complex, so the next section describes in detail how you can use it.

### CREATING CUSTOM HATCH PATTERNS WITH SUPER HATCH

You can access a number of hatch patterns from AutoCAD's Hatch And Gradient dialog box, but at times none of those patterns will fulfill your needs. This is where the Super Hatch tool comes in. With Super Hatch, you can create virtually any hatch pattern you want. You can use objects in your drawing as a basis for a hatch pattern, or you can import bitmap images and use them to form a hatch pattern, such as tiled wallpaper in the Windows Desktop background.

The following exercise shows you how to use Super Hatch:

1. Open the superhatch.dwg file. You see a block of an arrow on the left side of the screen and a rectangular area to the right. In this exercise, you'll turn the arrow into a hatch pattern.

**2.** Click the Super Hatch tool to open the SuperHatch dialog box.

**3.** Click the Select Existing button to close the SuperHatch dialog box.

**4.** Click the arrow. It becomes highlighted, and a magenta rectangle encircles the arrow.

At this point, you can indicate the area you want repeated in your pattern. The default is the extents of the selected item, as indicated by the magenta rectangle.

**5.** Click the two points shown in Figure 24.1 to indicate the area that you want repeated. The rectangle changes to reflect the new area. You can repeat the area selection as many times as you need until you get exactly the area you want.

**FIGURE 24.1**
Selecting the area
to be repeated

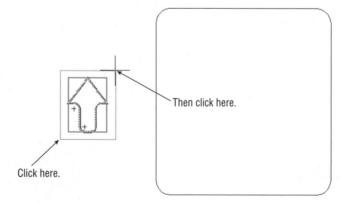

Then click here.

Click here.

**6.** Press ↵ to move to the next step.

**7.** Click the interior of the rectangle to indicate the area you want to hatch. If you have multiple hatch areas, you can continue to select them at this step.

**8.** Press ↵ to finish your selection of hatch areas. The arrow appears repeated as a pattern in the rectangle, as shown in Figure 24.2.

**FIGURE 24.2**
The custom hatch pattern

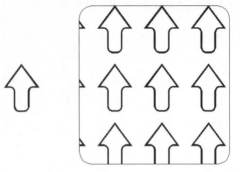

The object you select by using the Select Existing option in the SuperHatch dialog box must be a block. You can modify that block by using the techniques described in Chapter 7, and the changes will appear in the hatch pattern as shown in Figure 24.3.

**FIGURE 24.3**
The custom hatch pattern after the arrow block has been modified to include the diagonal hatch pattern

As you can see from the SuperHatch dialog box, you can incorporate Xrefs, blocks, and even image files into your custom hatch pattern. Each of these options prompts you to insert the object before you convert it into a hatch pattern. You use the usual insertion method for the type of object you select. For example, if you choose the Block option, you're prompted for an insertion point, the X and Y scale factors, and a rotation angle. For image files, you see the same dialog box that you see when you insert an image file, offering the options for insertion point, scale, and rotation. Figure 24.4 shows a sample hatch pattern with an image file used instead of an AutoCAD block.

**FIGURE 24.4**
A custom hatch pattern using a bitmap image

## Tools on the Express Drop-Down Menu

Most of the Express tools discussed so far are available as options in the AutoCAD menu bar on the Express menu. The Express menu offers some additional options that aren't in any of the toolbars. You won't want to miss these additional tools. They can greatly enhance your productivity on any type of project.

### CONTROLLING SHORTCUTS WITH THE COMMAND ALIAS EDITOR

Throughout this book, I've been showing you the keyboard shortcuts to the AutoCAD commands. In Windows XP, all these shortcuts are stored in a file called `Acad.pgp` in the `C:\Documents and Settings\`*User Name*`\Application Data\Autodesk\AutoCAD 2008\R17.1\enu\Support` folder. (Check the Working Support File Search Path option in the Files tab in the Options dialog box to find the exact location for the support files on your system.) In the past, you had to edit this file with a text editor to modify these command shortcuts (otherwise known as command *aliases*). But to make our lives simpler, Autodesk has supplied the Command Alias Editor, which automates the process of editing, adding, or removing command aliases in AutoCAD.

In addition, the Command Alias Editor lets you store your own alias definitions in a separate file. You can then recall your file to load your own command aliases. Here's how the Command Alias Editor works:

1. Choose Express ➤ Tools ➤ Command Alias Editor to open the AutoCAD Alias Editor dialog box.

2. As you can see from the button options, you can add, delete, or edit an alias. Click the Add button to open the New Command Alias dialog box.

In this dialog box, you enter the desired alias in the Alias input box and then select the command from the AutoCAD Command list box. You can also enter a command or macro name, such as Wipeout, in the input box. When you click the Edit option in the AutoCAD Alias Editor dialog box, you see a dialog box identical to this one with the input boxes already filled in.

3. After you create or edit an alias, click OK to return to the AutoCAD Alias Editor dialog box.

4. Click OK to exit the dialog box. A warning message tells you that you're about to overwrite the Acad.pgp file.

5. Click Yes to update the Acad.pgp file.

If you're a veteran AutoCAD user, you may be accustomed to your own set of command aliases. If so, you may want to create your own .pgp file containing just your custom aliases. Then, whenever you use AutoCAD, you can open the AutoCAD Alias Editor, choose File ➢ Import, and load your personal .pgp file. From then on, the aliases in your file will be included with those of the standard Acad.pgp file.

### USING EXTENDED CLIP TO CLIP A RASTER IMAGE TO A CURVED SHAPE

In Chapter 7, you saw how you can clip portions of an Xref or a raster image so that only a portion of these objects is visible. One limitation to the Raster Clip option is that you can clip only areas defined by straight lines. You can't, for example, clip an area defined by a circle or an ellipse.

Extended Clip is designed for those instances when you absolutely need to clip a raster image to a curved area. The following steps show you how it works:

1. Create a clip boundary by using a curved polyline or circle.

2. Choose Express ➢ Modify ➢ Extended Clip.

3. Click the boundary.

4. Click the Xref, block, or image you want to clip.

5. At the

   ```
   Enter maximum allowable error distance for resolution of arc segments <7-16">:
   ```

   prompt, press ↵. The Xref, block, or image clips to the selected boundary.

6. You can erase the boundary you created in step 1 or keep it for future reference.

Extended Clip doesn't really clip to the boundary you created, but instead approximates that boundary by creating a true clip boundary with a series of very short line segments. The prompt in step 5 lets you specify the maximum allowable distance between the straight-line segments it generates and the curve of the boundary you create (see Figure 24.5).

After you've created a boundary by using Extended Clip, you can edit the properties of the boundary by choosing Modify ➢ Clip➢ Xref for Xrefs and blocks or Modify ➢ Clip ➢ Image for raster images.

### USING MAKE LINETYPE TO CREATE A CUSTOM LINETYPE

Most of the time, the linetypes provided by AutoCAD are adequate. But if you're looking for that perfect linetype, you can use the Make Linetype tool to create your own. Here's how it works:

1. Open the customltype_completed.dwg sample file from the Figures folder. The sample drawing is made up of simple lines with no polylines, arcs, or circles. When you create your

own linetype prototype, make sure the lines are all aligned. Draw a single line, and break it to form the segments of the linetype (see Figure 24.6). Also make sure it's drawn to the actual plotted size.

**FIGURE 24.5**

Extended Clip enables you to set the maximum distance from your clip boundary and the one it generates.

Your clip boundary

The clip boundary produced by Extended Clip

**FIGURE 24.6**

Creating a custom linetype by using Make Linetype

Click here for the start point.

Click here for the endpoint.

2. Choose Express ➢ Tools ➢ Make Linetype to open the MKLTYPE dialog box. This is a typical file dialog box allowing you to create a new linetype file.

3. Enter **myltype** for the filename, select a location for the file, and then click Save.

4. At the Enter linetype name: prompt, enter **MyLinetype** or any name you want to use to describe the linetype. The name must be a single word.

5. At the Enter linetype description: prompt, enter a description for your linetype. This can be a sentence that best describes your linetype.

6. At the Specify starting point for line definition: prompt, pick one endpoint of the sample linetype.

7. At the Specify ending point for line definition: prompt, pick a point just past the opposite end of the sample linetype. Pick a point past the endpoint of the sample to indicate the gap between the end of the first segment of the linetype and the beginning of the repeating portion, as shown in Figure 24.6.

8. At the Select objects: prompt, select the sample linetype lines. When you're done, press ⏎. You now have a custom linetype.

If you send your file to someone else, you need to make sure you include your custom linetype files with the drawing file. Otherwise, anything drawn using your custom linetype will appear as a continuous line, and your recipient will get an error message saying that AutoCAD can't find a linetype resource.

The Make Linetype tool creates a single linetype file for each linetype you create. The linetype file is a simple ASCII text file. If you end up making several linetypes, you can combine your linetype files into one file by using a simple text editor such as Windows Notepad. Don't use WordPad or Word because these programs will introduce special codes to the linetype file.

### CREATING CUSTOM SHAPES AS AN ALTERNATIVE TO BLOCKS

*Shapes* are special types of AutoCAD objects that are similar to blocks. They're usually simple symbols made up of lines and arcs. Shapes take up less memory and can be displayed faster, but they're much less flexible than blocks, and they aren't very accurate. You can't use object snaps to snap to specific parts of a shape, nor can you explode shapes. They're best suited for symbols or as components in complex linetypes.

Shapes have always been difficult to create. In the past, you couldn't create a shape by drawing it. You had to create something called a *shape definition* by using a special code. A shape definition is an ASCII file that contains a description of the geometry of the shape. Creating such a file was a tedious, arcane process that few users bothered with.

With the introduction of complex linetypes in recent versions of AutoCAD, interest in shapes has revived. To make it easier for users to create shapes, AutoCAD 2008 provides a tool that creates a shape definition file for you based on a line drawing. Try this simple exercise to learn how to create and use a shape:

1. Open the `makeshape.dwg` sample file from the `Chapter 24` folder of the sample project files. This file contains a simple drawing of an upward-pointing arrow. It contains lines and arcs.

2. Choose Express ➤ Tools ➤ Make Shape to open the MKSHAPE dialog box. This is a typical file dialog box that enables you to specify a name and location for your shape definition file.

3. In the File Name input box, enter **Arrow**; then, locate the `My Documents` folder and place your new file there.

4. Click OK to create your file.

5. At the `Enter the name of the shape:` prompt, enter **Arrow**↵.

6. At the `Enter resolution <128>:` prompt, enter **512**↵. Shapes are defined with a square matrix of points. All the endpoints of lines and arcs must be on a point in that matrix. At this prompt, you can define the density of that matrix. A higher density will give you a better-looking shape, but you don't want to get carried away with this setting.

7. At the `Specify insertion base point:` prompt, select the tip of the arrow, as shown in Figure 24.7. This will be the insertion point of your shape, which is similar to the insertion point of a block.

8. At the `Select objects:` prompt, select the entire arrow, and then press ↵.

9. A series of messages tells you what AutoCAD is doing. The last message tells you whether AutoCAD was successful in creating the shape file, and it tells you the location and name of the new shape file:

```
Compilation successful.  Output file C:\Documents and Settings\User Name\My
    Documents\Arrow.shx contains 309 bytes.
Shape "ARROW" created.
```

**FIGURE 24.7**
Creating a shape from
an existing drawing

Click here for the insertion base point.

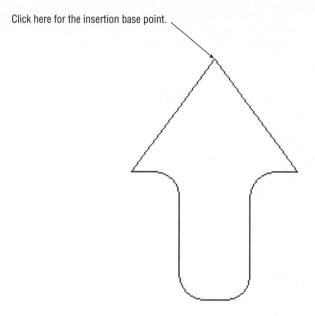

Use the SHAPE command to place shapes in your drawing.

To see how your shape came out, try the following. Here you'll learn how to load and insert a shape:

1. At the Command prompt, type **Load**↵ to open the Select Shape File dialog box. This is a typical file dialog box.

2. In the My Documents folder, locate the file Arrow.shx, and click Open to load it.

3. Type **Shape**↵.

4. At the Enter shape name or [?]: prompt, type **Arrow**↵. Now the arrow follows the cursor as you move it across the drawing area.

**NOTE**   If you've forgotten the name of a shape you're loading, you can enter a question mark (?) to see a listing of available shapes.

5. At the Specify insertion point: prompt, click to the right of the original arrow.

6. At the Specify height: prompt, press ↵ to accept the default of 1.

7. At the Specify rotation angle: prompt, enter **45**↵. The arrow appears at a 45° angle.

In many ways, a shape acts like a block, but you can't snap to any of its points. It's also less accurate than a block in its representation, although for some applications this may not be a great concern. Finally, you can't use complex shapes such as splines or 3D objects for your shape; you can use only lines and arcs.

Still, you may find shapes useful in your application. As mentioned earlier, you can include shapes in linetype definitions. See Chapter 26 for a description of how to create a linetype that includes shapes as part of the line.

**TIP** You may also notice a tool that converts shapes into AutoCAD blocks. Choose Express ➢ Blocks ➢ Convert Shape To Block, and then select a shape. A prompt asks for a name for the block. You can accept the default name, which is the same name as the shape you're converting.

### USING THE EXPRESS SELECTION TOOLS

Sometimes it seems that there aren't enough selection tools available in AutoCAD. In Chapter 2, you learned about the various methods you can use to select groups of objects to build a *selection set*, which is a set of objects selected for an operation such as a move or copy. The Express tools offer a few more ways to select objects.

The Get Selection Set tool sets up a selection set based on layers or types of objects. When you choose Express ➢ Selection Tools ➢ Get Selection Set, you're prompted to select an object whose layer contains all the objects you want to select. You can press ↵ to create a selection set of all the objects in the drawing. Next, you're prompted to select an object of the type you want. If you press ↵ at the first prompt and then select a line at the second prompt, all the lines in the drawing will be included in a new selection set. You won't see anything happen on the screen, but the next time you use a command that asks you to select objects, you can enter **P**↵ to select the lines.

The other selection tool is Fast Select. When you choose Express ➢ Selection Tools ➢ Fast Select, you're prompted to select an object. After you do so, the object you select plus any object touching it will be selected.

### USING DIMSTYLE EXPORT AND DIMSTYLE IMPORT

Most AutoCAD users need to set up their dimension styles only once and then make minor alterations for drawing scale. You can set up your dimension styles in a template file and then use that template whenever you create new drawings. That way, your dimension styles will already be set up the way you want them.

But frequently, you'll receive files created by someone else who may not have the same ideas about dimension styles as you do. Normally, this would mean you'd have to re-create your favorite settings in a new dimension style. Now, with the Express tools, you can export and import dimension styles at any time, saving you the effort of re-creating them.

### ATTACHING DATA TO OBJECTS

This set of options is less likely to get as much use as the others you've looked at so far, so I've included a brief description of them here without going into too much detail. They're fairly easy to use, and you shouldn't have any trouble trying them. You can access both tools by choosing Express ➢ Tools:

**Attach Xdata** Lets you attach extended data to objects. Extended data is usually used only by AutoLISP or ARX applications. You're asked to select the object that will receive the data, and then you're asked for an application name that serves as a tag to tell others who the data belongs to. You can then select a data type. After this is done, you can enter your data.

**List Object Xdata** Displays extended data that has been attached to an object.

### USING FILE TOOLS

AutoCAD has always made extensive use of external files for its operation. Everything from fonts to keyboard shortcuts depends on external files. The Express File tools (choose Express ➢ File Tools) offer options to simplify a few file-related operations. You may find some of these tools helpful on a daily basis, such as Save All Drawings and Close All Drawings. Others, such as Edit Image, may be useful to know about when you need to edit an image. The following is a list of these tools:

**Move Backup Files**  Lets you specify a location for AutoCAD `.bak` files for the current drawing session.

**Convert PLT To DWG**  Converts HPGL plot files to drawing files. You must first set up AutoCAD or Windows for an HPGL plotter and then specify that HPGL plotter in the Plot or Page Setup dialog box. You must also indicate that you want to plot to a file at the time you produce the plot (select the Plot To File check box in the Printer/Plotter group of the Plot dialog box).

**Edit Image**  Offers a quick way to open and edit an image file that has been inserted into an AutoCAD drawing. Choose Express ➢ File Tools ➢ Edit Image, and then select the image you want to edit. A File dialog box opens, showing the file in a list box. Click Open, and the program associated with the image file type will open the image file.

**Redefine Path**  Lets you redefine the path to external files that are referenced from the current drawing. This includes Xrefs, images, shapes, styles, and Rtext. You can strip a path from a referenced file by using the asterisk option (*) when you see the `Enter old directory (use '*' for all)`, or `? <options>:` prompt. When you see the `Replace "*" with:` prompt, press ↵. If you strip the path in this way, AutoCAD will use the support file search path specified in the Files tab of the Options dialog box. You can specify the type of external file you want to redefine by pressing ↵ at the first prompt to open the REDIRMODE dialog box. This dialog box contains a simple check box list of the types of support files whose path you want to redefine.

**Update Drawing Property Data**  Drawing property data can be a handy feature of AutoCAD, but using it requires some discipline. (See Chapter 19 for more on drawing property data.) For one thing, the amount of data you must enter can be a bit daunting. The Update Drawing Property Data Express tool offers a way to let you quickly add drawing property data by utilizing property data templates. Drawing property data is often the same for a set of drawings, so you can create a template and apply it to similar drawings in a set by using the Update Drawing Property Data tool.

To create a drawing property data template, choose Express ➢ File Tools ➢ Update Drawing Property Data. At the `Enter an option [Active template/Edit template/List/Remove/ Update] <Update>:` prompt, enter **E**↵ to open the Edit Propulate Template dialog box.

Fill in the data, and then choose File ➢ Save As. Use the Update option in the Update Drawing Property Data command prompt to apply the template to a drawing or to a set of drawings in a folder.

**Save All Drawings**  Saves all currently open files. The files remain open for additional editing.

**Close All Drawings**  Closes all currently open drawings. AutoCAD remains open.

**Quick Exit**  Closes all currently open drawings, and exits AutoCAD. You're asked whether you want to save changes to each file before it's closed.

**Revert To Original**  Causes a drawing to revert to its last saved state. It does so by closing the file without saving any changes (since the last Save) and then reopening the file.

### USING WEB TOOLS

AutoCAD enables you to add URL links to objects. This is a great feature that can help you link drawings to other types of data. The Express Web tools (choose Express ➢ Web Tools) add some enhancements to the URL linking features of AutoCAD:

**Show URLs**  Displays the URL link attached to an AutoCAD object.

**Change URLs**  Lets you quickly edit an object's existing URL. You must still choose Insert ➢ Hyperlink to attach a new URL to an object.

**Find And Replace URLs**  Replaces a set of existing URLs with a URL of your specification.

## Layout Express Tools

AutoCAD includes some Express tools that will help make your work with layouts a lot easier. These tools, found in the Express ➢ Layout Tools menu, address some of the more common operations you'll encounter as you work with layouts.

### ALIGNING MODEL SPACE OBJECTS WITH LAYOUT OBJECTS

If you've ever tried to align an object in a layout with objects in a Model Space viewport, you know how difficult it can be. This situation often arises when you accidentally pan or zoom a Model Space viewport, and objects drawn in Paper Space (such as break lines or dimensional notations) become misaligned with the underlying view.

The Align Space tool helps you quickly align objects in a Model Space viewport with objects in the layout Paper Space. Align Space can even rotate a viewport view to align objects that are at an angle. To see how it works, try the following exercise. You'll align a Plan view of a set of survey data points to a north arrow in Paper Space:

1. Open the `alignspace.dwg` sample file.

2. Choose Express ➢ Layout Tools ➢ Align Space. The viewport automatically becomes active.

3. At the `FIRST alignment point in MODEL space:` prompt, click the upper endpoint of the north arrow in the viewport, as shown in Figure 24.8.

4. At the `SECOND point in MODEL space or <Return> for none:` prompt, click the endpoint of the bottom end of the north arrow, as shown in Figure 24.8.

5. At the `FIRST alignment point in PAPER space:` prompt, AutoCAD automatically switches to Paper Space to allow for your next input. Click the upper endpoint of the layout Paper Space north arrow.

First alignment point
in Model Space

First alignment point
in Paper Space

Second alignment point in Model Space

Second alignment point in Paper Space

**6.** At the SECOND alignment point in PAPER space: prompt, click the lower end of the Paper Space arrow. The two arrows align, and a message tells you the scale of the viewport.

In this exercise, the two north arrows were aligned in both scale and direction. The object you're aligning to in Paper Space doesn't have to be in the area of the viewport, either.

If you prefer, you can align a single point without changing the scale or rotation of the viewport by pressing ⏎ in step 4 when you see the SECOND point in MODEL space or <Return> for none: prompt.

### ALIGNING MULTIPLE VIEWPORTS TO A SINGLE VIEWPORT

The Align Space tool lets you align a Model Space object to a Paper Space object—but what if you want to align two Model Space views? For example, suppose you want to overlap two viewports of the same view, with one viewport displaying graphics while the other displays just the power and signal symbols for a small region of the plan.

The Synchronize Viewports tool lets you do just that. It aligns one or more viewports to another *master* viewport. The Synchronize Viewports tool aligns the coordinates in one viewport with the coordinates and scale of another so the views are matched like pieces of a jigsaw puzzle. To get a better idea of what this means, try the following exercise. Suppose you have an enlarged plan showing a portion of a building. You want to include the grid lines in your plan, but you don't want to have to include other portions of the plan or redraw the grids. Synchronize Viewports makes easy work of this project:

**1.** Open the synchronize.dwg file, and then choose Express ➢ Layout Tools ➢ Synchronize Viewports.

**2.** At the Select objects: prompt, click the border of the viewport in the lower-right corner.

**3.** At the Select viewports to be aligned to master viewport Select objects: prompt, click the other two viewports, and press ⏎. The two viewports change to show the adjacent areas of the first viewport.

The three views of the layout combine to show a contiguous Plan view instead of three random views.

You could use Synchronize Viewports this way to piece together parts of a floor plan in a non-rectangular shape.

To finish adding the grid lines, do the following:

1. Double-click in the top viewport, and then click the Pan Realtime tool in the Standard toolbar.

2. Shift+click and drag the view downward to bring the grid lines into view. Then, Shift+click and drag, and keep the pan motion in an exact vertical direction. Pan downward until you see only the grids and dimensions.

3. Press Esc to exit the Pan tool; then, double-click the left viewport, and use the Pan tool to Shift+click and drag the view toward the right. Keep panning until just the grid lines show.

If you've ever tried to do this operation without the aid of the Synchronize Viewports tool, you can see how helpful a tool it is.

### FINDING VIEWPORT SCALES AND MERGING LAYOUTS

The Layout Tools category includes two more fairly simple tools: List Viewport Scale and Merge Layout. List Viewport Scale does just what its name says. Choose Express ➤ Layout Tools ➤ List Viewport Scale, and then click a viewport border to display the viewport scale. Merge Layout combines the contents of one layout with another. This tool is handy if you're exporting files to earlier versions of AutoCAD in which only one layout is possible. Choosing Express ➤ Layout Tools ➤ Merge Layouts opens the LAYOUTMERGE dialog box. This dialog box is a list showing the layouts in the current drawing.

You can select the layout that you want merged with the current layout. After you make your selection and click OK, another dialog box appears that looks identical to the first LAYOUTMERGE dialog box. This time, you select the destination layout for the merged layouts.

That covers the Express Layout tools. Like many of the other Express tools, you may find yourself using these tools more than the other standard AutoCAD commands; keep them in mind as you work on the layout of your next set of drawings.

# Putting AutoLISP to Work

Most high-end CAD packages offer a macro or programming language to help users customize their systems. AutoCAD has *AutoLISP*, which is a pared-down version of the popular LISP artificial intelligence language.

Don't let AutoLISP scare you. In many ways, an AutoLISP program is just a set of AutoCAD commands that help you build your own features. The only difference is that you have to follow a different set of rules when using AutoLISP. But this isn't so unusual. After all, you had to learn some basic rules about using AutoCAD commands too—how to start commands, for instance, and how to use command options.

If the thought of using AutoLISP is a little intimidating, bear in mind that you don't need substantial computer knowledge to use this tool. In this section, you'll see how to get AutoLISP to help out in your everyday editing tasks, without having to learn the entire programming language.

## Loading and Running an AutoLISP Program

Many AutoCAD users have discovered the usefulness of AutoLISP through the thousands of free AutoLISP utilities that are available from web sites and online services. It's common for users to maintain a toolbox of their favorite utilities on a disk. But before you can use these utilities, you need to know how to load them into AutoCAD. In the following exercise, you'll load and use a sample AutoLISP utility:

1. Start AutoCAD, and open the `24-unit.dwg` file.

2. Choose Tools ➢ Load Application to open the Load/Unload Applications dialog box.

3. Locate and select the GETAREA.LSP file.

4. Click the Load button. The message GETAREA.LSP successfully loaded appears in the message box at the bottom of the dialog box. If you scroll down the list in the Loaded Applications tab, you also see Getarea.lsp listed there, which tells you that it's loaded.

5. Click Close to close the Load/Unload Applications dialog box.

6. Enter getarea↵.

7. At the Pick point inside area to be calculated: prompt, click inside the unit plan.

8. At the Select location for area note: prompt, pick a point just above the door to the balcony. A label appears, displaying the area of the room in square feet.

You've just loaded and used an AutoLISP utility. As you saw in the Load/Unload Applications dialog box, you can load and try several other utilities. Next, you'll look more closely at the Load/Unload Applications dialog box.

**TIP** The functions of some of the more popular AutoLISP utilities have become part of the core AutoCAD program. Tools such as Match Properties and Make Object's Layer Current have been around as AutoLISP utilities since the earliest releases of AutoCAD.

## Managing Your AutoLISP and VBA Library

The Load/Unload Applications dialog box gives you plenty of flexibility in managing your favorite AutoLISP utilities. You can also manage your VBA and ARX applications. As you saw in the previous exercise, you can easily find and select utilities by using this dialog box. If you often use a custom application, you can include it in the History List tab of the Load/Unload Applications dialog box, as you'll see in the following steps:

1. Choose Tools ≻ Load Application to open the Load/Unload Applications dialog box.

2. Select the Add To History check box.

3. Click the History List tab.

4. Select GETAREA.LSP from the list of applications at the top of the dialog box.

5. Click Load. GETAREA.LSP now appears in the History List tab.

6. Click Close to close the Load/Unload Applications dialog box.

Now, when you exit AutoCAD, the dialog box retains the name of the Getarea.lsp utility in the History List tab. When you want to load GETAREA.LSP in a future session, you won't have to hunt it down. You can highlight it in the History List tab and then load it from there. You can add as many items as you want to your History List tab or remove items by highlighting them and clicking the Remove button. The History List tab works with all types of applications that AutoCAD supports.

## Loading AutoLISP Programs Automatically

As you start to build a library of AutoLISP and VBA applications, you may find that you use some of them all the time. You can set up AutoCAD to automatically load your favorite applications. To do this, you use the Startup Suite in the Load/Unload Applications dialog box:

1. Choose Tools ➤ Load Applications to open the Load/Unload Applications dialog box.

2. Click the Contents button or the suitcase icon in the Startup Suite group to open the Startup Suite dialog box. This dialog box contains a list box that shows any applications that are to be started whenever AutoCAD starts. You add applications with the Add button at the bottom. If there are applications in the list, you can use the Remove button to remove them.

3. Click the Add button to open the Add File To Startup Suite dialog box. This is a typical file dialog box that enables you to search for and select a file.

4. Locate and select the GETAREA.LSP file in the Chapter 24 folder, and click Add. The Startup Suite dialog box reappears, and GETAREA.LSP is listed.

5. Click Close, and then click Close again in the Load/Unload Applications dialog box.

From now on, GETAREA.LSP will be loaded automatically whenever you start AutoCAD. You can add several files to the Startup Suite list.

## Creating Keyboard Macros with AutoLISP

You can write simple AutoLISP programs of your own that create what are called keyboard macros. *Macros*—like script files—are strings of predefined keyboard entries. They're invaluable for shortcuts to commands and options you use frequently. For example, you might often use the Break command to break an object at a single point while editing a particular drawing. Here's a way you can turn this operation into a macro:

1. Close the 24-unit.dwg file without saving it, and then open it again and enter the following text at the Command prompt. Be sure you enter the line exactly as shown here. If you make a mistake while entering this line, you can use the I-beam cursor or arrow keys to go to the location of your error to fix it:

   ```
   (defun C:breakat () (command "break" pause "f" pause "@"))↵
   ```

2. Enter **breakat**↵ at the Command prompt. The Break command starts, and you're prompted to select an object.

3. Click the wall on the right side of the unit.

4. At the Specify first break point: prompt, click a point on the wall where you want to create a break, and make sure Osnap mode is turned off.

5. To see the result of the break, click the wall again. It's been split into two lines, as shown in Figure 24.9.

You've just written and run your first AutoLISP macro! Let's take a closer look at this simple program (see Figure 24.10). It starts with an opening parenthesis, as do all AutoLISP programs, followed by the word defun. Defun is an AutoLISP function that lets you create commands; it's followed by the name you want to give the command (Breakat, in this case). The command name is preceded by C:, telling defun to make this command accessible from the command prompt. If the C: were omitted, you would have to start Breakat by using parentheses, as in (Breakat).

**FIGURE 24.9**
With the grips exposed, you can see that the wall is split into two lines.

Break location

**FIGURE 24.10**
Breakdown of the Breakat macro

After the command name is a set of opening and closing parentheses. This set encloses what is called the *argument list.* The details aren't important; just be aware that these parentheses must follow the command name.

Finally, a list of words follows, enclosed by another set of parentheses. This list starts with the word command. Command is an AutoLISP function that tells AutoLISP that whatever follows should be entered just like regular keyboard input. Only one item in the Breakat macro—the word pause—isn't part of the keyboard input series. Pause is an AutoLISP function that tells AutoLISP to pause for input. In this particular macro, AutoLISP pauses to let you pick an object to break and the location for the break.

Most of the items in the macro are enclosed in quotation marks. Literal keyboard input must be enclosed in quotation marks this way. The pause function, on the other hand, doesn't require quotation marks because it's a proper function, one that AutoLISP can recognize.

The program ends with a closing parenthesis. All parentheses in an AutoLISP program must be in balanced pairs, so these final two parentheses close the opening parenthesis at the start of the command function as well as the opening parenthesis back at the beginning of the defun function.

### STORING AUTOLISP MACROS AS FILES

When you create a program at the Command prompt, as you did with the Breakat macro, AutoCAD remembers it only until you exit the current file. Unless you want to re-create this macro the next time you use AutoCAD, save it by copying it into an ASCII text file with an .lsp extension using the Windows Notepad application. Figure 24.11 shows a file named Keycad.lsp, which contains the saved Breakat macro, along with some other macros I use often.

**FIGURE 24.11**
The contents of
Keycad.lsp

```
(defun c:breakat ()  (COMMAND "break" PAUSE "f" PAUSE "@"))
(defun c:arcd    ()  (COMMAND "arc" pause "e" pause "d"))
(defun c:corner  ()  (COMMAND "fillet" "r" "@" "fillet"))
(defun c:ptx     ()  (COMMAND "pdmode" "3"))
```

The other macros are commands that include optional responses. For example, the third item, defun c:corner, causes AutoCAD to start the Fillet command, enter an **R**↵ to issue the Radius option, and finally enter a **0** for the fillet radius. Use the Windows Notepad application and copy the listing in Figure 24.11. Give this file the name Keycad.lsp, and be sure you save it as an ASCII file. Then, whenever you want to use these macros, you don't have to load each one individually. Instead, you load the Keycad.lsp file the first time you want to use one of the macros, and they're all available for the rest of the session.

After the file is loaded, you can use any of the macros in it by entering the macro name. For example, entering **ptx**↵ sets the point style to the shape of an X.

Macros loaded in this manner are available to you until you exit AutoCAD. Of course, you can have these macros loaded automatically every time you start AutoCAD by including the Keycad.lsp file in the Startup Suite of the Load/Unload Applications dialog box. That way, you don't have to remember to load it in order to use the macros.

Now that you have some firsthand experience with AutoLISP, I hope these examples will encourage you to try learning more about this powerful tool.

## The Bottom Line

**Using Enhancements Straight from the Source** The Express tools have been around for a while and were originally intended to show what could be done with customization. Many users have come to rely on some of these tools.

**Master It** Which of the toolbars described in this chapter is a former Express toolbar that became part of the main program?

**Solution** Layers II.

**Putting AutoLISP to Work** AutoLISP is a macro language that gives you the ability to create your own commands.

**Master It** Name the filename extension for AutoLISP programs.

**Solution** LSP.

# Chapter 25

# Exploring AutoLISP

In the previous chapter, you were introduced to AutoLISP, AutoCAD's macro and programming language. You learned that you can take advantage of this powerful tool without having to know anything about its internal workings. In this chapter, you'll see how you can take more control of AutoLISP and have it do the things you want to do for your own AutoCAD environment. You'll learn how to store information such as text and point coordinates, how to create smart macros, and how to optimize AutoLISP's operation on your computer system.

A word of advice as you begin this chapter: Be prepared to spend lots of time with your computer—not because programming in AutoLISP is all that difficult, but because it's so addicting! You've already seen how easy it is to use AutoLISP programs. I won't pretend that learning to program in AutoLISP is just as easy as using it, but it isn't as hard as you may think. And once you've created your first program, you'll be hooked.

Topics in this chapter include the following:

- ◆ Understanding the Interpreter
- ◆ Using Arguments and Expressions
- ◆ Creating a Simple Program
- ◆ Selecting Objects with AutoLISP
- ◆ Controlling the Flow of an AutoLISP Program
- ◆ Data-Type Conversions
- ◆ Storing Your Programs as Files
- ◆ Getting More Help with AutoLISP

## Understanding the Interpreter

You access AutoLISP through the AutoLISP *interpreter,* which is a little like a hand-held calculator. When you enter information at the Command prompt, the interpreter *evaluates* it and then returns an answer. *Evaluating* means performing the instructions described by the information you provide. You could say that evaluation means "find the value of." The information you give the interpreter is like a formula—called an *expression* in AutoLISP.

Let's examine the interpreter's workings in more detail:

1. Start AutoCAD, and open a new file called Temp25a. You'll use this file just to experiment with AutoLISP, so don't worry about saving it.

2. At the Command prompt, enter (+ 2 2)↵. The answer, 4, appears on the prompt line. AutoLISP has *evaluated* the formula (+ 2 2) and returned the answer, 4.

By entering information this way, you can perform calculations or even write short programs on the fly.

The plus sign you used in step 2 represents a *function*—an instruction telling the AutoLISP interpreter what to do. In many ways, it's like an AutoCAD command. A simple example of a function is the math function, Add, represented by the plus sign. AutoLISP has many built-in functions, and you can create many of your own.

## Defining Variables with Setq

Another calculator-like capability of the interpreter is its ability to remember values. You probably have a calculator that has some memory. This capability allows you to store the value of an equation for future use. In a similar way, the AutoLISP interpreter lets you store values using *variables*.

A variable is like a container that holds a value. That value can change many times in the course of a program's operation. You assign values to variables by using the Setq function. For example, let's assign the numeric value 1.618 to a variable named Golden. This value, often referred to as the *golden section*, is the ratio of a rectangular area's height to its width. Aside from having some interesting mathematical properties, the golden section is said to represent a ratio that occurs frequently in nature. Follow these steps:

1. At the Command prompt, enter **(setq Golden 1.618)**↵. The value 1.618 appears just below the line you enter. The value of the Golden variable is now set to 1.618. Let's check it to make sure.

2. Enter **!Golden**↵ at the Command prompt. As expected, the value 1.618 appears at the prompt.

The exclamation point (!) acts as a special character that extracts the value of an AutoLISP variable at the prompt. From now until you close the drawing, you can access the value of Golden at any time by preceding the variable name with an exclamation point.

In addition to using math formulas as responses to prompts, you can also use values stored as variables. Let's see how you can use the variable Golden as the radius for a circle:

1. Click the Circle button on the Draw toolbar.

2. At the Specify center point: prompt, pick a point in the center of your screen.

3. At the Specify radius of circle or [Diameter]: prompt, enter **!Golden**↵. A circle appears with the radius 1.618. Check this using the Properties palette (see Figure 25.1).

Numbers aren't the only things that you can store using Setq. Let's look at the variety of other data types that variables can represent.

## Understanding Data Types

**WARNING**   Understanding the various data types and how they differ is important because they can be a source of confusion if not carefully used. Remember that you can't mix data types in most operations, and quotes and parentheses must always be used in open-and-close pairs.

Variables are divided into several categories called *data types.* Categorizing data into types lets AutoLISP determine precisely how to evaluate the data and keep programs running quickly. Your computer has different ways of storing various types of data, so the use of data types helps AutoLISP communicate with the computer more efficiently. Also, data types aid your programming efforts by forcing you to think of data as having certain characteristics. The following list describes each of the available data types:

**FIGURE 25.1**
The circle, using the
Golden variable as
the radius

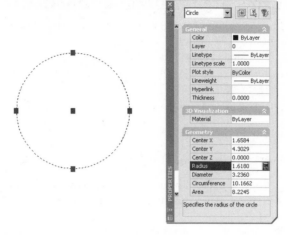

**Integers**  Integers are whole numbers. When a mathematical expression contains only integers, only an integer is returned. For example, the expression

    (/ 2 3)

means two divided by three. (The forward slash is the symbol for the division function.) This expression returns the value 0, because the answer is less than one. Integers are best suited for counting and numbering. The numbers 1, –12, and 144 are all integers.

**Real numbers**  Real numbers, often referred to as *reals,* are numbers that include decimals. When a mathematical expression contains a real number, a real number is returned. For example, the expression

    (/ 2.0 3)

returns the value 0.66667. Real numbers are best suited in situations that require accuracy. Examples of real numbers are 0.1, 3.14159, and –2.2.

**Strings**  Strings are text values. They're always enclosed in double quotes. Here are some examples of strings: "1", "George", and "Enter a value".

**Lists**  Lists are groups of values enclosed in parentheses. Lists provide a convenient way to store whole sets of values in one variable. There are two classes of lists: those meant to be evaluated, and those intended as repositories for data. In the strictest sense, AutoLISP programs are lists, because they're enclosed in parentheses. Here are some examples of lists: (6.0 1.0 0.0), (A B C D), and (setq golden 1.618).

**Elements**  There are two basic elements in AutoLISP: *atoms* and *lists.* I've already described lists. An atom is an element that can't be taken apart. Atoms are further grouped into two categories: *numbers* and *symbols.* A number can be a real number or an integer. A symbol, on the other hand, is often a name given to a variable, such as `point1` or `dx2`. A symbol can use a number as part of its name; however, its name must always start with a letter. Think of a symbol as a name given to a variable or function as a means of identifying it.

## Using Arguments and Functions

In the previous exercise, you used the Setq function to store variables. The way you used Setq is typical of all functions.

Functions act on *arguments* to accomplish a task. An argument can be a symbol, a number, or a list. A simple example of a function acting on numbers is the addition of 0.618 and 2. In AutoLISP, this function is entered as

    (+ 0.618 2)

which returns the value 2.618.

**TIP**  An expression is a list that contains a function and arguments for that function.

This formula—the function followed by the arguments—is called an *expression*. It starts with the left (opening) parenthesis first, then the function, then the arguments, and finally the right (closing) parenthesis.

Arguments can also be expressions, which means you can *nest* expressions. For example, here is how to assign the value returned by 0.618 + 2 to the variable Golden:

    (setq Golden (+ 0.618 2))

This is called a *nested expression*. Whenever expressions are nested, the deepest nest is evaluated first, then the next deepest, and so on. In this example, the expression adding 0.618 to 2 is evaluated first. On the next level out, setq assigns the result of the expression (+ 0.168 2) to the variable Golden.

Arguments to functions can also be variables. For example, suppose you use Setq to assign the value 25.4 to a variable called Mill. You can then find the result of dividing Mill by Golden, as follows:

1.  Enter **(setq Mill 25.4)**↵ to create a new variable called Mill.

2.  Enter **(/ Mill Golden)**↵. (As mentioned earlier, the forward slash is the symbol for the division function.) This returns the value 15.698393. You can assign this value to yet another variable.

3.  Enter **(setq B (/ Mill Golden))**↵ to create a new variable, B. Now you have three variables—Golden, Mill, and B—which are all assigned values that you can later retrieve, either in an AutoCAD command (by entering an ! followed by the variable) or as arguments in an expression.

---

### WATCHING PARENTHESES AND QUOTES

You must remember to close all sets of parentheses when using nested expressions. Take the same care to enter the second quotes in each pair of quotes used to enclose a string.

If you get the prompt showing a parenthesis or set of parentheses followed by the > symbol, such as

    (_>

then you know you have an incomplete AutoLISP expression. This is the AutoLISP prompt. The number of parentheses in the prompt indicates how many parentheses are missing in your expression. If you see this prompt, you must type the closing parenthesis the number of times indicated by the number. AutoCAD won't evaluate an AutoLISP program that has the wrong number of parentheses or quotes.

## Using Text Variables with AutoLISP

The examples so far have shown only numbers being manipulated, but you can manipulate text in a similar way. Variables can be assigned text strings that can later be used to enter values in commands requiring text input. For text variables, you must enclose text in quotation marks, as in the following example:

```
(setq text1 "This is how text looks in AutoLISP")
```

This example shows a sentence being assigned to the variable text1.

Strings can also be *concatenated,* or joined together, to form new strings. Here is an example of how two pieces of text can be added together:

```
(setq text2 (strcat "This is the first part and " "this is the second part"))
```

Here, the AutoLISP function strcat is used to join the two strings. The result is

```
"This is the first part and this is the second part"
```

Strings and numeric values can't be evaluated together, however. This may seem like a simple rule, but if not carefully considered, it can lead to confusion. For example, it's possible to assign the number 1 to a variable as a text string, by entering

```
(setq foo "1")
```

Later, you may accidentally try to add this string variable to an integer or real number, and AutoCAD will return an error message.

The Setq and the addition and division functions are but three of many functions available to you. AutoLISP offers all the usual math functions, plus many others used to test and manipulate variables. Table 25.1 shows some commonly used math functions.

**TABLE 25.1:** Math Functions Available in AutoLISP

| **FUNCTIONS THAT ACCEPT MULTIPLE ARGUMENTS** | |
| --- | --- |
| **Operation** | **Example** |
| Add | (+ *number number*) |
| Subtract | (− *number number* ) |
| Multiply | (* *number number* ) |
| Divide | (/ *number number* ) |
| Find largest number in list | (Max *number number* ) |
| Find smallest number in list | (Min *number number* ) |
| Find the remainder of a division | (Rem *number number*) |

**TABLE 25.1:** Math Functions Available in AutoLISP *(CONTINUED)*

| FUNCTIONS THAT ACCEPT SINGLE ARGUMENTS | |
|---|---|
| **Operation** | **Example** |
| (1 + *number*) | Add 1 to *number* |
| (1 - *number*) | Subtract 1 from *number* |
| (Abs *number*) | Find the absolute value of *number* |
| (Atan *angle in radians*) | Arc tangent of *angle* |
| (Cos *angle in radians*) | Cosine of *angle* |
| (Exp *n*) | e raised to the *n*th power |
| (Expt *number n*) | *Number* raised to the *n*th power |
| (Gcd *integer integer*) | Greatest common denominator |
| (Log *number*) | Natural log of *number* |
| (Sin *angle in radians*) | Sine of *angle* |
| (Sqrt *number*) | Square root of *number* |

## Storing Points as Variables

Like numeric values, point coordinates can also be stored and retrieved. But because coordinates are sets of two or three numeric values, they have to be handled differently. AutoLISP provides the Getpoint function to handle the acquisition of points. Try the following to see how it works:

1. At the Command prompt, enter **(getpoint)**↵. The Command prompt goes blank momentarily.

2. Pick a point near the middle of the screen. In the prompt area, you see the coordinate of the point you picked.

Here, Getpoint pauses AutoCAD and waits for you to pick a point. Once you do, it returns the coordinate of the point you pick in the form of a list. The list shows the X, Y, and Z axes enclosed by parentheses.

You can store the coordinates obtained from Getpoint using the Setq function. Try the following:

1. Enter **(setq point1 (getpoint))**↵.

2. Pick a point on the screen.

3. Enter **!point1**↵.

Here you stored a coordinate list in a variable called point1. You then recalled the contents of point1 using the !. The value of the coordinate is in the form of a list with the *x*, *y*, and *z* values appearing as real numbers separated by spaces, instead of the commas you've been used to.

# Creating a Simple Program

So far, you've learned how to use AutoLISP to do simple math and to store values as variables. Certainly, AutoLISP has enormous value with these capabilities alone, but you can do a good deal more. In this section, you'll examine how to combine these three capabilities—math calculations, variables, and lists—to write a program for drawing a rectangle:

1. Press F2 to flip to a text display.

2. At the Command prompt, enter (**defun c:rec ()**↵. You get a new prompt that looks like this:

   ```
   (_>
   ```

   This is the AutoLISP prompt. It tells you, among other things, that you're in the AutoLISP interpreter. While you see this prompt, you can enter instructions to AutoLISP. You'll automatically exit the interpreter when you have finished entering the program. A program is considered complete when you've entered the last parenthesis, thereby balancing all the parentheses in your program.

3. Very carefully enter the following several lines. If you make a mistake while typing a line, use the arrow keys to navigate to the location of the error, and then highlight and correct the error. Each time you enter a line and press ↵, you'll see the AutoLISP prompt appear. Once you've entered the final closing parenthesis, you can't go back to fix a line:

**TIP**   AutoLISP isn't *case sensitive*. It doesn't matter if you type entries in uppercase or lowercase letters; they will work either way. The only time you must be careful with uppercase and lowercase is when you use string data types.

```
(setq Pt1 (getpoint "Pick first corner point:" ))↵
(setq Pt3 (getpoint "Pick opposite corner:" ))↵
(setq Pt2 (list (nth 0 Pt3) (nth 1 Pt1)))↵
(setq Pt4 (list (nth 0 Pt1) (nth 1 Pt3)))↵
(command "Pline" Pt1 Pt2 Pt3 Pt4 "C")↵
) ↵
```

   Once you enter the last parenthesis, you return to the standard AutoCAD Command prompt.

4. Check the lines you entered against the listing in step 3, and make sure you entered everything correctly. If you find a mistake, start over from the beginning and reenter the program.

**TIP**   You can use AutoLISP programs transparently, as long as the program doesn't contain an embedded AutoCAD command.

When you're done, you get the message C:REC. This confirms that the rectangle-drawing program is stored in memory. Let's see it in action:

1. Enter **Rec**↵ at the Command prompt.

2. At the Pick first corner point: prompt, pick a point at coordinate 1,1.

3. At the Pick opposite corner: prompt, pick a point at 6,4. A box appears between the two points you picked (see Figure 25.2).

**FIGURE 25.2**

Using the rectangle-drawing program

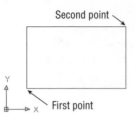

## Dissecting the Rectangle Program

The rectangle-drawing program incorporates all the things you've learned so far. Let's see how it works. First, it finds the two corner coordinates of a rectangle, which it gets from you as input; then, it extracts parts of those coordinates to derive the coordinates for the other two corners of the rectangle. Once it knows all four coordinates, the program can draw the lines connecting them. Figure 25.3 illustrates what the rec program does. Next, we'll look at the program in more detail.

**FIGURE 25.3**

The rec program draws a rectangle by getting two corner points of the rectangle from you and then recombining coordinates from those two points to find the other two points of the rectangle.

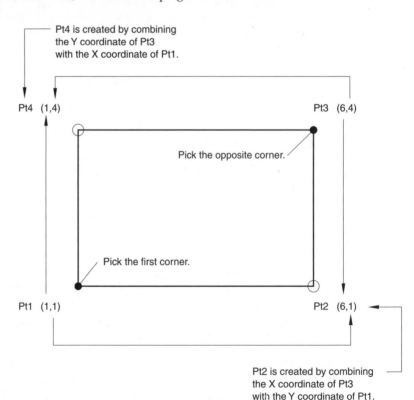

### Getting Input from the User

In the foregoing exercise, you started with the line

```
(defun c:rec ()
```

You may recall from Chapter 24 that the defun function lets you create commands. The name that follows the defun function is the name of the command as you enter it through the keyboard. The c: tells AutoLISP to make this program act like a command. If the c: was omitted, you'd have to enter (rec) to view the program. The set of empty parentheses is for an argument list, which I'll discuss later.

In the next line, the variable Pt1 is assigned a value for a point you enter using your cursor. Getpoint is the AutoLISP function that pauses the AutoLISP program and allows you to pick a point using your cursor or to enter a coordinate. Once a point is entered, Getpoint returns the coordinate of that point as a list.

Immediately following Getpoint is a line that reads

```
"Pick first corner point:"
```

Getpoint allows you to add a prompt in the form of text. You may recall that when you first used Getpoint, it caused the prompt to go blank. Instead of a blank, you can use text as an argument to the Getpoint function to display a prompt describing what action to take.

The third line is similar to the second. It uses Getpoint to get the location of another point and then assigns that point to the variable Pt3:

```
(setq Pt3 (getpoint "Pick opposite corner:" ))
```

Once AutoLISP has the two corners, it has all the information it needs to find the other two corners of the rectangle.

### Taking Lists Apart

The next thing AutoLISP must do is take apart Pt1 and Pt3 to extract their X and Y coordinates and then reassemble those coordinates to get the other corner coordinates. AutoLISP must take the X coordinate from Pt3 and the Y coordinate from Pt1 to get the coordinate for the lower-right corner of the rectangle (see Figure 25.3). To do this, you use two new functions: Nth and List.

Nth extracts a single element from a list. Because coordinates are lists, Nth can be used to extract an $x$, $y$, or $z$ component from a coordinate list. In the fourth line of the program, you see

```
(nth 0 Pt3)
```

Here the zero immediately following the Nth function tells Nth to take element number 0 from the coordinate stored as Pt3. Nth starts counting from 0 rather than 1, so the first element of Pt3 is considered item number 0. This is the $x$ component of the coordinate stored as Pt3.

To see how Nth works, try the following:

1. Enter **!point1**↵. You see the coordinate list you created earlier using Getpoint.

2. Enter **(nth 0 point1)**↵. You get the first element of the coordinate represented by point1.

Immediately following the first Nth expression is another Nth expression similar to the previous one:

```
(nth 1 Pt1)
```

Here, Nth extracts element number 1, the second element, from the coordinate stored as Pt1. This is the *y* component of the coordinate stored as Pt1. If you like, try the previous exercise again, but this time, enter **(nth 1 point1)** and see what value you get.

### COMBINING ELEMENTS INTO A LIST

AutoLISP has extracted the *x* component from Pt3 and the *y* component of Pt1. They must now be joined together into a new list. This is where the List function comes in. The List expression looks like this:

```
(list (nth 0 pt3) (nth 1 pt1))
```

You know that the first Nth expression extracts an *x* component and that the second extracts a *y* component, so the expression can be simplified to look like this:

```
(list X Y)
```

Here X is the value derived from the first Nth expression, and Y is the value derived from the second Nth expression. The List function recombines its arguments into another list, in this case another coordinate list.

Finally, the outermost function of the expression uses Setq to create a new variable called Pt2, which is the new coordinate list derived from the List function. The following is a schematic version of the fourth line of the rec program, so you can see what is going on more clearly:

```
(setq pt2 (list X Y))
```

Pt2 is a coordinate list derived from combining the *x* component from Pt3 and the *y* component from Pt1.

Try the following exercise to see how List works:

1. Enter **(list 5 6)**↵. The list (5 6) appears in the prompt.

2. Enter **(list (nth 0 point1) (nth 1 point1) )**↵. The X and Y coordinates of point1 appear in a list, excluding the Z coordinate.

The fifth line is similar to the fourth. It creates a new coordinate list using the *x* value from Pt1 and the *y* value from Pt2:

```
(setq Pt4 (list (nth 0 Pt1) (nth 1 Pt3)))
```

The last line tells AutoCAD to draw a polyline through the four points to create a box:

```
(command "Pline" Pt1 Pt2 Pt3 Pt4 "c")
```

The Command function issues the Pline command and then inputs the variables Pt1 through Pt4. Finally, it enters **c** to close the polyline. Note that in this expression, keystroke entries, such as **"Pline"** and **"C"**, are enclosed in quotes.

### GETTING OTHER INPUT FROM THE USER

In your rec program, you prompted the user to pick some points by using the Getpoint function. Several other functions allow you to pause for input and instruct the user what to do. Nearly all these functions begin with the Get prefix.

Table 25.2 shows a list of these Get functions. They accept single values or, in the case of points, a list of two values.

In Getstring, string values are case sensitive. This means that if you enter a lowercase letter in response to Getstring, it's saved as a lowercase letter; uppercase letters are saved as uppercase letters. You can enter numbers in response to the Getstring function, but they're saved as strings and can't be used in mathematical operations. Also, AutoLISP automatically adds quotes to string values it returns, so you don't have to enter any.

**TABLE 25.2:**     Functions That Pause to Allow Input

| FUNCTION | DESCRIPTION |
| --- | --- |
| Getint | Allows entry of integer values |
| Getreal | Allows entry of real values |
| Getstring | Allows entry of string or text values |
| Getkword | Allows filtering of string entries through a list of keywords |
| Getangle | Allows keyboard or mouse entry of angles based on the standard AutoCAD compass points (returns values in radians) |
| Getorient | Allows keyboard or mouse entry of angles based on the Units command setting for angles (returns values in radians) |
| Getdist | Allows keyboard or mouse entry of distances (always returns values as real numbers, regardless of the unit format used) |
| Getpoint | Allows keyboard or mouse entry of point values (returns values as coordinate lists) |
| Getcorner | Allows selection of a point by using a window* |
| Initget | Allows definition of a set of keywords for the Getword function; keywords are strings, as in (initget " Yes No ") |

*This function requires a base point value as a first argument. This base point defines the first corner of the window. A window appears, allowing you to select the opposite corner.*

Just as with Getpoint, all these Get functions allow you to create a prompt by following the function with the prompt enclosed by quotation marks, as in the expression

```
(getpoint "Pick the next point:" )
```

This expression displays the prompt Pick the next point: while AutoCAD waits for your input.

The functions Getangle, Getorient, Getdist, Getcorner, and Getpoint let you specify a point from which the angle, distance, or point is to be measured, as in the expression

```
(getangle Pt1 "Pick the next point:" )
```

Here, Pt1 is a previously defined point variable. A rubber-banding line appears from the coordinate defined by Pt1 (see Figure 25.4).

**FIGURE 25.4**
Using Getangle

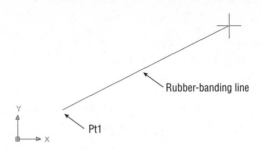

Once you pick a point, the angle defined by Pt1 and the point you pick are returned in radians. You can also enter a relative coordinate through the keyboard in the unit system currently being used in your drawing. Getangle and Getdist prompt you for two points if a point variable isn't provided. Getcorner always requires a point argument and generates a window rather than a rubber-banding line (see Figure 25.5).

**FIGURE 25.5**
Using Getcorner

## Selecting Objects with AutoLISP

You can easily create an AutoLISP expression that lets you select a single object and perform operation on it. Here is an example of a macro that rotates an object 90°:

```
(defun c:r90 () (command "rotate" pause "" pause "90"))
```

In this example, the pause after "rotate" allows you to make a selection. The double quotes that follow act like a ↵, and then another pause lets you select a rotation point. Finally, 90 is supplied to tell the Rotate command to rotate your selection 90°.

If you load this macro into AutoCAD and run it, you're prompted to select an object. You're then immediately prompted to pick a point for the rotation center. You won't be allowed to continue to select other objects the way you can with most AutoCAD commands.

But what if you want that macro to let you make several selections instead of just one? At this point, you almost know enough to create a program to do that. The only part missing is Ssget.

## The *Ssget* Function

So far, you know you can assign numbers, text, and coordinates to variables. Ssget is a function that assigns a set of objects to a variable, as demonstrated in the following exercise:

1. Draw a few random lines on the screen.

2. Enter **(setq ss1 (ssget))**⏎.

3. At the Select objects: prompt, select the lines using any standard selection method. You can select objects just as you would at any object-selection prompt.

4. When you're done selecting objects, press ⏎. You get the message <Selection set: *n*>, in which *n* is an alphanumeric value that identifies the selection set.

5. Start the Move command, and, at the object-selection prompt, enter **!ss1**⏎. The lines you selected previously are highlighted.

6. Press ⏎, and then pick two points to finish the Move command.

In this exercise, you stored a selection set as the variable ss1. You can recall this selection set from the Command prompt using the !, just as you did with other variables.

### USING *SSGET* IN AN EXPRESSION

You can also use the ss1 variable in an AutoLISP expression. For example, the R90 macro in the next exercise lets you select several objects to be rotated 90°:

1. Enter **(defun c:r90 (/ ss1)**⏎. The AutoLISP prompt appears.

2. To complete the macro, enter

```
(setq ss1 (ssget))(command "rotate" ss1 "" pause "90"))
```

and press ⏎.

3. Enter **r90**⏎ to start the macro.

4. At the Select objects: prompt, select a few of the random lines you drew earlier.

5. Press ⏎ to confirm your selection, and then pick a point near the center of the screen. The lines you selected rotate 90°.

The defun function tells AutoLISP this is to be a command called r90. A list follows the name of the macro—it's called an *argument list*. We'll look at argument lists a bit later in this chapter.

Following the argument list is the (setq ss1 (ssget)) expression you used in the previous exercise. This is where the new macro stops and asks you to select a set of objects to later be applied to the Rotate command.

The next expression uses the Command function. Command lets you include standard AutoCAD command line input in an AutoLISP program. In this case, the input starts by issuing the Rotate command. It then applies the selection set stored by ss1 to the Rotate command's object-selection prompt. Next, the two " " marks indicate an ⏎. The pause lets the user select a base point for the rotation. Finally, the value 90 is applied to the Rotate command's angle prompt. The entire expression when entered at the Command prompt would look like the following:

```
Command: Rotate↵
Select objects:!ss1↵
Select objects:↵
Specify base point: (pause for input)
Specify rotation angle or [Copy/Reference] <0>: 90↵
```

In this macro, the Ssget function adds flexibility by allowing the user to select as many objects as desired. (You could use the Pause function in place of the variable ss1, but with Pause, you can't anticipate whether the user will use a window, pick points, or select a previous selection set.)

### CONTROLLING MEMORY CONSUMPTION WITH LOCAL VARIABLES

Selection sets are memory hogs in AutoLISP. If you create too many of them, you'll end up draining AutoLISP's memory reserves. To limit the memory used by selection sets, you can turn them into *local variables*. Local variables are variables that exist only while the program is executing its instructions. Once the program is finished, local variables are discarded.

The vehicle for making variables local is the *argument list*. Let's look again at the set of empty parentheses that immediately follow the program name in the rec program:

```
(defun c:rec () ...)
```

If you include a list of variables between those parentheses, those variables become local. In the new r90 macro you just looked at, the ss1 selection-set variable is a local variable:

**WARNING**  The space after the / in the argument list is very important. Your macro won't work properly without it.

```
(defun c:r90 (/ ss1)...)
```

The argument list starts with a forward slash, then a space, followed by the list of variables. Once the r90 program is done with its work, any memory assigned to ss1 can be recovered.

Sometimes, you'll want a variable to be accessible at all times by all AutoLISP programs. Such variables are known as *global variables*. You can use global variables to store information in the current editing session. You could even store a few selection sets as global variables. To control memory consumption, however, use global variables sparingly.

# Controlling the Flow of an AutoLISP Program

A typical task for a program is to execute one function or another depending on an existing condition. This type of operation is often called an *if-then-else conditional statement:* "If a condition is met, then perform computation A, else perform computation B." AutoLISP offers the If function to facilitate this type of operation.

## Using the *If* Function

**TIP**  A common use for the if-then-else statement is to direct the flow of a program in response to a user's Yes or No reply to a prompt. If the user responds with a Yes to the prompt Do you want to continue?, for example, that response can be used in the if-then-else statement to direct the program to go ahead and perform some function, such as erasing objects or drawing a box.

The If function requires two arguments. The first argument must be a value that returns True or False—in the case of AutoLISP, *T* for true or *nil* for false. It's like saying "If True then do A." Optionally, you can supply a third argument, which is the action to take if the value returned is nil. ("If True then do A, else do B.")

Here is an example of an If expression:

```
(if Exst (+ a b) (* a b))
```

Here, the value of the Exst variable determines which of the two following expressions is evaluated. If Exst has a value, it returns T for true; that is, when AutoLISP evaluates Exst, the value returned is T. The expression then evaluates the second argument, (+ a b), which is itself an expression. If Exst doesn't have a value or is nil, the expression evaluates the third argument, (* a b).

Several special AutoLISP functions test variables for specific conditions. For example, you can test a number to see if it's equal to, less than, or greater than another number. In this expression, if A is equal to B, the second argument is evaluated:

```
(if (= A B) (+ A B) (* A B))
```

In this expression, if A is greater than B, the second argument is evaluated:

```
(if (> A B) (+ A B) (* A B))
```

The functions that test for T or nil are called *predicates* and *logical operators*. Table 25.3 shows a list of these functions.

**TABLE 25.3:** Predicates and Logical Operators

| FUNCTION | RETURNS T (TRUE) IF |
|----------|---------------------|
| < | One numeric value is less than another. |
| > | One numeric value is greater than another. |
| <= | One numeric value is less than or equal to another. |
| >= | One numeric value is greater than or equal to another. |
| = | Two numeric or string values are equal. |
| /= | Two numeric or string values aren't equal. |
| eq | Two values are exactly the same. |
| equal | Two values are the same (approximate). |
| atom | A symbol represents an atom (as opposed to a list). |
| listp | A symbol represents a list. |
| minusp | A numeric value is negative. |
| numberp | A symbol is a number, real or integer. |

**TABLE 25.3:** Predicates and Logical Operators (CONTINUED)

| FUNCTION | RETURNS T (TRUE) IF |
|---|---|
| zerop | A symbol evaluates to zero. |
| and | All of several expressions or atoms return non-nil. |
| not | A symbol is nil. |
| nul | A list is nil. |
| or | One of several expressions or atoms returns non-nil. |

Let's see how conditional statements, predicates, and logical operators work together. Suppose you want to write a program that either multiplies two numbers or adds the numbers together. You want the program to ask the user which action to take depending on which of the two values is greater. Follow these steps:

1. Enter the following program at the Command prompt, just as you did for the rec program:

```
(defun c:mul-add ()↵
(setq A (getreal "Enter first number:" ))↵
(setq B (getreal "Enter second number:" ))↵
(if (< A B) (+ a b) (* a b))↵
)↵
```

2. Run the program by entering **Mul-add**↵.

3. At the Enter first number: prompt, enter **3**↵.

4. At the Enter second number: prompt, enter **4**↵. The value 7.0 is returned.

5. Run the program again, but this time enter **4** at the first prompt and **3** at the second prompt. This time, you get the returned value 12.0.

In this program, the first two Setq expressions get two numbers from you. The conditional statement that follows, (< A B), tests to see if the first number you entered is less than the second. If this predicate function returns T for true, (+ a b) is evaluated. If it returns nil for false, (* a b) is evaluated.

You'll often find that you need to perform not just one but several steps, depending on some condition. Here is a more complex If expression that evaluates several expressions at once:

```
(if (= A B) (progn (* A B)(+ A B)(- A B) ))
```

In this example, the function Progn tells the If function that several expressions are to be evaluated if (= A B) returns True.

## Repeating an Expression

Sometimes, you'll want your program to repeatedly evaluate a set of expressions until a particular condition is met. If you're familiar with BASIC or Fortran, you know this function as a *loop*.

You can repeat steps in an AutoLISP program by using the `While` function in conjunction with predicates and logical operators. Like the `If` function, `While`'s first argument must be one that returns a T or nil. You can have as many other arguments to the `While` function as you like, as long as the first argument is a predicate function:

```
(while test (expression 1) (expression 2) (expression 3)...)
```

The `While` function isn't the only one that will repeat a set of instructions. The `Repeat` function causes a set of instructions to be executed several times; but unlike `While`, `Repeat` requires an integer value for its first argument, as in the following:

```
(Repeat 14 (expression 1) (expression 2) (expression 3)...)
```

In this example, `Repeat` will evaluate each expression 14 times.

A third function, `Foreach`, evaluates an expression for each element of a list. The arguments to `Foreach` are first a variable, then a list whose elements are to be evaluated, and then the expression used to evaluate each element of the list:

```
(foreach var1 ( list1 ) (expression var1))
```

`Foreach` is a bit more difficult to understand at first, because it involves a variable, a list, and an expression, all working together.

## Using Other Built-in Functions

**TIP**   In many of the examples in this section, you'll see numeric values or lists as arguments. As in all AutoLISP functions, you can use variables as arguments, as long as the variable's value is of the proper data type.

At this point, you've seen several useful programs created with just a handful of AutoLISP functions. Although I can't give a tutorial showing you how to use every available AutoLISP function, in this final section I'll demonstrate a few more. This is far from a complete list, but it should be enough to get you well on your way to making AutoLISP work for you. Experiment with the functions at your leisure—but remember, using AutoLISP can be addicting!

### GEOMETRIC OPERATIONS

These functions are useful for manipulating geometric data. (And don't forget the `Get` functions listed earlier, in Table 25.2.)

**TIP**   In some examples, an apostrophe (`'`) precedes a list. This apostrophe tells AutoLISP not to evaluate the list, but to treat it as a repository of data.

**Angle**   Finds the angle between two points, and returns a value in radians. For example,

```
(angle '(6.0 4.0 0.0) '(6.0 5.0 0.0))
```

returns 1.57. This example uses two coordinate lists for arguments, but point variables can also be used.

**Distance**   Finds the distance between two points. The value returned is in base units. Just like `Angle`, `Distance` requires two coordinates as arguments. This expression

```
(distance '(6.0 4.0 0.0) '(6.0 5.0 0.0))
```

returns 1.0.

**Polar**   Returns a point in the form of a coordinate list based on the location of a point, an angle, and a distance. This expression

```
(polar '(1.0 1.0 0.0) 1.5708 1.0)
```

returns (0.999996 2.0 0.0). The first argument is a coordinate list; the second is an angle in radians; and the third is a distance in base units. The point must be a coordinate list.

**Inters**   Returns the intersection point of two vectors, with each vector described by two points. The points must be in this order: the first two points define the first vector, and the second two points define the second vector. This expression

```
(inters
'(1.0 4.0 0.0)'(8.0 4.0 0.0)'(5.0 2.0 0.0)'(5.0 9.0 0.0)
)
```

returns (5.0 4.0 0.0). If the intersection point doesn't lie between either of the two vectors, you can still obtain a point, provided you include a non-nil fifth argument.

### STRING OPERATIONS

These functions allow you to manipulate strings. Although you can't supply strings for the text input of the text command, you can use the Command function with string variables to enter text, as in the following:

```
(Setq note "Hello World")
 (command "text" (getpoint) "2.0" "0" note)
```

In this example, note is first assigned a string value. Then, the Command function is used to issue the Text command and place the text in the drawing. Notice the (getpoint) function, which is included to obtain a point location.

Two other string functions, Substr and Strcat, let you manipulate text.

**Substr**   Returns a portion of a string, called a *substring*, beginning at a specified location. This expression

```
(substr "string" 3 4)
```

returns *ring*. The first argument is the string containing the substring to be extracted. The second argument, 3, tells Substr where to begin the new string; this value must be an integer. The third argument, 4, is optional and tells Substr how long the new string should be. The length must also be an integer.

**Strcat**   Combines several strings, and the result is a string. This expression

```
(strcat string1  string2  etc. )
```

returns *string1 string2 etc.* In this example, the

```
etc.
```

indicates you can have as many string values as you want.

# Data-Type Conversions

**TIP**   The Angtos and Rtos functions are especially useful for converting radians to any of the standard angle formats available in AutoCAD. For example, using Angtos, you can convert 0.785398 radians to 45d0´ 0˝, or N 45d0´0˝ E. Using Rtos, you can convert the distance value of 42 to 42.00 or 3´-6˝ (three feet six inches). Be aware that Angtos and Rtos also convert numeric data into strings.

While using AutoLISP, you'll often have to convert values from one data type to another. For example, because most angles in AutoLISP must be represented in radians, you must convert them to degrees before you can use them in commands. You can do so using the Angtos function. Angtos converts a real number representing an angle in radians into a string in the degree format you desire. The following example converts an angle of 1.57 radians into surveyor's units with a precision of four decimal places:

```
(angtos 1.57 4 4)
```

This expression returns N 0d2´44˝ E. The first argument is the angle in radians; the second argument is a code that tells AutoLISP which format to convert the angle to; and the third argument tells AutoLISP the degree of precision desired. (The third argument is optional.) The conversion codes for Angtos are as follows:

0 = Degrees

1 = Degrees/minutes/seconds

2 = Grads

3 = Radians

4 = Surveyor's units

Now that you've seen an example of what the Angtos data-type conversion can do, let's briefly look at similar functions:

**Atof and Atoi**   Atof converts a string to a real number. This expression

```
(atof "33.334")
```

returns 33.334.

Atoi converts a string to an integer. This expression

```
(atoi "33.334")
```

returns 33.

**Itoa and Rtos**   Itoa converts an integer to a string. The argument must be an integer. This expression

```
(itoa 24)
```

returns 24.

Rtos converts a real number to a string. As with Angtos, a format code and precision value are specified. This expression

```
(rtos 32.3 4 2)
```

returns "2´-8 ¼ \""

**NOTE**  You may notice the \ just after the ¼ in the returned value. This is an AutoLISP symbol indicating that the following "symbol is part of the string text and not the closing "that indicates the end of the string.

The first argument is the value to be converted, the second argument is the conversion code, and the third argument is the precision value. The codes are as follows:

1 = Scientific

2 = Decimal

3 = Engineering

4 = Architectural

5 = Fractional

**Fix and Float**  Fix converts a real number into an integer. This expression

```
(fix 3.3334)
```

returns 3.

Float converts an integer into a real number. This expression

```
(float 3)
```

returns 3.0.

## Storing Your Programs as Files

When you exit AutoCAD, the rec program will vanish. But just as you were able to save keyboard shortcuts in Chapter 24, you can create a text file on a disk containing the rec program. That way, you'll have ready access to it at all times.

To save your programs, open a text editor and enter them through the keyboard just as you entered the rec program, including the first line that contains the defun function. Be sure you save the file with the .lsp filename extension. You can recall your program by choosing Tools ➤ Load Applications, which opens the Load/Unload Applications dialog box.

If you prefer, you can use the manual method for loading AutoLISP programs. This involves the Load AutoLISP function. Just as with all other functions, it's enclosed by parentheses. In Chapter 24, you loaded the GETAREA.LSP file using the Load/Unload Applications dialog box. To use the Load function, instead, to load GETAREA.LSP, enter the following:

```
(Load "getarea")
```

Load is one of the simpler AutoLISP functions, becuaseit requires only one argument: the name of the AutoLISP file you want to load. Notice that you don't have to include the .lsp extension.

If the AutoLISP file resides in a folder that isn't in the current path, you need to include the path in the filename, as in the following example:

```
(Load "C:/AutoCAD2008/Projects/Chapter 24 /getarea")
```

The / is used to indicate folders instead of the usual Windows \. The forward slash is used because the backslash has special meaning to AutoLISP in a string value: It tells AutoLISP that a special character follows. If you attempted to use \ in the previous example, you'd get an error message.

As you may guess, the Load function can be a part of an AutoLISP program. It can also be included as part of a menu to load specific programs whenever you select a menu item. You'll learn more about customizing the menu in the next chapter.

## Getting More Help with AutoLISP

I hope you'll be enticed into trying some programming on your own and learning more about AutoLISP. You can find a wealth of information in the AutoCAD Help window:

1.  Choose Help ➢ Additional Resources ➢ Developer Help. The AutoCAD 2008 Developer Help window opens.

2.  In the panel on the left, expand the AutoLISP reference listing. You see an alphabetic listing of the AutoLISP functions, some of which were discussed in this chapter.

As you work with AutoLISP material in the AutoCAD Help window, you'll also see references to Visual LISP. This is a self-contained programming environment for AutoLISP. similar to the Visual Basic editor. Visual LISP is an excellent tool if you intend to make extensive use of AutoLISP in your work. Once you understand the basics of AutoLISP, you may want to explore Visual LISP through the tutorial in the AutoCAD Help system. You can find the Visual LISP tutorial by choosing Help ➢ Additional Resources ➢ Developer Help. In the AutoCAD 2008 Help: Developer Documentation window, look under the AutoLISP Tutorial section.

## The Bottom Line

**Understanding the Interpreter**   One of the simplest ways to start using AutoLISP is to enter an AutoLISP expression directly into the command line.

> **Master It**   Give an example of an AutoLISP formula that performs a simple math function.
>
> **Solution**   (+ 2 2).

**Using Arguments and Functions**   AutoLISP needs two elements, an argument and an expression, to do any work.

> **Master It**   Which is the function in the following AutoLISP expression?
>
> (+ 45 33)
>
> **Solution**   +.

**Creating a Simple Program**   You can input a simple program directly into AutoCAD by entering it through the command line.

> **Master It**   Name a function that pauses an AutoLISP program for user input.
>
> **Solution**   Getpoint or any of the Get functions.

**Selecting Objects with AutoLISP**    AutoLISP offers an expression that lets you select objects and then perform some operation on the set of objects.

**Master It**    What function lets you select objects, and what AutoLISP feature do you use to store your selection?

**Solution**    Ssget, variable.

**Controlling the Flow of an AutoLISP Program**    You can set up an AutoLISP program to test for conditions and perform different operations depending on the result.

**Master It**    Name some functions that test for a condition.

**Solution**    If, While, Foreach.

**Data-Type Conversions**    The functions in AutoLISP are designed to work with their own types of data. For example, math functions only work with numbers, and string operations only work with text. If you need to use the result of a math function in text, you can convert the number into text.

**Master It**    What is the name of the function that converts an angle in radians to text?

**Solution**    Angtos.

**Storing Your Programs as Files**    You can save your AutoLISP program in a text editor like Windows Notepad and then later have AutoCAD retrieve your program for use any time.

**Master It**    What is the filename extension for AutoLISP programs?

**Solution**    .LSP.

# Chapter 26

# Customizing Toolbars, Menus, Linetypes, and Hatch Patterns

AutoCAD offers a high degree of flexibility and customization, enabling you to tailor the software's look and feel to your requirements. In this chapter, you'll see how to customize AutoCAD so that it integrates more smoothly into your workgroup and office environment.

The first part of the chapter shows how to adapt AutoCAD to fit your particular needs. You'll learn how to customize AutoCAD by modifying its menus, and you'll learn how to create custom macros for commands that your workgroup uses frequently.

You'll then look at some general issues that arise when you use AutoCAD in an office. In this discussion, you may find help with problems you've encountered when using AutoCAD in your particular work environment. I'll also discuss how to manage AutoCAD projects.

Topics in this chapter include the following:

◆ Using Workspaces

◆ Customizing the User Interface

◆ Creating Macros in Tools and Menus

◆ Pausing for User Input

◆ Opening an Expanded Text Box for the Macro Option

◆ Editing Keyboard Shortcuts

◆ Saving, Loading, and Unloading Your Customizations

◆ Understanding the Diesel Macro Language

◆ Creating Custom Linetypes

◆ Creating Hatch Patterns

## Using Workspaces

Once you're comfortable with AutoCAD, you may find that you like a certain arrangement of toolbars and palettes or that you have several sets of toolbars that you like to use depending on your type of work. You've already worked with the two workspaces AutoCAD offers out of the box: 3D Modeling and AutoCAD Classic. You can also set up your own custom toolbar arrangements and then save those arrangements for later retrieval using the Workspace feature. Let's take a closer look at how you can customize this feature.

The Workspaces toolbar is shown in Figure 26.1. AutoCAD users see the Workspaces toolbar in its docked position in the upper-left corner of the AutoCAD Window, and LT users see the floating version. In Chapter 1, you saw how you can use this toolbar to save your AutoCAD Window layout. You can save multiple arrangements of toolbars and palettes and then recall them easily by selecting them from the Workspaces toolbar drop-down menu.

**FIGURE 26.1**

The Workspaces toolbar

My Workspace

Workspace Settings

Workspaces and Options drop-down list

**TIP** If you don't have your Workspaces toolbar open already, right-click any toolbar, and then select Workspaces from the shortcut menu.

Click the Workspace Settings tool on the Workspaces toolbar to open the Workspace Settings dialog box, as shown in Figure 26.2.

**FIGURE 26.2**

The Workspace Settings dialog box

Let's take a moment to look at this dialog box in detail. In Chapter 1, you created a workspace called My Custom Layout by using the Save Current As option in the Workspaces toolbar drop-down list.

With the Workspace Settings dialog box open, you can see the AutoCAD Classic, 3D Modeling, and the My Custom Layout settings. From here, you can control the behavior of the settings.

The check box next to each setting lets you control whether the item appears in the drop-down list on the Workspaces toolbar. For example, if you remove the check from the My Custom Layout setting, you'll only see 3D Modeling and AutoCAD Classic in the drop-down list on the Workspaces toolbar.

The My Workspace = drop-down list lets you select which workspace setting is activated when you click the My Workspace tool on the Workspaces toolbar. You can use this option for your most frequently used workspace settings.

The options in the When Switching Workspaces group at the bottom of the Workspace Settings dialog box let you determine whether workspace changes are saved automatically. For example, if you select Automatically Save Workspace Changes, then the next time you switch to a different workspace setting, AutoCAD will save any changes you've made to the current workspace.

The Workspaces toolbar is the easiest customization feature you'll find in AutoCAD, and it can go a long way toward helping you stay organized. But workspaces are just the tip of the iceberg when it comes to customizing AutoCAD. In the next section, you'll delve into the *Custom User Interface* (CUI) feature to see how you can customize the AutoCAD menus and toolbars directly.

# Customizing the User Interface

Out of the box, AutoCAD offers a generic arrangement of toolbars, tools, and palettes that works fine for most applications. But the more you use AutoCAD, the more you may find that you tend to use tools that are scattered over several toolbars. You'll probably feel that your work would go more easily if you could create a custom set of toolbars and menus to consolidate those tools. If you're to the point of creating custom macros, you may want a way to have easy access to them.

The Customize User Interface (CUI) is a one-stop location that gives you nearly total control over the menus and toolbars in AutoCAD. With the CUI feature, you can mold the AutoCAD interface to your liking. The main entry point to the CUI is the Customize User Interface dialog box.

The following section introduces you to the CUI by showing you how to add a tool to the Draw toolbar. You'll also get a chance to see how to create an entirely new toolbar and custom tools.

## Taking a Quick Customization Tour

The most direct way to adapt AutoCAD to your way of working is to customize the toolbars. AutoCAD offers new users an easy route to customization through the Custom User Interface dialog box. With this dialog box, you can create new toolbars, customize tools, and even create new icons. You can also create keyboard shortcuts.

To get your feet wet, try adding a tool to the Draw toolbar:

1. If it's still open, close the Workspace Settings dialog box.

2. Right-click in any of the control panels in the dashboard, and then select Customize Commands toward the bottom of the shortcut menu to open the Customize User Interface dialog box, as shown in Figure 26.3. You see five groups in this dialog box: Customizations In All CUI Files, Command List, Preview, and Properties.

3. In the Customizations In All CUI Files group, expand the Dashboard Panels list, and then select 2D Draw. A view of the 2D Draw control panel appears in the Preview group. A Button Image group appears, displaying the icon for the 2D Draw control panel along with thumbnail samples of other icons. This is where you can customize the icon for the control panel.

4. Expand the 2D Draw list, and you see three more items labeled Row 1, Row 2 and <PANEL SEPARATOR>. The give you access to the two rows of tools in the 2D Draw control panel.

5. Expand the Row 1 list. You see a list of the tools that appear in the top row of the 2D Draw control panel.

6. In the Command List group, scroll down the list, and locate and select Dimension, Linear. This is the Linear Dimension command. When you select Linear, the Properties group displays the properties of the Linear command. The Preview group changes to show the Button Image group, and you see the Linear Dimension icon, as shown in Figure 26.4.

7. Click and drag the Dimension, Linear item in the Command List group into the Customizations In All CUI files group, but don't release the mouse button yet. As you drag the item over the tool names in the Customizations In All CUI Files group, a bar tells you where your dragged item will appear. The list may scroll up or down depending on where you place the bar. This is to allow you to place the bar in an area of the list that isn't currently displayed.

**FIGURE 26.3**

The Customize User Interface dialog box

**FIGURE 26.4**

The Button Image and Preview groups change when you select an element from the Command List group or the Customizations In All CUI Files group.

**8.** Place the bar just below Line, and release the mouse button. Dimension, Linear appears below Line in the list.

**9.** Click OK. You'll see some disk activity, and in a moment the Dimension, Linear tool appears in the 2D Draw control panel just to the right of the Line tool.

You've just added a command to the 2D Draw control panel. You can follow these steps to add any command to any control panel, toolbar, or menu-bar menu.

Now, suppose you've changed you mind, and you decide to remove Dimension, Linear from the Draw toolbar. Here's how it's done:

**1.** Right-click the 2D Draw control panel, and choose Customize Commands from the shortcut menu.

**2.** In the Customizations In All CUI Files group of the Customize User Interface dialog box, expand the Dashboard Panels list, and continue to expand the list as you did before to get to the Dimension, Linear command you added earlier.

**3.** Right-click Dimension, Linear, and choose Remove from the shortcut menu. The Dimension, Linear command is removed from the list.

**4.** Click OK to close the dialog box.

Dimension, Linear has been removed from the 2D Draw control panel. As you've just seen, adding tools to a toolbar is a matter of clicking and dragging the appropriate item from one list to another. To remove tools, right-click the toolbar, and select Remove.

Before you go too much further, you may want to know a little more about the Customize User Interface dialog box and how it works. You saw briefly how each group displayed different elements of AutoCAD's interface from a listing of toolbar tools to the individual tool's icon. Let's look at each group independently to see how it's organized.

## Getting the Overall View

When you first opened the Customize User Interface dialog box by right-clicking the dashboard, you saw a listing of the AutoCAD interface elements in the Customizations In All CUI Files group. Each interface element in the list can be expanded to get to the individual commands for the element. If you expand the Toolbar list, for example, all the AutoCAD toolbars are available. Expand a toolbar, and the commands contained in the toolbar are displayed. As you saw earlier, you can expand the Dashboard Panel list to gain access to the dashboard control panels. Table 26.1 lists all the interface elements in the Customizations In All CUI Files group with a brief explanation of their contents.

**TABLE 26.1:** Main Headings in the Customizations In All CUI Files Group

| ITEM | WHAT IT CONTAINS |
| --- | --- |
| Workspaces | Workspaces that are currently available |
| Toolbars | Current toolbars |
| Menus | Current menu-bar menus |
| Dashboard Panels | Current dashboard control panels |
| Shortcut Menus | Menus shown with right-clicks |
| Keyboard Shortcuts | Current keyboard shortcuts, such as Ctrl+C and Ctrl+V |
| Double-Click Actions | Object-dependent double-click actions |
| Mouse Buttons | Mouse button options, such as Shift+click and Ctrl+click |
| LISP Files | Any custom LISP files that are used with your CUI |
| Legacy | Any legacy custom items you use, such as table or screen menus |
| Partial CUI Files | Custom CUI files that have been included in the main CUI file |

You can customize any of the interface elements. For example, if you want to create new keyboard shortcuts, you can expand the Keyboard Shortcuts listing and add new shortcuts or edit existing ones. Right-click any item to add or delete options. If you click an item, its properties appear in the Properties group, where you can modify the item's function. Just as you added the Dimension, Linear dimension command to the Draw toolbar, you can click and drag a command into one of the menus under the Menus listing to add a command there.

You also see some options in the Customizations In All CUI Files title bar. These options give you control over what is displayed in this group. You can also load and save CUI files from here.

My Load Partial Customization File

Save All Current Customization files

You'll learn more about these options later in this chapter.

## Finding Commands in the Command List

You've already seen how the Command List group contains all the commands in AutoCAD. You also saw that you can click and drag these items into options in the Customizations In All CUI Files group. This list also contains predefined macros, icons used for toolbars, and *Control Elements*, which are the drop-down lists you see in toolbars. The Layer drop-down list in the Layer toolbar is an example of a Control Element. The drop-down lists in the Properties and Styles toolbars are also examples of Control Elements. When you select an item in the Command List group, you see either its properties in the Properties group or its icon in the Button Image group, or both. The exception to this is the Control Elements, which have no editable features.

## Preview/Button Image/Shortcuts

If you click a dashboard control panel, toolbar, or toolbar tool in the Customizations In All CUI Files group, you see the Preview or Button Image group. Toolbars display the Preview group, which shows you how the selected dashboard or toolbar will appear. Previews aren't editable and are there for your reference

If you click a tool listing, or *element* as it's called in AutoCAD nomenclature, in the Customizations In All CUI Files group, you see the Button Image group. This group lets you select an icon for that tool by clicking a list of icons (see Figure 26.5), or you can edit an existing icon or create an entirely new icon. You'll get a chance to see this firsthand later in this chapter.

**FIGURE 26.5**
The Button
Image group

The Keyboard Shortcuts area in the Customizations In All CUI Files group shows the Shortcuts group, which lists the existing keyboard shortcuts.

## Getting to the Core of Customization in the Properties Group

Finally, when you're ready to do some serious customizing, you'll work with the Properties group. You see the Properties group in the lower half of the right side of the Customize User Interface dialog box when you select a command from the left side of the dialog box.

The Properties group is set up just like the Properties palette, and it works the same way. On the left side, you see a listing of options, and to the right of each option is a description or a text input box where you can make changes (see Figure 26.6).

If you go to the Customizations In All CUI Files group and select the Line tool under Draw Toolbar, you see the properties for that tool in the Properties group, as shown in Figure 26.6. You'll have to close the Button Image group to get a complete view of the Properties group. You can close any group by clicking the double arrow on the right side of the group's title bar.

**FIGURE 26.6**

The Properties group showing the properties for the Line tool

In the General category, you see the Line tool's name. You also see the description that is displayed in the status bar whenever you display its ToolTip. You can change this description here in the Properties group, and the description will change in the status bar.

In the Macro category, you see the command as it would be entered through the keyboard. The ^C^C that precedes the actual line command input is equivalent to pressing the Escape key twice. The Advanced category offers information regarding the ID of this particular tool. Finally, the Images category lists the name of the image files used for the Line tool icon. Two icons are listed: one for the large icon version and one for the small icon version of the tool.

You'll get a chance to work with the Properties group later in this chapter. Next, you'll try your hand at creating your own custom toolbar.

## Creating Your Own Toolbars and Menus

Earlier, I mentioned that you can collect your most frequently used tools into a custom control panel or toolbar. Now that you've gotten a chance to become familiar with the Customize User Interface dialog box, you can try the following exercise to create your own control panel:

1. If the Customize User Interface dialog box isn't open, right-click the Dashboard, and choose Customize Commands.

2. In the Customizations In All CUI Files group, right-click Dashboard Panel, and choose New Panel. The list expands, and you see a new panel called Panel1 at the bottom of the Dashboard Panel list.

3. Replace Panel1 by typing **My Panel** to give your panel a distinct name. As you type, the name changes. If you decide to change a panel name later, right-click a panel listing, and then choose Rename

**TIP**   You can create custom menus in the same way you create custom panels. The only difference is that you right-click Menus in step 1. Once you do that, you can perform the same operations described in the rest of this section to add commands to your custom menu.

You now have a custom toolbar. You'll want to start to populate your toolbar with some commands. You've already seen how this works, but for review, try adding a few commands:

1. In the Command List group, locate the Line tool.

2. Click and drag the Line command to your new panel so that you see an arrow pointing to the My Panel item.

3. Release the mouse button. The Line tool appears below My Toolbar.

4. Repeat steps 2 and 3 to add more commands to your panel.

Now, add an icon for the panel:

1. Click the My Panel listing to select the panel name.

2. Click any icon in the Button Image group. The icon appears in the Panel Preview, showing you how your panel will look.

3. Click OK to close the Customize User Interface dialog box. AutoCAD works for a moment and then displays the default workspace. In addition, your new custom panel appears.

**TIP** You can delete any tool from your custom panel by right-clicking the tool and choosing Remove while in the Customizations In All CUI Files group of the Customize User Interface dialog box. You can also delete your entire panel using this method. Take care not to delete any of the existing panels you want to keep.

## Customizing Control Panel Tools

Let's move on to more serious customization. Suppose you want to create an entirely new button with its own functions. For example, you might want to create a set of buttons that insert your favorite symbols. Or you might want to create a control panel containing a set of tools that open some of the other toolbars that are normally put away.

### CREATING A CUSTOM TOOL

Follow these steps to create a custom tool:

1. Open the Customize User Interface dialog box, expand the Dashboard Panel list, and then expand the My Panel list.

2. In the Command List panel title bar, click the Create A New Command button. A new command called Command1 appears at the top of the list of commands.

**3.** Click the Command1 item, and change the name to **Door**.

**4.** In the Properties group to the right, change Description to **Insert a 36″ door**.

**5.** Change the Macro option to the following:

```
^C^C-insert door;\36;;
```

**6.** Click and drag the Door element from the Command List into your My Panel item in the Customizations In All CUI Files group. If you look at the Panel Preview group, you see that the Door tool you just added shows a question mark. This question mark appears when no icon has been assigned to the tool.

**7.** Click OK to close the Customize User Interface dialog box. Your custom tool is added to your custom panel. It appears as a blank, however, because you haven't yet assigned an icon to the tool.

The series of keystrokes you entered for the macro in step 5 are the same as those you would use to insert the door, with the addition of a few special characters. The minus in front of the Insert command tells AutoCAD to bypass the Insert dialog box and use the command-line version of Insert. The semicolons are equivalent to a ↵, and the backward slash (\) is a special macro code that tells AutoCAD to pause the macro for user input. In this case, the pause allows you to select the insertion point for the door. The Properties group should look like Figure 26.7.

**FIGURE 26.7**
The Properties group for your new custom tool that inserts a door block

Next, try the custom tool to make sure it works:

**1.** Point to the custom tool. You see the Door ToolTip.

**2.** Click the Door tool. The door appears in the drawing area at the cursor. It may appear very small because it's being inserted at its default size of 1 unit.

**WARNING** The Door drawing must be in the default folder or in the Acad search path before the Door will be inserted. For easy access, copy the Door.dwg file from the Chapter 4 projects folder to the My Documents folder.

**3.** Click a location to place the door, and then click a point to set the door rotation. The door appears in the drawing.

In this example, you created a custom tool that inserts the door block. Later in this chapter, you'll learn more about creating macros for menus and tools. Next, you'll learn how to add a custom icon to your custom tool.

### CREATING A CUSTOM ICON

You have all the essential parts of the button defined. Now, you just need to create a custom icon to go with your Door button:

1. Open the Customize User Interface dialog box.

2. Expand the Dashboard Panel and My Panel lists.

3. Expand the Row1 list, and select Door.

4. Click any icon image in the Button Image group. The icon appears in the Panel Preview group, replacing the question mark for your Door tool.

5. In the Button Image group, click the Edit button to open the Button Editor dialog box. The Button Editor is like a simple drawing program. Across the top are the tools to draw lines, circles, and points, as well as an eraser. Along the right side is a color toolbar from which you can choose colors for your icon. At upper left, you see a preview of your button.

**TIP**   If you prefer, you can use any of the predefined icons in the scroll box to the right of the Button Image group in the Customize User Interface dialog box. Click the icon you want to use, and then click Apply.

6. Before you do anything else, click the Clear button, and then click the Save As button.

7. In the Create File dialog box, enter **Door** for the name, and click Save. You now have a blank custom icon in the form of a file called `Door.bmp`.

8. Draw the door icon shown here. Don't worry if it's not perfect; you can always go back and fix it.

9. Click Save, and then click Close.

10. In the Button Image group, scroll the image panel down to the bottom, and then locate and select the door icon you just created.

11. Click OK to close the Customize User Interface dialog box. You see your custom icon for the Door tool.

The Button Editor behaves like a simplified image editing tool and is fairly straightforward to use. The only part that may be confusing is that you have to clear the image and save any new image under a new name.

You can continue to add more buttons to build a panel of symbols. Of course, you're not limited to a symbols library. You can also incorporate your favorite macros or even AutoLISP routines that you accumulate as you work with AutoCAD. The possibilities are endless.

## Creating Macros in Tools and Menus

Combining existing commands into new toolbars can be useful, but you'll get even more benefit from the CUI by creating your own macros. *Macros* are predefined sets of responses to commands that can help automate your most frequently used processes.

Early on, you saw how a macro was included in a tool to insert a door. You added a special set of instructions in the Macro option of the Properties group to perform the door insertion and scale. You also saw how the Line command was formatted as part of a tool.

Let's take a closer look at how macros are built. Start by looking at the existing Line tool and how it's formatted.

The Macro option for the Line tool starts with two ^C elements, which are equivalent to pressing the Escape key twice. This cancels any command that is currently operative. The Line command follows, written just as it would be entered through the keyboard. Two Cancels are issued in case you're in a command that has two levels, such as the Edit Vertex option of the Pedit command (Modify ➤ Object ➤ Polyline).

The underscore character (_) that precedes the Line command tells AutoCAD that you're using the English-language version of this command. This feature lets you program non-English versions of AutoCAD by using the English-language command names.

You may also notice that there is no space between the second ^C and the Line command. A space in the line would be the same as ↵. If there were a space between these two elements, ↵ would be entered between the last ^C and the Line command, causing the command sequence to misstep. Another way to indicate ↵ is by using the semicolon, as in the following example:

```
^C^C_LINE;;
```

**TIP**   If a menu macro contains multiple instances of ↵, using semicolons instead of spaces can help make your macro more readable.

In this sample menu option, the Line command is issued, and then an additional ↵ is added. The effect of choosing this option is a line that continues from the last line entered into your drawing. The two semicolons following Line tell AutoCAD to start the Line command and then issue ↵ twice; the first ↵ starts the Line command, and then the second ↵ tells AutoCAD to begin a line from the endpoint of the last line entered. (AutoCAD automatically issues a single ↵ at the end of a menu line. In this case, however, you want two instances of ↵, so they must be represented as semicolons.)

## Pausing for User Input

Another symbol used in the macro option is the backslash (\); it's used when a pause is required for user input. For example, the following sample macro starts the Arc command and then pauses for your input:

```
^C^C_arc \_e \_d
```

The space between `^c^c_arc` and the backslash (\) represents pressing the spacebar. The backslash indicates a pause to enable you to select the starting endpoint for the arc. After you've picked a point, the _e represents the selection of the Endpoint option under the Arc command. A second backslash allows another point selection. Finally, the _d represents the selection of the Direction option. Figure 26.8 illustrates this. If you want the last character in a menu item to be a backslash, you must follow the backslash with a semicolon.

**FIGURE 26.8**

The execution of the Arc menu item

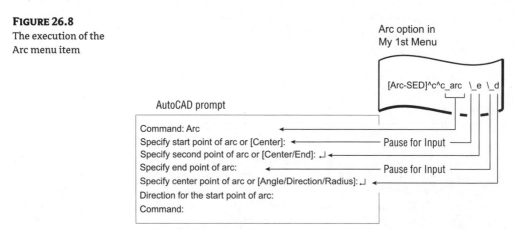

## Opening an Expanded Text Box for the Macro Option

As you become more expert at creating macros, you may find the line provided in the Macro option too small for your needs. Fortunately, you can open an expanded text box in which to write longer macros. For example, suppose you want to include the following macro in a tool:

```
(defun c:breakat ()
(command "break" pause "f" pause "@")
)
breakat
```

This example shows the Breakat AutoLISP macro. Everything in this segment is entered just as it would be from the keyboard at the Command prompt. You may find it a bit cumbersome to try to enter this macro in the text box provided by the Macro option in the Properties group of the Customize User Interface dialog box, but if you click the Macro text box, a Browse button appears to the right.

Click the Browse button to open the Long String Editor.

You can then enter the macro and see it clearly. The following shows how it would be entered:

```
^c^c(defun c:breakat ()+
(command "break" pause "f" pause "@")+
);breakat
```

It starts with the usual ^c^c to clear any current commands. The plus sign at the end of lines 1 and 2 tells AutoCAD that the macro continues in the next line without actually breaking it. The break is there to help make the macro easier to read as you enter it.

**TIP** It's okay to break an AutoLISP program into smaller lines. Doing so can help you read and understand the program more easily. LT doesn't support AutoLISP.

---

**LOADING AUTOLISP MACROS**

As you become a more advanced AutoCAD user, you may want many of your own AutoLISP macros to load with your custom interface. You can do so by combining all your AutoLISP macros into a single file. Give this file the same name as your menu file but with the .mnl filename extension. Such a file automatically loads with its menu counterpart. For example, say you have a file called Mymenu.mnl containing the Breakat AutoLISP macro. Whenever you load Mymenu.cui, Mymenu.mnl is automatically loaded along with it, giving you access to the Breakat macro. This is a good way to manage and organize any AutoLISP program code you want to include with a menu.

---

## Editing Keyboard Shortcuts

Another area of customization that can be useful is the keyboard shortcut. You probably already know about the standard Ctrl+C and Ctrl+V, which are shortcuts to the Windows Copy and Paste functions. In AutoCAD, Shift+Ctrl+A toggles groups on and off, and Ctrl+1 opens the Properties palette.

You can edit existing keyboard shortcuts or create new ones by opening the Keyboard Shortcuts list in the Customizations In All CUI Files group of the Customize User Interface dialog box. If you expand this list, you see Shortcut Keys and Temporary Override keys. These can be expanded to reveal their elements. Select an element to display its properties in the Properties group.

You can click and drag a command from the Command List group into the Shortcut Keys group and then edit its properties to set the shortcut keys you want to use for the command. For example, if you click and drag the 3D Orbit command from the Command list into the Shortcut Keys list and then select it from that list, you see its properties in the Properties group.

Click the Key(s) option in the Properties group and then click the Browse button that appears to the far right of the Keys option to open the Shortcut Keys dialog box.

Click in the Press New Shortcut Key input box, and then press the shortcut key you want to use for this command. For example, if you press Shift+Ctrl+Z, that sequence appears in the input box. If the shortcut you selected is already assigned to another command, you see a message that says so just below the input box. Click OK when you're done.

## Saving, Loading, and Unloading Your Customizations

You may want to save the custom menus and toolbars you create with the Customize User Interface dialog box so that you can carry them with you to other computers and load them for ready access. To save your customization work, you need to use the Transfer tab of the Customize User Interface dialog box. Here's how it works.

1. Open the Customize User Interface dialog box.

2. Click the Transfer tab. This tab contains two panels: The left panel shows the Customizations In Main CUI group, and the right panel shows a similar group called Customizations In New CUI File.

3. In the left panel, locate your custom component, such as a menu or a toolbar.

4. Click and drag it to the appropriate item in the right panel. In other words, click and drag a custom toolbar from the Dashboard Panel list of the left group to the Dashboard Panel section in the right group.

5. Repeat step 4 for each custom component you've created.

6. When you've copied everything from the left group to the right, click the drop-down list in the Customizations In New CUI File title bar, and select Save As.

**7.** In the Save As dialog box, enter a name for your customization file, and select a location.

**8.** Click Save to complete the process.

Your customization is saved as a `.cui` file. Once it's saved as a file, you can load it into another copy of AutoCAD by doing the following:

**1.** Open the Customize User Interface dialog box.

**2.** Click the Load Partial Customization File tool in the Customizations In All CUI Files group title bar.

**3.** In the Open dialog box, locate and select your `.cui` file, and then click Open.

**4.** Back in the Customize User Interface dialog box, click OK.

**5.** If your `.cui` file contains menus, enter **Workspace.⤶⤶⤶** at the Command prompt. Or, if you have the Workspaces toolbar open, select a workspace from the Workspace drop-down list. If it contains toolbars, right-click in a blank area next to an existing docked toolbar, and then select the name of your CUI file and the toolbar.

As an alternative to using the Customize User Interface dialog box, you can use the CUIload command. Enter **Cuiload.⤶** at the Command prompt to open the Load/Unload Customizations dialog box.

Click the Browse button to locate and select your CUI file. Once you've done this, the name of your file appears in the File Name input box. You can then click the Load button to import it into your AutoCAD session.

Finally, if you want to unload a CUI file, do the following:

**1.** Open the Customize User Interface dialog box.

**2.** Scroll down to the bottom of the list in the Customizations In All CUI Files group, and expand the Partial CUI Files item.

**3.** Right-click the partial CUI file you want to unload, and select Unload CUI File.

**4.** Close the dialog box by clicking OK.

## Understanding the Diesel Macro Language

If you browse through the `Acad.mnu` file, you'll see many menu options that contain odd-looking text beginning with a dollar sign ($). In some instances, the dollar sign tells AutoCAD to open a shortcut menu. But in many cases, it's used as part of the Diesel macro language. Diesel is one of many macro languages AutoCAD supports, and you can use it to perform simple operations. Like AutoLISP, Diesel uses parentheses to enclose program code.

In this section, you'll look at the different ways to use Diesel. You'll start by using Diesel directly from the command line. This will show you how a Diesel macro is formatted and will give you a chance to see Diesel in action. Then, you'll go on to see how Diesel can be used as part of a menu option to test AutoCAD's current state. In the third section, you'll see how Diesel can be used as part of the menu label to control what is shown in the menu. Finally, you'll learn how to use Diesel with Field objects to control text in your drawing.

## Using Diesel at the Command Line

You can use Diesel at the AutoCAD command line by using a command called Modemacro. The Modemacro command sends information to the status bar. Diesel can be used with Modemacro to perform simple tasks.

Try the following exercise to experiment with Diesel:

1. At the Command prompt, type **Modemacro**↵.

2. At the Enter new value for MODEMACRO, or . for none <" ">: prompt, enter **$(/,25,2)**↵. The answer to the equation appears at far left in the status bar.

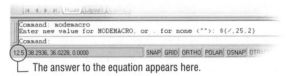

The answer to the equation appears here.

3. To clear the status bar, enter **Modemacro**↵.↵.

The equation you entered in step 2 is referred to as an *expression*. The structure of Diesel expressions is similar to that of AutoLISP. The dollar sign tells AutoCAD that the information that follows is a Diesel expression.

A Diesel expression must include an operator of some sort, followed by the items to be operated on. An *operator* is an instruction to take a specific action, such as adding two numbers or dividing one number by another. Examples of mathematical operators include the plus sign (+) for addition and the forward slash (/) for division.

The operator is often referred to as a *function* and the items to be operated on as the *arguments* to the function, or simply the arguments. In the expression (/,25,2), the / is the function, and 25 and 2 are the arguments. All Diesel expressions, no matter what size, follow this structure and are enclosed by parentheses.

Parentheses are important elements of an expression. All parentheses must be balanced; for each left parenthesis, there must be a right parenthesis.

You can do other things with Diesel besides performing calculations. The Getvar function is an AutoLISP function that you can use to obtain the drawing prefix and name. Try the following to see how Diesel uses Getvar:

1. Type **Modemacro**↵ again.

2. Type **$(getvar,dwgprefix)**↵. The location of the current drawing appears in the status bar.

3. Press ↵ to reissue the Modemacro command; then type **$(getvar,dwgname)**↵. The name of the drawing appears in the status bar.

In this example, the Getvar function extracts the drawing prefix and name and displays it in the status bar. You can use Getvar to extract any system variable you want. If you've been working through the tutorials in this book, you've seen that virtually all AutoCAD settings are also controlled through system variables. (The AutoCAD help window contains a list of all the system variables.) This can be a great tool when you're creating custom menus, because with Getvar, you can poll AutoCAD to determine its state. For example, you can find out what command is currently being used. Try the following exercise to see how this works:

1. Click the Line tool on the Draw toolbar.

2. Type ´**Modemacro**↵. The apostrophe at the beginning of Modemacro lets you use the command while in another command.

3. Type **$(getvar,cmdnames)**↵. The word *LINE* appears in the status bar, indicating that the current command is the Line command.

Diesel can be useful in a menu when you want an option to perform a specific task depending on which command is currently active.

**WARNING**   LT users can't use AutoLISP to find the location of AutoCAD resource files. However, you can use the Diesel macro language. For example, to find the log file path, enter **Modemacro** and then **$(getvar,logfilepath)**. The path is displayed at far left in the status bar.

## Using Diesel in a Custom Menu Macro

So far, you've been experimenting with Diesel through the Modemacro command. To use Diesel in a menu macro requires a slightly different format. You still use the same Diesel format of a dollar sign followed by the expression, but you don't use the Modemacro command to access Diesel. Instead, you use $M=. You can think of $M= as an abbreviation for Modemacro.

Here's a Diesel expression that you can use in a menu macro:

```
^C^C_Blipmode;$M=$(-,1,$(getvar,Blipmode))
```

This menu option turns Blipmode on or off depending on Blipmode's current state. As you may recall, Blipmode is a feature that displays point selections in the drawing area as tiny crosses. These tiny crosses, or *blips*, don't print and can be cleared from the screen with a redraw. They can be helpful when you need to track your point selections.

In this example, the Blipmode command is invoked, and then the $M= tells AutoCAD that a Diesel expression follows. The expression

```
$(-,1,$(getvar,Blipmode))
```

returns either 1 or a 0, which is applied to the Blipmode command to turn it either on or off. This expression shows that you can nest expressions. The most deeply nested expression is evaluated first, so AutoCAD evaluates

```
$(getvar,Blipmode)
```

to begin with. This returns either 1 or a 0, depending on whether Blipmode is on or off. Next, AutoCAD evaluates the next level in the expression

```
$(-,1,getvar_result)
```

in which *getvar_result* is either 1 or a 0. If *getvar_result* is 1, the expression looks like

```
$(-,1,1)
```

which returns 0. If *getvar_result* is 0, the expression looks like

```
$(-,1,0)
```

which returns 1. In either case, the end result is that the Blipmode command is assigned a value that is opposite of the current Blipmode setting.

## Using Diesel as a Menu Option Label

In the previous example, you saw how to use Diesel in a menu macro to read the status of a command and then return a numeric value to alter that status. You can also use Diesel as part of the menu option name so the text it displays depends on certain conditions. The following expression shows how to write a menu option name to display the current setting for Blipmode. It includes Diesel code as the menu option label:

```
$(eval,"Blipmode =" $(getvar,blipmode))
```

**TIP**   When Diesel is used as the menu name, you don't need the $M= code.

Normally, you would just have a menu name, but here you see some Diesel instructions. These instructions tell AutoCAD to display the message Blipmode = 1 or Blipmode = 0 in the menu, depending on the current Blipmode setting.

Here's how it works. You see the familiar $(getvar,blipmode) expression, this time embedded in a different expression. You know that $(getvar,blipmode) returns either 1 or a 0 depending on whether Blipmode is on or off. The outer expression

```
$(eval,"Blipmode =" getvar_result)
```

displays Blipmode = and then combines this with *getvar_result*, which, as you've learned, will be either 1 or 0. The eval function evaluates any text that follows it and returns its contents. The end result is the appearance of Blipmode = 1 or Blipmode = 0 in the menu, depending on the status of Blipmode. Here's how the option looks in a menu.

You can get even fancier by setting up the menu option label to read Blipmode On or Blipmode Off by using the if Diesel function. Here's that same menu listing with additional Diesel code to accomplish this:

```
$(eval,"Blipmode " $(if,$(getvar,blipmode),"Off","On"))
```

In this example, the simple $(getvar,blipmode) expression is expanded to include the if function. The if function reads the result of $(getvar,blipmode) and then returns the Off or On value depending on whether $(getvar,blipmode) returns 0 or a 1. Here's a simpler look at the expression:

```
$(if, getvar_result, "Off", "On")
```

If *getvar_result* returns 1, the if function returns the first of the two options listed after *getvar_result*, which is Off. If *getvar_result* returns 0, the if function returns On. The second of the two options is optional. Here's how the fancier Blipmode option appears in a menu.

You've just skimmed the surface of what Diesel can do. To get a more detailed description of how Diesel works, choose Help ➢ Help to open the AutoCAD 2008 Help dialog box. Click the Contents tab, expand the Customization Guide listing, and click the DIESEL listing that appears.

Table 26.2 shows some of the commonly used Diesel functions. Check the AutoCAD Help dialog box for a more detailed list.

**TABLE 26.2:** Sample of Diesel Functions. To Indicate True or False, Diesel Uses 1 or 0.

| CODE | FUNCTION | EXAMPLE | RESULT | COMMENTS |
|------|----------|---------|--------|----------|
| + | Add | $(+,202,144) | 346 | |
| − | Subtract | $(-,202,144) | 58 | |
| * | Multiply | $(*,202,144) | 29,088 | |
| / | Divide | $(/,202,144) | 1.4028 | |
| = | Equal to | $(=,202,144) | 0 | If numbers are equal, 1 is returned. |
| < | Less than | $(<,202,144) | 0 | If the first number is less than the second, 1 is returned. |
| > | Greater than | $(>,202,144) | 1 | If the first number is less than the second, 0 is returned. |
| ! | Not equal to | $(!,202,144) | 1 | If the numbers are equal, 0 is returned. |
| <= | Less than or equal to | $(+,202,144) | 0 | If the first number is less than or equal to second, 1 is returned. |
| >= | Greater than or equal to | $(+,202,144) | 1 | If the first number is less than or equal to the second, 0 is returned. |
| eq | Equal string | $(eq,"Yes", "No") | 0 | If both text strings are the same, 1 is returned. |
| eval | Evaluate text | $(eval,"Here I Am") | Here I Am | Returns the text in quotes. |
| getvar | Get system variable value | $(getvar,ltscale) | Current linetype scale | |
| if | If/Then | $(if,1,"Yes","No") | Yes | The second argument is returned if the first argument evaluates to 1. Otherwise, the third argument is returned. The third argument is optional. |

## Using Diesel and Fields to Generate Text

Using Diesel expressions in the status bar or in a menu can be helpful to gather information or to create a more interactive interface, but what if you want the results of a Diesel expression to become part of the drawing? You can employ field objects to do just that.

For example, suppose you want to create a note that shows the scale of the drawing based on the dimension scale. Further, you want the note to automatically update the scale whenever the dimension scale changes. You can add a field object and associate it with a Diesel expression that displays the dimension scale as it relates to the drawing scale. Try the following steps to see how it's done:

1. In the Draw toolbar, click the Multiline Text tool, and select two points to indicate the text location. The Text Formatting toolbar and Text Window appear.

2. Right-click in the Text Window, and select Insert Field to open the Field dialog box.

3. In the Field Category drop-down list, select Other; then, in the Field Names list box, select DieselExpression.

4. Add the following text in the Diesel Expression box to the right. If you need to expand the width of the dialog box, click and drag the right edge of the dialog box:

```
$(eval,"Dimension Scale: 1/")$(/,$(getvar, dimscale),12)$(eval," inch = 1 foot")
```

5. Click OK in the Field dialog box, and then click OK in the Text Formatting toolbar. The following text is displayed in the drawing:

```
Dimension Scale: 1/0.08333333 inch = 1 foot
```

The resulting text may not make sense until you change the dimension scale to a value that represents a scale other than 1-to-1. Here's how to do that:

1. Enter **Dimscale**⏎ at the Command prompt.

2. At the `Enter new value for DIMSCALE <1.0000>:` prompt, enter **96**. This is the value for a ⅛″ scale drawing.

3. Choose View ➤ Regen, or enter **Re**⏎. The text changes to read

```
Dimension Scale: 1/8 inch = 1 foot
```

In this example, several Diesel operations were used. The beginning of the expression uses the eval operation to tell AutoCAD to display a string of text:

```
$(eval "Dimension Scale: 1/")
```

The next part tells AutoCAD to get the current value of the Dimscale system variable and divide it by 12:

```
$(/,$(getvar, dimscale),12)
```

Notice that this is a nested expression: `$(getvar,dimscale)` obtains the value of the Dimscale system variable, which is then divided by 12. The end of the expression adds the final part to the text:

```
$(eval," inch = 1 foot")
```

When it's all put together, you get the text that shows the dimension scale as an architectural scale. Because it's an AutoCAD text object, this text is part of the drawing.

# Creating Custom Linetypes

As your drawing needs expand, the standard linetypes may not be adequate for your application. Fortunately, you can create your own. This section explains how to do so.

You'll get an in-depth view of the process of creating linetypes. You'll also learn how to create complex linetypes that can't be created by using the Express Make Linetype tool.

## Viewing Available Linetypes

Although AutoCAD provides the linetypes most commonly used in drafting (see Figure 26.9), the dashes and dots may not be spaced the way you would like, or you may want an entirely new linetype.

**FIGURE 26.9**

The lines in this list of standard linetypes were generated with the underscore key (_) and the period (.) and are only rough representations of the actual lines.

**TIP** AutoCAD stores the linetypes in a file called Acad.lin, which is in ASCII format. When you create a new linetype, you add information to this file. Or, if you create a new file containing your own linetype definitions, it too will have the extension .lin. You can edit linetypes as described here, or you can edit them directly in these files.

To create a custom linetype, use the Linetype command. Let's see how this handy command works, by first listing the available linetypes:

1. Open a new AutoCAD file.

2. At the Command prompt, enter **–Linetype**↵. (Don't forget the minus sign at the beginning.)

3. At the `Enter an option [?/Create/Load/Set]:` prompt, enter **?**↵.

4. In the dialog box, locate and double-click `Acad.lin` in the listing of available linetype files. You get a list which shows the linetypes available in the `Acad.lin` file along with a simple description of each line.

5. A message at the bottom says *Press ENTER to continue:*. Do so until you see the command prompt.

## Creating a New Linetype

Next, let's try creating a new linetype:

1. At the `?/Create/Load/Set:` prompt, enter **C**↵.

2. At the `Enter name of linetype to create:` prompt, enter **Custom**↵ as the name of your new linetype.

3. The dialog box you see next is named Create Or Append Linetype File. You need to enter the name of the linetype file you want to create or add to. If you select the default linetype file, Acad, your new linetype is added to the `Acad.lin` file. If you choose to create a new linetype file, AutoCAD opens a file containing the linetype you create and adds `.lin` to the filename you supply.

4. Let's assume you want to start a new linetype file. Enter **Newline**↵ in the File Name input box.

**TIP**   If you accept the default linetype file, Acad, the prompt in step 5 is `Wait, checking if linetype already defined....` This protects you from inadvertently overwriting an existing linetype you want to keep.

5. At the `Descriptive text:` prompt, enter a text description of your linetype. You can use any keyboard character as part of your description, but the actual linetype can be composed of only a series of lines, points, and blank spaces. For this exercise, enter

   ```
   Custom - My own center line _____ _ _____  ↵
   ```

   using the underscore key (_) to simulate the appearance of your line.

6. At the `Enter linetype pattern (on next line):` prompt, enter the following numbers, known as the *linetype code* (after the A that appears automatically):

   ```
   1.0,-.125,.25,-.125↵
   ```

**WARNING**   If you use the Set option of the –Linetype command to set a new default linetype, you'll get that linetype no matter what layer you're on.

7. At the New linetype definition saved to file. Enter an option [?/Create/Load/ Set]: prompt, press ↵ to exit the –Linetype command.

Remember, after you've created a linetype, you must load it in order to use it, as discussed in Chapter 4.

**TIP** You can also open the Acad.lin or other .lin file in Windows Notepad and add the descriptive text and linetype code directly to the end of the file.

## Understanding the Linetype Code

In step 6 of the previous exercise, you entered a series of numbers separated by commas. This is the linetype code, representing the lengths of the components that make up the linetype. The separate elements of the linetype code are as follows:

◆ The 1.0 following the A is the length of the first part of the line. (The A that begins the linetype definition is a code that is applied to all linetypes.)

◆ The first –.125 is the blank or broken part of the line. The minus sign tells AutoCAD that the line is *not* to be drawn for the specified length, which is 0.125 units in this example.

◆ Next comes the positive value 0.25. This tells AutoCAD to draw a line segment 0.25 units long after the blank part of the line.

◆ The last negative value, –.125, again tells AutoCAD to skip drawing the line for the distance of 0.125 units.

This series of numbers represents the one segment that is repeated to form the line (see Figure 26.10). You can also create a complex linetype that looks like a random broken line, as in Figure 26.11.

**FIGURE 26.10**
Linetype description with plotted line

**FIGURE 26.11**
Random broken line

You may be wondering what purpose the A serves at the beginning of the linetype code. A linetype is composed of a series of line segments and points. The A, which is supplied by AutoCAD automatically, is a code that forces the linetype to start and end on a line segment rather than on a blank space in the series of lines. At times, AutoCAD stretches the last line segment to force this condition, as shown in Figure 26.12.

**FIGURE 26.12**
AutoCAD stretches the beginning and the end of the line as necessary.

| Stretched | | Stretched |

**TIP** The values you enter for the line-segment lengths are multiplied by the Ltscale factor; so be sure to enter values for the plotted lengths.

As mentioned in the beginning of this section, you can also create linetypes outside AutoCAD by using a word processor or text editor such as Windows Notepad. The standard Acad.lin file contains addition of the code used by AutoCAD to determine the line-segment lengths.

Normally, to use a linetype you've created, you have to load it through either the Layer or the Linetype dialog box (choose Format ➢ Layers or Format ➢ Linetype). If you use one of your own linetypes frequently, you may want to create a button macro so it will be available as an option on a menu.

## Creating Complex Linetypes

A *complex linetype* is one that incorporates text or special graphics. For example, if you want to show an underground gas line in a site plan, you normally show a line with the intermittent word *GAS*, as in Figure 26.13. Fences are often shown with an intermittent circle, square, or *X*.

**FIGURE 26.13**

Samples of complex linetypes

For the graphics needed to compose complex linetypes, use any of the symbols in the AutoCAD font files discussed in Chapter 10. Create a text style by using these symbol fonts, and then specify the appropriate symbol by using its corresponding letter in the linetype description.

To create a linetype that includes text, use the same linetype code described earlier, with the addition of the necessary font file information in brackets. For example, say you want to create the linetype for the underground gas line mentioned previously by using just the letter *G*. You add the following to your Acad.lin file:

```
*Gas_line, -- G -- G -- G --
A,1.0,-0.25, ["G",STANDARD,S=.2,R=0,X=-.1,Y=-.1], -0.25
```

The first line serves as a description for anyone looking at this linetype code. The next line is the code itself. Note that the code should not contain spaces—spaces are used here for clarity.

The information in the square brackets describes the characteristics of the text. The actual text that you want to appear in the line is surrounded by quotation marks. Next are the text style, scale, rotation angle, X displacement, and Y displacement.

**WARNING**   You can't use the –Linetype command to define complex linetypes. Instead, you must open the Acad.lin file by using a text editor, such as Windows Notepad, and add the linetype information to the end of the file. Make sure you don't duplicate the name of an existing linetype.

You can substitute A for the rotation angle (the R value), as in the following example:

```
a,1.0,-0.25, ["G", standard, S=.2 A=0, X=-.1, Y=-.1], -0.25
```

This has the effect of keeping the text at the same angle, regardless of the line's direction. Notice that in this sample, the X and Y values are -.1; this will center the Gs on the line. The scale value of .2 will cause the text to be 0.2 units high, so –.1 is half the height.

In addition to fonts, you can also specify shapes for linetype definitions. Instead of letters, shapes display symbols. Shapes are stored not as drawings, but as definition files, similar to text-font files. Shape files have the same .shx filename extension as font files and are also defined similarly. Figure 26.14 shows some symbols from sample shape files. The names of the files are shown at the top of each column.

**FIGURE 26.14**

Samples of shapes

| ST.SHX | ES.SHX | PC.SHX | LTYPESHP.SHX |
|--------|--------|--------|--------------|
| opt-x | con1 | dip14 | track1 |
| obl-x | cap | dip18 | |
| pro-x | pnp | | |
| opt-m | mark | dip24 | box |
| bol-m | jump | | bat |
| pro-m | zener | dip8 | zig |
| opt-c | nor | dip16 | circ1 |
| obl-c | and | dip20 | |
| pro-c | buffer | | |
| opt-r | | | |
| obl-r | box | | |
| pro-r | | | |
| opt-p | res | dip40 | |
| obl-p | diode | | |
| pro-p | npn | | |
| opt-perp | arrow | | |
| obl-perp | con2 | | |
| pro-perp | or | | |
| opt-parallel | xor | | |
| obl-parallel | nand | | |
| pro-parallel | inverter | | |
| | neg | | |
| | feedthru | | |

To use a shape in a linetype code, you use the same format as shown previously for text. However, instead of using a letter and style name, you use the shape name and the shape filename, as in the following example:

```
*Capline, ====
a,1.0,-0.25,[CAP,ES.SHX,S=.5,R=0,X=-.1,Y=-.1],-0.25
```

This example uses the CAP symbol from the Es.shx shape file. The symbol is scaled to 0.5 units with 0 rotation and an X and Y displacement of –0.1.

Here is another example that uses the arrow shape:

```
*Arrowline, --|---|---|
a,1.0,-0.25,[ARROW,ES.SHX,S=.5,R=90,X=-.1,Y=-.1],-0.25
```

Just as with the Capline example, the ARROW symbol in this example is scaled to 0.5 units with 0 rotation and an X and Y displacement of –0.1. Here's what the Arrowline linetype looks like when used with a spline.

In this example, the Ltype generation option is turned on for the polyline. Note that the arrow from the `Es.shx` sample shape file is used for the arrow in this linetype.

## Creating Hatch Patterns

AutoCAD provides several predefined hatch patterns you can choose from, but you can also create your own. This section demonstrates the basic elements of pattern definition.

Unlike linetypes, hatch patterns can't be created while you're in an AutoCAD file. The pattern definitions are contained in an external file named `Acad.pat`. You can open and edit this file with a text editor that can handle ASCII files, such as Windows Notepad. Here is one hatch pattern definition from that file:

```
*square,Small aligned squares
0, 0,0, 0,.125, .125,-.125
90, 0,0, 0,.125, .125,-.125
```

You can see some similarities between pattern descriptions and linetype descriptions. They both start with a line of descriptive text and then give numeric values defining the pattern. However, the numbers in pattern descriptions have a different meaning. This example shows two lines of information. Each line represents a line in the pattern. The first line determines the horizontal line component of the pattern, and the second line represents the vertical component (see the image to the far right in Figure 26.15) A pattern is made up of line groups. A *line group* is like a linetype that is arrayed a specified distance to fill the area to be hatched. A line group is defined by a line of code, much as a linetype is defined. In the square pattern, for instance, two lines—one horizontal and one vertical—are used. Each of these lines is duplicated in a fashion that makes the lines appear as boxes when they're combined. Figure 26.15 illustrates this point.

Look at the first line in the definition:

```
0, 0,0, 0,.125, .125,-.125
```

**FIGURE 26.15**
The individual and combined line groups

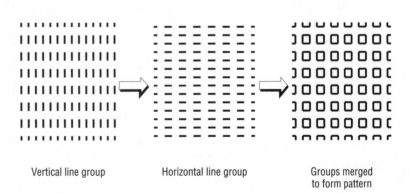

Vertical line group      Horizontal line group      Groups merged to form pattern

This example shows a series of numbers separated by commas; it represents one line group. It contains four sets of information, separated by blank spaces:

◆ The first component is the 0 at the beginning. This value indicates the angle of the line group, as determined by the line's orientation. In this case, it's 0 for a horizontal line that runs from left to right.

◆ The next component is the origin of the line group, 0,0. This doesn't mean the line begins at the drawing origin (see Figure 26.16). It gives you a reference point to determine the location of other line groups involved in generating the pattern.

**FIGURE 26.16**
The origin of the patterns

Polyline defining hatch area
Hatch pattern

Light pattern shows how the hatch relates to the drawing origin.
Origin of drawing (0,0)

**TIP** If you've forgotten the numeric values for the various directions, refer to Chapter 2, which explains AutoCAD's system for specifying angles.

◆ The next component is 0,.125. This determines the distance and direction for arraying the line, as illustrated in Figure 26.17. This value is like a relative coordinate indicating X and Y distances for a rectangular array. It isn't based on the drawing coordinates, but on a coordinate system relative to the orientation of the line. For a line oriented at a 0° angle, the code 0,.125 indicates a precisely vertical direction. For a line oriented at a 45° angle, the code 0,.125 represents a 135° direction. In this example, the duplication occurs 90° in relation to the line group, because the X value is 0. Figure 26.18 illustrates this point.

**FIGURE 26.17**
The distance and direction of duplication

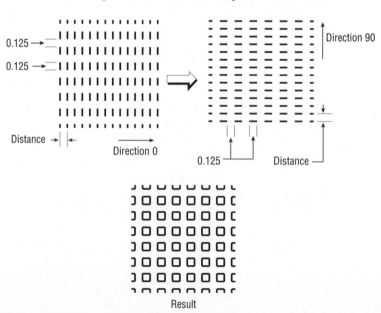

0.125 →
0.125 →

Distance →| |←
Direction 0

Direction 90

0.125
Distance

Result

**FIGURE 26.18**
How the direction of
the line group copy is
determined

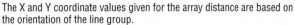

The X and Y coordinate values given for the array distance are based on
the orientation of the line group.

♦ The last component is the description of the line pattern. This value is equivalent to the value given when you create a linetype. Positive values are line segments, and negative values are blank segments. This part of the line-group definition works exactly as in the linetype definitions you studied in the previous section.

This system of defining hatch patterns may seem somewhat limiting, but you can do a lot with it. Autodesk managed to come up with 69 patterns—and that was only scratching the surface.

**TIP**    If you want to include thick lines in your hatch patterns, you have to build up line widths with multiple linetype definitions.

## The Bottom Line

**Using Workspaces**    Often with AutoCAD, you find that you have different sets of toolbars open to perform specific tasks. You might have one set of toolbars for editing text and dimensions, whereas another set is more useful for design. Workspaces are a great way to organize your different editing modes.

   **Master It**    Where do you find the Customize option for workspaces?

   **Solution**    The Workspace drop-down menu.

**Customizing the User Interface**    In addition to using workspaces to organize toolbars and control panels, you can also customize the AutoCAD interface to make it fit the way you like to work. You can add tools to control panels or even create your own tools for operations you perform frequently.

   **Master It**    What does the Customizations In All CUI Files group display?

   **Solution**    Interface elements like toolbars, menus, dashboards, and so on.

**Creating Macros in Tools and Menus**    A macro is a set of instructions that performs more complex operations than single commands. Macros are often built on commands with additional predefined responses to help speed data input.

   **Master It**    What does the ^C do in a macro?

   **Solution**    The ^C is equivalent to pressing the Escape key.

**Editing Keyboard Shortcuts**   Keyboard shortcuts can help improve your speed when drawing in AutoCAD. They can reduce several clicks of the mouse to a simple keystroke. AutoCAD lets you create custom shortcuts for your favorite commands.

**Master It**   What is the keyboard shortcut for Copy?

**Solution**   Ctrl+C.

**Saving, Loading, and Unloading Your Customizations**   To keep your customization organized, you can save new toolbars, menus, and dashboards as files that you can load on demand. When you save your custom elements as a file, you can move them to other computers.

**Master It**   Name the tab that contains the group you use to save your custom elements.

**Solution**   Transfer tab.

**Understanding the Diesel Macro Language**   If you're adventurous, you may want to try your hand at creating more complex macros. The Diesel macro language is an easy introduction to AutoCAD macro customization and is most useful in controlling the behavior in menu options.

**Master It**   What does the expression $(getvar, blipmode) do?

**Solution**   It returns 1 or a 0 depending on the current state of the Blipmode command.

**Creating Custom Linetypes**   AutoCAD offers a number of noncontinuous linetypes, and you may find them adequate for most of your work. But now and then, you may need a specific linetype that isn't available. Creating custom linetypes is easy once you understand the process.

**Master It**   What is the purpose of a negative value in the linetype code?

**Solution**   A blank or break in the line.

**Creating Hatch Patterns**   Like linetypes, the hatch patterns provided by AutoCAD will probably fill most of your needs. But now and then, you may need to produce a specific pattern.

**Master It**   How are a hatch pattern code and a linetype code similar?

**Solution**   They both use numeric values to describe lines.

# Chapter 27

# Managing and Sharing Your Drawings

Whether you're a one-person operation working out of your home or one of several hundred AutoCAD users in a large company, file sharing and file maintenance can become the focus of much of your time. In our interconnected world, the volume of messages and files crossing our paths seems to be constantly on the rise. In addition, the Internet has enabled us to be more mobile, adding complexity to file-management tasks.

In this chapter, you'll learn about some of the tools AutoCAD offers to help you manage your files and the files you share with others. You'll also examine some general issues that arise while using AutoCAD in a workgroup environment. In this discussion, you may find help with problems you've encountered when using AutoCAD in your particular work environment.

Topics in this chapter include the following:

◆ Sharing Drawings over the Internet

◆ ePublishing Your Drawings

◆ Managing Your Drawings with DesignCenter and the Tool Palettes

◆ Establishing Office Standards

◆ Converting Multiple Layer Settings

## Sharing Drawings over the Internet

The Internet has become a major part of our daily working lives. And the Internet provides AutoCAD users some real, practical benefits through its ability to publish drawings and other documents online. AutoCAD gives you tools that enable you to post drawings on the Internet that others can view and download. In the architecture, engineering, and civil (AEC) industry in particular, this can mean easier access to documents needed by contractors, engineers, cost estimators, and others involved in the design, bidding, and construction of architectural projects. Suppliers of products can post symbol libraries of their products or even 3D solid models.

In this section, you'll learn about the tools AutoCAD provides for publishing and accessing drawings over the Internet (and on any local or wide area network). You'll start by looking at one of the most common uses of the Internet: file transmission.

### Sharing Project Files with eTransmit

Perhaps the most common use of the Internet is sending and receiving files. Whether you're a one-person office or a member of a 50-person firm, you'll eventually have to share your work with others outside your building. Before eTransmit existed as a feature in AutoCAD, you had to carefully examine what you were sending to make sure you included all the ancillary files needed to view or work on your drawings. Xref, font, and custom linetype files all had to be carefully included with the drawings you sent to consultants or partners in a project, and often something was missed.

By using eTransmit, you can quickly collect all your project drawings into a single archive file, or you can store the files in a separate folder for later processing. This collection of files is included with a report file as a transmittal. Try the following to see how eTransmit works:

1. In AutoCAD, open a file you intend to send to someone; then, choose File ➢ eTransmit to open the Create Transmittal dialog box. In the dialog box, a tree structure lists the files that are included in the transmittal. If you need to add more files to the transmittal than are shown in the list, you can click the Add File button to open a file dialog box. To remove files, expand the listed item and remove the check mark that appears next to the file you want to exclude. You can also use the Files Table tab to view the files as a simple list.

**WARNING**    If you edited the file before choosing File ➢ eTransmit, you see a message telling you that you must save the drawing before continuing.

2. Click in the Enter Notes To Include With This Transmittal Package input box, and enter a description or other note.

3. In the Select A Transmittal Setup group, click the Transmittal Setups button to open the Transmittal Setups dialog box. From here, you can create a new transmittal or rename or modify an existing one.

**4.** Click the Modify button to open the Modify Transmittal Setup dialog box.

**5.** In the Transmittal Package Type drop-down list, select the format for your collection of files. You can create a Zip or self-extracting executable archive, or you can save the files in a folder. If you choose the Zip or executable option, you can also add a password by selecting the Prompt For Password check box near the bottom of the dialog box. The person receiving the transmittal file must then enter a password to extract the files. If you choose the Folder option, you can tell AutoCAD where to place the files by using the Browse button. For this exercise, choose the Folder option in the Transmittal Package Type list.

**6.** Click the Browse button to open the Specify Location Folder dialog box. This is a typical AutoCAD file dialog box that you can use to select a location for your files. You can use the Create New Folder tool to create a new folder for your files. You'll want to keep your transmittal files in a separate location from other files. After you select a location, you return to the Modify Transmittal Setup dialog box.

**7.** After you've set up your transmittal, click OK. Then, click Close in the Transmittal Setups dialog box.

**8.** Preview the report file by clicking the View Report button in the Create Transmittal dialog box. This report gives you a detailed description of the types of files included in the transmittal. It also alerts you to files that AutoCAD was unable to find but that are required for the drawing.

**9.** After you've set up the eTransmit options, click OK in the Create Transmittal dialog box.

**10.** If you selected the Zip option in step 5, you see the Specify Zip File dialog box. Enter a name and a location for the file, and AutoCAD collects the files into an archive folder or a Zip file. You can then send the files over the Internet or put them on a removable disk for manual transport.

You probably noticed that you have an option to create additional transmittal setup options in the Transmittal Setups dialog box. That way, you can have multiple transmittal options on hand that you don't have to set up each time a different situation arises. For example, you might have the Standard setup configured to create a Zip file and another setup configured to copy the files into a folder. A third setup might be created with a password.

Several options are available for configuring the transmittal setup. Table 27.1 gives a rundown of those options:

**TABLE 27.1:** Modify Transmittal Setup dialog box options.

| OPTION | PURPOSE |
| --- | --- |
| Transmittal package type | Lets you select Folder, Zip, or Executable Zip file. |
| File Format | Lets you select 2007, existing file format, or AutoCAD 2004 and AutoCAD 2000 file formats in case your recipient requires an earlier version. |
| Transmittal file folder | Lets you determine the location for your transmittal package. |
| Transmittal File Name | Not available if you select Folder as the transmittal package type. Options are Prompt For A File Name, Overwrite If Necessary, and Increment File Name If Necessary. |
| Use Organized Folder Structure | Preserves the folder structure for the files in the transmittal. This can be important when Xref and other files are located across several folder locations. |
| Place All Files In One Folder | Self-explanatory. |
| Keep Files And Folders As Is | Preserves the entire folder structure for the files in the transmittal. |
| Include Fonts | Tells AutoCAD to include the font files in the transmittal. |
| Include Textures from Materials | Lets you include bitmap files that are part of a file's material settings. |
| Include Files From Data Links | Lets you include external data-link files for tables. |
| Include Photometric Web Files | Lets you include photometric web files for 3D lighting models. |
| Send E-Mail With Transmittal | Lets you send an e-mail transmittal with the files included as an attachment. |
| Set Default Plotter To 'None' | Removes any reference to printers or plotters that you've set up for the drawing. (The type of printer you've set up for your files is stored with the drawing file.) |
| Bind External References | Lets you bind external references to the drawings that contain them if it isn't important for the recipient to maintain the external references as separate drawings. |
| Prompt For Password | Gives you the option to password-protect the transmittal file |
| Transmittal Setup Description | Lets you include a brief description of the current transmittal setup. |

eTransmit gives you a quick way to package a set of files to be sent to others working on the same project. But you may need to offer a wider distribution of your files. You might want to let others view and plot your drawings from a website without exposing your drawing database to anyone who might visit your site. If this sounds like something you're interested in, you'll want to know about the AutoCAD DWF file format, which lets anyone view AutoCAD files whether they own the program or not. You'll learn more about the DWF file format in the "ePublishing Your Drawings" section, later in this chapter.

## Protecting AutoCAD Drawing Files

Because AutoCAD drawings specify the methods and materials used to produce an object or a building, the drawings are often treated like legal documents. After an AutoCAD drawing is issued, it's often archived and guarded as a legal record of a design. For this reason, many AutoCAD users are concerned about possible tampering with drawings that are sent to third parties. Even minor, unauthorized changes to a drawing can have major repercussions to the integrity of a design.

AutoCAD 2008 offers tools that can help minimize file tampering. The eTransmit feature offers a password-protection option to reduce the possibility of unauthorized tampering with transmittal files. AutoCAD also offers password protection for individual files as well as a digital-signature feature that helps protect both the author of a drawing and the recipient in the event of file tampering.

### ADDING PASSWORD PROTECTION TO FILES

The basic type of file protection is the password protection of individual files. AutoCAD offers password protection through the Save Drawing As dialog box and the Options dialog box.

To add a password to a drawing when you save it, do the following:

1. Choose File ➢ Save As to open the Save Drawing As dialog box.

2. Choose Tools ➢ Security Options from the menu in the upper-right corner of the dialog box.

3. In the Security Options dialog box, enter a password or phrase in the input box.

4. Click OK. You're prompted to enter the password again.

5. Enter the password again, and click OK to return to the Save Drawing As dialog box.

6. Enter the name and location of your file, and then click Save.

In addition to the Save Drawing As dialog box, you can also add password protection through the Options dialog box:

1. Choose Tools ➢ Options to open the Options dialog box, and then click the Open And Save tab.

2. Click the Security Options button in the File Safety Precautions group to open the Security Options dialog box.

3. Enter your password, select other options as necessary, and then click OK.

As a third option, you can enter **Securityoptions**⏎ at the Command prompt to go directly to the Security Options dialog box.

After you've added a password, anyone attempting to open the file will be asked to provide the password before the file can be opened. This includes any attempt to use the file as an Xref or a file insertion.

**TIP** After you open a password-protected file and give the password, you can open and close the file repeatedly during that AutoCAD session without having to reenter the password. If you close and reopen AutoCAD, AutoCAD will prompt you for a password the next time you attempt to open the password-protected file.

### USING A DIGITAL SIGNATURE

In addition to password protection, you can use a digital signature to authenticate files. A digital signature can't prevent someone from tampering with a file, but it offers a way to validate whether a file has been modified after it has been saved. This protects you in the event that your file is unofficially altered. It also protects the recipient of your file by verifying the file's authenticity and by verifying that it was not altered from the time it left your computer.

The first time you attempt to use the digital signature feature, you see a message telling you that you need a digital ID.

As the message explains, a digital ID is required to use the digital signature feature. AutoCAD uses a digital ID issued by any certificate authority, such as VeriSign, a company that specializes in Internet security. The VeriSign ID is fee based, with prices ranging from about $15 for a basic one-year enrollment to nearly $700 for a professional-level ID. A free 60-day trial is also offered.

The following steps show how to acquire a digital ID:

1. Connect to the Internet. During the process, you'll log on to the VeriSign website.

2. From the Windows Taskbar, choose Start ➤ Programs ➤ Autodesk ➤ AutoCAD 2008 ➤ Attach Digital Signatures. Or, from AutoCAD, open the Security Options dialog box and click the Digital Signature tab. The Valid Digital ID Not Available warning dialog box appears.

3. Click the Get A Digital ID button. Your web browser opens at the VeriSign page.

4. Select the security services you want, and follow the rest of the instructions.

After you've obtained a digital ID, the signature resides in the Registry on your computer. You can then access the digital ID from AutoCAD by using the Digital Signature tab of the Security Options dialog box. Here are the steps:

1. Open the drawing to which you want to attach the digital signature, and then open the Security Options dialog box by entering **Securityoptions**↵ at the Command prompt.

**2.** Click the Digital Signature tab.

**3.** Select the Attach Digital Signature After Saving Drawing option. The Signature Information options become available. You can add a date stamp and a brief description.

**4.** Click OK to exit the dialog box.

The next time you save the file, depending on the level of security you choose during the digital ID setup, you may be prompted for a password. After you enter the password, the file is saved.

The next time the file is opened, you'll see the Digital Signature Contents dialog box, which verifies that the drawing hasn't been tampered with.

You'll also see a stamp icon in the lower-right corner of the AutoCAD Window. You can click this icon at any time to view the file's digital signature status. You can also issue the Sigvalidate command to view the status. If the file is modified in any way and then saved, a warning message will appear at the top of the Validate Digital Signatures dialog box the next time the file is opened.

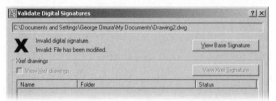

A file containing a digital signature also displays a warning when it's being modified, stating that saving a new version will invalidate the digital signature.

If you need to update a drawing that contains your digital signature, you can do so and then use the Security Options dialog box to reissue the digital signature.

### ADDING YOUR DIGITAL SIGNATURE TO MULTIPLE FILES

If you have multiple files to which you'd like to attach your digital signature, you should use the Attach Digital Signatures utility. This program runs outside AutoCAD, and it provides a convenient way to attach your digital signature to a set of drawings. Here's how it works:

1. From the Windows Taskbar, choose Start ➢ Programs ➢ Autodesk ➢ AutoCAD 2008 ➢ Attach Digital Signatures to open the Attach Digital Signatures dialog box.

**WARNING** If you haven't obtained a digital ID, you see a message telling you that no valid digital IDs are installed on your system. To proceed, you'll have to obtain a digital ID from a certificate authority such as VeriSign, as described earlier in "Using a Digital Signature."

2. Click the Add Files button to locate and select files. You can also search for files in a particular folder by clicking the Search Folders button. The files you add appear in the Files To Be Signed list box.

3. If you decide to remove a file from the list box, highlight it and then click Remove. You can also remove all the files from the list by clicking Clear List.

4. The rest of the dialog box is the same as the Digital Signature tab of the Security Options dialog box. You can enter the date and time and a comment for the files you've selected.

5. Click Sign Files when you're sure you've selected the correct files and entered an appropriate comment.

If you exchange AutoCAD drawings regularly with clients and consultants, you'll want to obtain a digital ID and use AutoCAD's digital signature feature. Be aware, however, that because this feature was new in AutoCAD 2004, it works only if you exchange files with others using AutoCAD 2004 or later. In fact, a quick way to remove a digital signature from a file is to save the file in the AutoCAD 2002 or earlier file format.

**WARNING**    If you intend to use the password feature in conjunction with your digital signature, you must add the signature first before adding the password.

## ePublishing Your Drawings

The features discussed so far are intended mostly for exchanging files with others who need to work directly with your AutoCAD files. But there are always associates and clients who need to see only your final drawings and don't care whether they get AutoCAD files. Or you might be working with people who don't have AutoCAD but still need to view and print your drawings. For those non-AutoCAD end-users, AutoCAD offers the DWF file format.

You can think of the DWF file format as a kind of Adobe Acrobat file for AutoCAD drawings. DWF offers a way to get your plans and design ideas in the hands of more people more easily. With the help of the free Autodesk DWF Viewer—equivalent to the Adobe Viewer for Acrobat documents—DWF files can be viewed using the same types of pan and zoom tools available in AutoCAD, thereby enabling greater detail to be presented in your drawings. In addition, you can embed URL links that can open other documents with a single mouse click. These links can be attached to objects or areas in the drawing.

You can also print DWF files by using your Windows system printer or plotter, all without having AutoCAD installed. A single DWF file can contain multiple drawing sheets, so you can combine a complete set of drawings into one DWF file.

### Exchanging Drawing Sets

Imagine that you're working on a skylight addition to a house and you need to send your drawings to your client for review. In addition to the skylight plans, you want to include some alternate floor plans that your client has asked you to generate. In this exercise, you'll put together a set of drawings that will become a single DWF file that you'll send as an e-mail attachment to your client:

1. Open the Sample house.dwg file. The file has several layout tabs, each representing a separate drawing sheet.

2. Choose File ➢ Publish to open the Publish dialog box. The dialog box lists all the layouts in its main list box, including Model, which is equivalent to the Model Space tab. (See

Chapter 8 for more on layouts.) LT users won't see the Plotter Named In Page Setup option at the bottom of the dialog box.

3. In the list box, Ctrl+click Sample House-Model, Sample House-Foundation Details, and Sample House-Skylite Details to select them. You don't want to include these layouts in your DWF file.

4. Right-click and choose Remove, or click the Remove Sheets button just below the list of sheets. The items you selected are removed from the list.

At this point, you could go ahead and create a DWF file; but suppose you want to include layouts from a file that isn't currently open. The following steps show you how to accomplish this:

1. Right-click and choose Add Sheets, or click the Add Sheets button to open the Select Drawings dialog box.

2. Locate and select the `sample house alt.dwg` file. You see two new items, Sample House Alt-Model and Sample House Alt-Alternate Plan, in the list box. These are the layout tabs that are in the `sample house alt.dwg` file.

**TIP** In this last step, the Model tab was imported. You can prevent Model tabs from being included in the Sheets To Publish list by turning off the Model Tab option. This option is located in the Include When Adding Sheets group in the lower-right corner of the dialog box.

All the sheets your client needs are listed in the list box. You're ready to create the DWF file:

1. Save the current list in case you want to reproduce it later. Click the Save Sheet List button. The Save List As dialog box appears, which is a standard file dialog box.

2. Select a location and name for the sheet list, and click Save.

3. Back in the Publish dialog box, in the Publish To group at lower left, make sure the DWF File radio button is selected.

4. Click the Publish button. The Select DWF File dialog box appears. This is a standard file dialog box in which you can find a location for your DWF file and also name it. Select a name and location for the DWF file. By default, AutoCAD uses the same name as the current file and the folder location of the current file. You can also set up a default location in the Publish Setup dialog box.

5. Click Select. AutoCAD displays the Processing Background Job message box and spends some time "printing" the selected layouts to a DWF file. The publishing occurs in the background, but you can tell whether it's taking place by the plotter icon in the far right of the AutoCAD status bar.

6. When AutoCAD is finished, you see the Plot And Publish Complete message bubble in the lower-right corner of the AutoCAD Window, indicating that you can view details of the publishing process.

7. Click the link in the bubble that says Click To View Plot And Publish Details. The Plot And Publish Details dialog box appears, offering detailed information about the sheets you published. You can then click the Copy To Clipboard button to export the list to a file as a record. If you want to recall this dialog box later, you can do so by choosing File ➢ View Plot And Publish Details.

You may notice that when you click the Publish button in the previous exercise, AutoCAD behaves as if it's printing the layouts in your list—and that is exactly what it's doing. AutoCAD uses its own DWF printer driver to "print" your drawings to a DWF file. AutoCAD uses the layout settings from the Plot dialog box for each layout to produce the DWF pages.

## Other Publish Options

A few more options are available when you use the Publish feature. Let's take a moment to review some of the options in the Publish dialog box toolbar:

- The Preview tool lets you preview a sheet based on the current settings.

- The Add Sheets tool lets you add sheets to the list. The Remove Sheets tool removes a selected item from the list.

- The Move Sheet Up and Move Sheet Down tools let you move an item in the list up or down. These are important options because the order of drawings in the list determines the order that the drawings will appear in the Autodesk DWF Viewer. The item at the top of the list appears first, the next one down the list is second, and so on.

- The Load Sheet List and Save Sheet List tools let you save and load the list you've compiled, respectively. It's a good idea to save your list in case you need to reproduce the DWF file at some future date.

- When the Include Plot Stamp option is turned on, you can use the Plot Stamp Settings tool to specify the data you want to include in the plot stamp. This tool opens the Plot Stamp dialog box. (See Appendix B for more on the Plot Stamp dialog box.)

### Shortcut Menu Options

If you right-click an item or a set of items in the Publish dialog box list box, you see a menu with the standard options mentioned earlier plus some additional options. You'll want to know about a few of these options.

By default, AutoCAD applies the existing layout settings for each layout when it produces the DWF file. These are the settings found in the Plot Or Page Setup dialog box and include settings such as the sheet size, scale, and page orientation. The Change Page Setup option lets you use a different set of layout settings for a selected layout in the list. To use this option, you must have saved a page setup in the file's Page Setup Or Plot dialog box. (See Chapter 8 for more on the Page Setup

## VIEWING DWF FILES

The Autodesk DWF Viewer offers a fast and simple way to view DWF files, and as I mentioned earlier, it's free. It's installed automatically when you install AutoCAD. Choose Start ➢ Programs ➢ Autodesk ➢ Autodesk DWF Viewer to get it started.

If the person receiving your DWF file doesn't have a copy of the Autodesk DWF Viewer, send them to the Products page of the Autodesk website (www.autodesk.com) to download their own copy. The download file is relatively small and is easily downloaded even with a slower dial-up connection.

dialog box and its options.) You can import a page setup from a different AutoCAD file, or you can assign a page setup to a sheet. Do this by clicking the sheet name and selecting a page setup from the list box that appears in the Page Setup column.

If you happen to have two layouts with the same name, right-click a layout name, and then select the Rename Sheet option on the shortcut menu to rename a layout. The Copy Selected Sheets option adds copies of selected layouts to the list. The copies have the word *copy* appended to their names. The last two items in the shortcut menu let you control what is displayed in the list box. Include Layouts When Adding Sheets controls whether layouts are automatically imported from a drawing into the list box. Include Model When Adding Sheets controls whether Model Space views are automatically imported from a drawing into the list box.

### THE PUBLISH OPTIONS DIALOG BOX

You can set up additional options by clicking the Publish Options button in the Publish dialog box. You'll then see the Publish Options dialog box.

This dialog box offers options for the location and type of output. The Default Output Location group lets you select the location for DWF files. The General DWF Options group lets you choose between a multisheet DWF file, which combines multiple sheets into one file, or single-sheet DWF files, which creates a file for each sheet. If you choose the Multi-sheet option, you have the added option to specify a default name for your DWF files or to have AutoCAD prompt you for a name each time you create a DWF file. You can also add password protection to the DWF file by using the Password option. The Multi-sheet DWF Options group lets you determine whether you're prompted for a DWF name each time you publish a set or use a predefined filename. In the DWF Data Options group, you have the option to include layer and block information with the DWF file.

## Creating a DWF File by Using the Plot Dialog Box

Another way to create DWF files is through the Plot dialog box. If you need to create a DWF file of only a single sheet, you may want to use the Plot dialog box, because it's a simple and familiar procedure.

Open the file that you want to convert to DWF, and then proceed as if you're going to plot the drawing. In the Plot dialog box, select DWF6 ePlot.PC3 from the Name drop-down list in the Printer/Plotter area. Proceed with the plot the normal way. When AutoCAD would normally send the drawing to the printer, you'll see a dialog box asking you to enter a name for your plot file and finish with the rest of the plot. You can control the DWF plot as you would any plot.

In addition to the settings available in the Plot dialog box, you can make some special configuration adjustments to the DWF plotter configuration file. Here is where to find those configuration settings:

1. Choose File ➤ Page Setup Manager to open the Page Setup Manager dialog box, select a setup from the Page Setups list, and then click Modify to open the Page Setup dialog box.

2. Make sure the DWF6ePlot.pc3 configuration file is listed in the Name list box of the Printer/Plotter group.

**3.** Click the Properties button to the right of the Name drop-down list to open the Plotter Configuration Editor dialog box.

**4.** Make sure the Device And Document Settings tab is selected; then, click Custom Properties in the list box.

**5.** Click the Custom Properties button that appears in the lower half of the dialog box to open the DWF6 ePlot Properties dialog box. Here, you can set the resolution, format, background color, and paper boundary for your DWF file. You can also specify whether to include layer and font information.

**6.** Click OK after selecting your settings. The Plotter Configuration Editor dialog box reappears. After you've set the custom properties, you can save any new settings in the DWF6 ePlot.pc3 file, or you can create a new DWF6 PC3 plot-configuration file. To save any setting changes, click the Save As button and select the PC3 file in which you want to save the settings.

**7.** Click OK in the Plotter Configuration Editor dialog box to return to the Page Setup dialog box.

**8.** Click OK to exit the Page Setup dialog box, and then close the Page Setup Manager.

**TIP** For more information about PC3 plot configuration files, see Chapter 8.

After you select your custom configuration settings in step 5, you needn't open the Plotter Configuration Editor dialog box again the next time you plot a DWF file. If you save your new settings as a new PC3 file, you can select it from the File drop-down list in the Plotter Configuration group. You needn't reenter the custom settings.

You can use either the Publish feature described in the previous section to create single or multiple DWF files or create DWF files directly through the Plot dialog box. You can post the output from either method to a website to offer a wide distribution of your drawings. Just create a link to the DWF file from your web page. Be aware that the person attempting to view your DWF file from a web browser will need a copy of the free Autodesk DWF Viewer program that lets you view AutoCAD DWF files. The Autodesk DWF Viewer is automatically installed with AutoCAD 2008.

---

**CREATING A WEB PAGE CONTAINING DWF FILES**

AutoCAD 2008 offers a tool that will automatically generate a web page containing your DWF files. The Publish To Web Wizard lets you create and edit web pages that contain single or multiple DWF files. You can then place the pages on your web server without any extra work.

To get to the Publish To Web Wizard, choose File ➢ Publish To Web from the AutoCAD menu bar. You can then follow the instructions in the wizard. The Publish To Web Wizard creates all the files needed for the page, including the JavaScript code to enable viewers of the page to drag and drop drawings from the page into their AutoCAD sessions.

If you feel creative, you can use the Publish To Web Wizard as a starting point to create custom web pages of your drawings, or you can use the pages as is. You can edit the pages by using any number of web programs.

---

## Adding Hyperlinks to Drawings

The Internet gave the world a tool that is so simple yet so powerful that it has permanently altered the way we look at information. Virtually every web page we view contains a hypertext link—a word, a sentence, or an image that takes us to another web page. Such links enable the viewer to explore the content of a web page or gather more information on a particular topic.

AutoCAD offers a similar tool that you can apply to your AutoCAD drawings, called *hyperlinks*. With AutoCAD hyperlinks, you can link any document to an AutoCAD object. Then, with a few clicks of your mouse, you can open these links to view other drawings, text files, spreadsheets, or web pages. After you create a hyperlink in an AutoCAD drawing, you can export the drawing to a DWF file, and that DWF file will also contain the same links. You can then post that DWF file on a web page where others can gain access to those links.

The inclusion of hyperlinks in drawings and DWF files opens a world of new possibilities in the way you work with drawings. You can link product specifications directly to the objects in the drawing that represent that product. You can also link to extended data beyond the simple symbol or graphic in a drawing, such as a database table or a spreadsheet.

You don't have to limit your links to HTML files containing AutoCAD drawings. You can link to all sorts of web documents, to drawings on your computer or your company network, and even to documents on other sites.

### CREATING HYPERLINKS

The following shows you how to add links to a sample floor plan:

1. In AutoCAD, open the file Houseplan.dwg.

2. Choose Insert ➢ Hyperlink.

3. At the Select objects: prompt, click all the hexagonal door symbols, as shown in Figure 27.1.

4. When you're done, press ↵. The Insert Hyperlink dialog box opens (see Figure 27.2).

5. Click the File button on the right side of the dialog box to open the Browse The Web – Select Hyperlink dialog box. It's a typical file dialog box.

6. Locate the doorsch.dwf file in the Projects subfolder, and select it.

**FIGURE 27.1**

The door symbol in the Houseplan.dwg file

**FIGURE 27.2**

The Insert Hyperlink dialog box

7. Click Open. The Insert Hyperlink dialog box reappears. Notice that doorsch.dwf appears in the list box at the top of the dialog box.

8. Make sure the Use Relative Path For Hyperlink option isn't selected, and then click OK.

The link you just created is stored with the drawing file. You can create a DWF file from this drawing, and the link will be preserved in the DWF file.

Now, let's see how you can use the link from within the AutoCAD file:

1. Move your cursor over the hexagonal door symbol. Notice that the cursor changes to the Hyperlink icon when it's placed on the symbol. It also shows the name of the file to which the object is linked. This tells you that the object is linked to another document somewhere on your system, on your network, or on the World Wide Web.

2. Click the hexagonal door symbol to select it.

3. Right-click a blank area of the drawing. In the shortcut menu, choose Hyperlink ➢ Open, to choose the link to the `doorsch.dwf file`. You can also Ctrl+click the door symbol.

Your default web browser opens and displays the file `doorsch.html`.

**WARNING**   If you installed the sample figures on another drive or folder location, the Hyperlink menu option will reflect that location.

You've used the `doorsch.html` file as an example in these exercises, but this could have been a text file, a spreadsheet, a database, or even another AutoCAD file. AutoCAD will start the application associated with the linked file and open the file.

### EDITING AND DELETING HYPERLINKS

You can edit or delete a hyperlink by doing the following:

1. Right-click the object whose link you want to edit, and then choose Hyperlink ➢ Edit Hyperlink from the shortcut menu to open the Edit Hyperlink dialog box, which offers the same options as the Insert Hyperlink dialog box (see Figure 27.2, earlier in this chapter).

2. You can now change the link, or you can click the Remove Link button in the lower-left corner of the dialog box to delete the link.

### TAKING A CLOSER LOOK AT THE HYPERLINK OPTIONS

You were introduced to the Insert Hyperlink dialog box, shown in Figure 27.2, in the previous exercises. Let's take a moment to study this dialog box in a little more detail.

To specify a file or a website to link to, you can enter either a filename or a website URL in the Type The File Or Web Page Name input box or use the Or Select From List area, which offers a list box and three button options. When you select one of the buttons, the list box changes to offer further, related options:

**Recent Files**   Displays a list of recently edited AutoCAD files, as illustrated in Figure 27.2. You can then link the object to a file in the list by clicking the filename.

**Browsed Pages**   Displays a list of websites that you recently visited using your web browser.

**Inserted Links**   Displays a list of recently inserted links, including files or websites.

You can also use the three buttons to the right of the list box to locate specific files, websites, or saved views in the current drawing. As you saw in the exercise, the File button opens the Browse The Web dialog box, which lets you locate and select a file from your computer, from your local area network, or even from an FTP site. This is a typical AutoCAD file dialog box with some additional features.

The buttons in the left column let you select the location of your file search. You can also select a location by using the file-navigation tools at the top of the dialog box.

The Web Page button on the right opens a simplified web browser that lets you locate a web page for linking (as shown earlier, in Figure 27.2). In this dialog box, you can use the standard methods for accessing web pages, such as using the Look In drop-down list to select recently visited pages or entering a URL in the Name Or URL input box. The page is then displayed in the main window of the dialog box.

The Target button in the Insert Hyperlink dialog box opens the Select Place In Document dialog box, which lists the saved views in the drawing that is selected in the Edit Hyperlink list box.

Views are subdivided by Layout tab. At the top is the Model Space tab listing, and below that are other Layout tab listings. If the current drawing contains saved views, you see a plus sign next to the Layout tab name. Click the plus sign to display a listing of the views in that layout.

At the top of the Insert Hyperlink and Edit Hyperlink dialog boxes is an input box labeled Text To Display. When a hyperlink is added to an object in AutoCAD, AutoCAD will display a hyperlink icon whenever the cursor passes over the object. You can also include descriptive text that will display along with the icon by entering a description in the Text To Display input box.

By default, the text is the name of the hyperlinked item that you select. You can change the text to provide a better description of the link.

There is a column of options at far left in the Insert Hyperlink dialog box, labeled Link To. The top button, Existing File Or Web Page, displays the options discussed so far in this section. The other two buttons change the appearance of the Insert Hyperlink dialog box to offer different but familiar options:

**View Of This Drawing**   This button changes the display to show just the views that are available in the current drawing. This option performs the same function as the Target button described earlier.

**E-Mail Address**   This button changes the Insert Hyperlink dialog box to enable you to link an e-mail address to an object. Clicking the object will then open your default e-mail application, enabling you to send a message to the address.

## Managing Your Drawings with DesignCenter and the Tool Palettes

As you start to build a library of drawings, you'll find that you reuse many components of existing drawing files. Most of the time, you'll probably be producing similar types of drawings with some variation, so you'll reuse drawing components such as layer settings, dimension styles, and layouts. It can be a major task to keep track of all the projects you've worked on. It's especially frustrating when you remember setting up a past drawing in a way that you know would be useful in a current project, but you can't remember that file's name or location.

AutoCAD offers DesignCenter to help you keep track of the documents you use in your projects. You can think of DesignCenter as a kind of super Windows Explorer that is focused on AutoCAD files. DesignCenter lets you keep track of your favorite files and helps you locate files, blocks, and other drawing components. In addition, you can import blocks and other drawing components from one drawing to another by using a simple click and drag. If you've been diligent about setting a unit format for each of your drawings, you can use DesignCenter to import symbols and drawings of different unit formats into a drawing, and the symbols will maintain their proper size. For example, a 90 cm door symbol from a metric drawing can be imported into a drawing in Imperial units, and the DesignCenter will translate the 90 cm metric door size to a 35.43″ door.

## Getting Familiar with DesignCenter

At first glance, DesignCenter looks a bit mysterious. But it takes only a few mouse clicks to reveal a tool that looks much like Windows Explorer. Try the following steps to get familiar with DesignCenter:

1. Open AutoCAD to a new file, and then click the DesignCenter tool on the Standard toolbar.

   DesignCenter opens as a floating palette (see Figure 27.3).

**FIGURE 27.3**
DesignCenter opens as a floating palette.

**TIP** If your DesignCenter view doesn't look like this, with the DesignCenter window divided into two parts, click the Tree View Toggle tool on the DesignCenter toolbar. The Tree view opens on the left side of the DesignCenter window. Click the Home tool to display the contents of the \Sample\DesignCenter folder.

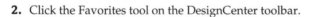

2. Click the Favorites tool on the DesignCenter toolbar.

   DesignCenter displays a listing of the Favorites folder. You're actually looking at a view into the C:\Documents and Settings\User Name\Favorites\Autodesk folder, where User Name is your login name. Unless you've already added items to the \Favorites\ Autodesk folder, you see a blank view in the right panel. You can add shortcuts to this folder as you work with DesignCenter. You may also see a view showing the tree structure of the files you have open in AutoCAD.

3. Place your cursor in the lower-right corner of the DesignCenter window so that a double-headed diagonal arrow shows; then, click and drag the corner out so you have an enlarged DesignCenter window that looks similar to Figure 27.4. The view on the right, containing the DesignCenter folder, is called the Palette view, and the view on the left is called the Tree view.

4. Place your cursor on the border between the Tree view and the Palette view until you see a double-headed cursor. Then, click and drag the border to the right to enlarge the Tree view until it covers about one-third of the window.

5. Use the scroll bar at the bottom to adjust your view of the Tree view so you can easily read its contents.

**FIGURE 27.4**
The components
of the DesignCenter
palette

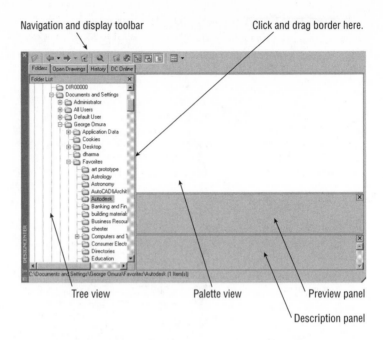

Navigation and display toolbar

Click and drag border here.

Tree view    Palette view    Preview panel

Description panel

**TIP** Like the Tool palettes and the Properties palette, DesignCenter has an Auto-hide feature. To use it, click the double-headed arrow icon near the bottom of the DesignCenter title bar. Design-Center will disappear except for the title bar. You can quickly open DesignCenter by placing the cursor on the title bar.

After you have it set up like this, you can see the similarities between DesignCenter and Windows Explorer. You can navigate your computer or network by using the Tree view, just as you would navigate Windows Explorer. There are a few differences, however, as you'll see in the following exercise:

1. Click the Home tool on the DesignCenter toolbar. The view changes to display the contents of the `DesignCenter` folder under the `\AutoCAD 2008\Sample\DesignCenter` folder.

2. Instead of the usual list of files, you see a sample image of each file. These are called *preview icons*.

3. Click the Views tool on the DesignCenter toolbar, and choose Details from the menu. The Palette view changes to show a detailed list of the files in the `DesignCenter` folder.

**4.** Click the Views tool again, and choose Large Icons to return to the previous view. The Views tool is similar to the various View options in Windows Explorer.

**5.** Click the `Basic Electronics.dwg` file to select it. You see a preview of the selected file in the Preview panel of DesignCenter. You can adjust the vertical size of the Preview panel by clicking and dragging its top or bottom border.

You can also open and close the Preview panel by clicking the Preview tool in the DesignCenter toolbar. The preview can be helpful if you prefer viewing files and drawing components as a list in the main part of the Palette view.

Below the Preview panel is the Description panel. This panel displays any text information included with the drawing or drawing element selected in the Palette view. To add a description to a drawing that will be visible here, choose File ➢ Properties in AutoCAD; to add a description to a block, use the Block Definition dialog box.

You can open and close this panel by clicking the Description tool on the DesignCenter toolbar. Because the `Basic Electronics.dwg` file doesn't have a description attached, the description panel shows the message `No description found`.

Both the Preview and the Description panels can offer help in identifying files that you may be looking for. After you find a file, you can click and drag it into a folder in the Tree view to organize your files into separate folders.

You can also add files to the `Favorites` folder by right-clicking and then choosing Add To Favorites. The file itself isn't moved to the `Favorites` folder; instead, a shortcut to the file is created in the `Favorites` folder. If you want to work on organizing your `Favorites` folder, you can open a window to the `Favorites` folder by right-clicking a file in the Palette view and choosing Organize Favorites. A window to the `Favorites` folder appears.

Because you'll be working with the sample drawings, go ahead and add the `Projects` folder to the `Favorites` folder:

**1.** Locate the `Projects` folder (the one created when you installed the sample files) in the left panel Tree view, and right-click it.

**2.** Choose Add To Favorites from the shortcut menu.

**3.** To go directly to the `Favorites` folder, click the Favorites tool on the DesignCenter toolbar. The `Favorites` folder appears in the right panel in Palette view.

**4.** Double-click the Projects shortcut in the Palette view. You see the contents of the `Projects` folder.

You can go beyond just looking at file listings. You can look inside files to view their components:

**1.** In the Palette view, locate the file named `16-unit.dwg` in the `Chapter 16` folder, and double-click it. You see a listing of its components in the Palette view. The Tree view also shows the file highlighted.

**2.** Double-click the Block listing in the Palette view. Now you see a listing of all the blocks in `16b-unit.dwg`.

From here, you can import any of the drawing components from the DesignCenter palette into an open drawing in AutoCAD. But before you try that, try a few other features of the DesignCenter.

## Opening and Inserting Files with DesignCenter

By using DesignCenter, you can more easily locate the files you're looking for because you can view thumbnail preview icons. But often that isn't enough. For example, you might want to locate all the files that contain the name of a particular manufacturer in an attribute of a drawing.

After you've found the file you're looking for, you can load it into AutoCAD by right-clicking the filename in the Palette view and then choosing Open In Window. Try it with the following exercise:

1. Click the Up tool in the DesignCenter toolbar twice. This takes you up two levels in the Palette view, from the view of the drawing blocks to the list of filenames.

2. In the Tree view, select the Chapter 12 folder. Then, in the Palette view of DesignCenter, locate the 12c-unit.dwg sample.

3. Click and drag 12c-unit.dwg to the AutoCAD 2008 title bar. The drawing appears in the AutoCAD Window.

If you want to insert a file into another drawing as a block, you can do so by clicking and dragging the file from the DesignCenter Palette view into an open drawing window. You're then prompted for the insertion point, scale, and rotation angle. If you prefer to use the Insert dialog box to insert a drawing from DesignCenter, right-click the filename in the Palette view and then choose Insert As Block. The Insert dialog box opens, offering you the full set of Insert options, as described in Chapter 3.

Finally, you can attach a drawing as an Xref by right-clicking a file in the Palette view of Design-Center and choosing Attach As Xref. The External Reference dialog box opens, offering the insertion point, scale, and rotation options similar to the Insert dialog box. This is the same dialog box described in Chapter 7.

## Finding and Extracting the Contents of a Drawing

Aside from the convenience of being able to see thumbnail views of your drawing, DesignCenter may not seem like much of an improvement over Windows Explorer. But DesignCenter goes beyond Windows Explorer in many ways. One of the main features of DesignCenter is that it enables you to locate and extract components of a drawing.

Imagine that you want to find a specific block in a drawing. You remember the name of the block, but you don't remember the drawing you put it in. You can search the contents of drawings by using DesignCenter's Search dialog box. In the following exercise, you'll search for a block named Kitchen2-metric among a set of files.

1. In the DesignCenter toolbar, click the Search tool to open the Search dialog box. It looks similar to the Search tool that comes with Windows.

2. Select the drive that contains your Projects folder from the In drop-down list.

3. Select Blocks from the Look For drop-down list. As you can see from the list, you can look for a variety of drawing component types.

4. Enter **Kitchen2-metric↵** in the Search For The Name input box, and then click the Search Now button to start the search. The magnifying glass icon in the lower-right corner moves back and forth, telling you that the Search function is working. After a minute or two, the name of the block appears in the window at the bottom of the dialog box.

5. Double-click the block name. DesignCenter displays the block in the Palette view and the file that contains the block in the Tree view.

### SEARCH OPTIONS

As you saw from the previous example, the Search dialog box can be helpful in finding items that are buried in a set of drawings. In the exercise, you searched for a block, but you can search for any named drawing component, including attribute data and text. For example, if you want to find all attributes that contain the name *ABC Manufacturing Company* in your drawings, you can do so with the DesignCenter Search dialog box. Table 27.2 shows a summary of its features. When you select Drawings from the Look For drop-down list, you see a set of additional tabs in the Search dialog box, as described in Table 27.3.

**TABLE 27.2:**    DesignCenter Search Dialog Box Options

| OPTION | PURPOSE |
| --- | --- |
| In | Lets you select the drive you want to search. |
| Look For Options | Lets you select the type of item to search for. The options are Blocks, Dimstyles, Drawings, Drawings And Blocks, Hatch Pattern Files, Hatch Patterns, Layers, Layouts, Linetypes, Tablestyles, Textstyles, and Xrefs. |
| Browse | Lets you locate a specific folder to search. |
| Search Subfolders | Lets you determine whether Search searches subfolders in the drive and folder you specify. |
| Search Now | Starts the search process. |
| Stop | Cancels the current search. |
| New Search | Clears all the settings for the current search so you can start fresh on a new search. |
| Help | Opens the AutoCAD help system to the Search topic. |

**TABLE 27.3:**    DesignCenter Search Dialog Box Tab Options When Drawings Is Selected from the Look For Drop-Down List

| DRAWINGS TAB | |
| --- | --- |
| Search For The Word(s) | Lets you specify the text to search for in the Drawing Properties fields. |
| In The Field(s) | Lets you specify the field of the Drawing Properties dialog box to search through, including filename, title, subject, author, and keyword. These are the fields you see when you choose File ➤ Drawing Properties. |

**TABLE 27.3:** DesignCenter Search Dialog Box Tab Options When Drawings Is Selected from the Look For Drop-Down List (CONTINUED)

| **DRAWINGS TAB** | |
| --- | --- |
| **Date Modified Tab** | |
| Radio buttons | Lets you limit search criteria based on dates. |
| **Advanced Tab** | |
| Containing | Lets you select from a list of data to search for, including block name, block and drawing description, attribute tag, and attribute value. |
| Containing Text | Lets you specify the text to search for in the types of data you select from the Containing option. |
| Size Is | Lets you restrict the search to files greater than or less than the size you specify. |

### AUTOMATICALLY SCALING BLOCKS AT INSERTION

After you've found a block by using DesignCenter, you can click and drag the block into your open drawing. In the following exercise, you'll do that, but with a slight twist. The block you've found is drawn in centimeters, but you'll insert the Kitchen2-metric block into a drawing named 12c-unit.dwg, which was created in the Imperial measurement system. If you were to insert the Kitchen2-metric block into 12c-unit.dwg, the kitchen would be exactly 2.54 times larger than it should be for 12c-unit.dwg. But as you'll see, DesignCenter takes care of scaling for you. Follow these steps:

1. In AutoCAD, make sure the 12c-unit.dwg sample drawing is loaded, if you haven't done so already. You can temporarily close DesignCenter to do this.

2. Back in DesignCenter, click and drag the Kitchen2-metric block from the Palette view into the 12c-unit.dwg window in AutoCAD. The kitchen appears at the appropriate scale.

3. To see that DesignCenter did indeed adjust the scale of the Kitchen2-metric block, click it in the 12c-unit window, and then right-click and choose Properties.

4. Check the Scale X, Scale Y, and Scale Z settings in the Geometry category. Notice that they show .3937 as the scale factor instead of 1.

5. After reviewing the Properties palette, close it.

You may recall from Chapter 3 that you have the opportunity to specify the type of units the drawing is set up for in the Drawing Units dialog box under the Drag-And-Drop Scale drop-down list. Design-Center uses this information when you drag and drop blocks from DesignCenter into an open drawing. This is how DesignCenter is able to correctly scale a block drawn in metric to a drawing that is drawn in the Imperial format. The same option is offered in the Block Definition dialog box.

Blocks aren't the only type of drawing component you can click and drag from the Palette view. Linetypes, layouts, dimension styles, and text styles can all be imported from files on your computer or network through DesignCenter's Palette view.

## Exchanging Data between Open Files

You've seen how you can extract a block from a file stored on your hard disk and place it into an open drawing, but what if you want to copy a block from one open drawing to another open drawing? You change the way the Tree view displays data so that it shows only the files that are loaded in AutoCAD. The following exercise demonstrates how this works:

1. In AutoCAD, make sure that `12c-unit.dwg` is still open; then, open the `12c-unit-metric.dwg` file.

2. In DesignCenter, click the Open Drawings tab above the Tree view. The Tree view changes to display only the drawings that are open.

3. Click the plus sign (+) to the left of the `12c-unit.dwg` filename in the Tree view. The list expands to show the components in `12c-unit.dwg`.

4. Click Blocks in the Tree view. The Palette view changes to show a list of blocks available in `12c-unit.dwg`.

5. Locate the Kitchen block in the Palette view.

6. Click and drag Kitchen from the Palette view into the open `12b-unit-metric.dwg` drawing in AutoCAD. The block moves with the cursor. Once again, DesignCenter has automatically scaled the block to the appropriate size, this time from Imperial to metric.

7. Click anywhere in the drawing to place the Kitchen block.

In this example, you inserted a block from one open drawing into another drawing. If you prefer to use the Insert dialog box, you can right-click the block name in step 6 and choose Insert Block. The Insert dialog box opens, enabling you to set the insertion point, scale, and rotation options.

Just as with drawings, you can see a preview and descriptive text for blocks below the Palette view. In Chapter 4, you had the option to save a preview icon with the block when you first created a block. This is where that preview icon can be really helpful. The preview icon gives you a chance to see what the block looks like when you use DesignCenter to browse through your drawing files. If you don't save a preview icon, you'll see the same block icon that was displayed in the previous Palette view.

You can also add the text description at the time you create the block. Before saving the block, enter a description in the Description input box of the Block Definition dialog box.

If you're updating older drawing files to be used with DesignCenter, you can add text descriptions to blocks by using the Make Block tool in the Draw toolbar. Click the Make Block tool, and then, in the Block Definition dialog box, select the name of a block from the Name drop-down list. Enter the description you want for this block in the Description input box toward the bottom of the Block Definition dialog box. When you're finished, click OK.

## Loading Specific Files into DesignCenter

You've seen how you can locate files through the Tree view and Palette view. If you already know the name and location of the file you want to work with, you can use a file dialog box to open files in DesignCenter. Instead of choosing File ➤ Open, you use the Load tool on the DesignCenter toolbar to open the Load dialog box. This is a standard file dialog box that lets you search for files on your computer or network.

If you want to open a file in DesignCenter that you've recently opened, you can use the History tab just above the Tree view. The Tree view closes, and you see a list of the most recent files you've worked on.

## Downloading Symbols from DesignCenter Online

In addition to obtaining files and blocks from your computer or network, you can also download symbols directly from Autodesk's DesignCenter Online website. This option offers thousands of ready-to-use symbols for a variety of disciplines. Follow these steps:

1. Connect to the Internet.

2. Click the DC Online tab that appears above the Tree view. The DesignCenter Online symbol categories appear in the Tree view, and the Palette view shows the same categories in a text view.

3. Expand the 2D Architectural listing in the panel to the left to display a set of subcategories.

4. Expand the Bathrooms category, and then click Bath Tubs. The Palette view displays a set of bathtubs.

5. Click one of the bathtubs. The i-drop icon appears.

6. Click a tub to display an enlarged preview of it in the display panel along with a description of the symbol.

7. Click and drag a symbol into the current open drawing. The i-drop cursor appears in the drawing. When you release the mouse button, the symbol appears at the cursor, waiting for you to select an insertion point.

8. Click a location to place the symbol.

9. To return to the opening page of DesignCenter Online, click the DesignCenter Online item at the top of the Tree view.

Because DesignCenter Online is a website, AutoCAD uses the i-drop feature to bring the symbols into your drawing. As you can see, the list of symbols is fairly extensive. Many of the symbols are samples from third-party vendors that offer expanded symbols libraries.

## Customizing the Tool Palettes with DesignCenter

Many AutoCAD users have built their own custom library of symbols and are accustomed to using them in conjunction with custom menus. But creating and editing menus is a bit cumbersome and can become difficult to manage. In Chapter 1, you saw how easy it is to drag and drop a symbol, known as a tool, from the Tool palettes. At first glance, there is no obvious way to add your own tools to the palettes. Adding tools and additional palettes to the Tool palettes is fairly simple once you're familiar with DesignCenter. The following exercise shows you how it's done:

1. If Tool palettes aren't open already, click the Tool Palettes Window tool in the Standard toolbar.

2. Right-click in the Tool palettes, and then choose New Palette from the shortcut menu.

3. Enter **My Tool Palette**.↵. A new, blank tab is added to the Tool palettes.

4. Go back to DesignCenter, make sure the Folders tab is selected, and click the Home tool.

**5.** In the Palette view to the right, double-click the `Landscaping.dwg` file, and then double-click the Blocks icon that appears in the Palette view.

**6.** Make sure that the Tool palettes are visible behind DesignCenter, and then Ctrl+click Clump Of Trees Or Bushes – Plan And North Arrow.

**7.** Click and drag the selection to the Tool palettes.

**WARNING** If you click a tool in a Tool palette, it's inserted in the current drawing; so take care when clicking around in the Tool palettes.

You've just created a Tool palette and added a symbol. You can continue to add symbols from other drawings to your custom Tool palette. Or, if you have a drawing that contains all the blocks you need for a Tool palette, you can quickly create a Tool palette directly from a file. Here's how that's done.

**1.** In DesignCenter, go up one folder level so you can select the `Landscaping.dwg` file.

**2.** Right-click `Landscaping.dwg` and then choose Create Tool Palette. After a few moments, a new Tool palette called Landscaping appears in the Tool palettes. This new palette contains all the blocks found in the `Landscaping.dwg` file.

This exercise showed that you can quickly create a palette of all the drawings from a file. You can do the same thing with entire folders of drawings, although you may want to make sure such folders don't contain too many files.

But what if you don't want some of the items in your custom palette? You can remove items easily by using a shortcut menu:

**1.** In the Landscaping palette, select the top three symbols by right-clicking the tool that is third from the top and then Shift+clicking the top tool. This is a little different from the typical Windows method for selecting items from a list.

**2.** Right-click, and choose Delete from the shortcut menu. Click OK to confirm the deletion.

You may have noticed the Cut and Copy options in the shortcut menu in step 2. You can use these options to move symbols from one palette to another. For example, instead of deleting the three symbols in step 2, you can choose Cut from the shortcut menu, open another palette, right-click, and choose Paste. The symbols move to the new palette location. In the next section, you'll see how you can use the Copy and Paste shortcut menu options to make a copy of a tool in the same palette.

### CUSTOMIZING A TOOL

Other shortcut menu options let you delete entire palettes or rename tools or palettes. You can also edit the properties of symbols in a palette. The following exercise shows how to use the shortcut menu options to create two scale versions of the same tool:

**1.** In the Landscaping tab of the Tool palettes, right-click the North Arrow tool, and choose Copy from the shortcut menu.

**2.** Right-click a blank area of the palette, and choose Paste. A copy of the North Arrow tool appears in the palette.

**3.** Right-click the copy of the North Arrow tool, choose Rename from the shortcut menu, and then enter **North Arrow Copy**.

4. Right-click the North Arrow Copy tool, and choose Properties to open the Tool Properties dialog box.

5. Click 1.0000 to the right of the Scale listing, and change the value to 4.

6. Click OK, and then click and drag the North Arrow Copy tool into the drawing.

7. Click and drag the original North Arrow tool into the drawing. Notice that the original North Arrow is smaller than the North Arrow Copy, whose scale you changed to 4.

This exercise demonstrated that you can have multiple versions of a tool at different scales. You can then use the tool appropriate to the scale of your drawing. And as you can see from the Tool Properties dialog box, you can modify other tool properties such as color and layer assignments. You can use this feature to create sets of tools for different scale drawings. For example, you can create a palette of architectural reference symbols for ¼″-scale drawings, and you can create another palette for ⅛″-scale drawings.

## ADDING HATCH PATTERNS AND SOLID FILLS

You've seen how you can turn blocks into Tool palette tools, but what about solid fills? In Chapter 1, you saw that sample hatch patterns and solid fills are available in the Tool palettes. Here's how you can add your own:

1. In DesignCenter, use the Tree view to locate the AutoCAD 2008 Support folder. In Windows XP, it's typically in

```
C:\Documents and Settings\User Name\Application Data\Autodesk\
AutoCAD 2008\R17.1\enu\Support
```

(*User Name* is your Windows login name.)

**TIP** To find out exactly where support files are located, choose Tools ➢ Options to open the Options dialog box. Click the Files tab. Expand the Support File Search Path item at the top of the list, and then place the cursor on the item just below Support File Search Path. You see the path to the Support folder. You can also enter **(findfile "acad.pat")** at the command prompt as a shortcut to find the support-file search path. If you use this shortcut, note that the directory names are separated with double hash marks (\\); this is an artifact of AutoLISP.

2. Double-click the `acad.pat` file shown in the Palette view. AutoCAD builds a list of the patterns and displays the list in the Palette view.

3. You can now click and drag a pattern into any Tool palette. You can also click and drag an entire `.PAT` file into the Tool palette to create a palette of all the patterns in a hatch pattern file.

In this exercise, you used the standard hatch patterns that come with AutoCAD. You can also create your own custom hatch patterns and import them to the Tool palettes by using the method described here. See Chapter 26 for more information on creating custom hatch patterns.

If you want to set up a set of solid fill colors, you can do the following:

1. Click and drag the solid fill pattern from the `Acad.pat` file into the Tool palette.

2. Right-click the new solid fill tool, choose Properties from the shortcut menu, and then select a color from the Color drop-down list in the Tool Properties dialog box.

You can select any color, including colors from the True Color or Color Book tab in the Select Color dialog box that you learned about in Chapter 4. You can also cut and paste an existing solid fill tool to make copies. You can then modify the color property for each copy to get a set of custom solid fill colors.

### MANAGING THE TOOL PALETTES

You can perform other types of Tool palettes maintenance operations by using the Customize dialog box. For example, you can change the order of the Tool palette tabs, or you can group tabs into categories that can be turned on or off. The following steps offer a glimpse of what you can do by showing you how to group palettes:

1. To open the Customize dialog box, right-click the Tool palettes, and choose Customize Palettes from the shortcut menu.

2. Right-click in a blank area of the Palette Groups panel, and choose New Group.

3. Enter **My Group** for the new group name.

4. Click and drag My Group to a position just above another group so it's its own group instead of a subgroup.

5. Click and drag Landscaping from the left panel to the right panel just below My Group. A black bar appears below My Group. Release the mouse button.

6. Click and drag My Tool Palette from the left panel to the right, just below Landscaping.

You've just created a new palette group and moved the two new palettes. You can view the palettes separately or all together:

1. Click Close to close the Customize dialog box. The Tool palette still displays all the tabs.

2. To display only the new tabs, click the Properties button at the bottom of the palette.

3. Select My Group. Now the Tool palette shows only the two tabs you just created.

You may have noticed that in the Properties menu, you also have the option to show just the new groups or all the palettes. This feature lets you keep the tabs in the Tool palettes organized.

The Tool Palettes tab of the Customize dialog box also lets you change the order of the tabs by clicking and dragging the tab names up or down in the left panel. If you select a palette in the left panel and right-click, you can rename, delete, import, or export a palette.

**WARNING**    If you use the Export or Import option to move a palette from one computer to another, be aware that you must also import or export the drawings that are the source files for the palette tools.

DesignCenter and Tool palettes offer great features that will prove invaluable to AutoCAD users. Although these examples show you how to use DesignCenter on a stand-alone computer, you can just as easily perform the same functions across a network or even across the Internet.

This ends our exploration of DesignCenter and Tool palettes. In the next part of this chapter, you'll look at AutoCAD's tools for maintaining layer-naming and other standards throughout an organization and for converting between your own layering system and those of clients or partners.

# Establishing Office Standards

Communication is especially important when you're one of many people working on the same project on separate computers. A well-developed set of standards and procedures helps to minimize problems that may be caused by miscommunication. In this section, you'll find some suggestions for setting up these standards.

## Establishing Layering and Text Conventions

The issue of CAD standards has always been difficult to resolve. Standardizing layers, dimensions, and text can go a long way toward making file exchange more seamless between different trades, and standards can also make files easier to understand. When everyone follows a standard, the structure of a drawing is more easily understood, and those who have to edit or interpret your work can do so without having to ask a lot of questions.

You've seen how layers can be a useful tool. But they can easily get out of hand when you have free rein over their creation and naming. With an appropriate layer-naming convention, you can minimize this type of problem (although you may not eliminate it entirely). A too-rigid naming convention can cause as many problems as no convention at all, so it's best to give general guidelines rather than force everyone to stay within narrow limits. As mentioned in Chapter 4, you can create layer names in a way that enables you to group them by using wildcards. AutoCAD allows up to 31 characters in a layer name, so you can use descriptive names.

Lineweights should be standardized in conjunction with colors. If you intend to use a service bureau for your plotting, check with them first; they may require that you conform to their color and lineweight standards.

**TIP** If you're an architect, an engineer, or in the construction business, check out some of the CAD layering standards set forth by the American Institute of Architects (AIA) and the Construction Specifications Institute (CSI). The AIA has a website at www.aia.org, and the CSI has a website at www.csinet.org.

## Checking Office Standards

**WARNING** The Standards command discussed in this section isn't available in AutoCAD LT.

AutoCAD offers an open-ended environment that lends itself to easy customization, but this also leaves the door wide open for on-the-fly creation of layer names, dimension styles, and other drawing format options. It's easy to stray from standards, especially when you're under pressure to get a project out on a deadline. To help you and your office maintain a level of conformity to office or industry standards, AutoCAD includes the Standards command.

The Standards command lets you quickly compare a drawing against a set of standard layer names, dimension style settings, linetypes, and text styles. A dialog box displays any item that doesn't conform to the standards you selected. You can then adjust the file to make it conform to your standards.

You can create several sets of standards for different types of files, and you can assign the standards directly to a file so that anyone editing that file can make periodic checks against your office standards while the drawing is being edited.

### SETTING UP STANDARDS FILES

The first step in using the Standards command is to set up a file to which other drawing files can be compared. Standards uses an AutoCAD drawing file with a .dws filename extension. Here are the steps to create a new DWS standards file:

1. Open AutoCAD, and choose File ➢ New.

2. Set up the file with the layers, linetypes, dimension styles, and text styles you want as your standards.

3. Choose File ➢ Save As.

4. In the Save Drawing As dialog box, choose AutoCAD Drawing Standards (*.dws) from the Files Of Type drop-down list.

5. Choose a convenient folder for the location of your standards file, and click Save.

As an alternative to creating a new file, you can open an existing file that contains all the typical settings you'll want to use on your projects. You can then delete all the graphics in the file and purge all its blocks and shapes. After you've done this, you can begin at step 3 of the previous exercise to save the file as a DWS standards file.

You can set up as many DWS files as you need for your office. Often, a single set of standards is too limiting if your office is involved in a diverse range of projects, so you may want to set up DWS files on a project basis, drawing on a core of generic DWS files.

**USING THE STANDARDS COMMAND TO ASSOCIATE STANDARDS**

After you've created your DWS standards files, you can begin to check other files for conformity. The next task is to assign your DWS file to the drawing file that you want to check:

1. In AutoCAD, open the file you want to check for standards conformity.

2. Choose Tools ➢ CAD Standards ➢ Configure to open the Configure Standards dialog box. This dialog box contains a list box and a description area. A row of buttons appears vertically between the list box and description.

3. Click the Add Standards File (F3) button in the middle column of the dialog box.

4. The Select Standards File dialog box opens. This is a typical AutoCAD file dialog box. Notice that the Files Of Type drop-down list shows the Standards (*.dws) file type.

5. Locate and select the standards file that you want to use to check the current file. After a moment, the name of the file you select appears in the list box of the Configure Standards dialog box. On the right side of the dialog box, you see a list of the items that will be checked whenever you check a file for conformity to the selected standards.

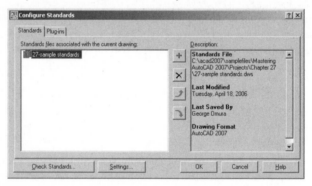

6. Check the current file against the DWS standards file. Click the Check Standards button in the lower-left corner of the Configure Standards dialog box. AutoCAD pauses while it checks the current file, and then you see the Check Standards dialog box.

If AutoCAD finds a discrepancy between the standards file and the current file, a description of the problem appears at the top of the dialog box. For example, if a dimension style name appears in the current file that isn't in the standards file, a message appears indicating that a nonstandard dimension style name exists in the current drawing. If this happens, take the following steps:

1. Below the Problem statement is the Replace With list box, which contains options related to the nonstandard item. You can replace the nonstandard item in your file with an option in the Replace With list box by selecting the option and clicking the check box to the right of the list. Or you can leave the problem alone for now.

2. Click the Next button in the bottom-right corner of the Check Standards dialog box to move to the next problem.

3. Repeat steps 1 and 2 until you see the statement `Checking is complete` in the Problem list box and the Checking Complete dialog box opens to display a summary of the checking results.

In this example, you entered the Check Standards dialog box directly from the Configure Standards dialog box. After you've used the Check Standards dialog box on a file, the DWS standards file is associated with the checked file. You can go directly to the Check Standards dialog box by choosing Tools ➤ CAD Standards ➤ Check during any subsequent editing session.

**TIP** After you've assigned a DWS standards file to a drawing, you'll need to save the drawing, or its association with the DWS file will be lost.

### CHECKING STANDARDS FOR MULTIPLE DRAWINGS

The Standards and Check Standards commands are great for checking individual files, but eventually you'll want a method to batch-check a set of files. AutoCAD 2008 provides a utility that does just that. The Batch Standards Checker is a stand-alone utility that audits a set of drawing files and checks them against their associated DWS files. The Batch Standards Checker can also check a set of drawings against a single DWS file of your choice. It then generates an audit report showing any problems it encounters.

Here's how it works:

1. From the Windows Desktop, choose Start ➤ Programs ➤ Autodesk ➤ AutoCAD 2008 ➤ Batch Standards Checker to open the Batch Standards Checker dialog box (see Figure 27.5).

**FIGURE 27.5**
The Batch Standards Checker dialog box

2. Click the Plus button in the middle of the dialog box to open the Batch Standards Checker – File Open dialog box. This is a typical AutoCAD file dialog box.

3. Locate and select the drawings you want to check. You return to the Batch Standards Checker dialog box, and, after a moment, a list of the drawings you selected appears in the Drawings To Check list box.

4. Click the Standards tab. This is where you can select the standards file against which your selection will be checked.

If the drawings you selected in step 3 already have a standards file associated with them, you can use the Check Each Drawing Using Its Associated Standards Files option to check each file. You can then skip to step 7.

5. If you select the Check All Drawings Using The Following Standards Files option, click the plus sign in the middle of the dialog box to open the Batch Standards Checker dialog box.

6. Locate and select a DWS standards file. The file then appears in the Standards Used For Checking All Drawings list box on the left of the Standards tab.

7. Click the Save button at the top of the Batch Standards Checker dialog box.

The Batch Standards Checker file dialog box opens to enable you to specify a Standards Check File name and location. This file has a .chx filename extension. The Batch Standards Checker file is an audit file that stores the drawing list and the list of standards files in the current session. It also stores the results of the audit.

8. After you've specified the location and name of a check file, click the Start Check button.

**TIP** The CHX file is an XML-based file. XML is a file format designed to allow data exchange over the World Wide Web.

AutoCAD proceeds to check each file listed in the Drawings tab list box. The progress is shown in the Progress tab of the Batch Standards Checker dialog box. If you decide to cancel the audit, you can click the Stop Check button (it looks like a stop sign), which cancels the current audit in progress.

When the checking is finished, the data from the audit is automatically saved in the check file you created in step 7. Then, the audit file is opened in your web browser, and you see the results of the audit.

The audit report file displays a number of options in a set of radio buttons:

**Overview** Displays a simplified view of the problems encountered by the audit. It lists the drawings audited and the number of problems encountered.

**Plug-ins**   Shows the standard plug-ins used to audit the drawings. Autodesk supplies these standard plug-ins, which test for layers, dimension styles, linetypes, and text styles. Third-party developers can create other plug-ins to check for additional problems.

**Standards**   Lists the DWS standards files used for the audit.

**Problems**   Displays a detailed description of the problems encountered in the audit. It gives the drawing name and the specific item name that is a problem. For example, if the audit discovers a nonstandard layer name, the layer name is listed under the drawing name as a nonstandard layer.

**Ignored Problems**   Displays problems that have previously been flagged as problems to ignore. You can flag problems to be ignored by using the Check Standards command in AutoCAD. (See the "Using the Standards Command to Associate Standards" section earlier in this chapter.)

**All**   Displays all the audit information.

### REVIEWING PREVIOUSLY SAVED STANDARDS AUDITS

After you've created a check file and completed a standards audit, you can always return to the audit by opening the Batch Standards Checker utility and clicking the Open tool in the toolbar.

This opens the Batch Standards Checker file dialog box, where you can locate and open a previously saved standards check file with the .chx filename extension. In this file, you see a list of the files that were checked in the Drawings tab and the DWS standards file used in the Standards tab.

You can then view the results of the audit by clicking the View Report tool in the toolbar. This opens a web browser and displays the audit results contained in the standards check file.

## Converting Multiple Layer Settings

As AutoCAD files flow in and out of your office, you're likely to find yourself working with layering standards from another system. You might, for example, receive files from an architect who uses the CSI standard for layer names, whereas your office prefers the AIA standard. If your job involves extensive reworking of such files, you'll want to change the layering system to one you're most familiar with. But converting layer settings is a painstaking and time-consuming process, especially if several files need conversion.

Fortunately, AutoCAD offers a tool that can make layer conversion from one standard to another much easier. The Layer Translator lets you map nonstandard layers (that is, those using a system different from your own) to your own set of standard layers. It can then convert those layers to match your office standards. After you've mapped a set of layers between two files, you can save the map settings in a drawing file. Then, any other files you receive that contain the same nonstandard layer settings can be converted to your own layer standards quickly. Let's take a closer look at how the Layer Translator works.

When using the Layer Translator, you must initially match the layers of your incoming file with those of a file whose layers are set up the way you want. Here are the steps to do this:

1.  Open the file whose layers you want to convert in AutoCAD. Choose Tools ➢ CAD Standards ➢ Layer Translator to open the Layer Translator dialog box, which lists the layers from the current file in the Translate From list box.

2.  Click the Load button in the Translate To group to open the Select Drawing File dialog box. Locate and select a file that contains the layer settings you want to use for this project. The file can be a standard DWG file, or it can be a DWS standards file or a DWT template file. After you've opened a file, its layer names appear in the Translate To list box.

3. Select a layer name in the Translate From list, and then select the layer you want to convert it to from the Translate To list box. After you've made your two selections, click the Map button in the middle of the dialog box. An item in the Layer Translation Mappings group shows you the old and new layer names and the layer settings for the conversion (see Figure 27.6).

**FIGURE 27.6**
The Layer Translator dialog box

4. Repeat step 3 for all the layers you want to convert. You can map several layers from the Translate From list to a single layer in the Translate To list if you need to.

5. If there are matching layers in the Translate From and Translate To list boxes, the Map Same button in the middle of the dialog box becomes active. You can then click this button to automatically map layers that have the same names in both the Translate From and the Translate To lists.

After you've completed your layer mapping, you can save the mapping for future use:

1. While still in the Layer Translator dialog box, click the Save button in the Layer Translation Mappings group to open the Save Layer Mappings dialog box. This is a typical AutoCAD file dialog box.

2. Enter a name for your saved settings, and click Save. You can save the layer-map settings as either a DWS standards file or a DWG file.

3. Click the Translate button, and AutoCAD will proceed to translate the mapped layers.

After you've saved the layer mapping in step 1, you can load the saved layer-map settings into the Layer Translator dialog box in future layer translations, saving you the effort of mapping each layer individually each time you want to perform a translation. This will work for incoming files that use the same layer settings, but you'll have to create another layer-map settings file for each different layer system you encounter.

To use a saved layer map, click the Load button in the Translate To group of the Layer Translator dialog box, and then select the saved layer-map file you saved in step 1. You can have several layer map files for each project involving files with nonstandard layer settings.

## Other Layer Translator Options

You'll often come across situations in which the layers in the Translate From list don't correspond directly to those in the Translate To list. For these situations, the Layer Translator offers a few additional options.

If you have difficulty finding a match for layers in the Translate From list, you can create a new layer by clicking the New button in the Translate To group. This opens the New Layer dialog box, in which you can enter the properties for your new layer.

After you create a new layer with this dialog box, it appears in the Translate To list box, enabling you to map Translate From layers to your new layer.

Another option you'll find useful is the Edit button in the Layer Translation Mappings group. You may find that after you've mapped a Translate From layer to a Translate To layer, the Translate To layer isn't exactly what you want. You can highlight the mapped layer in the Layer Translation Mappings group list box, and then click Edit to open the Edit Layer dialog box. From here, you can modify the new layer's settings from their original values.

Finally, the Layer Translator offers a set of options that give you some control over the way translations are performed. For example, you can control whether layer colors and linetypes are forced to the ByLayer setting or whether layer assignments for objects in blocks are translated. You can access these options by clicking the Settings button in the lower-left corner of the Layer Translator dialog box. Figure 27.7 shows the Settings dialog box. The options are self-explanatory.

**FIGURE 27.7**
The Layer Translator's
Settings dialog box

## The Bottom Line

**Sharing Drawings over the Internet**   As a drafter or designer, it's very likely that you'll be involved in collaborative efforts, which means you'll have to share your work with others. The Internet has made it much easier to do this.

**Master It**   Why is eTransmit important for sending AutoCAD drawings over the Internet?

**Solution**   An AutoCAD drawing can have many different external files associated with it, such as fonts, Xrefs, and image files. eTransmit offers a quick way to gather these files into one place or into a single archive files.

**ePublishing Your Drawings**   Autodesk offers the DWF drawing format, which lets non-CAD users view and add comments to your drawings. You can use the Publish feature to create a single DWF file from several drawings.

**Master It**   True or false: The Publish feature can be used to plot multiple drawings in the background.

**Solution**   True.

**Managing Your Drawings with DesignCenter and the Tool Palettes**   The DesignCenter is a great tool for managing your drawings' resources, like blocks, custom linetypes, and other elements.

**Master It**   True or false: The DesignCenter has the capacity to automatically scale a block to the correct size when moving from metric to Imperial drawings.

**Solution**   True.

**Establishing Office Standards**   AutoCAD allows for a wide range of settings in a drawing. For this reason, it's a good idea to create standards for the way drawings are set up.

**Master It**   Name the file extension for an AutoCAD drawing standards file.

**Solution**   .dws.

**Converting Multiple Layer Settings**   If you exchange files with another office, you may find that their layer scheme is different from yours. AutoCAD offers the Layer Translator to help you translate layer names from an unfamiliar drawing to names you're more comfortable with.

**Master It**   Name the filename extensions of the types of files that you can use as a template for layer-name translations.

**Solution**   .dwg, .dws, and .dwt.

## Chapter 28

# Keeping a Project Organized with Sheet Sets

It's rare to have a drawing project fit on one sheet. Most CAD projects require multiple sheets, sometimes numbering in the hundreds. With multiple sheets in a project, you often spend a fair amount of time checking cross-references between the drawings and making sure that sheet titles and other information are correct.

Even the smallest project requires some coordination of cross-references between drawings in a set and checking for consistency across sheets. For example, a floor plan of a house will have callout symbols that direct you to a sheet with building elevations, construction details, or door and window schedules. As a CAD user, you eventually spend a lot of time just making sure that you have your set of drawings in the proper order and labeled correctly. Checking a set of drawings for continuity and correctness is a time-consuming job, and errors can easily creep in.

To help make your sheet coordination efforts easier, AutoCAD 2008 offers the Sheet Set Manager. (If you're an LT user, you may be interested in the information presented here, but the Sheet Set Manager isn't available in AutoCAD 2008 LT.)

Topics in this chapter include the following:

◆ Understanding Sheet Sets

◆ Creating a Sheet Set from an Existing Project

◆ Managing Title Blocks and Cross-References

◆ Customizing Sheet Sets

◆ Archiving, Publishing, and eTransmitting Sheet Sets

## Understanding Sheet Sets

The Sheet Set Manager is a tool that keeps track of all the drawings in a project. It also helps maintain the integrity of cross-references between sheets in a set of drawings by automatically updating sheet numbers throughout a set as sheets are added or moved. The Sheet Set Manager won't replace a careful check of a set of drawings before they're released for consumption, but it will reduce the amount of time you spend on coordinating and checking a set of drawings.

Sheet sets and the Sheet Set Manager can be a bit difficult to understand clearly, so in this section you can take a moment to get a better idea of what sheet sets are all about.

## Organizing by Reference Files and Sheet Files

To better understand how sheet sets work, it helps to consider the methods used to organize AutoCAD files. One common method for organizing files is to separate drawings into two categories: reference files and sheet files. You can think of *reference files* as the data sources. These are the drawing files that contain the core drawing geometry of a project. For example, they might be the floor plan drawings that contain the paving, finish, ceiling, and power information, all drawn in Model Space.

*Sheet files* are files that represent the actual printed sheets or pages in the drawing set. Sheet files include title block information as well as the different views of the reference files needed for the sheet. View titles and scale information are also included.

You use one Layout tab in the sheet file for each physical sheet that eventually gets printed. The reference files are included as Xrefs in the sheet files with the appropriate views and layers set up for that sheet.

For example, you might have one sheet file called A1 Floor Plan.dwg that has a title block in its Layout tab. That Layout tab has a viewport containing a view of an Xref floor plan file. Another sheet file called A2 Enlarged Plan.dwg might contain the same Xref but with a Layout tab including multiple viewports to show a more detailed set of views of the plan.

The Sheet Set Manager can take this reference/sheet system of file organization and automate it. Without the Sheet Set Manager, you must create the sheet file, import the reference file, and then add a title block, viewport, and labels to produce a finished sheet. The Sheet Set Manager automates many of the fussy details of creating and maintaining the sheet files.

**NOTE**    The example given here illustrates one way that sheet sets can be used. You don't have to organize your drawings in this way to take advantage of sheet sets. The key point to remember is that the sheet sets focus on drawing layouts as the equivalent to drawing sheets. As long as you set up drawings to use layouts for your final output, you can use sheet sets successfully.

## Managing Your Files with Sheet Sets

Sheet sets also serve as a way to gain an overview of your drawing set in a way similar to the table of contents of a book. When you use the Sheet Set Manager, you can view a list of all the drawings in your project and quickly find and open the drawing you need to work on.

You can think of the Sheet Set Manager as a database that contains information about the drawings in the set. It uses a file with the .dst filename extension to store this information. Like a database, this file is updated automatically whenever you make changes to the sheet set. It doesn't wait for you to manually save the sheet-set data. In fact, you won't see a File ➢ Save option in the Sheet Set Manager.

The Sheet Set Manager can change multiple drawing files whenever a change affects the entire set. For example, if there is a change in the project information in the title block, you can update all the title blocks in the set by making a single change in the Sheet Set Manager. The Sheet Set Manager can keep track of title-block data such as submission dates, drawing titles, people who have worked on the individual drawings, and other title-block–related information.

Finally, the Sheet Set Manager can help simplify the printing of whole sets of drawings by automatically setting up AutoCAD's Publish feature. It can help automate your archiving tasks and help collect all the necessary files to send your set to a different location for editing.

# Creating a Sheet Set from an Existing Project

As an introduction to sheet sets, you'll first create a sheet set from an existing set of drawings. You'll then see how your sheet set can be used as a way to keep track of the files in a project.

This example is a small house remodel with some basic drawings. Although the project is small, it will show you the main elements of the Sheet Set Manager.

## Using the Create Sheet Set Wizard

The Create Sheet Set Wizard is the main tool you'll use when creating a sheet set. It offers a step-by-step method for setting up new sheet sets, and as with all wizards, you can back up and make changes along the way. Here's how to use it:

1. In AutoCAD, click the Sheet Set Manager tool on the Standard toolbar to open the Sheet Set Manager palette. (You may see the title bar and tabs reversed from the example shown here, depending on whether the palette is located on the left or right side of the AutoCAD Window.)

2. Click the drop-down list at the top of the palette, and select New Sheet Set to start the Create Sheet Set Wizard.

**WARNING** The Sheet Set Manager won't allow you to create a new sheet set unless a drawing is currently open.

3. Click the Existing Drawings radio button, and then click Next. The Sheet Set Details screen of the wizard appears.

4. Enter **My Existing Sheet Set** for the name of the sheet set.

5. Enter **My first sheet set using samples from Mastering AutoCAD** in the Description text box.

6. Click the Browse button to the right of the Store Sheet Set Data File (.dst) Here text box.

7. Browse to and open the location of the Sheet Set Sample 1 folder, which is in the \Projects\Chapter 28\ folder. This is a folder created when you installed the *Mastering AutoCAD* sample files.

8. Click Next. The Choose Layouts screen of the wizard appears.

9. Click the Import Options button to open the Import Options dialog box.

10. Make sure all three options are selected, and then click OK. You'll learn more about the options in this dialog box in the next section.

11. Click the Browse button, and then locate and select the Sheet Set Sample 1 folder you selected earlier. After you've selected the folder, you see the list of subfolders in that folder.

**TIP** You can set a default location for your sheet sets by using the Files tab of the Options dialog box. See Appendix A for more on the Options dialog box.

**12.** Click the plus signs to expand the listings for Architectural and Structural. You see the drawings in those folders. Expand the list for each drawing to see the layouts available in each drawing. You can select and deselect the layouts and drawings to include in the sheet set.

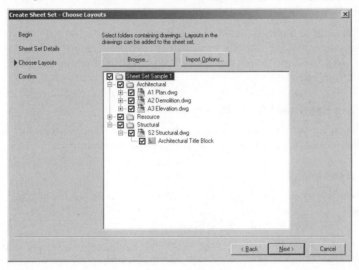

**WARNING** Your list may not be in the same order as shown here, but the contents will be basically the same.

**13.** Remove the check mark next to the Resource folder shown in the list. You don't want to include the Resource folder because that contains the files used as Xrefs in the Paper Space files. You want to select only the drawings and layouts that represent the sheets in your set.

**14.** Click Next. You see the last screen of the wizard, which shows you the statistics of your new sheet set. It shows only the layouts from the selected drawings, because the layouts are the focus of the Sheet Set Manager. Click Finish to exit the wizard. AutoCAD creates new sheet set.

**15.** Select the Sheet List tab in the Sheet Set Manager to view its contents. The Sheet Set Manager now shows a list of the drawings in the Sheet Set Sample 1 folder.

**WARNING** Your Sheet Set Manager may look slightly taller or narrower than the one shown here, because it can be resized by stretching its borders. The order of the drawings may also be different, but the same drawings will be shown. You can click and drag items in the list to change their order.

The Sheet List in the Sheet Set Manager shows the name of the existing drawing files with the layout name appended. This helps you identify both the filename and the layout associated with the sheet. As you become more familiar with the Sheet Set Manager, you can choose to display only the layout name.

## Exploring the Sheet Set Manager

Although you have more work to do before the sheet set becomes a useful tool, it's complete enough that you can explore some features of the Sheet Set Manager before you add the resource drawings.

### FORMATTING SHEET SETS WITH THE IMPORT OPTIONS

In step 9 of the preceding exercise, you saw the Import Options dialog box. This dialog box lets you control how files and folders are organized in the Sheet Set Manager and how the sheets are assigned names. Here is a list of these options:

**Prefix Sheet Titles With File Name** The Sheet Set Manager displays only the layout names in its Sheet List. With this option selected, the Sheet Set Manager adds the name of the file containing the layout as a prefix to the sheet name. If you want only the layout name to appear in the Sheet List, turn off this option.

**Create Subsets Based On Folder Structure** If you set up your file structure to separate your project folder into subfolders (such as architectural, mechanical, structural, and civil), you can retain that structure in the Sheet Set Manager by selecting this option. Turn off this option if you want the Sheet Set Manager to display all the sheets in your project in a single column with no subfolders.

**Ignore Top Level Folder** When you select a project folder containing your drawings for the sheet set, and subfolders are used to keep separate categories of drawings organized, this option causes the Sheet Set Manager to ignore the top-level folder and display only the subfolders. This is useful if you have one main folder that contains subfolders of your drawings.

The sample folders you used for the previous exercise were set up to demonstrate how these options work. All the options were turned on. As a result, the Sheet Set Manager displayed the sheets with two main categories, Architectural and Structural, reflecting the folder structure of the sample project files. It also didn't display the main folder called Sheet Set Sample 1 because you turned on the Ignore Top Level Folder option. Finally, the sheet names showed the layout names appended to the drawing filenames because the Prefix Sheet Titles With File Name option was turned on.

### PREVIEWING AND OPENING DRAWINGS IN THE SHEET SET MANAGER

You can view quite a bit of information about the drawings in your list. You can also open a file by double-clicking its name in the Sheets List. Here's how:

1. Select 1 - A1 Plan - 22x17 Arch Layout - Plan from the Sheet List. The Details group at the bottom of the palette displays a description of the sheet, including the name, location, and size of the file that contains the sheet.

**SETTING THE SHEET SET PROPERTIES**

In the Sheet Set Details screen of the Create Sheet Set Wizard was a button labeled Sheet Set Properties. If you click this button, the Sheet Set Properties dialog box opens, showing you some of the settings that are part of your new sheet set.

Much of this information describes the location of the that the Sheet Set Manager will use as you work with sheet sets. Also note the Edit Custom Properties button at the bottom of the dialog box. This enables you to add or edit some of the properties of the sheet set. This information can be edited in the Sheet Set Manager, as you'll see later.

2. Click the Preview button in the title bar of the Details group. The description changes into a thumbnail view of the drawing.

3. Double-click the 1 - A1 Plan - 22 x17 Arch Layout - Plan listing. AutoCAD opens the drawing.

**ADDING THE RESOURCE DRAWINGS**

Now, you'll add the resource drawings to the Sheet Set Manager's Sheet List. Remember that the resource drawings are the source Xref files for the sheet drawings. By adding them to the Sheet Set Manager, you'll have ready access to all the files in your project:

1. Select the Model Views tab in the Sheet Set Manager. The palette changes to show the Locations list. Right now, nothing is shown except the Add New Location listing.

**NOTE** You may recall that earlier, in the "Using the Create Sheet Set Wizard" section, I asked you not to include the Resource folder. That's because the Create Sheet Set Wizard attempts to create a sheet from all the files in your selection. You don't want to include your resource files as sheets, but you do want to include them as resources.

2. Double-click the Add New Location item. A standard file dialog box opens.

3. Locate and select the Resource subfolder under the Sheet Set Sample 1 folder that you've been using; then, click Open. The Sheet Set Manager palette displays the list of drawings in that folder.

4. Double-click plans.dwg. The plans file opens, showing you the source drawing for the 1 - A1 Plan drawing.

Your sheet set now contains a list of all the files in the project. You can use the Sheet Set Manager to keep track of your AutoCAD files as the project progresses. If you need to plot all your sheets, archive them, or move them, you can do so with relative ease by using options described toward the end of this chapter.

## Adding New Sheets to Your Sheet Set

Now that you've created a sheet set from an existing project, as the project continues you'll want to use the Sheet Set Manager to create any new sheets that you want to add to your set. Doing so ensures that the Sheet Set Manager knows about all the files in the project at all times.

But before you start to add new sheets, you need to do a bit of setup. You'll need to make sure the Sheet Set Manager knows which template file to use for any new sheet drawings you add to the set.

**POINTING TO A SHEET TEMPLATE**

The following exercise will show you how to tell the Sheet Set Manager which template file to use for new sheets:

1. Select the Sheet List tab of the Sheet Set Manager.

2. Right-click My Existing Sheet Set at the top of the Sheet List; then, select Properties. The Sheet Set Properties dialog box opens. (See the "Setting the Sheet Set Properties" sidebar, earlier in this chapter.) You see three groups of listings: Sheet Set, Project Control, and Sheet Creation. The Sheet Set group offers information about the current sheets and sheet set. The Project Control group lets you add information regarding the sheet set, such as the project name, number, and milestones. The Sheet Creation group lists information about new sheets.

3. Click the Sheet Creation Template option in the Sheet Creation group. If you can't read the names of the options, hover your cursor over the name, and the full option name will appear as a ToolTip. A Browse button appears to the right of the option.

4. Click the Browse button to open the Select Layout As Sheet Template dialog box.

   The Drawing Template File Name text box shows the location of the current default file from which a new sheet will be derived. That default location is as follows:

   ```
   C:\Documents and Settings\User Name\Local Settings
   \Application Data\Autodesk\AutoCAD 2008\R17.1\enu
   \Template\SheetSets\Architectural Imperial.dwt
   ```

**TIP**   You can change the default location for sheet set templates in the Files tab of the Options dialog box (choose Tools ➢ Options). In the Files tab, expand the list for Template Settings, select Sheet Set Template File Location, click Browse, and then locate and select your sheet-set template file location.

   Also note that a layout name is listed in the Select A Layout To Create New Sheets list box.

5. Continue to select a template file. Click the Browse button to the far right of the Drawing Template File Name text box to open the Select Drawing dialog box. This is a standard file dialog box.

6. Browse to the \Chapter 28\Sheet Set Sample 1\Resource folder, select the 22×17 Arch.dwt file, and then click Open. This is the template file used for the sheet drawings of the set you've been working with.

7. Back in the Select Layout As Sheet Template dialog box, select Architectural Title Block from the Select A Layout To Create New Sheets list; then, click OK. Click OK in the Sheet Set Properties dialog box.

8. A confirmation window asks whether you want to apply the change you made to all nested subsets. Click Yes.

You've just set up your sheet set to point to a custom template that contains the title block for any new sheet files you may create. The last step points out a feature you'll want to be aware of.

In this exercise, you set the 22x17 Arch.dwt template file to be the file the Sheet Set Manager uses for all new drawings. If you prefer, you can set up the Sheet Set Manager to use different template files for new sheets in the sheet subsets. For example, you can have one template for the Architectural subset and a different one for the Structural subset, if they require different title blocks.

To set up the template for the subsets, follow the steps in the previous exercise, but instead of right-clicking My Existing Sheet Set, select the subset name. In the Sheet Set Sample 1 sheet set, the name would be Architectural or Structural.

Another option is to select the Prompt For Template option near the bottom of the Sheet Set Properties dialog box. As the option name indicates, it prompts you for a template file whenever you create a new sheet.

### ADDING A NEW SHEET

You're ready to create new sheets that are based on the same title block as the existing sheets in the set:

1. In the Sheet Set Manager palette, right-click the Architectural subset listing, and select New Sheet to add a sheet under this heading. The New Sheet dialog box opens.

2. In the Number text box, enter **A4**; and in the Sheet Title text box, enter **Details**. As you type, the File Name text box is automatically filled in. You can enter a different sheet title if you like.

3. Click OK to finish creating your new sheet. Your new sheet appears in the Sheet List of the Sheet Set Manager palette.

4. Double-click the A4 - Details listing in the Sheet List. The A4 Details drawing opens to the Layout tab. The Layout tab has been given the name A4 Details.

5. After reviewing these steps, you can close all the drawings and the Sheet Set Manager.

Before you added the new A4 Details sheet, the Sheet Set Manager was only collecting data about your sheet set and displaying that data in the palette. It hadn't created any new files. In the preceding exercise, the Sheet Set Manager created the A4 Details file, although it didn't open it until you double-clicked it in step 4.

Now that the A4 sheet has been created, you can edit it as you would any other drawing to include Xref files, blocks, or other drawing data. You can then create a viewport in the layout to lay out the sheet the way you want.

**TIP** In addition to keeping track of existing and new drawing files in a project, the Sheet Set Manager can help you with plotting, archiving, and publishing your set. See the "Archiving, Publishing, and eTransmitting Sheet Sets" section, later in this chapter.

In a large project with many sheets, managing title-block information can be a lot of work. In the next section, you'll look at some other sheet-set features that can automate much of the work of maintaining title-block information. You'll also learn how the Sheet Set Manager can simplify the creation of callout bubbles and cross-references between drawings.

# Managing Title Blocks and Cross-References

You've just seen that at a basic level, you can use the Sheet Set Manager to keep track of files in a set of drawings. But other features can help reduce the time it takes to create and maintain sheets. In this section, you'll look at some of the more advanced sheet-set features by creating a sheet set based on an existing one.

The Sheet Set Manager can use specially designed template files to automate the creation and management of your sheets. You can include fields (see Chapter 11 for more on fields) that are *sheet set aware*, enabling the Sheet Set Manager to automatically update text whenever there is a change in the sheet set. In addition, the Sheet Set Manager can use blocks with field attributes to automate the process of adding drawing titles and reference symbols, called *callout blocks* in the Sheet Set Manager. You can customize these templates and callout blocks to fit your particular style of drawing and method of organization.

## Creating a New Sheet Set Based on an Existing One

To see firsthand how the Sheet Set Manager can help you manage title blocks and cross-references, you'll create a new sheet set based on an existing sample sheet set created by Autodesk. You'll use a sample sheet set found in the user template folder for new AutoCAD 2008 installations. This sample sheet set uses a template file that has the title block and callout blocks already set up and available for use.

Just as before, you'll start by opening the Create Sheet Set Wizard. Follow these steps:

1. If it isn't already open, click the Sheet Set Manager tool on the Standard toolbar.

2. Open a new, blank file. Click the drop-down list at the top of the palette, and select New Sheet Set to start the Create Sheet Set Wizard.

3. Make sure the An Example Sheet Set radio button is selected, and click Next. The Sheet Set Example screen appears. Here you can select from the standard sheet-set examples provided by Autodesk; or, if you have a custom sheet set or sheet sets from a third party, you can use the Browse To Another Sheet Set To Use As An Example option.

4. Make sure the Select A Sheet Set To Use As An Example radio button is selected. Then, select Architectural Imperial Sheet Set from the list box, and click Next. The Sheet Set Details screen appears.

5. Enter **My Sheet Set** in the Name Of New Sheet Set input box. You also have the opportunity to add a description of the sheet set in the Description box. The Store Sheet Set Data File (.dst) Here option lets you determine where the sheet-set data file is stored. You can see the current location by placing the cursor over the input box. A ToolTip displays the path to the location. This ToolTip is useful if the path is too long to read from the input box.

6. Click the Browse button to the right of the Store Sheet Set Data File input box, and browse to the location of the sample files for this chapter. Typically, this location is \Chapter 28\ Sheet Set Sample 2.

7. Back in the Sheet Set Details screen of the Create Sheet Set Wizard, click Next. The Confirm screen appears. This screen lets you review the settings before you confirm the creation of your sheet set. You've seen this information in the Sheet Set Properties dialog box.

8. Click the Finish button to create your new sheet set. A list of predefined sheet categories appears in the Sheet List tab of the Sheet Set Manager.

Now, if you check your sample file folder, `\Chapter 28\Sheet Set Sample 2`, you'll find the `My Sheet Set.dst` file that you've just created. As you've seen in prior steps, this file holds the information regarding the location of the files and custom settings for your sheet set.

In the first sheet set you created, you created a sheet set from drawings that already had Xrefs and views set up for the sheets. The next section shows you how to use the Sheet Set Manager to create a sheet from scratch, including views and Xrefs.

## Building a Set of Drawings

The sheet set you just created is like the framework of your set of plans. It isn't the actual set of drawings, but rather a structure onto which you can start to build your set of drawings. The Sheet Set Manager manages the coordination and continuity of the set as you add sheets to the set.

To see how these drawing components are managed by the Sheet Set Manager, you'll create some sheets from existing Model Space files. You'll start by adding a couple of floor plans to the sheet set.

You'll use the resource drawings that you saw in the first set of exercises in this chapter as the basis for the new sheets.

### SETTING UP SOME VIEWS

The Sheet Set Manager uses drawing views to help simplify the creation of viewports in a sheet, so you'll start by creating some views in a plan drawing. These views will define the areas and layer settings that will be needed later when you create the plan sheets. Follow these steps:

1. Open the `plans.dwg` file from the `Chapter 28\Sheet Set Sample 2\Resource` folder. You see two plans of the house. The top plan is a floor plan, and the lower plan is a combination of a floor plan and a site plan.

2. Click the Layer Properties Manager tool.

3. Click the Layer States Manager tool at upper left in the Layer Properties Manager dialog box.

4. In the Layer States Manager dialog box, select Plan_site from the list box, and click the Restore button.

5. Click OK in the Layer Properties Manager dialog box.

You've just restored a layer state that shows all the appropriate layers for the site plan. Next, you'll save a view of just the site plan, which you'll use a bit later when you create the site plan sheet:

1. Choose View ➢ Named Views to open the View Manager dialog box.

2. Make sure Current is selected in the list to the left. Then, click the New button.

3. In the New View dialog box, enter **Site Plan** for the View name. Click the Define View Window button. The dialog box temporarily closes to enable you to select a window to define the view area.

4. Place a selection window around the area shown in Figure 28.1. Press ↵ when you're satisfied with the boundary selection.

5. Back in the New View dialog box, make sure the Save Layer Snapshot With View option is select, and click OK.

6. Click OK in the View Manager dialog box to close it.

**TIP**    If you need to adjust the view area, open the View Manager dialog box again, select the view name from the list box, and click the Define View Window button. The dialog box closes temporarily, and the drawing displays with the view area highlighted. You can then reselect the view area with a selection window.

**FIGURE 28.1**
Selecting the
view area

You've just created a view for the site plan. Now, create another view for the floor plan:

1. Click the Layer Properties Manager tool again. Then, click the Layer States Manager tool in the Layer Properties Manager dialog box.

2. In the Layer States Manager dialog box, select Plan_finish from the list box, and click the Restore button.

3. Click OK in the Layer Properties Manager dialog box to close it.

4. Choose View ➢ Named Views to open the View Manager dialog box.

5. Make sure Current is selected in the left panel. Then, click New.

6. In the New View dialog box, enter **Floor Plan** for the View name. Click the Define View Window button. Then, place a selection window around the area shown in Figure 28.2. Press ↵ when you're satisfied with the area you've selected.

**FIGURE 28.2**
Selecting the
view area

7. Back in the New View dialog box, click OK. Then, click OK in the View Manager dialog box to close it.

8. Choose File ➢ Save to save the changes you've just made, and then close the `plans.dwg` file.

If you know that you want to use other views for your sheets, you can continue to define more views. But for this exercise, let's move on to creating a sheet from the views you just created.

### CREATING A SHEET

Now that you have some views defined, you're ready to create a sheet for those views:

1. If it isn't already open, click the Sheet Set Manager tool on the Standard toolbar.

2. Select Architectural from the list, right-click, and select New Sheet to open the New Sheet dialog box.

3. Enter **A1** in the Number input box. This defines the sheet number that will appear in the lower-right corner of the sheet. As you type, your entry appears in both the Number input box and the File Name input box.

4. Enter **Site Plan and Floor Plan** in the Sheet Title input box. Again, as you type, your entry appears in both the Sheet Title input box and the File Name input box.

5. Click OK. AutoCAD creates a new file called `A1 - Site Plan and Floor Plan`, and the new drawing name appears as a subhead below Architectural in the Sheet Set Manager.

6. Double-click the A1 - Site Plan And Floor Plan listing. The sheet appears in AutoCAD.

If you look closely, you'll notice that the sheet number is already in place in the lower-right corner of the drawing. The Sheet Set Manager was able to apply the sheet number you entered in step 3 to the new sheet because the template uses a field for the sheet-number text. You'll learn how to add such a field to your own title block later in this chapter. For now, you'll add the views you created in the `plans.dwg` file to this new sheet.

### ADDING YOUR VIEWS TO THE NEW SHEET

You've created views in your `plans.dwg` resource drawing, and you've created a new sheet for the Plan views. The next step is to insert those saved views into the sheet.

Start by adding the resource drawings to the sheet set:

1. Click the Model Views tab, and then double-click Add New Location in the Locations list.

2. Browse to and open the `\Chapter28\Sheet Set Sample 2\Resource` folder. The files in the Resource folder appear in the list of resource drawings.

With the resource files added to the Sheet Set Manager, you can add a view to the A1 sheet from the `plans.dwg` file you worked on earlier:

1. Click the plus sign next to the `plans.dwg` item. The list expands to show the Site Plan and Floor Plan views you created earlier in this chapter.

2. Make sure the A1 Site Plan And Floor Plan drawing is current; then, select Site Plan from the list, right-click, and choose Place On Sheet. Don't click your mouse yet; but as you move the cursor

over the A1 - Site Plan And Floor Plan layout, a rectangle appears at the cursor and covers most of the drawing.

3. Right-click in the Layout view to display a list of drawing scales.

4. Select ⅛″ = 1′ from the list. You see the Site Plan view of `plans.dwg` along with a title bubble, all following the cursor. You can also click and drag the Site Plan view from the list into the sheet to get the same result.

5. Place the view in the top half of the layout, and click. The Site Plan view is placed in the layout along with a title bubble, drawing scale, and view title.

6. Back in the Sheet Set Manager, select Floor Plan from the list. Right-click, and select Place On Sheet.

7. Right-click in the Layout view, and select ¼″ = 1′ from the list.

8. Place the view in the lower half of the layout, and click. The Floor Plan view is placed in the layout along with a title bubble, drawing scale, and view title.

9. Zoom in to the title bubble for the Site Plan view. It already has the proper view name and scale.

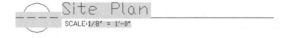

In the preceding exercise, the Sheet Set Manager performed several steps that you could have done manually with much more effort. It imported the `plans.dwg` file as an Xref into the A1 - Site Plan And Floor Plan layout. It then created a viewport in the layout, scaled the layout view according to your selections in steps 4 and 7, and finally added a title bubble and the title and scale for each view.

**EDITING THE VIEW NUMBERS**

You need to take care of one more item for this sheet. Although the view names and scales have been provided by the Sheet Set Manager, you still need the view numbers. Right now, they're just three dashes. Follow these steps:

1. In the Sheet Set Manager, select the Sheet Views tab.

2. Expand the list, and select Site Plan; then, right-click, and select Rename & Renumber to open the Rename & Renumber View dialog box.

3. Enter 1 in the Number input box. The name of the view is available for editing as well.

4. Click the Next or Previous button, whichever is available for selection. This advances the data in the dialog box to the next view, which is the Floor Plan view. Enter **2** in the Number input box. Once again, you see the name of the view.

5. Click OK, and then choose View ≻ Regen. The title bubbles change to show the numbers 1 and 2 for the two views.

The final task is to hide the viewport borders. You can do this by creating a layer just for the viewports and then turning off that layer:

1. Use the Layer Properties Manager to create a layer called Viewport.

2. Turn off the Viewport layer, and click OK to close the Layer Properties Manager.

3. Select the two viewports. Select Viewport from the Layer drop-down list in the Layers toolbar. A warning message tells you that the layer you've assigned to the selected objects is frozen or turned off. Click OK. The viewports disappear.

Adding the view numbers is important for two reasons. The obvious one is so you have a number you can refer to when referencing this plan sheet in the future. But the Sheet Set Manager also keeps track of this view number so that later, when you start to add callout blocks to your drawing set, the Sheet Set Manager knows which view goes with the callout block you're adding. The next section will show you how this works.

## Adding Callout Blocks as Cross-Reference Symbols

As mentioned earlier, in the process of building a set of drawings, you'll have to add cross-reference symbols. One common type of cross-reference indicates an elevation view of a building from a floor plan.

In a typical set of architectural drawings, you'll have a sheet or several sheets that show the sides of a building. The most common views are the north, south, east, and west sides of a building. Elevation drawings are used to indicate window locations, wall finishes, building heights, floor levels, and other key elements in the design. Reference symbols, called *callout blocks* in AutoCAD, are placed in the floor plan and tell the viewer which sheet contains these elevation drawings and show where the view is taken in relation to the plan.

In this section, you'll learn how to set up an Elevation view and place callout blocks in the floor plan that show which sheet contains the elevation. You'll see how callout blocks are tied to sheet numbers so that even if a sheet number changes, the callout block always indicates the right sheet number.

You'll use a sheet set similar to the one you just started, but with a few additions to save some work for you. The My Sheet Set 1.dst sheet set has the A1 Site Plan And Floor Plan sheet already created and an additional sheet called A2 Elevation Plan. This additional sheet contains two Elevation views. These Elevation views were created in the same way as the Plan views in the previous exercise, so no method was used to create them that you haven't already been shown.

In the following steps, you'll add a callout block to the A1 sheet that references the A2 sheet. Along the way, you'll become familiar with some of the other features of the Sheet Set Manager.

Start by closing the current sheet set and the files associated with it:

1. In the Sheet Set Manager, select the Sheet List tab.

2. Right-click My Sheet Set in the list, and click Close Sheet Set.

3. Close and save any drawing that may be open except the blank default drawing file.

Next, open the sample sheet set:

1. Click Open from the drop-down list. Then, in the Open Sheet Set dialog box, locate and select My Sheet 1.dst in the Chapter 28\Sheet Set Sample 3 folder. Click Open in the Open Sheet Set dialog box.

2. Make sure the Sheet List tab is selected; then, double-click A1 Site Plan And Floor Plan and A2 Elevations to open these two files.

Go ahead and add the callout symbol to the A1 sheet:

1. In the Sheet List tab of the Sheet Set Manager, double-click the A1 sheet again. Because it's already open, double-clicking the A1 sheet makes it the current drawing file.

2. Enlarge your view of the floor plan so it looks similar to Figure 28.3.

3. Click the Sheet Views tab; then, select and right-click 1 - South Elevation.

**FIGURE 28.3**

Enlarge your view, and place the callout block as shown.

Place the 2 - West Elevation callout block here.

Place the 1 - South Elevation callout block here.

4. Choose Place Callout Block ➢ Elev Indicator Ext - Up from the shortcut menu. As you move the cursor into the drawing area, a symbol appears at the cursor. This is the callout block for the exterior elevation.

5. Position the callout block as shown in Figure 28.3, and click. The callout block already shows the appropriate drawing number and sheet number.

6. Right-click 2 - West Elevation, and choose Place Callout Block ➢ Elev Indicator Ext - Right from the shortcut menu.

7. Place this callout block to the left of the floor plan, as shown in Figure 28.3.

When you inserted the callout blocks in steps 4 through 7, the Sheet Set Manager automatically added the appropriate sheet and view number to the block, saving you the effort of checking which drawing contained the Elevation view and making sure the numbers between the callout block and view matched.

**TIP** Later, when you learn how to create your own custom callout blocks, you'll learn about the hyperlink feature. The callout blocks you just added have this feature turned on; if you Ctrl+click the text of either of the callout blocks, AutoCAD will open the drawing containing the view that the callout block references—namely, the A2 Elevation drawing.

## Editing Sheet Numbers and Title Block Information

Suppose you need to change the sheet number of the elevation sheet from A2 to A3 to make room for a demolition plan. The following exercise demonstrates how the Sheet Set Manager can make quick work of such a change:

1. In the Sheet Set Manager, select the Sheet List tab.

2. Right-click the A2 Elevations sheet item, and choose Rename & Renumber.

3. In the Rename & Renumber Sheet dialog box, change the number from A2 to A3; then, click OK.

4. Choose View ➢ Regen. The Elevation callout blocks you added earlier now show the new sheet number for the Elevation sheet.

5. Double-click A3 Elevations from the Sheet List tab, and choose View ➢ Regen. The sheet number in the lower-right corner of the drawing changes to A3.

As you saw from this exercise, the drawing numbers are coordinated through settings in the Sheet Set Manager as long as you use the callout symbols from the Sheet Set Manager.

Drawing numbers aren't the only part that can be managed through the Sheet Set Manager. You have two sheets in the set now, but they were created without regard for the client name and address in the title block. You'll need to go back and add this information to the sheets. Here's a quick way to do it:

1. In the Sheet List of the Sheet Set Manager, right-click My Sheet Set 1 at the top of the list box; then, choose Properties to open the Sheet Set Properties dialog box.

2. Scroll down to the lower half of the Sheet Set Properties dialog box, where you see a set of options labeled Sheet Set Custom Properties. Click the Project Address 1 label, and enter **444 Crescent Way** for the first line of the address. (Or you can add anything you like.) You may need to widen the first column to read the label or hover over the label to see a ToolTip showing the full label.

3. In the next option, Project Address 2, enter **Big Bear, Ca**.

4. Enter **Smith Residence** for the Project Name.

5. Leave the Client, Project Number, and Project Address 3 options blank. Click OK.

6. Zoom in to the lower-right corner of the sheet so you can clearly see the title-block information; then, click View ➢ Regen to display the changes in the current sheet.

The changes you made in this exercise affect all the existing sheets in the set. If you add new sheets, they will also display the new address and project name.

## Closing a Sheet Set

By now, you have two sheet sets open: the one you created from an existing set of drawings, and the one you opened for the latest set of exercises. In the next section, you'll look at customizing sheet sets. You won't need both sheet sets open. Close the one you've been working on by following these steps:

1. Click the drop-down list at the top of the Sheet Set Manager.

2. Right-click My Sheet Set 1, and select Close Sheet Set.

3. In preparation for the next section, close all the drawings that are open in AutoCAD except the 22 ×17 Arch.dwt file; leave the Sheet Set Manager open. You'll need the 22 ×17 Arch.dwt file for a later exercise, so if it isn't open, open it now.

**WARNING**  Closing a sheet set doesn't automatically close the drawings associated with it.

As you can see, you can have multiple sheet sets open at any one time. This feature can facilitate the movement of drawing data from one project to another. For example, you may want to borrow construction details from one set to add to a new set. You can use the Sheet Set Manager to locate the detail sheet from the prior project and then cut and paste drawing data from that drawing into a drawing in your most current project.

# Customizing Sheet Sets

In the preceding section, you created and used a sheet set that was based on a canned sheet set from Autodesk. That sheet set included a title block with many of the field text objects already embedded in the title block so you could take advantage of the Sheet Set Manager's ability to control the text in the title block. The view title bubbles and callout blocks were also supplied, and they contained the field text objects to automate the insertion of view names and coordination of callout cross-reference numbers.

But not everyone will want to use the title blocks and symbols offered in the Autodesk samples. You aren't limited to using the canned sheet set from Autodesk. In this section, you'll look at how to customize your own title block to work with the Sheet Set Manager. You'll also learn how to create custom view titles and callout blocks.

## Customizing a Title Block

To begin your exploration of sheet-set customization, you'll add field objects to the sample title block you used at the beginning of this chapter. Remember that the first project included an existing set of drawings that wasn't set up to take full advantage of all the sheet-set features you saw in the latest set of exercises. The title block in that early exercise contained some attributes that could be used to include text information, but the title block was not *sheet-set aware*. To prepare a title block for use with the Sheet Set Manager, you'll need to convert those attribute values into field objects. This entails editing the title block and saving it as the template file for the sheet set.

**WARNING** In this section, I use the terms *title block* and *AutoCAD block*, which may cause confusion. *Title block* is a standard drafting term meaning the drawing border and drawing title information, including a business logo and other textual information about the drawing. *AutoCAD block* refers to the type of AutoCAD object known as a *block* that is a collection of objects combined into one object. See Chapter 4 for more on AutoCAD blocks.

### SETTING UP SHEET NUMBERS AND TITLES

The first thing you'll do is set up the title block to create a sheet-set aware number and title. This will enable the Sheet Set Manager to control the number and title that appears in the title block, as you saw in earlier exercises.

You could open the template file and start editing the title block without involving the Sheet Set Manager in any way. But in the following set of exercises, you'll edit the template file with a little help from the Sheet Set Manager. By using the Sheet Set Manager while editing your template file, you'll be able to get instant feedback on your edits.

Start by creating a new sheet in the sheet set you created in the beginning of this chapter. You'll use this new sheet to edit the title block. Follow these steps:

1. If it's closed, open the My Existing Sheet Set sheet set. Remember that this was the first sheet set in the \Chapter 28\Sheet Set Sample 1 folder.

2. In the Sheet List, right-click the sheet set name at the top of the list, and choose New Sheet.

3. In the New Sheet dialog box, enter **000** for the sheet number and **Template Edit** for the sheet title. Click OK. The sheet number and title can be anything because this isn't a sheet you'll save.

4. In the Sheet Set Manager, double-click 000 - Template Edit. The sheet you just created appears in the AutoCAD Window.

Remember that a new file based on a template is really just a copy of the template. As I mentioned earlier, the title block is an AutoCAD block that contains attribute definitions. To edit those definitions, you'll need to explode the block:

1. Click the title block to select it.

2. Click the Explode tool on the Modify toolbar.

Now, you're ready to edit the attribute definitions. Start by editing the definition for the sheet number in the lower-right corner of the title block:

1. Locate the attribute definition in the lower-right corner of the title block that shows a large *No.*, and double-click it. This is the attribute definition for the sheet number. The Edit Attribute Definition dialog box opens.

2. Double-click in the Default text box. Right-click it, and choose Insert Field to open the Field dialog box.

3. Select SheetSet from the Field Category drop-down list.

4. In the Field Names list box, select CurrentSheetNumber.

5. In the Format list box, select Uppercase. Then, click OK.

6. Back in the Edit Attribute Definition dialog box, the Default text box now shows 000, the number you assigned to this drawing. This tells you that your field attribute is working properly, because the default value shows the current sheet number. The gray background of the text tells you that the text is a field.

**7.** Click OK to exit the Edit Attribute Definition dialog box.

**8.** Press ↵ to exit attribute-editing mode.

In step 6, you received instant feedback when you assigned the CurrentSheetNumber attribute field to the attribute definition. The default value changed to the sheet number of the current drawing. Next, you'll make a similar change to add the project name to the title block:

**1.** Zoom in to the area of the title block that shows the project information.

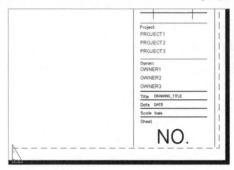

**2.** Double-click the DRAWING_TITLE attribute definition just below the OWNER3 attribute definition.

**3.** As in the preceding exercise, select the Default value, right-click, and choose Insert Field.

**4.** Select CurrentSheetTitle from the Field Names list, and select Title Case from the Format list.

**5.** Click OK. Now the Default value is the current sheet title, Template Edit.

**6.** Click OK to accept the changes in the Edit Attribute Definition dialog box.

**7.** Press ↵ to exit attribute-editing mode.

These two exercises demonstrated how you can add a field object to an attribute definition and have those definitions give you immediate feedback about their association to the sheet set. In the first case, the default sheet number in the Edit Attribute Definition dialog box reflected the current sheet number. In the second exercise, you saw that the sheet title appeared.

### ADDING CUSTOM SHEET-SET PROPERTIES

You've added two of the standard sheet-set fields to the title block. The standard fields are the ones that appear in the Field Names list in the Field dialog box. But what if you want to add custom sheet-set fields that aren't on the list? You can create your own field categories in the Sheet Set Manager. In the following set of exercises, you'll create some custom fields in the Sheet Set Manager properties dialog box and then add those fields to your title block.

First, set up some new custom fields:

**1.** In the Sheet Set Manager, right-click My Existing Sheet Set at the top of the Sheet List, and choose Properties.

**2.** At the bottom of the Sheet Set Properties dialog box, click the Edit Custom Properties button to open the Custom Properties dialog box.

**3.** Click the Add button to open the Add Custom Property dialog box.

**4.** In the Name text box, enter **Project 1**. This will be the first line for the project information area in the title block.

**5.** In the Default Value text box, enter **Project Line 1**.

**6.** In the Owner group at the bottom of the dialog box, make sure Sheet Set is selected. This tells the Sheet Set Manager that this value applies to all the sheets in the set, not just the individual sheets.

**7.** Click OK to return to the Custom Properties dialog box.

**8.** Repeat steps 3 through 7 to add two more custom properties called **Project 2** and **Project 3**, with the values **Project Line 2** and **Project Line 3**.

**9.** Click OK to close the Custom Properties dialog box, and then click OK in the Sheet Set Properties dialog box.

You've created some custom properties. Now, include those properties in your title block:

**1.** Pan up to the area in the title block that shows the project information.

**2.** Double-click the Project 1 attribute definition. In the Edit Attribute Definition dialog box, highlight the Default text box, right-click, and choose Insert Field.

**3.** In the Field Names list box, select CurrentSheetSetCustom.

**4.** Open the Custom Property Name drop-down list near the bottom of the dialog box, and select Project1. All the custom properties you created are listed here.

**5.** Click OK to return to the Edit Attribute Definition dialog box. The default field value shows Project Line 1, which is the default value you gave for the custom properties in the previous exercise.

6. Click OK, and then repeat steps 2 through 5 for the Project 2 and Project 3 attribute definitions.

7. Press ↵ to exit attribute-editing mode.

### SAVING YOUR NEW TITLE BLOCK AS A TEMPLATE

You've just seen how to include custom sheet-set properties in your title block. Now, you're ready to convert your newly edited title block back into the template file you're using for this sheet set. First, you need to turn your exploded title block back into an AutoCAD block object:

1. Zoom out so you can see all of the title block.

2. Click the Make Block tool on the Draw toolbar.

3. Select 22 × 17 Arch Block from the Name drop-down list.

4. Click the Select Objects button, and select the entire title block.

5. Make sure the Convert To Block radio button is selected in the Objects group.

6. Click OK. A warning message tells you that you're about to redefine the 22 × 17ArchBlock block. Click Yes.

7. The Edit Attributes dialog box opens. You don't need to change anything here, so click OK.

---

### TAKING ADVANTAGE OF OTHER FIELD OPTIONS

As you learned in Chapter 11, you can add field objects directly to a drawing if you want drawing data to appear as text. For example, you can add field text directly in a drawing layout to provide information about the author of a drawing, the date the drawing was printed, or the scale to which the layout is set for plotting.

This information can be included in small print on the border of the drawing to aid others when they need to know more about the drawing's origin. You can either add the field directly to the drawing by using the Field command or include it in Mtext or Dtext as part of a paragraph or sentence. Here is a list of field options from the Field Category list in the Field dialog box to help you get an idea of what you can include as text in a sheet:

**Date & Time**   Lets you add a date and time stamp to your drawing. You can select from a variety of date and time styles or show only a date or only a time.

**Document**   Lets you add data from the drawing properties that are stored in AutoCAD by using the Dwgprops command (choose File ➤ Drawing Properties). This includes information such as the author, filename and size, comments, title, and subject.

**Linked**   Lets you add a hyperlink to another file.

**Objects**   Lets you include the name or property of an object. For example, you can add a block name as a field text label, or you can add an object's layer.

**Other**   Lets you add Diesel expressions or system-variable values as field text.

**Plot**   Lets you display plot settings as text in your drawing. This can be useful to help others determine how a drawing was plotted.

**SheetSet**   Offers options to help automate many of the labeling chores you normally do when creating sheets.

The title block now shows the sheet number 000; if you look closely, you'll also see that the sheet title shows Template Edit. These are the name and number you assigned to this sheet when you first created it.

The next task is to save the file as the template file for the current sheet set:

1. Right-click in the Layout tab labeled 000 Template Edit, and choose Rename.

2. Rename the layout **My Title Block**.

3. Choose File ➢ Save As. In the Save Drawing As dialog box, select AutoCAD Drawing Template (*.dwt) from the File Of Type drop-down list.

   Browse to the location of the template file for this sheet set, select 2217 Arch.dwt, and click Save. This location is \Chapter 28\Sheet Set Sample 1\Resource. Click Yes in the warning message box.

4. Click OK in the Template Description dialog box.

**TIP** Normally, at this point you could close the newly saved template file and remove the 000 - Template Edit sheet from the Sheet List, but you'll use this file again later when you create other components of the sheet set.

### TESTING THE NEW TEMPLATE

Now, you can test the new template to make sure it's working. You'll start by creating a new sheet to check whether the sheet number and title appear correctly:

1. Right-click My Existing Sheet Set, and choose New Sheet.

2. Enter **A5** for the number and **Schedules** for the title; then, click OK.

3. Double-click A5 - Schedules from the Sheet List of the Sheet Set Manager to open it. The sheet shows A5 for the number and Schedules for the title.

You also added some custom sheet-set properties. Do the following to see if they're working properly:

1. Right-click My Existing Sheet Set at the top of the Sheet List in the Sheet Set Manager, and choose Properties.

2. Toward the bottom of the Sheet Set Properties dialog box, change the value for Project1 to **John Smith Residence**.

3. Change the value for Project 2 to 123 **Anystreet**. Change the value for Project 3 to **Roseville, California**.

4. Click OK.

5. Choose View ➢ Regen. The title block now shows the new project information you just edited.

You've customized the title block with custom properties and a sheet-set aware number and title. Armed with this information, you can customize any title block to take full advantage of the sheet-set features.

You can include a lot of information in the title block through the Sheet Set field option. Table 28.1 gives you a rundown of the sheet-set options to help you decide what you may want to include.

**TABLE 28.1:** Field Options Available for Sheet Sets

| FIELD NAME | PURPOSE |
| --- | --- |
| CurrentSheetCustom | Displays custom sheet data. Custom sheet data can be added and edited through the Sheet Set Properties dialog box. |
| CurrentSheetDescription | Displays the description for the current sheet found in the properties for the sheet. Select the sheet name from the Sheet Set Manager's Sheet List tab, right-click, and choose Properties. |
| CurrentSheetNumber | Displays the current sheet number. |
| CurrentSheetNumberAndTitle | Displays the sheet number and title combined into one line of text. |
| CurrentSheetSet | Displays the name of the current sheet set. |
| CurrentSheetSetCustom | Displays a custom value for the current sheet set. |
| CurrentSheetSetDescription | Displays the sheet set description, which can be found in the Sheet Set Properties dialog box. |
| CurrentSheetSetSubSet | Displays the name of a subset of the current sheet set. |
| CurrentSheetTitle | Displays the current sheet title. |
| SheetSet | Displays any standard sheet-set value (such as sheet number and title, sheet title, sheet number, or sheet description) from any sheet in the sheet set. |
| SheetSetPlaceholder | Displays standard sheet-set values from within callout blocks. |
| SheetView | Displays sheet-set view data such as view title, view number, or view scale. |
| CurrentSheetCategory | Displays a category field. |
| CurrentSheetIssuePurpose | Displays an Issue Purpose field. |
| CurrentSheetRevisionDate | Displays a Revision Date field. |
| CurrentSheetRevisionNumber | Displays a Revision Number field. |
| CurrentSheetProjectMilestone | Displays a Project Milestone field. |
| CurrentSheetProjectName | Displays a Project Name field. |
| CurrentSheetProjectNumber | Displays Project Number field. |
| CurrentSheetProjectPhase | Displays a Project Phase field. |

## Creating Custom View Labels and Callout Blocks

In the earlier section "Managing Title Blocks and Cross-References," you learned how to create a new sheet set from an existing one. You saw that the Sheet Set Manager was able to automatically create a viewport and add a view label, including a view number bubble, a view title, and the scale for the view. Just like the title block, the view label you used in the "Adding Your Views to the New Sheet" section was a block with field attribute values. You can create your own view-label block or edit an existing one by using the methods you've already seen for the title block. Callout blocks are also created and edited in the same way.

### CREATING THE COMPONENTS OF YOUR VIEW LABEL

In this section, you'll create a custom view label. This will help you to understand which field attributes are used for the view label. You'll also learn how to set up the Sheet Set Manager to use your custom block.

Just as with the title block, you could create the view-label block in AutoCAD without using the Sheet Set Manager, but using it simplifies your work and also helps verify that you're on the right track. You'll start by going back to the template file you edited earlier, and then you'll create the graphics and attribute definitions for your custom view label.

1. Return to the 22 ×17 Arch.dwt file that you updated in the earlier exercise. You can use the Windows menu in the menu bar to return to the file. You'll add the view label block to this drawing.

2. Make sure the current layer is set to 0; then, draw a circle with a 0.25″ diameter.

3. Add a line to the right of the circle that is 1″ long, as shown in Figure 28.4.

**FIGURE 28.4**
Beginning to create the view-label block

0.25″-diameter circle        1″ line

4. Choose Draw ➤ Block ➤ Define Attributes to open the Attribute Definition dialog box.

**5.** Enter **ViewNumber** in the Tag text box and **View Number** in the Prompt text box.

**6.** Click the Insert Field button to the right of the Value text box to open the Field dialog box.

**7.** Select SheetSet in the Field Category drop-down list; then, select SheetSetPlaceholder from the Field Names list.

**8.** Select ViewNumber from the Placeholder Type list and Uppercase from the Format list.

You've just added the field that this block will need for the view number. Next, you need to make sure the text is formatted correctly.

**9.** Click OK to return to the Attribute Definition dialog box. Set the Justification value in the Text Options group to Middle, and set the Height value to 0.15.

**10.** Turn on the Preset option in the Mode group.

**WARNING**    If you don't turn on this option, you'll be prompted for the attribute value when the view is inserted, even though the Sheet Set Manager supplies these values automatically.

**11.** Click OK. Then, use the Center osnap to place the attribute definition in the center of the circle. *VIEWNUMBER* appears in large letters, centered on the circle.

**TIP**    If you forgot a setting in the previous steps, you can always go back and use the Properties palette to modify the attribute definition settings. Select the attribute definition, right-click, and choose Properties.

Next, you need to add the view title and scale. The steps to add these parts of the view label are the same as for the view number you just added. You first create an attribute definition by using the Insert Field option for the attribute value. The only difference is the location and text options for the attribute definition. Here are the steps:

**1.** Choose Draw ➣ Block ➣ Define Attributes to open the Attribute Definition dialog box. Enter **ViewTitle** in the Tag text box and **View Title** in the Prompt text box.

2. Click the Insert Field button to the right of the Value text box to open the Fields dialog box. Select SheetSet in the Field Category drop-down list, and select SheetSetPlaceholder from the Field Names list.

3. Select ViewTitle from the Placeholder Type list and Title Case from the Format list.

4. Click OK. Then, in the Attribute Definition dialog box, set Justification to Left and Height to 0.15. Also make sure the Preset option in the Mode group is selected.

5. Click OK, and place the attribute definition approximately as shown in Figure 28.5.

**FIGURE 28.5**

The parts of the view-label block

Base point | View title attribute definition

VIEWNUMBER VIEWTITLE VIEWSCALE

View scale attribute definition

Finally, you need to add the scale information to the view title:

1. Choose Draw ➣ Block ➣ Define Attributes to open the Attribute Definition dialog box a third time. Enter **ViewScale** in the Tag text box and **View Scale** in the Prompt text box.

2. Click the Insert Field button to open the Fields dialog box. Make sure Sheet Sets is selected in the Field Category drop-down list and SheetSetPlaceholder is selected in the Field Names list.

3. Select ViewportScale from the Placeholder Type list, and select #″ = 1′-0″ from the Format list.

4. Click OK to exit the Field dialog box.

5. Set the Justification value in the Text Options group to Left, set the Height value to 0.1, and select the Preset option.

6. Click OK. Then, place the View Scale attribute definition approximately as shown in Figure 28.5.

### TURNING THE COMPONENTS INTO A BLOCK

You have all the attribute definitions you'll need. The next task is to turn the whole thing into a block:

1. Choose Make Block from the Draw toolbar.

2. In the Block Definition dialog box, enter **ViewTitle** for the block name.

3. Click the Select Objects button. Select all the objects you created in this set of exercises, including the circle and line you started with.

4. Click the Pick Point button in the Base Point group, and select the point indicated in Figure 28.5. This is important because the insertion point of the block will coincide with the lower-left corner of the viewport that the Sheet Set Manager creates when adding views to a sheet.

5. Click OK to finish the block. The block is now a part of your template file. All you need to do is save it to have the block available to the Sheet Set Manager.

6. If the ViewTitle block remains in the drawing, erase it. Then, zoom out so you see the entire layout.

7. Choose File ➤ Save to save the template file, which now includes your ViewTitle block.

You may notice that in step 5, the text in the block obscured the circle and line graphic. Fields always show a gray background to distinguish them from other types of text. The gray background doesn't print, so even though it appears to cover the line and circle, the fields won't interfere with the printing of those objects.

### INCLUDING YOUR VIEW LABEL IN THE SHEET SET

You must complete one more task to let the Sheet Set Manager know that your ViewTitle block is available. To do this, you need to open the Sheet Set Manager Preferences dialog box and point to the ViewTitle block. Here's how that's done:

1. Right-click My Existing Sheet Set in the Sheet List, and choose Properties.

2. In the Sheet Set Properties dialog box, click Label Block For Views in the Sheet Set group.

3. Click the Browse button to the far right of Label Block For Views.

4. In the Select Block dialog box, click the Browse button to the far right of the Enter The Drawing File Name text box. In the Select Drawing dialog box, locate and select the 22 × 17 Arch.dwt template file you've been working with for this sheet set. Remember to choose AutoCAD Drawing Template (*.dwt) in the File Of Type drop-down list at the bottom of the Select Drawing dialog box.

5. Back in the Select Block dialog box, click the Choose Blocks In The Drawing File radio button. Select ViewTitle from the list box just below the option. Click OK after you've made the selection, and then click OK in the Sheet Set Properties dialog box.

Remember that you created the ViewTitle block inside the `22 × 17 Arch.dwt` template file, so when you saved that file, the block became a part of that template file. In steps 4 and 5, you selected the template file and then selected the block in that file. If you prefer, you can save your view-title blocks as individual files. If you choose this route, make sure you select the Select The Drawing File As A Block option in step 4.

**TIP** If you would rather use a drawing as a block, you don't have to turn the circle-and-line drawing and attribute definitions into a block. Leave them unblocked in the file, and save the file with a name indicating that it's a file for the view title. Also make sure you specify a base point for the drawing by using the Base command (choose Draw ➤ Block ➤ Base).

Now, you're ready to test the block by adding a sheet and inserting a view. Remember that the Sheet Set Manager uses views to determine the contents of new viewports. Follow these steps:

1. Right-click My Existing Sheet Set in the Sheet List, and choose New Sheet.

2. Enter **001** for the number and **View Test** for the sheet name, and click OK.

3. Double-click 001 View Test in the Sheet List to open the file.

4. Click the Model Views tab of the Sheet Set Manager; then, expand the list for the `elevations.dwg` listing.

5. Right-click South Elevation in the list, and choose Place On Sheet.

6. Right-click the layout drawing area, and choose ⅛″ = 1′. Click in the layout to place the view. The view appears along with the view-title block you created in the beginning of this section.

You've seen how to create a custom view-label block. The process for creating a callout block is basically the same.

### CREATING A CALLOUT BLOCK

You may recall that you were able to insert a callout block in a Plan view that was linked to an elevation drawing on another sheet. You can create a custom callout block by using the same steps you used to create the view-title block in the preceding section. The only difference is that you select a different set of field values for the block's attribute definitions.

A callout block typically shows a circle with a view number on top and a sheet number on the bottom, as shown in Figure 28.6.

**FIGURE 28.6**
A typical callout block inserted in a drawing

Figure 28.7 shows an exploded version of the callout block with the attribute definitions labeled with the appropriate field values. Those field values are found under the SheetSetPlaceholder field names in the Field dialog box.

**FIGURE 28.7**

The attribute definitions of a callout block and their associated field values

ViewNumber field

SheetNumber field

In addition, you'll want to select the Associate Hyperlink option in the Field dialog box.

With this option selected, a hyperlink is created between the callout block and the view associated with it. This hyperlink will enable you to go directly to the sheet and the view being referenced by the callout block by Ctrl+clicking the field value in the callout block.

Just as with the view-title block, you can include the callout block inside the template file, or you can create individual files for each of your callout blocks. You can also have several callout blocks for different purposes.

For example, in the My Sample Sheet Set you created toward the beginning of this chapter, several callout blocks were available in the View List shortcut menu.

In that example, there was a callout block for the arrow directions. You can create a similar set of callout blocks for your drawings. You can also include callout blocks for details and finishes. You can even invent some uses on your own.

**TIP** If you like the callout blocks and label blocks that are already available in the My Sample Sheet Set exercise, you can find them as blocks in the template file used for that project. The location of that template file is C:\Documents and Settings\*User Name*\Local Settings\ Application Data\Autodesk\AutoCAD 2008\R17.1\enu\Template\ SheetSets\ Architectural Imperial.dwt. You can customize the graphics for that template file and use them for your own projects.

### REVIEWING THE STEPS FOR CREATING CUSTOM CALLOUT AND VIEW-LABEL BLOCKS

The callout block and view-label feature will save you a lot of time when you're building your set of drawings, but you must go through a lot of steps when creating them. To help you get a better overall grasp of the process, here is a checklist of the general steps you need to take:

◆ Create the graphics for the callout blocks.

◆ Create the attribute definitions for the text in the callout blocks.

◆ Assign the appropriate fields for the attribute definition values. For callout blocks and view titles, this is usually a SheetSetPlaceholder field.

◆ Convert the graphics and attribute definitions into a block. Place the insertion point of view-title blocks in the upper-left corner of the block to coincide with the location of the lower-left corner of the viewport it will be associated with.

◆ Use the Sheet Set Properties dialog box to indicate the file location of your callout and view-title blocks. These can be blocks in a file or individual files.

Also remember to turn on the Associate Hyperlink option when selecting the fields for your callout blocks.

## Archiving, Publishing, and eTransmitting Sheet Sets

The sheet-sets feature is a great way to keep your project files organized while you're creating your drawings. You can also use the Sheet Set Manager to turn your set into a package that can be easily sent to others who may need to work on the drawings or view them. Or you can use the Sheet Set Manager to create an archive of your set for safekeeping at the end of the project.

You may have noticed that the Sheet Set shortcut menu contains several options. Right-click the main title of your sheet set in the Sheet Set Manager's Sheet List, and you see the Archive, Publish, and eTransmit options:

◆ The Archive option lets you collect your sheet set files into a Zip archive file.

◆ The Publish option offers a convenient way to convert your set into a format that can be easily read by others who don't have AutoCAD.

◆ The eTransmit option offers a way to easily transport your sheet set to others who may need to work on the set.

In this section, you'll take a closer look at these three sets of features for sharing your sheet set.

## Archiving Your Sheet Set

One of the more important housekeeping jobs you'll do is archiving completed projects. If you organize your projects by folders, you could archive the entire folder for a project; but in so doing, you might archive many files that weren't part of the set.

The sheet-set Archive option lets you be more selective about the files you archive. You can exclude files in the sheet set or include other files that aren't necessarily AutoCAD drawings.

When you're ready to archive your sheet set, save all the files in your archive, and then open the Archive dialog box by doing the following:

**1.** Right-click the name of your sheet set in the Sheet List of the Sheet Set Manager.

**2.** Choose Archive from the shortcut menu to open the Archive A Sheet Set dialog box.

The Archive A Sheet Set dialog box has three tabs. The Sheets tab shows you the name of the sheets that will be archived. The check boxes by the sheet names indicate the sheets that will be archived. If you decide that you want to leave a sheet out of the archive, you can remove the check mark. The unchecked file and its associated Xref aren't archived.

The Files Tree tab offers a slightly different view of the archive. Instead of just showing you the sheet names, the Files Tree tab shows you the filenames that will be archived. These include support files such as the sheet-set data file and the template file associated with the sheet set.

The Files Table tab shows you even more detail about the files that will be archived, such as the path, the AutoCAD version, and similar information; it also includes information about the resource files that are Xrefs in the sheet files.

In both the Files Tree and Files Table tabs, the Add A File button enables you to include other files with the archive that aren't necessarily AutoCAD related but are part of the overall project. You can use this option to include Excel or Word documents that represent correspondence or worksheets.

### MODIFYING THE ARCHIVE SETUP

By default, the sheet-set Archive feature saves files in the .zip archive format. You can change the way the archives are saved, as well as the location of the archive, the archive name, and several other settings through the Modify Archive Setup dialog box.

Click the Modify Archive Setup button in the Archive A Sheet Set dialog box to open the Modify Archive Setup dialog box.

Here you can make adjustments to the properties of the archive file, including the type of file to create and whether to preserve the file structure.

### SAVING THE VITAL STATISTICS OF YOUR ARCHIVE

You can also view and save pertinent information about your archived sheet set by clicking the View Report button in the Archive A Sheet Set dialog box. Clicking this button opens the View Archive Report dialog box.

You can view the vital statistics regarding your sheet set archive. You also have the option to save the information in a file by clicking the Save As button. This opens a standard save-file dialog box where you can assign a name and location for the information file. It's stored as a plain-text file with the .txt filename extension.

## Batch-Plotting and -Publishing Your Sheet Set

Another advantage of using sheet sets is that you can print all the sheets in a set at once and in the background. The Publish option in the Sheet Set shortcut menu enables you to turn the Sheet Set Manager into a batch-plot utility.

When you right-click the sheet-set title in the Sheet List of the Sheet Set Manager, you see the Publish option. Click Publish, and another set of options appears, offering several plotting and publishing options.

The following list gives a rundown of these options. More detailed descriptions are offered in Chapters 7 and 27. See Appendix B for more on plot stamps:

**Publish To DWF**   Publishes your sheet set to a DWF file. This option uses the Publish command's current default settings for the Publish feature and the Sheet Set Publish Options command. Before you use this option, make sure your settings are correct by using the Sheet Set Publish Options command in the Sheet Set shortcut menu.

**Publish To Plotter**   Sends your sheet set to a printer or plotter. This option uses the Publish command's current default settings for the Publish feature and the Sheet Set Publish Options command. Before you use this option, make sure your settings are correct by choosing Publish ➢ Sheet Set Publish in this shortcut menu.

**Publish Using Page Setup Override**   Enables you to override the default layout settings in your sheets with a named page setup. See Chapter 8 for more on page setups. This can help to unify the plotter settings for all the sheets in your sheet set.

**Publish in Reverse Order**   Sends the drawing sheets to the printer or plotter starting with the last sheet and adding subsequent sheets from back to front.

**Include Plot Stamp**   Turns on the plot-stamp feature in AutoCAD. A check mark appears next to this option when it is turned on. See Appendix B for more on plot stamps.

**Plot Stamp Settings**   Opens the Plot Stamp dialog box. You can then make setting changes to your plot stamps. See Appendix B for more on plot stamps.

**Manage Page Setups**   Lets you edit or create a page setup that you want to apply to your sheets as they're published. When you click this option, the Page Setup Manager dialog box opens, which is the same dialog box you see when you right-click a Layout tab and choose Page Setup Manager. See Chapter 8 for more on page setups.

**Sheet Set Publish Options**   Opens the Sheet Set Publish Options dialog box, which is essentially the same as the Publish Options dialog box described in Chapter 27. This dialog box lets you set the type of DWF file to create, the file location, and security options.

**Publish Dialog Box**   Opens the Publish dialog box, and populates the Sheets To Publish list with the sheets in the sheet set. See Chapter 27 for more on the Publish dialog box.

## Packaging Sheet Sets with eTransmit

In Chapter 27, you learned that you can use the eTransmit feature to package a set of AutoCAD files into a Zip file in order to send the files to someone else who may need to edit them. eTransmit is similar to the sheet-set Archive feature, but it also makes sure all the supporting files, including fonts, font maps, and plotter configuration files, are included in the Zip file.

When you select eTransmit from the sheet-set shortcut menu, the list of files to include in the eTransmit file is automatically populated with the files from the current sheet set. This means that you don't have to manually build the list of drawings for the eTransmit file.

If you need to make setting changes for the eTransmit feature, you can do so by selecting the Transmittal Setups option in the sheet-set shortcut menu.

## Preparing Your Project Files

Now that you've seen how sheet sets work, you can start to use them on your own projects. Sheet sets work best when your project files are organized and you have some additional files prepared and on hand. Here's a checklist of things to keep in mind when you start to use sheet sets:

◆ Organize your files so that when you import your project into a sheet set, the files will be automatically organized by discipline or sheet number.

◆ Use only one layout per sheet-set drawing file. The Sheet Set Manager uses only one drawing per sheet and one layout per drawing.

◆ Create a template file containing the title block that you want to use for your project. Make sure to include any sheet-set fields you want to use in the title-block attribute definitions. You can also include your callout blocks in the template file for convenience.

◆ Because all the sheets in your project will most likely be printed on the same size sheet with the same plot specifications, it helps to create a sheet setup that you can apply to all your sheets. You can store the sheet setup in any drawing file and then use the Sheet Set Properties option to locate that file to assign the page setup to the entire sheet set.

**NOTE** If you want to repeat the exercises in this chapter, you can reset the sheet-set sample folders to their original state by copying them from the \Chapter 28\Backup folder into the \Chapter 28 folder.

## The Bottom Line

**Understanding Sheet Sets** The Sheet Set feature is like a database that automatically keeps track of drawings and drawing resources for your projects. To use sheets sets successfully, you need to make sure the Sheet Set Manager is aware of all the drawings and resources used in a project.

**Master It** Name the two main categories of files mentioned at the beginning of this chapter that sheets sets use.

**Solution** Reference files and sheet files.

**Creating a Sheet Set from an Existing Project** If you have existing project files, you can set up a sheet set to work with them.

**Master It** Name the option on the first page of the Create Sheet Set Wizard that lets you set up a sheet set for an existing project.

**Solution** The Existing Drawings radio button.

**Managing Title Blocks and Cross-References** When the Sheet Set Manager is aware of a drawing or drawing resource, you can automate the creation of sheets such as elevations and sections. You can also control the naming and numbering of drawings in a set through the Sheet Set Manager.

**Master It** What is the name of the right-click option that lets you change the name and number of a drawing?

**Solution** Rename & Renumber.

**Customizing Sheet Sets** To use sheets sets to their full potential, you should create title blocks and callout blocks that are sheet-set aware so they can communicate with the Sheet Set Manager.

**Master It** What is the name of the object you must include in a block to store data?

**Solution** Attribute definition.

**Archiving, Publishing, and eTransmitting Sheet Sets**   As a project starts to grow, you'll have to keep track of sheet and reference drawings, as well as other drawing resources. Because the Sheet Set Manager is already aware of all the files needed for a project, you can use the Sheet Set Manager to help keep track of project files.

**Master It**   Name the three AutoCAD features that help you manage your files.

**Solution**   Archive, Publish, and eTransmit.

# Appendix A

# Installing and Setting Up AutoCAD

This appendix gives you information about installing AutoCAD 2008 on your system and describes the system parameters you should set to configure AutoCAD to meet the needs of your operating environment. Throughout this appendix, the system variable associated with a setting, when available, is included at the end of an option description, enclosed in brackets. System variables are settings that enable you to control AutoCAD's behavior when using commands and features. You'll find a detailed description of the AutoCAD system variables in the AutoCAD Help window.

## Before Installing AutoCAD

Before you begin the installation process, be sure you have at least 750MB of free disk space on the drive on which you intend to install AutoCAD. You should also have at least an additional 100MB of free disk space for AutoCAD temporary files and swap files, plus another 20MB for the tutorial files you'll create. AutoCAD will work with Microsoft Windows Vista, Windows XP (Home, Professional or Tablet edition) with Service Pack 2, or Windows 2000 Professional with Service Pack 4. AutoCAD also works with Internet Explorer 6 with Service Pack 1 or Internet Explorer 7.

For 2D work, you'll also need a Pentium IV-CPU or better at least 512MB of RAM, and a video card that supports at least $1024 \times 768$ resolution and TrueColor.

For serious 3D work, Autodesk recommends 2GB of RAM, 2GB of free disk space not including the AutoCAD installation, and a 128MB or greater OpenGL/Direct3D-capable workstation class graphics card. Autodesk has a list of certified graphics cards for 3D modeling. This list is always being updated, so check the Autodesk website for the latest information.

Finally, have your AutoCAD vendor's name and phone number ready. You'll be asked to enter this information during the installation. Single-user systems have a 30-day grace period, so you can install and use AutoCAD without entering your authorization code right away. You can obtain an authorization code by fax, by phone, or over the Internet as indicated when you first start AutoCAD. The trial software that comes with this book can't be authorized, so be sure that you have a good block of free time to study AutoCAD before you install it.

## Proceeding with the Installation

AutoCAD 2008 installs like most other Windows programs, but you should know a few things before you start. This section provides some information that can be helpful as you begin your installation.

### Installing the AutoCAD Software

Installing AutoCAD is simple and straightforward; AutoCAD uses an installation wizard like most other Windows programs. Here are some guidelines to follow during the installation process:

◆ Before you start, make sure you have enough disk space, and also make sure no other programs are running. You'll need your AutoCAD serial number, which is usually on the package label. If you're installing the trial version from the companion CD, use the serial number 000-00000000.

◆ Typically, the AutoCAD installation program starts automatically when you insert the AutoCAD 2008 CD into your computer, but in the event that it doesn't, do the following:

1. In Windows, choose Start ➢ Run to open the Run dialog box.

2. In the Open box, enter **D:setup**. Enter the letter of your CD drive in place of the D in this example. Click OK when you're ready. The AutoCAD 2008 Master Setup dialog box opens.

3. You see a row of tabs at the top of the Install dialog box labeled Documentation and Support. Select the Install tab, and select Stand Alone Installation. The rest of the dialog box changes to show the Install options. Click Install under Install AutoCAD 2008.

4. After the installation starts, follow the directions in the installation wizard. On the Personal Information screen, you're asked for your name, company, and AutoCAD vendor's name and telephone number. This information will be displayed on the opening AutoCAD screen, so don't enter anything you'll regret later.

5. You're also asked to select the location for your AutoCAD files. The tutorials in this book assume that you have AutoCAD on drive C and in a folder called \Program Files\ Autodesk\AutoCAD 2008\—these are the defaults during the installation.

6. You're given the choice of Typical or Custom installation. Choose Typical.

7. You're also asked if you want to install the Express tools and sample files. Go ahead and install them.

8. If you don't have enough disk space, the installation wizard lets you know exactly how much room you need on each drive involved in the installation. You can take steps to make more room by using Windows Explorer or the Windows Disk Cleanup utility. If you do this, make sure you close those programs when you've finished making room and before you return to the AutoCAD setup.

After the installation is complete, you see the AutoCAD 2008 Setup dialog box, which may ask whether you want to restart your computer. It's usually better to restart your computer immediately after installing AutoCAD, if it requests that you do so.

## Configuring AutoCAD

In this section, you'll learn how to configure AutoCAD to work the way you want it to. You can configure AutoCAD at any time during an AutoCAD session by using the Options dialog box.

The tutorials in this book assume that you're using the default Options settings. As you become more familiar with the workings of AutoCAD, you may want to adjust the way AutoCAD works, using the Options dialog box. You can also set many of the options in the Options dialog box through system variables.

Choose Tools ➤ Options or type **options.↵** at the Command prompt to open the Options dialog box, which has the following tabs and settings.

**TIP**   Many of the options in the Options dialog box show an AutoCAD file icon. This icon indicates that the option's setting is saved with the file, as opposed to being saved as part of AutoCAD's default settings.

## The Files Tab

You use the options on the Files tab to tell AutoCAD where to place or find files it needs to operate. It uses a hierarchical list, similar to the one presented by Windows Explorer. You first see the general topics in the Search Paths, File Names, and File Locations list box. You can expand any item in the list by clicking its plus sign.

The following explanations describe each item in the list box. Chances are you won't have to use most of them, but you may change others occasionally.

**TIP**   The related system variable is shown in brackets at the end of the description of each item.

### SUPPORT FILE SEARCH PATH

AutoCAD relies on external files for many of its functions. Menus, text fonts, linetypes, and hatch patterns are a few examples of features that rely on external files. The Support File Search Path item tells AutoCAD where to look for these files. You can add folder paths to this listing by clicking the Add button and entering a new path or using the Browse button. It's probably not a good idea to delete any of the existing items under this heading unless you really know what you're doing.

If you're familiar with using environment variables, you can include them in the search paths.

### WORKING SUPPORT FILE SEARCH PATH

The Working Support File Search Path item contains a read-only list of the support-file search path for the current session, including any special settings that may be included with command switches and environment settings.

### DEVICE DRIVER FILE SEARCH PATH

The Device Driver File Search Path item locates the device drivers for AutoCAD. *Device drivers* are applications that enable AutoCAD to communicate directly with printers, plotters, and input devices. In most cases, you don't have to do anything with this setting.

### PROJECT FILES SEARCH PATH

Eventually, a consultant or other AutoCAD user will provide you with files that rely on Xrefs or raster images. Often, such files expect the Xref or raster image to be in a particular folder. When such files are moved to another location with a different folder system, Xref-dependent files won't be able to find their Xrefs. The Project Files Search Path item enables you to specify a folder where Xrefs or other dependent files are stored. If AutoCAD is unable to find an Xref or other file, it will look in the folder you specify in this listing.

To specify this folder, highlight Project Files Search Path, and then click the Add button. AutoCAD suggests Project1 as the folder name. You can change the name if you prefer. Click the plus sign next to Project1, and then click Browse to select a location for your project-file search path. The project-file search path is stored in a system variable called Projectname [Projectname].

### CUSTOMIZATION FILES

If you're customizing AutoCAD with your own menu files and icons, you can use this setting to locate your files. This option makes it convenient to keep your customization files in a place that is separate from the built-in AutoCAD files. You can specify a location for the main customization files like your CUI menu files, enterprise customization files for files you want to share, and your custom icons.

### HELP AND MISCELLANEOUS FILE NAMES

This item lets you set the location of a variety of support files including menu, help, automatic save, log, and configuration files. It also lets you set the default Internet address for the Launch Browser button on the AutoCAD Standard toolbar. If you have a network installation, you can also set the License Manager location on your network.

### TEXT EDITOR, DICTIONARY, AND FONT FILE NAMES

Use this item to set the location of the text editor [mtexted], the Custom and Standard dictionaries [Dctmain, Dctust], and the alternate font and font-mapping files [Fontalt]. Chapter 10 describes these tools in more detail.

### PRINT FILE, SPOOLER, AND PROLOG SECTION NAMES

You can specify a print filename other than the default that is supplied by AutoCAD whenever you plot to a file. The Spooler option lets you specify an application intended to read and plot a plot file. The Prolog option is intended for PostScript export. It lets you specify the Prolog section from the Acad.psf file that you want AutoCAD to include with exported Encapsulated PostScript files. See Chapter 19 for more information on exporting PostScript files and the Acad.psf file [Psprolog].

### PRINTER SUPPORT FILE PATH

Several support files are associated with the AutoCAD printing and plotting system. This item enables you to indicate where you want AutoCAD to look for these files.

### AUTOMATIC SAVE FILE LOCATION

You can indicate the location for AutoCAD's automatic save file by using this item [Savefilepath].

### COLOR BOOK LOCATIONS

This item lets you specify the locations for the PANTONE color book. This is an optional installation item, so if the PANTONE color books aren't installed, you can install them through your AutoCAD 2008 Installation CD.

### DATA SOURCES LOCATION

This item lets you specify the location for Open Database Connectivity (ODBC) Data Link files for linking AutoCAD drawings to database files.

### TEMPLATE SETTINGS

When you select the Use A Template option in the Create New Drawing dialog box, AutoCAD looks at this setting for the location of template files. You can modify this setting, but chances are you won't need to.

### TOOL PALETTES FILE LOCATIONS

This item lets you specify a location for your custom Tool palettes resource files. When you create custom palettes, AutoCAD stores its data regarding those palettes in this location.

### AUTHORING PALETTE FILE LOCATIONS

If you're creating custom dynamic blocks, you can designate a folder location where you keep your custom block settings and files.

### LOG FILE LOCATION

With this item, you can indicate where log files are to be placed [Logfilepath].

### PLOT AND PUBLISH LOG FILE LOCATION

With this item, you can indicate where plot and publish log files are to be placed [Logfilepath].

### TEMPORARY DRAWING FILE LOCATION

AutoCAD creates temporary files to store portions of your drawings as you work on them. You usually don't have to think about these temporary files unless they start crowding your hard disk or unless you're working on a particularly large file on a system with little memory. This item lets you set the location for temporary files. The default location is the `C:\Documents and Settings\ User Name\Local Settings\Temp\` folder. *User Name* is your login name. If you have a hard disk that has lots of room and is very fast, you may want to change this setting to a location on that drive to improve performance [Tempprefix, read-only].

### TEMPORARY EXTERNAL REFERENCE FILE LOCATION

If you're on a network and you foresee a situation in which another user will want to open an Xref of a file you're working on, you can set the Demand Load Xrefs setting in the Open And Save tab to Enabled With Copy. This causes AutoCAD to make and use a copy of any Xref that is currently loaded. This way, others can open the original file. The Temporary External Reference File Location item lets you specify the folder where AutoCAD stores this copy of an Xref [Xloadpath].

### TEXTURE MAPS SEARCH PATH

This item specifies the location for AutoCAD Render texture maps. In most cases, you won't have to change this setting. You can, however, add a folder name to this item for your own texture maps as you acquire or create them.

### WEB FILE SEARCH PATH

Although you may think this is for Internet files, it's really for photometric web files that are used to control the way lights behave in 3D models. These files have an .ies filename extension.

### I-DROP ASSOCIATED FILE LOCATION

This is where you specify the location of files imported to your computer through the i-drop function in AutoCAD. By default, no location is specified, so the i-drop imported DWG file is placed in the same folder location as the current drawing.

**NOTE** While in AutoCAD, you may want to quickly find the location of a resource file such as a log file or the automatic save file. You can do so by using the system variable associated with the resource. For example, to quickly find the location of the log-file path, enter **logfilepath.**↵ at the Command prompt. For the automatic save file, enter **savefilepath.**↵. LT users can employ the Modemacro command as in **Modemacro.↵$(getvar,logfilepath).↵** or **Modemacro.↵$(getvar,savefilepath).↵**. See Chapter 26 for more on Modemacro.

## The Display Tab

The settings on this tab let you control AutoCAD's appearance. You can make AutoCAD look completely different with these settings if you choose. Scroll bars, fonts, and colors are all up for grabs.

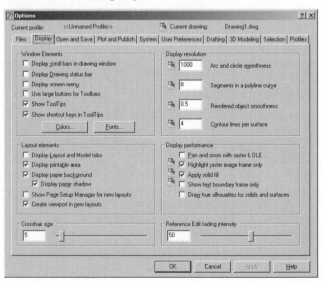

### THE WINDOW ELEMENTS GROUP

These options control the general settings for AutoCAD windows:

**Display Scroll Bars In Drawing Window**   Lets you turn the scroll bars on and off. If you have a small monitor with low resolution, you may want to turn off the scroll bars for a larger drawing area.

**Display Drawing Status Bar**   When turned on, displays the Annotation Scale settings at the bottom of the drawing area instead of at the bottom of the AutoCAD Window.

**Display Screen Menu**   Turns on the old AutoCAD Format Screen menu that once appeared on the right side of the screen. If you must have it displayed, this is where you can turn it back on.

**Use Large Buttons For Toolbars**   Controls whether large icon buttons are used in toolbars.

**Show ToolTips**   Controls whether ToolTips are shown when you hover the mouse over tools.

**Show Shortcut Keys In ToolTips**   Controls whether shortcut keys are displayed in ToolTips.

**Colors**   Opens a dialog box that lets you set the color for the various components of the AutoCAD window. This is where you can change the background color of the drawing area if you find that black doesn't work for you.

**Fonts**   Opens a dialog box that lets you set the fonts of the AutoCAD window. You can select from the standard set of Windows fonts available in your system.

### THE DISPLAY RESOLUTION GROUP

These options control the way objects are displayed in AutoCAD. You can choose between display accuracy and speed:

**Arc and Circle Smoothness**   Controls the appearance of arcs and circles, particularly when you zoom in on them. In some instances, arcs and circles appear to be octagons, even though they plot as smooth arcs and circles. If you want arcs and circles to appear smoother, you can increase this setting. An increase also increases memory use [Viewres].

**Segments In A Polyline Curve**   Controls the smoothness of polyline curves. Increase the value to make curved polylines appear smoother and less segmented. Decrease the value for improved display performance [Splinesegs].

**Rendered Object Smoothness**   Controls the smoothness of curved solids when they're rendered or shaded. Values can range from 0.01 to 10 [Facetres].

**Contour Lines Per Surface**   Lets you set the number of contour lines used to represent solid, curved surfaces. Values can range from 0 to 2047 [Isolines].

### THE LAYOUT ELEMENTS GROUP

These options control the display of elements in the Paper Space Layout tabs. See Chapters 8 and 16 for more information. Most of these options are self-explanatory. The Show Page Setup Manager For New Layouts option opens the Page Setup Manager dialog box whenever a layout is first opened. The Create Viewport In New Layouts option automatically creates a viewport in a layout when it's first opened.

### THE DISPLAY PERFORMANCE GROUP

You can adjust a variety of display-related settings from this group:

**Pan And Zoom With Raster & OLE**   Controls the way raster images react to real-time pans and zooms. If this option is selected, raster images move with the cursor. Turn off this option for better performance [Rtdisplay].

**Highlight Raster Image Frame Only**   Determines how raster images appear when selected. Turn on this option for better performance [Imagehlt].

**Apply Solid Fill**   Controls the display of filled objects such as wide polylines and areas filled with the solid hatch pattern. This option is also controlled by the Fillmode system variable. See Chapter 18 for more information on filled polylines and the solid hatch pattern. Turn off this option for better performance [Fillmode].

**Show Text Boundary Frame Only**   Controls the way text is displayed. Turn on this option to display text as rectangular boundaries [Qtextmode].

**Draw True Silhouettes For Solids And Surfaces**   Controls whether surface meshes for solid models are displayed. Turn off this option for better performance [Dispsilh].

### THE CROSSHAIR SIZE SLIDER

This slider controls the size of the crosshair cursor. You can set this to 100 percent to simulate the full-screen crosshair cursor of earlier versions of AutoCAD [Cursorsize].

### THE REFERENCE EDIT FADING INTENSITY SLIDER

This slider controls the display of nonselected objects during in-place reference editing. See Chapter 7 for more information on in-place reference editing [Xfadectl].

## The Open And Save Tab

The Open And Save tab offers general file-related options such as the frequency of the Automatic Save and the default file version for the Save and Save As options.

### THE FILE SAVE GROUP

You can control how AutoCAD saves files by using the options in this group:

**Save As**   Lets you set the default file type for the File ➤ Save and the File ➤ Save As options. If you're working in an environment that requires Release 14 files as the standard file type, for example, you can use this option to select Release 14 as the default file type. You can also set up AutoCAD to save DXF files by default.

**Maintain Visual Fidelity For Annotative Objects**   Ensures that annotative scale is preserved in layouts when you save drawings to earlier versions of AutoCAD. If you work primarily in Model Space, leave this setting off.

**Thumbnail Preview Settings**   Lets you determine whether a preview image is saved with a drawing. Preview images are used in the AutoCAD File dialog box and in DesignCenter to let you preview a file before opening it [Rasterpreview]. You can also control the display of the sheet-set preview [Updatethumbnail].

**Incremental Save Percentage**   Controls the degree to which the Incremental Save feature is used when you choose File ➤ Save or File ➤ Save As. An incremental save improves the time required to save a file to disk, but it also makes the file size larger. If you have limited disk space, you can set this value to 25. A value of 0 turns off incremental save altogether but reduces AutoCAD performance [Isavepercent].

### THE FILE SAFETY PRECAUTIONS GROUP

These options control AutoCAD's automatic backup features:

**Automatic Save**   Offers control over the Automatic Save features. You can turn it on or off by using the check box or set the frequency at which files are saved by using the Minutes Between Saves input box. You can set the location for the automatic-save files by using the Automatic Save File Location item in the Files tab of the Options dialog box. You can also set the frequency of automatic saves through the Savetime system variable [Savefilepath, Savefile].

**Create Backup Copy With Each Save**   Lets you determine whether a BAK file is saved along with every save you perform. You can turn off this option to conserve disk space [Isavebak, Tempprefix].

**Full-Time CRC Validation**   Controls the cyclic-redundancy-check feature, which checks for file errors whenever AutoCAD reads a file. This feature is helpful in troubleshooting hardware problems in your system.

**Maintain A Log File**   Lets you record the data in the AutoCAD Text Window. See Chapter 19 for more on this feature. You can set the location for log files in the Files tab of the Options dialog box [Logfilemode, Logfilename].

**File Extension For Temporary Files**   Lets you set the filename extension for AutoCAD temporary files. These are files AutoCAD uses to store drawing data temporarily as you work on a file. If you're working on a network where temporary files from multiple users may be stored in the same folder, you may want to change this setting to identify your temporary files.

**Security Options**   Opens the Security Options dialog box, in which you can either password-protect a file or add a digital signature. See Chapter 27 for more on these features.

**Display Digital Signature Information**   When a file containing a digital signature is opened, this option will display a warning message alerting you to the presence of the signature [Sigwarn]. See Chapter 27 for more on the digital signature feature.

### THE FILE OPEN GROUP

You can control how AutoCAD displays filenames in the File menu or the drawing title bar:

**Number Of Recently-Used Files To List**   Lets you specify the number of files listed in the File menu history list. The default is 9, but you can enter a value from 0 to 9.

**Display Full Path In Title**   Controls whether the full path is included in the title bar with a drawing's name.

### THE EXTERNAL REFERENCES (XREFS) GROUP

These options let you control memory and layer features of Xrefs:

**Demand Load Xrefs**   Lets you turn on the Demand Load feature of Xrefs. Demand Load helps to improve the performance of files that use Xrefs by loading only those portions of an Xref drawing that are required for the current open drawing. This option is a drop-down list with three options: Disabled turns off demand loading, Enabled turns on demand loading, and Enabled With Copy turns on demand loading by using a copy of the Xref source file. This last option enables others on a network to edit the Xref source file while you're working on a file that also uses the file [Xloadctl].

**Retain Changes To Xref Layers**   Lets you save layer settings of Xref files in the current drawing. This doesn't affect the source Xref file. With this setting turned off, the current file imports the layer settings of the Xref file when it loads that file [Visretain].

**Allow Other Users To Refedit Current Drawing**   Lets you specify whether others can simultaneously edit a file that you're editing. This option is intended to enable others to use the Modify ➢ Xref And Block Editing option (the Refedit command) on files you currently have loaded in AutoCAD [Xedit].

### THE OBJECTARX APPLICATIONS GROUP

AutoCAD allows users and third-party developers to create custom objects that usually require the presence of a custom ObjectARX application to support the object. These options control the way AutoCAD treats custom objects and their related ObjectARX applications:

**Demand Load ObjectARX Apps**   Controls when a supporting third-party application is loaded if a custom object is present in a file. This option offers several settings that you can select from a drop-down list. The available settings are Disable Load On Demand, Custom Object Detect, Command Invoke, and Object Detect And Command Invoke. Disable Load On Demand prevents AutoCAD from loading third-party applications when a custom object is present. Some standard AutoCAD commands won't work if you select Disable Load On Demand because AutoCAD itself uses ObjectARX applications. Custom Object Detect causes AutoCAD to automatically load an ARX application if a custom object is present. Command Invoke loads a custom application when you invoke a command from that application. The Object Detect And Command Invoke option loads an ARX application when either a custom object is present or when you invoke a command from that application [Demandload].

**Proxy Images For Custom Objects**   Offers a drop-down list with three settings that control the display of custom objects when the objects supporting ARX applications aren't present on your system. Do Not Show Proxy Graphics turns off the display of custom objects. Show Proxy Graphics displays the custom object. Show Proxy Bounding Box shows a bounding box in place of the custom object.

**Show Proxy Information Dialog Box**   Lets you determine whether the Show Proxy Information warning dialog box is used. When this option is selected, the Show Proxy Information warning appears when a drawing with custom objects is opened but AutoCAD can't find the objects' associated ARX application [Proxynotice].

## The Plot And Publish Tab

The Plot And Publish tab in the Options dialog box offers settings related to printing and plotting. See Chapter 8 and Appendix B for a description of these options.

## The System Tab

These options in the System tab offer control over some of AutoCAD's general interface settings such as display drivers and pointing devices.

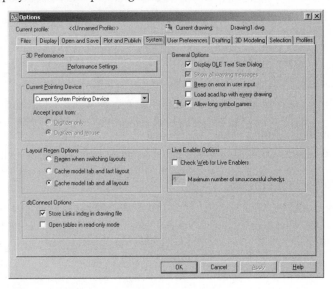

### THE 3D PERFORMANCE GROUP

Clicking the Performance Settings button in this group displays a variety of settings to help you fine-tune the performance of your 3D graphics. When you click this option, the Adaptive Degradation And Performance Tuning dialog box opens. *Adaptive degradation* refers to the way AutoCAD's display behaves as you change views such as camera or orbital. AutoCAD degrades the view to keep up with real-time changes in a view (thus the term *adaptive degradation*.) You can control how the view degrades using these options. The Hardware And Performance Tuning section gives you information about your current graphic system and allows you to make setting changes. See the "Adjusting AutoCAD's 3D Graphics System" section later in this appendix.

### THE CURRENT POINTING DEVICE GROUP

You can choose the type of pointing device you want to use with AutoCAD through the options in this group. The drop-down list offers Current System Pointing Device and Wintab Compatible Digitizer ADI 4.2 – by Autodesk. If you want to use the default Windows pointing device, choose Current

System Pointing Device. If you have a digitizer that uses the Wintab driver, you can select Wintab Compatible Digitizer.

You can further limit AutoCAD's use to the Wintab Compatible Digitizer by selecting the Digitizer Only radio button. If you select the Digitizer And Mouse radio button, AutoCAD will accept input from both devices.

### THE LAYOUT REGEN OPTIONS GROUP

This set of radio buttons enables you to specify how regens are applied when working with Layout tabs:

**Regen When Switching Layouts**   Causes AutoCAD to force a regen when you select a Layout or Model tab. Use this option when your computer is limited in RAM.

**Cache Model Tab And Last Layout**   Causes AutoCAD to suppress regens when switching to the Model tab or the most recently opened Layout tab. Other layouts will regen when selected.

**Cache Model Tab And All Layouts**   Causes AutoCAD to suppress regens when selecting any Layout tabs or the Model tab.

### THE dbCONNECT OPTIONS GROUP

The check boxes in this group offer controls over the dbConnect feature:

**Store Links Index In Drawing File**   Lets you specify where database link data is stored. If this check box is selected, link data is stored in the drawing that is linked to a database. This increases file size and file-loading time.

**Open Tables In Read-Only Mode**   Lets you limit access to database files.

### THE GENERAL OPTIONS GROUP

This set of check boxes enables you to set options related to the general operation of AutoCAD:

**Display OLE Text Size Dialog**   Lets you control the display of the OLE Text Size dialog box, which normally appears when you insert OLE text objects into an AutoCAD drawing by choosing Edit ➤ Paste.

**Show All Warning Messages**   If you turn off a warning message with the Don't Display This Warning Again option, this option enables you to turn all warning messages back on. If no warning messages have been turned off, this option is grayed out.

**Beep On Error In User Input**   Turns on an alarm beep that sounds whenever there is an input error.

**Load Acad.lsp With Every Drawing**   Lets you determine whether an Acad.lsp file is loaded with every drawing. If you're used to using an Acad.lsp file with your AutoCAD system, you can select this option; otherwise, AutoCAD will load only the Acaddoc.lsp file [Acadlspasdoc].

**Allow Long Symbol Names**   Enables you to use long names for items such as layer, block, linetype, and text-style names. With this option turned on, you can enter as many as 255 characters for names [Extnames].

### THE LIVE ENABLER OPTIONS GROUP

Since AutoCAD 14, third-party developers have had the ability to create custom objects, also known as *proxy objects*, through a programming tool known as ObjectARX. When this feature was first introduced, you had to have the third-party application installed on your computer in order to view or edit such custom objects. *Object enablers* are small programs, like plug-ins to AutoCAD, that enable you to view and edit custom third-party objects without having the full third-party application present. These object enablers may be available on the Web for free download if the third-party producer has posted them.

**Check Web For Live Enablers**   Causes AutoCAD to look for enablers over the Internet. For example, if you receive a file created in Architectural Desktop that contains a custom object, AutoCAD can automatically go to the Autodesk website and download the Architectural Desktop Object Enabler so you can edit and view the file. The Live Enabler options let you control how the Object Enabler feature is engaged when AutoCAD encounters custom objects.

**Maximum Number Of Unsuccessful Checks**   Lets you specify the number of times AutoCAD checks the Internet for object enablers after an attempt to make a connection has failed.

## The User Preferences Tab

The options in the User Preferences tab enable you to adjust the way AutoCAD reacts to user input.

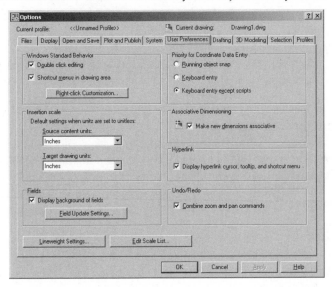

### THE WINDOWS STANDARD BEHAVIOR GROUP

These settings enable you to control how AutoCAD reacts to keyboard accelerators and mouse right-clicks:

**Double Click Editing**   Controls whether a double-click on an object automatically starts an editing command for the object. If this option is turned off, double-clicking objects has no effect [Dblclkedit].

**Shortcut Menus In Drawing Area**   Lets you see the shortcut menu when you right-click. When this check box isn't selected, AutoCAD responds to a right-click with a ↵ [Shortcutmenu].

**Right-Click Customization**   Opens the Right-Click Customization dialog box, which offers further options for the behavior of the right-click in AutoCAD.

The Turn On Time-Sensitive Right-Click option causes AutoCAD to respond differently depending on whether you right-click quickly or hold the right mouse button down momentarily. With this option, a rapid right-click issues a ↵ as if you press the Enter key. If you hold down the right mouse button, the shortcut menu appears. You can further adjust the time required to hold down the mouse button.

### THE INSERTION SCALE GROUP

These settings control how the DesignCenter or i-drop feature determines the scale of blocks when blocks are given a unitless setting for their DesignCenter unit type. Each drop-down list offers the standard set of unit types that are available in the Block Definition dialog box under the Insert Units drop-down list. See Chapter 7 for more information on blocks and Chapter 27 for information on DesignCenter [Insunits].

### THE FIELDS GROUP

These settings offer control over the display and refresh of fields. Display Background Of Fields lets you control the display of the gray background on fields. This background lets you see at a glance which text object in a drawing is a field. The background doesn't print. Clicking the Field Update Settings button opens a dialog box that lets you select the action that updates fields.

### THE PRIORITY FOR COORDINATE DATA ENTRY GROUP

These options control the way AutoCAD responds to coordinate input:

**Running Object Snap**   Forces AutoCAD to use Running Osnaps at all times [Osnapcoord].

**Keyboard Entry**   Enables you to use keyboard entry for coordinate input [Osnapcoord].

**Keyboard Entry Except Scripts**   Enables you to use keyboard entry for coordinate input, except in scripts [Osnapcoord].

### THE ASSOCIATIVE DIMENSIONING GROUP

This area has one option, Make New Dimensions Associative, which you can toggle on or off. This option lets you control whether AutoCAD uses the true associative dimension feature. With true associative dimension, a dimension follows changes to an object whenever the object is edited. In the old method, you have to include a dimension definition point during the editing process in order to have the dimension follow changes in an object.

### THE HYPERLINK GROUP

The one option in this group turns on or off the display of the Hyperlink cursor, ToolTip, and shortcut menu.

### THE UNDO/REDO GROUP

This option controls how Undo and Redo react with the Zoom and Pan commands.

### LINEWEIGHT SETTINGS

Click the Lineweight Settings button to open the Lineweight Settings dialog box. See Chapters 8 and 16 for more information about the Lineweight Settings dialog box.

### EDIT SCALE LIST

Click the Edit Scale List button to open the Edit Scale List dialog box. You can add your own custom scales, which appear in the Plot dialog box.

## The Drafting Tab

The Drafting tab offers settings that relate to the drawing cursor, including the AutoSnap and AutoTrack features.

### THE AUTOSNAP SETTINGS GROUP

The options in this group control the AutoSnap features that are engaged when you use osnaps:

**Marker**   Turns on the small, square graphic that appears on the osnap location. If you prefer not to see this marker, clear this check box [Autosnap].

**Magnet**   Causes the osnap cursor to jump to an osnap location as the cursor moves close to that location [Autosnap].

**Display AutoSnap Tooltip**   Controls the display of the Osnap ToolTip [Autosnap].

**Display AutoSnap Aperture Box**   Displays a square over the cursor whenever osnaps are active. If you're familiar with earlier versions of AutoCAD, you'll recognize the Aperture Box as the graphic used to indicate osnaps before the AutoSnap feature was introduced [Apbox].

**Colors**   Lets you determine the color for the AutoSnap marker. Opens the Drawing Window Colors dialog box.

### THE AUTOSNAP MARKER SIZE SLIDER

Move the slider to control the size of the AutoSnap marker.

### THE AUTOTRACK SETTINGS GROUP

These options offer control over the tracking vector used for Polar Tracking and Osnap Tracking:

**Display Polar Tracking Vector**   Turns the Polar Tracking vector on or off [Trackpath].

**Display Full-Screen Tracking Vector**   Lets you control whether the tracking vector appears across the full width of the drawing window or stops at the cursor location or the intersection of two tracking vectors [Trackpath].

**Display AutoTrack Tooltip**   Turns the Osnap Tracking ToolTip on or off [Autosnap].

### THE ALIGNMENT POINT ACQUISITION GROUP

This option lets you determine the method for acquiring Osnap Tracking alignment points.

### THE APERTURE SIZE SLIDER

Move the slider to set the size of the osnap aperture pickbox [Aperture].

### THE OBJECT SNAP OPTIONS GROUP

This group offers the Ignore Hatch Objects and Replace Z Value With Current Elevation options. When Ignore Hatch Objects is turned off, osnaps attempt to snap to geometry in hatch patterns. When turned on, Replace Z Value With Current Elevation causes AutoCAD to use the current UCS default Z value instead of the Z value of the selected point. Ignore Negative Z Object Snaps For Dynamic UCS causes osnaps to ignore locations with negative Z values while using the DUCS feature.

### THE DRAFTING TOOLTIP SETTINGS

These options give you control over the color, size, and transparency of ToolTips.

### THE LIGHT GLYPH SETTINGS

These options give you control over the color and size of the spot and point light glyphs.

### THE CAMERA GLYPH SETTINGS

These options give you control over the color and size of the camera glyph.

## The 3D Modeling Tab

The options on this tab control the behavior and display of your drawing when you're working in 3D modes. You can adjust the appearance of the crosshair and the UCS icon. You can specify the default method for displaying 3D objects, and you can specify the default settings for Walk And Fly and Animation features.

### 3D CROSSHAIRS

These settings control the behavior and appearance of the crosshair cursor when viewing your drawing in 3D:

**Show Z Axis In Crosshairs**   Displays the Z axis in the crosshair.

**Label Axes In Standard Crosshairs**   Displays the X, Y, and Z axis labels on the crosshair.

**Show Labels For Dynamic UCS**   Displays the axis labels during the use of Dynamic UCS regardless of the Label Axes In Standard Crosshairs setting.

**Crosshair Labels**   Lets you select from three label styles: Use X, Y, Z; Use N, E, z; or Use Custom Labels. If you select Use Custom Labels, you can enter the labels you want to display for the X, Y, and Z axes in the boxes provided.

### DISPLAY UCS ICON

These three options pretty much explain themselves. Each option determines when the UCS icon is displayed. By default, they're all turned on, so the UCS icon always displays.

### DYNAMIC INPUT

When turned on, the Show Z Field For Pointer Input option offers a Z coordinate for input when using Dynamic Input mode.

### 3D OBJECTS

These settings affect the display of 3D objects. Visual Style While Creating 3D Objects is self-explanatory. Deletion Control While Creating 3D Objects lets you determine whether defining objects used to create 3D objects are saved or deleted.

The U and V isoline settings let you set the number of isolines on 3D solids and surface meshes. Isolines are the lines you see on a mesh or solid that help you visualize their shape. You see them in wireframe and realistic visual styles.

### 3D NAVIGATION

If you want to adjust the way AutoCAD behaves when you're navigating a 3D view, these settings will help. Reverse Mouse Wheel Zoom is self-explanatory. The remaining two buttons give you control over the behavior of the Walk And Fly feature and the Animation settings:

**Walk And Fly Settings**   Click this button to open the Walk And Fly Settings dialog box.

When you first start the 3DWalk or 3DFly feature, you see an instructional window that tells you how to use the feature. You use the options in the Settings group of the Walk And Fly Settings dialog box to specify when that instructional window appears. After using these features a few times, you may find the instructional window annoying and turn it off. You can turn it back on in this dialog box. You can also set the Position Locator window to automatically appear or not appear.

The Current Drawing Settings group lets you set the step size and steps per second when you're "walking" or "flying" through your model. These are the same settings you see in the Navigate control panel for Step Size and Steps Per Second.

**Animation Settings**   Click this button to open the Animation Settings dialog box. Here you can control the default visual style, resolution, frame rate, and animation file format when using the Motion Path Animation (anipath) feature.

## The Selection Tab

The options in the Selection tab of the Options dialog box control the way you select objects in AutoCAD. You can also make adjustments to the Grips feature.

### THE PICKBOX SIZE SLIDER

This control lets you adjust the size of the pickbox [Pickbox].

### THE GRIP SIZE SLIDER

This control lets you adjust the size of grips [Gripsize].

### THE SELECTION PREVIEW GROUP

These options let you control the behavior of the selection preview when you hover over objects. Click the Visual Effect Settings button to fine-tune the visual effects of the object selection, including the color and pattern of auto-select windows.

### THE SELECTION MODES GROUP

These options let you control the degree to which AutoCAD conforms to standard graphical user interface (GUI) methods of operation:

**Noun/Verb Selection**   Makes AutoCAD work more like other Windows programs by letting you select objects before you choose an action or command [Pickfirst].

**Use Shift To Add To Selection**   Lets you use the standard GUI method of holding down the Shift key to select multiple objects. When the Shift key isn't held down, only the single object picked or the group of objects indicated with a window will be selected. Previously selected objects are deselected, unless the Shift key is held down during selection. To turn on this feature by using system variables, set Pickadd to 0 [Pickadd].

**Press And Drag**   Lets you use the standard GUI method for placing window selections. First, click and hold down the Pick button on the first corner of the window; then, while holding down the Pick button, drag the other corner of the window into position. When the other corner is in place, you let go of the Pick button to finish the window. This setting applies to both Verb/Noun and Noun/Verb operations. In the system variables, set Pickdrag to 1 for this option [Pickdrag].

**Implied Windowing**   Causes a window or crossing window to start automatically if no object is picked at the Select objects: prompt. This setting has no effect on the Noun/Verb setting. In the system variables, set Pickauto to 1 for this option [Pickauto].

**Object Grouping**   Lets you select groups as single objects [Pickstyle].

**Associative Hatch**   Lets you select both a hatch pattern and its associated boundary by using a single pick [Pickstyle].

### THE GRIPS GROUP

These options control the Grips feature:

**Unselected Grip Color**   Lets you select a color for grips that are exposed but not selected [Gripcolor].

**Selected Grip Color**   Lets you set the color for grips that are exposed and selected [Griphot].

**Hover Grip Color**   Lets you set the color for grips when the cursor hovers over the grip [Griphover].

**Enable Grips**   Turns on grips.

**Enable Grips Within Blocks**    Turns on the display of grips in blocks. Although you can't edit grips in blocks, you can use grips in blocks as selection points [Gripblock].

**Enable Grip Tips**    Turns on the display of grip ToolTips for custom objects that have them [Griptips].

**Object Selection Limit For Display Of Grips**    Controls the display of grips based on the number of objects selected. If set to 1, grips aren't displayed if more than one object is selected. You can select a range from 1 to 32,767. The default is 100 [Gripobjlimit].

## The Profiles Tab

In Windows XP Professional, a user profile is saved for each login name. Depending on the login name you use, you can have a different Windows setup. The Profiles tab offers a similar function for AutoCAD users. You can store different settings from the Options dialog box in a profile and recall them at any time. You can also save them to a file with the .arg extension and then take that file to another system. It's a bit like being able to take your Options settings with you wherever you go.

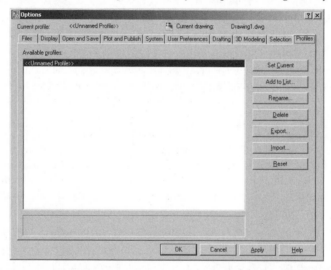

The main part of the Profiles tab displays a list of available profiles. The default profile is shown as <<Unnamed Profile>>. As you add more profiles, they appear in the list.

To create a new profile, highlight a profile name from the list, and then click Add To List. The Add Profile dialog box opens, enabling you to enter a profile name and a description of the profile. The description appears in the box below the list on the Profiles tab whenever that profile is selected.

After you've created a new profile, you can modify the settings on the other tabs of the Options dialog box, and the new settings will be associated with the new profile. Profiles store the way menus are set up, so you can use them as an aid to managing both your own custom schemes and third-party software. Here is a brief description of the options on the Profiles tab:

**Set Current**    Installs the settings from the selected profile.

**Add To List**    Creates a new profile.

**Rename**    Enables you to rename a profile and change its description.

**Delete**    Removes the selected profile from the list.

**Export**   Lets you save a profile to a file.

**Import**   Imports a profile that has been saved to a file.

**Reset**   Resets the values for a selected profile to its default settings.

## Configuring the Tablet Menu Area

If you own a digitizing tablet and you would like to use it with the AutoCAD tablet menu template, you must configure your tablet menu. You can open the `Tablet.dwg` file in the `Sample` folder of the AutoCAD 2008 folder and print the tablet menu template drawing to a size that will fit your digitizing tablet. Then, do the following:

1. Securely fasten your tablet menu template to the tablet. Be sure the area covered by the template is completely within the tablet's active drawing area.

2. Choose Tools ➤ Tablet ➤ Configure. The following prompt appears:

```
Enter number of tablet
menus desired (0-4) <0>:
```

Enter **4**↵. For the next series of prompts, you'll be locating the four tablet menu areas, starting with menu area 1 (see Figure A.1).

1. Follow the instructions provided by the Command prompt.

2. When you're asked if you want to re-specify the fixed screen-pointing area, enter **Y**↵, and then select the corners of the pointing area as indicated by the prompts.

**FIGURE A.1**

How to locate the tablet menu areas

## Turning On the Noun/Verb Selection Method

If, for some reason, the Noun/Verb Selection method isn't available, follow these steps to turn it on:

1. Choose Tools ➤ Options. Then, in the Options dialog box, click the Selection tab.

2. In the Selection Modes group, click the Noun/Verb Selection check box.

3. Click OK.

You should now see a small square at the intersection of the crosshair cursor. This square is actually a pickbox superimposed on the cursor. It tells you that you can select objects, even while the Command prompt appears at the bottom of the screen and no command is currently active. As you saw earlier, the square momentarily disappears when you're in a command that asks you to select points.

You can also turn on Noun/Verb Selection by entering **'Pickfirst.**↵ at the Command prompt. At the Enter new value for PICKFIRST <0>: prompt, enter **1.**↵. (Entering **0** turns off the Pickfirst function.) The Pickfirst system variable is stored in the AutoCAD configuration file. See Appendix C for more on system variables.

## Turning On the Grips Feature

If, for some reason, the Grips feature isn't available, follow these steps to turn it on:

1. Choose Tools ➤ Options. Then, in the Options dialog box, click the Selection tab.

2. In the Grips group, click the Enable Grips check box.

3. Click OK, and you're ready to proceed.

The Selection tab of the Options dialog box also lets you specify whether grips appear on objects that compose a block (see Chapter 4 for more on blocks), as well as set the grip color and size. You can also set these options by using the system variables.

You can also turn the Grips feature on and off by entering **'Grips.**↵ At the Enter new value for GRIPS <0>: prompt, enter **1** to turn grips on or **0** to turn grips off. Grips is a system variable that is stored in the AutoCAD configuration file.

## Setting Up the Tracking Vector Feature

If AutoCAD doesn't display a tracking vector as described in the early chapters of this book, or if the tracking vector doesn't behave as described, chances are this feature has been turned off or altered. Take the following steps to configure the tracking vector so it behaves as described in this book:

1. Open the Options dialog box by choosing Tools ➤ Options.

2. Click the Drafting tab.

3. Click all three options in the AutoTrack Settings group.

4. Make sure the Marker, Magnet, and Display AutoSnap Tooltip check boxes are selected in the AutoSnap Settings group.

5. Make sure the Automatic radio button in the Alignment Point Acquisition group is selected.

6. Click OK to exit the dialog box.

# Adjusting AutoCAD's 3D Graphics System

You can adjust the performance of AutoCAD's 3D graphics system through the Adaptive Degradation And Performance Tuning dialog box. To open this dialog box, click the System tab in the Options dialog box, and then click the Performance Settings button in the 3D Performance group.

This dialog box offers control over the way AutoCAD displays 3D models when you use the 3D Orbit tool or when you're using a visual style. Here is a list of the options for the Adaptive Degradation And Performance Tuning dialog box.

## The Adaptive Degradation Group

The 3D navigation tools enable you to adjust your view in real time, which places high demands on your display system. To maintain the smoothness of the real-time update of your 3D views, AutoCAD degrades the display while performing the view transformations.

The options in the Adaptive Degradation group let you set the level to which the view is degraded while you're navigating your model in real time. You can turn off this feature completely by deselecting the Adaptive Degradation check box. If you prefer, you can determine the specific feature to be degraded on an individual basis by removing the check box next to an item name in the Degradation Order list box. The Degrade When Fps Is Below setting lets you set when, in frames per second, the degradation takes effect.

## The Hardware And Performance Tuning Group

The Hardware And Performance Tuning group lets you view and adjust your display system's performance. The View Tune Log button displays the vital statistics for your display system. The Manual Tune button opens the Manual Performance Tuning dialog box. The Check For Updates button takes you to the Autodesk website to allow you to see if new drivers are available for your graphics display card.

## The Manual Performance Tuning Dialog Box

When you click the Manual Tune button, the Manual Performance Tuning dialog box opens.

The Hardware Settings group lets you determine whether to use hardware acceleration. If you turn on Hardware Acceleration, the Driver Name option becomes available, and the available features for the selected type of acceleration are displayed in the list box.

The General Settings group offers two options:

**Discard Back Faces**   In most 3D rendering systems, surfaces have just one visible side. The back sides of surfaces are invisible. This doesn't matter for objects such as cubes and spheres because you see only one side of a surface at any given time; but in some situations, you can see both sides of a surface, such as a single surface used as a wall.

If your drawing is composed of mostly closed objects such as cubes and spheres, and you'll see only one surface, you can select the Discard Back Faces check box to improve system performance. If you have many single surfaces that will be viewed from both sides, you should leave this option turned off.

**Transparency Quality**   This option lets you control the visual quality of transparent objects in your model when viewing your model in a realistic visual style. You can set transparency to a high-, medium-, or low-quality level. Low-quality levels show transparent objects with a screen-door effect, whereas medium and high options give transparent objects a smoother appearance. The low-quality level allows faster view changes.

The options in the Dynamic Tessellation group determine the smoothness of 3D objects when you use a visual style other than a Wireframe or Hidden view. To simulate smoothness, the graphic system divides curved surfaces into triangles called *tessellations.* You can turn all these features on or off by using the check box next to the group title:

**Surfaces**   Controls the amount of detail shown for surfaces. Greater detail requires more surface tessellation, which in turn requires more system memory.

**Curves**   Controls the amount of detail shown for curved surfaces. Greater detail requires more surface tessellation, which in turn requires more system memory.

**Number Of Tessellations To Cache**   Controls the number of tessellations that are cached. A *cache* is a part of memory reserved to store frequently used data. AutoCAD always caches one tessellation. Caching two tessellations improves the appearance and performance of 3D objects when you use multiple viewports.

## Finding Hidden Folders That Contain AutoCAD Files

Many of AutoCAD's features rely on external files to store settings and other resources. Many of these files reside in hidden folders. These folders are as follows:

```
C:\Documents and Settings\User Name\Application Data\Autodesk\AutoCAD 2008\R17.1\enu
C:\Documents and Settings\All Users\Application Data\Autodesk\AutoCAD 2008\R17.1\enu
```

If you attempt to user Explorer to browse to these locations, you may not find the \Application Data folder. You can unhide this folder by doing the following:

1. Right-click the Start button in the lower-left corner of your screen, and then choose Explore to open Windows Explorer.

2. Choose Tools ➢ Folder Options from the menu bar.

3. In the Folder Options dialog box, select the View tab.

4. In the Advanced Settings list, look for the Hidden Files And Folders option. You see two radio buttons just below this option.

5. Select the Show Hidden Files And Folders radio button.

6. Click OK to close the Folder Options dialog box.

After you've done this, the Application Data folder will be visible, and you'll be able to browse to AutoCAD folders that are found there. Once you're able to explore these folders, you may want to create a shortcut to them (right-click the folder and choose Create Shortcut) and then place the shortcut on your desktop or other convenient location. That way, you can get to these folders without having to navigate through several layers of folders.

# Appendix B

# Hardware and Software Tips

Because some of the items that make up an AutoCAD system aren't found on the typical desktop system, I have provided this appendix to help you understand some of them. This appendix also discusses ways you can improve AutoCAD's performance through software and hardware.

## The Graphics Display

There are two issues to consider concerning the graphics display: *resolution* and *performance.* Fortunately, nearly all computers sold today have display systems that are more than adequate for AutoCAD, thanks to the popularity of 3D games. You do need to make sure that your resolution is set to at least 1024 × 768, preferably higher. The higher your resolution, the more detail you'll be able to see in your drawings.

If you have an older system that needs a graphics display upgrade, you should consider the following factors in choosing a new display.

Contemporary motherboards use high-speed PCI Express (PCIe) slots that offer the fastest video throughput available. Check that yours is a system of this type. If you're only doing 2D work, you can get by with an older Accelerated Graphics Port (AGP) graphics card. Windows XP also provides options for using multiple monitors, an approach that has been popular among AutoCAD users. Multiple monitors enable AutoCAD users to view multiple or large documents more easily.

If you want to take full advantage of AutoCADs new 3D features, you'll want one of the Autodesk certified graphics cards in your system. To get the most up-to-date information on the latest graphic-card support, check the Autodesk Service and Support website by doing the following:

1. Enter **3dconfig** at the Command prompt.

2. In the Adaptive Degradation and Performance Tuning dialog box, click the Check for Updates button. Your default browser opens to the Autodesk Service and Support page, where you'll find a description of general hardware issues.

3. Click the Graphics Hardware List option in the left column of the page to go to the page that gives you more detailed information about available graphics hardware drivers.

Even if you already have one of these cards, make sure you have the latest drivers. You can go to the Autodesk web page and download the appropriate driver by doing the following:

1. Choose Tools ➢ Options, and select the System tab.

2. Click the Performance Settings button. Then, in the Adaptive Degradation And Performance Tuning dialog box, click the Check For Updates button.

    The Autodesk AutoCAD Certified Hardware XML Database page opens; you can locate driver updates on this page.

# Pointing Devices

The basic means of communicating with computers are the keyboard and pointing device. Most likely you'll use a mouse, but if you're still in the market for a pointing device, choose an input device that generates smooth cursor movement. Some of the lesser-quality input devices cause erratic movement. Because AutoCAD relies on precise input, you may want to upgrade to an optical mouse, which is less likely to wear out or accumulate dirt in its mechanism.

If you need to trace large drawings, you may want to consider a digitizing tablet. It's usually a rectangular object with a penlike *stylus* or a device called a *puck,* which resembles a mouse. It has a smooth surface on which to draw. The most common size is 4″ × 5″, but digitizing tablets are available in sizes up to 60″ × 70″. The tablet gives a natural feel to drawing with the computer because the movement of the stylus or puck is directly translated into cursor movement.

AutoCAD supports Wintab-compatible digitizers. If your digitizer has a Wintab driver, you can use your digitizer as both a tracing device (to trace drawings on a tablet) and a general pointing device for Windows to choose program menu items.

Your Wintab digitizer must be installed and configured under Windows. Make sure it's working in Windows before enabling it in AutoCAD, or you won't be able to use the digitizer as a pointing device (mouse). To enable the digitizer in AutoCAD, choose Tools ➤ Options to open the Options dialog box, and click the System tab. Open the Current Pointing Device drop-down list, and select Wintab-Compatible Digitizer ADI 4.2 – by Autodesk, Inc.

# Output Devices

Output options vary greatly in quality and price. Quality and paper size are the major considerations for printers. Nearly all printers give accurate drawings, but some produce better line quality than others. Some plotters give merely acceptable results, whereas others are impressive in their speed, color, and accuracy.

AutoCAD can use the Windows Vista, XP, or 2000 system printer, so any device that Windows supports is also supported by AutoCAD. You can also plot directly to an output device, although Autodesk recommends that you set up your plotter or printer through Windows and then select the device from the Plot Configuration group in the Plot Device tab of the Plot dialog box or the Page Setup dialog box.

# Fine-Tuning the Appearance of Output

In Chapter 8, you were introduced to AutoCAD's printing and plotting features. You learned about the AutoCAD features you can use to control the appearance of your output, including layouts and lineweights. This section covers some of the finer points of printer and plotter setup. You'll find information about controlling how lines overlap, how to include more media sizes, adding plot stamps, adjusting the aspect ratio or your printer, and more.

### Making Detailed Adjustments with the Printer/Plotter Configuration Options

If you open the Plot dialog box or the Page Setup dialog box, you see the option groups that offer control over how your plotter or printer works. These groups seem innocent enough, but behind two of them lies a vast set of options that can be quite intimidating. You've already seen in Chapter 8 how the Plot Style Table options work. This section covers the options available when you click the Properties button in the Printer/Plotter group.

The Printer/Plotter Configuration options enable you to adjust those printer or plotter settings that you may want to change only occasionally. These settings are fairly technical and include such items as the port your printer is connected to, the quality of bitmap-image printing, custom paper sizes, and printer calibration, which lets you adjust your plotter for any size discrepancies in output. You won't use most of these settings often, but you should know that they exist just in case you encounter a situation in which you need to make some subtle change to your printer's configuration. You can also use these options to create multiple configurations of the same plotter for quick access to custom settings.

All the settings in this group are stored in a file with the `.pc3` filename extension. You can store and recall any number of configuration files for situations that call for different plotter settings. PC3 files are normally stored in the `Plotters` folder under the `C:\Documents and Settings\`*User Name*`\Application Data\Autodesk\AutoCAD 2008\R17.1\enu\` folder. *User Name* is your login name. You can access this folder by choosing File ➢ Plotter Manager from the AutoCAD menu bar.

The Printer/Plotter group in the Plot and Page Setup dialog boxes offers a drop-down list from which you can select a printer or file output configuration. If a PC3 file exists for a plotter configuration, the drop-down list displays it, and the list displays any Windows system printer. After you've selected an output device from the list, you can click the Properties button to access the Plotter Configuration Editor dialog box.

**TIP** You can configure AutoCAD to create bitmap files in the most common file formats (such as TIFF, Targa, and PCX) or to create Autodesk's DWF file format for the Internet. After you've configured AutoCAD for these types of output, this is where you select the file output type.

The Plotter Configuration Editor dialog box has three tabs: General, Ports, and Device And Document Settings. The General tab displays a list of Windows drivers that this configuration uses, if any, and there is a space for your own comments.

**TIP** You can access and edit the plotter configuration settings without opening AutoCAD. To do this, locate the PC3 file in the `Plotters` subfolder under the `C:\Documents and Settings\`*User Name*`\Application Data\Autodesk\AutoCAD 2008\R17.1\enu\Plotters` folder (*User Name* is your login name), and double-click it.

The Ports tab lets you specify where your plotter data is sent. This is where you should look if you're sending your plots to a network plotter or if you decide to create plot files. You can also select the AutoSpool feature, which enables you to direct your plot to an intermediate location for distribution to the appropriate output device.

The Device And Document Settings tab is the main part of this dialog box. It offers a set of options ranging from OLE output control to custom paper sizes. The main list box offers options in a hierarchical list, similar to a listing in Windows Explorer. Toward the bottom of the dialog box are the Import, Save As, and Defaults buttons. These buttons let you import configuration settings from earlier versions of AutoCAD, save the current settings as a file, or return the settings to their default values.

The list has four main categories: Media, Graphics, Custom Properties, and User-Defined Paper Sizes & Calibration. Not all the options under these categories are available for all plotters. When you select an item from this list, the area just below the list displays the options associated with that item. The following describes each category and its options, using the Xerox Engineering Systems XES8855 as an example.

### THE MEDIA CATEGORY

Some plotters, such as the Xerox Engineering Systems 8800 series, offer options for the source and size of printer media and for the media type. If the Source And Size option is available, the dialog box offers a listing of the source, such as sheet feed or roll, and the sheet size. The Media Type option lets you choose from bond, vellum, or glossy paper or any other medium that is specifically controlled by the plotter. Duplex Printing, when available, controls options for double-sided printing in printers that support this feature. Media Destination, when available, lets you select a destination for output such as collating or stapling in printers that support such features.

### THE PHYSICAL PEN CONFIGURATION CATEGORY (SHOWN ONLY FOR PEN PLOTTERS)

Pen plotters have features that diverge from the typical laser or ink-jet printers or plotters. When these options are present, they let you control some of the ways that AutoCAD generates data for pen plotters. Here is a listing of those pen-plotter feature settings:

**Prompt For Pen Swapping**   Stops the plotter to enable you to switch pens. This feature is designed primarily for single-pen plotters.

**Area Fill Correction**   Tells AutoCAD to compensate for pen width around the edges of a solid-filled area in order to maintain dimensional accuracy of the plot.

**Pen Optimization Level**   Sets how AutoCAD sorts pen movement for optimum speed. AutoCAD does a lot of preparation before sending your drawing to the plotter. If you're using a pen plotter, one of the things it does is optimize the way it sends vectors to your plotter, so your plotter doesn't waste time making frequent pen changes and moving from one end of the plot to another just to draw a single line.

**Physical Pen Characteristics**    Lets you assign plotter pen numbers to AutoCAD colors, adjust the speed of individual pens, and assign pen widths.

### THE GRAPHICS CATEGORY

These settings give you control over both vector and raster output from your plotter. The Vector Graphics settings let you control resolution and color depth, as well as the method for creating shading. If you want to configure your printer for virtual pens, select 255 Virtual Pens under the Color Depth option.

The Raster And Shaded/Rendered Viewports slider gives you control over the quality of any bitmap images. If this slider is placed all the way to the left, raster images aren't plotted. As you move the slider to the right, the raster image quality increases, the speed of printing decreases, and memory requirements increase. The OLE slider controls the quality of OLE linked or embedded files. With the slider all the way to the left, OLE objects aren't printed. As you move the slider farther to the right, OLE image quality and memory requirements increase while speed is reduced.

The Trade-Off slider lets you choose how the Raster and OLE sliders improve speed. You can choose between lower resolution and fewer colors.

For printers and plotters that support TrueType fonts, the TrueType Text options enable you to select between plotting text as graphics or as TrueType text.

### THE CUSTOM PROPERTIES CATEGORY

Select Custom Properties from the Device And Document Settings tab, and the Custom Properties button appears in the lower part of the dialog box. This button gives you access to the same printer or plotter settings that are available from the Windows system printer settings. You can also access these settings by choosing Start ➢ Printers And Faxes, right-clicking the desired printer, and choosing Properties from the shortcut menu.

**TIP**    The options offered through the Custom Properties button often duplicate many of the items in the Device And Documents tab. If an option isn't accessible from the Device And Documents tab, select the options under Custom Properties.

### THE INITIALIZATION STRING

Some plotters require preinitialization and postinitialization codes, in the form of ASCII text strings, to get the plotter's attention. If you have such a plotter, this option lets you enter those strings.

### USER-DEFINED PAPER SIZES & CALIBRATION

The options in the User-Defined Paper Sizes & Calibration category offer some of the more valuable options in this dialog box. In particular, the Plotter Calibration option can be useful in ensuring the accuracy of your plots.

#### *Plotter Calibration*

If your printer or plotter isn't producing an accurate plot, focus on the Plotter Calibration option. If your plotter stretches or shrinks your image in one direction or another, this option lets you adjust the width and height of your plotter's output. To use it, click Plotter Calibration.

A Calibrate Plotter button appears. Click this button to start the Calibrate Plotter Wizard. You're asked first to select a paper size and then to select a width and height for a rectangle that will be plotted with your printer. Figure B.1 shows the wizard screen that asks for the rectangle size.

**FIGURE B.1**

The Calibrate Plotter Wizard lets you adjust the width and height scaling of your plotter output in order to fine-tune the accuracy of your plots.

You can use the Calibrate Plotter Wizard to plot a sample rectangle of a specific size. You then measure the rectangle and check its actual dimensions against the dimensions that you entered. If there are any discrepancies between the plotted dimensions and the dimensions you specified, you can enter the actual plotted size and print another test rectangle. You can repeat this process until your plotted rectangle exactly matches the dimensions entered into the wizard.

Toward the end of the Calibrate Plotter Wizard's steps, you're asked to give a name for a Plot Model Parameter (PMP) file that will store your calibration data. The PMP file also stores any custom paper-size information that you input from other parts of the User-Defined Paper Sizes & Calibration options. This file is then associated with the PC3 file that stores your plotter configuration data.

If you have more than one PC3 file for your plotter, you can associate the PMP file with your other PC3 files by using the PMP File Name option in the Device And Document Settings tab. You need only one calibration file for each plotter or printer you're using. This option appears under the User-Defined Paper Sizes & Calibration category.

To associate a PMP file with a PC3 plotter configuration file, select the PC3 file from the Name drop-down list in the Printer/Plotter section of the Plot dialog box. Click the Properties button, and then, in the Device And Document Settings tab, click the PMP File Name listing. The PMP options appear in the bottom of the dialog box. Click the Attach button, and then select the PMP file from the Open dialog box. Click OK. You'll see that the PMP file has been added to the PMP filename listing.

### Custom Paper Sizes

Some plotters offer custom paper sizes. This feature is usually available for printers and plotters that you've set up to use the AutoCAD drivers instead of the Windows system drivers. If your plotter offers this option, you see a list box and a set of buttons when you select Custom Paper Sizes.

Clicking the Add button starts the Custom Paper Size Wizard, which lets you set the sheet size and margin, as well as the paper source. This information is then saved in a PMP file. You're asked to provide a specific name for the custom paper size, which will be listed in the Custom Paper Size list box.

After you've created a custom paper size, you can edit or delete it by clicking the Edit or Delete button in the Custom Paper Sizes options.

### Modify Standard Paper Size

The last item in the Device And Document Settings tab is the Modify Standard Paper Size option. If this option is available, you can adjust the margins of a standard paper size.

**TIP**    If you're using an older pen plotter, you'll see the Physical Pen Configuration options in the Device And Document Settings tab. These additional options give you control over pen speed, pen optimization, and area fill correction.

### IMPORT, SAVE AS, AND DEFAULTS

The Import, Save As, and Defaults buttons at the bottom of the Plotter Configuration Editor let you import or save your plotter settings as PC3 files, which you can then load from the Plot Device tab of the Plot dialog box and the Page Setup dialog box, as described earlier in this appendix. The Import button lets you import PCP and PC2 files from earlier versions of AutoCAD. Save As lets you save your current settings under an existing or a new PC3 filename. The Defaults button restores the default settings, if any, for the current plotter configuration.

## Adding a Plot Stamp

To help cross-reference your printer or plotter output to AutoCAD drawing files, it's a good idea to add a *plot stamp* to your drawings that identifies the date, time, and filename of the drawing that generated your plot. To accomplish this, the Plot Stamp feature lets you imprint data onto your plotted drawings, usually in the lower-left corner. In addition, Plot Stamp lets you keep a record of your plots in a log file.

To use Plot Stamp, type **Plotstamp**↵ at the AutoCAD Command prompt. You can also turn on the Plot Stamp On option in the Plot dialog box and then click the Plot Stamp Settings button that appears to the right of the option. The Plot Stamp dialog box opens (see Figure B.2).

**FIGURE B.2**

The Plot Stamp
dialog box

The Plot Stamp dialog box offers several options that let you determine what to include in the stamp.

**TIP**    If the options are grayed out, click the Save As button to save Plot Stamp settings under a new file.

The Plot Stamp Fields group lets you include seven predefined options in your stamp, including drawing, layout, and output device name. The User Defined Fields group lets you add custom text to the stamp. To use this feature, click the Add/Edit button in the User Defined Fields group. The User Defined Fields dialog box opens, as shown in Figure B.3.

You can use the Add, Edit, or Delete button to add or make changes to the user-defined fields. After you add a field, it appears in both the list boxes in the User Defined Fields group of the Plot Stamp dialog box.

**FIGURE B.3**

The User Defined
Fields dialog box

To control the location, orientation, font, and font size of the plot stamp, click the Advanced button in the lower-left corner of the Plot Stamp dialog box to open the Advanced Options dialog box, shown in Figure B.4.

**FIGURE B.4**

The Advanced Options dialog box

This dialog box lets you specify the orientation of the stamp on the page as well as the exact location of the stamp in relation to either the printable area or the paper border. In addition, you can specify whether to save a record of your plotting activities in a log file by using the Log File Location group.

## Controlling How Lines Overlap

Some output devices let you control how overlapping lines and shaded areas affect one another, a feature known as *merge control*. In versions of AutoCAD prior to 2000, merge control was handled through additional commands such as Hpconfig or OCEconfig. AutoCAD 2008 includes merge control as part of the Plotter Configuration Editor dialog box.

You can gain access to merge control by opening the Plotter Configuration Editor and, in the Graphics area of the Device And Document Settings tab, clicking the plus sign next to Graphics to expand the list of Graphics options.

If your device supports merge control, you'll see it listed under Graphics, as shown in Figure B.5.

**FIGURE B.5**

The location of the Merge Control setting in the Plotter Configuration Editor

## Filtering Paper Sizes

AutoCAD displays all the available paper sizes for a selected output device in the Page Setup dialog box or the Plot dialog box. For some plotters, the list can be a bit overwhelming. You can filter out paper sizes that you don't need by using the Filter Paper Sizes option in the Plotter Configuration Editor.

Open the Plotter Configuration Editor, and click the plus sign next to the User-Defined Paper Sizes & Calibration item. You see Filter Paper Sizes as an option. After you select this option, you see the Filter Paper Sizes area in the lower half of the Plotter Configuration Editor. Remove the check mark in the box next to any size you won't need.

## Filtering Printers

In some instances, you may want to hide the Windows system printer from the list of printers shown in the AutoCAD Plot dialog box. For example, there may be several shared system printers on a network that aren't intended for AutoCAD use, so you wouldn't want those printers to appear in your list of available printers. You can do this by turning on the Hide System Printers option at the bottom of the General Plot Options group in the Plot And Publish tab of the Options dialog box (choose Tools ➤ Options). This limits the selection of printers and plotters to those that have a PC3 plotter configuration. You can further limit the plotter selections by moving any unneeded PC3 files out of the AutoCAD Plotters folder and into another folder for storage.

## Controlling the Plot-Preview Background Color

If you prefer to use a color other than white for the plot-preview background, you can set the plot-preview background color by using the Color Options dialog box:

1. Choose Tools ➤ Options to open the Options dialog box.

2. Select the Display tab.

3. In the Windows Elements group, click the Colors button to open the Drawing Window Colors dialog box.

4. Select Plot Preview from the Context list.

5. Select a color from the Color drop-down list.

6. Click the Apply & Close button.

### Controlling the Windows Metafile Background Color

If you prefer using the Windows metafile file type to export AutoCAD drawings to other programs, you can control the background color of your exported file. The AutoCAD Wmfbkgnd system variable lets you control the background color of exported Windows metafiles. Wmfbkgnd offers two settings: off generates a transparent background, and on generates the background color of the current view. The initial default value is off.

## Memory and AutoCAD Performance

Next to your computer's CPU, memory has the greatest impact on AutoCAD's speed. How much you have, and how you use it, can make a big difference in whether you finish that rush job on schedule or work late nights trying. This section will clarify some basic points about memory and how AutoCAD uses it.

AutoCAD is a virtual memory system. This means that when your RAM resources reach their limit, part of the data stored in RAM is temporarily moved to your hard disk to make more room in RAM. This temporary storage of RAM to your hard disk is called *virtual memory paging*. Through memory paging, AutoCAD continues to run, even though your work may exceed the capacity of your RAM. The Windows operating system manages this virtual memory paging. If you have several programs open at once, Windows determines how much memory to allocate to each program. AutoCAD always attempts to store as much of your drawing in RAM as possible. When the amount of RAM required for a drawing exceeds the amount of physical RAM in your system, Windows pages parts of the data stored in RAM to the hard disk. Your drawing size, the number of files you have open in AutoCAD, and the number of programs you have open under Windows affect how much RAM you have available. For this reason, if your AutoCAD editing session is slowing down, try closing other applications you may have open or closing files that you're no longer using. This will free up more memory for AutoCAD and the drawing file.

### AutoCAD and Your Hard Disk

You'll notice that AutoCAD slows down when paging occurs. If this happens frequently, the best thing you can do is add more RAM. But you can also improve the performance of AutoCAD under these conditions by ensuring that you have adequate hard-disk space and that free hard-disk space has been *defragmented* or *optimized*. A defragmented disk offers faster access, thereby improving paging speed.

Windows dynamically allocates swap-file space. However, make sure there is enough free space on your hard disk to allow Windows to set up the space. A good guideline is to allow enough space for a swap file that is twice the size of your RAM capacity. If you have the minimum 512MB of RAM, you need to allow space for a 1024MB swap file (at a minimum). This will give your system 1024MB of virtual memory. Also consider setting the minimum and maximum swap file space to be equal.

Fast, high-capacity hard disks are fairly inexpensive, so even if you aren't running out of space, you may want to consider adding another hard disk with as much capacity as you can afford. You can greatly improve your system speed by upgrading from an old hard drive to a new one. Consider upgrading to an SATA or SATA2 hard-drive controller and drive. You may also consider a Raid0 hard-drive setup if your system supports it. Raid0 can greatly improve the speed of your system by dividing hard-drive access between two drives. Such a system can nearly double access speeds.

### Keep Your Hard Disk Clean

If you aren't in the habit of emptying your Recycle Bin, you want to get into the habit of doing so. Every file that you "delete" using Windows Explorer is actually passed to the Recycle Bin. You need to clear this out frequently. If you're a regular Internet user, check your Internet cache folder for unnecessary files. You can employ one of the many hard-disk cleaning utilities to do this. Finally, it's a good idea to perform regular maintenance on your hard disk to keep it clear of fragmentation and unused files. The Tools tab of the Properties dialog box for your hard disk offers error-checking and defragmenting options.

## AutoCAD Tools to Improve Memory Use

AutoCAD offers some tools to help make your use of system memory more efficient. Partial Open and the Spatial and Layer indexes let you manage the memory use of large drawings and multiple open files by reducing the amount of a file that is loaded into memory. Using these tools, you can have AutoCAD open only those portions of a file that you want to work on.

### Using Partial Open to Conserve Memory and Improve Speed

Use the Partial Open option in the File dialog box when you know you're going to work on only a small portion or a particular set of layers of a large drawing. Choose File ➢ Open, and then locate and select the file you want to open. At the bottom-right corner of the dialog box, click the down arrow next to the Open button, and select Partial Open to open the Partial Open dialog box. Note that this option is available only for files created and edited in AutoCAD 2000 and later.

You can use this dialog box to open specific views of your drawing by selecting the view name from the View Geometry To Load list box. Only the geometry displayed in the selected view is loaded into memory. This doesn't limit you to only that view as you edit the drawing. Subsequent views cause AutoCAD to load the geometry of those views as needed.

You can further limit the amount of a drawing that is loaded into memory by selecting only those layers you want to work with. Place a check mark next to the layers you want in the Layer Geometry To Load list box.

After you open a file by using the Partial Open option, you can always make further adjustments by choosing File ➤ Partial Load. This opens the Partial Load dialog box, which offers the same options as the Partial Open dialog box. The Partial Load dialog box isn't available for files that are opened normally without using the Partial Open option.

### Using Spatial and Layer Indexes to Conserve Memory

The Spatial and Layer indexes are lists that keep a record of geometry in a drawing. A *Spatial index* lists a drawing's geometry according to the geometry's location in space. A *Layer index* lists the drawing's geometry according to layer assignments. These indexes offer more-efficient memory use and faster loading times for drawings that are being used as Xrefs. They take effect only when Demand Load is turned on. (See Chapter 7 for more on Demand Load.) The Layer index enables AutoCAD to load only those layers of an Xref that aren't frozen. AutoCAD uses the Spatial index to load only objects in an Xref that are within the boundary of a clipped Xref.

You can turn on the Spatial and Layer indexes for a file through the Indexctl system variable. Indexctl has four settings:

◆ 0 is the default. This turns off Spatial and Layer indexing.

◆ 1 turns on Layer indexing.

◆ 2 turns on Spatial indexing.

◆ 3 turns on both Layer and Spatial indexing.

To use the Indexctl system variable, type **Indexctl⏎**. Then, at the `Enter new value for INDEXCTL <0>:` prompt, enter the number of the setting option you want to use.

**TIP**   The Partial Open option in the Select File dialog box includes the Index Status button group, which offers information on the index status of a drawing. If the drawing you're opening has Spatial or Layer indexing turned on, you can use it by selecting the Spatial Index check box.

### Using the Incremental Save Percentage to Conserve Disk Space

If your disk is getting crowded and you need to squeeze as many files as you can onto it, you can reduce the amount of wasted space in a file by adjusting the Incremental Save value in the Open And Save tab of the Options dialog box. By setting Incremental Save to a lower value, you can reduce the size of files to some degree. The trade-off is slower performance when saving files. See Appendix A for more information on this setting.

Another related option is to turn off the BAK file option, also located in the Open And Save tab of the Options dialog box. Each time you choose File ➤ Save or File ➤ Save As, AutoCAD creates a backup copy of your file with the .bak file extension. When you turn off the Create Backup Copy With Each Save option, BAK files aren't created, thereby saving disk space.

## Setting Up Architectural Desktop to Act Like Standard AutoCAD

Many users who have Architectural Desktop 2008 (ADT) would like to use this book to learn AutoCAD 2008. However, the interface to ADT is quite different from the standard AutoCAD interface. Still, underneath the ADT menus and palettes lies the basic AutoCAD program discussed in this book. If you have Architectural Desktop 2008, the following instructions show you how to set up a shortcut on your Windows Desktop to launch standard AutoCAD 2008.

1. Make a copy of the ADT windows desktop shortcut. Right-click the Architectural Desktop 2008 shortcut, and choose Copy.

2. Right-click a blank spot on the Desktop, and choose Paste.

3. Right-click the copy of the ADT shortcut, and choose Properties.

4. In the Target text box, change the value to read as follows:

   ```
   "C:\Program Files\Autodesk Architectural Desktop 2008\acad.exe" /t "acad.dwt"
   /p "Standard AutoCAD"
   ```

   The /t is a command switch that tells AutoCAD to use a specific template file, which in this case is acad.dwt. The /p is a command switch that tells AutoCAD to use the Standard AutoCAD profile when starting AutoCAD. Note that the Standard AutoCAD profile doesn't exist. AutoCAD creates it when you attempt to start AutoCAD from the shortcut. Click Apply after you've made the change to the Target text box.

5. Click the Change Icon button, and then click the Browse button in the Change Icon dialog box. From here, you can select a different icon from the Change Icon dialog box.

6. Click OK to exit the Shortcut Properties dialog box. Then, right-click the shortcut copy again and choose Rename.

7. Rename the shortcut to **AutoCAD 2008**.

Double-click your new AutoCAD 2008 Desktop shortcut to start AutoCAD 2008. You'll see a warning message that the Standard AutoCAD profile doesn't exist and that AutoCAD will create it using the default AutoCAD settings. Once AutoCAD has started, the title bar will still show Autodesk Architectural Desktop 2008, but the program will behave like standard AutoCAD 2008. You can still start the full version of Architectural Desktop by using the Architectural Desktop 2008 shortcut or if you launch AutoCAD by double-clicking an AutoCAD file.

## When Things Go Wrong

AutoCAD is a complex program, and at times AutoCAD doesn't behave in a way you expect. If you run into problems, chances are they won't be insurmountable. Here are a few tips on what to do when AutoCAD doesn't work the way you expect.

### Starting Up or Opening a File

The most common reason you'll have difficulty opening a file is a lack of free disk space. If you encounter errors attempting to open files, check whether you have adequate free disk space on all your drives.

If you've recently installed AutoCAD but you can't start it, you may have a configuration problem. Before you panic, try reinstalling AutoCAD from scratch. Particularly if you're installing the CD version, this doesn't take long. (See Appendix A for installation instructions.) Before you reinstall AutoCAD, use the Uninstall program to remove the current version of AutoCAD.

After you've uninstalled AutoCAD, delete the `AutoCAD 2008` folder from the `Program Files` folder and also delete the `AutoCAD 2008` folders under the following two locations:

`C:\Documents and Settings\`*UserName*`\Application Data\Autodesk`
`C:\Documents and Settings\`*UserName*`\Local Settings\Application Data\Autodesk`

Make sure you have your authorization code, serial number, and CD key handy. Make sure you've closed all other programs when you run the AutoCAD installation. As a final measure, restart your computer when you've completed the installation.

## Restoring Corrupted Files

Hardware failures can result in data files becoming corrupted. When this happens, AutoCAD is unable to open the drawing file. Fortunately, there is hope for damaged files. In most cases, AutoCAD runs through a file-recovery routine automatically the next time you open AutoCAD after a crash. You'll see a panel on the left side of the AutoCAD window listing files that are available for recovery, including BAK files. You can double-click the file you want to recover and then save it.

If you have a file you know is corrupted, but it doesn't appear in the panel described in the previous paragraph, you can start the file-recovery utility by choosing File ➢ Drawing Utilities ➢ Recover. This opens the Select File dialog box, enabling you to select the file you want to recover. After you enter the name, AutoCAD goes to work. You'll see a series of messages, most of which have little meaning to the average user. Then, the recovered file is opened. You may lose some data, but a partial file is better than no file at all, especially when the file represents several days of work.

Another possibility is to attempt to recover your drawing from the BAK file—the last saved version before your drawing was corrupted. Rename the drawing BAK file to a DWG file with a different name, and then open it. The drawing will contain only what was in your drawing when it was previously saved.

If you want to restore a file that you've just been working on, you can check the alphanumeric file with the `.sv$` file name extension. This is the file AutoCAD uses to store your drawing during automatic saves. Change the `.sv$` filename extension to `.dwg`, and then open the file.

In some situations, a file is so badly corrupted it can't be restored. By backing up frequently, you can minimize the inconvenience of such an occurrence. You may also want to consider a third-party utility that performs regular disk maintenance.

## Troubleshooting Other Common Problems

AutoCAD is a large, complex program, so you're bound to encounter difficulties from time to time. This section covers a few of the more common problems experienced while using AutoCAD:

**You can see but can't select objects in a drawing someone else has worked on.** This may be happening because you have a Paper Space view instead of a Model Space view. To make sure you're in Model Space, type **Tilemode.**↵ and then type **1.**↵ Or you can turn on the UCS icon (by typing **Ucsicon.**↵**On.**↵). If you see the triangular UCS icon in the lower-left corner, you're in Paper Space. You must go to Model Space before you can edit the drawing. Another item to check is the layer lock setting. If a layer is locked, you can't edit objects on that layer.

**Grips don't appear when objects are selected.** Make sure the Grips feature is enabled (choose Tools ➢ Grips). See Appendix A for details.

**Selecting objects doesn't work as described in this book.** Check the Selection settings to make sure they're set the same way as the exercise specifies. See Chapter 2 for details. Also check the Selection tab in the Options dialog box (choose Tools ➢ Options). See Appendix A for more on the Selection tab of the Options dialog box.

**Text appears in the wrong font style, or an error message says AutoCAD can't find font files.**
When you're working on files from another company, it's not uncommon that you'll encounter a file that uses special third-party fonts you don't have. You can usually substitute standard AutoCAD fonts for any fonts you don't have, without adverse effects. AutoCAD automatically displays a dialog box that lets you select font files for the substitution. You can either choose a font file or press the Esc key to ignore the message. (See Chapter 10 for more on font files.) If you choose to ignore the error message, you may not see some of the text that would normally appear in the drawing.

**You can't import DXF files.** Various problems can occur during the DXF import, the most common of which is that you're trying to import a DXF file into an existing drawing rather than a new drawing. Under some conditions, you can import a DXF file into an existing drawing by using the Dxfin command, but AutoCAD may not import the entire file.

To ensure that your entire DXF file is safely imported, choose File ➤ Open, and select *.DXF from the File Type drop-down list. Then, import your DXF file.

If you know that the DXF file you're trying to import is in the ASCII format and not a binary DXF, look at the file with a text editor. If it contains odd-looking lines of characters, chances are the file is damaged or contains extra data that AutoCAD can't understand. Try deleting the odd-looking lines of characters, and then import the file again. (Make a backup copy of the file before you attempt this.)

**A file can't be saved to disk.** Frequently, a hard disk will fill up quickly during an editing session. AutoCAD can generate temporary and swap files many times larger than the file you're editing. This may leave you with no room to save your file. If this happens, you can empty the Recycle Bin to clear some space on your hard disk or delete old AutoCAD BAK files you don't need. *Don't delete temporary AutoCAD files.*

**The keyboard shortcuts for commands aren't working.** If you're working on an unfamiliar computer, chances are the keyboard shortcuts (or command aliases) have been altered. The command aliases are stored in the Acad.pgp file. Use the Windows Search utility to locate this file, and make sure the Acad.pgp file is in the C:\Documents and Settings\*User Name*\ Application Data\Autodesk\AutoCAD 2008\R17.1\enu\Support folder.

**Plots come out blank.** Check the scale factor you're using for your plot. Often, a blank plot means your scale factor is making the plot too large to fit on the sheet. Try plotting with the Scale To Fit option. If you get a plot, you know your scale factor is incorrect. See Chapter 8 for more on plotting options. Check your output before you plot by using the Full Preview option in the Plot Configuration dialog box.

**You can't get your drawing properly oriented on the sheet.** If you want to change the orientation of your drawing on a plotted sheet, and the Plot Configuration orientation options don't seem to work, try rotating the UCS to align with your desired plot view and then type **Plan**↵. Adjust the view to display what you want plotted, and then use the View command (choose View ➤ Named Views) to save this view. When you're ready to plot, use the View option in the Plot Configuration dialog box and plot the saved view, instead of rotating the plot.

**Dimensions appear as objects, or lines and text and don't act as described in this book.**
The Dimassoc system variable has been set to 0 or was 0 when the dimension was created. Another possibility is that the dimension was reduced to its component objects by using the Explode command. Make sure Dimassoc is on by typing **Dimassoc**↵**2**↵. Unfortunately, an exploded dimension or one that was created with Dimassoc turned off can't be converted to a true dimension object. You must redraw the dimension.

**A file containing an Xref appears to be blank, or parts are missing.**   AutoCAD can't find the Xref file. Use the Xref Manager dialog box (choose Insert ➢ Xref Manager) to reestablish a connection with the Xref file. After the Xref Manager dialog box is open, select the missing Xref from the list, and then click the Browse button and locate and select the file by using the Browse dialog box.

**As you draw, little marks appear on your screen where you have selected points.**   The Blipmode system variable is on. Turn it off by typing **Blipmode↵off↵**.

**A file you want to open is read-only, even though you know no one else on the network is using the file.**   Every now and then, you may receive a file that you can't edit because it's read-only. This frequently happens with files that have been archived to a CD. If you have a file that is read-only, try the following:

1. Locate the read-only file with Windows Explorer, and right-click its filename.

2. Choose Properties from the shortcut menu to open the Properties dialog box.

3. Click the General tab.

4. Click the Read-Only check box to remove the check mark.

**Tracking vectors don't appear in the drawing as described in this book.**   Make sure that the AutoTrack features are turned on. See the discussion of the Drafting tab in the Options dialog box in Appendix A.

**The Hyperlink icon doesn't appear as described in Chapter 27.**   Make sure the Hyperlink options are turned on in the User Preferences tab in the Options dialog box.

**When you open new files, the drawing area isn't the same as described in this book.**   Make sure you're using the correct default unit style for new drawings. In the Create New Drawing dialog box, click the Start From Scratch button, and select the appropriate unit style from the Default Settings button group. If you're using feet and inches, select Imperial (feet and inches). If you're using metric measurements, select Metric. AutoCAD uses the Acad.dwt file template for new Imperial measurement drawings and the Acadiso.dwt template for metric measurement drawings. You can also use the Measureinit system variable to set the default unit style.

**When you offset polylines, such as rectangles or polygons, the offset object has extra line segments or rounded corners.**   Set the Offsetgap system variable to 0. Offsetgap controls the behavior of the line segments of offset polylines. When Offsetgap is set to 0, the individual line segments of a polyline are extended to join end to end. When Offsetgap is set to 1, the line segments retain their original length and are joined with an arc. If Offsetgap is set to 2, the line segments retain their original length and are joined by a straight-line segment.

**Your older AutoCAD file contains filled areas that were once transparent, but in AutoCAD 2008 the text and line work are obscured by solid fills.**   Earlier versions of AutoCAD let you adjust the Merge Control feature of your plotter, which in turn allowed solid filled areas to appear transparent. The Merge Control feature is still available, but it has been moved to the Plotter Configuration Editor. See the section on merge control earlier in this appendix for more information.

Another option is to use the Draworder command to move the solid filled area behind other objects in the drawing. See Chapter 14 for more on the Draworder command.

**Filled, non-TrueType fonts appear to have extraneous lines around the edges.**   If your font looks distorted and lines appear around the edges, it may be due to a setting in the plot-style table. Open the plot-style table for your drawing (see Chapter 9), and make sure the Line End Style setting for the text's layer or plot style is set to Use Object End Style.

# Appendix C

# System Variables and Dimension Styles

AutoCAD is a complex program with a bewildering set of options and settings. You don't need to know everything about AutoCAD to be a productive user, but it does help to be aware of some of the inner workings that let you fine-tune AutoCAD.

This appendix covers a few of the details that can help you get tighter control over the way AutoCAD works. You'll find a brief discussion of system variables that give you direct control over options and features. That discussion is followed by a detailed look at Dimension Styles settings.

## System Variables

System variables let you fine-tune your AutoCAD environment. Most of the system variables control the same options you find in AutoCAD's dialog boxes and palettes. The main advantage of system variables is that you can set them without having to dig through a series of dialog boxes.

To set a system variable, you enter the variable name at the Command prompt. Or, if you're in the middle of another command, you can set a system variable by entering the variable name preceded by an apostrophe. For example, if you're drawing a series of line segments, you can enter 'Snapang.⌐ at the Specify next point or [Undo}: prompt to change the Snapang system variable on the fly.

Because system variables are command-line driven and don't require access to a dialog box, you can use them in your custom macros to control settings. You can also access system variables through AutoLISP by using the Getvar and Setvar functions, as well as through ActiveX automation. LT users can use the Modemacro command and the Diesel macro language to obtain information from the system variables. (See Chapter 26 for more on Modemacro and Diesel.)

A list of the system variables and their functions could take up a full chapter. A detailed look at system variables is beyond the scope of this book, but you have an excellent resource for information about system variables in the AutoCAD Help window. Choose Help ➤ Help to open the AutoCAD 2008 Help window. Select the Contents tab, and expand the Command Reference option in the left panel. There you see the system variables listed in alphabetical order.

You can also find system variables through the features and commands they control. For example, if you search for *Grip* in the AutoCAD 2008 Help window's Search tab, you'll see "Understand Grip

Tool" at the top of the left panel. Select this option, and a list of system variables related to the Grip feature appears under the Quick Reference tab in the right side panel.

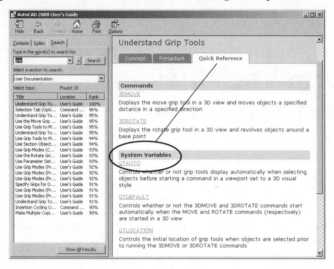

# Taking a Closer Look at the Dimension Style Dialog Boxes

As you saw in Chapter 12, you can control the appearance and format of dimensions through dimension styles. You can create new dimension styles or edit existing ones. This section describes all the components of the dialog boxes you use to create and maintain dimension styles.

## The Dimension Style Manager Dialog Box

The Dimension Style Manager dialog box is the gateway to dimension styles. With this dialog box, you can create a new dimension style, edit existing dimension styles, or make an existing dimension style current. To open the Dimension Style Manager dialog box, choose Dimension ➢ Dimension Style.

**TIP**   You can use the DesignCenter to import dimension styles from one drawing into another.

The following sections describe the options in the Dimension Style Manager dialog box.

### PREVIEW OF *STANDARD*

The image in the right half of the Dimension Style Manager dialog box gives you a preview of your dimension style. It shows a sample of most of the types of dimensions you'll use, formatted the way you specified when you created or modified your dimension style.

### THE STYLES LIST BOX

The Styles list box displays the available dimension styles. You can highlight the dimension style names in the Styles list box to indicate a style to be used with the Set Current, New, Modify, and Override options. You can also right-click a style name and then rename or delete the selected style.

### THE LIST DROP-DOWN LIST

The List drop-down list lets you control what is listed in the Styles list box. You can display either all the styles available or only the styles in use in the drawing.

### DON'T LIST STYLES IN XREFS

The Don't List Styles In Xrefs check box lets you specify whether dimension styles in Xrefs are listed in the Styles list box.

### THE SET CURRENT BUTTON

The Set Current button lets you set the dimension style highlighted in the Styles list box to be current.

### THE NEW BUTTON

The New button lets you create a new dimension style. The New button uses the dimension style that is highlighted in the Styles list box as the basis for the new style. Clicking New opens the Create New Dimension Style dialog box.

In the Create New Dimension Style dialog box, you can enter the name for your new dimension style. You can also select the source dimension style on which your new dimension style will be based.

**New Style Name**   Lets you specify the name for your new dimension style.

**Start With**   Lets you select an existing style on which to base your new dimension style.

**Use For**   Lets you choose a dimension type for your new dimension style. For a completely new dimension style, use the All Dimensions option in the Use For drop-down list. If you want to modify the specifications for a particular dimension type of an existing dimension style, select a dimension type from this list. Your modified dimension type will appear in the Styles list box under the main style you specify in the Start With drop-down list. After you've modified a dimension type, the new type will be applied to any new dimensions.

After you've entered your options in the Create New Dimension Style dialog box, click Continue. You see the New Dimension Style dialog box described in the next section. When you're finished setting up your new style, it's listed in the Styles list box.

### THE MODIFY BUTTON

The Modify button lets you modify the dimension style that is selected in the Styles list box. Clicking this option opens the Modify Dimension Style dialog box described in the next section.

### THE OVERRIDE BUTTON

The Override button lets you create a temporary dimension style based on an existing style. You may want to use this option if you need to create a dimension that differs only slightly from an existing style.

To use the Override option, select a style from the Styles list box, and then click Override. You'll see the Override Current Style dialog box described in the next section. After you create an override, it's listed as <style overrides> in the Styles list box, right under the style you used to create the override.

The override then becomes the default dimension style until you select another one from the Styles list. When you select a different style to be current, a message tells you that the unsaved style will be discarded. To save an override style, select the override from the Styles list box, and click New. Then, click Continue in the Create New Dimension Style dialog box, and click OK in the New Dimension Style dialog box. You can also merge the Override style with its source style by right-clicking <style overrides> and selecting Save To Current Style.

### THE COMPARE BUTTON

The Compare button lets you compare the differences between two dimension styles. When you click the Compare button, the Compare Dimension Styles dialog box opens.

You can select the two styles you want to compare from the Compare and With drop-down lists. The differences appear in the list box. Just above the upper-right corner of the list box is a Copy button; this copies the contents of the list box to the Windows Clipboard, enabling you to save the comparison to a word-processed document.

## The New/Modify/Override Dimension Style Dialog Box

When you click the New button in the Dimension Style Manager dialog box and then click Continue in the Create New Dimension Style dialog box, the New Dimension Style dialog box opens.

You'll also see this same dialog box under a different name when you click the Modify or Override button in the Dimension Style Manager dialog box. The options in this dialog box let you determine all the characteristics of your dimension style. This section provides detailed descriptions of each available option.

**TIP** The equivalent dimension style variables are shown in brackets at the end of the description of each option.

### THE LINES TAB

The options in this tab give you control over the appearance of dimension and extension lines. Figure C.1 shows an example of some of the dimension components that are affected by these options. The values you enter here for distances should be in final plot sizes and will be multiplied by the dimension scale value in the Fit tab to derive the actual extension distance in the drawing.

**FIGURE C.1**

Examples of how some of the options in the Lines tab affect dimensions

### The Dimension Lines Group

The following options let you control the general behavior and characteristics of the dimension lines:

**Color**   Lets you set the color of the dimension line [Dimclrd].

**Linetype**   Lets you set the linetype for dimension lines.

**Lineweight**   Lets you set the lineweight for dimension lines [Dimlwd].

**Extend Beyond Ticks**   Lets you set the distance that the dimension line extends beyond the extension lines. The value you enter here should be in final plot sizes and will be multiplied by the dimension scale value in the Fit tab to derive the actual extension distance in the drawing [Dimdle].

**Baseline Spacing**   Lets you specify the distance between stacked dimensions [Dimdli, Dimbaseline].

**Suppress**   Check boxes let you suppress the dimension line on either side of the dimension text [DimLine1, DimLine2].

### The Extension Lines Group

The following options let you control the general behavior and characteristics of the extension lines:

**Color**   Lets you set the color for extension lines [Dimclre].

**Linetype Ext Line 1**   Controls the linetype for the first extension line.

**Linetype Ext Line 2**   Controls the linetype for the second extension line.

**Lineweight**   Lets you set the lineweight for extension lines [Dimlwe].

**Extend Beyond Dim Lines**   Lets you set the distance that extension lines extend beyond dimension lines [Dimexe].

**Offset From Origin**   Lets you set the distance from the extension line to the object being dimensioned [Dimexo].

**Fixed Length Extension Lines**   Lets you set the extension lines to a fixed length. The Length input box provides a space to enter the length you want.

**Suppress**   Check boxes let you suppress one or both extension lines [Ext Line1, Ext Line2].

#### THE SYMBOLS AND ARROWS TAB

The options in this tab give you control over the appearance of arrowheads and center marks. The value you enter in this tab for distances should be in final plot sizes and will be multiplied by the dimension scale value in the Fit tab to derive the actual extension distance in the drawing.

### Arrowheads

The following options let you select the type and sizes of arrowheads for dimensions and leaders:

**First**   Lets you select the type of arrowhead to use on dimension lines. By default, the second arrowhead automatically changes to match the arrowhead you specify for this setting [Dimblk1].

**Second**   Lets you select a different arrowhead from the one you select for First [Dimblk2].

**Leader**   Lets you specify an arrowhead for leader notes [Dimldrblk].

**Arrow Size**   Lets you specify the size for the arrowheads [Dimasz].

### The Center Marks Group

The following options let you set the center mark for radius and diameter dimensions:

**None/Mark/Line**   Let you select the type of center mark used in radius and diameter dimensions. The Mark option draws a small cross mark, Line draws a cross mark and center lines, and None draws nothing [Dimcen].

**Size**   Lets you specify the size of the center mark [Dimcen].

### The Arc Length Symbol Group

This set of radio buttons controls the display of the arc-length symbol in arc-length dimensions:

**Preceding Dimension Text**   Places the symbol before the dimension text.

**Above Dimension Text**   Places the symbol above the dimension text.

**None**   No symbol.

### The Radius Dimension Jog Group

You can set the angle of the radius-dimension jog with this setting. The radius-dimension jog is the short line in the radius dimension that indicates the dimension is measured to a point out of view.

## THE TEXT TAB

The options in the Text tab give you control over the appearance of the dimension text. You can set the text style and default location of text in relation to the dimension line. If the text style you select for your dimension text has a height value of 0, you can set the text height from this tab.

### The Text Appearance Group

The following options give you control over the appearance of text:

**Text Style**   Lets you select an existing text style for your dimension text. You can also create a new style for your dimension text by clicking the Browse button [Dimtxsty].

**Text Color**   Lets you select a color for your dimension text [Dimclrt].

**Fill Color**   Lets you select a color for your dimension background.

**Text Height**   Lets you specify a text height for dimension text. This option is valid only for text styles with 0 height [Dimtxt].

**Fraction Height Scale**   Lets you specify a scale factor for the height of fractional text. This option is available only when Architectural or Fractional is selected in the Primary Units tab [Dimtfac].

**Draw Frame Around Text**   Draws a rectangle around the dimension text when selected [Dimgap].

### The Text Placement Group

The following options give you control over the placement of text, including the ability to specify the distance of text from the dimension line:

**Vertical**   Lets you set the vertical position of the text in relation to the dimension line. The options are Centered, Above, Outside, and JIS. Centered places the text in line with the dimension line; the dimension line is broken to accommodate the text. Above places the text above the dimension line, leaving the dimension line unbroken. Outside places the text away from the dimension line at a location farthest from the object being dimensioned. JIS places the text in conformance with the Japanese Industrial Standards [Dimtad].

**Horizontal**   Lets you set the location of the text in relation to the extension lines. The options are Centered, At Ext Line 1, At Ext Line 2, Over Ext Line 1, and Over Ext Line 2. Centered places the text between the two extension lines. At Ext Line 1 places the text next to the first extension line but still between the two extension lines. At Ext Line 2 places the text next to the second extension line but still between the two extension lines. Over Ext Line 1 places the text above the first extension line and aligned with the first extension line. Over Ext Line 2 places the text above the second extension line and aligned with the second extension line [Dimjust].

**Offset From Dim Line**   Lets you determine the distance from the baseline of text to the dimension line when text is placed above the dimension line. It also lets you set the size of the gap between the dimension text and the endpoint of the dimension line when the text is in line with the dimension line. You can use this option to set the margin around the text when the dimension text is in a centered position that breaks the dimension line into two segments [Dimgap].

### The Text Alignment Group

The following options give you control over the alignment of text in relation to the dimension line:

**Horizontal**   Keeps the text in a horizontal orientation, regardless of the dimension line orientation.

**Aligned With Dimension Line**   Aligns the text with the dimension line.

**ISO Standard**   Aligns the text with the dimension line when it's between the extension lines; otherwise the text is oriented horizontally [Dimtih, Dimtoh].

### THE FIT TAB

The options in the Fit tab let you fine-tune the behavior of the dimension text and arrows under special conditions. For example, you can select an optional placement for text and arrows when there isn't enough room for them between the extension lines.

### The Fit Options Group

The Fit Options radio buttons let you determine which dimension component is moved when there isn't enough room between the extension lines for either or both the text or the arrows:

**Either Text Or Arrows (Best Fit)**   Automatically determines whether only text, only arrows, or both text and arrows will fit between the extension lines, and then places them accordingly. For example, if there isn't enough room for both text and arrows, and the text is wider than the two arrows combined, the text is placed outside the extension lines. If the width of the arrows is greater than the width of the text, the arrows are moved outside the extension lines. If the gap between the extension lines is too narrow for either the text or arrows, both the arrows and the text are moved outside the extension lines [Dimatfit].

**Arrows**   Moves the arrows outside the extension lines when there isn't enough room for both arrows and text between the extension lines. If the gap between the extension lines is too narrow for either the text or the arrows, both the arrows and the text are moved outside the extension lines [Dimatfit].

**Text**   Moves the text outside the extension line when there isn't enough room for both arrows and text between the extension lines. If the gap between the extension lines is too narrow for either the text or the arrows, both the arrows and the text are moved outside the extension lines [Dimatfit].

**Both Text And Arrows**   Moves both the text and the arrows outside the extension line when there isn't enough room for both arrows and text between the extension lines [Dimatfit].

**Always Keep Text Between Ext Lines**   Places the text between the extension lines, regardless of whether the text fits there [Dimtix].

**Suppress Arrows If They Don't Fit Inside Extension Lines**   Removes the arrows entirely if they don't fit between the extension lines [Dimsoxd].

### The Text Placement Group

The Text Placement radio buttons determine how the dimension text behaves when it's moved from its default location:

**Beside The Dimension Line**   Keeps the text in its normal location relative to the dimension line [Dimtmove].

**Over Dimension Line, With Leader**   Lets you move the dimension text, independent of the dimension line. A leader is added between the dimension line and the text [Dimtmove].

**Over Dimension Line, Without Leader**   Lets you move the dimension text, independent of the dimension line. No leader is added [Dimtmove].

### The Scale For Dimension Features Group

These options offer control over the scale of the dimension components. You can set a fixed scale, or you can allow the dimension components to be scaled depending on the Paper Space viewport in which they're displayed:

**Annotative**   Turns on the Annotative Scale feature, which lets you quickly set the size of text to correspond with your drawing's annotation or viewport scale setting [Annotativedwg].

**Use Overall Scale Of**   Lets you determine the scale of the dimension components. All the settings in the Dimension Style dialog box are scaled to the value you set in the input box if this radio button is selected [Dimscale].

**Scale Dimensions To Layout**   Scales all the dimension components to the scale factor assigned to the Paper Space viewport in which the drawing appears [Dimscale].

### The Fine Tuning Group

The following two check boxes offer miscellaneous settings for dimension text and dimension lines:

**Place Text Manually**   Enables you to manually place the dimension text horizontally along the dimension line when you're inserting dimensions in your drawing [Dimupt].

**Draw Dim Line Between Ext Lines**   Forces AutoCAD to draw a dimension line between the extension lines no matter how narrow the distance is between the extension lines [Dimtofl].

### THE PRIMARY UNITS TAB

The options in the Primary Units tab let you set the format and content of the dimension text, including the unit style for linear and angular dimensions.

### The Linear Dimensions Group

The following options give you control over the unit style and the formatting of dimension text for linear dimensions:

**Unit Format**   Lets you determine the unit style of the dimension text. The options are Scientific, Decimal, Engineering, Architectural, Fractional, and Windows Desktop. You must set this option independent of the overall drawing units setting (choose Format ➣ Units) if you want the dimension text to appear in the appropriate style [Dimunit].

**Precision**   Lets you set the precision of the dimension text. This option rounds off the dimension text to the nearest precision value you set. It doesn't affect the actual precision of the drawing [Dimdec].

**Fraction Format**   Available only for Architectural and Fractional unit formats. This option lets you select between vertically stacked, diagonally stacked, and horizontal fractions [Dimfrac].

**Decimal Separator** Lets you select a decimal separator for dimension unit formats that display decimals. You can choose a period, a comma, or a space. If you want to use a dimension separator not included in the list, you can use the Dimsep system variable to specify a custom dimension separator [Dimsep].

**Round Off** Lets you determine the degree of rounding applied to dimensions. For example, you can set this option to 0.25 to round off dimensions to the nearest .25 or ¼ of a unit [Dimrnd].

**Prefix** Lets you include a prefix for all linear-dimension text. For example, if you want all your linear dimension text to be preceded by the word *Approximately,* you can enter **Approximately** in this input box. Control codes can be used for special characters. See Chapter 10 for more information on character codes [Dimpost].

**Suffix** Lets you include a suffix for all linear-dimension text. Control codes can be used for special characters. See Chapter 10 for more information on character codes [Dimpost].

### The Measurement Scale Group

This group offers options that can convert dimension values to different scale factors. For example, dimensions in Imperial units can be scaled to metric, and vice versa. The options are as follows:

**Scale Factor** Lets you set a scale factor for the dimension text. This option scales the value of the dimension text to the value you enter. For example, if you want your dimensions to display distances in centimeters, even though the drawing was created in inches, you can enter **2.54** for this option. Your dimension text will then display dimensions in centimeters. Conversely, if you want your dimension text to show dimensions in inches, even though you've created your drawing using centimeters, you enter **0.3937** (the inverse of 2.54) for this option [Dimlfac].

**Apply To Layout Dimensions Only** Causes AutoCAD to apply the measurement scale factor to Paper Space layouts only. With this check box selected, the Dimlfac dimension variable gives a negative value [Dimlfac].

### The Zero Suppression Group

Lets you suppress zeros so they don't appear in the dimension text. For dimensions other than architectural, you can suppress leading and trailing zeros. For example, 0.500 becomes .500 if you suppress leading zeros. It becomes 0.5 if you suppress trailing zeros. For architectural dimensions, you can suppress zero feet or zero inches, although typically you wouldn't suppress zero inches [Dimzin].

### The Angular Dimensions Group

The following options enable you to format angle dimensions:

**Units Format** Lets you select a format for angular dimensions. The options are Decimal Degrees, Degrees Minutes Seconds, Gradians, and Radians [Dimaunit].

**Precision** Lets you set the precision for the angular dimension text [Dimadec].

**Zero Suppression** Lets you suppress leading or trailing zeros in angular dimensions [Dimazin].

### THE ALTERNATE UNITS TAB

The Alternate Units tab lets you apply a second set of dimension text for dimensions. This second set of text can be used for alternate dimension styles or units. Typically, alternate units are used to display dimensions in metric if your main dimensions are in feet and inches.

Select the Display Alternate Units check box to turn on alternate units. This causes AutoCAD to include an additional dimension text in the format you specify in the Alternate Units tab [Dimalt].

#### *The Alternate Units Group*

The following options offer control over the unit style and the formatting of dimension text for linear dimensions:

**Unit Format**   Lets you determine the unit style of the dimension text. The options are Scientific, Decimal, Engineering, Architectural Stacked, Fractional Stacked, Architectural, Fractional, and Windows Desktop. You must set this option independent of the overall drawing units setting (choose Format ➤ Units) if you want the dimension text to appear in the appropriate style [Dimaltu]. You can adjust the size of fractions relative to the main dimension text by using the Dimfac dimension variable.

**Precision**   Lets you set the precision of the dimension text. This option rounds off the dimension text to the nearest precision value you set. It doesn't affect the actual precision of the drawing [Dimaltd].

**Multiplier For Alt Units**   Lets you set a multiplier value for the dimension text. This option multiplies the value of the dimension text by the value you enter. For example, if you want your alternate dimensions to display distances in centimeters even though the drawing was created in inches, you can enter **2.54** for this option. Your alternate dimension text will then display dimensions in centimeters. Conversely, if you want to have your alternate dimension text show dimensions in inches, even though you've created your drawing by using centimeters, you enter **0.3937** (the inverse of 2.54) for this option [Dimaltf].

**Round Distances To**   Lets you determine the degree of rounding applied to alternate dimensions. For example, you can set this option to 0.25 to round off dimensions to the nearest .25 or ¼ of a unit [DImaltrnd].

**Prefix**   Lets you include a prefix for all linear alternate dimension text. For example, if you want all linear-dimension text to be preceded by the word *Approximately,* you can enter **Approximately** in the Prefix input box. Control codes can be used for special characters. See Chapter 10 for more information on character codes [Dimpost].

**Suffix**   Lets you include a suffix for all linear alternate dimension text. Control codes can be used for special characters. See Chapter 10 for more information on character codes [Dimapost].

### The Zero Suppression Group

The check boxes in this group let you suppress zeros so they don't appear in the alternate dimension text. For dimensions other than architectural, you can suppress leading and trailing zeros. For example, 0.500 becomes .500 if you suppress leading zeros. It becomes 0.5 if you suppress trailing zeros. For architectural dimensions, you can suppress zero feet or zero inches, although typically you wouldn't suppress zero inches [Dimaltz].

### The Placement Group

The following options let you determine the location for the alternate units:

**After Primary Value**   Places the alternate dimension text behind and aligned with the primary dimension text [Dimapost].

**Below Primary Value**   Places the alternate dimension text below the primary dimension text and above the dimension line [Dimapost].

### THE TOLERANCES TAB

The options in the Tolerances tab offer the inclusion and formatting of tolerance dimension text.

### *The Tolerance Format Group*

The following options offer control over the format of tolerance dimension text:

**Method**   Lets you turn on and set the format for the tolerance dimension text. The options are None, Symmetrical, Deviation, Limits, and Basic. None turns off the tolerance dimension text. Symmetrical adds a plus/minus tolerance dimension; this is a single dimension preceded by a plus/minus sign. Deviation adds a stacked tolerance dimension showing separate upper and lower tolerance values. The Limits option replaces the primary dimension with a stacked dimension showing maximum and minimum dimension values. The Basic option draws a box around the primary dimension value. If an alternate dimension is used, the box encloses both primary and alternate dimension text [Dimtol, Dimlim, (minus) Dimgap].

**Precision**   Lets you set the precision of the tolerance dimension text. This option rounds off the dimension text to the nearest precision value you set. It doesn't affect the actual precision of the drawing [Dimtdec].

**Upper Value**   Lets you set the upper tolerance value for the Symmetrical, Deviation, and Limits tolerance methods [Dimtp].

**Lower Value**   Lets you set the lower tolerance value for the Deviation and Limits tolerance methods [Dimtm].

**Scaling For Height**   Lets you adjust the size for the tolerance dimension text as a proportion of the primary dimension text height [Dimtfac].

**Vertical Position**   Lets you determine the vertical position of the tolerance text. The options are Top, Middle, and Bottom. The Top option aligns the top tolerance value of a stacked pair of values with the primary dimension text. Middle aligns the gap between stacked tolerance values with the primary dimension text. Bottom aligns the bottom value of two stacked tolerance values with the primary dimension text [Dimtolj].

### *Tolerance Alignment Group*

These radio buttons set the alignment of stacked tolerance values. The two options, Align Decimal Separators and Align Operational Symbols, are self-explanatory.

### *The Zero Suppression Groups*

These options let you suppress zeros so they don't appear in the tolerance dimension text. For dimensions other than architectural, you can suppress leading and trailing zeros. For example, 0.500 becomes .500 if you suppress leading zeros. It becomes 0.5 if you suppress trailing zeros. For architectural dimensions, you can suppress zero feet or zero inches, although typically you wouldn't suppress zero inches [Dimtzin].

### *The Alternate Unit Tolerance Group*

The Precision drop-down list lets you set the precision of the alternate tolerance dimension text. This option rounds the dimension text to the nearest precision value you set. It doesn't affect the actual precision of the drawing [Dimalttd]. You can also control zero suppression (see "The Zero Suppression Groups," mentioned previously).

## Notes on Metric Dimensioning

The AutoCAD user community is worldwide, and many of you may be using the metric system in your work. As long as you aren't mixing Imperial (feet and inches) and metric measurements, using the metric version of AutoCAD is fairly easy. In the Drawing Units dialog box (choose Format ➤ Units), set your measurement system to decimal, and set the Units To Scale Inserted Content option to the appropriate metric option; then, draw distances in millimeters or centimeters. At plot time, select the MM radio button (millimeters) under Paper Size and Paper Units in the Plot dialog box.

If your drawings are to be in both Imperial and metric measurements, you'll be concerned with several settings, as follows:

**Dimlfac**  Sets the scale factor for dimension values. The dimension value will be the measured distance in AutoCAD units times this scale factor. Set Dimlfac to 25.4 if you've drawn in inches but want to dimension in millimeters. The default is 1.0000. If you want to scale dimension values from millimeters to inches, use a value of 0.03937.

**Dimalt**  Turns the display of alternate dimensions on or off. Alternate dimensions are dimension text added to your drawing, in addition to the standard dimension text.

**Dimaltf**  Sets the scale factor for alternate dimensions (that is, to metric from Imperial). The default is 25.4, which is the millimeter equivalent of 1″. If you're using metric ISO units, the default is 0.03937, which is the inch equivalent of 1 mm.

**Dimaltd**  Sets the number of decimal places displayed in the alternate dimensions.

**Dimapost**  Adds a suffix to alternate dimensions, as in 4.5 mm.

### USING THE AUTOCAD METRIC TEMPLATE

If you prefer, you can use the metric template drawing supplied by AutoCAD:

1. Choose File ➤ New. If you see the Select Template dialog box, go to step 2; otherwise, skip to step 3.

2. Select the Acadiso.dwt file, and click Open. You can also select acadISO – Named Plot Styles.dwt if you want to use a named plot style.

3. In the Create New Drawing dialog box, click the Template button. Then, select the filename Acadiso.dwt and click OK to open a new drawing based on the template. You can also select ACADISO – Named Plot Style.DWT if you want to use a named plot style.

These templates are set up for metric/ISO standard drawings.

You can also click the Metric radio button in the Start From Scratch option of the Create New Drawing dialog box. When you do so, subsequent new files will be set to metric by default.

If the AutoCAD 2008 Startup dialog box doesn't appear when you open AutoCAD, or if you don't see the Create New Drawing dialog box when you choose File ➤ New, you can turn on these dialog boxes by using the Startup option in the System tab of the Options dialog box. Choose Tools ➤ Options, and then click the System tab in the Options dialog box. In the General Options group, select Show Startup Dialog Box from the Startup drop-down list.

## Drawing Blocks for Your Own Dimension Arrows and Tick Marks

If you don't want to use the arrowheads supplied by AutoCAD for your dimension lines, you can create a block of the arrowheads or tick marks you want, to be used in the Arrowheads group of the Dimension Styles/Geometry dialog box.

**TIP**    To access the Arrowhead options, open the Symbols And Arrows tab of the New, Modify, or Override Dimension Style dialog box.

For example, suppose you want a tick mark that is thicker than the dimension lines and extensions. You can create a block of the tick mark on a layer you assign to a thick pen weight and then assign that block to the Arrowhead setting. To do so, choose Dimension ➤ Styles from the menu bar to open the Dimension Styles dialog box; then, select a style from the Style list, and click the Modify button. In the Symbols And Arrows tab, select User Arrow from the First drop-down list in the Arrowheads group. In the User Arrow dialog box, enter the name of your arrow block.

When you draw the arrow block, make it 1 unit long. The block's insertion point will be used to determine the point of the arrow that meets the extension line, so make sure you place the insertion point at the tip of the arrow. Because the arrow on the right side of the dimension line will be inserted with a zero rotation value, create the arrow block so that it's pointing to the right (see Figure C.2). The arrow block is rotated 180° for the left side of the dimension line.

**FIGURE C.2**

The orientation and size of a block used in place of the default arrow

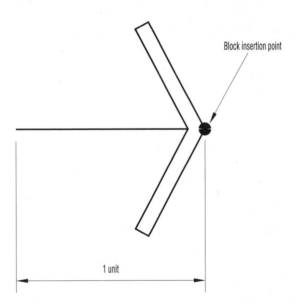

Block insertion point

1 unit

If you want a different type of arrow at both ends of the dimension line, create a block for each arrow. In the Dimension Styles/Geometry dialog box, choose User in the drop-down list for the first arrowhead and enter the name of one block. Then, choose User in the drop-down list for the second arrowhead, and enter the name of the other block.

# Index

**Note to the Reader:** Throughout this index **boldfaced** page numbers indicate primary discussions of a topic. *Italicized* page numbers indicate illustrations.

Align option, 310, *310*
Align tool, 640
Align Space tool, 758
Aligned tool, 363
Aligned With Dimension Line
    option, 342, 947
aligning
    dimensions, 363, *364*, 947
    multileader notes, 373
    objects
        in 3D space, **640–642**, *641*
        with layout objects,
            **758–759**, *759*
        with Osnap tracking,
            **97–102**, *98–102*
    with Sweep, 628, *628*
    text, **301–302**, *301*, **309–310**,
        *309–310*, 327, *327*
    viewports, **759–761**, *760*
Alignment option, 628, *628*
Alignment Point Acquisition
    option, 910
All options
    selecting objects, 48
    zooming, 198, 200
All Borders option, 330
All Cross Sections option, 638
All Used Layers option, 148, 150
Allow Exploding option, 110
Allow Long Symbol Names
    option, 906
Allow Other Users To Refedit
    Current Drawing option,
    232, 904
Allow reverse Lookup option, 494
Alt key for accelerator keys, 15
alternate dimensions, adding and
    removing, **362–363**
alternate units, 346, *346*
Alternate Units tab, 346, *346*, 362,
    **951–952**, *951*
Always Keep Text Between Ext
    Lines option, 948
American Institute of Architects
    layer naming convention,
    152–153
AND operations
    AutoLISP, 782
    grouping, 433
    searches, 63
Ang function, 445
Angbase system variable, 75

Angdir system variable, 75
Angle function, **783**
Angle Of Line Defined By Two
    Points tool, *436*, 437, 439, *439*
angles
    arcs, 40, *40*
    circular copies, 168
    dimension lines, *365*, **368**, *368*
    dimension text, 355, 358
    dimensions for, **365–367**, *365*
    direction for, 73–74, *73*
    falloff, 670–671, *670–671*
    hatch patterns, 207, 815
    linetypes, 813
    with Loft, *639*, 640
    moving objects, **46–48**
    multileaders, 370
    Polar Tracking, 79, **80**
    precision for, 73
    QuickCalc calculator for,
        **437–439**, *437–439*
    revolving polylines, 713
    row and column copies, 169
    shapes, 755
    specifying, **34**, *35*
    styles for, 74–75
    text, 296, *296*, 308
    units for, 76
    Xlines, 190
Angtos function, **785**
Angular tool, 365
animation
    settings, 912
    walk-throughs, **690–692**, *690*
Animation Preview window, 691
Animation Settings button, 912
Annotation Object Scale dialog
    box, 123–124, *123*
annotation scale, **122–125**,
    *123–125*, **294–295**
Annotative option
    blocks, 110
    hatch patterns, 217
    scales, 948
ANSI format, templates for, 164
Aperture Size option, 910
apostrophes ('), 541
Apparent Intersection Osnap
    option, 95
Append to Current Selection Set
    option, 435

Application Data folders
    option, 919
Apply Changes To Existing
    References option, 397
Apply Global Scale Factor to
    Non-ISO Linetypes option, 278
Apply Material To Objects tool,
    657, *657*, 678
Apply Selected Visual Style To
    Current Viewport tool, 588, *588*
Apply Solid Fill option, 510, 902
Apply To option, 435
Apply To All Active Viewports
    option, 604
Apply To Layout Dimensions
    Only option, 473, 730, 950
Ar command, 385
Arc And Circle Smoothness
    option, 156, 901
Arc tool, 29, 39, 89, *89*
Arc Length tool, 368
Architectural Desktop 2008
    (ADT), **933–934**
Architectural units, 73–74
Archive A Sheet Set dialog box,
    890–891, *890*
archiving sheet sets, **889–891**,
    *890–891*
arcs, **88–93**, *90–91*
    dimensions, **365–368**, 946
    distances along, **191–192**,
        *191–192*
    length, 192, 368
    moving, 50
    options, 38–42, *40–42*
    for polylines, 508, *509*
    properties, **67–68**, *67*
    smoothness, **651**, 901
    with UCS, 605
Area command, **534–538**
Area Fill Correction option, 924
area of objects, **534–535**
    complex, **536–538**, *536*, *538*
    hatch patterns for,
        **535–536**, *536*
Area system variable, 541
Area tool, 534
argument lists, 765
arguments
    AutoLISP, **770–771**
    Diesel, 805
    functions, 765